# Praise for *Certified Enterprise Architect All-in-One Exam Guide*

The only way we can stay on top of this world's accelerating rates of change and complexity is via architecture. Building buildings, airplanes, gig economies, and enterprise-minded businesses require structured methods, proven techniques, and practical lessons learned from the trenches. All this is bound in this complete *Certified Enterprise Architect All-in-One Exam Guide*. Beryl Bellman, Prakash Rao, and Ann Reedy continue to extend their EA best practices to advance this comprehensive, must-read guide for all enterprise architects.

*Patrick Bolton*, CEA, TOGAF, Zachman
Practice Leader for Management | Business Consulting, Integrated Systems, Inc.
Founding faculty and instructor of the FEAC Institute and TOGAF

There is no better *decision-making rubric* than this modern approach to EA! Apply these principles to create and dramatically improve *enterprise-grade evolution and optimization*. Prakash Rao, Beryl Bellman, and Ann Reedy show you practical and implementable EA methods that capture your organization's most important and audacious ideas—ensuring adoption and full realization. Without an EA mindset, you can't deliver the goods—the continuous and cross-cutting strategic pivots required by today's complex and evolving businesses and government organizations. Keep this book away from your competition! Especially if your organization is facing complex and difficult strategic and transformation decisions. Only EA can see you through!

*Robert Moore*, Vice President
NTT DATA Federal, Inc.

All-age students and learners of enterprise architecture and systems engineering will find state-of-the-art viewpoints and answers to most questions in this well-structured, up-to-date book. The foundations of enterprise innovation and learning for realization of future customizable digital solutions and active models and architectures are described by approaches, methods, and tools. Examples from government, defense, and commercial sectors improve comprehension.

*Frank Lillehagen*, Manager R&D
Commitment AS
Oslo, Norway

D1319090

## ALL·IN·ONE

# Certified Enterprise Architect

## EXAM GUIDE

ALL · IN · ONE

# Certified Enterprise Architect
## EXAM GUIDE

Prakash C. Rao
Ann Reedy
Beryl Bellman

New York   Chicago   San Francisco
Athens   London   Madrid   Mexico City
Milan   New Delhi   Singapore   Sydney   Toronto

**Library of Congress Cataloging-in-Publication Data**

Names: Rao, Prakash C., author. | Reedy, Ann, author. | Bellman, Beryl,
    author.
Title: Certified enterprise architect all-in-one exam guide / Prakash C. Rao,
    Ann Reedy, Beryl Bellman.
Description: New York : McGraw-Hill Education, [2019] | Includes index.
Identifiers: LCCN 2018030974 | ISBN 9781260121483 (alk. paper)
Subjects: LCSH: Industrial organization (Economic
    theory)—Examinations—Study guides.
Classification: LCC HD2326 .R367 2019 | DDC 338.6076—dc23 LC record available at
https://lccn.loc.gov/2018030974

McGraw-Hill Education books are available at special quantity discounts to use as premiums and sales promotions, or for use in corporate training programs. To contact a representative, please visit the Contact Us pages at www .mhprofessional.com.

### Certified Enterprise Architect All-in-One Exam Guide

1 2 3 4 5 6 7 8 9   QFR   21 20 19 18

ISBN    978-1-260-12148-3
MHID        1-260-12148-8

| | | |
|---|---|---|
| **Sponsoring Editor**<br>Wendy Rinaldi | **Copy Editor**<br>Lisa Theobald | **Composition**<br>Cenveo Publisher Services |
| **Editorial Supervisor**<br>Janet Walden | **Proofreader**<br>Claire Splan | **Illustration**<br>Cenveo Publisher Services |
| **Project Manager**<br>Snehil Sharma,<br>    Cenveo® Publisher Services | **Indexer**<br>Claire Splan | **Art Director, Cover**<br>Jeff Weeks |
| **Acquisitions Coordinator**<br>Claire Yee | **Production Supervisor**<br>James Kussow | |

As just compensation for the times I have been AWOL from my parental and husbandly duties because of the book, I want to dedicate this work to my loving wife of more than three decades, Malathi; our two lively and lovely children, Vikram and Rajni; and our new additions, daughter-in-law Lauren and son-in-law to-be Brian. No one can ask for a better family! My professional and personal friends and well-wishers are too many to name but you know who you are—our debates and discussions, your advice and inputs helped shape this book! To John Zachman whom I have personally known for more than two decades, you have always been an inspiration with your energy, enthusiasm, and wisdom! Cort Coghill, your breadth and depth of knowledge has outstripped that of all your teachers and you make us proud!

*—Prakash Rao*

I wish to express my thanks to my husband, Dr. Christopher L. Reedy, for his patience and support during the development of this book and to my co-authors for their continuing encouragement and support. I would like to thank the other FEAC instructors and staff for their insights and support as well as the FEAC DoDAF students from whom I have learned perhaps more than they have learned from me. Finally, I would like to thank my colleagues, past and present, especially Kathie Sowell, at the MITRE Corporation, with whom I have enjoyed stimulating conversations about architecture and related issues over the years.

*—Ann Reedy*

I also thank those Prakash mentioned along with colleagues in the **Association for Enterprise Architects** and especially Ken Griesi of MITRE, with whom I have jointly published and presented on emergent enterprise architecture. I also thank my former business partners and co-founders of FEAC, Felix Rausch, and Barbara Charuhas Rausch, for their support and friendship. I am most grateful to colleagues in the EA and related professional associations with whom I am affiliated and am honored by being given leadership roles. I also thank John A. Zachman for his close personal friendship and support and his son, John P. Zachman. In addition, I thank my colleagues and students at California State University Los Angeles as well as those at California State University East Bay and National University for their support of our programs; and also I thank colleagues in Norway, including Frank Lillehagen, John Krogstie, and Soba Peterson, who work with Active Knowledge Models at the National Science and Technology University in Trondheim. Most importantly, I express my deepest gratitude to my wife, Dr. Suzanne Regan, who provides support and encouragement in all of my work and teaching, and to my children, Sarah and Che, who continually make me proud.

*—Beryl Bellman*

# ABOUT THE AUTHORS

**Prakash C. Rao** is a Certified Enterprise Architect with a graduate degree in Computer Science from the University of Minnesota and an undergraduate in Electronics and Telecommunications Engineering. Since starting as a research scientist in the Corporate Computer Science Center at Honeywell in the early 1980s, he has been active as a researcher, program manager, and line manager, and he has also worked in systems business development at Honeywell. He is the co-founder of InfoSpan Corporation, one of the developers of the industry's first open standard repositories.

Prakash has been teaching classes in enterprise architecture at the FEAC Institute as a faculty member for many years and has also co-trained more than 1000 staff members of the United States Air Force at various USAF locations worldwide. He is also a practicing enterprise architect, with more than 15 years of experience in EA, including participating in one of the earliest EA implementations at USAF Air Mobility Command with EA pioneers John Zachman and Dr. Steven Spewak in the mid-1990s. He has been active as an invited speaker, facilitator, trainer, consultant, and architecture subject matter expert in several engagements during the past 15 years. He is currently the chief executive officer of architecture consulting firm Enterprise Sherpas LLC located in Fairfax, Virginia. He continues to research actively and also develop innovative architecture tools to jump start the architecting effort in step with the changing enterprise.

As a co-founder of a venture-funded startup, Prakash realizes, first hand, the applicability and usefulness of enterprise architecture techniques to the organizing, management, evolution, and governance of a startup as well as ongoing enterprises. As a practitioner for more than 15 years, he brings real-world experience to his teaching and training methods.

**Ann Reedy** has a PhD in Computer Science, with more than 40 years of experience in academia, federal research, and contracting communities. She taught courses in computer science at the University of Iowa and the University of Nebraska, Lincoln. After working with analyst support systems and software development environments in the federal contracting community, she focused on enterprise architecture. While working for the MITRE Corporation, a federally funded research and development center, she was one of the principal developers and editors of the C4ISR Architecture Framework and worked on its evolution into the DoD Architecture Framework (DoDAF).

She has adapted the DoDAF for various federal organizations and agencies and supported a wide variety of DoDAF-based enterprise architecture startups as well as helping agencies develop enterprise architecture governance processes. These federal agencies included Treasury, Customs, IRS, and FAA, as well as DoD projects. While at MITRE, her research topics have included the integration of security concerns and the use of pattern-based approaches in enterprise architecture.

She taught enterprise architecture to groups supporting the U.S. government through the MITRE Institute and through the Federated Enterprise Architecture Certification (FEAC) Institute for more than 10 years and co-authored a textbook for the FEAC.

Now retired from MITRE, Ann continues to pursue research into new enterprise architecture concepts and approaches.

**Beryl Bellman** is Emeritus Professor of Communication at California State University at Los Angeles, was co-founder and Academic Director of the FEAC Institute, and is a frequent TOGAF trainer. He has been involved in teaching, research, publishing, consulting, and project management in the fields of enterprise architecture, knowledge management, and organizational communications/behavior for more than 45 years and has an excellent reputation in both academe and professional consulting. He has held faculty and research positions at the University of California at San Diego, Stony Brook University, City University of New York Graduate Center, and California Institute of the Arts, and was research director of the Western Behavioral Sciences Institute prior to his current university position.

In addition to academic positions, Beryl has some 30 years of concurrent consulting experience in both the government and private sectors, and he has been a principal consultant and project manager with three major enterprise architecture consulting and tool vendor companies. He has consulted in enterprise architecture–related programs in the public sector for the DoD; Departments of Agriculture, Energy, and Justice/INS; U.S. Forest Service; and the Executive Office of the President. And he served as a contract consultant for NCR, AT&T, ASK, RAND, and Digital Equipment Corporation, working for internal and external customers. This included working as an EA in the aerospace, financial, banking, pharmaceutical, entertainment, and manufacturing sectors. He has published several books and numerous articles and is a frequent presenter at national and international professional and academic conferences. He is also the co-author of the *FEAC Certified Enterprise Architect CEA Study Guide* with Prakash Rao and Ann Reedy.

# CONTENTS AT A GLANCE

# CONTENTS

# FOREWORD

Seven years ago, I wrote the foreword to the first version of this book and, actually, I haven't changed my mind appreciably since that time. I was tempted simply to reproduce that earlier foreword with a few adjustments and submit it to Prakash, Ann, and Beryl. They are probably so stressed out trying to get the book completed that they may not have even noticed!

But I do have some observations I would share with you about how significant this book really is. I do not think many people have any idea the profound implications of Enterprise Architecture. My opinion is, this is not simply an Enterprise issue. I believe it has everything to do with the destiny of humanity for the foreseeable future.

The game has CHANGED! We no longer are in the Industrial Age, although many people, notably Information people, are still walking around with Industrial Age glasses on. Those of us who come from the Information Community tend to interpret everything we see in the context of the Industrial Age, where we have lived for the last 60 or 70 years, the total history of the stored programming computing technologies.

Peter Drucker, in a *Forbes* periodical, *ASAP*, on August 24, 1998, said, "The next information revolution is well underway. But it is not happening where information scientists, information executives, and the information industry in general are looking for it. It is not a revolution in technology, machinery, techniques, software or speed. It is a revolution in CONCEPTS."

Those of us from the Information community are well-conversant with the technology, machinery, techniques, software, and speed; however, Drucker continues to observe that in the Information Age, it is the "I" in IT that becomes dominant. It is the CONTENT owners that prevail. In the previous three Information Revolutions (Papyrus, Scrolls, Gutenberg Press), initially, the technologists were hailed by kings and princes. However, within 50 years or so, the technologists (the "T" in IT) became common laborers. The content owners, in our case, the Enterprise, is now the focus of power and authority.

Ask a building architect what he does for a living, and his response will be, "We design buildings."

Ask an aeronautical engineer what she does for a living, and she will say, "We design airplanes."

If you ask systems engineers or people from IT what they do for a living, you will typically hear something like, "We build and run systems." That would be a manufacturing idea. You never hear anyone say, "We design enterprises." In contrast, designing enterprises would be an engineering idea.

Fred Brooks, the author of the seminal work, *The Mythical Man Month* (Addison Wesley, 1975), is attributed to the saying, "Programming is manufacturing, not engineering."

But, "the systems ARE the Enterprise!" People used to get frustrated with me when I would say that! Typically, people would respond, "Oh, no! The systems are NOT the Enterprise. The systems … aahhh, eerrrrraahhh, hmmmm, aaaahh … the systems SUPPORT the Enterprise." When I hear that, I usually say, "You have been replacing the people of the Enterprise with systems for the last 60 or so years. What were those people doing? Weren't they the Enterprise? If they weren't the Enterprise, you shouldn't have bothered replacing them with systems! No—you made the systems the Enterprise instead of the people. If there is any question in your mind as to whether the systems are the Enterprise or not, turn the systems off for 15 or 20 minutes!! The Enterprise will come to a screeching halt!! Everybody will be sitting on their hands waiting for the systems to come back up!"

Therefore, IT has been "manufacturing" the (your) Enterprise for the last 60 or so years.

BUT the Enterprise was never designed!! The Enterprise happens—little by little, iteratively and incrementally, as it grows in complexity. And, by the way, it doesn't have to get very big to get very complex.

Therefore, actually, IT hasn't been manufacturing the Enterprise; they have been manufacturing PARTS of the Enterprise—and the parts don't fit together!

If you were building airplanes (or buildings, or locomotives, or computers, or whatever) and you built a bunch of parts that didn't fit together, what do you do with them?

SCRAP AND REWORK!!

Nobody wants to hear that, but if you want the parts to fit together, you have to engineer the parts to fit together BEFORE you manufacture them. If you manufacture them and THEN try to fit them together, you can't get there from here! Oh, in some cases, if the clearances are not too great, you can stick shims in to make them fit, but that destabilizes the product and inhibits change and it costs more for maintenance, and so on.

In a speech at Seville University in 1998, Jay Forrester, the author of *Industrial Dynamics* (Pegasus Communications, 1999), said, "Organizations built by committee and intuition perform no better than an airplane built by the same methods…. As in bad airplane design, which no pilot can fly successfully, such badly designed corporations lie beyond the ability of real-life managers…. A fundamental difference exists between an enterprise operator and an enterprise designer. A manager runs an organization just as a pilot runs an airplane. Success of a pilot depends on an aircraft designer who created a successful airplane…. Who designed the corporation that a manager runs?"

That's the point: nobody.

There is a plethora of business books and research that observe that the characteristics of the Information Age that we presently understand are twofold: complexity and change. In fact, Alvin Toffler's books on change (*Future Shock*, *The Third Wave*, and *Powershift*) provide theoretical explanations of why both complexity and the rate of change are dramatically and continuously escalating.

Seven thousand years of known history would suggest that the only device humanity has identified to address complexity and change is ARCHITECTURE!

If it, whatever it is you are creating, gets so complex that you can't see it at the level of definition required to create it, then you are going to have to formally describe it—that is, Architecture.

And if you ever want to change whatever it is you have created, you have to retain the descriptive representations that were required to create it, to serve as a baseline for changing it—that is, once again, Architecture.

Therefore, in an Enterprise, if you want to accommodate complexity and extreme rates of change, you are going to have to create and retain its ARCHITECTURE.

A few years ago, a friend of mine interviewed 108 CEOs around North America, including Lee Iococca (Chrysler), Sandy Weill (CitiBank), Jack Welch (GE), and others, and I was shocked! Every one of them, to a person, said that the biggest problem facing the Enterprise was CHANGE! I thought I had to explain to the CEOs of the world, "Chief! Change is a BIG problem!" It turns out, they already knew that! They are obviously a lot smarter than I was giving them credit for being.

The question is NOT "Is complexity and the rate of change increasing?" The question IS "What are YOU going to do about the dramatic escalation of complexity and the rate of change?" And the question is NOT a technical question. It is an ENTERPRISE question: "What are you, CHIEF, going to do about the dramatic escalation of complexity and change?"

There is only one possible answer: ENTERPRISE ARCHITECTURE!

I hope this short discussion is sufficient to help you understand why this book is so significant.

No! One more point.

If you build a bunch of parts and the parts don't fit together, you can try to compensate by inserting "shims" and things to force a fit—if the discontinuity is somewhat limited. In Enterprises, these "shims" are called middleware, or cross-references, or interfaces, or MBAs with Excel spreadsheets running on PCs reconciling discontinuities, and so on. This is ENTROPY—the price you pay just to keep the Enterprise running. It is not contributing to the "bottom line." It is general and administrative expense.

Management has lamented for decades about the costs of IT. I haven't seen any numbers lately but, historically, around 80 percent of the IT budget was spent on "maintenance." And the more lines of code there are, the more dis-integration, the more compensation, the more entropy, the more "maintenance."

Fred Brooks observed, "All repairs tend to destroy the structure, to increase the entropy and disorder of the system. Less and less effort is spent on fixing the original design flaws and more and more is spent fixing flaws introduced by earlier fixes.... Although in principle [the system is] usable forever, the system has worn out as a base for progress. Furthermore, machines change, configurations change, and user requirements change so the system is not in fact useable forever. A brand new, from-the-ground-up redesign is necessary."

## SCRAP AND REWORK

(e.g., Windows 3, Windows XP, Windows 2000, …Windows 7, 8, 9, …Windows "n")
(e.g., Version 1.0, v1.2, v1.3, v1.31, v1.32, v1.33, v2.0, v3.0, v4.0, …version "n")

Notice: The end objective is NOT to get the code to run. That is what we have been doing for the last 60 or so years. The result is what we have: lines of code, LOTS of lines of code, the "legacy," dis-integration, dis-continuity, entropy.

The end objective IS to design the Enterprise such that there is NO discontinuity, NO disorder, NO dis-integration, NO de-normalization. Its "parts" are "integrated." That is, ENTERPRISE ARCHITECTURE!

Now we have the *Certified Enterprise Architect All-in-One Exam Guide!*

I have known the authors of this book for 35 years (Beryl Bellman), 25 years (Prakash Rao), and 15 years (Ann Reedy). They are consummate enterprise architecture practitioners and they have been DOING enterprise architecture for all the years that I have known them. Each of them brings his or her own particular focus and experience: culture change, modeling and repository products, and methodology development, and so on, to give a comprehensive understanding of the Enterprise and its architecture.

They have gathered together in one volume, a comprehensive summary of state-of-the-art practical issues that an enterprise architect has to address, elaborated in a Six-Step methodology derived from the Department of Defense Architecture Framework (DoDAF): 1. Planning, 2. Developing, 3. Disseminating, 4. Sustaining, 5. Governing, and 6. Using … Enterprise Architecture.

All of the authors were extensively involved in developing and teaching DoDAF.

They develop a comprehensive case study employing the DoDAF artifacts to serve as practical illustrations of architectural representations.

Personally, I would pay attention to their "lessons learned," the first one of which, by the way, is INTEGRATION!

I would make one more foreword point for you:

We do not have 1000 years of accumulation of wisdom around the subject of Enterprise Architecture. We have only a few decades. I have spent 40 or 50 years myself trying to learn as much as I can, and the more I know, the more I don't know! We have a LOT more to learn.

The authors allude to the next critical (in my estimation) intellectual hurdle: We need a theoretical context to define the physics, the Laws of Nature relative to Enterprises, and in this, I am confident, lies the domain of ontologies.

The authors graciously refer to my Framework in the book and acknowledge that it is an ontology—NOT a methodology. To tell you the truth, I didn't even know what an ontology was, or even that my Framework was an ontology until just a few years ago!

Actually, I did not even invent my Framework. It kind of fell on my desk one day. I was just trying to figure out how to transform the Enterprise Business Strategy into implementations such that the implementations somewhat resembled the strategies. Those of us who were working together thought that Architecture might have something to do with this, but we had no idea what Architecture looked like for Enterprises.

One day, I had a bright idea. I have an architect friend who designs buildings, and I thought that if he would talk to me about creating a building (like a 100-story building) architecture, maybe I could figure out what Enterprise Architecture might look like.

My friend sketched out a "creating Building Architecture" scenario, and I began to see a pattern. At that time, I was doing some strategy consulting in several airplane manufacturing enterprises, where I could do some research and validation of the pattern I discovered, and voila! The pattern recurs! It is the same! Then we looked at ships, computers, automobiles—whatever we could get access to—and all confirmed the pattern. Subsequently, all I did was put Enterprise names on the same descriptive representations that were created for designing and building Industrial Age, complex engineering products. The result is what you might now know as the "Zachman Framework."

I appreciate my friends Beryl, Prakash, and Ann. They have taught me invaluable lessons about Enterprise Architecture and helped me refine my understanding of the ontological structure.

At the very beginning of this foreword, I made the observation, "I do not think many people have any idea the profound implications of Enterprise Architecture. My opinion is, this is not simply an enterprise issue. I believe it has everything to do with the destiny of humanity for the foreseeable future."

I also suggested that the next intellectual barrier to progress in the Enterprise Architecture state of the art lies in the domain of ontologies.

To give you a sense of this significance, I suggest a chemistry metaphor:

For six or seven thousand years, there were chemists, actually alchemists, who were learning how to create chemicals by trial and error, "best (or worst) practices." They were very creative and very innovative, but it was only after Dmitri Mendeleev published the Periodic Table, an ontology, around 1890, that they began to understand the molecular physics of chemical engineering, REUSING the elements of the Periodic Table to create an infinite variety of compounds. Up until that time, they had created only a relative few chemical compounds by using other chemical compounds they had available. They only had a suspicion that something like atoms existed. But within a mere 50 years or so after the publication of the Periodic Table, they were splitting atoms!

With the advent of an ontology of elements theoretically classified, research was no longer constrained to practice, trial and error. It became scientific, with results being predictable and repeatable. Friction went to zero. Every ALCHEMIST who began to USE the Periodic Table became a CHEMIST.

The Periodic Table is the foundation for understanding the physics of elements. The compounds are specific implementations of combinations of elements to fulfill a specific purpose. There is ONE Periodic Table. There are "n" different compound (implementations) and maybe "n-squared" processes (methodologies) for creating them. The elements (Periodic Table) are timeless. The compounds (implementations) are temporal.

The breakthrough was the acknowledgement of and the employment of the ontology by the practitioners.

I would also suggest that the key to the INDUSTRIAL AGE was ARCHITECTURE, in that case, Industrial Product Architecture.

For example, if someone hadn't figured out how to describe buildings, we'd be having our meetings in log cabins. If someone hadn't figured out how to describe airplanes, we'd be traveling in covered wagons. If someone hadn't figured out how to describe automobiles, we'd be riding horses (et cetera). The key to the Industrial Age was ARCHITECTURE, Product Architecture!!! Learning how to describe (and create) the tangible objects to which we are so accustomed that we tend to take them all for granted.

I submit that the key to the Information Age also is ARCHITECTURE, but ENTERPRISE ARCHITECTURE. Whereas the Industrial Age was focused on tangible PRODUCTS, I believe the Information Age will be characterized by the focus on groups of PEOPLE collaborating in pursuit of a common mission or purpose—that is, on ENTERPRISES!

If we don't figure out how to describe Enterprises and AGREE to REUSE the ontological structures for architecting them, we are relegated to producing more of what we already have now: legacy, code, and an inability to accommodate the escalation of complexity, and "Future Shock," the inability to accommodate extreme change—that is, paralysis.

We need the breakthrough of an explosion in the body of knowledge in Enterprise Architecture. We need the release into the molecular physics of Enterprise Design. We need to start thinking about splitting the atoms of Enterprise "primitives" (elements).

In this book, Ann, Beryl, and Prakash introduce us to the domain that opens the door to the future: ontologies.

Thank you, Ann, Beryl, and Prakash!

Keep this book beside your bed! Read some every day!! Do what they say!!! You'll be happy.

In seven years, I am planning to be around to write the foreword to the THIRD edition, the ontological version of the *Certified Enterprise Architect All-in-One Exam Guide*!!!

*John A. Zachman*, CEO
Zachman International
Bakersfield, CA, 2018

# PREFACE

A good friend of mine has been telling me for years that if something is so complicated that the whole thing cannot be viewed once, or if it is subject to dramatic change, then you must have explicit descriptive representations to be able to manage it. I have heard John A. Zachman make that assertion in countless conferences and training sessions regarding the value proposition of enterprise architecture. However, the reality is that people still seem to think that they have their enterprise under control. There is a widespread denial about the complexity of our enterprises. We do not want to accept that our enterprises are in fact complex adaptive systems, with emergent behavior arising from the interactions of not only internal operations, but of external factors such as shifts in business markets, the increasingly intertwined regulatory landscape, or the ever-growing rate of technological change. These are only a few of the variables impacting how our enterprises work.

In a 1993 *Harvard Business Review* article, "Predators and Prey: A New Ecology of Competition," John F. Moore provides, in my humble opinion, one of the most salient arguments about the need for enterprise architecture. Moore emphasizes the organic nature of our enterprises as parts of an ecosystem, and the fact that they are born and must evolve or risk possible death. Moore's discourse on business as an ecosystem concerns the complexity of tasks related to gaining and maintaining a competitive advantage. This is where enterprise architecture is relevant. There is a need to understand not only how the parts of our enterprises are connected but to gain an appreciable understanding of how a change impacts the enterprise before it is implemented. The required shift is from the ad hoc "let's see what sticks" silver bullet mentality to one of engineering the enterprise. The commitment to continuous renewal requires a means to ensure that change occurs by design and not by mere happenstance.

Enterprise architecture has never been more crucial than in today's increasingly connected and complex world. Our connectedness to other enterprises, ecosystems, and industries creates ever more demand for strategic coherence around decision-making, resource allocation, and risk management. Enterprise architecture is recognized as a means to help create understanding between and among the various parts of an organization. A comprehensive knowledge base, such as that found in this book, is needed by practitioners at all levels.

I have known the authors of this book for more than a decade. I continue to teach at the FEAC Institute, but first I was a student there. The authors were my teachers when I went through the course of instruction, and I learned a great deal from each of them. I realized that they have bestowed on me an honor in allowing me to talk about their collective wisdom and knowledge regarding enterprise architecture and how their contributions are still an active part of the FEAC Institute itself. I still count them among my current teachers. I am constantly amazed by their insight, their continued drive to learn, and more importantly their desire to share knowledge with others.

When this book was first published in 2011, it represented a comprehensive desk reference providing a lucid discussion about concepts of enterprise architecture, the impact of culture, as well as the development and integration of architecture models and diagrams. The authors' contributions added to the body of knowledge on enterprise architecture, providing examples of architecture diagrams while using a running example that helped practitioners gain an understanding of how to communicate stakeholder concerns between one another using enterprise architecture. The book contributed not only to the mechanics of constructing diagrams from a framework model but also addressed the issue of culture and its impact on enterprise operations. Fast-forward to this revised edition, and you see expanded discussions on culture, the use of multiple frameworks, and the continued use of a running example that provides an integrated context for practitioners at all levels to think about how to plan for and solve all types of challenges that an enterprise may face. This revised book is another contribution in moving the rock of knowledge forward. The body of knowledge around enterprise architecture continues to evolve. The authors are all active practitioners who know that the body of knowledge for enterprise architecture, like enterprises themselves, needs continual renewal.

For me, this book touches on the topic of enterprises as complex adaptive systems. Enterprise architecture is not merely about collecting and documenting the structural and behavioral relationships between an enterprise's components (people, processes, technologies, and so on). An enterprise is greater than the sum of its parts. Even a perfect set of models will not convey a perfect understanding of an enterprise. The authors of this book have sought to address the complexity of enterprises and their dynamic networks of interactions to include the impact that social science (such as culture) has on stakeholder perceptions. This book explores the reality that no enterprise is static, but instead is subject to constant change and stresses, both internal and external. The authors look at factors such as complexity, emergence, and self-organization. They examine the role of enterprise architecture frameworks and put them in context as a means to an end. This book thus becomes a very useful reference for the practical development of knowledge concerning EA concepts (such as integration versus federation), and it also enables the reader to reflect on how the elements of an enterprise interact dynamically. The authors provide a springboard for additional research and encourage the reader to think beyond any specific framework, while keeping the examples and knowledge grounded with tangible and practical guidance and examples.

This book is important because of its holistic treatment of the practice of enterprise architecture practice—it does not merely seek to explain the values and virtues of any specific framework, methodology, or notation. A quick inquiry with any search engine using phrases such as "nobody could have seen the impact of regulatory change" or "we could not have anticipated the shift in technology" (or any type of assertion stating that "we could not know") generally reveals a real lack of knowledge of how one's own enterprise works and how change in one part will impact another aspect that is seemingly unrelated. Problems are often expressed as a single variable, but the truth is that they always have multiple variables. This book provides insight on the use of the Zachman Enterprise Ontology as a means of separating the independent variables to be able to do engineering-level analysis as a part of enterprise change management.

There are a great many references for the practicing enterprise architect to choose from. As a committed lifelong learner, I appreciate the effort that Prakash, Beryl, and Ann have put into this book. I see it as a substantive contribution to the current body of enterprise architecture knowledge. I also see it as a relevant book for other disciplines looking to make sense of their functional domain of expertise. Process improvement alone will not help an enterprise renew itself—this must be done in the context of people and technology. Technology alone will not fix things, no matter how big the latest silver bullet being marketed is. People alone cannot fix things because, as stated in the *Rigveda*, one of the sacred texts of Hinduism, "Reality is one, though wise men speak of it variously." We have different perceptions of what the enterprise is. Without a body of knowledge such as the one presented in this book, we will not be able to renew our enterprises effectively and further their evolution. I hope this book finds a cherished place in your library.

*Cort Corghil,* D.Eng., ZCEA, CEA, PMP
Director of Education Operations
FEAC Institute

# ACKNOWLEDGMENTS

John Locke said, "The improvement of understanding is for two ends: first, our own increase of knowledge; secondly, to enable us to deliver that knowledge to others." In this, our second co-authored book, we are trying to do just that. The field and discipline of enterprise architecture has come a long way from its roots in the early 1990s with the seminal work of John Zachman, Stephen Spewak, and many other pioneers. Different types of enterprises such as the U.S. federal government; the military in the United States, Canada, United Kingdom, Australia, and the North Atlantic Treaty Organization (NATO); The Open Group; and several EA consultants and practitioners have borrowed from one another's discoveries, learning, and bodies of knowledge. As a result, though there is much diversity, a common base of core knowledge is emerging that transcends the diversity. This book is an attempt to capture, represent, and convey that core knowledge while recognizing and discussing the diversity that still remains.

Sir Isaac Newton once famously stated, "I reach further because I stand on the shoulders of giants." We encourage the reader to supplement this book with readings from other sources and to constantly renew their understanding and implications of developing and applying enterprise architecture concepts to their worlds—constantly reaching farther. Given the vast body of knowledge and the broad range of theories, conceptual frameworks, and terminologies for the detail-oriented student or researcher, we recommend supplemental readings from a specific framework or domain or modeling technique of interest.

In a growing body of knowledge, it is hard to pin down the invariants. In this book, we have concentrated on the communication of core concepts as well as a discussion to introduce the reader to the importance of architectural representations both as communication tools and as analysis tools. Doubtlessly, you as readers will contribute in some manner to this growing body of knowledge.

The authors express deep gratitude to many people who made this book possible. The very first group we want to thank are the people at McGraw-Hill Education who gave birth to this project and were behind the earlier book that was the foundation for this one. Wendy Rinaldi, Claire Yee, and their team have been encouraging and reinforcing in their support for our efforts. McGraw-Hill's commitment to the highest standards of publishing quality has been a large part of the success of the previous EA work. We want to thank Snehil Sharma whose role as Project Manager demanded an unreasonable amount of patience and understanding as we went through the drafts, editors Janet Walden, Lisa Theobald, Claire Splan, artwork by Jeff Weeks and production supervision by James Kussow. There is definitely no "I" in "BOOK"!

To the previous key people at the FEAC Institute, where all three of the co-authors taught for several years, thank you for providing a forum for us to grow our thoughts, test our ideas, and experience tens of student enterprise architecture projects over the years. Felix Rausch and Barbara Charuhas Rausch—thank you for your support of the original book. To the current key people at the FEAC Institute, thank you John A. Zachman and Cortland Coghill for graciously writing the Foreword and Preface. John Zachman has been a friend, a mentor, a well-wisher, and a wise advisor throughout our journey in EA that started more than two decades ago.

Thank you for all the shoulders that we stood on, to reach farther in the field of enterprise architecture over 20-plus years. Thank you to our FEAC colleagues—Dan Spar, Bob Moore, Patrick Bolton, Rob Thomas, Ken Griesi, Francisco Loiza, Mike Tiemann, and Kathy Sowell. A big thank you to John Zachman, the late Steve Spewak, Joe Butchko, Paula Pahos, Lieutenant Colonel Edmund Kera USAF (Retired), Cyndi Marler, Jeff Akers, Terry Balven, and Christine Dear for many years of EA learning and heated and lively arguments and debates in classrooms, offices, and at *biergartens* since 1994! Thank you to all the students of FEAC who gave us as much in learning as they received from us. Space does not allow us to list all the people who have helped us through the past journey and who still continue to do so for the future!

# INTRODUCTION

This book is about enterprise architecture (EA). To paraphrase the IEEE definition, an EA, or more properly, an EA description, is a representation of the components and their relationships, the structure and the behavior of an enterprise, and the evolution of these elements over time. An EA is created to support planners and decision-makers in aligning the processes and technical infrastructure of the enterprise with the enterprise's business strategy. An EA provides the enterprise business context that supports the decisions about what processes, systems, and technologies should be developed or acquired to achieve the enterprise's strategic goals and objectives. So, EA informs and precedes systems engineering and its representations are distinct. Systems engineering is concerned with the building of solutions and draws context and constraints from EA. The EA also provides the information on the overall integration of the enterprise's systems and the orchestration of system development projects. EA and SE interface with each other and are both critical parts of organizational transformation. EA models and artifacts are sometimes referred to as conceptual blueprints, whereas SE models are more detailed representations for the construction of solutions the EA identifies. (Both EA and SE are complemented by the disciplines of program and project management.)

Today, the discipline of EA is multifaceted and interacts with multiple other disciplines, ranging from business, management, IT, and systems engineering, to the social sciences. It is taught by a number of training organizations as well as academic departments. In addition, a growing number of universities offer certifications and professional master's degrees in EA in the United States, England, and Australia. In contrast to many professional certifications, there is no single exam across the industry and discipline; rather, various training organizations provide their own branded forms of certification. For this reason, many enterprise architects hold several simultaneous EA certifications from different sources, including the Federal Enterprise Architecture Certification (FEAC) Institute (in both Federal Enterprise Architecture Framework, or FEAF, and Department of Defense Architecture Framework, or DoDAF) in conjunction with California State University, East Bay; The Open Group Architecture Framework (TOGAF); Zachman; the Enterprise Architecture Center for Excellence (EACOE); Pragmatics; and others. In addition, there are certifications and courses from universities including the National Defense University, Penn State, Carnegie Mellon University Software Engineering Institute, Kent State, National University, Griffith University, and more.

This book, as part of the McGraw-Hill All-in-One Series, provides exam preparation relevant to each of these certifications and is also a practitioner's reference guide addressing different frameworks, types of models and artifacts used, and differences in terminologies and EA development methodologies employed. Our intent is to provide generic information relevant to any certification or academic course examination on enterprise architecture.

Although there are differences in the certifications and course curricula and the language and dialects of EA, we provide an orientation toward EA that is analogous to what sociologist C. Wright Mills attempted in his classic *The Sociological Imagination* (1959) for the social sciences. He advocated a theoretical intentional stance providing a vision or way of looking at the world that characterized a discipline. Taking this analogy, we advocate what might be called an *Enterprise Architecture Imagination* or, better, an *Enterprise Architecture Attitude* proffering a vision that underlies the various forms of inquiry about enterprises and their respective architectures relevant to all training and educational programs. A similar approach to business strategy and strategic planning was recommended by Kenichi Ohmae in his seminal book, *The Mind of a Strategist* (1991): "Recognize that strategy begins with analysis. The strategist analyzes a set of facts, in the sense of taking the set apart, and then reassembling it in an order that makes sound strategic sense. The purpose of strategy is to maximize one's advantage. On a battlefield, this means picking the right place to fight, the right time to attack, the right time to retreat—weighing and re-assessing as circumstances change, but always with maximum advantage in mind. Strategy is intuitive, but it is also analytical; it is analytical, but also intuitive."

Enterprises have intuitive patterns that are variously called business models, operating models, technology models, service concepts, business concepts, etc. (Hohpe and Woolf, 2003) Once having adopted this EA attitude stance, most architects are successful at passing the varying certification examinations and academic courses as they grasp core concepts and common truths despite the varied languages and techniques used to express them!

For instance, one of the authors with EA experience was among the first to get certified in TOGAF 9, when it was first introduced at The Open Group conference in San Diego in 2009. The Open Group offered volunteers willing to try out the exams a full day of testing; beginning with the TOGAF 8 transition to TOGAF 9 exam, followed by the TOGAF 9 Foundation, and then the TOGAF 9 Certification exam. Although the TOGAF 9 publications were not generally available at that time, he and others passed their TOGAF 9 certification based on their having what we call here an "EA mindset."

A goal of this book is to introduce and reinforce the EA attitude by providing practitioners with a full set of case study–based examples of the kinds of artifacts, products, and models that constitute an architecture and by highlighting EA as an approach that supports management decision-making and organizational transformation efforts. With the EA attitude and the basic concepts and patterns of EA, readers will have the requisite background knowledge and confidence for any type of certification examination.

We do not claim that this book will replace any specific training, educational program, or detailed treatise on any one specialized architecture topic such as process modeling. However, we attempt to clarify and cross-reference different frameworks and approaches to EA to emphasize the "enterprise architecture imagination" that underlies any and all programs, and in so doing enable the enterprise architect to leverage the wealth of knowledge to satisfy certification and course exams on the basics of EA. This includes the following:

- Modeling techniques
- Architecture artifacts, building blocks, and deliverables

- Business strategy
- Business pattern
- Governance
- Mined information about primary drivers for businesses such as laws, policies, and regulations for government and industry

As authors of this practitioner's guide, we emphasize how our approach can be used to reduce the time to a first draft of the EA. Too often, especially in project-inspired attempts at developing the EA, schedule urgency far outstrips the need for detailed EA development, and many EA developments are too little, too late. This book shows you how to leverage knowledge to reduce the time drastically to understand and communicate the anatomy of the enterprise.

# Today: Current Enterprise Challenges

In today's environment, enterprises both large and small have become more and more dependent on information to fuel and information technology to propel their businesses. These enterprises face a number of challenges that affect their planning environment; their ability to make decisions; their ability to assess, evaluate, and prioritize many alternative proposals; and their ability to face new pressures from regulation, globalization, intense competition, and dramatic changes in their business environments. Many enterprises have not been able to address these challenges successfully as the evidence of a long list of failed multimillion-dollar IT initiatives seems to convey. The complexity and scale of some of these IT projects, though comparable to large civil engineering works or the building of airframes, do not appear to have benefited from a holistic, structured planning approach combined with an integrated, well-managed implementation approach that mitigates risks and results in good design tradeoffs. In short, these enterprises need a new approach for supporting their decision-making in both strategic and investment planning to manage the complexity and scale of the implementation. A systematic application of architecture, which is such an approach, is therefore a major subject of this book.

Enterprises face many challenges today, including the following:

- *Failure of large IT projects.* Failure results not only in the inability to support the business but also robs the enterprise of resources for future opportunities, forces the need to keep systems and solutions built on obsolete or aging technology, and introduces new vulnerabilities.

- *Faster tempo of operations, which results in the need to detect and eliminate latencies and reduce the time of delivery to the customer.* Military operations, for example, need to reduce latency in the delivery of intelligence, imagery, and other situational assessment and operating picture elements to support better operational planning and execution capabilities. Often in military operations, the ability to act is predicated on the availability of accurate and timely situational information. The ability to collaborate and cooperate is predicated on the establishment of a common operating picture.

- *Mergers and acquisitions, where new parts of the IT environments acquired from merged enterprises increase the diversity in standards, information representations, architectures and equipment, and operational costs.* Mergers also have cultural implications, and the way forward involves resolving inconsistencies, mismatches, gaps, and consolidations in business processes as well as in IT.

- *Globalization, where parts of the workforce are located in different regions of the world.* Workers bring their own cultures, languages, and local constraints on power, equipment, communications, and other factors. Operating a global enterprise involves mediating among cultures, languages, mindsets, work practices, and world views.

- *Changing workforce skills and environments driven by new ways of interaction and collaboration and increased automation and use of computers, applications, information, and networking.* With new technologies comes the need for new skills. Existing skills become obsolete or less useful than in the past, while the need for new skills becomes imperative. Understanding, representing, and forecasting skill needs in the face of constantly changing labor needs is imperative.

- *Increasing expenses in information technology as a whole, despite dramatic decreases in per-unit cost of processing and memory.* Expenses can increase as a result of labor costs, the need to control obsolescence, the evolution of standards and technologies, and the need to constantly increase the speed of processing and increase the availability of memory. Though the per-unit cost of information technology investment is decreasing year after year, the scope and scale of the systems keeps increasing, which means enterprises do more and more with their IT every year at significant expense. One of the big disrupters is the advent of cloud technology that promises elasticity, demand computing, expensing rather than capital investment, and the opportunity to offload non-core IT assets to service providers and use IT as a service.

- *Increases in complexity and scale of IT projects.* Complexity includes scope and reach and the consequent need for orchestrating work outputs of large numbers of professionals located all over the globe to complete projects successfully.

- *Inability to fully assess impact of complexity and scale at the planning or at the implementation level.*

- *Rampant adoption of technology driven by marketplace competition and vendor push as well as the pressure to align to contemporary standards.* As customers and consumers get used to advanced technology in their products and services, they begin to demand more from their suppliers. Enterprises, including federal government agencies, have had to retrofit or adapt their legacy systems to meet this new demand.

- *Rampant outsourcing, based on financial analyses, competitive price pressures, and the current enterprise focus on the core mission and the decision to outsource all non-critical supporting services.* Outsourcing brings its own challenges related to lack of day-to-day control and the reliance on service agreements to enforce contractual obligations.

- *Dramatic opportunities posed by evolving IT architecture style that change the way systems are built and introduce new planning and transformational challenges.* Changing to a new style of architecting, such as service-oriented architecture and cloud computing, can change the way business is performed, often disrupting existing methods of connecting supplier to consumer or customer.

# The Case for Enterprise Architecture

The famous Finnish architect Eero Saarinen recommended a design principle: "Always design a thing by considering it in its next larger context—a chair in a room, a room in a house, a house in an environment, an environment in a city plan." This design principle reminds us that changes to the enterprise, such as changes in systems, business processes, or organizations, need to be considered in the context of the entire enterprise, including the enterprise strategy, goals, and objectives. Given this design principle, developing an EA is an exercise of common sense.

What are some of the key high-level concepts of an enterprise architecture?

- An enterprise architecture has three components: a current or as-is understanding of the enterprise, a target or to-be vision of the enterprise, and a transition plan.

- An enterprise architecture needs to provide traceability or line of sight from the IT infrastructure through the business processes and organization to the strategy, goals, and measurable objectives of the enterprise. In other words, the EA shows how well the IT infrastructure and business processes align with the enterprise strategy. Line of sight is essential to provide governance and course correction.

- An enterprise architecture needs to include the artifacts and models that can address the issues or expected problems the enterprise is facing.

- An enterprise architecture can focus on different levels of the enterprise. The enterprise may need multiple levels of architecture to understand and resolve its problems. A common set of levels of architecture are Enterprise Level, Segment Level, and Solution Level.

These concepts and some of the challenges they help address are discussed next.

## Three Components of an Enterprise Architecture

Enterprises are constantly transforming, either proactively as part of a planned improvement, or reactively, struggling and kicking as a response to changes in environment or competition. In either case, any successful transformation is predicated on the following:

- A clear understanding of *the current state,* which we call the baseline or as-is state. This understanding needs to be documented and based on verifiable fact, not supposition.

- A clear understanding of *the objective,* or *target state,* which we call the to-be or target state. The to-be state of the enterprise must also be represented in the same dimensions, artifacts, and models as is the as-is state. From this representation comes an understanding of what remains the same, what cannot change easily or must stay, and what must change.

- A clear *transformation plan/roadmap* that will transform the enterprise from the as-is state to the to-be state. This plan requires a timeline that is acceptable within the window of change; otherwise, you risk a transformation that is too late, usually calling for enterprise triage measures. The roadmap will generally consist of a number of concurrent initiatives or projects that must all support one another and join together to provide the net transformation effect that the enterprise desires.

Even this simple concept can address many of the challenges identified. In all cases, having these three components of the EA can boost the chances of successful transformation if used as the basis of communication and buy-in for all the parties involved.

## IT Failures

You need a good understanding of the current state of the architecture to understand the impact of proposed changes on the enterprise, not only in terms of process and IT but also in terms of the impact on enterprise personnel, their required skills, and their organization. Some planners and managers don't want to spend time and money on developing this "as-is" understanding of the enterprise, since this is something they will be changing. Yet some of the most expensive IT system failures have resulted from attempts to install enterprise resource planning (ERP) systems without any understanding of the complicated nature of the enterprise's existing payroll processes. ERP systems need to be customized to support the business rules of the enterprise. If you don't know the number of rules that need to be addressed, you won't be able to correctly estimate to cost of customization or the length of time it will take to perform the customization process, leading to potentially uncontrolled cost and schedule overruns. In fact, if you don't understand these business rules, you won't be able to customize the ERP system successfully and the effort will be a failure.

Other expensive failures have resulted, at least in part, from the failure of planners and management to understand the impact of the proposed changes on the existing workforce or their resistance to change. For example, if operational workers discover that the new process or system supports only part of their job and leaves them struggling to get through their workload with two unintegrated systems that require duplicated effort, they may refuse to use the new system and the transition effort with fail. The importance of getting buy-in on changes from all affected stakeholders cannot be underestimated.

## Mergers and Acquisitions

If both of the merging enterprises have an EA, then the as-is component of each architecture can be used to identify disjoints in policy, process, and IT infrastructure. Given the disjoints, a vision of the merged enterprise and a potentially phased transition plan can be developed. Given the existing EAs, this planning process may not take a long time, and, done correctly, it will ensure that valuable enterprise assets, such as critical business data, are not lost in a rush to consolidate. The new vision and transition plan can be communicated to the new management and the employees and used to get buy-in. Clashes in corporate cultures can be identified and reasonable plans made to resolve them. However, changes that mean lost jobs are always resisted and have to be handled carefully.

## Globalization

An as-is architecture identifies current operating requirements and documents existing processes, business rules, and aspects of corporate culture. For enterprises thinking of global expansion, the underlying assumptions of the work environment need to be explicitly documented. This information can be used to perform risk analysis on the expansion into new global regions and to develop mitigation strategies. The as-is and to-be architectures aid identification of potential conflicts with new culture, languages, mindsets, work practices, and world views.

Some IT failures have resulted from failing to recognize the difference in communications and electrical power stability in areas of the world where systems installations are planned. One U.S. agency developed an online timecard system and tested it in a lab located within the United States, where electrical power and communications are usually stable. They forgot that in many other "austere" locations where the system would be installed, communications and electricity availability are unstable and unpredictable. Needless to say, the system had to be scrapped in those locations.

Failure to understand differences in laws and regulations, such as privacy laws, in overseas areas have also led to serious IT problems.

## Off-loading Non-core Assets, IT as a Service, and Outsourcing

Careful analysis of the as-is and to-be architectures in conjunction with the transition plan can identify risks and issues with off-loading non-core assets, treating IT as a service, and outsourcing. The usual issues to consider are the availability and control of critical business information, fallback plans if service providers fail or payment disputes arise with service providers or outsourcing contractors, and security, as well as the impact on current business processes and personnel in the face of these types of changes.

## New Styles of IT Architecture

Frequently, when an IT department sees new IT architecture technologies that promise performance or cost improvements, the department lobbies for permission to employ or install these new approaches. However, with the EA approach, a new to-be architecture reflecting the new IT infrastructure will need to be developed together with any changes in the current business processes and organizations that result from the adoption of the new IT architecture. Then the new to-be architecture and transition plan will need to be analyzed to determine whether the new IT architecture will actually bring the benefits promised in terms of improved business performance and cost. It may be that the new IT architecture does not really provide much benefit to the enterprise or that the new architecture must meet certain requirements or criteria before its use will be beneficial. EA evolved to combat this expensive tendency to adopt new technologies for technology's sake.

# Alignment

If an enterprise has an as-is architecture with good performance measures and current measure values on its business processes and IT infrastructure, then the line of sight that the architecture provides from infrastructure to strategy gives the enterprise a perfect model for identifying latencies and their probable causes. When the time to delivery needs to be decreased, many enterprises simply attempt to add more automation and computer support. However, in some cases, it is the business processes that are broken and no amount of additional automation will fix the problem. The business processes and organizations need to be optimized and then new IT support provided to meet the desired business performance requirements. Implementing change in business processes and organizations can be tricky; if a set of middle managers perceive that their "turf" is being impacted or their importance in the management chain is being decreased, they will band together to resist the changes and derail the improvement effort.

The case of the "common operating picture" is, in fact, an example of a need to change the business process. If an EA exists for each of the organizations that need to share a common operating picture, then an analysis of all the relevant as-is business processes and the data they use should reveal the data needed in the common operating picture. Once the common operating picture is defined, the business processes need to be restructured to use and update the common data source and, finally, the IT adjusted to support the new business processes.

## A Rich Set of Artifacts and Models

An enterprise architect needs a rich and flexible set of artifacts and models to document an enterprise's architecture. The set needs to be able to capture data to support decision-making with respect to the questions and issues of the architecture stakeholders. One of the areas that must be addressed is the tracking of emerging technologies, evolving standards, and marketplace trends and their potential impacts on the IT infrastructure and workforce skills of the enterprise. Comparison of the as-is architecture to the to-be architecture shows changes in business processes resulting from the expected inclusion of new technologies and standards and highlights the new skills and organizations that may be needed if the new to-be architecture is adopted. The new IT base and changed business processes and personnel needs can be checked for alignment with enterprise strategy, goals, and objectives. A return-on-investment analysis can determine whether the new technology is worth the overall investment.

The tracking of marketplace trends along with other emerging technologies must be included. Sometimes unexpected changes in the marketplace, such as the emergence of a popular cell phone, can cause major impacts on an enterprise's plans. With an EA in place, an enterprise can perform rapid "what if" analyses to understand potential impacts and to make corrections in everything from its strategy to its IT base and security approaches.

## Levels of Architecture

Enterprise architectures can be developed at many levels of abstraction. If increasing complexity and scope of IT projects drive a need to orchestrate work outputs from multiple sets of widely separated workers, then two levels of architecture can be employed.

There should be one lower level of abstraction architecture for each project. The focus of these architectures should be on the development and delivery of the work products. A single higher level architecture can focus on the orchestration of these work products. This higher level architecture documents dependencies among the work products and how they fit together to provide functionality to operational organizations. Schedules from the projects are compared and analyzed to ensure that work products from one project that are input to work products from another project arrive in good time and that the delivered functionality is completed in a timely manner to avoid gaps in functionality coverage.

Similarly, if complexity and scope are impacting planning and implementation, several levels of architecture need to be used to separate detailed concerns from higher level issues.

# Enterprise Architecture Skills and Expertise

People entering the EA field come from a variety of backgrounds. Many come from systems and software engineering, because EA impacts and interacts with these disciplines and many of the modeling techniques used in the various architecture frameworks are familiar to them. However, managers and executives are also interested in the field because they want to understand firsthand and directly exploit the information available for management decision-making that is available from an EA. Managers will also need to manage EA program offices and the development, sustainment, and governance of the EA.

An EA development team also uses expertise from a variety of other disciplines, including business and social sciences. Business experts are key to providing both generic and specific business knowledge to domain-specific architectures. Those with a social science background are needed to understand organizational and cultural issues such as corporate culture and emergent groups that are resistant to change and can seriously impact the success of transformations.

An important skill needed by all members of the architecture team is the ability to communicate ideas and concepts, both to other team members and to architecture stakeholders. The medium of communication within the team is a uniform set of organized artifacts and models provided by an architecture framework. The architecture framework provides the language used to capture and document the enterprise's architecture. While specific modeling experts on the team may develop the artifacts and models, all members of the team need to understand these artifacts and models and be able to use them to "tell the story of the enterprise" and the transformation that is being planned for it. The architects need the analytical skills to understand how to use the architecture framework artifacts and models to address stakeholder questions.

Enterprise architects also need to be able to translate the framework artifacts and models into reports, presentations, simple graphs, or other representations that are easily understandable to the architecture stakeholders and enterprise decision-makers who need the input from the architecture. Architects also need to work with business, simulation, and performance analysts to provide the architecture information they need to complete their work. Example types of business analysis that need architecture input include business case analysis, return on investment, and activity based costing.

So, enterprise architects, regardless of background, need the following skills:

- Good communication skills
- Good analytical skills
- Good understanding of the architecture framework they are using

Since communication skills and analytical skills are difficult to teach and are gained mainly through experience, most EA education focuses either general concepts or on architecture frameworks.

## Architecture Frameworks

The main tool of EA is the architecture framework. The framework establishes a common vocabulary for architecture elements and defines an organized set of artifacts and models that use these architecture elements. Further, these artifacts and models should be integrated—that is, the artifacts and models all show a different view of the same reality and provide that line of sight from strategy to IT infrastructure, enabling the alignment of IT and business investments with the strategy of the enterprise.

An architecture framework establishes a set of terms that describe the various types of architecture elements. For example, the DoD Architecture Framework (DoDAF) defines architecture elements such as *activity, performer, location,* and *capability*. The use of a single architecture framework across an enterprise means that all the architects will be using the same set of well-understood terms.

# Enterprise Architecture Certification

EA has developed as a practitioner-based and practice-driven discipline rather than being grounded in any specific academic discipline. A prime driver for EA was the U.S. government's search for a way to ensure that large investments in IT would create actual improvements in business performance and outcomes. Though this effort began with requiring agencies to have an integrated IT architecture that encompassed multiple views of the enterprise, it soon became apparent that a more holistic enterprise view was required. EA provided the ability to establish traceability or "line of sight" from automation and IT infrastructure through business process performance to strategic goals and objectives (desired business outcomes). Independently, the Department of Defense had also turned to EA to solve its interoperability problems in its move from single military service war-fighting to a Joint Task Force approach. The DoD needed an enterprise approach to ensure that complex weapons systems, planning systems, and communications from multiple military services would work together in a Joint Task Force environment.

As industry also adopted EA approaches, both government and industry wanted some form of assurances that the people they hired to develop their EAs had the skills, expertise, and experience to do the job. As demand increased, various certification approaches evolved.

## What It Means to Be Certified

Certification in most areas refers to a formal procedure to recognize the knowledge, skills, and experience of members of a profession. This is most often done in part by asking candidates to demonstrate their knowledge through some form of examination procedure. In most, but not all instances, certification is done through some external body or organization that is recognized as a credible body to assess capabilities. In many disciplines, such as medicine, education, and law, this certification is under the authority of major professional organizations and/or governmental entities. There are also a number of technical certifications that are promoted by industrial organizations that test for competencies with a defined body of knowledge and skill sets. These range from certifications in specific products such as those offered by Microsoft, CISCO, and Oracle to the mastery of a set of approaches that are often incorporated into the curricula of various university departments. These include such fields as program management, Six Sigma, information assurance, and the like.

Because EA is an emerging discipline, no single professional organization has yet materialized with the necessary prestige and acknowledged professionalism to establish a single certification examination or process. So far, the government has not established any standards for EA education or training, although a few very preliminary attempts at these standards have been made. Since professionals seeking to enter the EA field may come from a variety of backgrounds, the certification approaches typically focus on either general EA concepts or on a specific architecture framework. EA certifications can come from a variety of sources, as mentioned earlier:

- Universities and colleges—master's degree programs, certifications from specific programs (independent of a degree program), or passing of single courses
- Certification bodies associated with organizations that control the development of specific frameworks such as the Zachman Framework or TOGAF, which offer both training courses and certification examinations
- Independent training vendors offering certification courses, which range from professional short courses on EA overview and concepts to more in-depth courses that focus on a specific framework or approach, and which may or may not include a certification examination

Thus, professionals seeking certification must decide what type of certification they want. The choice may depend on their background and the requirements of the job they are currently working in or would like to work in. This book provides both overview and in-depth materials relevant to certification examinations.

# Learning Objectives for this Book

The goal of this book is to prepare the reader for certification by covering major EA concepts and helping readers to demonstrate competencies in areas such as the following:

- Selection of the correct level of architecture (such as Enterprise Level, Segment Level, or Solution Level) needed to address a specific enterprise problem
- Planning for the development of useful architecture by selecting appropriate views and artifacts depending on the problems the architecture needs to address and the stakeholder issues
- Understanding and using reference models such as the Federal Enterprise Architecture Consolidated Reference Model
- Understanding the TOGAF Architecture Development Methodology (ADM), FEAF Collaborative Planning Methodology (CPM), and DoDAF Six-Step methodologies
- Engaging in EA analysis and building actual customer deliverables
- Identifying the enterprise's corporate tribes, conducting stakeholder interviews, and developing EA analyses
- Using EA for organizational transformation

# How to Use This Book

Table 1 provides an overview of the organization of this book and its contents. Parts II and III have a primary focus on DoDAF details to provide the initial introduction to a complete framework. DoDAF was chosen because of its extensive influence on defense-oriented architecture frameworks worldwide; its influence on U.S. government federal and agency architecture frameworks, including FEAF; and because its views and viewpoints are compatible with TOGAF.

| Part | Chapters | Contents |
|---|---|---|
| Part I: Foundation Concepts | Chapters 1–2 | Provides basic EA concepts and vocabulary used throughout the book and an introduction to cultural concepts of importance to EA |
| Part II: Architecture Development and Use | Chapters 3–10 | Chapter 3 introduces the RMN Airport Case Study used in examples throughout Parts II and III; Chapter 4 introduces the DoDAF; Chapters 5–10 introduce EA planning, management, and governance concepts |
| Part III: Viewpoints and Views | Chapters 11–20 | Provides details of DoDAF viewpoints and views through an integrated set of examples based on the case study |
| Part IV: Comparative Frameworks | Chapters 21–24 | Provides introduction to the Zachman Framework, TOGAF, and FEAF2 with a comparison of these with DoDAF |

**Table 1**  Overview of Organization of this Book

# Reading Advice

Readers should read or at least skim Part I to understand the EA vocabulary used throughout the book and the basic cultural concepts important to EA, such as corporate tribes. If readers want to read any other chapters in Parts II and III, they should read Chapter 3 to understand the discussions and examples involving the RMN Airport Case Study. Readers who want to know about planning for an EA development, developing an EA, setting up an EA project office, and EA management, governance, dissemination, and use should read the rest of Part II. Readers who want a detailed introduction to DoDAF viewpoints and views with examples should read Part III. A study of the examples in Part III will provide an introduction to the concept of integration that is one of the keys to a useful architecture. Readers interested in a framework other than the DoDAF or with a general interest in architecture frameworks should read Part IV.

At the end of most chapters is a "Questions" section. These questions are designed to reinforce the meaning of concepts presented in the book. These questions often require self-examination of your own enterprise in the light of the concepts presented in order to deliver value to you in the understanding of your own enterprise. Thus, the questions at the end of each chapter are to be taken more as a study guide to assist in the understanding of the concepts involved and therefore no answer keys have been provided.

# Questions

1. Discuss what motivates (or hinders) EA development in your organization. What are the key drivers for EA in your enterprise? What are the key demotivators?

2. What are the early reasons for the emergence of EA? Are those reasons still valid? Are there new reasons driving the need for EA? What are they?

3. What is the relationship between enterprise architecture and enterprise transformation?

4. What is the role of project management as a discipline in enterprise architecture? Think of two roles—projects that are related to the development of the EA itself and projects that represent transformation initiatives or investments.

5. Why is EA certification beneficial to enterprises? What are the elements of EA certification? How does EA certification described in this book differ from or resemble other certification processes such as product certifications from, say, a Microsoft or professional certifications such as the Project Management Institute?

6. Should EA be restricted to use in information technology planning or is it applicable to all aspects of the enterprise such as the value-added business processes, inbound logistics, outbound logistics, and aspects of sales and marketing, for instance? Discuss why, or why not, and present examples of how EA can be used in the IT realm as well as in the business realm.

# References

Gregor, Hohpe, and Bobby Woolf. 2004. *Enterprise Integration Patterns: Designing, Building, and Deploying Messaging Solutions.* New York: Addison-Wesley Professional.

Lankhorst, Marc. 2017. *Enterprise Architecture at Work: Modelling, Communication and Analysis.* Berlin: Springer.

Mills, C. Wright. 1959. *The Sociological Imagination.* Oxford, U.K.: Oxford University Press.

Ohmae, Kenichi. 1991. *The Mind of a Strategist: The Art of Japanese Business.* New York: McGraw-Hill Education.

Rao, Prakash, Ann Reedy, and Beryl Bellman. 2011 *FEAC Certified Enterprise Architect CEA Study Guide.* New York: McGraw-Hill Education.

# PART I

# Foundation Concepts

# Enterprise Architecture Concepts

The purpose of this chapter is to lay the groundwork of terminology that is used throughout the book and to provide a grasp of the fundamentals of enterprise architecture (EA). This chapter informally introduces the concepts through the prism of a hypothetical airport. Chapter 3 elaborates on Richard M. Nixon Municipal Airport, the primary case study used throughout this book.

This chapter provides a general discussion of the terms used in enterprise architecture. Specific architecture frameworks may use additional or variants of terminology unique to their scope. The terms presented here are a direct reflection of the current state of practice of enterprise architecture. Understanding of the foundational concepts is essential before you tackle the actual process of planning, developing, using, and sustaining architecture representations in subsequent chapters.

## High-Level Concepts

The high-level concepts are enterprise, architecture, and enterprise architecture.

## Enterprise

The term *enterprise* can be defined in several ways. Here are some examples:

- "One or more organizations sharing a definite mission, goals, and objectives to offer an output such as a product or service." [ISO 2000–06]

- "Any collection of organizations that has a common set of goals. (Also) The highest level (typically) of description of an organization and typically covers all missions and functions. An enterprise will often span multiple organizations." [The Open Group 2009]

- "An organization (or cross organizational entity) supporting a defined business scope and mission that includes interdependent resources (people, organizations and technologies) that must coordinate their functions and share information in support of a common mission (or set of related missions)." [CIO Council 1999]

3

- "The term enterprise can be defined in one of two ways. The first is when the entity being considered is tightly bounded and directed by a single executive function. The second is when organizational boundaries are less well defined and where there may be multiple owners in terms of direction of the resources being employed. The common factor is that both entities exist to achieve specified outcomes." [OMB 2012]

An enterprise, informally, is a group of people engaged in purposeful activities with a common motive. All the definitions associate the people who form an enterprise into one or more organizational structures. The motive or purpose of the enterprise is defined in terms of the mission, goals, objectives, or vision, and the achievement of such motives enables the enterprise to continue to operate. This broad definition includes large corporations, such as IBM and AT&T, small businesses, the Executive Branch of the United States government, and small municipal entities such as an airport. In a viable enterprise, the motivation must be common and the activities must be collaborative in support of the common purpose.

The Merriam-Webster dictionary defines enterprise as "a project or undertaking that is especially difficult, complicated or risky." Transformations of large corporations or organizations involve several difficult, complicated, and risky projects. Each of these individual projects as well as the collection of projects may be deemed to be enterprises in their own right.

Why is the enterprise concept important? The enterprise concept raises the collaboration and common motivation aspects that people tend to forget in their preoccupation with daily activities. An enterprise exists for a purpose larger than the output of daily activities. Threads link the activity and output of one person or organization with the activity and output of others. Understanding these linkages is a very important aspect of streamlining the collection of activities that together fulfill the purpose of the enterprise. Linkages between people and activities involve handshakes, sequencing, orchestration, and the flow of resources.

Enterprises can be defined at any level of abstraction. As an enterprise, General Motors, for example, supplies automotive products and solutions to the world. But a manufacturer that supplies General Motors with transmission assemblies for automobile manufacturing is also an enterprise. The supplier that provides hardware parts to the transmission manufacturer is also an enterprise. The first order of business, therefore, is to describe carefully the scope or extent of the enterprise that is being analyzed. It is important that you understand the relationships among the component enterprises of a larger enterprise as well as relationships among partner enterprises. These relationships may be of a command and control (directive) nature, as in the case of reporting organizations, or they may be based on agreements and contracts for organizations that do not have formal direct reporting relationships. Some of the issues related to culture are discussed in Chapter 2, as well as styles of influencing that may be brought to bear in managing these interenterprise relationships.

## Airport Example

An airport is an enterprise. At a minimum, it must provide a capability for repeatable and safe aircraft landings and takeoffs. It must also provide capabilities for loading and unloading aircraft cargo, passengers, and crew; for staging them prior to takeoff; and for processing them after landing. Optionally, the airport may provide capabilities for refreshments and food, automobile parking, vending, shopping, and many other possibilities. On the organization side, a major airport may have an airport authority managing the operations, an air traffic management managing traffic, and multiple airline operations centers where the airlines using the airport stage their operations, to cite a few examples.

## Architecture

Simply put, an *architecture*—or, more correctly, an *architecture description*—is a representation of the elements and the relationships among those elements as well as the rules that guide the behavior of those elements. Formally, an architecture is defined by the ANSI/IEEE Standard 1471-2000 as "The fundamental organization of a system, embodied in its components, their relationships to each other and the environment, and the principles governing its design and evolution."

An architecture includes the following:

- Components that form a whole, including structural and/or behavioral elements, which are both types of architectural components
- Relationships among the components
- Principles that govern the design of the components
- Principles that govern the evolution of the components and their relationships in the context of the system they create

John Zachman argues that "Architecture" IS the set of descriptive representations relevant for describing a complex object (actually, any object) such that an instance of the object can be created and such that the descriptive representations serve as the baseline for changing an object instance (assuming that the descriptive representations are maintained consistent with the instantiation)." [Zachman 2015]

Many of the things around us, such as buildings, the highway system, and airports, have implicit architectures that we can observe, at least in terms of components and relationships. However, some components may be hidden, some relationships may be unclear to the casual observer, and the principles that govern the design and evolution of the components and their relationships may be entirely unclear. For example, when I was working for a large commercial building HVAC-control supplier, a local joke was that the Empire State Building was being held up by all the copper wiring inside! Each succeeding contractor ran their own wires because they did not have the wiring plans (that is, an explicit electrical architecture description) and simply cut off the end points of the old wire, leaving the old wire in the building. Anyone who watches the remodeling shows on HGTV knows that house remodelers, who must work from the implicit—that is, the externally observable—architecture of a house, often find unexpected and expensive problems when they open walls and find the hidden components and relationships of the house's architecture. In the same way, implicit architectures are not very useful to people who have to remodel all or part of an enterprise. Thus, we focus on explicit architectures, or architecture descriptions.

## Architecture Descriptions

An *architectural description* is an electronic or paper representation of all aspects of an architecture. This book will use the term "architecture description" synonymously with the word "architecture" from this point on. The DoD Architecture Framework Version 2.0 defines an architectural description as "a strategic information asset that describes the current and/or desired relationships between an organization's business, mission and management processes, and the supporting infrastructure." [DoD 2007] Other sources go farther and include aspects of transformation in the definition of architecture descriptions:

- Architectural descriptions may include a strategy for managing change, along with transitional processes needed to evolve the state of a business or mission to one that is more efficient, effective, current, and capable of providing those actions needed to fulfill its goals and objectives.

- Architectural descriptions may illustrate an organization, or a part of it, as it presently exists; any changes desired (whether operational or technology driven); and the strategies and projects employed to achieve the desired transformation.

- An architectural description also defines principles and goals and sets direction on issues that facilitate enterprise decisions, such as the promotion of interoperability, intra- and interagency information sharing, and improved processes.

- Architecture descriptions represent structural aspects of the enterprise, such as organization structures, physical locations, and equipment and systems, as well as behavioral aspects, such as activities, events, and changes of state of structural elements in the face of such activities and events.

**Benefits of an Explicit Architecture Description**    Why is an explicit architecture concept so important? An architecture (description) is an explicit representation of the elements of an enterprise or part of an enterprise and the relationships among them. Without this explicit representation, the enterprise is unable, for example, to do the following:

- Prioritize resource allocations among the various competing demands for resources.

- Determine the viability of transformation in terms of the impact, the need for resources and change, and the ability to achieve the desired end states.

- Govern the expenditure of current resources and determine whether they are being correctly applied in achieving the enterprise's mission.

- Organize the transformational objectives crisply into initiatives (and projects that follow) that focus on aspects of the enterprise for change.

- Develop roadmaps for modernization.

- Develop roadmaps for orderly replacement of obsolete technology and infrastructure.

- Develop roadmaps for acquiring skills and specialties in the workforce required to operate the enterprise for the future.

# Enterprise Architecture

Informally, an *enterprise architecture* is the concept of "architecture" applied to the concept of "enterprise." There are many competing formal definitions for enterprise architecture, depending on the interest and viewpoint of the defining organizations:

- An enterprise architecture provides a clear and comprehensive picture of the structure of an entity, whether an organization or a functional or mission area. It is an essential tool for effectively and efficiently engineering business processes and for implementing and evolving supporting systems. [GAO 2003] The interest of the Government Accountability Office (GAO) is accountability in terms of effectiveness of investments.

- Simply stated, enterprise architectures are "blueprints" for systematically and completely defining an organization's current (baseline) or desired (target) environment. Enterprise architectures are essential for evolving information systems, developing new systems, and inserting emerging technologies that optimize their mission value. [CIO Council 2001] The interest of the Federal Chief Information Officer (CIO) is Information Technology and information processing systems.

- Enterprise architecture is a management practice to maximize the contribution of an agency's resources, IT investments, and system development activities to achieve its performance goals. Architecture describes clear relationships from strategic goals and objectives through investments to measurable performance improvements for the entire enterprise or a portion (or segment) of the enterprise. [OMB 2012] The interest of the Office of Budget and Management (OMB) is management and financial governance.

- Enterprise architecture is the principle structural mechanism for establishing a basis for assimilating high rates of change, advancing the state of the art in enterprise design, managing the knowledgebase of the enterprise, and integrating the technology into the fabric of the enterprise. Enterprise architecture is cross-disciplinary, requiring diverse skills, methods, and tools within and beyond the technology community. [FEAF 1999] The interest of the CIO council in this area is the need for a common Federal Enterprise Architecture Framework (FEAF).

- "Enterprise architecture is the organizing logic for business processes and IT capabilities reflecting the integration and standardization requirements of the firm's operating model." [MIT CISR]

- "Enterprise Architecture is a management engineering discipline that presents a holistic, comprehensive view of the enterprise including strategic planning, organization, relationships, business process, information, and operations. The organization must be viewed as fluid—changing over time as necessary based on the environment and management's response to that environment." [NASCIO 2017] NASCIO's definition is broader than simply the IT perspective and encompasses a more holistic view of the enterprise. This definition starts with the strategic plan as the foundation for the architecture.

As you can see, the many definitions of enterprise architecture stem from the concerns that make it useful rather than actually defining what it is! Here's a new definition that borrows from the IEEE definition of architecture, adds the enterprise context, and removes the specificity of concerns: Enterprise architecture is a knowledgebase of the behavioral and structural elements of an enterprise, the relationships between these elements, and their evolution over time." The knowledgebase that the enterprise architecture represents can be applied equally well to designing new, complex systems; planning technology insertion; incorporating innovations; or governing expensive investments.

## As-Is and To-Be Architectures

An enterprise is constantly changing. An enterprise architecture description developed at one point in time may no longer be a valid representation of reality at some future point in time. We use the term "as-is," or baseline, to describe the currently modeled representation of the enterprise. At the same time, we may also want to represent what we want the enterprise to look like at a future date using architecture representations as well. This representation of the enterprise architecture at a future date is called the "to-be," or target, enterprise architecture.

The analysis of the differences between the as-is architecture and the to-be architecture is a form of gap analysis. The sum total of changes that need to be effected in various elements of the as-is architecture to achieve the state described by the to-be architecture represents the transformations that needs to be made to the enterprise. The identified gaps are therefore addressed by a transformation that is undertaken in steps. The step-by-step plan that describes the evolution of the enterprise from the baseline state to the target state is called an *Enterprise Transition Roadmap*. As discussed in later chapters, the roadmap may be broken down into different layers related to transformation in multiple aspects of architecture.

In enterprises whose charters are enduring, such as those of federal agencies established by law or the Department of Defense, where doctrine, policy, organization, and force structures and training determine the enterprise's characteristics, the development of an as-is, the formulation of a to-be or target state, and an orderly transformational plan comprising initiatives and projects is a very viable strategy. For enterprises that are founded and based on laws, regulation, and policy, we sometimes talk about an idealized "should-be" state that is predicated on compliance of the laws, regulations, and policies. Such an enterprise state is arguably what is benchmarked during investigations by third-party investigators, such as the Office of Inspector General or the Government Accountability Office (GAO).

## Transformation

Sometimes it is said that every act of construction must begin with an act of engineering analysis. It is only through such analysis, sometimes requiring destruction, that we can divine or verify original intent. We can determine if future intent differs from the original intent and make architectural changes accordingly. Analysis of current operations, systems, and technology infrastructure results in a baseline, or as-is architecture.

Considerable debate has occurred within the architecture community on the value of baselining enterprise states. The argument is that in a constantly changing world, the architecting enterprise gains more benefit from modeling and moving the enterprise to the target state rather than in spending large amounts of architecting resources in looking back at the current state of operations. Yet in areas such as civil engineering projects, any remodeling effort has to ride on the back of an understanding of the current construction. Any act of demolition requires an understanding of what and how to demolish in order to limit the impact of the demolition.

The fact of the matter is that many transformational initiatives in large organizations have failed by failing to take into account traumatic changes that may be imposed upon the enterprise or by failing to realize the inability to reach the target state from the current state within time and cost constraints. Cultural impacts may result in (often unwitting) sabotage of those initiatives by human beings who are unwilling to change. A lack of understanding of complexities of current business rules and processes has left some modernization efforts with failed transformation after exceeding the scheduled time frame by years and scheduled cost by millions. A successful transformation plan must reflect an understanding of the current state and cultural factors of the enterprise. It needs to set realistic transformational initiatives that are phased according to the enterprise's ability to absorb and finance change.

Some recent documented and spectacular complex project failures such as the U.S. Air Force's Expeditionary Combat Support System (ECSS)—a write-off of more than $1 billion—illustrate the need to represent and socialize architectural representations and impacts and anticipate problems before diving into implementation. ECSS represents a class of failed complex enterprise resource planning systems, where multiyear investments continued to flow into a large program plagued by failure to adhere to principles of business process reengineering, cultural resistance to change within the Air Force, and lack of leadership to implement needed changes. The replacement of existing systems or families of systems by new integrated enterprise resource planning (ERP) systems are especially prone to issues of organizational and cultural factors that need to be addressed as well as issues of understanding how the business currently operates.

The time needed to develop a baseline architecture is often perceived as a luxury in the commercial world, where the pace of change is often forced by competition and alternatives that are outside the control of the architecting enterprise. In this world, in situations where new products and services are offered, entire new enterprises are created by founding, mergers, or acquisitions. These new enterprises exhibit complex behaviors that must be factored into the transformation plan. Often, these new enterprises behave like startups—an area where traditional enterprise architecture study has not generally focused. They are driven by extreme financial goals under extreme time constraints, often with extreme resource constraints, and where common motivation for individual profit and reward outweigh all other cultural considerations, at least for a few years.

Here's an example: Most airports are constantly in transition. They face pressures of increasing traffic of departures and arrivals, increasing passenger traffic through the airport, upgrading of technology to meet passenger and stakeholder expectations of performance, convenience and amenities—and all of these pressures drive the need for change. Once an airport is operational, it is essential that it make incremental transformations while staying open for business. A large transformation will therefore have to be broken down into small increments that disrupt the operations of the airport to the smallest extent possible. The airport master plan is the instrument for describing the planned transformation increments to the airport. It contains a sequence of to-be states that describe the intermediate steps within the planned transformation.

**Emergence**    There is one further complication for enterprise transformation: *emergence*. Because nothing stands still as the enterprise is being transformed, both external and internal forces may change enterprise elements in unplanned ways. Unexpected shifts in the marketplace, new competitors, and breakthrough technology may require changes to the transformation roadmap and change the enterprise's strategic vision and target state. Workers may find that planned new processes don't work well and may develop new ones on their own. In short, we must be ready for a new version of the enterprise to emerge from the old in response to unplanned, reactive evolution of the enterprise.

The approach to architecting for the emergent enterprise involves careful attention to the sustainment and maintenance of the architecture (discussed in Chapter 8). The enterprise architecture in such enterprises serves as a knowledgebase for option exposure and exploration rather than as a compass for transformation planning. Architecting is performed on the things that matter, rather than attempting a comprehensive representation of every aspect of the enterprise. In the airport, temporary emergent behavior occurs when a single or a few airlines have scheduling problems and passengers desperately try to reroute their travel via other airlines. The planning factors that have established the size of the check-in counters, the number of booking agents, and the ability to move passengers through the reservation, ticketing, and boarding processes are severely restricted by available capacity. If this is a normal occurrence, airlines will adapt over time to an unexpected rush of passengers with routine responses that are permanently built into their enterprise.

## Reference Architectures

A *reference architecture* is a special form of enterprise architecture that provides a template architecture for enterprises or partitions of enterprises, such as segments, that have observed or desired similarities. For example, U.S. government agencies called "commissions" have organizational structures, functions, and processes dictated by law. Examples of these agencies are the Securities and Exchange Commission and the Nuclear Regulatory Commission. This means that you could build a reference architecture with template organization charts, template high-level activity models, and other template views that could be refined to provide at least a should-be architecture for a new commission. Similarly, if a company had a specific way it wanted a regional office to be set up and run, it could develop a reference architecture for regional offices that could be used to describe any regional office or to set up a new regional office.

# Architecture Frameworks

One of the key decisions prior to developing an enterprise architecture is the selection of an *architecture framework*. In general, architecture frameworks provide guidance on what to include in an enterprise architecture and how to structure and organize the information. An architecture framework provides guidance and rules for structuring, classifying, and organizing architectures [DoD 2007].

Architecture frameworks use organizing concepts such as levels of enterprise, viewpoints and views, integrated metamodels, and methodologies and processes, each of which is discussed in general in the following sections. Not all frameworks use all of these concepts, but when they do use a concept, the terminology, organization, and structure may be very different from what is used in another framework. The concepts used in each of today's four major frameworks are summarized in the chapter that addresses that specific framework: the Zachman Framework in Chapter 21, the U.S. Department of Defense Architecture Framework (DoDAF) and its related defense frameworks in Chapter 4, The Open Group Architecture Framework (TOGAF) in Chapter 22, and the Federal Enterprise Architecture Framework Version 2.0 (FEAF2) in Chapter 23.

# Levels of Enterprise

As mentioned, the definition of enterprise is very flexible; enterprises come in many sizes and shapes. Because many enterprises are too large to be fully described in one document, there are ways of breaking them up into pieces that can be described separately and in such a way to be integrated or related to each other at a later time. One of the first steps in developing an enterprise architecture is to set the scope and level of detail of an architecture. Various levels of enterprise detail ranges from an extended enterprise down to solutions and initiatives.

## Extended Enterprise

Few enterprises, if any, are self-sufficient or self-contained. One enterprise may have a network of partner enterprises that provides various capabilities and resources needed to run the first enterprise. The *extended enterprise* is a representation of this network of partnerships. Extended partners may include supplychain participants, information technology service providers, marketing and sales partners, and others.

Our airport example includes capabilities for security checks (provided by the Transportation Safety Agency and local law enforcement), capabilities for air traffic control (provided by the Federal Aviation Administration), and capabilities for refreshments, food, drinks, and sustenance of airport employees, passengers, crew members, and airline staff (provided by a food concessionaire corporation). As we extend the scope of capabilities that we want to include within an architecture, we see that the extended enterprise begins to proliferate!

## Partitioning the Enterprise

How do we break up the complexity of enterprises into smaller units? In the commercial world, a large complex enterprise can be broken down into smaller business units, each responsible for some area of business or "product lines." In the government, often this breakdown of the enterprise is in the form of functional organizations responsible for various business functions. In holding companies, each of the businesses that form a conglomerate is a smaller enterprise that has a financial (profit-and-loss) relationship with the parent enterprise.

**Segments**    In any case, governing a large enterprise involves partitioning the enterprise into smaller enterprises called *enterprise segments*, or *segments* in short. At each stage of the partitioning, one or more criteria may be used to determine the scope of the segments:

- **Partitioning along business areas**    Widely differing business areas are partitioned into widely different subenterprises. An area of business may therefore be an enterprise segment. If the business areas are large and complex, a further partitioning may be required.

- **Partitioning along product lines or service areas**    In product- or service-based enterprises, each product line or service area may have differing characteristics and therefore different "enterprise patterns" for fulfillment. An area of business, line of business, or product line or service area may be a legitimate segment of an enterprise architecture. If the product line is too broad or complex, further partitioning into smaller segments may be required.

- **Partitioning along functional boundaries**    Areas such as marketing, sales, engineering, and manufacturing may all be segments of the larger enterprise architecture. Functional architectures, without the integrating mechanism that unifies the functions and cross-thread processes that are performed by individual functions, results in stovepipe processes that may be optimized for the function but not for the enterprise. For example, if the process producing hubcaps efficiently produces 200 hubcaps a minute for an assembly line assembling one car per minute that consumes only four of the hubcaps, producing more hubcaps faster will not improve the overall throughput of cars coming off the assembly line.

- **Partitioning along physical boundaries**    Large and complex organizations that are geographically distributed can be partitioned into subsets that are physically colocated as independent partitions that are connected by collaboration and coordination.

- **Partitioning along subpatterns**    In enterprises that have undergone standardization efforts such as the military or the federal government, parts of the enterprise are built along some common architecture pattern. For example, Air Force bases are constructed and staffed using a common pattern as are Navy bases and Army bases. Field offices in certain federal agencies such as the one for the Securities and Exchange Commission exhibit the same four functions of corporation finance, market regulation, investment management, and enforcement. Regulatory enterprises that are regulated by laws, such as the Federal Administrative Procedures Act, for example, are forced to have a common organizational structure and apply high-level processes such as rulemaking in a common way. Recognizing these subpatterns enables us to decompose the larger complex enterprise into smaller subenterprises that can be individually modeled for analysis. These architecture patterns can also be translated into reference architectures.

Why is partitioning complex enterprises into segments useful? *Decomposition* is a common technique to address complexity analysis. By decomposing a large enterprise into segments, the architecture development and the analysis become easier. Also, the large, complex enterprise is an abstract concept for most stakeholders involved in the day-to-day operations of the enterprise. Decomposing an enterprise into something smaller also brings closeness of the issues and architecture elements to such stakeholders. Arguably, the enterprise stakeholder pyramid has a small but very influential group at the top, for which the enterprise vantage point is both important and useful. But a larger group of stakeholders in the middle and at the bottom of the stakeholder pyramid have a stake in the daily operations of the enterprise. Without bringing the detail down to their level of abstraction, the enterprise architecture simply becomes a theoretical exercise targeted solely for upper management.

Segments also provide direct visibility of operations that can be tied to specific projects and initiatives. This direct tie-in enables portfolio managers who are balancing the investments in projects and initiatives to make a more accurate impact assessment of the project or initiative on the specific operational activities undertaken within an enterprise segment.

**Solutions**  A *solution architecture* is the lowest level of enterprise architecture, or the finest partition of an enterprise. What is a solution? A solution is a system that provides automated or nonautomated support for business processes. We use the word "system" in the general sense as a set of components that together provide the functionality support and desired outputs for a business process. A system may comprise smaller systems, called a system of systems, or cooperate and collaborate with other systems in a family of systems.

An initiative or a project is responsible for delivering a single solution, a family of solutions, or some aspect of a solution. An *initiative* is a collection of resources aimed at achieving an explicit purpose or outcome. A *project* is a schedule of activities that will implement an initiative and expend the resources allocated to that initiative. Together, initiatives and projects are used to transform an enterprise to a desired end state. Enterprise architecture provides the knowledgebase for planning this transformation in an orderly manner, recognizing dependencies, risks, and issues before actual transformation projects are undertaken.

An example initiative that is currently being implemented at larger airports everywhere is the rapid processing of prescreened passengers through security checkpoints. The scope of the solution for each airport is restricted to processing prescreened passengers with credentials that are validated before rapid processing commences. TSA Pre is an example of this type of prescreening. This initiative divides the current single long queues at airport security checkpoints into two groups: one that contains only prescreened passengers and another for the general traveling public.

**Airport Example**  In our airport example, following are some of the levels of architecting that we could potentially undertake, given the needs of the sponsor and the scope of the problem set being addressed:

- The entire *extended airport enterprise*
- The *airport enterprise* for core functions of the airport performed internally without partners

- *Vertical segment* architectures for capability groups such as passenger management, aircraft maintenance, air-traffic control, and concession management

- *Horizontal segments* such as financial management and human resource management

- *Solutions* for specific problems such as passenger or employee identification, concession revenue improvement, and airport expansion planning

### Federated Architectures

*Federated architectures* are enterprise architectures assembled or made up from the separately developed architectures of the enterprise's component parts. A federated architecture could be an architecture for an extended enterprise, where the independent architectures have been developed by a large enterprise and its various partners. Or it could be an enterprise architecture for a very large enterprise, such as the U.S. Executive Departments, assembled from the architectures developed by the set of partitions of the enterprise. Clearly, there would have to be detailed guidance provided to each architecture development group in order for these subarchitectures to be compatible enough to assemble into a coherent whole. For example, all the component architectures would have to use the same framework and interfaces, or relationships between elements in different subarchitectures would have to be agreed upon. Terms and vocabularies would also have to be agreed upon. This is a place where reference models (see the "Reference Models" section later in the chapter) are useful.

## Viewpoints

One of the organizing structures that most architecture frameworks provide is called a viewpoint. *Viewpoints* are key to connecting the people who need to see the architecture to those parts of the architecture in which they are most interested.

### Stakeholders

Who is an enterprise architecture stakeholder? Informally, an *architecture stakeholder* is any organization, role, or group that uses the architecture to support decision-making or understanding. One definition of enterprise architecture stakeholder is "an individual, team, or organization (or classes thereof) with interests in, or concerns relative to, the outcome of the architecture. Different stakeholders with different roles will have different concerns." [TOGAF 2009]

One of the first tasks while architecting the enterprise, after defining the purpose and scope of the architecting exercise, is to identify the stakeholders and their concerns related to the architecture. What are the issues that they want to solve through understanding the architecture representation and the connections between the architecture elements?

**Airport Example**   In the airport, there are multiple stakeholders, as is usual in most enterprises. When the airport is being constructed or expanded, stakeholders may include those who are involved in the land acquisition, financing, environmental impact analysis, municipal and local government, airport management, construction companies and contractors, and many others.

After the airport is operational, some of these initial stakeholders' roles are diminished or irrelevant, and the architect has to deal with many new stakeholders such as passengers, airlines, airline employees, airport employees, airline crew members, concession owners and operators, cargo and baggage handlers, parking ramp operators, medical service providers, and many others.

Depending on the scope of the architecting effort, not all stakeholders of the enterprise need to be considered as factors. Solution architectures, for example, will involve a subset of stakeholders. Automation architectures such as a system for automated baggage handling will introduce stakeholders who must operate and sustain the automation.

Chapter 5 includes a more thorough discussion of stakeholders.

## Stakeholders and Viewpoints

The difficulty in representing architecture descriptions in a universal format stems from the fact that different stakeholders of the enterprise have different viewpoints and interests. The need to support multiple viewpoints is fundamental for architecture. During architecture development, the architect must determine which viewpoints will be supported by architecture representations. In general, architecture frameworks have tried to codify the types of viewpoints that are supported by the framework. Due to the traditional evolution of enterprise architecting, these viewpoints, such as applications, data, and infrastructure and technology tend to be IT-centric. However, the concept of a viewpoint is very general and can be used to describe the common concerns of any group of stakeholders.

Here are some examples of typical viewpoints:

- A viewpoint for enterprise management, strategy, and planning
- A viewpoint for business process designers, managers, and operators
- A viewpoint for IT/automation designers, managers, developers, and maintainers
- A viewpoint for data managers and users

Viewpoints are very useful in architecture work:

- Viewpoints provide visibility of architecture elements that are important from that viewpoint; however, architecture elements that are of no concern are invisible from that viewpoint!
- Viewpoints reduce the scope of architecting by restricting the architect only to elements that are important from that viewpoint.
- Viewpoints generally reflect common concerns from a specialized group of stakeholders who have well-established models, artifacts, and techniques. The stakeholders' familiarity with the terms and definitions of these representations makes it easy to communicate with these stakeholders.
- Viewpoints that are codified by an architecture framework provide a standardized way to represent architectures. Implementing standardized ways to represent the architecture for specific groups of stakeholders makes it possible to aggregate, compare, and analyze architectures using common methods.

## Views

A *view* is used to address a subset of the concerns of a specific viewpoint and is specific to a single viewpoint. In the world of buildings, architecture is represented in several standardized views, including a floor plan that describes the layout of various parts of the building and a front elevation drawing that describes how the building looks from the front. Each of these methods of representation uses symbols for denoting architectural elements. For example, in a floor plan, walls and openings are drawn in a consistent manner that is comprehensible to any architect who is trying to understand the building design.

Views may be represented informally as pictures and unstructured documents, formally as mathematical models, or semiformally as relationship matrices and timeline charts. Though the definition of a model is quite rigorous in the mathematical and computer science domains, frameworks may refer to views of any form as a model or to views in general as architecture artifacts or products. A viewpoint is defined using one or more views.

## Artifacts

*Artifact* is a general term that describes any type of architecture representation in document form. The TOGAF 9 Standard describes an artifact as "an architectural work product that describes an aspect of the architecture. Artifacts are generally classified as catalogs (lists of things), matrices (showing relationships between things), and diagrams (pictures of things). Examples include a requirements catalog, business interaction matrix, and a use-case diagram. An architectural deliverable may contain many artifacts." [The Open Group 2009]

Multiple views may be required to represent all aspects of the viewpoint. For example, a business process model, a resources flow model, and an organizational chart might be included to represent a business operational viewpoint.

**Pictures**   A *picture* is an informal graphical representation that is not governed by any specific rules of construction. The primary criterion for a picture is that it "convey the information that the architect is trying to convey." Because of the variety of architects and audiences alike, the effectiveness of the picture in conveying information is also varied. Different architects could draw different pictures of the same object they are architecting, resulting in no consistency in communicating understanding. Understanding the representation becomes a hit-or-miss exercise!

**Semiformal Views**   *Structured documents* (that is, documents that have a prescribed outline or content requirements), matrices, and graphics with limited syntax and semantic rules are all examples of semiformal views. Syntaxes are rules for physical representation that tell when a view is properly formed or, in technical terms, *well-formed*. For example, structured documents such as reports have outlines that specify required section headings and their order. Such a report will be rejected if it is not in the correct format. However, it takes a human to decide whether the content of the sections actually makes sense—that is, whether it has meaningful semantics.

**Formal Models**     *Models* are formal representations, graphical or otherwise, that are constructed according to a set of specific syntax and semantics rules. These rules determine, for example, which symbol can be connected to which other symbol and describe what the meaning of the links and symbols are in a consistent manner. By controlling the construction (syntax) as well as the meaning (semantics) of model objects and interconnections through a set of well-established and agreed-upon rules, architects can use the models to communicate with one another in a consistent manner. By formalizing the semantics and structures of the models, formal models can be used to perform mathematical analyses and drive simulations used to estimate measures of performance and the effectiveness of the architecture in the face of requirements that drove that architecture's design.

Architecture models are electronic or paper representations of some aspect of an architecture for some specific audience. Models comprise model elements, which are also architecture elements. Model elements have relationships based on some defined semantics—that is, they are not haphazard assemblies of architecture elements but follow constraints described by a methodology or an accepted set of practices. These semantics may be driven by the laws of nature, existential relationships, human creations, or abstractions. Architecture models are therefore pictorial or other representations that have structure and meaning to specific audiences. The organization of the types of elements and their relationships contained within a model or a set of models is called a *metamodel.* The metamodel controls what elements and relationships are valid in the context of a model or a set of models. It acts as a rulebook for a modeler.

Models are also blueprints for audiences who understand what they are trying to communicate. Just as a floor plan conveys the layout of various parts of a building to a number of audiences, from the homeowner to the architect to the city inspector, a carefully constructed model that is compliant with conventions and well laid out conveys a wealth of meaning in an unambiguous manner to the right people.

## Reference Models

*Reference models* are taxonomies that are associated with frameworks and usually serve to control vocabularies so that architectures developed by different organizations can be federated or more easily compared. Examples are taxonomies of business functions and standards. At the enterprise level, reference models may stand in for viewpoint views. For example, at the highest enterprise level, the business process view may simply consist of a reference model containing the taxonomy of business functions for the enterprise rather than any detailed view of actual business processes or activities.

## Integration

We encounter two problems when we are looking at an architectural description or representation organized into a set of viewpoints and views. We need to ensure that the description provides both a complete and a consistent description of reality or target vision. We also need to ensure that the views are integrated both within and across the viewpoints. That is, we need to know that all the architectural elements needed appear in some view and that these architectural elements appear in all the views and viewpoints where they are appropriate. Each architectural element must be identified by the same name in all the views in which it appears and all of the relevant aspects of the architectural element must be described. The views should not be disjoint. That is, a view should always contain some elements that also appear in or are easily related to elements in other views. Achieving this integration leads us to a topic in the next section: integrated metamodels.

## Repositories and Metamodels

Frameworks may provide two additional related structuring and organizing concepts: repositories and metamodels.

### Repositories

Frameworks may have explicit or implicit requirements for architecture repositories. These repositories contain information about the architecture elements and views. Some frameworks, such as TOGAF, may require several different types of repositories for different types of architecture components, as described in Chapter 22.

There may be a special view called a *dictionary* that contains the definitions and other relevant information about all of the terms and architecture elements used in the architecture. The "other relevant information" may include relationships between architecture elements or information about views or elements that does not appear on relevant view diagrams or graphics. This information may be omitted from the view diagrams or graphics because of space and readability considerations, or it may reflect relationships between views or view elements that are only implied by the diagrams or graphics. Formal models often have requirements for what information should be provided about elements of the model. For example, the ICAM Definition for Functional Modeling (IDEF0) has specific requirements about what must be documented.

The need for a repository is implicit, because the difficulty of developing and maintaining a non-trivial architecture without some form of a dictionary and repository management system makes such an approach impractical. Repository concepts are discussed further in Part II.

### Metamodels

The organization of the types of elements and their relationships contained within a view or a set of views is called a *metamodel*. The metamodel controls what elements and relationships are valid in the context of a view or a set of views. It acts as a rulebook for the architect. An integrated metamodel recognizes that all the views are describing different facets of a single reality.

The biggest risk with a large set of viewpoints and views is the risk of defining the same architecture elements differently in different viewpoints and views and thereby creating multiple versions of reality. Without a unifying framework and an integrated metamodel that is defined by the framework, this is a very real risk. The integrated metamodel provides a schema for any dictionary and ensures that if an element appears in more than one architecture representation, it must be defined in the same way. The flaws in nonintegrated architecture representations become very obvious during the analysis and use phase of the architecture, as different analyses of the representation can bring up conflicting answers.

This chapter has discussed the concept of views as architecture representations that have symbols and linkages between symbols. Each of the symbols represents a certain type of architecture element. For example, if the model represents the logical organization of a database as one aspect of the architecture, the symbols on the diagram represent database entity types. The links between the entity type symbols represent the allowable types of relationships between the participating entity types. The collection of symbol types and linkage types allowable in a specific view are considered the metamodel for that type of view. Each formal modeling technique is usually associated with a metamodel, usually defined by a standards body such as American National Standards Institute (ANSI), Federal Information Processing Standards (FIPS), Object Management Group (OMG), or the Institution for Electrical and Electronics Engineers (IEEE), to cite a few examples, or in the mathematical literature. The metamodel is, in effect, the language with which the model speaks to its audience.

As illustrated in later chapters, architecting a complex entity such as an enterprise requires the development of many types of views. Many of these views are formal models developed using their own methodologies and associated metamodels. If the metamodels of the various models are not integrated—that is, are not compatible in their languages—the models developed will be disjointed. Like the reports of the five unsighted men attempting to describe an elephant, the models, when taken together, will not provide a coherent picture of the enterprise. Many frameworks have recognized this issue and resolved metamodel inconsistencies in their collection of views by using an ontological approach to describe how architecture element types are defined as well as the types of relationships they can participate in.

## Ontology

*Ontology* is the study of existence or reality: what kinds of things exist (in our case, types of architectural elements) and the types of relationships between them. Ontology is associated with a domain of discourse. Terms that describe objects that exist are commonly understood within a domain of discourse, although they may have synonyms and antonyms outside that domain of discourse. Architecture frameworks may include an ontology to support their integrated metamodel.

For example, in the domain of discourse of defense architecture descriptions, the Department of Defense Architecture Framework (DoDAF) and Ministry of Defense (United Kingdom) Architecture Framework (MODAF) have established a joint set of standard ontological concepts and relationships, such as activity, performer, and resource flows, that are abstract and can encompass the terms of specific modeling methodologies such as IDEF0. Thus, an IDEF0 *mechanism* is interpreted as a *performer* in the ontology, since the mechanism performs/enables an *activity*. Ontology is used as semantic shorthand in describing large numbers of concrete relationships compactly using a few specifications and enables the integration of metamodels.

# Methodologies and Process

Architecture frameworks may include a methodology or process to guide the development and evolution of architecture. A 2012 Office of Management and Budget report defines architecture methodology as "the repeatable process by which architecture documentation will be developed, archived, and used; including the selection of principles, a framework, modeling tools, artifacts, repository, reporting, and auditing." [OMB 2012] However, the process included with a framework may be a detailed, phased, or step-by-step methodology to developing and evolving architecture, or it may be something simpler. Some frameworks do not supply any process advice. The discussions of the major architecture frameworks in Chapters 4, 21, 22, and 23 provide details of the methodology or process features of these frameworks.

## Summary

In this, the first chapter of this book, we introduce concepts of the enterprise and the description of its architecture that we call the enterprise architecture. We have introduced an understanding that the architecture is a basis for planning for change. We have introduced the concept of viewpoints that show different people in the enterprise, different views of the enterprise based on their own motivations, languages, background knowledge, and skill sets. We have also introduced the concept of architecture frameworks to show how diverse architecture descriptions can be normalized through a set of constructs that force commonality of description while preserving the diversity of viewpoints. We have introduced modeling as a fundamental practice in architecting as a way to represent architecture descriptions using pictorial, both structured and unstructured, representations as well as formal methods both to capture an understanding of the architecture as well as to provide a platform for performing analyses.

We want to stress that this book is intended to capture the overall concepts of enterprise architecting that are common to all EA frameworks in much the same way a book on Relational Database Management captures salient features of commercially available vendor products. We stress the commonality of EA concepts, techniques, and procedures.

## Questions

1. What is an enterprise? What are the fundamental characteristics of an enterprise? How would you describe the scope of your specific enterprise? Based on the narratives of the levels of architecture scope, which level of scope does your enterprise fall into?

2. What are some methods to reduce the complexity of analyzing a large and complex enterprise?

3. What is enterprise transformation? What are initiatives and projects in the context of enterprise transformation? What is an enterprise transformation roadmap? Why is it useful in guiding the transformation process?

4. A forecast is a prediction of the state of something at a particular point in time. How does the enterprise transformation roadmap align with anticipated business forecasts, technology forecasts? What viewpoints are needed to ensure such an alignment?

5. What is the definition of architecture? Discuss, using your definition, various characteristics of architecture that are related to the quality of an architecture. What are some of the architecture attributes that are needed to understand the context of the architecture such as creation, modification, ownership, duration, cost, and so on?

6. What is an architecture description? Discuss the existence of implicit and explicit architecture representations inside your specific enterprise. What is the usefulness of having explicit architecture descriptions? How can architecture descriptions be kept up to date? Discuss the differences in frequency of change of different types of architecture descriptions.

7. What is the purpose of building or representing the as-is state of an enterprise? How would you justify the building of an as-is architecture description for your own enterprise? What information would you need to build the as-is architecture representation of your enterprise?

8. What is the purpose of building a target or to-be state of an enterprise? How would you go about building a to-be state of your enterprise? Where would you start and what information would you need? How would you address architecting a constantly changing enterprise?

9. What are the viewpoints that are important to your enterprise? What stakeholders' needs are addressed by those viewpoints? What views within those viewpoints will address the challenges of the stakeholders for that viewpoint?

# References

Architecture Working Group (AWG). 1997. "C4ISR Architecture Framework Version 2.0." www.afcea.org/education/courses/archfwk2.pdf.

CIO Council. 2001. "A Practical Guide to Federal Enterprise Architecture, Version 1.0." www.gao.gov/assets/590/588407.pdf.

CIO Council. 1999. "Federal Enterprise Architecture Framework, Version 1.1." www.bettergovernment.jp/diki?files_download&filename=fedarch1.pdf.

Department of Defense. 2007. DoD Architecture Framework Version 1.5. "Volume I: Definitions and Guidelines." dodcio.defense.gov/Portals/0/Documents/DoDaF/DoDAF_Volume_I.pdf.

Department of Defense. 2007. DoD Architecture Framework Version 1.5. "Volume II: Product Descriptions." dodcio.defense.gov/Portals/0/Documents/DODAF/DoDAF_Volume_II.pdf.

Department of Defense. 2007. DoD Architecture Framework Version 1.5. "Volume III: Architecture Data Description." dodcio.defense.gov/Portals/0/Documents/DODAF/DoDAF_Volume_III.pdf.

Department of Defense. 2010. "DoD Architecture Framework 2.02—DoD Deputy Chief Information Officer." http://dodcio.defense.gov/Library/DoD-Architecture-Framework/

FEA Program Office, U.S. Office of Management and Budget. 2007. "FEA Practice Guidance." www.fsa.usda.gov/Assets/USDA-FSA-Public/usdafiles/SDLC-non-secure/Enterprise-Architecture-Program-/Training/Docs/FEA_Practice_Guidance_Nov_2007.pdf.

Federal Enterprise Architecture Program Management Office. 2007. "FEA Consolidated Reference Model Document Version 2.3." www.reginfo.gov/public/jsp/Utilities/FEA_CRM_v23_Final_Oct_2007_Revised.pdf.

Federal Segment Architecture Methodology (FSAM), Version 1.0. 2008. http://bettergovernment.jp/resources/FSAMv1.pdf.

Government Accountability Office. 2003. "Information Technology. A Framework for Assessing and Improving Enterprise Architecture Management. Version 1.1." (GAO-03-584G)

Greefhorst, Danny, and Erik Proper. 2011. *Architecture Principles: The Cornerstones of Enterprise Architecture*. New York: Springer.

Harrison, Rachel. 2016. *TOGAF 9 Foundation Study Guide*, 3rd Ed. The Netherlands: Van Haren Publishing.

International Organization for Standardization (ISO). 2000–06. "15704:2000: Industrial automation systems: Requirements for enterprise-reference architectures and methodologies."

Merriam-Webster Dictionary online. nd. www.merriam-webster.com/dictionary/enterprise.

MIT Center or Information Systems Research (CISR). nd. "Enterprise Architecture." https://cisr.mit.edu/research/research-overview/classic-topics/enterprise-architecture/.

MODAF—United Kingdom Ministry of Defense Architecture Framework. https://www.gov.uk/guidance/mod-architecture-framework.

National Association of State Chief Information Officers (NASCIO). 2007. "Building Better Government through Enterprise Architecture." www.nascio.org/Publications/ArtMID/485/ArticleID/218/Building-Better-Government-through-Enterprise-Architecture.

Office of Management and Budget. 2012. "The Common Approach to Federal Enterprise Architecture." https://obamawhitehouse.archives.gov/sites/default/files/omb/assets/egov_docs/common_approach_to_federal_ea.pdf.

Office of the DoD CIO. Office of the Assistant Secretary of Defense, Networks and Information Integration (OASD/NII). 2010. "Reference Architecture Description. dodcio.defense.gov/Portals/0/Documents/DIEA/Ref_Archi_Description_Final_v1_18Jun10.pdf.

Permanent Subcommittee on Investigations of the Committee on Homeland Security and Governmental Affairs, United States Senate. 2014. "The Air Force's Expeditionary Combat Support System (ECSS): A Cautionary Tale on the Need for Business Process Reengineering and Complying with Acquisition Best Practices." www.gpo.gov/fdsys/pkg/CPRT-113SPRT89869/pdf/CPRT-113SPRT89869.pdf.

Spewak, Steven H. 1993. *Enterprise Architecture Planning: Developing a Blueprint for Data, Applications, and Technology.* New York: Wiley.

The Open Group. 2006. "The Open Group Architecture Framework Version 8.1.1, Enterprise Edition." pubs.opengroup.org/architecture/togaf8-doc/arch/.

The Open Group. 2009. "TOGAF Version 9: An Open Group Standard." pubs.opengroup.org/architecture/togaf9-doc/arch/index.html.

Zachman, John A. 2015. "Enterprise Physics 101." Zachman International blog. www.zachman.com/resources/zblog/item/enterprise-physics-101.

# The Importance of Culture, Climate, and Tribes in the Context of Enterprise Architecture

In this chapter, we consider the influences of culture and the related concepts of tribes and organizational climate on enterprise architecture (EA). As described in Chapter 1, the essence of EA involves planning and transformation of enterprises. However, no matter how carefully we plan for change and account for the nature of the systems we are concerned with, we face emergent and unexpected consequences resulting from human factors. Such factors can, however, be understood based on the culture of the enterprise and the metacultures (occupational, regional, national, and beyond) in which it is situated.

Cultures are like nested dolls or layers of an onion: as we peel or open one culture, we find that others are nested within, and each of those layers concomitantly provide a wider universe in which they are embedded. This is the dilemma: How do we characterize the culture of the enterprise or the portions of the culture that impact the transformation projects we propose? This chapter discusses approaches to culture and proposes how they can be modeled and incorporated into a project for the purposes of creating EA. It examines various ways of viewing, characterizing, and analyzing culture and documenting it within an architecture. Culture is an important concept, because it influences the attitudes and behaviors of members of organizations and enterprises and thus impacts their reactions to attempts at organizational or enterprise transformation.

## Introduction to Culture

It is a common assertion that although all humans have culture, it is something we learn, and in the case of national and ethnic cultures, it is passed down between generations. In addition to such macro notions of culture, we recognize its relevance to virtually all forms of human collectivity, including those we identify as enterprises and organizations.

## Origins of Culture Study

The formal study of culture emerged from the disciplines of anthropology and sociology during the colonial period of European and American political expansions over different populations with intent to administer and control them better. This introduced a variety of functionalist and structural theories for understanding different types of organization, from highly controlled hierarchical bodies, to self-adapting structures such as African segmentary lineage, or tribal, systems. These systems can be described as "tribes without rulers," where lineages have formed into larger entities based on need and circumstances to manage some external risk. They are sometimes called "ordered anarchies."

In the late 1970s, the concept of culture was first introduced to the study of formal organizations [Pettigrew 1979]. This led to ethnographic studies of organizations, such as Edgar Schein on the Digital Equipment Corporation (2004), Gideon Kunda (2006) on engineering culture, Michael Lynch (1985) on laboratory culture, and Eric Livingston (2016) on mathematical reasoning. Concomitant with qualitative based organizational culture studies, particularly within the management and organizational behavior disciplines, a more quantitative approach focused on attitudes and behaviors across organizations, forming the basis for studies in organizational climate.

## Organizational Climate and Organizational Culture

In the introduction to their handbook of organizational climate and culture studies, Schneider and Barbera (2014) provided the following working definition for *organizational climate*: "the meaning organizational employees attach to the policies, practices, and procedures they experience and the behaviors they observe getting rewarded, supported and expected." This is contrasted with *organizational culture*: "the values and beliefs that characterize organizations, as transmitted by the socialization experiences newcomers have, the decisions made by management, and the stories and myths people tell and re-tell about their organizations." These definitions suggest that climate is at a conscious and behavioral level and is more easily changed than the underlying value and belief structures of culture that underlie such behavior. According to Schein, organizational climate can be considered a visible artifact of the underlying taken-for-granted assumption system constituting the basis of culture.

## Corporate Tribes

In addition to culture and climate is the concept of corporate tribes. Joanne Martin (2002) describes organizational cultures as being simultaneously integrated, differentiated, and fragmented. A tribe can be considered a differentiated part of a larger cultural manifestation that maintains its own identity and political foundation [Wilcock 2004]. As with the anthropological characterization, a corporate culture can be organized into a number of clans or tribes. These share common cultural assumptions but are corporate entities that often compete with one another. In organizational contexts, tribes are usually groups of between 20 and 150 people. When networks scale, they produce phase transitions common to all organisms, cities, economies, or companies.

As described in Malcom Gladwell's *The Tipping Point* (2000), tribes adapt and shift in how they exercise power. For the purposes of this book, we consider tribes to be politicized cohorts (that is, groups) that can either facilitate or impede organizational initiatives. Tribes can function either formally or informally as communities of practice, and they can also function across organizational boundaries. An example of tribal influence can be seen in the analysis of the over $1.1 billion failure of an ERP (Enterprise Resource Planning) Oracle implementation: the Expeditionary Combat Support System (ECSS) for the Air Force. The Government Accountability Office and Congress eventually determined that the most significant issues underlying that failure were cultural. This finding is particularly telling, because defense organizations, such as the Air Force, have a highly organized command and control hierarchy, yet efforts to implement ECSS were impeded by a highly fragmented and diversified organizational cultural reality. Tribal cohorts led resistance to change and negatively impacted the success of the project. In this book, we consider how culture, tribes, and organizational climate differences impact enterprise architecture, and we suggest approaches for their effective management.

Chapter 3, in the case study of an airport, introduces a variety of architecture viewpoints. These viewpoints are representative of differentiated subcultures or tribal perspectives including air operations, cargo, security, TSA, and air traffic management. As of this writing, the administration has advanced the privatization of air traffic control as the first major infrastructure proposal. We can anticipate cultural response and forms of resistance from NATCA (National Air Traffic Control Association). In 2006, the FAA imposed drastic cuts in their contract with NATCA, resulting in lower salaries for new employees and changes in working conditions. This led to a significant staffing crisis, increases in runway incursions, and an increase in delays. A shift toward privatization has both supporters and detractors within the union, and depending on location, the implementation of such a plan must address the cultural acceptance of such a transformation.

Likewise, an airport's decision of whether to use TSA or outsource security screening to security contractors proffers both advantages and challenges to FAA employees, who form a cohort that can coalesce into tribal resistance to change. Such challenges can present themselves as opportunities if the cultural assumptions of the tribal entities are understood and incorporated into EA planning and structure. The natures of such underlying assumption systems are discussed in this chapter.

# Understanding Culture: Language Perspective

Culture is like *language* (and is expressed within it), in that every human society has language, and its possession as a symbolic mode of representation is one of the distinguishing features of being human. Like language, cultural structure functions at an underlying level and is, as organizational culture theorist Geert Hofstede included in a title of one of his books, the "software of the mind." As he explains, culture involves unwritten rules of a social game, and "is the collective programming of the mind that distinguishes the members of one group or category of people from another." [Hofstede 2010] This "collective programming" obtains at every level of culture. One way of understanding culture is as a system, and systems science recognizes that systems exist within systems. We must identify the boundaries of the cultural system that interests us in our architectural analysis.

If we understand a system as being composed of two or more subsystems oriented toward a common purpose, we can situate cultures within cultures within cultures. In this manner, we can argue that there is an organizational culture to continuous larger groupings, the largest of which would be human culture. Understanding the underlying systems constituting human culture or human nature was a primary motivation of structuralists such as Levi-Strauss, who deconstructed cross-cultural symbol systems of myth, ritual, art, and other processes looking for underlying and universal patterns.

We can distinguish between those whose interests are to peel back the layers of culture to locate invariant properties, and those who focus on what distinguishes groups from one another. For our purposes, we are concerned with cultural differences and how they affect organizational behavior.

Although we recognize differences in organizational culture, they are most often attributed to negative experiences, such as encounters with not-invented-here attitudes and turf battles between and among functional stovepipe organizations. So initiatives such as EA may be challenged as unwelcome intrusions by management to put another bureaucratic obstacle in the way of those who do the real work. From this point of view, culture can be seen as an impediment and something that has to be managed, dealt with, and changed. As Hofstede observed, "Culture is more often a source of conflict than of synergy. Cultural differences are a nuisance at best and often a disaster."

Yet culture, like language, is neutral. It is not defined in terms of content; rather it exists at the underlying deep structural level that gives rise to surface behavior. Consider the parallels of language and culture. Every language has an underlying structure of an essentially finite number of rules that give rise to a virtually infinite number of possible expressions in the language. The underlying rule system is often referred to as "deep structure," and the way the application of the rules appears in discourse is called "surface structure." These underlying systems are not always apparent to speakers and need to be discovered in linguistic analysis.

There is no language superior to another in being able to express information. In this manner, languages represent metaphoric parallel universes. Culture, likewise, can be understood according to an underlying system of rule-like structures. One way of considering culture is to characterize it as a form of social cognition. Ray Jackendoff (2007) provides an important comparison between language and social cognition, showing how both comprise underlying rule patterns that are not directly available to consciousness. In his book *Language, Consciousness, Culture* he provides a table, illustrated in Figure 2-1, to show these relationships.

Both language and culture (characterized as a type of social cognition or thought process) have finite underlying structures or combinational rule systems that generate a virtually infinite number of displays: sentences and understandable social situations that are at the surface or surface structures. Although these underlying systematic structures generate meaning, the latter is independent of them. We can communicate any number and kind of messages with language, as we can perform any number and kind of culturally relevant behavior. In this manner, we reserve judgment on cultural performance in the same way that we do on what might be said.

Using language, we can complement or insult, make promises, offers, or threats using the similar language principles. As anthropologist Dell Hymes (1977) showed, culture

| | |
|---|---|
| •Unlimited number of understandable sentences | •Unlimited number of understandable social situations |
| **•Requires combinational rule system in mind of language user** | **•Requires combinational rule system in mind of social participant** |
| •Rule system not available to consciousness | •Rule system only partly available to consciousness |
| •Rule system acquired with only imperfect evidence in environment – virtually no teaching | •Rule system acquired with only imperfect evidence, only partially taught |
| •Learning requires inner unlearned resources, perhaps partly specific to language | •Learning requires inner unlearned resources, perhaps partly specific to social cognition |
| •Inner resources determined by genome interacting with process of biological development | •Inner resources determined by genome interacting with process of biological development |

Parallels between Language and Social Cognition
(Ray Jackendoff – Language, Consciousness, Culture)

**Figure 2-1**  Parallels between language and social cognition (used with permission from MIT Press)

is a "system of ideas that underlies and gives meaning to behavior in society, and what is distinctively cultural is a question of capabilities acquired or elicited in social life rather than the behavior or things that are shared." This allows for the same underlying system of rules to elicit outcomes that are in conflict with one another. This potential for conflict was the basis for Schein's observation regarding the culture at the Digital Equipment Corporation, which entailed both "a positive innovative culture that could at the same time grind out 'fabulous new products' and develop such strong internal animosities that groups would accuse one another of lying, cheating and misuse of resources." According to Schein (2004), the underlying cultural grammar at DEC was responsible for both its meteoric rise to success and its eventual downfall.

## Classifying Cultures

Although we characterize deep structure as a finite set of rules that generates a virtually infinite variety of surface structures (sentences in language and social situations in culture), these rules are highly complex. They are self-adaptive, nonlinear, and complex. For culture, there are invariant structures contained in its universal presence in all human societies, and variant structures that enable us to classify cultures according to various value and other dimensions. The comparison and measuring of differences in cultural value orientation is a significant advance in the study of intercultural communications.

Approaches to this type of classification give us a way of understanding the corporate culture and subcultures of the enterprise we are dealing with and a way of predicting at least some of the conflicts that will arise.

## Power Distance Index

Hofstede developed a framework for this in his comparative study of IBM in different countries to locate what dimensions differ in behavior, by observing and interviewing persons at the same level in the corporate hierarchy around the world. He developed a value dimensions comparison: power distance, uncertainty avoidance, individualism/collectivism, and masculinity/femininity.

His Power Distance Index (PDI) focuses on the degree of equality, or inequality, between people in society. High power distance indicates that inequalities of power and wealth exist and are tolerated within the society. Such societies often have caste systems that do not allow upward mobility. In low power distance societies, there is a de-emphasis on structural differentiation, and equality along with opportunity for everyone is emphasized. Hofstede measured power distance according to how those he interviewed responded to such questions as, "how frequently does the following occur: employees being afraid to express disagreement with managers," and subordinates' perception and then preference for a boss's decision-making style, choosing between autocratic, paternalistic, or consultative.

Hofstede's distinction between individualism and collectivism focuses on how much a society emphasizes individual versus collective achievement and interpersonal relationships. High individualism stresses individuality and individual rights, and individuals tend toward looser relationships. Low individualism societies emphasize collectivist natures and closer ties between individuals. In such cultures, extended families are emphasized and everyone assumes responsibility for fellow group members. Hofstede contrasts locus of control and evaluation between these types. If this focus is external to the individual, as is found in more collectivistic societies, there is a greater emphasis on fatalism and lack of individual responsibility, whereas an internal focus tends to emphasize a rejection of submission to authority.

In Hofstede's interviews, he determined the contrast of individualism versus collectivism according to how his respondents answered several questions. Answers that included a desire for personal time, freedom to adopt an individual approach to a job, and challenging work indicate an orientation toward individualistic. On the other hand, answers that emphasized a desire for training, physical conditions, and use of one's skills tended toward the collectivistic.

Hofstede's Masculinity (MAS) ranking focuses on how much a society reinforces traditional masculine work role models of achievement, control, and power. High MAS indicates the cultural experiences in gender differentiation, where males maintain a hegemonic role in the power structure. In low masculinity cultures, there is less discrimination between genders and women are treated with greater equality. Hofstede contrasted Masculine versus Feminine cultures according to how respondents ranked a series of preferences regarding work environments. Masculine emphasizes earnings, recognition, advancement, and work challenges; Feminine emphasizes having good working relationships with managers, cooperation with co-workers, living in a desirable area, and employment security.

His next area of contrast was the level of uncertainty avoidance (UAI). UAI focuses on the amount of tolerance for ambiguity and uncertainty or unstructured situations. High uncertainty avoidance rankings that show a low tolerance for uncertainty and ambiguity create a rule-oriented society that stresses laws, rules, regulations, and controls to reduce the amount of uncertainty. A low ranking indicates less concern about ambiguity and more tolerance for differences of opinion. Low uncertainty avoidance societies are less rule oriented, more acceptable of change, and readier to take risks.

Hofstede's final contrast involved time orientation—high long term (LTO) versus low. This measure looked at the amount of focus on traditional versus forward-thinking values. High LTO shows a commitment and respect for tradition with a strong work ethic, where long-term rewards are anticipated for today's work. In such societies, business often takes longer to develop for outsiders.

One of the authors found a curious example of this several years ago when he learned about a benefit that Canon Business Machines, a Japanese firm, wanted to make to its American managers at a facility in the United States. They offered to pay for the tuition of all of their managers' children in college so that the cost of education would not be a barrier to entry into any university. Interestingly, the American managers almost universally rebelled against the offer, saying they would prefer receiving the compensation now and they would take care of their children's education. This offer was made during a period when Japanese industry expected workers to remain loyal to their company throughout their career. This contrasted to American business experience, where advancing in one's career more often involved lateral moves to other companies, and lifelong loyalty to an organization was rare.

Hofstede, and those making similar contrasts between cultures, hypothesized the ability to predict types of interactive styles between those expressing such value orientation differences, such as exemplified in the case of Canon Business Machines just cited. Where Hofstede emphasized intercultural distinctions between national cultures, different organizations, and professions also differ in their expression of these differences. For instance, one might contrast the academic profession and government service that provide tenure and more job security with the uncertainty, short-term project orientation, and individual advancement stressed in contract-based consulting professions and in highly competitive industries. Consider how Dan Bricklin and Bob Frankston, the inventors of the first killer application (VisiCalc), as university professors, published the source code as standard for the academic profession. Their reward was tenure and a well-deserved reputation, but they did not become computer billionaires like Bill Gates, Steve Jobs, or Larry Ellison.

## Grid and Group

Contrasts of macro-national cultural differences with micro-organizational distinctions are also strongly exemplified in anthropologist Mary Douglas's distinction between grid and group. Douglas first discussed this contrast in her book *Natural Symbols* (1970), based on research in Central Africa. Douglas was concerned with how people ordered their universe and proposed a system of classification for how they went about doing so. She developed a typology to account for the distribution of values within society. She proposed a connection between kinds of social organization and the values that maintain them.

Douglas developed a schema based on two dimensions: ground (referring to a general boundary around a community) that forms the basis of a horizontal axis, and grid (or regulation) on the vertical axis. Members of a society or an organization move across the matrix according to choice or to circumstances. Douglas's grid/group diagram appears as Figure 2-2.

The ground, or group, dimension is a measure of how much people are controlled by their social group. Individuals need to accept constraints on behavior when they are affiliated with a group. Groups require collective pressures to demonstrate loyalty. Douglas points out that these constraints obviously vary in strength. She gives the example of how at one end of the spectrum an individual might belong to a religious group and attend services only on major holy days, while at the other end of the spectrum are those who join convents and monasteries.

The other variable on the grid is the differences in amount of control or structure members of a group accept. On one hand, individuals live free of group pressures and structural constraints, where everything "has to be negotiated ad hoc"; on the other hand, others live in highly structured hierarchical environments. The grid creates four opposed and incompatible types of social control, with various mixtures between the extremes.

Douglas provides a characterization of three ideal types of persona associated with the grid (see Figure 2-2). She describes these as "The smug pioneer with his pickaxe, the stern bureaucrat with his briefcase, the holy man with his halo," each exemplifying

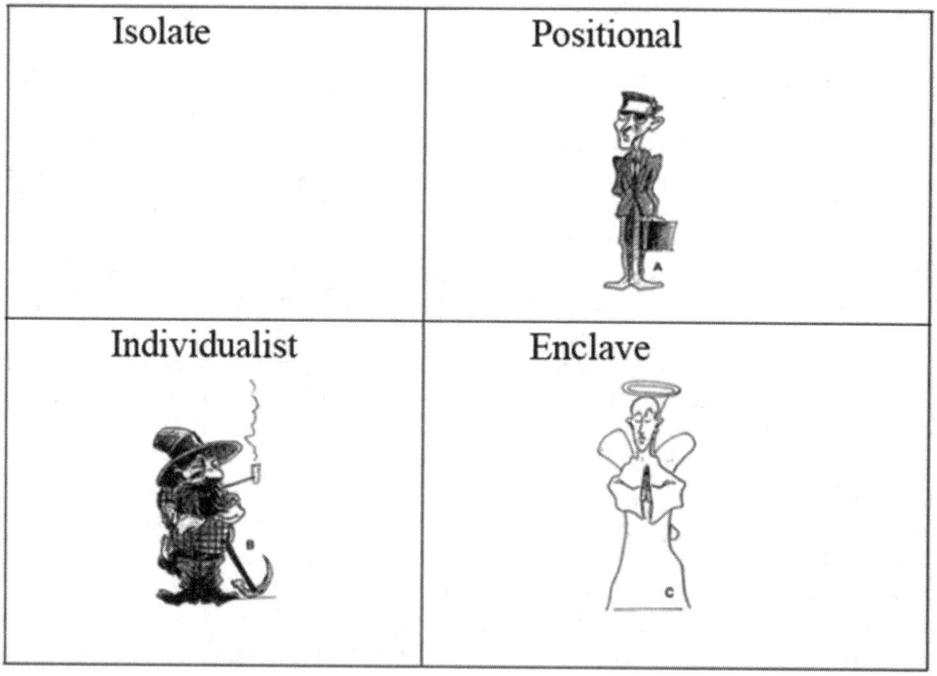

**Figure 2-2** Matrix with associated ideal types of personas

German sociologist Max Weber's types of rationality: bureaucracy, market, and religious charisma. These reflect the three grid-group cultures of positional, individualist, and sectarian enclave.

She describes how the positional society at the top right is strong on grid and group. This reflects societies and concomitantly organizations in which all roles are ascribed and behavior is governed by positional rules. The cultural biases are tradition and order. In culture, the roles are ascribed by birth, gender, or family and ranked according to tradition. She refers to this as "positional," as a form of society that uses "extensive classification and programming for solving problems of co-ordination." In the organizational domain, the positional enterprise might be the family owned and controlled business where employees can expect to achieve only a certain level of power within the enterprise.

At the lower right-hand (enclave) position are strongly bounded groups with little or no ranking or grading rules for the relationships among its members. Douglas considers this to be descriptive of a community of dissidents or sects. This might also pertain to lattice design organizations [Papa et al. 2008], where there are no bosses. New members are not assigned to departments but find teams that they volunteer to join. The lattice organization encourages direct communication with few intermediaries or little approval seeking. Instead of a defined authority structure, team members commit to objectives to make them happen. Lattice organizations have sponsors rather than bosses. According to Papa, such organizations involve a heterarchy, with self-organizing, non-hierarchical systems characterized by lateral accountability and by organizational heterogeneity. Lattice organizations involve distributed intelligence and diversity. They comprise multiple communities of knowledge and practice with diverse evaluative and performance criteria and answer to different constituencies and principles of accountability.

At the lower left is extreme individualism. This type of society or organizations is defined in terms of both weak group and grid controls. The primary form of control is competition. Dominant positions are open to merit. Douglas sees this as a commercial society, where the individual is concerned only with private benefit. This type of society also exhibits a "greed is good" mentality and the extremism that led to the collapse of banking in the recent recession.

The fourth quadrant (upper right) is the world of the total isolate, and it is populated by those who withdraw from society. As an organizational form, this might be the independent researcher and entrepreneur.

Douglas later described the grid as the basis for understanding how organizations think. This approach reflected an alternative view of corporate culture. In such a schema, we may be tempted toward a Goethe type of prediction regarding interactions between the systems in these quadrants. However, rather than being predictive, we may instead consider characterizations to be elements of cultural grammars that can yield any number of types of surface structures. Thus, as Douglas argued, culture is not a thing; it is not static but instead is "something which everyone is constantly creating, affirming and expressing." From this perspective, culture is not imposed but rather emerges. Organizational culture is the result of continuing negotiations regarding values, meanings, and proprieties among members of an organization and within its environment. Culture is the consequence of interactions and negotiations among members of organizations. To change culture may require that we change the nature of those conversations. This type of change is not trivial.

As Harold Garfinkel (1967) argued for health clinical records, there are "good organizational reasons" for bad organizational behavior. That is, at the macro level, we can easily see "organizational problems," but as we move to what he refers to as the "shop floor," we tend to "lose the phenomenon." Thus, when we try to investigate some macro organizational problem, we often find good rationales for what is being done at the local level. That is, asking "why do you do things in that way?" yields responses that make good sense in the situation and setting where the work actually gets done.

## How Culture Affects the Enterprise Architecture

Organizational psychologist Karl Weick describes how every organization, including the most effective ones, are essentially "garrulous, clumsy, superstitious, hypocritical, monstrous, octopoid, wandering and grouchy" (1977). This is because organizations organically emerge out of the communication patterns that develop in the course of doing business and in response to the host of environmental variables in dynamically changing business landscapes. Enterprises are instances of complex adaptive systems having many interacting subcomponents whose interactions yield complex behaviors. Complexity involves a "duality of interactive complex systems," in which "duality" refers to the idea that every action produces a ripple effect, on interdependent actors—that is, the "structure." This ripple effect, in turn, shapes "actions."

Enterprises are by their very nature disorganized. Russ Ackoff argued that all organizations are a mess. It is the architect's job to support the transformation of the organization by rolling up our sleeves and defining the mess and proposing solutions. Ackoff described the nature of the problem of messes that faces us:

> In a real sense, problems do not exist. They are distractions from real situations. The real situations from which they are abstracted are messes. A mess is a system of interrelated problems. We should be concerned with messes, not problems. The solution to a mess is not equal to the sum of the solution to its parts. The solution to its parts should be derived from the solution of the whole; not vice versa. Science has provided powerful methods, techniques and tools for solving problems, but it has provided little that can help in solving messes. The lack of mess-solving capability is the most important challenge facing us. [Ackoff 1994, pp 210–12]

Ackoff advocates five steps for solving these messes: formulating the mess, ends planning, means planning, resource planning, and the design of implementation and control systems. In one way or other, most business process renewal or reengineering efforts involve some version of this approach.

The first step is to formulate the mess: "A corporation's mess is the future implied by it and its environment's current behavior. Every system contains the seeds of its own deterioration and destruction. Therefore, the purpose of formulating the mess is to identify the nature of these often-concealed threats and to suggest changes that can increase the corporation's ability to survive and thrive." Figuring out that mess involves three types of work. The first is an analysis of the state of the organization (or corporation) and how it interacts with the environment. Next is an "obstruction analysis" to identify the obstructions to development. Then we prepare reference projections engaging in the four stages leading to the transformation.

These tasks are often easier said than done. Consider most instances when we decide to clean up some mess, such as spring cleaning or cleaning up our offices after the conclusion of a major project. When I do so, I normally get a number of big black garbage or lawn bags with the intent to toss away what I no longer need. However, by the end of the day, I am always taken back by the small amount of trash I actually have. It seems that with each file or paper I pick up, I find "strange connections" to other files and projects that are ongoing or have perceived potential to next projects I will be involved with. So I end up throwing away perhaps copies of documents and a few other non-relevant materials, but for the most part I just refile or sort what I already have.

This description of the "mess" fits what we have recently learned about the nature of chaotic systems. In spite of perceived disorganized chaos, there seems to be what John Holland (1996) calls a "hidden order" to things. Rather than systems being totally random and chaotic, they are better understood as highly complex and self-adapting. In such systems, components become associated with one another by what complexity theorists call "strange attractors," which lead to new patterns entailing the emergence of new organizational forms.

There is a distinction between complication and emergence. In the latter, we may understand what components make up some situation or event. However, in such systems there are often interconnections between components that are almost impossible to take into account. Consider, for instance, the phenomenon of weather. Although understanding the dynamics of weather and the range of variable involved, we are, despite the literally billions spent on predictive technologies, unable to fully predict it. This leads to the concept of what has become known as the "butterfly effect," which was originally conceived by MIT meteorologist Edward Lorenz, who created a mathematical model of the weather. He suggested how minute changes, as minimal as the flap of the wing of a butterfly, could have impacts on other molecules that are forming together to create weather patterns. That is, the wing flap is associated with other molecules through strange attraction and lead to unexpected events. His model led him to realize that long-term forecasting was doomed to failure. The butterfly effect suggests that a butterfly flapping its wings can affect the world's weather, and upon the suggestion of another colleague, Lorenz titled a paper he presented to the AAAS in 1972 "Does the flap of a butterfly's wings in Brazil set off a tornado in Texas?" that emphasized such interaction [Lorenz 1993].

We are, however, not condemned to incomprehensible complexity. We can, after all, make approximate predictions of weather along with a wide range of natural, cultural, and organizational behavior. We may not be precise, but we can approximate a "for-all-practical-purposes" mode of description. In a very real sense, that is what we intend in modeling the complexity of an enterprise. We can establish relationships between operational, systems, and technical nodes in a highly complex organization that enables us to plan for organizational transformation. Such modeling is far superior to no planning at all. This again brings up Ackoff's point about plan or be planned for. It is important to be proactive and enact the organizational changes we want rather than be reactive to events as they chaotically unfurl.

# Social Networks

Weick's portrayal of organizations as wandering and octopoid characterizes how we encounter them. Despite such ubiquitous chaos, we seem to find order. However, order is something we do to organizations rather than it being an inherent property of them. We create order through our beliefs about organizations. These beliefs constitute "cause maps" that we impose on the world and, once imposed, characterize our view of organizations.

This imposition of order is also known as the "process of structuration" [Giddens 1986]. Repeated interactions are the foundation of social structure. Interacting individuals whose activities are in turn constrained by that perceived constructed structure produce structure. This Giddens calls the "duality of structure." This duality describes how social structures constrain choices and at the same time how social structures are created by the activities they constrain.

Structure does not exist in its own right. Rather, it is through enactments that we produce organization as ongoing accomplishments and reify their structure. The kind of sense that an organization makes of its thoughts and of itself has an effect on its ability to deal with change. An organization that continually sees itself in novel images that are permeated with diverse skills and sensitivities is equipped to deal with altered surroundings when they appear. Weick argues that organizational transformation continually involves enactment. Enactment is a form of social construction in social networks.

*Connectedness* in an organization characterizes the social networks within the organization. The study of social networks has led to a field within organizational and communications studies known as *social network theory*, which analyzes social relationships according to nodes and types that define them. There are three types of nodes:

- Operational nodes are the individual actors in networks that have ties that characterize the resources/information that they exchange.
- Systems nodes are the structures or systems individuals use in their communication.
- Technical nodes are the technical components of those systems.

In enterprise architecture, each of these types of nodes can be represented in different views that document the types of ties and information flows that occur between them.

The study of social networks in organizations or organizational network analysis offers an approach to understand the internal workings of an organization. Organization charts prescribe how work and information flow in a hierarchy, but network mapping reveals that they actually flow through a web of informal channels. These informal channels point to significant differences between the formal organizational structural view and what is actually occurring in the daily life of the enterprise. These differences have important impacts on how work gets done, and knowledge of the informal channels enables analysis of bottlenecks, inefficiencies, and gaps in business processes. The organization's enterprise architecture captures and documents these informal channels and information flows to enable this analysis of business processes.

An important discovery in the study of social networks is the importance of applying graph theory to understand the complexity involved. Graph theory is the substance of contemporary network analysis, and it formulates the basis for the range of network type diagrams used in different enterprise architectural products. Social network theorist Rob Cross describes ONA (Organizational Network Analysis) as "a powerful means of making invisible patterns of information flow and collaboration in strategically important groups visible." Cross and his colleagues interviewed members of organizations to uncover the types of links that existed between them and graphed these relationships, connecting the members as nodes. This often led to some quite surprising results. In every social network, different people played different roles, ranging from central, peripheral, boundary spanner, and isolates. Architects do the same and document using the views of the framework they are using.

There is no single network structure or role positioning that is best for all organizations. For instance, in some organizations, a few individuals may be in a highly interactive role connecting different subgroups together. In a close examination of what is occurring, sometimes we find that these individuals function more as bottlenecks than enablers. Once their functions within the organization are shared with other positions, information and workflow is made more efficient. However, in some instances, such boundary spanning positions are relevant, allowing close management of projects.

What is important in network analysis is to uncover whether the structure is intentional and functional, or whether the networks are emergent structures that impede the work and communication flows within the enterprise. Cross, Liedtka, and Weiss (2005) characterized three types of organizational networks: customized response networks, modularized response networks, and routine response networks. Each represents a different value proposition that affects the patterns of collaboration that occur. The authors propose that managers should not force collaboration onto all employees and must take into account the appropriate proposition and organizational mission.

Customized response networks exist in organizational contexts where there is ambiguity in both problems and solutions. Examples could include new product-development companies, high-end investment financial institutions, early-stage drug development teams, and strategy consulting firms. They require networks that allow rapid definition of problems and coordination of expertise in response. The quick framing and problem solving in an innovative manner derive value.

Modular response networks exist in contexts where parts of a problem and solution are known, but the sequencing of these components is not known. Cross and his colleagues give as examples surgical teams, business-to-business sales, and mid-stage drug development teams. These types of organizations have networks to identify problem elements and to deal with them using modularized expertise. Value comes from delivering a unique response based on types of expertise required by particular problems such as a lawsuit or surgical procedure.

Routine response networks are found in standardized work contexts. Here problems and solutions are well defined and predictable. This includes call centers, claims processing, and late-stage drug development. Value is derived by efficient and consistent response to established problems.

Each of these three network types requires different types of communication flows. In highly innovative and creative contexts, it is important for those directly involved to be in close, frequent communication where expertise is redundant, as well as having boundary spanning access to other networks dealing with related issues. However, it is also important for some experts, such as scientists, to have independence and not always be closely managed such that their creativity is impeded. In the modular response networks, there is more interchangeability of roles and more structured approach to boundary spanning. In routine response networks, there are defined and structured boundaries with clear lines of authority and role relationships. Figure 2-3 shows the parameters for each network type [Cross et al. 2006].

As discussed, some see culture as very inclusive and define it in ways in which it is hard to conceive of what might be outside the boundaries of culture: "Culture is the deposit of knowledge, experiences, beliefs, values, attitudes, meanings, hierarchies, religion, timing, roles, spatial relations, concepts of the universe (world view), and material objects and possessions acquired by a group of people in the course of generations through individual and group striving." [Gudykunst and Kim 2002] Anthropological and sociological ethnographers spend years doing ethnographic fieldwork to write up their studies of culture. As enterprise architects, we surely cannot undertake such an effort.

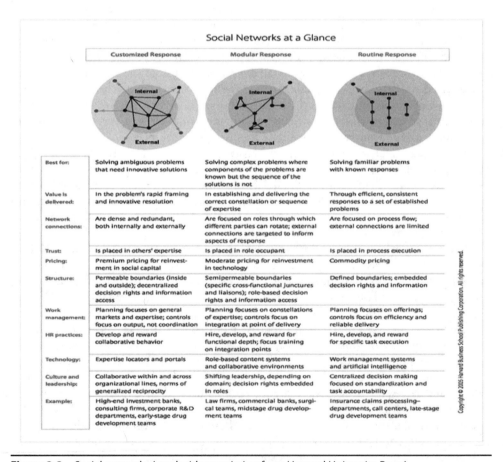

**Figure 2-3** Social networks (used with permission from Harvard University Press)

So, the bad news is that a full ethnographic account of culture can take a significant investment of time and effort. The good news is that a full, comprehensive analysis of culture is not required to understand the cultural features that we require in enterprise architecture. Schein (2010) suggests a clinical ethnographic approach. Rather than being concerned with researching the complexity of organizational culture, a clinical perspective entails an action research perspective. Here, the goal is to undertake cultural analysis to uncover the basic systemic cultural assumptions that give rise to particular problems, issues, and concerns within an organization. For example, Schein used this approach in analyzing the DEC culture, locating those cultural principles or assumptions that led both to its meteoric success and to its eventual decline. He argues we need to understand culture as the "pattern of shared basic assumptions that the group learned as it solved its problems of external adaptation and internal integration that has worked well enough to be considered valid and ... to be taught to new members as the correct way to perceive, think and feel in relation to those problems." (2004) These assumptions are not simply lists; rather they are interconnected, networked, and systemic, forming the underlying bases for corporate behavior.

These assumptions are at the deepest level of culture and constitute what might be considered a grammar of cultural principles that gives rise to two higher levels in organizational culture: its artifacts and espoused values. The artifacts are the visible products of the group or, for our purposes, some of the primitives or basic elements included in the EA. The espoused values "focus on what people say is the reason for their behavior, what they ideally would like those reasons to be and ... their rationalizations for behavior," including the mission and vision, strategies, values, goals, and objectives that are their conscious guides. Basic assumptions are the underlying theories of practice in use that actually (rather than assertively) guide behavior and inform group members about how to perceive, think about, and feel about things. Unless we dig down to the level of basic assumptions we cannot decipher artifacts, norms, and values. These assumptions are identified only through an analysis of anomalies between observed visible artifacts and the espoused beliefs and values.

As you will see, the representation of performers in the enterprise architecture currently is based on the explicit nature of organizations—representations of formal organizational charts, roles, internal and external players, and their interactions based on formal and informal agreements. In our discussions on social networks, we have distinguished espoused values from intrinsic beliefs. While building stakeholder charts tabulating various stakeholders of the enterprise and their concerns, we tend to focus on the espoused beliefs. Understanding tribal behavior requires understanding of the intrinsic assumptions and beliefs of tribes, as demonstrated in the work of Schein.

# Schein's Three Levels of Culture

In his book *DEC is Dead, Long Live DEC* (2004), Schein posited three levels of culture: artifacts, espoused values, and tacit values, as illustrated in Figure 2-4. The following sections provide examples of the espoused and tacit values and assumptions from Schein's analysis of two actual companies: DEC and Novartis.

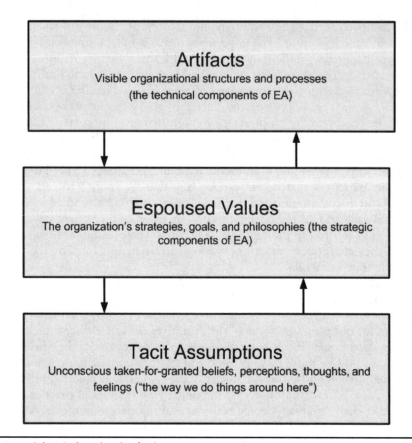

**Figure 2-4**   Schein's three levels of culture

## Clinical Cultural Analysis Example: DEC

Schein analyzed five tacit assumptions forming a systemic pattern in DEC's internal relationships, as illustrated in Figure 2-5.

Each of these assumptions was originally advocated by DEC founder Ken Olsen and then was eventually incorporated into that assumption system. At the center was the assumption that work is fun and DEC was a culture of innovation. Related to this central assumption were four additional basic assumptions. At the upper left in Figure 2-5 is the entrepreneurial spirit or "rugged individualism," where every member of the organization was in a sense an internal entrepreneur coming up with new ideas. When a new idea was proposed, there was the assumption of personal responsibility, where, in the words of Olsen and often quoted by DEC's senior management, "he who proposes does" and that everyone can be trusted to "do the right thing."

The entrepreneurial spirit was also linked to the assumption that truth would arise through conflict. Employees were expected to be highly volatile and even combative for their ideas. At DEC, engineers received financial rewards when their project was chosen, so there was a tremendous competition among employees to promote their ideas. Olsen established off-site meetings, or "woods meetings," where engineers would fight

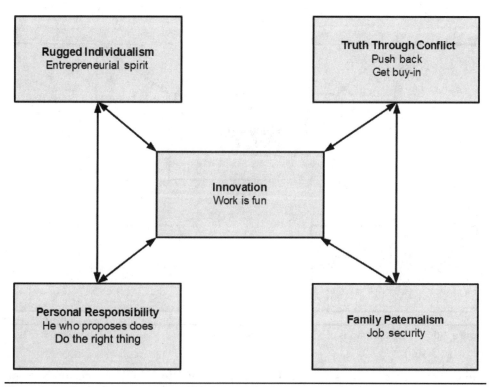

**Figure 2-5** Five tacit assumptions of DEC's internal culture

each other for their ideas. The volatile nature of these meetings was the first reason why Olsen hired Schein as his consultant. However, once a concept was accepted, participants whose ideas were not selected would buy into the winners and push back on their ideas. This argument system for obtaining buy-in on ideas was supported by a kind of tenure system at DEC, where once hired, an engineer was assumed job security and a strong sense of family paternalism.

Along with the internal system was an external assumption system for how DEC interacted with its environment for survival, as diagrammed in Figure 2-6.

At the center of the external assumptions is arrogance, this being engineering arrogance, the idea that engineers, scientists and (myself being one) academics "know what is best." With this central assumption are four associated assumptions. One that was indigenous to DEC management was that there is central control and the operations committee manages budgets for all projects. That being said, the three other major assumptions address how, through "arrogance," problems can be solved. There is the concept of organizational idealism that reasonable people of goodwill can solve any problem. Engineers can resolve anything. This assumption is strongly linked to a commitment to customers and a dedication to solving customers' problems. At DEC, this commitment

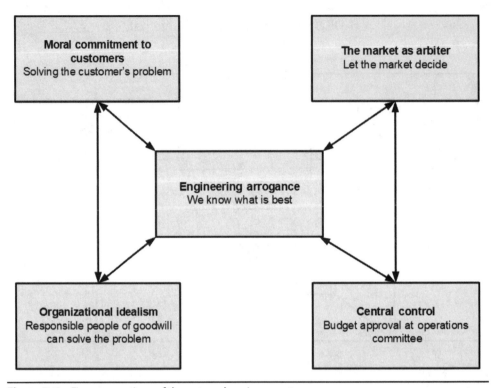

**Figure 2-6**   Five assumptions of the external environment

and dedication was expressed in yearly conferences such as DECUS, a customer membership organization where customers presented both problems and ideas for DEC engineers to take on.

Finally, there was the assumption about markets as arbiter. This involved the belief that if good products were made, they would demonstrate their value without having to be strongly promoted. The latter involved a basic assumption of engineering culture that "good work speaks for itself" and that an engineer "should not have to sell himself." Olsen directly expressed this in his attitude about sales and marketing: "Public relations and image building are forms of 'lying' and are to be avoided." This idealism of engineering and dominance over sales resulted in what Schein described as a lack of "the money gene" in the cultural DNA of DEC that countered DEC's ability to adapt to growth and changes in the business and technological landscapes. Consequently, the same assumptions that resulted in the meteoric success of DEC also underlay its eventual demise.

## Clinical Cultural Analysis Example: Novartis

Schein also provides an analysis of the pharmaceutical company Novartis that stands in interesting contrast to DEC. Where DEC emphasized informality and rank and status were based on the actual job being performed by individuals, Novartis had a system of managerial ranks based on length of service, overall performance, and personal background of the individual rather than on job being performed at a given time. Thus, rank and status had a more permanent quality at Novartis; whereas at DEC one's fortunes could rise and fall based on project.

The value set at DEC versus Novartis was seen in the contrast for how meetings were perceived. At DEC, they were places where work got done; at Novartis they were necessarily evils where announcements got made. Both corporations placed high value on individual contribution, but at Novartis one never went outside chain of command or did things out of line with what one's boss suggested.

The tension between organizational artifacts and espoused values provides an avenue to discover the underlying assumptions of culture. In the case of Novartis, the artifact of central importance, as Schein worked with the corporation under mandate to help them be more innovative, was the problem in the distribution of his suggestions. These were sent only after they were requested rather than by the manager he gave them to in order to distribute. The rationale for this is that when a manager is given a job, it becomes the private domain of that individual. Hence, there was a strong sense of turf or ownership and an assumption that each owner of a piece of the organization would be in charge and on top of his area. Only if information was asked for was it acceptable to offer an idea. This led Schein to model the assumption system of Novartis, illustrated in Figure 2-7.

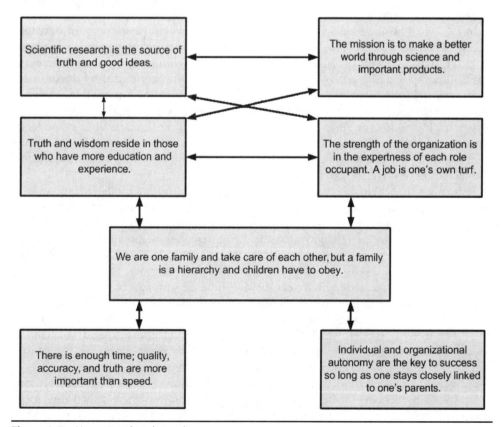

**Figure 2-7**  Novartis cultural paradigm

The important point here is how Schein was able to locate an underlying systematic that constituted what Jackendoff (2007) described as an underlying set of grammatical rules for social cognition, or what we consider here to be culture. Also significant is that these rule sets can be modeled, and they are consistent with a particular set of products included in some EA frameworks: operational or business rules.

# Representing Culture as Business Rules

A *business rule* is guidance that there is an obligation concerning conduct, action, practice, or procedure within a particular activity or sphere. One definition of business rule specifies that operational or business rules are constraints on the way that business is done in the enterprise. At lower levels, rule models may describe the rules under which performers behave under specified conditions. Such rules can be expressed in a textual form, for example, "If (these conditions) exist, and (this event) occurs, then (perform these actions)."

Some business rules can be found in policy and other organizational policy and business process documentation. However, while many business rules are expressed as formal, documented rules of the business, others are hidden from view and need to be uncovered. Both types of rules constrain activity and provide schema for culturally appropriate organizational behavior.

In EA, when business rules constrain processes or activities, these rules can be associated with activity models. That is, business or operational rules can be modeled relevant to each activity, and cultural rules can thus be expressed within activities. Such activities can be decomposed into sets of constitutive activities with inheritance and documented in an activity hierarchy or tree diagram. The flow of information among these activities can then be modeled using one of the standard activity modeling methodologies such as Integrated Definition for Functional Modeling 0 (IDEF0) or Business Process Modeling Notation (BPMN). The rules can also be documented directly using one of the many rules modeling languages, although the independently modeled rules must be associated with activities through an activity model.

Returning to Schein's example of DEC culture, we might model the process of becoming a project manager as follows using the IDEF0 technique: First, we construct a context diagram with inputs, outputs, controls, and mechanisms for the highest level activity in an activity hierarchy, which can be represented as shown in Figure 2-8. In this technique, rules are modeled as controls because they constrain the processes and component activities.

The top-level process or activity can be decomposed into component activities and documented in a hierarchy diagram, as illustrated in Figure 2-9.

The flow of information among the component activities can be documented in an IDEF0 activity model, which includes inputs, outputs, controls, and mechanisms (ICOMS) (distributed to the component activities from those shown on the context diagram) for each component activity, as illustrated in Figure 2-10.

An example of such modeling can be made from an observation from DEC culture as described by Schein. In the 1980s, one of the authors was the research director at Western Behavioral Sciences Institute (WBSI) in La Jolla, California, which focused on

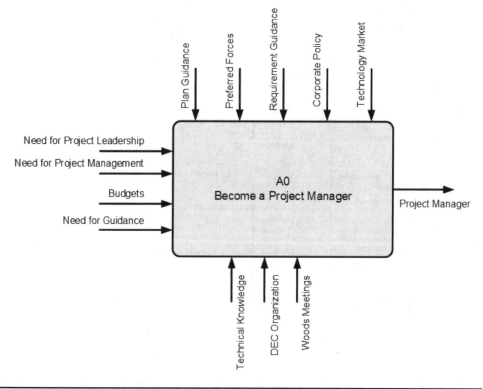

**Figure 2-8** Context diagram for becoming a project manager

computer communications and included the formation of The School of Management and Strategic Studies (SMSS). The school was a program for senior executives from the public and private sectors who attended twice a year, weeklong workshops and then continued their discussions online using computer conferencing and messaging.

## Operational Activity Decomposition Tree (OV-5a)

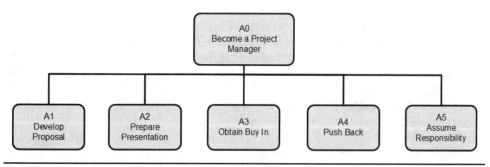

**Figure 2-9** Decomposition diagram

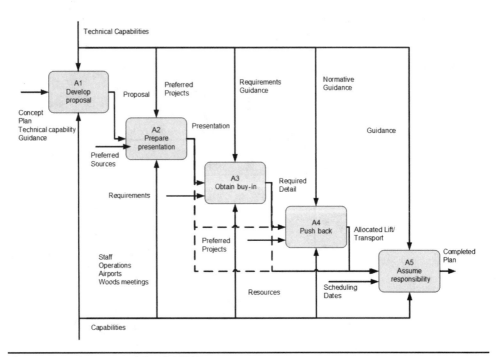

**Figure 2-10** Activity model with ICOMs

An interesting perk of being on the WBSI staff was often being invited to lunch with several of the management teams from the participating organizations. After a short time, Beryl Bellman, professor in the Department of Communications at California State University at Los Angeles, noticed an interesting pattern, where at lunch, when the check was presented, a number of executives got up and went to the restroom. He interviewed several of his DEC associates and learned that there was a "cultural" business rule that the highest ranking person attending such an event is responsible to pay the bill. In this case, there often were several members of DEC with equal rank within the corporation (VP level) attending the sessions, which potentially created a dilemma or competition for paying the check. This was resolvable by an associated business rule that seniority is established by project rather than rank. That is, the highest ranking person at the table was the individual of high rank that had been attending the WBSI program for the longest period of time. Thus, those at the table contextually evaluated their relative rank to others in attendance. If others were of higher rank, they remained at the table. However, if others at the table were of equal rank within the company, the person to pay the bill was the person who had been attending the SMSS program the longest. In this case, those of equivalent rank often left the table when the bill was presented, allowing the most senior among them to take out his or her credit card. This cultural business rule structure could be modeled as illustrated in Figure 2-11. This rule could be associated with the (informal) process of Having Lunch.

This business rule corresponds to the assumption system structural schema Schein described for internal integration in the interaction between the two cultural assumptions

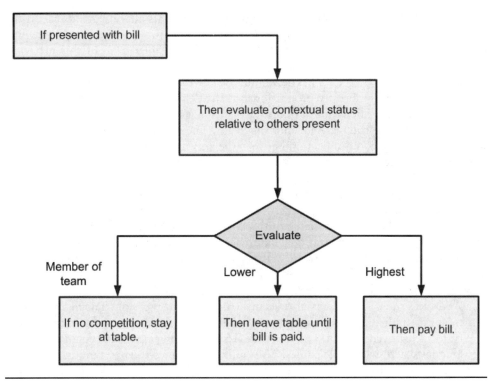

**Figure 2-11**   Cultural business rule

of family paternalism and truth through conflict. On the one hand, there is the strong integrative function expressed in the assumption about the DEC family, and on the other hand, of the "truth through conflict" when decisions are made. In this case, there is a "pushing back" and "buying in" rather than openly negotiating status in the presence of non-family members.

# Culture as a Emergent Phenomenon

An enterprise arises from local interaction of often independent units that exist within a common environment. Each unit or entity interacts with its immediate environment according to a set of low order rules. The combined effects of these lower order interactions within an environment give rise to higher order organizational phenomenon or organizational culture. Culture emerges from localized interactions. As culture is grounded at the local level, culture is highly resistant to change.

So organizational culture is an emergent phenomenon. It resembles the process of *stigmergy*, which is a kind of indirect communication and learning in the environment found in social insects. It is a well-known example of self-organization, providing vital clues to understanding how the components can interact to produce a complex pattern. Stigmergy is a form of coordination through changes in an environment. Following an example by Depickère et al. (2004), if we were to take a bucket of dead ants and scatter them about in a room and then throw in a bucket of live ants afterward and seal off the room, in a few days when we look inside we would find all the dead ants in a single pile. Depickère and her associates conjectured a probabilistic explanation of this behavior: Faced with a dead ant, an ant picked it up with probability inversely proportionate to the number of other dead ants in the vicinity. While carrying a dead ant, the ant put it down with probability directly proportional to the density of dead ants in the vicinity. Thus, the coordinated behavior of piling dead ants in a single pile resulted from a simple local rule controlling the behavior of a single ant. The piling behavior is accounted for without postulating communication between the ants. Researchers developed an experiment using robotic ants programmed with a swarm instruction based on the living ants and produced similar consequences.

Since enterprise culture emerges from local interactions, changing culture entails respecifying local level rules rather than simply imposing change from the top. Creating EA proffers a mechanism to initiate positive change. The underlying local level rules giving rise to an emergent organizational culture can be modeled to help us understand the implications they have on enterprise culture at every level and to identify the rules that need to be modified to effect change.

We have discussed how the behavior of individuals can be described as sets of cultural "business rules." These sets of rules make up different types of strategic interaction games, as exemplified in the classic example of the prisoner's dilemma. However, in game theory, focus has been on one game at a time. Using evolving automata, cognitive behavior is modeled across multiple games. This points to a games-theoretic model of culture as simultaneously playing out a series of games as constituting ensembles that impact the strategy for any particular game.

In this context, Axelrod (1997) characterized cultures as vectors with agent attributes. By vectors, he considered cultural diffusion as a simple model capable of complex behaviors. This entails the effects of empirical opinion vectors promoting cultural diversity in cultural models. As described in a Wikipedia entry "we find that a scheme for evolving synthetic opinion vectors from cultural 'prototypes' shows the same behavior as real opinion data in maintaining cultural diversity in the extended model; whereas neutral evolution of cultural vectors does not."

The development of a shared culture of common attributes emerges when these agents become more like those with whom they interact and also when they interact with those who share similar attributes. This recommends a new type of explanation for social and cultural phenomenon. As Epstein and Axtell (1996) argue, we should reinterpret the question of explanation by asking "can we grow it?" They maintain that such modeling "allows us to 'grow' social structures ... demonstrating that certain sets of *micro-specifications* are sufficient to generate the *macro-phenomena* of interest." They argue, with this in mind, that social scientists "are presented with 'already emerged' collective phenomena and ... seek *micro-rules* that can generate them." The point here is that by locating the underlying business rule schema that drives social contextualized behaviors, we can, in a sense, run computational models that allow the traceability suggested earlier between business process proposals and cultural assumptions that are entailed and informed and can be incorporated into EA.

# Culture from Multiple Perspectives

A full understanding of any organizational/enterprise culture involves seeing it from multiple perspectives. Organizational theorist Joanne Martin (2002) argues for a three-perspective view of culture. First is the integration view, where every member of the organization shares culture in an enterprise-wide consensus. When there is lack of consensus, either remedial actions are taken or there are suggestions that those who do not agree leave the organization. This view is expressed in solidarity and esprit de corps. Next, there is the differentiation or subcultural view. This involves a focus on inconsistent interpretations based on subculture and stakeholder perspectives and entails a loose coupling between representations of the culture as expressed to outsiders versus insiders. We refer to this perspective as tribal views. Then there is the fragmentation perspective that focuses on ways in which organizational cultures are inconsistent, ambiguous, and multiplicitous and in a state of flux. This fragmentation addresses the multiplicities of interpretation that do not coalesce into a collectivity-wide consensus of an integration view nor create subcultural consensus of the differentiation perspective.

Each view entails different sets of assumptions, and though each is simultaneously present in every culture, at any given time one of the perspectives can have prominence over others. So when presenting itself to the outside, the integration view shows esprit de corps, and enables members to see themselves as part of a common culture despite the differences within. In the differentiation view are the organizational stovepipes and internal competition. There is always a danger of subcultures becoming hostile and fighting against each other, turning themselves in contra cultures.

In the airport example discussed throughout this book, we need to keep in mind these perspectives and that each entails a different level of emergence through interlocking sets of game ensembles. There are the integrated emergent properties of the coherent culture of the airport as an entity, the divergent subcultures emerging in the context of the various functional organizations of the airport (management, flight control, concessions, TSA, and so on) that represent different tribes within the organization, and the emergence of fragmented cultures at the shop floor, with the local level politics and "how we are going about doing things around here." There is a concatenation of these at any given time, yet they can be modeled with the effects of culture to better understand how they impact the EA of an airport.

# Summary

We have shown here that organizational culture can be incorporated into an EA project using both business rules and activity or process models. These rules form the logic or grammar for the rules set that, like grammar, are finite but provide for virtually an infinite variation of surface representations, like the sentences of a language form deep structure. Likewise, these rules are syntactical and have form and function. These syntactical rules are the grammatical and transformational rules that enable us to determine whether and how an architectural artifact can be interpreted, accepted, or rejected. We will return to this concept in the following chapters as we observe the impacts of culture, climate, and tribes in our case study.

# Questions

1. Describe the organizational or corporate culture that you must deal with to obtain information relevant to your enterprise architecture.

2. Describe cultural constraints—social, political, interpersonal, value systems, and so on—that impact your ability to obtain information, and how you plan to deal with them.

3. Using the grid/group model for measuring culture, how would you place the organizational culture of your enterprise?

4. How is culture represented in the different architecture viewpoints?

5. Be able to differentiate the organizational climate or atmosphere in your enterprise from its organizational culture.

6. What is the relationship between communication networks and organizational culture?

7. We discussed how culture assumption systems could be modeled as a special instance of business rules. Such rules can be expressed in a textual form, for example, "If (these conditions) exist, and (this event) occurs, then (perform these actions)" or graphically shown using a flow diagram. Identify some cultural assumption relationships within your or a client's organization and provide a rule schema for some cultural activity scenario using either a textual or a graphical representation.

8. What steps would you engage in to diagnose organizational culture problems, and how would you begin to change them?

# References

Ackoff, Russell L. 1981. *Creating the Corporate Future: Plan or Be Planned For.* New York: Wiley.

Ackoff, Russell L. 1994. *The Democratic Corporation: A Radical Prescription for Recreating Corporate America and Rediscovering Success.* New York: Oxford University Press.

Ackoff, Russell L., Herbert J. Addison, and Andrew Carey. 2010. *Systems Thinking for Curious Managers: With 40 New Management F-Law.* Axminster, UK: Triarchy Press.

Axelrod, Robert. 1997. "The Dissemination of Culture: A Model with Local Convergence and Global Polarization" *Journal of Conflict Resolution* (41) 2: 203–26.

Bendor, Jonathon, and Piotr Swistak. 2001. "The Evolution of Norms." *American Journal of Sociology,* 106(6): 1493–1545.

Bittner, E., and H. Garfinkel. 1967. "'Good' organizational reasons for 'bad' clinical records," in Garfinkle, *Studies in Ethnomethodology.* Englewood Cliffs, NJ: Prentice-Hall.

Cross, Rob, Tim Laseter, Andrew Parker, Guillermo Velasquez. 2006. "The Basis for Creating Network Links." *Harvard Business Review*, November 2006.

Cross Rob, J. Liedtka, and L. Weiss. 2005. "A practical guide to social networks." *Harvard Business Review* (3): 124–32.

Depickère S., D. Fresneau, and J.L. Deneubourg. 2004. "A basis for spatial and social patterns in ant species: dynamics and mechanisms of aggregation." *Journal of Insect Behavior*, 17(1): 81–97.

Douglas, Mary. 1970. *Natural Symbols: Explorations in Cosmology*. New York: Pantheon Books.

Douglas, Mary, and Aaron Wildavsky. 1983. *Risk and Culture*. Berkeley: University of California Press.

Epstein. Joshua. M., and Robert L. Axtell. 1996. *Growing Artificial Societies: Social Science from the Bottom Up*. Cambridge, MA: MIT Press.

Garfinkle, Harold. 1967. *Studies in Ethnomethodology*. Cambridge, UK: Polity Press.

Giddens, Anthony. 1986. *The Constitution of Society: Outline of the Theory of Structuration*. Berkeley: University of California Press.

Gladwell, Malcom. 2000. *The Tipping Point: How Little Things Can Make a Big Difference*. Boston: Little Brown & Co.

Gudykunst, William, and Young Yun Kim. 2002. *Communicating with Strangers: An Approach to Intercultural Communication*. New York: McGraw-Hill Humanities/ Social Sciences/Languages.

Hofstede, Geert, Gert Jan Hofstede, and Michael Minkov. 2010. *Cultures and Organizations, Software of the Mind: Intercultural Cooperation and Its Importance for Survival*, 3rd Ed. New York: McGraw-Hill.

Holland, John H. 1996. *Hidden Order: How Adaptation Builds Complexity*. New York: Perseus Books.

Hymes, Dell. 1977. *Foundations of Sociolinguistics: An Ethnographic Approach*. London: Tavistock Press.

International Phonetic Association. 1999. "Phonetic description and the IPA chart," in International Phonetic Association, *Handbook of the International Phonetic Association: A Guide to the Use of the International Phonetic Alphabet*. Cambridge, UK: Cambridge University Press.

Jackendoff, Ray. 2007. *Language, Consciousness, Culture: Essays on Mental Structure*. Cambridge, MA: MIT Press.

Kunda, Gideon. 2006. *Engineering Culture: Control and Commitment in a High-Tech Corporation*. Philadelphia: Temple University Press.

Livingston, Eric. 2016. *Ethnographies of Reason*. New York: Routledge Kegan & Paul.

Lorenz, Edward N. 1963. "Deterministic Nonperiodic Flow." *Journal of the Atmospheric Sciences*, (20): 130–41.

Lorenz, Edward N. 1993. *The Essence of Chaos*. Seattle: University of Washington Press.

Lynch, Michael. 1985. *Art and Artifact in Laboratory Science: A Study of Shop Work and Shop Talk in a Research Laboratory*. New York: Routledge Kegan & Paul.

Martin, Joanne. 2002. *Organizational Culture: Mapping the Terrain*. Thousand Oaks, CA: Sage Publications.

Papa, M.J., T.D. Daniels, and B.K. Spiker. 2008. *Organizational Communication: Perspectives and Trends*, Rev. Ed. Thousand Oaks CA: Sage Publications.

Pettigrew, Andrew M. 1979. "On Studying Organizational Cultures." *Administrative Science Quarterly* (24) 4: 570–81.

Romney, Kimball, and Roy D'Andrade. 1964. "Cognitive Aspects of English Kin Terms." *American Anthropologist*, (66)3: 146–70.

Rumelhart, David E., James L. McClelland, and PDP Research Group. 1986. *Parallel Distributed Processing: Explorations in the Microstructure of Cognition, Vol. 1: Foundations*. Cambridge, MA: MIT Press.

Schein, Edgar. 2001. *Organizational Culture: Mapping the Terrain*. Thousand Oaks, CA: Sage Publications.

Schein, Edgar. 2004. *DEC is Dead, Long Live DEC: The Lasting Legacy of Digital Equipment Corporation*. Oakland, CA: Berrett-Koehler Publishers.

Schein, Edgar. 2010. *Organizational Culture and Leadership,* 4th Edition. San Francisco: Jossey-Bass.

Schneider, Benjamin, and Karen Barbera, eds. 2014. *The Oxford Handbook of Organizational Climate and Culture*. New York: Oxford University Press.

Seel, Richard. 2000. "Culture and Complexity: New Insights on Organisational Change," in *Organizations & People* (7) 2.

United States Senate, Staff Report. 2014. *The Air Force's Expeditionary Combat Support System (ECSS): A Cautionary Tale on the Need for Business Process Reengineering and Complying with Acquisition Best Practices*.

Weick, Karl. 1977. "On Re-Punctuating the Problem in New Perspectives on Organizational Effectiveness," in Paul S. Goodman and Johannes Pennings, eds., *New Perspectives in Organizational Effectiveness*. San Francisco: Jossey-Bass.

Wilcock, Keith. 2004. *Hunting and Gathering in the Corporate Tribe: Archetypes of the Corporate Culture*. New York: Algora Publishing.

# PART II

# Architecture Development and Use

# Introduction to the Case Study

This chapter provides background and context for the case study that is used for examples in Part II and Part III. The case study focuses on the transformation of a hypothetical airport in an alternative Southern California, as it grows from a civil aviation field to an alternative airport to Los Angeles International Airport (LAX). For purposes of the case study, the details have been somewhat simplified, but there are references at the end of the chapter for those interested in further details and requirements for airports.

## RMN Airport Today

Our hypothetical RMN Airport is strategically located in (an alternative) Southern California, south and east of LAX, surrounded by the hypothetical towns of Tornton, Brownsville, and Petersboro. The airport is near major freeways, but there is undeveloped land surrounding it, as shown in Figure 3-1.

Like other airports in the United States, our RMN Airport is governed by a port authority. A port authority is a governmental commission empowered to manage or construct port facilities. In this case, the RMN Airport Authority is a separate governing agency created under a joint powers agreement from the three surrounding towns for the sole purpose of owning and operating the airport. The authority consists of nine commissioners, three from each city. Each city's commissioners are appointed by the city council. The airport's day-to-day operations are managed by an executive director selected by the commissioners.

### Background

RMN Airport started life as a civil air patrol airport in World War II. After the war, it evolved into a regional civil aviation field. It was named after Richard M. Nixon, the 37th President of the United States, in the late 1960s through the efforts of a local congressman who was a loyal supporter of the Southern California native.

RMN Airport provides services for smaller private planes, including some small private jets, a small plane charter company, a flight training school, and the local civil air patrol. The airport has one runway, fueling facilities, aircraft parking space, some hanger and repair facilities, and an administration building that includes space for a crew and

**Figure 3-1**
Location of
the airport

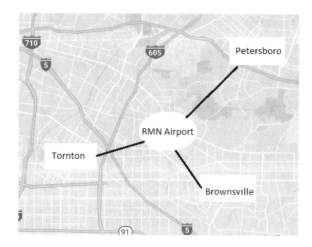

passenger lounge, space for the executive director's office and (currently very limited) staff, and air traffic management facilities. There is a parking lot in front of the Administration Building for those working at or using the airport.

# Opportunities and Aspirations

The Airport Authority has noted increasing opportunities for expansion of RMN Airport. With the increasing congestion at LAX and other Southern California airports, RMN Airport is beginning to get inquiries from intrastate commuter airlines and even some West Coast commuter airlines about the possibility of using it as one of their destinations for Southern California flights. The Federal Aviation Administration (FAA) is interested in a strategic alternative to LAX that is very close and is viable in the event of LAX closure due to unforeseen events, so the FAA would be very supportive of expansion at RMN Airport.

The airport could stand to receive subsidies from the State of California as part of a state initiative to reduce congestion at LAX and incentivize smaller airports to offload the peak traffic over the skies of Los Angeles. These subsidies are offered on a sliding scale, with a large amount being available initially to jumpstart operations and tapering off over a 15-year period, with the assumption that the airport's natural increase of revenues would be able to sustain operations after 15 years without the state subsidies. There is general agreement between the local municipalities as well as the nine-member board of commissioners that the expansion of RMN Airport would bring new jobs, new trade, new passenger traffic, and potentially a lot of beneficial effects on nearby farming communities in terms of eco-tourism and farm-to-table produce sales.

In light of this increasing evidence of opportunities for expansion, the Airport Authority has seriously begun to consider plans to transform RMN Airport into a full-service international airport so it can ultimately become a *reliever airport* (the FAA term) or viable passenger and cargo alternative to LAX. The commissioners also see opportunities to draw additional traffic from other Southern California airports such as Orange County, Burbank, and Ontario airports. The commissioners are looking at a 15-year growth plan

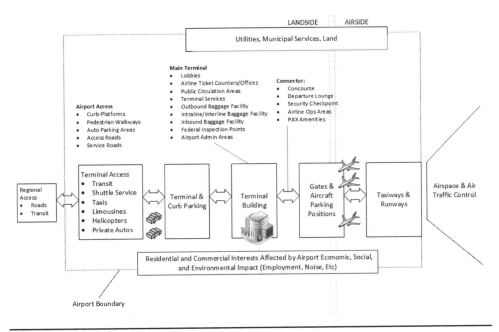

**Figure 3-2**   Conceptual image of RMN Airport

to take advantage of aggressive subsidies from California while developing the 20-year master plan required to be filed with the FAA and updated regularly. The commissioners don't want to count on state money, but they want to be in a position to compete for it, should the money become available.

Figure 3-2 shows a conceptual image of the airport, with the typical components divided into airside components and landside components. The airport is serviced by regional access roads and transit systems.

# Challenges

Major transformations of any enterprise are always fraught with issues and risks. From a strategic viewpoint, the transformation of a small airport into a reliever airport for a major air traffic hub creates a number of new challenges related to dealing with external players in areas of environmental impact, energy footprint, neighborhood and local governments, federal regulators, transportation security, and others.

The transformation of the airport has additional challenges, because the airport needs to remain operational (and keep its existing revenue stream stable) during large-scale construction of runways and terminals. For example, the FAA has strict regulations on the size of runways needed to handle wide-body jets. If RMN Airport is to handle wide-body airliners and some of the larger cargo aircraft, its existing runway will have to be both widened and lengthened. Modifications to the runway cannot be undertaken without an additional runway to absorb the load while the construction operations are in process. Even with a new runway, the construction on the old runway will severely limit operations because the presence of construction equipment close to another operating runway needs close supervision and extra procedures for safety. In addition, funding a new runway is a serious financial investment and a serious risk if the planned-for air-traffic growth does not materialize as expected. All these issues mean that changes must be carefully coordinated throughout the entire transformation period. Figure 3-3 shows the factors and stakeholders that RMN must address if it is to grow into the role of a reliever airport for LAX.

The subsections that follow provide a rough overview of at least some of the changes that need to be made to achieve RMN Airport's transformation.

## Regulations

As RMN Airport grows, it will have to conform to an increasing number of regulations that did not previously apply.

### FAA Regulations

Civil aviation in the United States is federally regulated because of the safety issues, coordination and collaboration challenges that are posed to passengers, airline industry players, partners and the general public, and the use of shared resources such as the airspace over the United States. The FAA is responsible for managing traffic inside U.S.

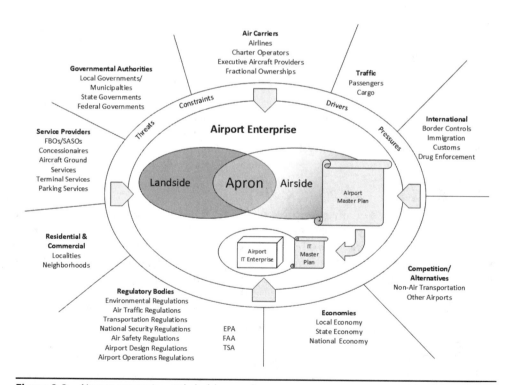

**Figure 3-3** Airport enterprise, stakeholders, and concerns

domestic airspace. The FAA has authority to promulgate and enforce a wide range of regulations on the airport. Some of these regulations restrict the scope and design/selection of the following:

- **Runways**   FAA regulates the width and length of runways needed to handle different classes of aircraft. The FAA has established standard categories for airports based on the types of aircraft they can handle.

- **Airport equipment and instrumentation**   The FAA has requirements on the system of weather and other sensing equipment along with automation and information requirements for the air traffic management operations, including tower operations, radio equipment for communications between aircraft and ground controllers, and terminal radios for gate personnel.

- **Air traffic personnel**   The FAA has requirements for skills, training, and certification of personnel involved in air traffic management.

- **Airline staff and aircrew**   The FAA has requirements for skills, training, certification, and experience maintenance of airline operations staff and aircrew.

In addition, the FAA has regulations on what airport planning documents must be developed and approved prior to changes at an airport.

## Local Regulations

Any physical improvements to the airport must conform to local zoning, noise, and traffic regulations as well as local safety regulations.

## Other Federal and State Regulations

The airport must conform to federal and state security, safety, and health regulations. The airport has to conform to Department of Homeland Security (DHS) and Transportation Security Agency (TSA) regulations for aviation security, such as rules for passenger, checked bag, and carry-on baggage screening; carriage of permissible items in checked baggage and luggage; and confiscation of banned items. Instead of part-time TSA agents or use of local law enforcement for occasional passenger screening, as it expands operations, the RMN Airport will need full-time TSA agents in growing numbers to staff the checkpoints that they must install.

In addition, as the airport staffs its expansion through contracts and outsourced deliverables, the airport must follow the Small Business Administration regulations for reserving a percentage of contracts for small minority- and woman-owned businesses. This regulation related to preference of small businesses for set-asides applies primarily to concession vendors' contracts.

# Stakeholders

As it grows, RMN Airport will need to interact with additional stakeholders and increased stakeholder presence at the airport. Increased presence means that space and facilities will need to be supplied. The increased workforce that will need access to RMN Airport facilities means that identifications of valid employees will be an issue. Badging with photos and biometrics, implementation of access controls to secured facilities, and tracking of movement within the sensitive areas of the airport will all have to be addressed. Some of the stakeholders include the following:

- **TSA**   Passenger and baggage screening, sky marshals
- **United States Immigration and Customs Enforcement (ICE)**   Immigration screening of incoming foreign nationals
- **United States Customs and Border Protection (CBP)**   Customs processing and border controls enforcement of incoming passengers from foreign originating ports on first entry to the United States at RMN Airport
- **U.S. Department of Agriculture – Agriculture Public Health Inspection Service (APHIS)**   Screening of baggage for dairy, plants, and farm products
- **U.S. Drug Enforcement Agency (DEA)**   Screening of passengers and baggage for illegal drugs
- **Contractors**   Vendors providing landside (terminal) passenger services
- **Unions**   Organized airport, contractor, and facility workers
- **Airlines**   Checking in passengers and managing local airline operations landside and airside through the airline operations centers

## Larger Management Staff

As the RMN Airport grows, the executive director will need to enlarge his or her staff, possibly at each phase in the transformation process, as new functions and responsibilities are created that need to be staffed. The executive director will need deputies, including one general deputy and potentially multiple deputies for some specialized functions, such as finance administration, engineering, maintenance, operations, and airline relations. Eventually, a second level of management may be needed, such as directors for financial services, business, property, administrative services, public affairs, communications, human resources, information, communications technologies, operations, maintenance, and public safety. Positions for a chief of airport police and a chief of the airport fire department will also become necessary at some time as the scale of airport security and emergency operations demand dedicated staff.

## More Functions, Facilities, and Capabilities

As RMN Airport transforms into a full-service international airport, it will need to support more functions and provide more facilities for those functions. In addition, new capabilities will need to be added.

### Landside Functions and Facilities

Figure 3-4 illustrates some of the core functions that must be available and certified by the FAA before an airport requests a license to operate. Not all of these functions are the responsibility of the airport authority—some of them are the responsibility of other partners such as the airline, or the fixed base operator (FBO), or the specialized aviation service operator (SASO).

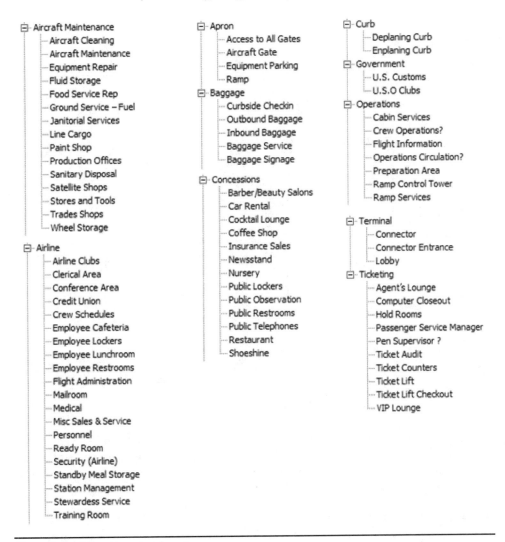

Airport Terminal Functions
(FAA AC 150_5630_13 1987)

**Figure 3-4**   Airport terminal functions

Landside facilities include the terminal areas comprising gates, baggage stations, concourses, concessions, automobile parking, airline counters, airline operational centers, roads and public access, general aviation facilities, cargo facilities, passenger facilities, and major utilities. All these facilities will need to be scaled up as the airport transforms.

## Airside Functions and Facilities

Figure 3-5 provides a summary of necessary airside functions.

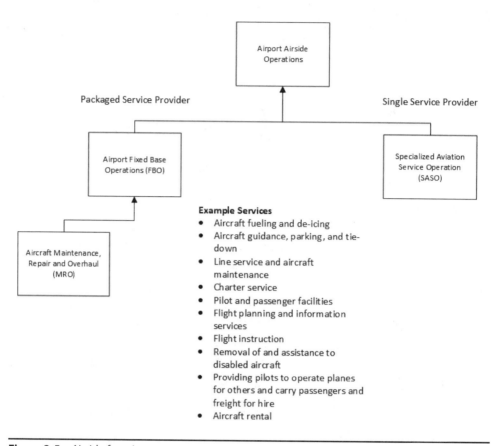

**Figure 3-5**  Airside function summary

Airside facilities include landing areas such as runways and helipads; aircraft movement areas such as taxiways; aircraft parking areas such as aprons; aircraft and airside safety areas such as runway protection zones, runway and taxiway safety areas, runway and taxiway object-free zones, and runway obstacle-free zones.

## Passenger Processing Capabilities

To be an attractive alternative to LAX, RMN will have to enhance its capabilities significantly for passenger management, passenger comfort, passenger convenience, and passenger safety from current levels.

- **Passenger management**   This includes processing passengers from point of check-in to the point of boarding the aircraft, or from debarking to collecting their baggage and being on their way to their final destination. Passengers may also use RMN Airport to connect to other flights. Passenger management includes completion of customs and immigration requirements, safety screening procedures, guided access through airport public areas, requirements for identification, and authorization to travel at all times at permitted locations of the airport.

- **Passenger comfort**   This involves providing environmental conditions for temperature control and management of passenger areas, adequate seating and resting facilities, provision of amenities such as clean restrooms, baby changing areas, potable water sources such as coolers in hallways, and fatigue-resistant flooring and moving areas such as elevators, escalators, and corridors.

- **Passenger convenience**   The provision of facilities inside the airport itself must be adequate for passengers' travel and work-related needs. These can range from providing in-airport services for wireless Internet and e-mail connections; electrical outlets for passengers to recharge their electronics equipment; facsimile and printing services for business documents; and help desks with maps and personnel to assist passengers, to help locate and use rapid transit transport to downtown Los Angeles and other points through partnerships with local authorities and rapid transit organizations. Providing facilities for passenger baggage storage, in-airport post offices, and other conveniences are intended to make RMN Airport an inviting departure, destination, and transit hub for airlines and passengers alike.

- **Passenger safety**   Safety is a very important concern in the post 9/11 world. The fear of plane hijacking and terrorism has rippled through U.S. airports. The increased alert posture of airports has also affected RMN Airport. From the entrance ramps of the highway that provides access to the airport to an array of equipment used for baggage and passenger screening, RMN Airport is deeply committed to providing passenger safety by upgrading its facilities to overcome or mitigate known vulnerabilities. RMN is also concerned with privacy and antidiscrimination laws that prevent passenger profiling. Law enforcement capabilities for the airport's security needs are provided by a detachment of local law enforcement precincts assigned to RMN Airport. Airport authorities, screeners, and other personnel involved in passenger screening and detection of explosives and lethal weapons in hand-carried and checked baggage refer cases of the violations of law to these local law enforcement authorities for apprehension and prosecution.

  Another important part of passenger safety is the need for well-established personnel support, processes and services for evacuation, fire protection, medical care and triage services, ambulance services, sick bays, and other equipment needed to respond immediately and decisively to medical and other emergencies. Each of these services reaches back to the broader system of hospitals, firefighting forces, and other state, local, and county resources in the tri-city area around RMN Airport. Given its current limited financial capabilities, RMN Airport has a limited standing army of first responders. RMN Airport has established the principle of a minimum presence in first response, recognizing that its capabilities are also limited by the staff available. But RMN Airport has also stipulated that escalation of first response will be the preferred approach to handling emergencies. RMN Airport has routinely run drills and exercises to test the principle though no major event has occurred. Given the planned escalation of the size and capacity and scope of the airport, it is anticipated that some of the assumptions related to escalation may need to be revisited.

## Cargo Processing Capabilities

In addition to the ability to manage passengers in a way that will attract travelers, RMN also needs capabilities to manage cargo operations in a way that will satisfy airlines and, by extension, their cargo shipping and receiving customers. These capabilities include the following:

- **Cargo handling capabilities**   These capabilities require acquisition and operation of equipment such as forklifts, pallets, containerized handling equipment, roll-on and roll-off containers, materials handling equipment, and so on.

- **Cargo tracking capabilities**   These capabilities require automated identification technologies such as radiofrequency ID (RFID) tagging and bar codes as well as a system of tracking that enables these identifiers to be captured at various points of the cargo processing cycle.

- **Cargo inspection capability**   This capability requires that various cargo items be checked against U.S. laws. These laws are enforced by various federal agencies. The Department of Agriculture and APHIS enforce laws that control importation of plant and animal products. The Department of Commerce enforces laws related to the International Arms Trade (ITARS). The Department of Customs and Border Protection enforces laws related to the assessment, charging, and collection of customs duty.

- **Cargo storage and cargo management capabilities**   These capabilities require space and segregated areas within the airport. For example, a bonded warehouse is required for customs-cleared cargo. A quarantine area is required when cargo suspected of containing harmful plant or animal material needs to be sequestered before being destroyed. Cargo storage also requires the need for security and fire protection forces.

- **Hazardous material cargo (hazmat) handling capabilities**   These capabilities require clear identification of hazardous materials and management of their storage to prevent potential CBRNE (chemical, biological, radiation, or nuclear explosion) events.

Cargo processing capabilities require space and facilities for cargo operations in addition to the passenger terminal operations. Although some of the capabilities needed to support cargo processing are the primary responsibility of the carriers, such as a package express company or the cargo operations arm of an airline, RMN Airport management and facilities need to be able to support cargo operations in a sustainable, safe, efficient, and effective manner. RMN Airport is a platform that enables cargo carrier operations in much the same way that it enables air transportation of passengers.

## Information Technology Capabilities

To bring RMN Airport up to the standards of LAX and newer major airports, information technology features and functions will have to be included in each phase of the transformation. Here are examples of the types of technologies and capabilities that will be needed:

- Terminals need to be equipped with wireless hubs to enable passengers to connect to the Internet. Wireless access points, electric charging points, and desks and stations for laptops and notebooks need to be provided in the terminal areas for passengers.

- Surveillance capabilities need to be integrated into the digital infrastructure. Storage needs to be provided for the large amounts of surveillance data picked up by terminal- and cargo-area cameras. The capability to index and recall this data for forensic and operational analysis is also needed.

- Airport back-office operations need to be integrated into loosely coupled, service-oriented systems that are at once flexible and agile and that can support a variety of orchestrated functions. Service orientation, loose coupling, separation of concerns, and reusability are fundamental architecture principles that RMN Airport has selected for adoption based on the promise of being able to upgrade in a rapid and modular way, increasing scale and tempo of operations as the airport expands.

- The airport IT infrastructure needs to provide a backbone platform to run the various federal agency system components such as those required by Department of Agriculture APHIS; Customs and Border Protection; Department of Homeland Security/Transportation Security Administration systems for flight manifests, no-fly lists, name searches, and other security measures; and the FAA's system of equipment and instrumentation.

- The airport needs to provide the technical capabilities of an enterprise service bus and an Internet transport layer as well as services for connectivity, data exchange, and a network of networks. These need to comply with existing and emerging standards within the aviation industry for internetworking computers; data exchange; data formats; and voice, data, and video networks.

- The airport will develop, implement, and use cloud-based services wherever possible to take advantage of scalability and demand elasticity and as a way to expense operations instead of investing in capital equipment.

- RMN Airport needs to allocate IT data centers at various strategic locations inside the airport perimeter, along with alternative sites for continuity of operations (COOP) support.

## Continuous Interactions with Communities of Interest

As RMN Airport transforms and grows, RMN management will have to interact with federal, state, and local groups on a regular basis. Federal and state approvals will be necessary for the plans that the airport develops (see the upcoming section, "Plans"). The city councils of the surrounding three communities will also need to approve the airport's plans and will need to be constantly updated on developments and issues. There will be many national, state, and local groups, such as environmental groups, business groups, and unions, that will want to be updated on the airport's plans and will want to provide input. Local groups will be most focused on noise, traffic, and land acquisition topics. As the airport grows, the number of these groups will also grow.

## Cultural Issues

A major cultural change at RMN Airport will be change from people-oriented operations to process-oriented operations. For a small airport, a combination of training and hiring the right people is sufficient to ensure that the right decisions will be made for smooth operations. However, as the airport grows and transforms to a vibrant aviation hub, the pace of operations will introduce a need for documented, enforced, and monitored processes to supplement the traditional human resource–based approach of hiring the right people. The transformation from people-oriented, relatively autonomous decision-making to a process-centric, command and control decision-making environment is a big change that may cause friction with longtime managers and employees. The addition of unionized workers introduces additional influences. Management will have to understand and manage these cultural issues.

# Plans

The FAA recommends the development of an Airport Master Plan (AMP) to provide guidance for the evolution of an airport. Figure 3-6 provides an overview of the contents of the AMP and two related plans: the Airport Layout Plan and the Integrated Project Roadmap.

Following are the objectives of the AMP:

- Document the issues that the proposed development will address. (Note that an enterprise architecture will help identify issues.)

- Justify the proposed development through the technical, economic, and environmental investigation of concepts and alternatives. (An enterprise architecture can provide support for these justifications and the analyses that backs them up.)

- Provide an effective graphical presentation of the development of the airport and anticipated land uses in the vicinity of the airport. (An enterprise architecture can provide input to these graphical presentations.)

- Establish a realistic schedule for the implementation of the development proposed in the plan, particularly the short-term capital improvement program. (An enterprise architecture, in terms of phased to-be architectures, can provide details of all changes to be made for each step of the transformation.)

- Propose an achievable financial plan to support the implementation schedule. (An enterprise architecture, in terms of phased to-be architectures, can provide details of all changes to be made for each step of the transformation for the costing analysis.)

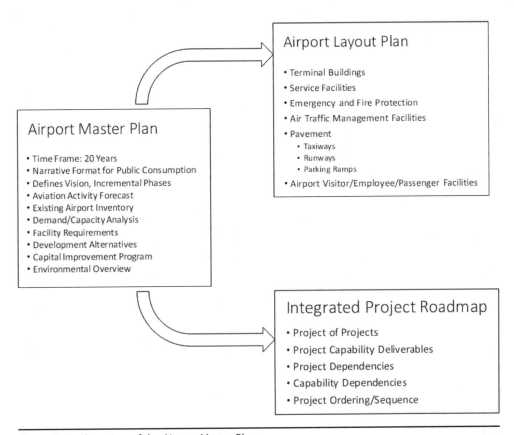

**Figure 3-6**  Overview of the Airport Master Plan

- Provide sufficient project definition and detail for subsequent environmental evaluations that may be required before the project is approved. (An enterprise architecture, in terms of phased to-be architectures with identified projects, can provide details of all changes to be addressed by each project.)

- Present a plan that adequately addresses the issues and satisfies local, state, and federal regulations. (An enterprise architecture can provide input to this analysis.)

- Document policies and future aeronautical demand to support municipal or local deliberations on spending, debt, land use controls, and other policies necessary to preserve the integrity of the airport and its surroundings.

- Set the stage and establish the framework for a continuing planning process. Such a process should monitor key conditions and permit changes in plan recommendations as required. (An enterprise architecture should be a key part of the enterprise planning process.)

RMN Airport management has prepared an AMP for the transformation of the airport but has focused on a 15-year view for this version of the plan, versus the 20-year time frame suggested by the FAA. RMN management will update the AMP every 5 years during the 15-year time frame of this plan.

From an enterprise architecture viewpoint, the AMP outline requires much of the same content as an enterprise architecture:

- Defines the vision and incremental steps with explicit annual progress measures—a target architecture, phasing architectures, and strategic viewpoint
- Describes the existing airport inventory—an as-is architecture
- Describes facility requirements, provides development alternatives, and describes the capital improvement program—other parts to the to-be architectures

The AMP requires aviation activity forecast and demand/capacity analysis, which would be needed as input to to-be architectures. However, the AMP wants narrative descriptions, whereas an enterprise architecture provides specific views and mathematical models, many of which are graphical in nature. The more detailed and structured views of the enterprise architecture can be used to support the required analyses required by the AMP.

Elements of the AMP and its two associated plans will need approval by the commissioners, the city councils of the three surrounding communities, and the FAA. Other approvals may be needed from the State of California Department of Transportation, the Environment Protection Agency, or local environmental organizations.

## Summary

The transformation of RMN Airport from a civil aviation field to a reliever airport for LAX will involve several phases and take at least 15 years. We have provided a brief overview of some of the challenging changes that must be accomplished in this transformation. The "References" section provides more information for anyone interested in airport regulations and requirements.

The chapters of Part II and Part III of this book will make reference to this case study in examples, especially in the example DoDAF views in Part III. Most of these examples focus on an enterprise-level architecture for RMN Airport with strategic and project viewpoints, a segment-level architecture for a passenger management segment as the airport starts to handle international passengers, and a solution-level architecture for passenger identification technology upgrades that are part of the passenger management segment.

## References

Federal Aviation Administration. 1988. Advisory Circular No 150/5360-13, Change 1. "Planning and Design Guidelines for Airport Terminal Facilities." www.faa.gov/regulations_policies/advisory_circulars/index.cfm/go/document.information/documentID/22618.

Federal Aviation Administration. 2014. Advisory Circular No 150/5300-13A, Change 1. "Airport Design." www.faa.gov/airports/resources/advisory_circulars/index.cfm/go/document.current/documentNumber/150_5300-13.

Federal Aviation Administration. 2015. Advisory Circular No 150/5070-6B, Change 2. "Airport Master Plans." www.faa.gov/airports/resources/advisory_circulars/index.cfm/go/document.current/documentNumber/150_5070-6.

Federal Aviation Administration. 2015. Advisory Circular No 150/5070-7, Change 1. "The Airport System Planning Process." www.faa.gov/documentLibrary/media/Advisory_Circular/150-5070-7-change1.pdf.

Federal Aviation Administration. 2016. "Airport Categories." www.faa.gov/airports/planning_capacity/passenger_allcargo_stats/categories/.

McKinney National Airport Master Plan, FAQ. nd. http://mckinney.airportstudy.com/files/FAQs-for-Study-Website1.pdf.

# Basic Concepts for Defense Frameworks

The focus of this chapter is on the details of the Department of Defense Architecture Framework (DoDAF) and related defense frameworks. We use the DoDAF as the basis for our examples in both Parts II and III of this book. We chose the DoDAF for these examples because it is one of the oldest frameworks (only the Zachman Framework is older), its views are compatible with the TOGAF and form a subset of the Federal Enterprise Architecture Framework Version 2 (FEAF2) views, and it is the basis for many other defense frameworks.

There are many reasons why military organizations have tried to unify architectures through the definition of overarching architecture frameworks. Defense architecture frameworks are specified in general terms that enable them to be equally easily applied to developing weapons systems as to developing force structures and military missions and operations during wartime and peacetime. The need for coalition partners to inter-operate and collaborate during coalition operations also requires that military partners have comparatively consistent, interoperable and well-documented architectures. The need for joint operations requires that the U.S. Navy, U.S. Army, U.S. Air Force, U.S. Marine Corps, and the U.S. Coast Guard all have compatible architectures. The primary purpose of defense architecture frameworks is to provide a common format and seman-tics for comparison, aggregation, and analysis of multiple architectures. With a common framework, classes of complex problems in a theater or on the battlefield such as joint asset visibility, joint mission threads, common operating picture, and others can be tack-led by federating multiple architectures during the planning, acquisition, and resourcing phase to ensure that collaboration, interoperability, single operating picture, and unity of actions are accomplished under critical war-fighting conditions. One of the most impor-tant needs met by the DoDAF was an integrated view of architecture elements through many views that share subsets of the same architecture elements. The requirement of an integrated dictionary to be provided for every architecture presses out redundancy and ensures that integration is built into the architecture from the very beginning.

Work on what became the DoDAF started in the mid-1990s, as DoD's Intelligence, Surveillance, and Reconnaissance (ISR) community struggled with trying to compare the architectures proposed by various contractors in response to requests for proposals

(RFPs). The DoD as a whole was also struggling with interoperability issues for various processes and systems as it moved toward integrated task force strategies, which required the military services to work together. The DoDAF was designed to provide a common language for describing architectures and provided a flexible set of basic building blocks—that is, views—for telling the story of each architecture. The DoDAF provided a necessary basis for comparing architectures and for identifying critical interfaces.

Other defense organizations adopted and refined the DoDAF into their own frameworks. Examples of related defense frameworks are the United Kingdom's Ministry of Defense Architecture Framework (MODAF), the Department of National Defense/Canadian Armed Forces Architecture Framework (DNDAF), the Australian Defense Architecture Framework (DAF), and the North Atlantic Treaty Organization (NATO) Architecture Framework (NAF), to name a few. In addition, the DoDAF views have been the basis for multiple U.S. federal agency architecture frameworks that have adopted the approach, viewpoints, and views as an integrated way of architecting. Extensions first developed in the MODAF have been integrated back into the DoDAF. Additional features developed in these related defense frameworks will undoubtedly be integrated back into DoDAF as it continues to evolve. Efforts are currently underway to specify a unified architecture framework ontology based on these defense architecture frameworks with assistance from standards bodies such as the Object Management Group (OMG).

We address the DoDAF concepts in the same order that generic enterprise architecture concepts were introduced in Chapter 1.

## Levels of Enterprise

There are three basic levels of enterprise architecture usually used in DoDAF: Enterprise, Segment, and Solution. These levels are illustrated in Figure 4-1.

Enterprise Level architectures are used to support strategic decision-making for the enterprise. Segment Level architectures are used to manage coherent sets of related capabilities or business services to ensure coordination and interoperability of related business processes, systems, and data. Solution Level architectures are used to support and manage business process and related system development and acquisition efforts. The Solution Level includes the concepts of System of Systems (SoS) and Family of Systems (FoS). (SoS and FoS are defined in the upcoming "Solution Level" section.) We will examine each of these levels in this chapter.

**Figure 4-1**
Levels of enterprise architectures

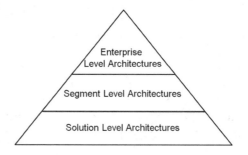

# Enterprise Level

The Enterprise Level includes architectures of enterprises with top-level strategic plans, goals, and objectives as well as multiple projects and a portfolio of IT investments to manage. At the Enterprise Level, management includes investment or project selection, control, and evaluation (as described in Chapter 10). The goal of an Enterprise Level architecture is to provide traceability from the enterprise strategic vision, goals, and objectives to the capabilities needed to achieve those objectives, to the projects (and their managing organizations) that implement those capabilities and to the organizations that use the capabilities. Phasing and timelines are key parts of this traceability.

Defense enterprises undertake complex, large multiyear acquisition programs from aircrafts and ships to worldwide software applications. These applications are deployed across thousands of personnel and require design constraints for security, survivability, performance, scalability, and deployability in austere environments. Much of this material is durable and has a service life of many years. (For example, a typical airframe may be used for more than 40 years with periodic upgrades.) By focusing on the capability needed rather than the specific solution requirement of the day, planners are able to architect these types of items to remain useful over their expected life-times. By applying a program-driven strategy for acquisition, military senior leaders are able to track the health of the acquisition through various milestones. The enterprise architecture aligns the capability requirements against the portfolio of programs that acquire the capability.

Here some example questions or issues that an Enterprise Level architecture might address:

- How do the business functions or capabilities relate to the enterprise's strategy and goals?
- Are there dependencies among the capabilities or business functions?
- How will business function or capability performance be measured?
- When will the capabilities or business functions be implemented and what projects will provide them?
- What organizations will use the capabilities or business functions?
- What organizations are in charge of which projects?
- What are the timelines for the projects and what are the dependencies among them?

An example of Enterprise Level architecture is outlined for the RMN Airport Case Study in Chapter 5.

When an enterprise is so large that a single architecture is impractical, a Federated Architecture approach may be used. A Federated Architecture for an enterprise is made up of an integratable set of independently developed lower-level architectures. The set of lower-level architectures may be a set of Segment Level architectures together with corresponding Solution Level architectures, or a set of domain architectures, each oriented toward an architectural domain such as business, data, application, and technology. The enterprise has to provide sufficient guidance, such as enterprise-level reference models (described in Chapter 1), to ensure that the lower-level architectures use consistent terminology and can be integrated. The reference models most often used in conjunction with the DoDAF in the U.S. are the Federal Enterprise Architecture (FEA) reference models discussed in Chapter 23.

Another type of notional architecture used by defense organizations (especially in the infrastructure and technology area) is reference architecture. A reference architecture "is an authoritative source of information about a specific subject area that guides and constrains the instantiations of multiple architectures and solutions." [OASD 2010] With the formulation of the DoDAF, it was possible to articulate notional architectures that serve as starting blueprints for specific enterprises to implement their own instances and variations using a common language, architecting paradigm, and suggested approach. Following are some of the reference architectures that have been developed using the DoDAF and provide specific guidance:

- **U.S. Army Identity and Access Management (IdAM) Reference Architecture**    Specifies how a standard architecture for identification and access management across the U.S. Army can be used by Army commands and agencies to implement their own IdAM strategies with the assurance that they will be conformant with the Army's overall approach. [Army IDAM RA 2014a]

- **U.S. Army Network Security Enterprise Reference Architecture**    Specifies an overall Army approach to providing network security that can be used by Army commands and agencies to implement their own network security architectures conformant with the overall Army approach. [Army Network Security RA 2014b]

- **DoD Joint Information Enterprise Reference Architecture**    An overarching view of how DoD information, IT, and the cyber environment will be transformed for the future through a collection of visions, reference architectures, and ways forward. [DeVries 2013]

- **DoD Core Data Center Reference Architecture**    Defines the DoD cloud. Existence of core data centers and modularized and containerized data centers (data center in a box) will enable synchronized data and services within tactical edge environments. [DeVries 2013]

- **Unified Capabilities Reference Architecture**    Provides a framework intended to guide and align DoD component instantiation of respective UC implementation plans and solutions. It provides a common language and reference for DoD components' implementation of UC technology, supports implementation of DoD component solutions, and directs adherence to common standards and specifications to support the Joint Information Environment (JIE) goal of establishing effective, secure, and common UC. [Takai 2013]

## Segment Level

One way of decomposing an Enterprise Level architecture into integratable component architectures is to use Segment Level architectures. Each Segment Level architecture addresses a core mission area of the enterprise, a subset of the Enterprise Level architecture capabilities, or a common or shared service that supports core mission areas. The common or shared services may be either business services, such as human resources management or financial management, or enterprise services (such as IT services, knowledge management or communications.

The core mission areas associated with Segment Level architectures may have strategic plans, goals, and objectives that are consistent with the strategic plans, goals, and objectives of the top-level enterprise. These core mission areas may also manage a subset of the top-level enterprise's projects and a subset of the IT investment portfolio. Thus, Segment Level architectures may address the same types of questions as Enterprise Level architectures.

For DoD, examples of Segment Level architectures are Joint Capability Areas (JCAs). Segment Level architectures for other federal agencies are frequently aligned with an agency's lines of business (LOBs). For example, some Health and Human Services (HHS) segments are healthcare administration (a core mission area segment) and IT management (a business service segment). Segment Level architectures may also be used for cross-agency government missions such as international trade. IT management and human resources management are often treated as segments in commercial enterprises. In other words, there is uniform management of these operations and services, and often a centralized organization that supplies these services to an entire enterprise. Specific product lines may also be treated as segments in commercial enterprises.

An example of a Segment Level architecture is outlined for the RMN Airport Case Study in Chapter 5. The Passenger Management Segment is used to manage and coordinate multiple Solution Level architectures that support passenger management processes at the airport.

When segments are commonly shared across multiple business units, reference architecture concepts can be used to define notional architectures for segments that are instantiated and specialized by each business unit. These reference architectures provide common blueprints that facilitate integration or federation of segments across business units or collaborating enterprises.

## Solution Level

Solution Level architectures are focused on a specific business/mission process solution involving a system or service or set of systems or services. These architectures provide guidance for system/service development projects and are the level of enterprise architecture most closely related to systems architectures. The system development project guidance includes concept of operations, required support for business processes, system interface and interoperability requirements, and technical standards. Solution Level architectures are frequently used as a way of comparing proposed solutions during an acquisition process. The goal of a Solution Level architecture is to provide traceability from performers to the operational activities they perform and to the IT that supports those activities. The resources or information exchanged are a key part of this traceability. Solution Level architectures may address SoS or FoS.

An SoS is a set of systems that are the components of a more complex system that shows emergent properties. That is, the capabilities of the whole exceed the capabilities of the component systems. Typically, the component systems are distributed and independently operated and managed. For example, the Global Earth Observation System of Systems (GEOSS) will be a global and flexible network of content providers providing information to decision-makers for the benefit of society. GEOSS will link together existing and planned observing systems around the world, using common technical standards so that data from thousands of different instruments can be combined into coherent data sets.

An FoS is a set of separate systems that can be integrated in different ways to provide a variety of mission-related capabilities. For example, consider a set of systems that supports search and rescue efforts. These systems would include basic command and control systems and communications systems, together with specialty support systems, including mountain search and rescue, sea search and rescue, and desert search and rescue. These systems could be combined as needed for specific search and rescue missions.

Here are some of the basic questions or issues that Solution Level architectures address:

- What are the key elements of the operational concept?
- How are the business/mission operations performed?
- Who performs the business/mission operations and what resources are exchanged?
- What are the systems/services and what are their interfaces (both internal and external)?
- How do the systems/services support operations?
- What are the technical standards for the systems/services?

Examples of Solution Level architectures include architectures for specific business processes or business services. The RMN Airport Case Study Solution Level architecture for passenger identification is a specific example of a business service architecture. In DoD, architectures for specific weapons systems are Solution Level architectures.

The concepts of reference architectures are also applicable to solutions. A family of solutions that share similar characteristics but are used in different enterprise components can all be rationalized and harmonized by specifying a solution reference architecture for the family of solutions, where each solution is an instance with specializations as required. The reference architecture is especially useful for products that form a product line or family. The architecture of the product line is notional and is specialized and instantiated by each product that belongs to the product line.

# DoDAF Viewpoints

The DoDAF organizes its views into a set of eight viewpoints, defined in Figure 4-2. These viewpoints tend to map to abstract classes of stakeholders: executives, business managers, operational personnel, and IT personnel.

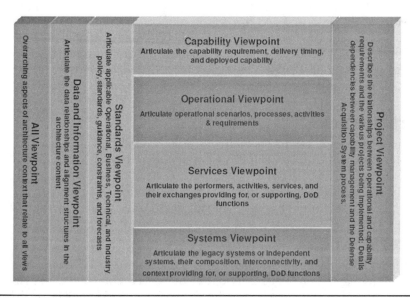

**Figure 4-2** DoDAF viewpoints (graphic from the DoDAF)

# All Viewpoint

The All Viewpoint provides an overview of the entire architecture. Its views provide both a living executive summary of the architecture, including conclusions and recommendations, and the detailed definitions for all terms used in the architecture. This viewpoint is used by all architecture stakeholders.

# Capability Viewpoint

The Capability Viewpoint focuses on the strategic aspects of the enterprise, such as the vision of the enterprise, its goals and objectives, capabilities that are necessary to achieve those goals and objectives, relationships among the capabilities, how the delivery of these capabilities will change over time, and organizations that will use these capabilities. This viewpoint is of primary interest to executive management.

# Data and Information Viewpoint

The Data and Information Viewpoint focuses on descriptions of the shared, structured enterprise data. Views in this viewpoint provide representations of the conceptual, logical, or physical models of this shared data. This viewpoint may be of interest to any of business managers, operational personnel, and IT personnel, depending on the level of detail included.

# Operational Viewpoint

The Operational Viewpoint provides information on the operations of the enterprise, such as the business or mission concept of operations, the business or mission processes and who performs them, the information flows between these performers and between the activities of the processes, and the organizations involved. The Operational Viewpoint also provides information on the operational behaviors of the enterprise: the operational elements that have interesting state behavior, the key operational scenarios, and the business or operational rules. This viewpoint is of primary interest to the business manager and operational personnel.

## Project Viewpoint

The Project Viewpoint has to do with the various development projects current or planned for the enterprise. Views in this viewpoint identify what organizations manage which projects, what the delivery timelines are for sets of projects and what the dependencies among the deliveries are, and which projects provide components for which capability. This viewpoint is of primary interest to executives and business managers.

## Services Viewpoint

The Services Viewpoint provides information on the business or IT services of the enterprise. This information can include service functions, service interfaces, and service level agreements (SLAs); how the services are interconnected; what resources are exchanged; and when services will be available. The behavioral aspects of the services can also be described. This viewpoint is of primary interest to business managers (for business services) and IT personnel (for IT services).

## Standards Viewpoint

The Standards Viewpoint focuses on the technical standards and the systems or services these standards should apply to. The technical standards are usually organized based on a technical reference model (TRM). Standards may have dates associated with them: when the standard must be met and when the standard will no longer apply and what emerging standard will replace it. This viewpoint is of primary interest to IT personnel and to business managers involved in acquisition.

## Systems Viewpoint

The Systems Viewpoint provides information on the enterprise's systems. Information includes what the systems are, how they are interconnected, what resources flow between them, when they become available, and what activities they support. The behavioral aspects of the systems can also be described. This viewpoint is of primary interest to IT personnel.

## Viewpoint Relationships

Figure 4-3 shows some of the relationships among the viewpoints and provides a foundation for understanding how the views in these viewpoints need to integrate across the viewpoints. The Systems and Services Viewpoints map to the Operational Viewpoint by showing how the information technology (IT) supports operations. The Standards

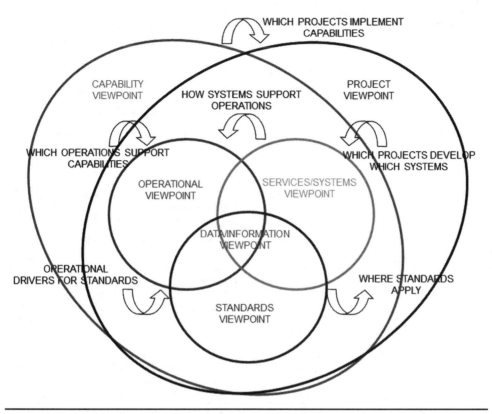

**Figure 4-3**  Relationships among the DoDAF viewpoints

Viewpoint maps to the Systems and Services Viewpoints by showing where the standards apply or should apply. The Operational Viewpoint maps to the Standards Viewpoint by providing operational needs for interoperability standards. This last relationship is not currently supported directly in the DoDAF views but can easily be added by tailoring views. The Capability Viewpoint maps to the Project Viewpoint through the projects that implement the capabilities. The Capability Viewpoint maps to the Operational Viewpoint in terms of the operational activities that implement the capabilities. The Project Viewpoint maps to the Systems or Services Viewpoints in terms of the projects that develop the systems or services. The Data Viewpoint is shown in the middle, since enterprise data can be important to understanding any of the other viewpoints.

# DoDAF Views

We introduce the set of DoDAF views, organized by viewpoint, for reference in Table 4-1. These DoDAF views are compatible with TOGAF and are a subset of the views/models contained in the FEAF2. Thus, the DoDAF views provide an integrated, basic set. Details of each view and examples related to the airport case study are provided in Part III.

| Viewpoint | Short Name | View Name | View Description |
|---|---|---|---|
| All | AV-1 | Overview and Summary Information | Describes a project's visions, goals, objectives, plans, activities, events, conditions, measures, effects (outcomes), and produced objects. |
| | AV-2 | Integrated Dictionary | An architectural data repository with definitions of all terms used throughout the architectural data and presentations. |
| Capability | CV-1 | Vision | The overall vision for transformational endeavors, which provides a strategic context for the capabilities described and a high-level scope. |
| | CV-2 | Capability Taxonomy | A hierarchy of capabilities that specifies all the capabilities that are referenced throughout one or more architectural descriptions. |
| | CV-3 | Capability Phasing | The planned achievement of capability at different points in time or during specific periods of time. The CV-3 shows the capability phasing in terms of the activities, conditions, desired effects, rules complied with, resource consumption and production, and measures, without regard to the performer and location solutions. |
| | CV-4 | Capability Dependencies | The dependencies between planned capabilities and the definition of logical groupings of capabilities. |
| | CV-5 | Capability to Organizational Development Mapping | The fulfillment of capability requirements shows the planned capability deployment and interconnection for a particular Capability Phase. The CV-5 shows the planned solution for the phase in terms of performers and locations and their associated concepts. |
| | CV-6 | Capability to Operational Activities Mapping | A mapping between the capabilities required and the operational activities that those capabilities support. |
| | CV-7 | Capability to Services Mapping | A mapping between the capabilities and the services that these capabilities enable. |
| Data and Information | DIV-1 | Conceptual Data Model | The required high-level data concepts and their relationships. |
| | DIV-2 | Logical Data Model | The documentation of the data requirements and structural business process (activity) rules. In DoDAF V1.5, this was the OV-7. |
| | DIV-3 | Physical Data Model | The physical implementation format of the Logical Data Model entities, such as message formats, file structures, physical schema. In DoDAF V1.5, this was the SV-11. |

**Table 4-1**   DODAF Views Organized by Viewpoint

| Viewpoint | Short Name | View Name | View Description |
|---|---|---|---|
| Operational | OV-1 | High-Level Operational Concept Graphic | The high-level graphical/textual description of the operational concept. |
| | OV-2 | Operational Resource Flow Description | A description of the need to exchange resources among performers in the performance of activities. |
| | OV-3 | Operational Resource Flow Matrix | A description of the resources exchanged and the relevant attributes of the exchanges. |
| | OV-4 | Organizational Relationships Chart | The organizational context, role, or other relationships among organizations. |
| | OV-5a | Operational Activity Decomposition Tree | The capabilities and activities (operational activities) organized in a hierarchal structure. |
| | OV-5b | Operational Activity Model | The context of capabilities and activities (operational activities) and their relationships among activities, inputs, and outputs; Additional data can show cost, performers, or other pertinent information. |
| | OV-6a | Operational Rules Model | One of three models used to describe activity (operational activity); identifies business rules that constrain operations. |
| | OV-6b | State Transition Description | One of three models used to describe operational activity (activity); identifies business process (activity) responses to events (usually, very short activities). |
| | OV-6c | Event-Trace Description | One of three models used to describe activity (operational activity); traces actions in a scenario or sequence of events. |
| Project | PV-1 | Project Portfolio Relationships | Describes the dependency relationships between the organizations and projects and the organizational structures needed to manage a portfolio of projects. |
| | PV-2 | Project Timelines | A timeline perspective on programs or projects, with the key milestones and interdependencies. |
| | PV-3 | Project to Capability Mapping | A mapping of programs and projects to capabilities to show how the specific projects and program elements help to achieve a capability. |

**Table 4-1**   DODAF Views Organized by Viewpoint *(continued)*

| Viewpoint | Short Name | View Name | View Description |
|-----------|-----------|-----------|------------------|
| Services | SvcV-1 | Services Context Description | The identification of services, service items, and their interconnections. |
| | SvcV-2 | Services Resource Flow Description | A description of the infrastructure, such as communications links and mechanisms, that enable the resource flows among the services. |
| | SvcV-3a | Systems-Services Matrix | The relationships among or between systems and services in a given architectural description. |
| | SvcV-3b | Services-Services Matrix | The relationships among services in a given architectural description; can be designed to show relationships of interest (such as service-type interfaces, planned vs. existing interfaces). |
| | SvcV-4 | Services Functionality Description | The functions performed by services and the service data flows among service functions (activities). |
| | SvcV-5 | Operational Activity to Services Traceability Matrix | A mapping of services (activities) back to operational activities (activities). |
| | SvcV-6 | Services Resource Flow Matrix | Provides details of service resource flow elements being exchanged between services and the attributes of that exchange. |
| | SvcV-7 | Services Measures Matrix | The measures (metrics) of Services Model elements for the appropriate time frame(s). |
| | SvcV-8 | Services Evolution Description | The planned incremental steps toward migrating a suite of services to a more efficient suite or toward evolving current services to a future implementation. |
| | SvcV-9 | Services Technology and Skills Forecast | The emerging technologies, software/hardware products, and skills expected to be available in a given set of time frames and that will affect future service development. |
| | SvcV-10a | Services Rules Model | One of three models used to describe service functionality; identifies constraints that are imposed on systems functionality due to some aspect of service design or implementation. |
| | SvcV-10b | Services State Transition Description | One of three models used to describe service functionality; identifies responses of services to events. |

**Table 4-1**  DODAF Views Organized by Viewpoint *(continued)*

| Viewpoint | Short Name | View Name | View Description |
|---|---|---|---|
| | SvcV-10c | Services Event-Trace Description | One of three models used to describe service functionality; identifies service-specific refinements of critical sequences of events described in the Operational Viewpoint. |
| Standards | StdV-1 | Standards Profile | The listing of standards that apply to solution elements. |
| | StdV-2 | Standards Forecast | The description of emerging standards and potential impact on current solution elements, within a set of time frames. |
| Systems | SV-1 | Systems Interface Description | The identification of systems, system items, and their interconnections. |
| | SV-2 | Systems Resource Flow Description | A description of the infrastructure, such as communications links and mechanisms or the transport links and mechanisms, that enable resource flows among the systems. |
| | SV-3 | Systems-Systems Matrix | The relationships among systems in a given architectural description; can be designed to show relationships of interest (such as system-type interfaces, planned vs. existing interfaces). |
| | SV-4 | Systems Functionality Description | The functions (activities) performed by systems and the system data flows among system functions (activities). |
| | SV-5a | Operational Activity to Systems Function Traceability Matrix | A mapping of system functions (activities) back to operational activities (activities). |
| | SV-5b | Operational Activity to Systems Traceability Matrix | A mapping of systems back to capabilities or operational activities (activities). |
| | SV-6 | Systems Resource Flow Matrix | Provides details of system resource flow elements being exchanged between systems and the attributes of that exchange. |
| | SV-7 | Systems Measures Matrix | The measures (metrics) of Systems Model elements for the appropriate time frame(s). |
| | SV-8 | Systems Evolution Description | The planned incremental steps toward migrating a suite of systems to a more efficient suite, or toward evolving a current system to a future implementation. |

**Table 4-1**   DODAF Views Organized by Viewpoint *(continued)*

| Viewpoint | Short Name | View Name | View Description |
|---|---|---|---|
| | SV-9 | Systems Technology and Skills Forecast | The emerging technologies, software/hardware products, and skills that are expected to be available in a given set of time frames and that will affect future system development. |
| | SV-10a | Systems Rules Model | One of three models used to describe system functionality; identifies constraints that are imposed on systems functionality due to some aspect of system design or implementation. |
| | SV-10b | Systems State Transition Description | One of three models used to describe system functionality; identifies responses of systems to events. |
| | SV-10c | Systems Event-Trace Description | One of three models used to describe system functionality; identifies system-specific refinements of critical sequences of events described in the Operational Viewpoint. |

**Table 4-1**  DODAF Views Organized by Viewpoint *(continued)*

The label in the Short Name column is the shorthand name for the view in the DoDAF. The set of letters preceding the "V" is an acronym for one of the DoDAF viewpoints and the number is an arbitrary number assigned to the view within the viewpoint. The view descriptions provided in the table are based on the official definitions from the DoDAF with small changes to enhance clarity. More detailed and specific descriptions of the views are provided in Part III.

## Integration of Views

Multiple views may share the same architecture elements or concepts. For example, performers appear in the OV-2: Operational Resource Flow Description, OV-3: Operational Resource Flow Matrix, OV-5b: Operational Activity Model, and OV-6c: Event-Trace Description. As discussed earlier, viewpoints are related to one another by shared architecture elements, so views in different viewpoints may also share architecture elements. For example, activities appear in the OV-5b: Operational Activity Model and in the SV-5b: Operational Activity to Systems Traceability Matrix. Within the same architecture, the activities that appear in the OV-5b should be the same activities that appear in the SV-5b. These activities should map to the same dictionary entries in the AV-2: Integrated Dictionary. In this way, a consistent version of reality is reflected across a single architecture. An architecture whose views are disjoint—that is, whose views should share the same elements but instead reference disjoint or partially disjoint sets of dictionary entries—is useless because the reality it represents is logically inconsistent. Such an architecture can be used only to raise issues and questions as to why it is inconsistent.

Examples in Part III will illustrate and discuss how views should integrate.

# Repository and Metamodel

DoDAF has an implicit repository concept in the AV-2: Integrated Dictionary. The AV-2 requires the cataloging of every architecture element and relationship along with its role in the architecture (such as performer, operational activity, system function, information exchange requirement, or needline). The various types of architecture elements form the schema (metamodel) elements of a repository and the relationships between them form schema relationships.

The DoDAF originally provided a DoDAF Metamodel (DM2) to define all the types of DoDAF architecture elements and their intended relationships. The metamodel was useful not only to provide architecture developers with guidance on how the architecture elements in views should fit together and how the views should integrate, but also to provide architecture tool vendors with guidance regarding what syntactic rules their tools should enforce and how to organize the repositories for their tools.

The metamodel for a framework is used to represent a vocabulary of elements that are commonly used and shared across all communities that use the same framework. When architects are using automated tools, the metamodel is implemented inside the tool by the vendor, and the user can only construct diagrams that have symbols and links that can be converted into conformant metamodel object instances inside the tool's repository. Tools based on the Unified Modeling Language (UML) use a UML mechanism, called a *profile*, to restrict the scope of class instances. A class is restricted using a stereotype. The DoDAF DM2 metamodel class types and MODAF class types are implemented in a UML tool as a profile called the Unified Profile for DoDAF and MODAF (UPDM). The UPDM is being evolved into an ontology that covers more of the defense related frameworks as discussed later in this chapter.

The following subsections provide an introduction to key elements of the DM2. These elements have been divided up into two main groups—business domain and IT and infrastructure domain—for ease in understanding.

## Elements of the Business Domain

The business domain deals with concepts and terms that address operations and business value. This domain focuses on what gets done and how it is managed rather than on IT and automation details. We first present the basic concepts of interest to an Enterprise Level architecture and then the basic concepts for Solution Level architectures. Segment Level architectures may contain a combination of these concepts.

Enterprise Level architectures tie together enterprise vision, strategy, goals, and objectives to the capabilities that support them, the projects that deliver the capabilities, and the organizations that own the projects or use the capabilities. Both objectives and capabilities may have performance measures associated with them. These concepts and their relationships enable the Enterprise Level stakeholders to see how proposed or existing projects align with business objectives. The performance measures provide criteria for evaluating whether the capabilities being delivered by existing projects are meeting expectations. This information enables the enterprise to manage its investments and coordinate its projects.

Figure 4-4 shows basic Enterprise Level concepts and their relationships. The concepts are the items inside the rounded rectangles and the relationships are indicated by the arrows of any style. For example, a Capability is part of a Desired Effect. Dashed arrows represent optional relationships. The concepts and their relationships are discussed next.

Most enterprises have *vision* statements that summarize their missions and views of current or future business objectives. The enterprise has a *strategy* for achieving its future vision that can be realized by achieving stated *goals* and measurable *objectives*. Thus, business objectives are achieved if they meet their *performance measures*. Another term for these goals and objectives is *desired effects*. A *capability* is the ability to perform a desired business function that creates business value and is part of a *desired effect*. That is, the capability is necessary to achieving the desired effect of the strategy. Capabilities may be organized in a specialization hierarchy (from most general to most specialized), and one capability may be dependent on other capabilities. Capabilities may also have associated performance measures.

Here are some Enterprise Level business domain concept examples from the RMN Airport Case Study. These concepts are relevant to the mid-phase to-be architecture that applies to the first five-year period of the transformation.

- **Vision**   RMN Airport becomes a viable alternative to LAX.

- **Desired effect (goal/objective) that realizes the vision**   Within five years, RMN Airport will have passenger flights to Mexico.

**Figure 4-4**
Enterprise Level
business domain
concepts and
relationships

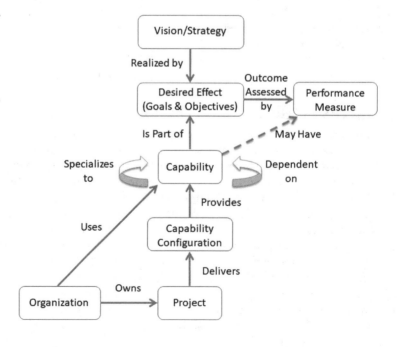

- **Performance measure for the objective**   Number of flights to and from Mexico per time period. Here are the performance goals for this measure:
  - At year 5 of the transformation, RMN Airport will have at least one weekly passenger flight to and from Mexico.
  - At year 7 of the transformation, RMN Airport will have daily flights to and from destinations in Mexico.
  - At year 9 of the transformation, RMN Airport will have daily flights to and from all major Mexican airports and tourist locations (at least five flights daily).
- **Capability that is part of the desired effect**   RMN Airport will be able to handle passenger management processes for international flights (such as customs and immigration).
- **Performance measure (for the capability)**   Number of passengers that can be handled by customs and immigration per time period on average. Here are the performance goals for this measure:
  - At year 5 of the transformation, RMN Airport will handle customs and immigration for one incoming international flight (about 200 passengers) per week at an average.
  - At year 7 of the transformation, RMN Airport will handle customs and immigration for one incoming international flight (about 200 passengers) per day at an average.
  - At year 9 of the transformation, RMN Airport will handle customs and immigration for five incoming international flights (about 1000 passengers) per day at an average.

Capabilities are provided by a *capability configuration* of personnel, systems, and software that are developed, delivered, and maintained by *projects*. *Organizations* within the enterprise use capabilities in their business processes to create business value. Organizations also own—that is, manage and control—projects. The organizations that use capabilities may not own the projects that deliver the corresponding capability configurations. Both organizations and projects may be decomposed into subordinate organizations and subprojects, respectively, although these decompositions are not indicated in Figure 4-4.

In the business domain, Solution Level architectures are focused on the business processes, the roles and organizational structures that perform the processes, and the resources managed and exchanged during the execution of the business processes. These concepts and their relationships enable the enterprise to evaluate current operations, select the best solution alternatives for increasing efficiency or providing new capabilities, and manage transition for business process improvement. Figure 4-5 shows some basic Solution Level concepts and their relationships. This figure uses the same notation as Figure 4-4. The concepts and their relationships are discussed next along with some additional concepts that are not shown in the figure.

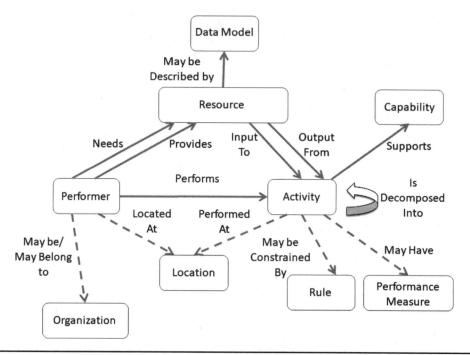

**Figure 4-5** Solution Level business domain concepts and relationships

*Performers* are those who perform the activities of a business process. A performer may be a role or an organization—or, in the case of activities that are fully automated, such as a sensor or agent software, a performer may be IT. An *activity* may be an entire business process or a task within a business process. Activities may be decomposed down to the needed level of detail. An activity or business process may have associated *performance measures* that provide the criteria for judging the effectiveness of the activity. Activities support *capabilities*. Activities may be constrained by business *rules* based on policy, operational standards and guidelines, or corporate culture. Performers perform activities at *locations*. Each activity may be performed at one or more locations. Locations may be abstract or logical, such as "Regional Office," if all regional offices are sufficiently alike for the purposes of the architecture, or concrete, such as "St. Louis, MO, Regional Office." Locations are increasingly mobile. Examples of mobile locations are the combat information center aboard an aircraft carrier and the more abstract "personal office" carried by a traveling salesman in his briefcase or car.

To perform their operations, performers may need to exchange *resources* with other performers. As part of their operations, performers may produce resources that they provide to other performers. These resources may be data, information, personnel types, or materiel (that is, non-personnel physical resources). If the resources are data or information that are sufficiently complex in terms of structure or relationships, they may be modeled in a conceptual or logical *data model*.

Here are some Solution Level business domain concept examples from the RMN Airport Case Study:

- **Performer**   Check-in agent
- **Performer**   Passenger
- **Organization**   Airline
- **Activity**   Check-in passenger
- **Resource**   Identity documents

Check-in agent (performer) employed by airline (organization) performs check-in passenger (activity). Check-in agent needs identity document (resource) from passenger (performer) to perform check-in passenger.

Additional Solution Level concepts relate to the dynamic behavior of the architecture and are not covered in Figure 4-5. These concepts are the *state* behavior and the *scenario* behavior.

State behavior is usually a characteristic of data entities or information elements. The state of a data entity or information element changes in response to events caused by the execution of business processes. Typically, a data entity or information elements will transition through a sequence of states, from some initial state to some terminal state, during the course of normal business operations. For example, in the RMN Airport Case Study, the passenger has state or status that changes as the passenger is processed through the airport and onto the airplane. This state or status is included in the passenger record and is queried and updated by various passenger management processes. Some examples of status for a passenger are checked-in, screened, and boarded. Not all information or data entities will have interesting state behavior, so this type of behavior is modeled in an architecture only when understanding state behavior is important to understanding the enterprise's business.

An operational scenario shows business behavior in terms of interactions among the performers in response to the specific sequence of events contained in the scenario. The scenario highlights the resource exchanges among performers in response to a specific sequence of events generated by the execution of one or more business processes. The scenarios chosen for an architecture usually relate to key operational concepts or performance or security-critical sequences.

As usual, in the business domain, Segment Level architectures can have elements that can appear in both Enterprise Level architectures and Solution Level architectures.

## Elements of the IT and Infrastructure Domain

The IT and infrastructure domain deals with concepts and terms that address systems, services, standards, and communications and how they support the business domain. This domain focuses on the details of systems or services and infrastructure functions, interfaces, performance, and resource exchanges, and how all these items support business process needs. Here, systems and services are usually provided by automation, but, as automation continues to become more sophisticated and the infrastructure becomes more capable and pervasive, systems may be viewed in the traditional systems engineering way, by inclusion in organizational structures and personnel. The inclusion of the relationships between system or services and the business domain is critical. Without this connection, a basic purpose of EA—that is to ensure that IT supports business needs and goals—cannot be achieved. Because of the need to show this connection, it is hazardous to develop business domain and IT domain architectures independently. There needs to be a strong coordination between the developments of these two domain architectures to achieve an integrated, useful EA.

The IT and infrastructure details are usually of more concern for Solution Level architectures, although Enterprise Level architectures are concerned with the overall IT and infrastructure interoperability and integration issues, including technical standards and delivery and retirement dates for capability configurations. The IT and infrastructure domain can be viewed from either a system-oriented or a service-oriented approach. We first present the basic concepts for a system-oriented viewpoint and then the basic concepts for a service-oriented viewpoint. Last, we discuss some basic concepts for communications infrastructure.

## System Viewpoint Elements

A system viewpoint looks at the IT and infrastructure domain as a set of systems with interfaces, where each system performs a set of system functions, exchanges resources (usually data), and has performance measures. Figure 4-6 shows some basic IT and infrastructure domain system viewpoint concepts and their relationships that will be discussed next along with some additional concepts that are not shown in the figure.

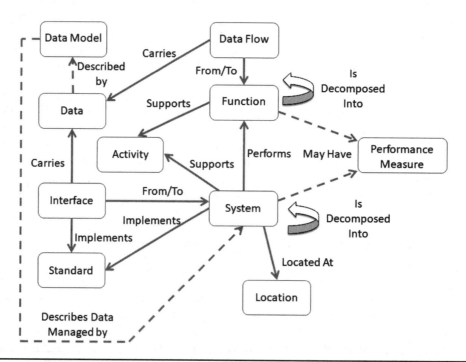

**Figure 4-6**   IT and infrastructure domain system viewpoint concepts and relationships

A system can be decomposed into component systems (in cases of SoS or FoS), subsystems, or system components. A system (or decomposed system) has interfaces to other systems. Each interface carries data between (out of and into) systems. Both systems and interfaces may have standards that apply to them. That is, systems and their interfaces may implement standards. Each system is located at one or more locations. A location may be logical or physical, and it may be mobile.

A system performs a set of functions, each of which can be decomposed into subfunctions. Each function has one or more logical data flows that carry data from or to that function. Each system can be mapped to the business activities it supports either directly or indirectly through the functions the system performs. Both systems and functions may have Performance Measures associated with them.

Data models can be used to describe the data managed by a system. For example, a data model can be used to describe the logical or physical schema of a shared database managed by a system. A data model can also be used to describe the data that flows between functions or between systems on interfaces, if this data is sufficiently complex.

Here are some solution level IT and infrastructure concept examples from the RMN Airport Case Study:

- **System**   Airline Reservation and Ticketing System (ARTS) client and server
- **Function**   Verify passenger identity
- **Location**   Check-in counter
- **System**   Passenger Intelligence Services (PaxIS)
- **Location**   RMN operations center
- **Interface**   ARTS to PaxIS
- **Activity**   Check-in passenger

The ARTS client (system), located at the check-in counter (location), supports check-in passenger (activity) by performing verify passenger identity (function) among other functions. The ARTS server has an interface to PaxIS.

Additional concepts associated with the systems viewpoint include system and standard availability, updates, and retirement dates and behavior concepts. Like the business domain, there may be system rules that constrain system structure, interfaces, and function. Systems may have internal states. In fact, this is usual for control and similar systems. Unlike business objects, system behavior is frequently continuous. Systems start in an initial state, transition state based on external system inputs, and cycle back to an initial state, ready to begin performing the set of functions again.

A common example of a control system that has state is the control system for a vending machine. In this case, in its initial state, the machine is ready to accept money. After sufficient money is inserted, the machine transitions to a state where input from the item selection buttons can be accepted. After a legitimate product code (whose cost is equal to or less than the amount previously inserted) is selected and the selected item is dispensed, the machine transitions to a state where change may be calculated and, if necessary, dispensed. Then the machine returns to its initial state.

System scenarios are also important for modeling system behavior. A system scenario shows the interactions of systems (or system components) in terms of data exchanges in response to a specific sequence of system events or external inputs, such as sensor inputs. The scenarios selected for an architecture usually relate to key performance or security critical sequences.

## Service Viewpoint Elements

A service viewpoint looks at the IT and infrastructure domain as a set of usually web accessible services that can be quickly configured to create new or updated applications. In the service viewpoint, much of what is considered a system, including the platform and operating system, becomes infrastructure for the services. Each service is defined with a standard interface. Ideally, multiple implementations of this service may be available, either from multiple vendors or for multiple platforms. Each implementation has an SLA that spells out such items as the performance characteristics promised by the service provider. Figure 4-7 shows some basic IT and infrastructure domain service viewpoint concepts and their relationships, which will be discussed next along with some additional concepts that are not shown in the figure. Sometimes services are not just IT services, but business services, in the cases where the enterprise relies on outside parties to perform these services. For example, a government agency or corporation may decide to outsource payroll services. The following discussion relates primarily to IT services.

Each abstract service may specialize to more specific abstract services. For example, in the case of search and rescue services (which are business services), there may be specialized

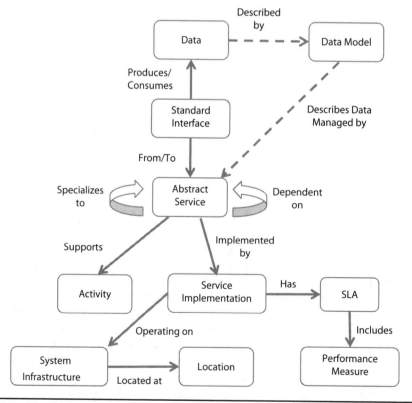

**Figure 4-7**   IT and infrastructure domain service viewpoint concepts and relationships

water search and rescue and mountain search and rescue services. Each abstract service may also depend on—that is, call upon—other abstract services. For example, a payment-handling service may call on a credit card service and a check-handling service. Each abstract service has a *standard interface* as part of its service definition. The standard interface describes the data consumed by the service (that is, required as input) and the data produced by the service (that is, produced as output). A data model may be used either to describe the data produced and consumed by services, if this data is complex, or to describe the data managed by a service, if the service is managing a database of shared data.

Each abstract service has one or more service implementations. Implementations may differ in terms of their development and maintenance organizations (that is, different vendors), in terms of the platforms they run on, or in terms of their performance characteristics. Each implementation typically has an SLA that includes the performance characteristics that are guaranteed for the service implementation. Like systems, service implementations run at one or more locations. For services, the concept of location also includes the concept of platform, or system infrastructure that is supporting the service. The location of the platform may be abstract, physical, or mobile. Unlike most systems, the number and location of implementations for a given service may change dynamically. That is, if a service implementation at a specific location becomes overloaded with service requests, then additional implementations of that service may be brought up at that location or other locations to maintain response performance. If a service implementation at a specific location becomes inaccessible because of communications problems, additional implementations of that service may be started up in locations that remain accessible.

Like systems, services need to be mapped to the business activities they support. Each service will support one or more business activities.

Additional concepts associated with the service viewpoint include service implementation availability, update, and retirement dates and behavior concepts. A service or service implementation may have associated rules. For example, a service implementation may have criteria for deciding when that implementation is becoming overloaded with requests. The related abstract service may have rules for deciding where additional implementations should be instantiated if an implementation becomes overloaded. Like systems, services may have internal state. Service scenarios are also important for modeling the behavior of sets of services. A service scenario shows the interactions of services in terms of data exchanges (that is, service requests and responses) in response to a specific sequence of events or external inputs caused by the execution of an application that uses the set of services. The service scenarios included in an architecture may be selected to demonstrate the effectiveness of the set of services in supporting critical applications, or they may be selected based on key performance or critical security issues.

## Communications Infrastructure Elements

The communications infrastructure is the network and communication systems, such as satellite relays, radio repeaters, routers, and gateways, whose purpose is to move data rather than to process it for operational purposes. The communications infrastructure implements the system interfaces shown in Figure 4-6 and the communication aspects of service standard interfaces shown in Figure 4-7. The communication infrastructure concepts and relationships are shown in Figure 4-8 from a systems viewpoint perspective.

**Figure 4-8**
Communications
infrastructure
concepts and
relationships

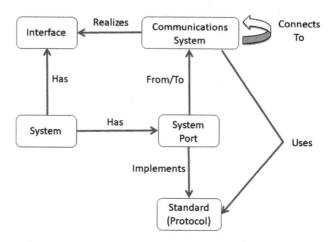

Communications infrastructure information is of interest to stakeholders who focus on reliability and availability of data and security issues.

A system sends data to external systems through one or more system ports. Each system port implements a standard protocol that is used to send the data via a sequence of communications links and communications systems that use the protocol to reach the system port on the receiving system. Frequently, there are multiple possible paths in a communications network that realize system interfaces, especially when the Internet is used.

## Ontology

Once other defense organizations started to develop their own frameworks based on DoDAF, the original metamodel was not sufficient for this larger community. Defense organizations in allied countries sometimes wanted to share architecture information but had difficulties moving the data between tools because the metamodel vocabulary for their frameworks was no longer consistent. Thus, the DM2 evolved into an ontology: the Unified Profile for DoDAF and MODAF (UPDM). This evolution was fueled both by government interest and by tool vendors under the auspices of the OMG, a commercial and technology industry–based standards-making body. UPDM was represented in a UML profile that offered a way for UML tools to exchange architecture data via XML.

Since UPDM is based on DM2, the impact of UPDM on architecture developers is to make it easier to find tools that will enforce the syntactic rules for views in a consistent way and that will be able to exchange architecture data easily. The concepts of DM2 discussed previously still hold true for architecture developers.

UPDM has evolved through several iterations and is currently being extended to additional defense frameworks under the proposed OMG standard Unified Architecture Framework (UAF) and to SysML under the proposed OMG standard Unified Architecture Framework Profile (UAFP). This work is aimed at allowing a wider range of

DoDAF-related defense architecture frameworks to exchange architecture data between both UML and SysML tools using XML.

Note that, despite their names, the UAF and UAFP are not frameworks, but ontologies. Confusingly, UAFP introduces additional "views" not included in the DoDAF to reflect relationships in its ontology. Understanding of the details of UAF and UAFP is not necessary for architects using tools based on these ontologies. The point of these profiles is that these tools will enforce the ontology and keep the architecture integrated.

## Process: The Six-Step Process

The Six-Step Process is a high-level or metaprocess for architecting. It does not provide a specific, detailed process for developing architecture artifacts, products, or data, but rather sets the context for this more detailed architecture development process. This approach lets the development organization select and use its own detailed architecture development process. Other comprehensive approaches, such as the Architecture Development Methodology (ADM) from TOGAF and the Collaborative Planning Methodology from FEAF2, discussed in Part IV, cover similar topics.

The Six-Step Process is the metaprocess provided by the DoDAF and the *Practical Guide to Federal Enterprise Architecture*. This process is illustrated in Figure 4-9. Although the steps are followed in numerical order, the process tends to be highly iterative. For simplicity, only one iteration arrow (from step 5 to step 3) is included in the figure. The architecture team gains more insight into the architecture domain with each step of the process, and each new insight may cause the team to return to an earlier step to refine previously developed material or add new material. Each step of the Six-Step Process will be discussed briefly here and in detail in Chapters 5 and 6. Note that step 1, determine the intended use of the architecture, is a critical, and too often skipped, step that drives all the other steps.

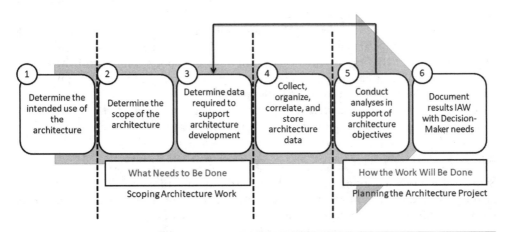

**Figure 4-9** The Six-Step Process

## Step 1: Determine the Intended Use of the Architecture

Step 1 focuses on identifying why the architecture is being built: what problem or problems the architecture should address, including who the architecture stakeholders (the users of the architecture) are and what decisions they are going to use the architecture to support. Each stakeholder will have a set of specific questions that the architecture will need to provide the answers to or analyses that the architecture will need to support. The architecture stakeholders considered here go above and beyond the usual set of stakeholders considered in system development, because a wide range of decision-makers in addition to system or even business process sponsors, owners, or users may use the architecture information in decision-making processes. For example, for all federal departments and agencies, the Office of Management and Budget (OMB) uses architecture information to decide which proposed projects get funding or which continuing projects get additional funding. In DoD, the Battle Integration Laboratories use architecture information to support integration testing across multiple, independently developed systems.

In the case study, the purpose of the RMN Airport Enterprise Level architecture is to support the transformation of RMN Airport from a civil aviation airport to a viable alternative to LAX. Stakeholders in the Enterprise Level architecture (users of this architecture) include the appropriate port authority, the RMN Airport management, and, potentially, the local governments of the communities surrounding the airport and the local citizens. The port authority and RMN Airport management need the architecture to identify and document the additional capabilities or business services that RMN Airport needs and to support the transition planning and projects for implementing these additional capabilities. The local governments and citizens will use the Enterprise Level architecture to analyze and understand how and when the airport changes will impact their communities in terms of noise, additional traffic, and expanded airport space and facilities.

Step 1 is critical since architecture is a decision-making tool, so it is vital to understand the decisions the architecture will be used to support. Many organizations jump immediately to step 4 and start collecting data and building models without careful consideration of what data is actually needed and how the data will be used. As a result, these organizations, after having expended large amounts of money, have found themselves with extensive models and mountains of data but with no real idea of how any of this data will support their key decision-making processes.

The material developed in step 1 will drive the selection of data and artifacts for the architecture, the level of detail needed, and completion criteria for the architecture.

## Step 2: Determine the Scope of the Architecture

Step 2 focuses on identifying the boundaries of the architecture—what is internal to the architecture and what is outside the scope of the architecture. Scope includes the level of the architecture (enterprise, segment, or solution), mission or organizational boundaries, technology and time frame constraints, or other scoping issues.

In the case study, the example Segment Level architecture is limited to business processes and organizations at RMN Airport that are involved with passenger management, including passenger-related business services. For example, some of these passenger-related business processes could be supplying information to RMN Airport financial systems so that the airport can bill airlines for services based on the number of passengers that enter or leave the airport on that airline's flights. However, the financial business processes and systems would be considered outside the scope of the passenger management segment architecture even though the passenger management segment would need interfaces to these financial business processes and systems.

## Step 3: Determine the Data Needed to Support Architecture Development

Step 3 focuses on identifying the types of data needed to answer the problems and issues identified in step 1, within the scope limitations set out in step 2. Each of the architecture stakeholder questions from step 1 should lead to a set of data types that will be involved in answering the question. For example, if one of the questions is "What changes will the new systems bring to our business processes?" then the architecture will need to include the current (as-is) and new (to-be) business process data for the business processes within the mission or organizational and time frame scope provided by step 2.

## Step 4: Collect, Organize, Correlate, and Store Architecture Data

In step 4, the set of architecture views is selected and developed. The views are selected to cover the data identified in step 3. Mathematical modeling techniques may be used to ensure that the data collected is consistent, complete, and correctly correlated. The development organization's specific architecture development process guides the techniques to use and the order in which the views are built. The specific architecture development process also guides the tools and data storage approach used.

## Step 5: Conduct Analyses in Support of Architecture Objectives

In step 5, the data resulting from the various view development efforts in step 4 are analyzed. There are two types of analyses that may be employed in this step. One type is the analysis needed to address issues involved in the development of the architecture, such as which of several operational process or system support options is most effective, based on the overall performance measures associated with the architecture. Another type is analysis that directly addresses the decision-making processes that the architecture is designed to support. This type of analysis often involves both architectural and, potentially, other types of data such as financial data. Examples of this second type of analysis include business case analysis, return on investment analysis, and various types of performance and sensitivity analyses based on executable architecture modeling.

In all cases, the analysis processes may uncover the need for additional types of data that were not originally identified in step 3. Thus, Figure 4-9 shows an iteration arrow going from step 5 to step 3. The need for additional types of data will also cause iteration of step 4 so that this additional data can be collected, correlated, and integrated with the current architecture data set, and stored, so it can be used for further analysis, sharing, and future use and reuse.

## Step 6: Document Results in Accordance with Decision-Maker Needs

In step 6, the data developed in step 4 and refined through step 5 is used to develop artifacts and products, also called fit-for-purpose views, which are used to communicate the results of the architecture process to the stakeholders and provide direct support to their decision-making processes. For some stakeholders and questions, the results can be documented using the same models the architecture development team developed in step 4. For other stakeholders, the results must be provided in other formats that are more easily understood by non-architects, such as bar or pie charts, dashboards, or combinations of simple graphics and text. The fit-for-purpose views or non-mathematical models are based on the consistent, correlated data stored during step 4. For example, to support the local government and citizen stakeholders, the data developed during steps 4 and 5 for the RMN Airport Enterprise Level architecture might be used to generate a fit-for-purpose view that was a bar chart showing the planned increase in air traffic for the airport by year. This relationship of mathematically based models or architect's views to the consistent, integrated, architectural knowledge base, to the stakeholder-oriented fit-for-purpose views, is illustrated in Figure 4-10.

For communicating the architecture contents to other architecture teams that are working on related architectures, a standard set of artifacts may be used. For example, the

**Figure 4-10**

Relationship of data and views in architecture (figure based on DoDAF graphic)

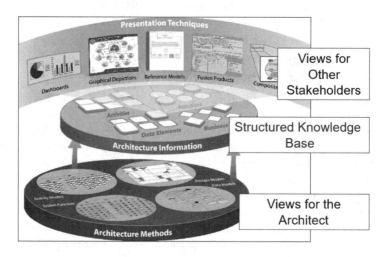

DoDAF provides a standard set of viewpoints and views for communicating architecture results within the DoD architecting community. From the implementation perspective, the knowledge base, built on a common data model, can be shared, and tools can be used to generate the standard views. With standard views, the architects do not have to learn all possible modeling techniques but only those involved with the standard views.

## Summary

This chapter introduced the basics of the DoDAF. It covered the three levels of enterprise architecture (Enterprise Level, Segment Level, and Solution Level), their relationships, and the contexts in which they are used. It introduced the DoDAF viewpoints and views and discussed the concept of view integration.

This chapter introduced the DM2 and some of its key concepts and their relationships. These concepts and relationships underlie all the architecture views and form the basis for many tool repositories. It discussed the evolving "deep structure" ontologies derived from DM2 that make it possible to have tools that can exchange architecture data easily.

The chapter also introduced a metaprocess for developing a DoDAF architecture: the Six-Step Process. The Six-Step Process sets the context in which an organization's specific enterprise architecture development process can be applied. The focus on the Six-Step Process is on understanding the purpose and uses of the enterprise architecture so that the development effort can be concentrated on useful data and views and the architecture can be formulated in standard ways for sharing with the community of interest. More detail on the Six-Step Process will be presented in other chapters.

## Questions

1. What is the relationship between an organization's specific architecture development process and the Six-Step Process?

2. Why should the Six-Step Process be considered as an iterative process?

3. What architecture concepts are common between the Solution Level business domain and the IT and infrastructure domain system? What do these common concepts imply about the relationships between the business domain and the IT and infrastructure domain?

4. What architecture concepts are common between the Enterprise Level business domain and the Solution Level business domain?

5. What are the different architecture concepts that can have performance measures associated with them? Why are these performance measures important?

6. What are the different concepts that can be related to a data model?

# References

Department of Defense. 2009. Department of Defense Architecture Framework Version 2.0. http://dodcio.defense.gov/Library/DoD-Architecture-Framework.

DeVries, David. 2013. "DoD Joint Information Enterprise," DoD Deputy Chief Information Officer for Information Enterprise. http://c4i.gmu.edu/eventsInfo/reviews/2013/pdfs/AFCEA2013-DeVries.pdf.

Director, Architecture & Interoperability Office of the DoD Chief Information Officer. 2012. "DOD Enterprise Architecture: Core Data Center Reference Architecture, Version 1.0." http://dodcio.defense.gov/Portals/0/Documents/DIEA/CDC%20 RA%20v1_0_Final_Releaseable%20Version.pdf.

Object Management Group. 2013. Unified Profile for DoDAF and MODAF Specification Version 2.1. www.omg.org/spec/UPDM/2.1/.

Object Management Group. 2016. Unified Architecture Framework Profile, Version 1.0 – FTF Beta 1. OMG Document Number dtc/16-08-01. www.omg.org/spec/UAF/1.0/Beta1/About-UAF/.

Object Management Group. 2016. Unified Architecture Framework (UAF): The Domain Metamodel, Version 1.0, Appendix A.

Office of the Assistant Secretary of Defense, Networks and Information Integration (OASD/NII), Department of Defense. 2010. Reference Architecture Description. http://dodcio.defense.gov/Portals/0/Documents/DIEA/Ref_Archi_Description_ Final_v1_18Jun10.pdf.

Takai, Teresa. 2013. "DOD Enterprise Architecture: Unified Capabilities Reference Architecture, Version 1.0." http://dodcio.defense.gov/Portals/0/Documents/DIEA/ Approved%20DoD%20UC%20Reference%20Architecture.pdf.

U.S. Army. 2014a. Identity and Access Management (IdAM) Enterprise Architecture Reference Architecture (RA), Version 4.0.

U.S. Army. 2014b. Network Security Enterprise Reference Architecture, Version 2.0.

# Planning the Enterprise Architecture

Planning is critical for achieving a useful enterprise architecture (EA). Key to remember is that EA is a decision support tool, not an end unto itself. To achieve success, you need to have a good understanding of the decisions stakeholders make and the data needed to support this decision-making.

There are two parts to architecture planning: identifying the scope of the architecture work, and planning for the project or projects to do this work. This chapter focuses on aspects of planning the architecture work, specifically scoping the architecture work.

An enterprise is dynamic and continuously evolves in response to business and technology drivers. Thus, the EA must be an evolutionary document driven by stakeholder decision-making needs and priorities. The architecture is developed in an iterative manner, with each release being responsive to priority decision-making needs and providing data in a timely manner. This means that planning for the architecture, especially scoping the work, is also an iterative process.

The architect needs to identify stakeholders (users of the architecture) and work with them to identify their needs and priorities. The top priority issue or set of related issues drives the initial EA release(s), while a priority organized backlog of issues needs to be maintained as input to the next planning iteration. Managing the scope of each architecture release is critical. Attempts to develop an architecture in one large project and without proper attention to stakeholder needs and priorities tend to result in an expensive and unmanageable mountain of data that stakeholders have no idea how to use.

We use the DoDAF Six-Step Process, described in Chapter 4, to guide our architecture planning process, as this is the general process associated with the defense-related frameworks. Other comprehensive and relatively more prescriptive approaches, such as the TOGAF Architecture Development Methodology (ADM) and the FEAF2 Collaborative Planning Methodology, both discussed in Part IV, cover similar topics.

Figure 5-1 shows the Six-Step Process from the planning perspective. Steps 1, 2, and 3 and part of step 4 need to be performed to scope the architecture work for a given architecture release and are the focus of this chapter. This part of planning needs to be done prior to developing or issuing a statement of work (SOW) for architecture development. Planning for the rest of step 4 and steps 5 and 6 is part of planning for an architecture development project and is addressed in Chapter 6.

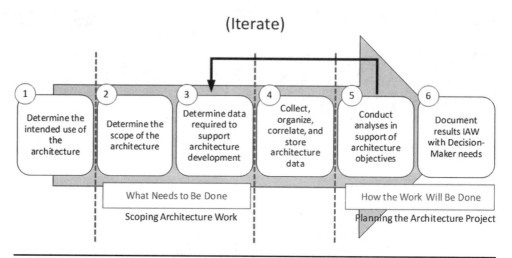

**Figure 5-1**  The Six-Step Process from a planning perspective

Since EAs evolve over time, the work identified in the scoping process may be addressed in more than one project. The approach to breaking up the EA work into projects (selecting among the needs and priorities of the various enterprise tribes) and the approach to planning in general is driven by enterprise culture.

# Scoping the Architecture Work

The first few steps of the Six-Step Process identify what needs to be done in terms of the scope and deliverables of an EA release, as illustrated in Figure 5-2. The goal of the planning exercise is to establish traceability from the stakeholder-selected issues driving

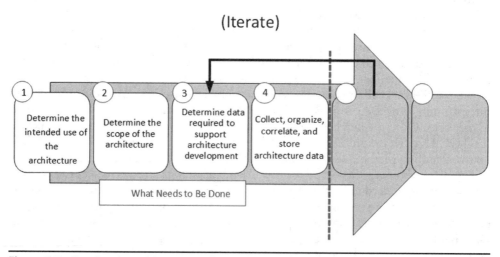

**Figure 5-2**  Scoping the architecture work

the EA release to the selected architecture artifacts and the data that they contain. This traceability ensures that the architecture release contains the data needed to support the stakeholders' decision-making in a timely manner, based on enterprise priorities. This traceability also provides a useful communications tool for getting stakeholder support for the architecture as it shows directly how the architecture will be useful.

The information developed in these first few steps also includes information needed for the DoDAF Summary and Overview Information (AV-1). We review each of the first four steps of the Six-Step Process in detail in the following sections, provide examples, and summarize success factors before moving on to planning for an architecture development project in Chapter 6.

## Purpose

Step 1 of the Six-Step Process focuses on identifying the reasons why the architecture release is being developed. Figure 5-3 lists some common items that need to be considered. Identifying the purpose of the architecture involves both framing the high-level problem or issue that the architecture release is being built to address as well as identifying all the users of the architecture release and their specific questions and time constraints. Identifying the high-level problem serves to align the architecture with strategic business or mission needs, while identifying the stakeholders and their specific questions ensures that the data needed to address specific decisions is included in the architecture release with the right level of detail. The architecture stakeholders considered here go beyond the usual set of stakeholders considered in system development, because a wide range of decision-makers in addition to system or even business process sponsors, owners, or users may use the architecture information in decision-making processes.

The material developed in step 1 will drive the selection of data and artifacts for the architecture, the level of detail needed, and completion criteria for the architecture. For example, a common problem is deciding how far to decompose an activity model (DoDAF OV-5). A typical question that architectural modelers often ask is, "We've decomposed the activity model down five levels. Are we done?" The answer depends on the intended use of the information, based on the specific needs of stakeholders.

**Figure 5-3**
Determining the intended use of the architecture

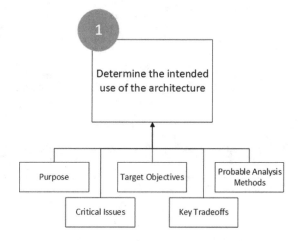

Suppose the architecture purpose is to develop an understanding of the current operations of an organization's headquarters offices. This information will be needed to perform impact analysis for proposed changes. Then the activity model needs to decompose organizational activities down to the level where the activities performed by the headquarters offices can be separated from the activities performed by other organizational entities, regardless of the number of modeling levels involved.

## Identifying the High-Level Purpose

The development of an architecture is normally driven by some important business need related to strategic business goals and objectives. The architecture usually supports some combination of transition planning and analysis. For example, in the case study (Chapter 3), the architecture supports transition planning and helps keep the changes and investments aligned with strategic goals.

Business transformation in the commercial world [KPMG 2017] is based on transforming the business model (such as managing revenues) or transforming the operating model (such as managing costs). An additional transformation that today is becoming an essential one is technology and infrastructure model transformation. The technology and infrastructure model serves not only as an operating platform in the traditional manner, but also connects the enterprise to the markets and customers, and provides a competitive advantage. Transforming the business model involves looking at markets, brands or business propositions, and customers. Transforming the operating model entails looking at core business processes, operational infrastructure and technology, organizational structures, governance and risk controls, people, and culture. Figure 5-4 shows the various types of transformation with the factors that must be examined.

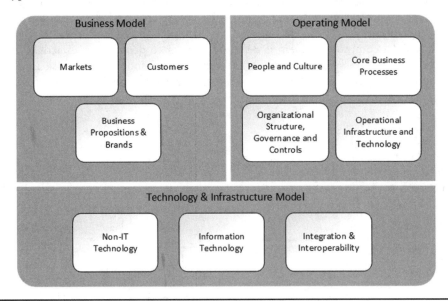

**Figure 5-4** Transformation target types

The technology and infrastructure model in its own right provides both a platform for the operational model and competitive differentiators in the business model. Adoption of disruptive technologies can afford competitive advantage on the one hand and self-disruption on the other.

Transition planning drives transition of the enterprise from the current (as-is) state to the desired target (to-be) state. Typically, two architectures are built: an as-is and a target architecture. Gap analysis between the target and the current states will provide clarity on the changes to be made. A transition plan or roadmap involves transformation of architecture elements from the as-is state to the target state. The transition plan will indicate what architecture elements will be deleted, which will be carried forward, which will be transformed or modified to be consistent with the target state, and when and how the transformation will take place. Typical examples of strategic changes that drive the need for transition include new capabilities, innovations, mission/business process reengineering, modernization, reorganization, and mergers and acquisitions.

Additional business needs that require architecture analysis include selection of projects for funding, joint/mission interoperability, and legacy system integrations. When multiple competing projects are requesting funding, determination of importance, "fit," priority, and continued longevity within the business context can be accomplished by building an architecture within which the competing projects can be compared and their relative impacts analyzed.

Joint or mission interoperability in defense enterprises is key to the operation of joint task forces. In the commercial world, mission interoperability is key to successful mergers and acquisitions as well as to consolidations or downsizings. Joint operations involve coordinating activities from multiple organizations with different processes, skills, training, operational structures, and organizational cultures. Mission interoperability requires "threading" together activities from these multiple organizations. Having architectures depicting the operational activities for each of these organizations is useful to support the definition of these mission "threads" and to ensure that data and information can pass seamlessly across organizational interfaces.

Integration of legacy systems is frequently a part of other types of enterprise changes such as mergers, acquisitions, and business process reengineering. Legacy systems are information systems implemented in technologies that are either obsolete or becoming obsolete but that continue to exist because the business value these systems provide cannot be provided easily or conveniently with newer systems built on more contemporary technologies. Integration of legacy systems involves orchestrating a set of system functions, some belonging to the legacy system and others belonging to newer systems. This orchestration also touches platform interactions, data exchanges, and connectivity issues as well as timing- and execution-related parameters. An architecture description depicting the legacy and new systems in a common way allows for the depiction of these issues and provides a means to achieving successful orchestration.

The high-level problem driving an architecture release may also involve at least one of the following: specific strategic objectives, key tradeoffs, critical issues, critical decision points, or specific analyses. An example program strategic objective might be a capability improvement, such as increasing the overall efficiency of a mission process by a certain percentage or improving the quality of the process output. An example of a strategic objective for the Federal Aviation Authority (FAA), for example, is to increase air traffic three times. The Next Generation Air Traffic System (NGATS) Architecture is being built both to guide transition and decide the appropriate measures for air traffic. An example key tradeoff is the one between centralized data management and distributed, replicated data with the synchronization management issues it entails. This tradeoff is frequently a key issue with the intelligence community. The tradeoff involves both operational issues regarding which approach best supports operations and technology issues regarding the current technology support for data replication and synchronization. An example critical issue is air defense command and control in the context of a joint task force. Since any of the military services may staff the air defense position in a joint task force, the solution must allow flexibility for the different services' approaches to this process.

Each problem may involve specific analyses of architecture information or analyses to which architecture information provides critical input. For example, answering questions about process improvement may involve activity-based costing analysis that will require both architecture information, such as an activity model, and financial/cost information. Support for selection of projects for funding may involve business case analysis. Tradeoffs may require performance modeling or simulation.

## The Challenges of Transition

Any change can be disruptive. Many types of changes create ripple effects, impacting areas of the enterprise that do not initially seem involved. Gap analysis supports impact analysis, enabling the identification of all the potential disruptions so that they can be anticipated and dealt with successfully. Changes that impact enterprise culture, such as mergers, acquisitions, or reorganizations, and enterprise tribal cultures, such as changes that impact a specific tribe's activities, roles, skills, or responsibilities, are most difficult to address. These cultural changes need to be identified early and managed carefully since they may result in fierce resistance unless management gets buy-in from the impacted stakeholders, regardless of the technical merits of the intended change.

Many large federal government "modernization" initiatives at the Internal Revenue Service, the Securities and Exchange Commission, the United States Air Force, and other agencies have failed for a variety of reasons, all of which involved cultural issues. Over time, a particular system or way of doing business becomes integrated into the culture, and attempts to change it are met with resistance and lack of will to change.

Part of transition planning includes an impact analysis of the planned changes on the enterprise and its organizations, locations, work force, business processes, systems, and infrastructure.

## Identifying Stakeholders and Their Issues

Although there is usually a single high-level purpose for building an architecture release, there are usually multiple users of the architecture, or *stakeholders*, with each having unique expectations of what the architecture will do for them. Each of these stakeholders has specific purposes for the architecture: decisions they need the architecture to support and specific issues and questions that they want the architecture to address. Not only are there multiple stakeholders with multiple purposes and time constraints, but many times these purposes are in conflict with one another. It is important to identify all the stakeholders and to address conflicts among the purposes. Stakeholder needs may have to be prioritized in the face of resource constraints in developing the architecture release. Reconciliation of multiple stakeholder needs into a single set of purpose statements for the architecture may involve tradeoffs and compromises.

Determining the full set of stakeholders and their architecture purposes may require detective work, some of which involves identifying the relevant "informal" enterprise tribes, as discussed in Chapter 2. Internal enterprise stakeholders entail all architecture users including the architecture owners and the organizations sponsoring the architecture work. However, in government or large organizations, success in achieving the owning organization's goals may include satisfying the needs of external architecture user groups, as illustrated next.

One way of identifying internal stakeholders is to consider the levels of stakeholders by function as identified by the key abstract roles described by the Zachman Framework (see Chapter 21). Figure 5-5 summarizes the top level of these types of stakeholders.

In defense enterprises, as in every other enterprise, there are often important external stakeholders. It is important that you consider the various levels of governmental decision-makers who may be using the architecture. For example, in DoD, the owning organization may need the architecture to address a service-specific program objective, but the Joint Requirements Oversight Council (JROC), which approves program funding, needs the architecture to determine how the proposed solution supports DoD-wide capability improvement goals and objectives. Additional architecture users would include service-specific investment/budget decision-makers, Battle Integration Laboratories, and

**Figure 5-5**
Levels of stakeholders from the perspective of the Zachman Framework (graphic from the DoDAF)

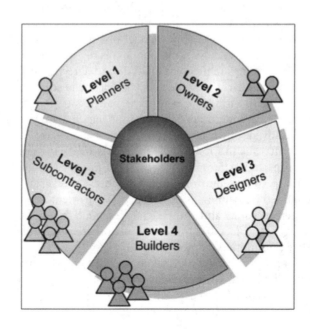

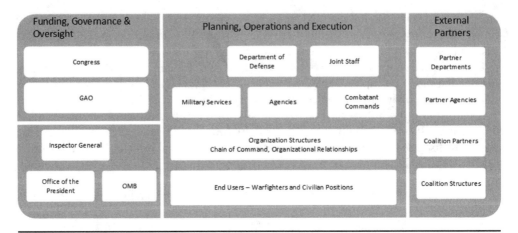

**Figure 5-6**  Levels of stakeholders for DoD within the government

service training organizations. Architecture users also include the groups that will perform the analysis of the architecture information. Figure 5-6 illustrates the various levels of stakeholders who may be involved with a DoD architecture.

The high-level stakeholders, such as the Government Accountability Office (GAO) and Office of Management and Budget (OMB), identified in Figure 5-6, also need to be considered for non-DoD federal departments, since the financial governance and legislative oversight is the same for all federal departments and agencies. OMB has very specific requirements regarding the architecture information it needs before it will approve funding for projects. (For example, see the "Enterprise Performance Life Cycle Framework" overview document published by the Department of Health and Human Services, at www.hhs.gov/sites/default/files/ocio/eplc-lifecycle-framework.pdf.)

For both government and commercial organizations, external partners may also be stakeholders. For example, working out details of "just-in-time" delivery of parts or supplies will involve joint architecture analysis and agreements between manufacturers and their suppliers. Similarly, commercial enterprises need careful architecture analysis to support agreements with any outsourcing partners to ensure security, privacy, and data ownership issues, among others. These arrangements are becoming increasingly important with the advent of the cloud.

Government organizations may need to work with commercial organizations or international partners. For example, the FAA needs to coordinate with the corresponding agencies in many countries and with international aviation organizations as well as with commercial airlines. The Treasury Department needs to coordinate procedures with commercial banks and the Federal Reserve System. The Securities and Exchange Commission accepts fees and filings from regulated companies. Additional discussion of stakeholders is found in Chapter 7.

A useful artifact for tracking stakeholders, their concerns and constraints, and the views that will be used to document the architecture data needed in response to their concerns is a *stakeholder matrix*. This type of matrix is useful not only for planning, but also for getting buy-in from stakeholders, because the matrix can be used to show

Adapted from: http://catsr.ite.gmu.edu/pubs/ICNS_Schaar_AirportStakeholders.pdf

**Figure 5-7**　Potential stakeholder types for RMN Airport

the value added by the architecture to a stakeholder's decision-making. Examples of the planning version of the stakeholder matrix are included in the examples at the end of this chapter. A slightly different form of the stakeholder matrix can also be used to track the political issues associated with the stakeholders and each stakeholder's importance to success of the architecture effort. This form of the stakeholder matrix is discussed in Chapter 6.

For RMN Airport, the types of stakeholders are identified in the references. Figure 5-7 shows an example set of stakeholder types. During a specific project activity or while architecting a segment of the airport, this taxonomy is instantiated with specific players or organizations.

## Scope

While step 1 of the Six-Step Process identifies the purposes of the architecture release, step 2 sets the scope of the release. The scope determines what is considered internal to the architecture release and what is external. Scope includes the level of the architecture (enterprise, segment, or solution), mission or organizational boundaries, technology and time frame constraints, and other scoping issues. (See Chapter 23 for a standard list of enterprise scopes as defined by the Federal Enterprise Architecture Framework Version 2 [FEAF2].)

Frequently, an architecture release may be focused on a specific aspect of a larger enterprise. Step 2 determines how to decide whether specific information should be included in the architecture. This step is critical to keeping the architecture release focused and ensures that the resulting architecture is developed in a timely manner to support decision-making.

Typically, the scope is determined by the context of the architecture, as summarized in Figure 5-8 and discussed in the following list.

- *What's the span of the enterprise?* There needs to be a clear understanding of what level of enterprise architecture will be developed. Setting an architecture's operational bounds starts with a clear statement of any overarching enterprise and the aspect of that enterprise that is to be the subject of the architecture. For example, within a multinational corporation, an architecture might be a *segment-level architecture* restricted to European operations. Within the U.S. DoD, *a solution-level* architecture might be specific to a single military service. Or a *solution-level architecture* may be part of the DoD Business Enterprise Architecture but be restricted to the Army-specific aspect of that architecture.

- *What are the operational bounds?* What missions, enterprise core functions, business support functions, or organizations are included? For example, within DoD, the architecture may be restricted to a specific warfare mission, to a specific support service, or to military operations other than war. Within a given operation, the architecture may be restricted to specific operational processes or to specific organizations. For example, an architecture might be limited to a specific combat service support process as carried out by a specific Army organization. For a corporation, the architecture might be limited to corporate financial operations or to a specific operation required by state law for all offices within that state.

- *Are there geographic bounds?* What georegions of the world, countries of the world, parts of the United States, or types of facilities and installations will be covered by the architecture effort? For example, the architecture may be focused on operations that are specific to the United States or specific states or territories, or it may involve worldwide operations. Some architectures may be restricted to a specific country or international geographic area, such as the Middle East, Africa, or Southeast Asia. A defense architecture may be restricted to in-theater operations. An architecture may have more generic geographic limits such as land, sea, littoral, air, or space.

**Figure 5-8**
Determining the scope of the architecture

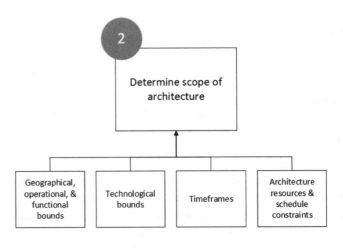

- *What time frames does the architecture address?* The time frame for an architecture release is the range of dates for which the architecture applies. A current, objective, or as-is baseline architecture documents the current state of the enterprise and can be used to support decisions having to do with sustainment. Sometimes these architectures are called "as-planned architectures" if they include information on the changes that are planned and funded within the current budget cycle. "Target" or "to-be" architectures address the anticipated architecture of the enterprise at some future point in time. To-be architectures need to have a specific date attached that indicates when the architecture is expected to become the as-is state of the enterprise. An enterprise may have multiple to-be, phased, architectures that show transitional stages toward a target or vision architecture. For example, a vision architecture is used to support strategic decision-making for the longer term, while the to-be architecture for the next budget cycle documents the proposed improvements to the current architecture for which funding is being sought. This near-term to-be architecture should be achievable within the fiscal years covered by that next budget cycle. These transitional architectures typically contain varying levels of information and detail. The vision architecture may focus only on high-level concepts, while the to-be architecture for the next budget cycle needs to be very detailed and concrete. The budget cycle to-be architectures should move the enterprise in the direction of the current vision architecture. The vision architecture will itself evolve over time to reflect changes in business strategy and technology.

- *Are there constraints on the technology to be considered?* The scope should identify any assumptions and constraints on the technology aspects of the architecture. As-is architectures may be limited in the extent of the information technology (IT) considered. The architecture may focus on applications only, or it may include infrastructure aspects of the technology, such as platforms and communications. Sometimes an as-is architecture may simply consist of a technology inventory. To-be architectures may be limited in terms of specific technology assumptions and constraints. Near term to-be architectures may need to be limited in the technology included by the need to remain interoperable with a specified set of external legacy systems or standards. Enterprise policy may limit technology for some parts of the enterprise, such as business operations, to available commercial-off-the-shelf (COTS) technology. Other parts of an enterprise may expect the use of innovative technology to meet operational capabilities. For example, the Internal Revenue Service (IRS) needs to restrict its operational IT to COTS technologies that have the proven capability to handle large amounts of data and transactions, while the intelligence community usually has requirements that "push the envelope" and will necessitate innovation in terms of integration of COTS or development of new algorithms and solutions.

- *Are there specific schedule and resource constraints?* For an architecture release to be useful, it must provide information in a timely manner to a prioritized set of stakeholders. This means that there will be schedule constraints on the completion of the release or at least on the completion of some set of views in the release. For example, specific enterprise milestones may need to be met.

Architecture guidance for key system development projects may be needed by specific dates (driven by the system development schedule), or other types of architecture information may be needed in time for an annual investment review at a specific time of year. In addition, there are always constraints on the resources available for the development of the architecture. There are usually budgetary constraints that limit the level of effort available to meet the architecture requirements based on identified milestones or schedules. These schedule and resource constraints make it important to focus the scope of the architecture carefully to get timely and useful results. Given the schedule and resources constraints, other aspects of the architecture scope, such as operational and geographic bounds and time frames, may need to be revisited and stakeholder priorities reconsidered. For example, the operational bounds of the architecture may be further restricted to the operations supported by the system or systems for which architecture guidance is needed. Stakeholder issues that cannot be addressed in the current release need to be added to a maintained backlog and reconsidered for the next release.

## Identifying Needed Data Types

Step 3 focuses on identifying the types of data needed to address the architecture purposes and stakeholder questions, within the bounds of the architecture scope and without explicit consideration of which architecture views or artifacts will be used to document the information. Figure 5-9 summarizes the focus of this step. To identify the needed types of data and their relationships, each purpose or stakeholder question should be examined to see what types of architecture data are needed to address the problem or answer the question and how these types of data are related. The concepts and relationships introduced in Chapter 4 provide a basic set of data types and relationships that can be used.

Sometimes the stakeholder questions may be too high-level or complex to analyze directly. In this case, each high-level question must be decomposed into a set of simpler questions whose answers provide the architecture information needed to address

**Figure 5-9**
Determine the data required to support architecture development

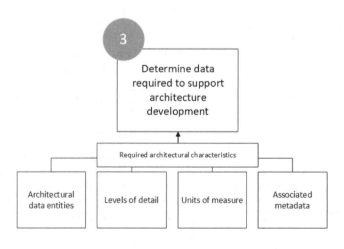

the original question. Further, not all the types of data needed by a purpose or problem are architectural in nature. For example, questions involving cost may need substantial financial input, and most financial information is not usually captured in an enterprise architecture.

A specific example of a question involving cost is determining the return on investment (ROI) for a proposed project. ROI analysis is frequently used in answering questions having to do with selecting projects for funding. The type of data needed to calculate ROI includes the cost of current operations, cost of the change process, and cost of the reengineered operations. The architecture inputs to this calculation are the details of current operations (as-is activities and systems support), the phasing of changes (new business process and system availability timelines), and the details of the reengineered operations (to-be activities and system support). The architecture would not usually include the salary data or facility cost data that is used to calculate operational costs. This financial data would have to come from a different source such as Human Resources or a financial planning group. However, the architecture could include information on the staff size and skills (roles and skills of performers in organizations) needed for current and reengineered operations. The architecture could also include summary information on operations and maintenance costs for the automated support for operations. The architecture could also include the performance measures used to evaluate the efficiency of the business process, the values of those measures for the current process, and the goals for the values of those measures for the reengineered process. So, the following types of data, at a minimum, are needed to answer questions about ROI: as-is and to-be business process activities, their supporting systems, to-be business processes and supporting systems availability timelines, as-is and to-be roles and skills required by performing organizations, and performance measures that relate to the activities and processes.

Performance measures are one type of data that should not be overlooked. Many architectures have as a purpose the improvement of some business process or business outcome. For U.S. government departments and agencies, the Office of Management and Budget (OMB) guidance requires performance measures to be associated with mission outcomes. Some guidance on performance measures can be found in the Federal Enterprise Architecture Performance Reference Model (PRM), which is part of the Consolidated Reference Model. The PRM has a standard taxonomy for classifying types of performance measures and advice for creating a "line of sight" from improvements in IT performance to improvements in business outcome performance. Performance measures can be associated with (related to) capabilities, business processes, or systems and services. Note that the performance measures included in the architecture are not the management performance measures applied to an architecture development project.

It is very important to determine the data needed up front prior to jumping into the architecture effort. By determining what is needed—and, more appropriately, what is not needed—the architecture team can focus on collecting needed data and developing useful architecture artifacts or views. The planning examples at the end of this chapter show stakeholder questions and their corresponding required data and relationships.

## Determine What Views to Use: How to Organize and Correlate Data

From the perspective of scoping the work, we limit our consideration of step 4 activities to determining how to organize and correlate the types of data identified in step 3. In planning, the architect selects views that cover the needed types of data identified in step 3. These views are usually selected from an integrated set of views and modeling techniques based on a corporate methodology or a standard framework such as the DoDAF. The development organization's specific architecture development process guides the modeling techniques to use and the order in which the views are built. The specific architecture development process also guides the tools and data storage approach used. The sets of views used to organize and correlate data usually use mathematical modeling techniques and the framework ontology to ensure that the data collected is consistent, complete, and correctly correlated in the structured knowledgebase or architecture repository.

In the following discussions and examples, we use the DoDAF-described views organized in the DoDAF set of viewpoints as our integrated set of views from which to choose. Note that the DoDAF doesn't require that the views described in it are used to develop the architecture; it just requires that the needed data (from step 3) be represented in those standard view formats for sharing among DoD architects. In this way, DoD architects don't have to learn everyone else's methodologies and models to understand shared DoD architectures.

Figure 5-10 summarizes all the activities to be accomplished in step 4. The activities covered in this section are marked with asterisks.

Planning activities in step 4 complete the traceability from architecture purpose and stakeholder questions to the architecture data needed to answer the question to the views needed to capture that data and ensure it is consistent and complete. This traceability ensures a useful architecture with integrated views and data. Figure 5-11 illustrates the importance of establishing this traceability to the development of a useful architecture.

**Figure 5-10**

Organize
and correlate
architecture data

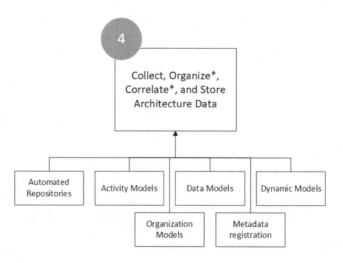

**Figure 5-11**
Traceability to
stakeholder
needs ensures
useful
architectures.

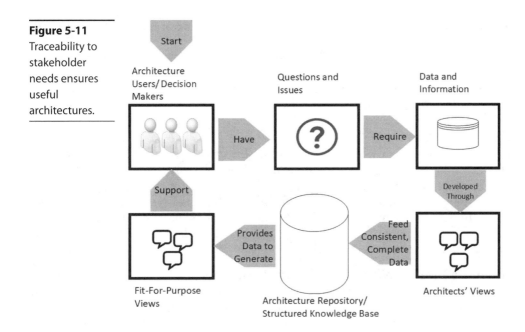

Many people jump straight to step 4 when planning an architecture and end up wasting time and effort. They spend resources on false starts and in building views that are not useful because they are not related to stakeholder (decision-maker) needs. Any time spent in performing steps 1 through 3 is more than made up for by the improved and more complete decisions made in step 4. These better decisions, in turn, ensure useful architecture results.

The process of selecting views is not a simple step. The architect must select the appropriate viewpoints and views together with the options and tailoring needed for each view. Each of these steps is discussed in the following sections.

## Selecting Viewpoints

The DoDAF organizes its views into a set of eight viewpoints, as discussed in Chapter 4. While the All View (AV) products are always included in an architecture, the inclusion of other viewpoints are determined by the types of data identified in step 3. As an architecture evolves and matures, additional viewpoints and views may be added. It is not necessary to build all the views in the same release.

As an enterprise initiates its architecture efforts, the viewpoints needed may be limited, depending on the immediate needs of the enterprise as reflected by prioritized stakeholder questions and issues. For example, an enterprise's immediate need may be a better understanding of its current operations. Fairly newly formed organizations, such as the Department of Homeland Security (DHS), may need to start with the Operational Viewpoint. An older enterprise's immediate need might be to gain control over its technology inventory in order to manage software licensing problems. Such enterprises may need to start with the Systems Viewpoint, although the Systems Viewpoint's view links to Operational Viewpoint views must remain to-be-determined (TBD) in the initial architecture release. Other enterprises may decide to focus early architecture efforts on interoperability issues. These enterprises might start with a Standards Viewpoint. In this case, the Standards Viewpoint's view links to Systems Viewpoint products must remain TBD until the Systems Viewpoint is developed. Any of these enterprises may include a Capability Viewpoint or Project Viewpoint to provide a basis for focusing new projects on strategic needs.

## Selecting Views

In general, you want to select views to address the types of architecture data identified in step 3. However, because there are many potential DoDAF views to pick from, we provide some general guidance on where to start. For each of the levels of architecture (enterprise, segment, and solution), we have identified a set of *core* views that we recommend for that level. The core views for a given level of architecture are the basic set of views that we recommend architectures at that level include. Each of these sets of core views is presented next together with its rationale.

**Enterprise Level Architecture Core Views**    The Enterprise Level architecture goal is to provide traceability from the enterprise strategic vision, goals, and objectives to the capabilities needed to achieve those objectives and to the projects (and their managing organizations) that implement those capabilities and to the organizations that use the capabilities. Phasing and timelines are a key part of this traceability. The core set of views for Enterprise Level architectures follows:

- AV-1: Overview and Summary Information
- AV-2: Integrated Dictionary
- CV-1: Vision
- CV-3: Capability Phasing
- CV-4: Capability Dependencies
- CV-5: Capability to Organizational Development Mapping
- PV-1: Project Portfolio Relationships
- PV-2: Project Timelines
- PV-3: Project to Capability Mapping
- OV-4: Organizational Relationships Chart

These views are primarily from the Capability and Project Viewpoints and support the type of basic information that is needed for Enterprise Level decision processes such as portfolio management and investment management. Figure 5-12 illustrates the integration of these core views for Enterprise Level architectures.

**Segment Level Architecture Core Views**    A Segment Level architecture may manage a subset of capabilities from an Enterprise Level architecture as well as coordinate the set of solution architectures that will provide those capabilities. Thus, Segment Level architectures may have the characteristics of both Enterprise Level architectures and Solution Level architectures. If the Segment Level architecture is to be used for

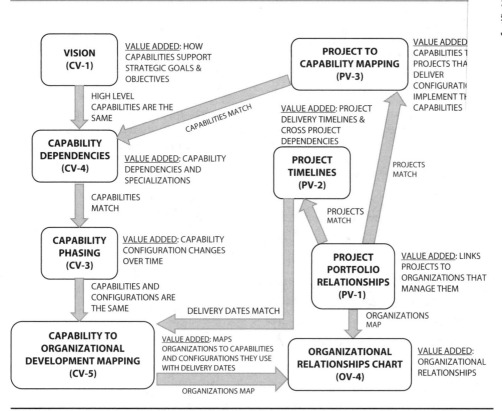

**Figure 5-12** Integration for Enterprise Level architecture core views

investment management or portfolio management for the capabilities included in the segment, then the core views for the segment should include the same views identified as core for an Enterprise Level architecture. In the case of a Segment Level architecture, those core views will be restricted to the subset of capabilities, projects, and organizations that fall within the scope of the segment. If the Segment Level architecture is to be used to coordinate a set of Solution Level architectures, then the core views for the segment should include the same views identified as core for a Solution Level architecture. However, in the case of a Segment Level architecture, these views will be focused on providing business context, documenting the support of the systems to the high-level business processes, and documenting business process and system interfaces necessary to ensure interoperability across the systems in all the solution architectures within the scope of the segment.

In addition to views, reference models (RMs) may also be included or associated with architectures. Enterprise Level and Segment Level architectures may use the various types of RMs to provide consistency and continuity of vocabulary and content across all the related Segment and Solution Level architectures. For example, a business reference model (BRM) can be used to further define the business areas and missions included in the scope of the enterprise. Each related Segment and Solution Level architecture can identify its relevant sets of business areas and missions. Enterprise and Segment Level architectures can use a technical reference model (TRM) to define the superset of standards that will constrain and help define the standards included in all the related Solution Level architectures.

**Solution Level Architecture Core Views**  The goal of a Solution Level architecture is to provide traceability from performers to the operational activities they perform and to the IT that supports those activities. The resources or information exchanged is a key part of this traceability. The core set of views for Solution Level architectures follows:

- AV-1: Overview and Summary Information
- AV-2: Integrated Dictionary
- OV-1: High-Level Operational Concept Graphic
- OV-2: Operational Resource Flow Description
- OV-3: Operational Resource Flow Matrix
- OV-5a: Operational Activity Decomposition Tree
- OV-5b: Operational Activity Model
- SV-1: System Interface Description
- SvcV-1: Services Context Description
- SvcV-4: Services Functionality Description
- StdV-1: Standards Profile
- CV-6: Capability to Operational Activity Mapping (optional)

The core set for the Solution Level architectures includes different options depending on which of the Systems or Services Viewpoints is included. (If the as-is portion of a solution architecture uses the Systems Viewpoint and the to-be portion of the Solution Level architecture uses the Services Viewpoint, then both sets of views will be included in the overall architecture.) The Services Functionality Description is included if the Services Viewpoint is used.

The integration of these core views is well defined, as illustrated in Figure 5-13, which shows only the Systems Viewpoint core view (instead of both the Systems and Services Viewpoints core views). The Capability To Operational Activities Mapping is not included in the figure because it is optional and should be included in the Solution Level core set only when the Solution Level architecture has an overarching Enterprise or Segment Level architecture that includes capabilities.

The views that are not designated "core" for the Solution Level architecture are sometimes called "supporting" views. The supporting views are included in the architecture as required by the purpose of the architecture.

## General Guidance on Selecting Views

For each needed viewpoint, build the core views for the appropriate level of architecture. These views cover the information commonly needed in that level architecture and provide commonality needed for comparisons across architectures developed by

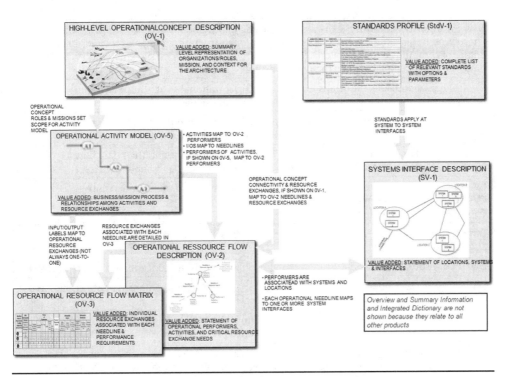

**Figure 5-13**   Integration for the Solution Level architecture core views

different organizations. If any needed data from step 3 is not addressed by the core views, select supporting views that cover that data—that is, select appropriate additional views that are not included in the core set for the given level architecture. Some corporate methodologies or government regulations, such as DoD directives, may require certain of the supporting views.

To select supporting views, you need to know the information addressed by or covered in the view. The three critical aspects of this information are the view template that provides the format for the view's graphic component, the information required by the dictionary entries for the view, and the view options. This information is covered in Part III of this book.

As an example, Table 5-1 provides a list of the views that are "supporting" for Solution Level architectures. Because the DoDAF view numbers are strictly arbitrary, this list is organized into categories that may help in selecting views. (More detail on these views is provided in Part III of this book.) However, some Capability and Project Viewpoint views listed may not be appropriate for a Solution Level architecture. For example, the Project Timelines view (PV-2) is designed to compare and relate project timelines over multiple projects. It is not appropriate to use PV-2 for one project. The timeline for a specific project by itself is of interest only to the immediate project management and sponsor and is part of the program management plan. The Project Timelines view is to support coordination and management of multiple projects.

**New Information Category**   These views include information that is not found in other views. These products include information on organizational structures, roles, and responsibilities; details of communications networks that support system interfaces; system functions and their data flows; and capabilities and their relationships.

| | |
|---|---|
| OV-4: Organizational Relationships Chart | Organizational structures, roles, and responsibilities |
| SV-2: Systems Resource Flow Description<br>SvcV-2: Services Resource Flow Description | Details of communications networks that support system or services interfaces |
| SV-4: Systems Functionality Description<br>SvcV-4: Services Functionality Description | System functions and their data flows/services functions, SLAs, and dependencies |
| CV-1: Vision<br>CV-2: Capability Taxonomy<br>CV-4: Capability Dependencies | Capabilities and their relationships |

**Data Model Category**   Views focus on representations of shared, structured enterprise concepts and data.

| | |
|---|---|
| DIV-1: Conceptual Data Model | Shared enterprise concepts and their relationships |
| DIV-2: Logical Data Model | Shared, structured enterprise data entities and relationships |
| DIV-3: Physical Data Model | Implementation of shared, structured enterprise data |

**Sequence and Timing Model Category**   Views are models that capture dynamic aspects of the enterprise and support executable architectures. The "a" options are Rules Models, the "b" options are State Transition models, and the "c" options are scenario-based models. Each type of model is the same, regardless of viewpoint, although the focus of the model will be different, depending on viewpoint.

| | |
|---|---|
| OV-6a: Operational Rules Model<br>SV-10a: Systems Rules Model<br>SvcV-10a: Services Rules Model | Rules constrain behavior |
| OV-6b: State Transition Description<br>SV-10b: Systems State Transition Description<br>SvcV-10b: Services State Transition Description | State or status flow for objects |
| OV-6c: Event-Trace Description<br>SV-10c: Systems Event-Trace Description<br>SvcV-10c: Services Event-Trace Description | Scenarios that show sequences of events, messages, and actions |

**Transition Planning Category**   Views contain information about transition strategy and plans. These views contain information on project timelines and relationships, how capabilities are supported over time, when new or upgraded automated systems will become operational, the performance improvements expected based on these system changes, and the status of new technology and standards needed for the new systems and upgrades.

| | |
|---|---|
| SV-7: Systems Measures Matrix<br>SvcV-7: Services Measures Matrix | Performance measures and time-phased performance goals |
| SV-8: Systems Evolution Description<br>SvcV-8: Services Evolution Description | Timeline for system/service availability |

**Table 5-1**   Supporting Views for Solution Level Architecture, by Category

| | |
|---|---|
| SV-9: Systems Technology & Skills Forecast<br>SvcV-9: Services Technology & Skills Forecast | Forecasts of systems/services technology in selected areas together with the skill sets needed for the new technology |
| StdV-2: Standards Forecast | Forecasts of standards changes |
| CV-3: Capability Phasing | Dates when new capabilities become available and which projects provide the capability over time (not recommended for Solution Level architectures) |
| PV-2: Project Timelines | Project start and stop dates and dependencies (not recommended for Solution Level architectures) |
| **Matrix Views Category**   Views share the same matrix style format and link together information found in other views, sometimes with additional new information. | |
| SV-3: Systems-Systems Matrix<br>SvcV-3b: Services-Services Matrix | Interfaces between systems or services (summarizing information on System Interface Description or Services Context Description) |
| SV-5a: Operational Activity to Systems Function Traceability Matrix<br>SvcV-5: Operational Activity to Services Traceability Matrix | Maps systems functions or services to the operational activities they support |
| SV-6: Systems Resource Flow Matrix<br>SvcV-6: Services Resource Flow Matrix | Identifies system/service resource exchanges and their attributes |
| CV-5: Capability to Organizational Development Mapping | Planned (by phase) capability deployment to organizations |
| CV-7: Capability to Services Mapping | Mapping from capabilities to the services that support them |
| PV-1: Project Portfolio Relationships | Maps projects to portfolios and the organizations that manage them |
| PV-3: Project to Capability Mapping | Maps projects to the capabilities that the project's products support |

**Table 5-1**   Supporting Views for Solution Level Architecture, by Category *(continued)*

If additional needed data cannot easily be addressed by any standard DoDAF views, even with tailoring, you may need to add Fit-for-Purpose views that are not included in the set of DoDAF views. Other frameworks, such as The Open Group Architecture Framework (TOGAF) and the Federal Enterprise Architecture Framework Version 2 (FEAF2) may be useful sources for additional types of views. (In addition, other defense frameworks related to DoDAF are relevant here. These include the MODAF [Ministry of Defense Architecture Framework] and NAF [NATO], which are now being merged. See Part IV for details about these other frameworks.) Additional views may range from reports based on information already captured in the dictionary (AV-2) to complex models for executable architectures. You may choose to include some additional Fit-for-Purpose views, such as dashboards, pie charts, bar charts, or fusion diagrams that draw on the data developed by more formal views and present that data in a form that supports the specific needs of decision-makers. In other words, the views used by architects may not be the best format for presenting data to decision-makers.

Added Fit-for-Purpose views should be documented in the Overview and Summary Information (AV-1). This documentation includes a discussion the semantics of any graphic notation or a reference to readily available texts or web sites that discuss the new view. In addition, the data to be included in the added views will need to be identified for inclusion in the dictionary (AV-2), and the relationship of the Fit-for-Purpose view to the standardized DoDAF views will need to be defined. The resulting set of views needs to remain integrated.

# Planning Examples

Following are some examples of the results of applying the previously described planning process to architectures at each architecture level. These examples are based on the case study in Chapter 3 of this book. The view examples in Part III of this book relate to these three architectures.

## Enterprise Level Architecture Planning Example

Here is an example of the documentation resulting from planning for an Enterprise Level architecture, based on the case study in Chapter 3.

**Purpose**   Provide guidance on what additional capabilities/business services will be necessary to achieve RMN Airport's strategic goals of becoming a viable alternative to LAX. The initial phase of the architecture will document the current baseline and starting point for any transition plan.

**Stakeholders**   Port Authority (especially the Planning Committee), RMN management.

**Stakeholder Questions and Issues**   The members of the appropriate county Port Authority Planning Committee have the following questions:

- What business services do we currently offer?
- Do these business services have any dependencies or relationships?
- How are these business services grouped into segments for management purposes?
- How do the current business services relate to the RMN Airport strategic vision and goals? That is, how important will the current business services be to achieving our strategic goals?
- What project/programs or contracts do we have that provide these business services, and what organizations oversee these projects or contracts?
- What organizations use the business services?
- When does the current funding for the existing projects/contracts expire? That is, for how long have the funds for these projects/contracts been committed?
- What are the current performance measures and values?

**Scope**

- Enterprise Level architecture for RMN Airport
- Covers all missions and organizations within RMN Airport

- Geographical bounds: RMN Airport grounds, airspace, and associated business offices
- Technology constraints: N/A (Enterprise Level)
- Time frame: As-is

**Required Data and Selected Views**    Table 5-2 identifies the data needed to answer these questions and the views (with selected options/tailoring) used to capture the data. There is no "stakeholder" column in this table because all the stakeholders have the same questions in this example.

| Question | Required Data | Views |
|---|---|---|
| What business services does RMN Airport currently offer? | Existing business services/capabilities | CV-2: Capability Taxonomy |
| Do these business services have any dependencies or relationships? | Relationships among business services | CV-4: Capability Dependencies |
| How are these business services grouped into segments for management purposes? | Management relationships among business services | CV-4: Capability Dependencies, tailored to highlight segment groupings |
| How do the current business services relate to the RMN Airport strategic vision and goals? | Strategic vision, goals, and desired effects<br>Relationships to current business services | CV-1: Vision, tailored to show to-be strategic vision and goals but just as-is business services/capabilities |
| What project/programs or contracts do we have that provide these business services? | Existing project/programs or contracts<br>Relationship of projects/programs/ contracts to business services | PV-3: Project to Capability Mapping |
| What RMN Airport organizations oversee these projects or contracts? | Organizational chart of RMN Airport | OV-4: Organizational Relationships Chart |
|  | Relationships of organizations to projects/programs/contracts they own/manage | PV-1: Project Portfolio Relationships |
| What organizations use the business services? | Organizations, including both internal and external organizations, that use the business services | OV-4: Organizational Relationships Chart, tailored to include all performers including external performers |
|  | Relationships of organizations to business services they use | CV-5: Capability to Organizational Development Mapping |
| When does the current funding for the existing projects/contracts expire? That is, for how long have the funds for these projects/contracts been committed? | End points (based on current funding commitments) of projects/programs or end dates on contracts | CV-3: Capability Phasing, tailored to show only existing projects/programs/contracts, (showing as-is phase only) |

**Table 5-2**    Mapping of Enterprise Level Questions to Required Data and Views

## Segment Level Architecture Planning Example

The following is an example of the documentation resulting from planning for a Segment Level architecture based on the case study in Chapter 3.

**Purpose**    Passenger Management is a segment of the RMN Airport enterprise architecture. This Segment Level architecture will provide the basis for transitioning RMN Airport passenger management services over the next five years to meet RMN Airport strategic goals. The strategic goals involve the addition of new capabilities that affect passenger services.

**Stakeholders**    Port Authority, RMN Airport management, RMN Airport employees and unions, local county and cities, western state commuter airlines and cargo carriers/delivery services, TSA, FAA, current and potential vendors for passenger-related services

**Stakeholder Questions and Issues**    The following is a sample subset of the stakeholders' questions and issues.

The Port Authority and RMN Airport management have the following questions:

- What additional passenger management business services will we need to offer within the next five years?
- What are the performance measures and their five-year goal values for all the passenger management services (both existing business services and new business services)?
- What existing passenger management business services will have to be expanded?
- What are the dependencies and other relationships among the passenger management business services (both existing and new)?
- What existing projects and contracts will be impacted by the expansion of existing passenger management business services?
- What new projects will be needed for the new passenger management business services?
- What are the major business processes that support passenger management business services?
- How many personnel will RMN Airport need to execute the passenger management business processes? What skills will these personnel need?
- What are the major systems that will be needed to support passenger-related business services in five years?
- Which of these systems will be new and which are existing systems?

- Will any of the existing passenger management systems need to be upgraded?
- What are the major interfaces among these passenger management systems with other RMN Airport segments, and with external systems?
- What infrastructure will these systems use?
- What are the standards that all the systems (new and existing) need to support five years from now?

The members of the Port Authority have the following questions:

- What passenger management business services should we offer in five years?
- Will these business services have any dependencies or relationships?
- How do these passenger management business services relate to the RMN Airport strategic vision and goals?
- What project/programs or contracts should we have to provide these passenger management business services?
- What organizations should oversee these projects or contracts?
- What organizations will use the passenger management business services?
- When do new projects/programs or contracts need to start to ensure there are no gaps in passenger management services over the next five years? Do any existing projects/programs need to be extended or upgraded?
- What are the performance measures and values for passenger management business services?

RMN Airport Management, TSA, local county and cities, and airlines have the following question:

- How many passengers can the future business processes handle per hour and per day?

**Scope**

- Segment Level architecture for RMN Airport
- Covers all missions and organizations related to passenger management business services at RMN Airport
- Geographical bounds: RMN Airport grounds and associated business offices
- Technology constraints: COTS, compatibility with systems in other RMN Airport enterprise architecture segments
- Time frame: To-be (present to five years)

**Required Data and Selected Views**    Table 5-3 identifies the data needed to answer some of these questions and the views (with selected options/tailoring) used to capture the data. This table includes a "Stakeholder" column since there are multiple stakeholders with different but overlapping questions and is an example of one form of stakeholder matrix. The table does not include all the questions.

| Question | Stakeholder | Required Data | Views |
|---|---|---|---|
| What are the performance measures and their five-year goal values for all the passenger management services (both existing business services and new business services)? | Port Authority, RMN Airport management | Business services with performance measures and goals | CV-2: Capability Taxonomy, with performance measures and tailored to include performance goals for five years in the future |
| What are the major business processes that support passenger management business services? | Port Authority, RMN Airport management | Business processes | OV-5a: Operational Activity Decomposition Tree |
| | | Business services | CV-2: Capability Taxonomy, restricted to scope of the segment |
| | | Mapping of business services to business processes | CV-6: Capability to Operational Activities Mapping |
| What are the major systems that will be needed to support passenger-related business services in five years? | Port Authority, RMN Airport management | Systems and interfaces (high-level) | SV-1: Systems Interface Description, with highest level perspective |
| | | Mapping of systems to business services | CV-7: Capability to Services Mapping, tailored to show systems instead of services |
| What are the major interfaces among these passenger management systems with other RMN Airport segments, and with external systems? | Port Authority, RMN Airport management | System interfaces | SV-1: Systems Interface Description, with high-level perspective, including external interfaces, tailored to show which externals are to other RMN segments and which are to outside externals |
| What infrastructure will these systems use? | Port Authority | Systems and interfaces | SV-1: Systems Interface Description |
| | | Communications systems and networks | SV-2: Systems Resource Flow Description |
| | | Standards | StdV-1: Standards Profile, with map to where the standards apply |
| What project/programs or contracts should we have to provide these passenger management business services? | Port Authority | Business services | CV-2: Capability Taxonomy |

**Table 5-3**    Mapping of Segment Level Questions to Required Data and Views

| Question | Stakeholder | Required Data | Views |
|---|---|---|---|
| | | Mapping of projects to business services | PV-3: Project to Capability Mapping |
| What organizations should oversee these projects or contracts? | Port Authority | Mapping of projects to organizations that own them | PV-1: Project Portfolio Relationships |
| What organizations will use the passenger management business services? | Port Authority | Organizations | OV-4: Organizational Relationships Chart, including all involved organizations both internal to RMN and external |
| | | Business services | CV-2: Capability Taxonomy |
| | | Mapping from organizations to the business services they will use | CV-5: Capability to Organizational Development Mapping; may be tailored to remove references to systems |
| How many passengers can the future business processes handle per hour and per day? | RMN Airport Management, TSA, local county and cities, airlines | Resource exchanges | OV-3: Operational Resource Flow Matrix, with throughput column |
| | | Business processes with performance measures and goals | OV-5a: Operational Activity Decomposition Tree, tailored with performance measures and goals |

**Table 5-3**    Mapping of Segment Level Questions to Required Data and Views *(continued)*

## Solution Level Architecture Planning Example

The following is an example of the documentation resulting from planning for a Solution Level architecture based on the case study in Chapter 3.

**Purpose**    One of the Passenger Management Segment business services that will need to be upgraded for RMN Airport is passenger identification. This Solution Level architecture will define upgraded passenger identification business processes and provide guidance on the acquisition of the required set of applications and common databases to support these upgraded business processes.

**Stakeholders**    Port Authority, RMN Airport management, DHS, RMN Airport employees (IT group), passenger airlines, FAA

**Stakeholder Questions and Issues**    The following is a sample subset of the stakeholders' questions and issues.

Port Authority, RMN Airport management, and DHS have the following questions:

- Will the new business processes and applications meet government regulations and requirements? That is, what types of passenger identification data is required?
- Who needs what passenger identification data and who should provide the data?
- How do the new processes improve confidence in passenger identification? (Measures include speed, availability, and consistency of data.)

RMN Airport management has the following questions:

- When will the upgraded processes and their supporting applications be ready for use?
- What performance, in terms of passengers per hour, should be expected from the new processes?

RMN Airport management and DHS have the following questions:

- How many personnel will be needed for the new business processes?
- Will the personnel need additional skills?
- When will any additional personnel be needed?
- Will new facilities be required? If so, when will they become available for use?

RMN Airport IT employees and management have the following questions:

- What are the upgraded business processes?
- How do the new applications support the business processes?
- How do the new applications, services, and databases integrate with other RMN Airport IT?
- What infrastructure will be required?
- What standards will the new applications, systems/services, and databases use?

DHS, airlines, and FAA have the following questions:

- What are the upgraded business processes?
- How do we use the new business processes and applications to get the data we need?

**Scope**

- Solution Level architecture for the Passenger Management Segment of the RMN Airport enterprise
- Covers passenger identification business services for RMN Airport
- Geographical bounds: RMN Airport grounds and associated business offices

- Technology constraints: COTS components and infrastructure with overall compatibility with the RMN Airport enterprise IT standards and federal (DHS/FAA) data standards
- Time frame: To-be (for 10 Year-plus time frame; includes international passenger travel)

**Required Data and Selected Views**    Table 5-4 identifies the data needed to answer some of these questions and the views (with selected options/tailoring) used to capture the data. The table does not include all the questions. This table is also an example of one form of stakeholder matrix.

| Question | Stakeholders | Required Data | Views |
|---|---|---|---|
| What types of passenger identification data are required? | All | Data model | DIV-2: Logical Data Model modeling information exchanges/activity I/Os |
| | | Information exchanges | OV-3: Operational Resource Flow Matrix with basic columns |
| | | I/Os from activities | OV-5b: Operational Activity Model |
| | | Government regulations and standards | StdV-1: Standards Profile, tailored to include regulations |
| Who needs what data and who should provide the data? | All | Performers, and relationships of performers to activities | OV-2: Operational Resource Flow Description |
| | | Information exchanges | OV-3: Operational Resource Flow Matrix |
| | | I/Os from activities | OV-5b: Operational Activity Model |
| How do the new processes improve confidence in passenger identification? (Measures include speed, availability, and consistency of data) | Port Authority, RMN Airport management, DHS | Business processes | OV-5b: Operational Activity Model, tailored to include performance measures and goals |
| When will the upgraded processes and their supporting applications be ready for use? | RMN Airport management | Timeline for application and process availability | SV-8: Systems Evolution Description and SvcV-8: Services Evolution Description, both tailored to include process definition and training completion dates |
| What performance, in terms of passengers per hour, should be expected from the new processes? | RMN Airport management | Business processes | OV-5b: Operational Activity Model, tailored to include performance measures and goals |
| | | Information exchanges | OV-3: Operational Resource Flow Matrix with Periodicity column (average and worst case numbers) |

**Table 5-4**    Mapping of Solution Level Questions to Required Data and Views *(continued)*

| Question | Stakeholders | Required Data | Views |
|----------|-------------|---------------|-------|
| How many personnel will be needed for the new business processes? | RMN management, DHS | Performers | OV-2: Operational Resource Flow Description |
| | | Organizations and number of personnel who are performers per organization | OV-4: Organizational Relationships Chart, tailored to include number of personnel per performer group |
| | | Relationship between performers and organizations | Map between organizations and performers |

**Table 5-4**   Mapping of Solution Level Questions to Required Data and Views

# Success Factors in Scoping the Architecture Work

The most critical success factor in scoping architecture work is getting agreement on the purpose of the architecture. Without this agreement, the various architecture user tribes may have false expectations and various groups of architecture developers may work at cross purposes. Without a clear purpose, the architecture work may be poorly defined and produce results that are not useful to any of the architecture users. Part of getting agreement on the purpose of the architecture is finding all the users of the architecture; identifying their issues, questions, and architecture data needs; and gaining their buy-in with the changes the architecture describes.

If there is a large set of architecture user tribes with a diversity of different issues, then it is important to prioritize the groups of users and issues. It is important to focus the architecture development efforts and generate timely and useful results. Each release of the architecture can focus on an additional group of users until all are getting the information they need.

The proof of a properly scoped (and executed) architecture effort is that the architecture data is actually used in decision-making processes.

# Summary

Here is a summary of advice for scoping the architecture work based on the Six-Step Process:

- Know why you are developing the architecture. Identify the full set of architecture users—the stakeholders—and the ways in which they plan to use the architecture.

- Expect to tailor the standard views to capture the data critical to your stakeholders.

- Be prepared to add to or modify the set of views as your experience with the architecture domain evolves.

- Do not develop views you can't find a customer (a user) or a purpose for. In some cases, the architecture team itself may be the principle user of some views to support analysis, conclusions, and recommendations.

- Do not develop more detail than your architecture users need.

# Questions

1. Why is it important to establish traceability from stakeholder issues to architecture data and views?

2. In your enterprise, who are the users of EA (the stakeholders) and how do they use EA information in decision-making?

3. This chapter provides suggestions for core sets of views to be included in each of the three levels of architecture. How are additional views selected?

4. Examine the views that have been selected by the partial planning analyses for the RMN Airport Enterprise, Passenger Management Segment, and Passenger Identification Solution Level architectures (Tables 5-2, 5-3, and 5-4). Have all the recommended core views been identified? Do the missing views give you any ideas for the stakeholders or stakeholder issues that might have been overlooked in the analysis?

5. The example Enterprise Level architecture for RMN Airport doesn't include local governments and citizens as stakeholders (users of the architecture), yet these stakeholders will want information about increased noise and traffic and expansion of airport grounds and facilities to analyze for impact on their communities. Formulate some of their questions and issues and redo the analysis in the Enterprise Level architecture example to identify any additional data and views that need to be included for these stakeholders.

6. The Solution Level example in this chapter handles only a subset of the stakeholder questions. Complete the traceability table and identify the complete set of data and views needed for the Solution Level architecture. Do you see any additional questions that need to be added to the analysis? Do you see any additional data or views that can be added to the existing part of the traceability table?

7. Why is an understanding of corporate/enterprise culture and enterprise tribes important in planning an architecture to support any enterprise change?

8. Company A is a large enterprise that has decided it needs an enterprise architecture. However, management has decided not to release the architecture until it is "complete." What are the pitfalls of this approach?

9. How might RMN Airport use the Passenger Management segment architecture in managing transition of passenger management capabilities and services? Will this Segment Level architecture be used to manage a subset of capabilities and services from the Enterprise Level architecture, or will it be used to coordinate the set of solution architectures that will provide those capabilities and services, or both? What core views should be included?

**10.** Here are the purpose, scope, and stakeholder questions for a Solution Level architecture. Develop the matrix to trace the questions to the data types needed to answer the questions and to the views (with options and tailoring) to develop and document the required data. Reference Chapter 4 of the text for more information on views.

**Purpose:** Define the operational processes and IT necessary to support data sharing for a newly formed cross-agency security incident management community of interest (COI).

**Scope**

- Cross-agency Solution Level architecture
- Function: Airspace security incident management
- Geographic: CONUS but coordination needed with internationals
- Time frame: To-be 2020
- Technology constraints: COTS integration; must integrate with existing agency systems

**Issues and Questions**

- What is the overall operational concept?
- Who are the potential members of the COI in terms of the following:
  - Organization, their owning agency, and reporting hierarchy
  - Their data sharing needs—what information they can provide and what data they need; what data they need but currently don't have access to
- What are the COI's shared vocabulary concepts?
- What are the current relevant operational processes of the COI?
- What are the relevant legacy systems, interfaces, and standards?
- What are nominal scenarios for key incident types?
- What is the common information model for supporting information sharing?
- What are the COI standards for interoperability, security, and privacy in data sharing?
- What is the data quality, timeliness, and media (video, audio, telephonic, and Internet) attributes necessary for shared data?
- What are the rules (based on policy) that define data creation, update, and access authorizations based on incident type?

# References

Department of Defense. 2009. Department of Defense Architecture Framework Version 2.0. http://dodcio.defense.gov/Library/DoD-Architecture-Framework.04.

Federal Enterprise Architecture Program Management Office. 2007. "FEA Consolidated Reference Model Document Version 2.3." www.reginfo.gov/public/jsp/Utilities/FEA_CRM_v23_Final_Oct_2007_Revised.pdf.

Hong Kong International Airport. 2014. "Sustaining Our Capacity: Addressing Emerging Constraints. Sustainability Report 2013/14." http://www.hongkongairport.com/iwov-resources/html/sustainability_report/eng/pdf/media/publication/sustainability/13_14/E_Sustainability_Report_Full.pdf, pp. 16–17.

KPMG. 2017. "Approach: The Global Strategy Group's proprietary 9 Levers of Value approach focuses on value creation, protection, and delivery from Innovation to Results." https://home.kpmg.com/cn/en/home/services/advisory/strategy/approach1.html.

North Atlantic Treaty Organization (NATO). 2007. "NATO Architecture Framework, v3.0." www.nafdocs.org.

Office of Management and Budget. 2012. "The Common Approach to Federal Enterprise Architecture." https://obamawhitehouse.archives.gov/sites/default/files/omb/assets/egov_docs/common_approach_to_federal_ea.pdf.

Schaar, David, and Lance Sherry. 2017. "Analysis of Airport Stakeholders, Paper Number 109." www.academia.edu/20996936/Analysis_of_airport_stakeholders.

SEA Network (SEA) Letter to the Stakeholder "Stakeholders Map." http://sea2013csr.rep.message-asp.com/en/sustainability-sea/stakeholders-map#start. Retrieved on 5/1/2018.

The Open Group. 2011. "TOGAF Version 9.2." The Netherlands: Van Haren Publishing.

United Kingdom Ministry of Defense (MOD). 2012. "Ministry of Defense Architecture Framework (MODAF)." www.gov.uk/guidance/mod-architecture-framework.

U.S. Department of Transportation. "Modernization of U.S. Airspace." https://www.faa.gov/nextgen/.

Zachman, John A. "About the Zachman Framework." www.zachman.com/about-the-zachman-framework.

# Developing the Architecture

In this chapter, we address planning for architecture development projects. Topics include an overview of the project plan and a discussion of important project implementation issues, such as the statement of work (SOW) for an enterprise architecture (EA) project, EA implementation steps as identified in the selected EA development methodology, and the EA life cycle, tools, and repositories. Corporate culture influences an enterprise's approach to each of these topics.

## Overview of the Project Plan

Planning for the last few steps of the Six-Step Process, illustrated in Figure 6-1, focuses on planning the architecture development project or program and how the work will be done. The scope of the work, identified in the initial steps of the Six-Step Process, must be determined in order to develop the SOW for a project. This SOW may take one or more fiscal years or budget funding cycles to accomplish. It is important to plan the architecture project and prioritize the development of views and data into multiple releases as necessary.

Some of the decisions made in planning the details of the architecture project may cause the initial decisions about the views (project deliverables) to be revisited. The methodologies, techniques, and tools selected for the management and technical approaches used in a project may impact or constrain the data and views to be developed. For example, a decision to use a service-oriented architecture (SOA) approach for system/software development means that steps 3 and 4 of the Six-Step Process will need to be reviewed to ensure that the data and views that focus on services have been included. The selected tools may limit the views that can be developed and constrain the options and tailoring that can be used.

Some tools have specific forms of tailoring for views built-in. If such a tool is selected one must use a specific format for each of those views. Other tools may have limitations on the views and tailoring they can support. If such a tool is selected, compromises may have to be made regarding the original set of views or tailoring selected in step 4.

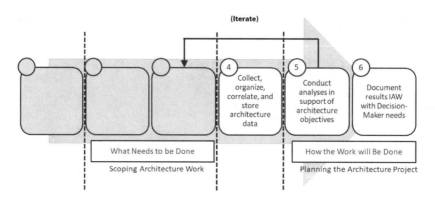

**Figure 6-1** How the work will be done

## The Project Plan

In this section, we focus on the elements of the architecture project plan.

Rather than use a specific outline for the project plan, sometimes also called a project or program management plan, we review the key topics that any project plan needs to cover:

- **What is to be done?** SOW, work breakdown structure (WBS), deliverables, reviews
- **Who is involved?** Stakeholders and project members with roles identified
- **How the work will be done?** Management and technical processes, methods, techniques, tools, computer resources and facilities
- **When will the work be done?** Project schedule and milestones

Each of these key topics is discussed in the following sections.

### What Is to Be Done

A key element of the project plan is a discussion of the work that is to be accomplished. Typically, a project will start with the development of a SOW or the receipt of a SOW from a customer who may be internal or external to the development group. The SOW spells out the work to be done in terms of deliverables (both management and technical), high-level schedule, and required reviews. Figure 6-2 provides a list of elements for an EA project SOW. A discussion of the contents of each of the suggested SOW sections is provided later in the chapter.

The usual response to a SOW is developing a WBS, which outlines the tasks necessary to manage and create the deliverables identified in the SOW and identifies dependencies among these tasks. These tasks include both technical and management tasks and may be

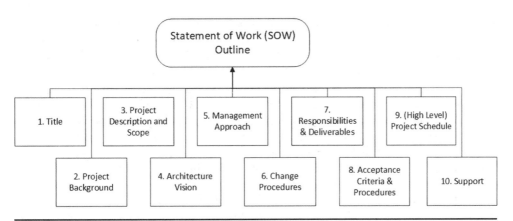

**Figure 6-2**   Suggested EA project SOW elements

guided by the specific methodology or process that will be used to perform the work. The WBS is input into the detailed project work plans and schedules. Many types of system and software development projects have generic WBSs that can be used as starting places for specific projects in these areas. Typically, generic WBSs can be found in textbooks or are part of corporate or enterprise management standards. Unfortunately, EA is a discipline that lacks generic WBSs. Some corporations or EA development departments may have such WBSs for use in-house, but they have not been generally accepted as standard approaches. A generic EA project WBS is something an EA development group may want to develop for themselves after experience with several EA projects or several iterations of releases for an evolving EA.

The deliverables listed in the SOW and addressed by tasks in the WBS will include the views and related data identified in steps 3 and 4 of the Six-Step Process, as well as any necessary management reports, technical briefings, and management processes such as configuration management. Since the DoDAF (and many other architecture frameworks) provides only high-level guidance, the description of the EA views needs to include any required options and tailoring as determined in step 4 of the Six-Step Process. The list of views also needs to include any selected Fit-for-Purpose views, with explicit descriptions of the desired format and integration requirements of these views.

Technical deliverables may also include the results of analyses, which may include analyses needed to develop the architecture as well as additional types in which the developed architecture data is just one of the sources of input. Many types of analysis needed to support decision-makers include both architecture and financial data. Examples of such analyses include return on investment (ROI), business case analysis, and activity based costing. Other types of technical analyses include performance or sensitivity analysis based on simulations.

The reviews of the technical deliverables also need careful identification and description. There are no standard reviews for EA views and data during development such as there are for systems and software. Each development organization will have to evolve its own way toward a reasonable set of reviews. However, there are at some known pitfalls that should be avoided. A common mistake is to try a review of "final" operational views and data prior to the development of systems or services views and data. The DoDAF views need to form an integrated set. Development of systems or services views will uncover data that will cause changes in operational views and data. Placing the operational views under formal configuration management (CM) too early (that is, accepting a set of operational views and corresponding data as "final" through a review process prior to the development of system or services views) may significantly slow down the development process, since development of the systems or services views will predictably result in a fair number of needed changes. Review of draft views and data by viewpoint may be appropriate, but premature CM of single viewpoints should be avoided.

## Who Is Responsible

The project plan needs to identify all the participants in the development process together with their roles and responsibilities. The organizational structure of the development team needs to be spelled out and the skills needed by the various team roles identified. As EA development is a collaborative process involving both members of the enterprise and the development team, the business or mission personnel and IT personnel of the enterprise in question have roles to play as well as the members of the EA development team. The "owners" of the EA need to provide overall enterprise vision and direction. While the EA development team can help facilitate the development of an enterprise strategy, ultimately, it is the executives and business or mission leaders who must buy into and own the vision and strategy. Otherwise the EA effort is wasted. Executives, business leaders, and subject matter experts (SMEs) must also participate in the review and validation of the architecture. This review and validation can be part of the development process and also part of the governance process discussed in Chapter 9.

An enterprise engaged in developing and using an EA should have an organization that is charged with the development, maintenance, and evolution of the EA. In government, this organization is usually called the EA program office and is usually headed by a chief architect. Whatever the name, best practice says that this organization needs to report directly to the enterprise's chief information officer (CIO) or equivalent. If the EA program office is removed, in terms of the organizational structure, from the CIO's office, this is an indication that the EA program does not have an appropriate level of buy-in or support from the enterprise high-level management. Note that the EA program office should report to the CIO rather than the chief technology officer (CTO) since the EA needs the active participation of the mission or business management and cannot be treated as simply an IT matter if the EA program is to be successful.

Best practice also indicates that an EA executive steering committee (EAESC) should be established to review and formally accept each architecture release. The EAESC includes representatives of senior management and business unit executives. A technical review committee and a business review committee are usually established to assist the EAESC with reviewing IT and business aspects of the architecture, respectively. The EAESC may also approve the appointment of the chief architect.

The EA program office needs adequate staff and resources in order to be credible, even if most of the development or update work is outsourced to an outside contractor. The EA program office may have dedicated staff or may depend on staff matrixed in from other organizations. Integrated product teams (IPTs) composed of SMEs and development team members can be used to help jumpstart as-is portions of architectures, to brainstorm to-be portions of architectures, and for short-term architecture validation activities. However, IPTs are not effective for long-term activities because the SMEs have other jobs and cannot usually devote large amounts of their time on the architecture tasks.

The roles and skills needed by the EA program office include management, technical and business expertise, architecture development specialists, reviewers and validators, tool support, and liaison with external enterprise organizations.

The chief architect's job requires a number of skills, as illustrated in Figure 6-3. The chief architect is usually the manager of the EA project, so he or she needs managerial skills and the ability to handle both in-house development and contract issues. The chief architect needs a good understanding of the enterprise missions and business as well as sufficient understanding of technical issues to know what is appropriate and feasible from a technical point of view with respect to the enterprise's domain. The chief architect needs a good understanding of architecture frameworks, views, methodologies, and tools, as well as the uses to which EA data will be put within the enterprise. The chief architect needs strong communications skills to interface with executive management, business management, and IT management. Because all these skills and knowledge are rarely found in a single individual, a chief architect will typically have deputies to provide expertise is areas where the chief architect is not as strong.

The development specialists have expertise in the various modeling techniques and views needed for the viewpoints involved in the architecture. In addition, the development specialists may include architect's assistants who manage the input of architecture data into complex architecture development tools. The architect's assistants enable the other development specialists to focus on modeling issues and view content and free them from having to deal with the details of the tools.

**Figure 6-3**
Chief architect
skills

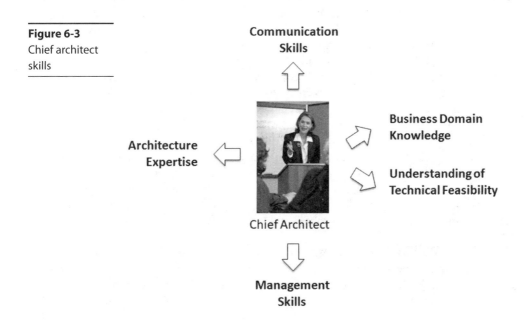

Architecture reviewers, who check the views and data for correctness, consistency, completeness, adherence to enterprise standards, and other quality issues, may include members of the development team, business and technical managers, and SMEs. Architecture validators determine whether the views and data appropriately reflect the current enterprise status (for as-is views) or the desired enterprise state (for to-be views). Validators need to include managers and SMEs. Carefully select validators, because SME groups may include multiple tribes (see Chapter 2) and may have conflicting opinions and priorities. Representatives from all relevant corporate tribes need to be included. If conflicting options arise, the architects should use the views and data of the architecture to illustrate the underlying issues to the appropriate level of enterprise management as soon as possible, so that the issues can be resolved and any risks appropriately managed and mitigated.

The development team will need access to IT specialists for installation, customization, and maintenance of the architecture development and analysis tools and their integration, as well as for general computing and communications support. Complex architecture development tools frequently have customization features that enable the tool to be adjusted to support specific view tailoring. This customization needs to be set up initially for the tailoring selected in step 4 of the Six-Step Process and specified in any enterprise EA standards. The customization will need adjustment as the EA project progresses and the tailoring is refined. In addition, the various tools used in the EA development project, including development, repository, analysis, management, and presentation tools, frequently need additional custom software to support their integration. These IT specialists may be dedicated members of the development team for large EA projects, or they may be available from some centralized support organization within the enterprise.

The EA project team needs the support of additional personnel to handle tasks associated with the CM process. These personnel act as the secretariat for the configuration control board (CCB) and handle such tasks as setting up CCB meetings and agendas and publishing reports on CCB activities. These personnel may be directly associated with the EA project team or may be organized in other ways, depending on corporate practices. The EA project team will need the support of quality assurance (QA) personnel. Again, these personnel may be directly associated with the EA project team or with a separate QA organization. Best practice directs that the head of QA reports to someone other than the chief architect.

Finally, the EA project team will need to maintain liaisons with other organizations or groups within the enterprise whose decisions may impact the architecture. While the architecture provides information to groups such as strategic planning and investment management, decisions or changes made by these groups directly impact the architecture. Although one of the chief architect's roles is to be the primary liaison with executive and management groups within the enterprise, the chief architect may want to appoint team members as special liaisons to critical external groups.

## How Work Will Be Done: Managerial and Technical Approaches

In laying out how the work will be done in a systems or software project, you would typically use a standard life cycle to identify the phases involved in the scope of the project and lay out your WBS tasks against the technical phases and the cross-phase categories.

Ideally, you would develop a filled-in version of the chart similar to that in Figure 6-4 to help you understand the order in which tasks will be accomplished and views and data will be developed, which techniques and tools will be used, and what reviews will be accomplished.

The challenge with an EA project is that there are no EA life cycle standards available. This means no accepted standard definitions for the phases, and no standards for where to start or for reviews (including what to review, when to review, and entry and exit criteria). This also means that an EA project organization needs to make its own decisions in terms of how the work will be done with only its selected methodology being its basic guidance. Frameworks vary widely in the amount of methodology or process guidance they provide. While the TOGAF provides a life cycle methodology (see Chapter 22), the DoDAF provides only minimal process guidance other than the Six-Step Process. The DoDAF leaves the development organization free to select its own process or methodology and life cycle.

At a minimum, the EA project plan should outline both the management approach and the technical approach. The management approach includes tasks that need to be executed continuously across all of the technical tasks. These include estimating, scheduling, tracking, reporting, configuration management, and quality assurance. The project plan must discuss specific methods, techniques, and tools that will be used for each of these management tasks. For example, the project plan needs to include a description of the CM processes and tools, or at least provide a pointer to a configuration management plan. Similarly, the QA processes and tools can be described or the project plan can point to a QA plan. Additional management tasks include risk management and data strategy.

| | PHASE I | PHASE II | PHASE III | PHASE IV | PHASE V | PHASE VI |
|---|---|---|---|---|---|---|
| TASKS | | | | | | |
| VIEWS | | | | | | |
| METHODS | | | | | | |
| TOOLS | | | | | | |
| REVIEWS | | | | | | |

| MANAGEMENT | | | |
|---|---|---|---|
| TASKS | PRODUCTS | METHODS | TOOLS |

| CONFIGURATION MANAGEMENT | | | |
|---|---|---|---|
| TASKS | PRODUCTS | METHODS | TOOLS |

| QUALITY ASSURANCE | | | |
|---|---|---|---|
| TASKS | PRODUCTS | METHODS | TOOLS |

**Figure 6-4**   Basic life cycle chart

Risk management is an important, but frequently avoided, part of project management. Risk management is the practice of planning for potential future adverse events or impacts on the project and its products. For architecture development projects, this practice involves the identification of potential issues with the architecture that may significantly impact the improvements to be implemented based on the architecture. Risk management is a field in itself and will not be further addressed in this book.

Because data is so important in architecture, architecture project management also needs to develop a set of data-related strategies to complement and support the view-development process. These data-related strategies include data management (usually for the architecture data repository), data validation, and data dissemination. Again, the details of these data management issues form a field of their own and are not addressed in this book. (See *DAMA-DMBOK: Data Management Body of Knowledge*, 2nd Edition, by Dama International, Technics Publications, 2017.) Some of these topics will be covered on a broad level later in this chapter and in Chapter 7.

The technical approach includes a discussion of the process or methodology and tools that will be used to develop, manage, and maintain the architecture views and data. The process or methodology will include the order in which to develop views and data and the specific modeling techniques and tools used to do so. An enterprise may develop its own EA development methodology or use a "name-brand" process such as that provided by TOGAF. The development methodology or process needs to include or be coordinated with the following:

- Architecture validation strategy
- Architecture evolution strategy
- Architecture maintenance strategy
- Architecture dissemination strategy
- Enterprise transition planning

These topics are discussed in more detail in the following chapters. The technical process description should also include the process for architecture view and data reviews and the nominal schedule for these reviews with respect to other development tasks and events.

## When Will the Work Be Done

An important part of planning is the development of project schedules, and a key part of developing schedules is level of effort (LOE) estimating for the various tasks that need to be done. Schedules for architecture development are complicated by the fact that EA data is used to support decision-making in major enterprise processes, and decisions made during these processes may in turn impact the EA. Estimating LOE is based primarily on experience. EA is still a new field and experience is limited for most enterprises.

**Scheduling Milestones**   Typical internal milestones include task completion dates, view draft delivery dates, and review dates. Scheduling must also deal with dependencies among EA development tasks. Example dependencies for as-is portions of architectures include the need to complete at least some portion of document review and SME interviews prior to beginning view development. These are typical scheduling problems, and approaches for dealing with them don't vary from those usually employed in most system or software projects.

One of the complicating issues of scheduling EA development or evolution activities is that there are many external process milestones that may constrain the EA development schedule. Examples of these external processes include the following:

- Enterprise budgeting process
- Investment review process
- System development life cycle process
- System of systems integration testing process

Each of these external processes may require types of EA data to support decision-making at key milestones. Budgeting and investment review processes usually have yearly cycles and require EA data to support decisions about which systems to select for initial funding, continuing funding, or retirement. Systems under development may require sufficient EA data to provide compliance criteria and guidance at key life cycle milestones. Planning for System of Systems (SoS) integration testing requires EA data such as internal and external interfaces for each system involved. Enterprise executives may decide that the EA development or evolution schedule needs to be adjusted so that the required data is available to meet key milestone dates for any of these processes. For system development life cycle and SoS integration testing processes, these milestone dates are usually those associated with critical systems.

In turn, decisions made during the processes described may impact the EA. Budgeting and investment review decisions may impact the planned timing of systems, business process, or capability evolution and architecture transition. Budgeting and investment review decisions, as well as EA decisions driven by system development needs, may also impact the speed of technology and standards introduction. SoS integration testing process results may impact key interfaces. All of these interactions complicate the scheduling of EA development, maintenance, and evolution.

Schedules also, as always, need to take into account management reserve based on risk analysis and planning.

**LOE Estimating Issues**    LOE estimates per EA development task or possibly per EA view are necessary to support the development of reliable schedules. Because experience is a large factor in LOE estimating, planners must review organizational experience with EA development with respect to the following:

- The EA development process or methodology being used, including the views being developed
- The level of detail required in the architecture under development, including the types of architectures (as-is or to-be) under development
- The development tools being used

If the process, view set, or development tools are new to the development organization, additional time will be required for appropriate training and the learning curve. Additional time will also be necessary to get new tools in place and integrated and for training to be completed.

There are no generic industry guidelines for LOE estimates for EA development. Government projects typically do not keep detailed enough records to provide meaningful guidance. Commercial firms that do keep detailed records usually consider their experience data a competitive advantage and treat it as proprietary. Few reports with detailed data are published. If the development organization has no experience with EA development, or most of the personnel on the development team are not experienced with EA, then the best way to generate some initial LOE estimates is through a pilot effort. Pilot efforts are best focused on a small subset or "sliver" of the full EA that concerns a limited but well-defined mission performed by a small, well-defined, and cooperative set of operators who have a specific architecture issue. A successful pilot project can result in two beneficial outcomes: an example of an early success in the use of EA and estimates on the minimum LOE for the involved architecture tasks.

## Summary of Project Planning

Organizations planning for architecture development projects should follow their standard planning procedures with attention to the following differences:

- There is no standard EA life cycle or standard set of reviews.
- The EA life cycle or development process must interact or interface with other key enterprise processes.
- There is less organizational experience with EA processes and views.
- There are fewer experienced personnel for EA development.
- For U.S. government organizations, there have been steadily increasing and changing federal requirements with respect to EA.

Standard planning should result in the following characteristics:

- A clear assignment of responsibilities
- A clear identification of deliverables
- A clear description of the processes, both managerial and technical, to be used
- A detailed schedule with identification of task dependencies

# Details of Project Planning

This section focuses on important details of project planning, including specific details of the SOW for architecture projects and methodology/process, tool, and repository issues.

# Statement of Work

All projects, whether internal or contracted, are based on some understanding of the work the project is to undertake. This understanding is usually documented in a written SOW. Architects need to have a good understanding of the elements of a SOW for an EA project since they may be required to develop or to respond to SOWs. The following subsections cover a generic SOW for an EA development project and highlight issues that are specific to EA projects.

Figure 6-2 provides an outline for an EA development project SOW. This outline is similar to that provided by The Open Group. Each of the items on the outline is discussed in a separate subsection next. Key information included in the SOW is provided by the first few steps of the Six-Step Process discussed in Chapter 5, and the relationships of items of the outline will be related back to the Six-Step Process.

## Title

The title for the SOW usually includes the EA name in some form.

## Project Background

The SOW should include a discussion of the sponsoring organization(s) and the context necessary for understanding their reasons for needing an EA.

## Project Description and Scope

The SOW should include a discussion of the purpose of the EA and the EA scope as identified in steps 1 and 2 of the Six-Step Process. The entire list of stakeholder questions needs not be included, but the stakeholders (the users of the architecture) need to be identified as well as all the scope boundaries from step 2. This section of the SOW should identify the level of architecture that is being developed (such as enterprise, segment, or solution).

## Architecture Vision

This section might be better called "Strategic Vision." The SOW should include the drivers for the architecture from step 1 of the Six-Step Process, especially any strategic visions and plans, strategies, goals, or objectives that the EA is to support. Especially for solution architectures, it is always important to link the architecture back to the high-level business and mission needs that are driving the need for the architecture.

## Management Approach

The SOW should spell out the required project management approach in terms of the management reporting that is expected of the executors of the SOW. This section should outline the types of estimating, scheduling, tracking, and reporting that will be expected. Configuration or version management, quality assurance, and risk management tasks and reporting requirements should also be identified.

## Change Procedures

During the course of the project, the details of the SOW may change. This is especially true of EA projects where the specific views, required data, and options or tailoring tends to evolve as the understanding of the architectural domain matures during EA development. Because the SOW is the written basis for the project, it needs to be updated to reflect these and other types of changes. If it is not updated, there is an opportunity for the different parties involved to have divergent expectations on what the outcomes of the project should be. This type of misunderstanding can be quite serious, especially in a contractual situation or when management personnel turn over during the duration of the project.

The Change Procedures section of the SOW should outline the procedures for updating the SOW, including a description of how changes are proposed and the identification of who has the authority to approve proposed changes. There may be a committee or board that needs to approve proposed changes. Note that this section specifically addresses the change procedures for the SOW itself, not any configuration management procedures for the EA views and data.

## Responsibilities and Deliverables

The SOW needs to outline clearly what products, artifacts, data, and other outcomes need to be generated by the project and who is responsible for which outcomes. In a contractual situation, the SOW includes identification of the responsibilities of the issuers of the SOW as well as the responsibilities of the executors of the SOW. The responsibilities of the issuers of the SOW may include providing timely access to documents and SMEs for as-is portions of an EA and access to critical business and technical SME groups for to-be portions of an EA. These responsibilities need to be spelled out in the SOW so that the impacts of delays in gaining access to needed data and experts on the outcomes of the project are clear. The responsibilities of the executors of the SOW include both the management and technical deliverables.

The management deliverables will include required status reports and briefings with the contents based on the work identified in the Management Approach section of the SOW. The technical deliverables include the EA views and data that are identified in step 4 of the Six-Step Process and possibly the standard views and data identified in step 6. The options (such as the types of models) and tailoring needed for the EA views and data, identified in step 4 of the Six-Step Process, need to be spelled out in the SOW. These options and tailoring choices can be updated with changes via the procedures in the Change Procedures section of the SOW. The electronic format for these EA deliverables should also be specified. The issuers of the SOW don't want the EA views only in a paper format, and the data is not useful except in an electronic format. It is important that the issuers and executors of the SOW agree on what electronic format is to be delivered. This format may be driven by a standard or by the tools the issuer of the SOW plans to use. The electronic format may also be driven by a requirement to deliver portions of the architecture to a government or other external repository. As an alternative to including the view options and tailoring in the SOW, the SOW can include a process for agreeing on and documenting the selected options and tailoring as part of the EA development process.

Failure to agree on view options and tailoring or on an acceptable electronic delivery format can cause serious problems, especially in contractual situations. Failure to agree on view options and tailoring can result in the delivery of architecture views and data that don't address the specific data needs of the stakeholders or that can't support required analysis. Failure to agree on an electronic delivery format early in the project can result in a large amount of unexpected work for the executors of the SOW at the end of the project, when the developers need to translate their views and data into an electronic format that is radically different from that provided by the tools they used.

Other items related to the technical deliverables that need to be specified in the SOW include required reviews and additional analysis tasks. Since there is no standard life cycle for EAs, there are no standard reviews with well-known entry and exit criteria. The issuers of the SOW must identify and describe any technical views and data reviews that they want. The descriptions of any required reviews need to include when, with respect to the architecture development process, the reviews should take place and what the entry and exit criteria are. A common problem with EA projects is the request for review of operational or business views prior to the development of technical views. Since EAs have integrated views, based on a common set of data, this type of review is unrealistic. Development of technical views will impact the business or mission views since they are related. A better approach is to ask for a review to validate draft business or mission views to the extent possible prior to the development of technical views.

Analysis tasks associated with EA development include types of analysis necessary to develop the architecture as well as types of analysis that use data from a completed portion (as-is or to-be for a specific date) or release of the architecture. Types of analysis that might be included as parts of architecture development are tradeoff analyses and capability gap analysis. Types of analysis that use data from a completed portion of the architecture include ROI analysis, business case analysis, and performance analysis. SOWs can include requirements for any of these types of analysis.

A SOW can also spell out requirements for technical briefings and additional products such as interview notes resulting from interviews of SMEs.

## Acceptance Criteria and Procedures

The SOW needs to specify how the technical EA deliverables will be judged acceptable. Acceptance criteria and procedures are critical in contractual situations and are different from organizational acceptance of the EA. That is, there is a difference between contractual acceptance and organizational acceptance of the EA as part of the governance process. The governance acceptance process is discussed in Chapter 9. Contractual acceptance criteria need to be considered carefully and spelled out explicitly in the SOW.

Acceptance criteria can include such items as compliance or conformance with a standard and consistency and completeness of views. However, note that requiring conformance with a standard may not be sufficient to ensure useful views. For example, the DoDAF provides guidance and as long as the EA data is defined in accordance with the DoDAF metamodel concepts, associations, and attributes, the EA is in conformance with DoDAF. However, conformance with the DoDAF doesn't mean that the data is sufficient to address stakeholder issues or support key decision-making. Acceptance criteria can also be based on the ability of the EA data to support key decisions.

In addition to acceptance criteria, the SOW should contain acceptance procedures. Who gets to apply the criteria to the deliverables and what is the process by which the criteria are applied? Procedures may involve review of the deliverables by a board.

### High-Level Project Schedule

A SOW should include a high-level project schedule containing the major milestones for deliverables from the SOW issuer's point of view. It will be up to the executors of the SOW to develop detailed project development schedules in response to the high-level schedule in the SOW. The high-level schedule should not require the delivery of final views and data from one viewpoint of the EA prior to the development of views and data from the other viewpoints. The EA views and data form an integrated set, and development of additional viewpoints, views, and data will impact the existing views and data.

### Support/Automated Environment and Tools

The SOW should identify any tools or facilities that the issuer of the SOW will provide to the executor of the SOW, plus any tool interfaces, such as an interface to the issuer's CM system or repository, that the issuer expects the executor of the SOW to deliver data or deliverables to. Any restrictions or conditions on the use of tools and facilities should be specified.

## Project Implementation Details

This section covers some of the basic elements needed for EA development. Included are discussions of stakeholder management; EA development methodologies; EA life cycle issues; and the relationships among methodologies, tools, and repositories.

### Stakeholder Management

In planning the scope of the EA release, the focus is on architecture users. However, in planning the project as a whole, all classes of stakeholders need to be considered. The stakeholders who play various roles in the sponsorship, initiation, development, and management as well as use of the architecture must be identified. A good way to track all of these groups is to develop a politically oriented form of a stakeholder matrix that identifies each stakeholder by class and lists both their concerns and a priority. The priority given a stakeholder should be determined by the stakeholder's criticality to the success of the EA project. So, for example, sponsors should get a high priority in terms of attention to their concerns. Another key item that assists in managing stakeholders is an EA marketing strategy and dissemination plan. This plan is discussed further in Chapter 7.

### Architecture Development Methodology/Process

What is an EA development methodology or process? It provides an ordered set of technical tasks for developing the views and data and usually the models and techniques to choose from for the views, as well as the relationships among the views. The architecture development methodology may include a repository approach and a validation approach. The development methodology that a development group chooses to use may differ depending on the level of architecture being developed. The development methodology may also differ depending on the domain of the architecture. For example, a solution architecture development process for command and control domain architecture might differ from a process for a logistics- or data-centered domain architecture. Not only might different views be involved, but the development order of those views could differ. The command and control domain development process might focus on process, event response, and performance, while the data-centered domain development process might focus on operational data prior to considering process, and performance would be much less critical.

## EA Life Cycle Issues

As discussed previously, the EA discipline is too new to have existing life cycle standards. Each development organization has had to develop its own life cycle. Right now, various government agencies, contractors, and commercial corporations have developed EA life cycles, and these life cycles tend to be quite different. Many focus on the early part of the EA life cycle and don't yet handle maintenance in detail. Unfortunately, maintenance of the EA is the most difficult area to deal with, because EA interacts with most of the other enterprise processes and life cycles. Any EA life cycle has to address a large set of challenges:

- Does the EA life cycle handle problem-oriented, incremental architecture development?

- How does the EA life cycle fit with the concept of federated architectures and reference models?

- How does the EA life cycle coordinate with other related enterprise life cycles and processes, such as strategic planning, investment management, and system engineering and system development life cycles?

A promising EA life cycle for large enterprises with a relatively slow business tempo (see Chapter 8) and a reactive approach to change, such as government agencies, is discussed briefly next. The TOGAF ADM, which supplies an architecture development methodology and implies an EA life cycle, is discussed in Chapter 22.

**OMB Life Cycle** The Office of Management and Budget (OMB) and Government Accountability Office (GAO) started to develop EA life cycles so that the agencies could use them in further development of EA guidance and assessment tools for U.S. government agencies. The GAO life cycle is still very primitive (develop, use, maintain), but the OMB life cycle is starting to evolve into a useable outline for government agencies and larger, established enterprises. However, it is not clear that this style of life cycle will be useful for smaller enterprises with a rapid business tempo and a need for rapid response to a constantly changing marketplace and technology.

Figure 6-5 shows the OMB life cycle, which focuses more on how to use the EA to transition the enterprise than on the details of EA development, which is why OMB calls it an "Information and IT-enabled Performance Improvement Life Cycle." This is a useful approach because it emphasizes the role of three levels of architecture (enterprise, segment, and solution) in enterprise evolution and transition and does not address the EA as an end in itself. However, more detail will be needed in the areas of EA development and maintenance to provide best practice guidance for EA development organizations

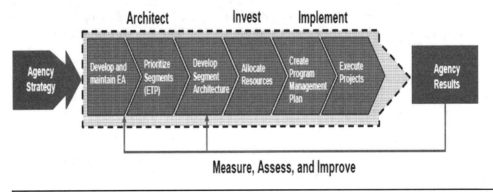

**Figure 6-5** OMB EA life cycle (graphic from the OMB)

and to enable comparison of EA development status in standardized terms. This additional development guidance will have to address development for each of the three levels of architecture. The life cycle diagram in Figure 6-5 is simplified and doesn't show the number of different segment, program, and project activities that can be ongoing within an enterprise simultaneously. However, it provides a good idea of how the different levels of architecture need to be involved to support enterprise transition. Obviously, the OMB EA life cycle will need to evolve to show additional feedback loops and phasing details.

The OMB life cycle shows EA as being driven by the enterprise strategy and yielding enterprise results, which, after assessment and analysis, provide additional feedback for another cycle of EA development aimed at further improvements.

The architecture addressed in the "develop and maintain EA" phase is the Enterprise Level architecture and will include the Capability Viewpoint and both as-is and one or more to-be architectures. The to-be architectures will usually include a vision or long-term target architecture as well as multiple intermediate transition stage architectures. The Enterprise Level architecture includes the identification of segments for which Segment Level architectures are needed. Segments could be captured in the Capability Taxonomy (CV-2) or Capability Dependencies (CV-4) if they were tailored to identify which capabilities belonged to which segment. This phase ends with the approval of the Enterprise Level architecture by the EAESC or other appropriate governance group, as discussed in Chapter 9.

In the "prioritize segments" phase, the enterprise prioritizes and schedules the segments identified in the Enterprise Level architecture and develops an enterprise transition plan (ETP). This process involves careful coordination with the enterprise strategic planning. The development of the ETP may also result in the development of additional Enterprise Level architectures that reflect changes in the intermediate steps in the transition toward the long-term vision. This phase ends with the approval of the ETP and any additional intermediate Enterprise Level architectures by the EAESC or appropriate governance authority.

The Segment Level architectures are developed in the priority order determined in the previous phase. Part of developing the Segment Level architecture will be identification of the Solution Level architectures needed to describe all the component parts of the segment. The various systems that are associated with each Solution Level architecture can be identified in a tailored, high-level Systems Interface Description (SV-1) in the Segment Level architecture. This phase ends with the approval of the Segment Level architecture by the EAESC or appropriate governance authority.

The "allocate resources" phase allocates resources for all the programs/projects identified for a segment. The process used for this phase will usually involve the investment review board (IRB) (or equivalent) approving budgets for these programs/projects, based on information provided by the enterprise architecture and included in business case analysis and ROI type documents (per program). Note that during this phase, the exact set of projects and Solution Level architectures included in the segment may change, based on IRB decisions. The Segment Level architectures may need to be updated as a result of these decisions.

Once a program or project has been approved, the "create program management plan" phase develops the project management plan (PMP). The PMP for a Solution Level architecture should contain all the information identified earlier in the chapter in "The Project Plan." The approval authority for the PMP will vary by enterprise, based on culture, but will frequently be the head of the organization who owns the program or project in question.

In the "execute projects" phase, the program/projects develop Solution Level architectures that align with the Segment Level architecture for their segment. These Solution Level architectures will need to be reviewed and approved by the appropriate governance authority, which may vary depending on the enterprise culture. The programs/projects then perform the necessary system and infrastructure development, testing, and installation.

Once the enterprise has been transitioned, the new processes and capabilities will be measured and assessed while the programs and projects continue to maintain the new systems and infrastructure. Further needs for improvement that impact existing segments can be fed back into the "develop segment architecture" phase. In the appropriate Segment Level architecture, these needs can be allocated to the appropriate program/project or a new program/project can be identified. The Segment Level architecture can be updated and the improvements implemented through the rest of the phases of the life cycle. Alternatively, if the identified improvement needs impact the existing segment priorities, these needs can be fed back to the "prioritize segments" phase. The existing priorities can be reexamined and the Enterprise Level architecture, ETP, and segment priorities and schedules can be updated to reflect these additional enterprise needs. New segments may be identified in this process. Then work on existing segments and program/projects can be readjusted and the additional needs implemented via the rest of the life cycle. Figure 6-6 summarizes the OMB life cycle in the format of the generic "Basic Life Cycle Chart" in Figure 6-4. Figure 6-6 shows the basic architectures and products per phase, along with the major reviews.

| Phase / Details | Develop & Maintain EA | Prioritize Segments | Develop Segment Architecture | Allocate Resources | Develop PMP | Execute Projects |
|---|---|---|---|---|---|---|
| TASKS | | | | | | |
| VIEWS/PRODUCTS | Enterprise Level Architecture (with Segments identified) | Enterprise Transition Plan (ETP) | Segment Level Architecture (with Programs/Projects identified) | Business Case Analysis | Program Management Plan (PMP) | Solution Level Architecture |
| METHODS | | | | | | |
| TOOLS | | | | | | |
| REVIEWS | Enterprise Level Architecture Acceptance by EAESC | ETP Acceptance by EAESC | Segment-Level Architecture Acceptance by EAESC | Approval of Programs by IRB | Approval of PMP | Acceptance of Solution Level Architecture |

**Figure 6-6**  Life cycle chart for OMB EA life cycle

Of the EA life cycle challenges discussed, the OMB EA life cycle addresses at least two. It embeds the concept of Federated Enterprise Architecture through segment development. It defines how the EA life cycle fits in with investment management and the system development life cycle. It shows input from enterprise strategic planning but doesn't address the full feedback issues involved in changing enterprise strategies. However, it is not clear how the OMB EA life cycle is adaptable to incremental architecture development as it clearly takes a full top-down approach.

## Methodologies, Tools, and Repositories

Automated tools and repositories are necessary for developing architectures because of the amount of data involved and the amount of data correlation and consistency checking that is needed to support an integrated architecture. Tools are necessary to support productivity, especially during maintenance and updates.

**Lessons Learned**  The EA development community is using some valuable lessons about automated tool support from the software and system development communities and their experiences with computer-aided software environment (CASE) and computer-aided design (CAD) tools. These lessons have to do with the integration of tools and development processes, with tool and process training and with repository issues.

The first lesson is that if different methods or techniques are used on different architecture views or in different architecture levels, these different methods or techniques need to integrate. That is, the data generated by the method or technique for one view must provide appropriate input for the next method or technique for the next view in the development process and for any method or technique that will be used to develop a view that shares data with the first view. Failure to have integrated methods and techniques will result in an inconsistent and un-integrated architecture. This need for data integration is what has driven DoD and the wider defense community to work on developing and standardizing an ontology to go with DoDAF and the related defense frameworks. This work is culminating in the standardizing of the Unified Architecture Framework (UAF), as discussed in Chapter 4.

The second lesson is that tools and development processes interact and must be integrated. Tools must be selected to support your development process. It may be tempting to try to use an inexpensive tool or one for which your organization already has a license, but if the tool and your process are a forced fit, experience shows use of the tool will be a serious mistake and will cause far more development problems and delays than is worth the cost. Forced fits include trying to use a tool that supports one specific method or technique to support a different method or technique and trying to use a tool that enforces a specific set of policies in an organization that has a different set of policies. Even a process-appropriate tool will usually have some features that may cause you to alter your process to achieve a smooth fit. Note that this lesson implies that if separate tools are used for different views or levels of architecture, then these tools must integrate. This need to integrate development tools has driven many EA development organizations to gravitate toward tools that provide support for all DoDAF views. Since the Unified Modeling Language (UML) provides a customizing technique (stereotyping) used in the definition of the Unified Architecture Framework Profile (UAFP), a current trend is to choose a UML tool that supports stereotyping as the key EA development tool. More tool integration issues are discussed in the upcoming sections.

The third lesson is that training is necessary both for new development tools and for new development processes and methods. The learning curve for both of these items is steep and needs to be accommodated in project schedules. The best way to compensate for the impact of these new techniques and tools on project schedules is training. Best practice includes having process or tool experts readily available, especially during the early days of use for new tools and techniques. Projects will encounter issues that weren't addressed in training, and prompt experienced help can prevent serious delays or missteps that can have serious impacts later on. Program or project guides for the specific options and tailoring required for architecture views are also helpful.

The fourth lesson is that any tool environment that includes multiple repositories, either internal to development tools, standalone, or external to the development organization, needs careful management, as many of these repositories may have proprietary data formats or specialized interfaces. Many of these repositories will need two-way exchange of data to support local processes, so it is imperative that the data import and export interfaces support easy and error-free exchange of data. An overall data strategy needs to be in place to define and support the flow of architecture data throughout the entire tool environment. More about repositories is discussed in the upcoming sections.

**Additional Processes and Tools** In addition to an architecture development process, the architecture group needs processes to support additional analysis, project management, and the automation environment. Further processes may be required to provide direct support to the enterprise decision-making processes that require EA-based input and provide EA-impacting output. All these processes may require additional automated tools.

As discussed, analysis may be required during architecture development to select the best approaches or after architecture development to provide input to decision-making processes. Some of these processes use only EA data, while others require a combination of architecture with financial or other types of data. Examples of these types of analysis include activity-based costing analysis, business case development, ROI analysis, and performance analysis based on executable architectures or simulations. In many cases, specialized tools will be needed to support this analysis.

An architecture development effort also requires basic management and other cross-phase or "umbrella" processes such as configuration management and quality assurance. Management processes include estimating, scheduling, planning, tracking, and reporting. Most organizations have tools to support all these processes. Some sophisticated organizations may have management tools that integrate with the development tools to support tracking of progress against assigned tasks. Risk management is an additional area that can fit under the general management category, or it can be considered an additional process area.

Configuration management (CM) is a tricky issue with architecture tools that manage integrated sets of architecture data—that is, repositories. Architecture development organizations are going to have to modify their corporate CM policies and processes to deal with this issue of repository data and to mesh with their evolving EA governance structures. Architecture development tools frequently support some form of version control, but additional processes and tools will be necessary to support full CM, which includes configuration identification, change control, configuration status accounting, and configuration auditing. Aligning the policies implicit in development tools' version control implementation with the organizational policies for full CM may also be a challenge and may cause serious problems with some development tools. Many development tools with repositories have embedded control policies that assume that the tool has the authoritative copy of the architecture data, while the CM processes and tools assume that they have the authoritative copy.

If quality assurance is defined in the currently accepted way as "process police," then the high-level processes and concepts used for software and systems development should be easily adaptable to EA. However, these processes may place additional requirements on architecture development tools or require additional tools.

Architecture development organizations shouldn't forget the processes needed to support the architecture development tools themselves and the organization's automated environment. The more complex architecture development tools often require specialized "care and feeding." These tools frequently allow for customization to support required tailoring both for views and for the development process. This customization may need frequent updating as the tailoring evolves and tool upgrades are released. All the development organization's tools, as well as its infrastructure, need to be kept up to date with both technology improvements and security enhancements. In addition, if the organization has developed special code to support the integration of any of the tools, this integration code will need to be updated if the infrastructure changes and as new tool releases arrive. Some of these issues are addressed by the move to UML-based tools that support the emerging standard ontology (UAF) and exchange of standardized data types using XML.

**Integration of Tools** One of the persistent challenges faced by architecture development organizations is getting their automated tools to integrate properly. This issue can cause development teams lots of problems. Solutions can be expensive, and a lack of solutions can severely impact project productivity and product quality. Two general types of problems occur: integration of the various architecture development tools with one another and integration of architecture development tools with the other tools in the project's environment. The architecture development tools may also need to integrate with other tools that are external to the architecture development organization's enterprise. Figure 6-7 illustrates an example architecture tool environment and the types of tool integration involved.

Architecture development organizations quickly learn that, regardless of the methodology and modeling techniques they select, it seems that no single tool exists that will completely meet their needs. Some architecture development tools support only a limited number of the techniques the project wants to use. Other tools support most of the techniques, but there are specialty tools that do a better job on specific types of models. With the advent of DoDAF-related profiles (discussed in Chapter 4), some UML-based tools have the promise of providing a single tool that can address all the DoDAF views. However, specialty tools, such as data modeling tools and executable state transition modeling tools, may still be needed to assist in the development of types of models critical for a given enterprise. Although the UML tools can be used to represent the output

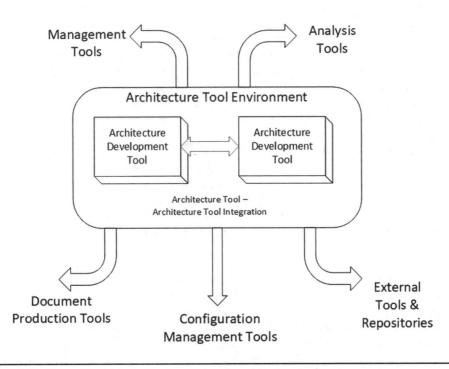

**Figure 6-7** Types of tool integration in an example architecture tool environment

of these specialty tools in a standard format, the UML tools may not have the capability to help develop certain views.

As a result, most architecture development organizations are faced with the continuing challenge of integrating multiple architecture development tools or repositories. This is not a new problem; software development projects have long faced similar issues in trying to integrate tools to support the entire software life cycle. However, because architecture views or models are integrated, all the tool interfaces must be two-way, which further complicates matters.

An expensive solution is to build custom interfaces between the tools. This is not always possible if the tools have proprietary databases and data formats that they use to store the architecture data. Another approach is standardization of the architecture data ontology coupled with a standard import/export format. This is the approach that the defense community has been evolving toward and is the basis of the current standardization of the UAF and UAFP.

Yet another approach to the development tool integration problem is based on the notion of a central architecture data repository that provides a standard import/export interface. In this approach, the repository is an independent tool, not an internal part of a tool that directly supports model or view development. View development tools must support the import/export standard in order to integrate with the repository. These tools can take repository data as input and output data to the repository. Basically, the development tools use the repository for sharing data. The repository approach has additional advantages. Tools can be simpler if they don't need to have an internal repository. The repository can support an ad hoc reporting capability, metadata to support metrics, and version control. A repository can also support sharing of architecture data across an enterprise and the reuse of architecture data and artifacts in related architectures.

This sharing of architecture data across the enterprise is the reason why DoD has been so interested in a repository approach that would enable sharing of architecture data across the DoD. The repository approach has been advocated for a long time, but it has proven difficult to implement. Repository tools are commercially available, but they typically require customization, so they are expensive for small organizations and projects. In addition, there has been limited success both in getting tools to support the repository interface standards and in developing effective standards. Figure 6-8 shows the different approaches to tool integration and how the repository approach makes the number of interfaces much smaller. The independent repository approach is less attractive if a single architecture development tool is used, but there may still be a requirement for an independent repository (not development tool–dependent) for sharing of architecture data, and the development environment may still include multiple repositories that must be dealt with.

Not only do the architecture development tools need to be integrated, but these tools also need to be integrated with analysis tools, management tools, and document and presentation tools, as shown in Figure 6-7. That is, the architecture development tools or repositories need to be able to provide input to analysis tools and, potentially, to management tracking tools and CM tools. In addition, the architecture development tools (or repository) should be able to provide text and graphics to document and

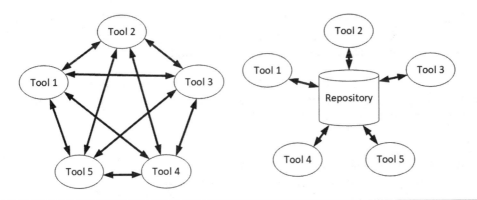

**Figure 6-8**   Two different approaches to tool integration

presentation tools. Failure to provide useable input for documents and presentation tools is a critical problem, because documents and presentations are one of the ways of making architecture data accessible to stakeholders. Sometimes problems with graphics can be subtle. Some tools provide exportable graphics, but although these graphics are suitable for wall charts for the architects' use, the graphics are not readable when inserted into documents and presentations. Extracting readable subsets of the larger graphics can be difficult and time consuming. Usually, the interfaces from architecture development tools to nonarchitecture tools are one-way, so integration may be easier than integrating between architecture development tools.

Sometimes, architecture development tools in a development organization will have to integrate with tools from other organizations. For example, architecture development tools may have to integrate with requirements tools when Solution Level architectures are being developed. In other cases, the architecture development tools from organizations building Segment or Solution Level architectures may need to integrate with repositories owned by organizations responsible for the Enterprise Level architecture. In DoD, Segment and Solution Level architecture organizations need to be able to post architecture data to DoD Enterprise Level repositories such as the DoD Architecture Registry System (DARS). In TOGAF Segment and Solution Level architectures are incorporated into the Enterprise Continuum. The nature of these repository interfaces is dependent on enterprise processes and requirements.

No matter what nature of tool integration challenges are faced by a development organization, the best way to test this integration, especially if the integration approach depends on COTS product support for integration, is to establish a test configuration in a laboratory environment prior to attempting to use the tools in an actual development project. This is a lesson learned from problems with software development environments. Often, COTS product support for various interfaces and standards has unforeseen limitations that severely impact the ability of the tool to integrate as expected. In general, best practice is to test the integration capabilities of the tool with the rest of the architecture development environment prior to purchasing the product, if possible. Tools that won't integrate are of very limited value.

The costs of integrating tools should be controlled as well. Although tools can be made to integrate using custom code or by maintaining customized repositories, the continuing costs of such an approach are frequently more than an organization or enterprise is prepared to pay. Though such a customized environment may be ideal in terms of architecture development and maintenance ease, usually less expensive approaches need to be investigated. These alternative approaches may require changes in the architecture development methodology or process.

## Success Factors for Planning

Several factors affect successful execution of an architecture effort:

- **Clear and common objectives/purpose**   The objectives and benefits for embarking on an architecture development must be clear, both to the sponsors and to the architecture team itself.

- **Clear definition of stakeholders and expectations**   At the outset and during the course of an architecture development, stakeholders must be clearly identified and involved in the communications process. Stakeholders need to be reidentified during the course of development because tribes can emerge, especially as planned enterprise changes become clearer.

- **Clear and demonstrated architecting skills**   Training and competence in the mechanics of modeling and view development as well as familiarity with the vocabulary, ontology, and semantic concepts used in your EA development methodology and framework are essential.

- **Clear work plan and risk mitigation strategy**   A step-by-step WBS along with a clear SOW, clearly identified deliverables, and identification and mitigation strategy for anticipated risks is essential.

- **Clear analysis and recommendations (and follow-up)**   In architecture projects that include findings and conclusions based on analysis, documenting findings clearly and communicating the impact of issues is essential. A follow-up plan to track actions based on findings and recommendations enhances the success of the architectural effort.

- **Clear communications**   Architectures tell a story. The development of the architecture involves parts of the story. The effort is akin to plotting a cast of characters, determining events and actions, and sweeping a timeline forward. Any architecture effort that tells the story in a manner that is clear to an audience garners instant support.

- **Crisp execution**   Ultimately, the success of architecture development efforts hinges on the crispness of the execution—in terms of quality of effort and timeliness.

# Summary

This chapter has focused on aspects of EA development that include project planning and implementation issues. Much of this material is planning for the last few steps (4–6) of the Six-Step Process and is directed toward EA project planning. The basic project plan needs to include the usual topics addressing what, who, how, and when. Data strategies for management, validation, and dissemination need to be included, as well as risk-management approaches. Personnel issues are particularly critical. The chief architect role requires a combination of a large number of skills and may require a small team of people to execute. EA projects also require involvement of or coordination with external or customer roles to function successfully. Many of the details of this type of planning depend on corporate culture and experience, especially with EA projects.

Projects need to be based on a clear SOW. Because EA is a new discipline, there is limited guidance available on such topics as WBS for EA projects and EA life cycle, although OMB has a promising EA life cycle for government agencies. Architecture development processes or methodologies may vary widely among organizations, although the TOGAF provides a methodology-based approach that has been developed by an industrial consortium. Automated tools will be necessary to support EA development, and lessons learned from software and systems development emphasize the need for development tools to be integrated with one another, with development processes, and with other automated project tools. This need for integration drives the importance of an ontology and the desire for a single EA development tool and repository that covers the maximum number of viewpoints and views.

Planning and executing EA development must be done carefully because of the limited overall experience with EA and the resultant limited guidance.

# Questions

1. How does your organization address the tool integration problem? How many architecture development tools do you use on a single project and how are they integrated?

2. How many other tools (management, document production, and analysis) do your architecture development tools need to integrate with on architecture projects? How is this integration achieved?

3. How does your EA life cycle address the three challenges identified in this chapter: problem-oriented, incremental architecture development; federated architectures and reference models; and integration with other enterprise life cycles and processes (including strategic planning, CPIC, and SDLC)?

4. How does your EA life cycle map or compare to the OMB EA life cycle?

5. See if you can find some SOWs for EA development projects. Compare the content of each SOW to the suggested SOW outline in this chapter. How are they similar and how are they different?

6. How does your organization deal with risk management? Do you have a methodology for risk assessment for EA projects?

7. What is your organization's approach to EA data validation? How are the personnel who perform EA data validation integrated with the rest of the EA project team?

8. Does your organization have a standardized WBS for EA projects? If yes, how do the tasks align with your EA life cycle?

9. Does your organization have a job description for the chief architect's position? What skills are required and how do they align with the skills identified in this chapter?

10. How is your organization's EA project team organized? To whom does the chief architect report?

11. What architecture development process does your organization use? What order are the data and views developed in?

# References

Bersoff, E., V. Henderson, S. Siegel. 1980. *Software Configuration Management: An Investment in Product Integrity.* Upper Saddle River, NJ: Prentice Hall PTR.

CIO Council. 2001. "A Practical Guide to Federal Enterprise Architecture, Version 1.0." www.gao.gov/assets/590/588407.pdf.

Department of Defense. 2009. Department of Defense Architecture Framework Version 2.0. http://dodcio.defense.gov/Library/DoD-Architecture-Framework.

Object Management Group. 2016. Unified Architecture Framework Profile, Version 1.0 – FTF Beta 1. OMG Document Number dtc/16-08-01. www.omg.org/spec/UAF/1.0/Beta1/About-UAF/.

Office of Management and Budget. 2009. "Improving Agency Performance Using Information and Information Technology (Enterprise Architecture Assessment Framework v3.1)."

The Open Group. 2018. "TOGAF Version 9.2, revised educational edition." The Netherlands: Van Haren Publishing.

# Disseminating the Enterprise Architecture

When we look at disseminating enterprise architecture information, we need to consider what information we need to disseminate, to whom we need to disseminate it, when we need to disseminate it, and how we are going to disseminate it. All of this is driven by why we need to disseminate this EA information.

## Preparing for Dissemination

We can disseminate three states of EA architecture representations: draft views, stable views, and accepted releases. Like software, EA data needs to be version controlled in the draft phase, placed under configuration management when it becomes verified and stable, and released as an integrated set of views after the whole has been accepted as correct, complete, and consistent via a formal process.

Though informal processes guide configuration management of architecture representations in very small enterprises, large and complex enterprises require formal configuration management processes. Formal processes are needed because communicating an architecture change has a cascading impact on so many other elements of the enterprise and affects so many stakeholders of the enterprise that inadvertent mistakes or oversights can be very disruptive. Notification of an architecture change involves understanding the implications of the change and requires a plan that incrementally implements the change and provides stakeholders the dates and schedules for events that will impact them.

Formal configuration management implies the need for a configuration control board (CCB), which is usually the EA executive steering committee (EAESC) or equivalent, with the CIO or other appropriate high-level executive as the change authority (the person with signature authority to place submitted draft material under configuration management, approve change requests, and approve an architecture for release, usually with the recommendation of the rest of the CCB). The CCB is supported by a business review board or committee (BRB/BRC) and a technical review board or committee (TRB/TRC). The BRC consists of business or operations managers. The BRC reviews EA artifacts or change requests that impact operations and provides recommendations to the CCB. The TRC consists of IT managers. The TRC reviews EA artifacts or change requests that impact the technical infrastructure of the enterprise and provides recommendations to the CCB. Both of these supporting groups may need security specialists as consultants. All three of the boards should have formal charters and formal processes for their activities.

Key features of configuration management process include the following:

- *A controlled baseline must be maintained for the released version and read-only access provided to all users to prevent corruption of the EA.* In other words, the configuration management repository or tool will contain the authoritative version of the controlled material and changes can be made only via formal change request processes. Formal configuration identification must be maintained to identify the specific release of the EA that will be disseminated. A controlled baseline is a formally identified release of enterprise architecture with a date and an identifier.

- *A formal process must be identified for validation of the EA information before considering a release.* The accuracy and validity of the disseminated EA release is essential for continued credibility and trust in the reliability of the EA information. If the latency of validation is a hindrance to the use of EA information, markings must be made that indicate the reliability status of the information as well as an indication of when a validated product will be available.

- *The formal approval process for an EA release must have a designated signature authority.* This signature authority is usually the chair of the CCB/EAESC.

- *Access controls must be in place for the CM repository.* There must be a formal process for authorizing access to the various classes of EA information in the repository, such as stable drafts, full releases, and parts of releases. Access will usually be based on roles. Although it is possible that an EA may not have any confidential information, the aggregation of the information may present a security risk. In the wrong hands, the compilation of enterprise information in the EA could create a vulnerability to the enterprise by providing sufficient information for infiltration and disruption. Some of the information (or an aggregation of that information) may need to be controlled and accessed on a "need-to-know" basis (such as network models, critical performance factors, system interfaces, and so on). The access controls must enable the incorporation of EA information into people's everyday duties. For example, executive and managerial staff should be able to incorporate EA information into communications, briefings, and directives. Application architects should be able to use the information to analyze artifacts against their own reality and identify opportunities for improvements. Enterprise architects should be able to use the information to apply what-if analysis against the baseline and use the baseline information as a basis for the next release.

## Marketing and Communications Plan

One of the key steps in preparing for disseminating the EA is the development of an EA marketing strategy and communications plan during the planning phase of the EA program. The purpose of the plan is to keep senior executives and business units continually informed, to disseminate EA information to management teams, and to secure continued support from subject matter experts and analysts and to get them to act as a target audience.

The CIO's staff, in cooperation with the chief architect and support staff, defines a marketing and communications plan consisting of constituencies, level of detail, means of communication, participant feedback, schedule for marketing efforts, and method of evaluating progress and buy-in.

One of the recommended means for marketing the EA is a primer to inform business executives and stakeholders of the EA strategy and plan. The primer can be used to express the enterprise's senior management's vision and the role of EA in accomplishing that vision.

An EA marketing and communications plan may divide the dissemination strategy into multiple phases. Each of these phases needs different types of dissemination. Table 7-1 shows an example.

| Phase | Purpose | Potential Dissemination Tools |
|-------|---------|-------------------------------|
| Preinception | Raise general awareness among decision-makers on the benefits of EA in general and to the enterprise in particular | Bring in EA evangelists and luminaries to raise awareness and excite top management |
| Inception | Brief sponsors on the EA program management plan, architecture development phases, expected deliverables, and required support | Presentation slides<br>Project management plan<br>Deliverable mockups<br>Resourcing plan |
| In-process | Disseminate models to elicit feedback from SMEs<br>Presentations of the in-process EA models and analysis at program management reviews (PMRs)<br>Prebriefings to validate direction of EA program | Presentation slides<br>EA project web site<br>EA project wiki<br>Tool generated web sites |
| Validation and finalization | Prebrief sponsors on the EA models, analysis, findings, and recommendations to determine any needed course changes and wording of critical findings and recommendations | EA program problem statement and summary<br>EA analysis reports<br>EA deliverable models<br>Navigable web sites of the EA<br>Presentation slides<br>EA project web site<br>EA project social network<br>EA project wikis<br>EA reports<br>EA documentation<br>HELP documentation<br>Training materials |
| Post release | Provide ongoing support for all stakeholders in using, navigating, downloading, and exploiting the EA for business use and as a communications tool for orientation and support for planning and decision-making efforts | EA deliverable views<br>Navigable web sites of the EA<br>Presentation slides<br>EA project web site<br>EA project social network<br>EA project wikis<br>EA reports<br>EA documentation<br>HELP documentation<br>Training materials |

**Table 7-1**  Sample EA Marketing and Communications Plan

# Identifying the Audience for Architecture Dissemination

Table 7-1 shows the purpose of disseminating information, when some information might be disseminated and how the information could be disseminated. But it is also important that you know the roles of the stakeholders to whom information should be disseminated and what information should be disseminated to these roles. The common type of stakeholders and their information needs are discussed in the following sections.

## Architecture Sponsors

The architecture sponsors are senior management people who have understood the need for architecture, have underwritten the cost of development, and are interested in solving the set of problems that drove that initial need. Unfortunately, in many enterprises, the unspoken need to undertake the development of EA is to comply with regulatory mandate or the demands of a higher power—an oversight office such as the Office of Management and Budget in the federal government. Sponsors generally include the chief information officer, executive management, and executive teams charged with effecting enterprise transformation. These stakeholders need to see the Enterprise Level architecture information and any management status reports on progress.

## Architecture Team Members

Members of the architecture team, as facilitators of transformation, are the "evangelists" and proponents of the architecture they are building. Dissemination of the EA in the development or draft stages also enables team members to share information using collaborative techniques through the project social network. The architecture team includes the chief architect, modelers, business analysts, technical specialists, and others, as described in Chapter 6. The extended architecture team includes SMEs who provided the data for the architecture development. The SMEs will need to see draft views to correct and validate them. However, each SME will need to see only the small set of views for which they are providing input.

## Architecture Stakeholders

Other stakeholders are business, systems, IT infrastructure, and operations staff who are affected by the analysis, findings, and recommendations that are generated by the architecture effort. Sometimes members of this audience may be hostile to the EA effort because of threats to current ways of doing business. Members of each stakeholder tribe need to see the portions of the architecture that will directly impact them. To ensure project buy-in, you may need to show these stakeholders early drafts as well as the views as they are being entered into the configuration management repository.

## Executive Management

The EA represents the anatomy and physiology of the enterprise. Executive management has a stake in understanding the implications that analysts arrive at by analyzing the EA. Management is responsible for being at the helm of transformations and therefore makes up a very interested audience—especially if the enterprise is looking at transformation as a survival technique. These stakeholders are interested in the high-level transformation or sequencing plans and the Enterprise Level architecture information.

## Business Partners, Suppliers, Customers, Agents

The EA exposes the operational, systems, services, and data "plumbing" of the enterprise. This is of interest to business partners who need to interface with the enterprise at each of these plumbing levels. Operational interfaces involve handshakes between business processes. Interfaces between systems and services involve orchestration of services among enterprises as well as contracts that preserve the interface structure durably. Data interfaces between partner enterprises have to rely on semantic data standards as well as messaging and format standards. The architecture is an explicit representation of these factors and is therefore very useful for planning interfaces at all levels. However, external partners need access only to the elements of the architecture that directly impact their interfaces with the enterprise. Sometimes they will require more detailed information if they need to certify that the enterprise has sufficient security controls in place to provide a safe and secure interface.

## Reusers

Dissemination of architecture models in a manner that can be used by the receiver for facilitating their own tasks is essential to the adoption of the EA as a valuable enterprise asset. For example, planners of a new initiative may want to describe the context of their planned initiative in terms of locations served, organizations involved, key business processes to be automated, key capabilities to be acquired, and key systems to interface with for data supply. All of this information may be available inside the architecture. By downloading and tailoring the data that comes from the EA, the team planning the initiative can produce an early concept of operations that has taken a small effort but is rooted in enterprise reality. In some cases, such as in the DoD or federal government, the sharing of EA information will be done through a central repository available, with appropriate access controls, to a larger enterprise.

## Communities of Interest/Communities of Practice

In recent years, with awakening interest in collaborative workspaces, wikis, and social networking has demonstrated the importance of forming communities of interest and communities of practice—people with shared motivation, working collaboratively on interleaved tasks with similar interests and skills. COIs and COPs are natural targets for architecture dissemination. Architecture content can be dramatically improved by employing facilitated wikis and managed social networking interfaces, in which members of the COI/COP who are familiar with the subject matter can provide corrections and improvements. However, these COI/COP represent emergent enterprise tribes who need to be handled carefully in order to get and preserve their buy-in.

# Architecture Presentation Techniques

Dissemination of architecture information to human beings is complex as it involves cultural, semantic, and clarity issues among others. Questions about presentation include the following:

- How is the information presented? Is it easily comprehensible by the target audience based on past experience and knowledge and familiarity?

- Does the information presentation conform to applicable standards?

- How dense is the information representation? Is the display making good use of whitespace?

- Is the information disseminated in a useable format? Can the information be readily used to build value-added presentations and perform analysis without the user having to retype or manipulate the disseminated data?

- What kinds of information patterns provide the most leverage? Sometimes, certain layouts of data tend to naturally represent a model. For example, comparisons of numeric data can use commonly understood pie and bar chart graphics. Taxonomical representations lend themselves to a hierarchical or tree diagramming patterns.

Although information is the lifeblood of enterprise architecture, it can be overwhelming to decision-makers when presented in a raw format. Many of the architecture views and models standardized by frameworks can be shared among trained architects and are useful for analysis. However, architects must be able to communicate architectural information in a meaningful way to process owners and other stakeholders who are not trained architects. The results of architectural-related data collection need to be presentable to nontechnical senior executives and managers at all levels. Many managers are skilled decision-makers but have not had technical training in architectural description development. Presentation views are always dependent on the quality of the architectural information that is collected through the rigor of architecture methods. As Figure 7-1 illustrates, presentation techniques pull from the architectural information store and display the data in a variety of meaningful ways to stakeholders.

Presenting architecture data to managers often means complex technical information has to be translated into a form for presentation that is useful to management. An "information bridge," built by the various presentation techniques such as those shown in Figure 7-1, is the link between the architect and management. The bridge provides the means to recast technical information in graphical or textual terms that are consistent with the culture of the management organization (see Figure 7-2).

## Choosing an Appropriate Presentation Technique

In any business, decisions must be made at multiple levels of the organization. Whether some one is a senior level executive, a process owner, or a system developer, he or she will need to make judgment calls based upon the available data. Each level of decision-making, in turn, has both a unique purpose and understanding of architectural description, making it important to tailor the data to maximize its effectiveness. The presenter,

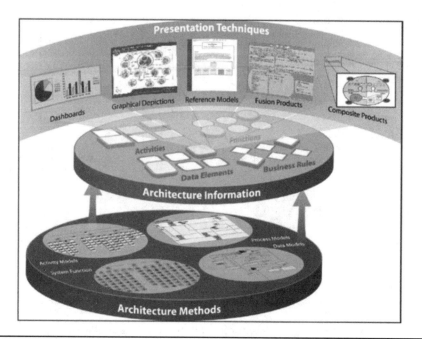

**Figure 7-1** Architecture data collection versus presentation (graphic from the DoDAF)

with the help of an experienced architect, must determine the audience of a presentation before choosing the type of presentation technique to use. Figure 7-3, based on the rows of the Zachman Framework, summarizes the multiple levels of decision-makers within a typical organization that make up an audience.

Each level has differing requirements for presentation of data. Level 1 planners may find a graphical wall chart more useful in making decisions, whereas a level 4 builder will most likely require a more technical presentation that relates more directly to the architectural description. Level 5 subcontractors are the workers who will perform the work required and generally need varying levels of technical data and other information to accomplish their task.

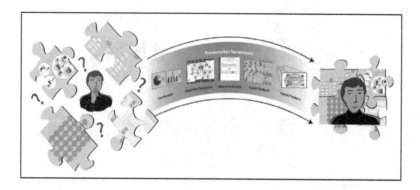

**Figure 7-2** Dissemination as an information bridge (graphic from the DoDAF)

**Figure 7-3**
Zachman
Framework
perspectives of
an enterprise
(graphic from
the DoDAF)

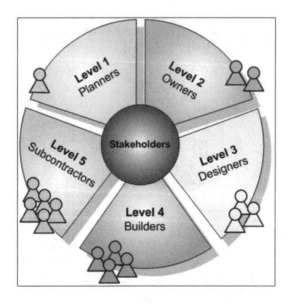

To narrow down the type of presentation required, ask the following question: What information does the decision-maker need to make a data-supported decision? For each decision level, there is a data set that can be manipulated using a presentation technique. After analyzing the audience and type of information, the presenter should consider the various types of techniques discussed in this section.

Figure 7-4 provides a simplified representation of the presentation development process.

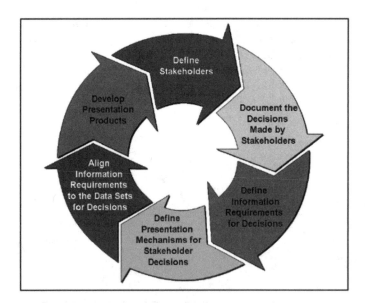

**Figure 7-4**   Presentation/dissemination development cycle (graphic from the DoDAF)

It is imperative to realize that when you choose how to present data sets, there is no limit on what views to use. There are countless ways to display information to decision-makers, and it is up to the presentation developer to determine the most effective way to accomplish this task.

## Fit-for-Purpose View Display Formats

This section describes a basic set of view development techniques to start from. Each technique was created to serve a unique purpose. Details are provided on five different presentation techniques that have proven to be useful in engaging various audiences.

Remember that some stakeholders may not necessarily want to see information in the way that the architect represents it in architecture views. Dissemination often involves building composite views that may be different from the original supplying views.

If there is one thing this book has stressed, it is the importance of building integrated architectures where all the views consistently share the same common architecture elements. Building an integrated architecture unifies the data consistently and enables the building of new composite views from the same data without compromising accuracy and faithfulness of semantics and structure of the originally modeled elements. These composite displays, or Fit-for-Purpose views, are built to suit the viewpoint of the audience rather than to conform to some view technique the audience does not understand.

Fit-for-Purpose views can be created using the architecture data from an integrated architecture to provide forms of graphical presentation other than those used to build the architecture models such as activity model, logical and physical data models, and business process models. Fit-for-Purpose views use presentation techniques that are more common to briefings and decision analysis.

The following five techniques commonly used:

- **Composite views**   Display multiple pieces of architectural data in formats that are relevant to a specific decision-maker

- **Dashboards**   Integrate abstracted architectural information for a given business context

- **Fusion views**   Display multiple pieces of architectural data and incorporate disparate pieces of information that are not captured within the architectural description

- **Graphics**   Visually represent manipulated data

- **Reference models**   Capture the elements of the architectural data and translate those elements into text

Fit-for-Purpose views provide wide flexibility for the architect and process owner to create architectural views easily understood and useful to management for decision-making purposes.

## Standardized View Display Formats

Part III of this book discusses the details of the standardized DoDAF views that are recognized and understood by a large community of architects. These views have been used for more than a decade and stand upon tried, proven, and heavily adopted modeling techniques and methodologies such as structured analysis and design, ICAM Definition for Functional Modeling (IDEF), state transition descriptions, and business process modeling notation (BPMN). The representation of views for each of these methodologies is generally standardized by the methodology. For example, IDEF0 uses the activity node tree, context diagram, and decomposition diagrams to represent activity models in a graphical way based on a recognized standard.

Standard model layouts generally fall into the categories shown in Table 7-2.

Although the DoDAF provides a set of standardized views, views from other frameworks such as TOGAF (Chapter 22) and FEAF2 (Chapter 23) can also be used either for architects or for presentation to other stakeholders.

## Audience Presentation Tips

Presenting multiple architecture views to mixed audiences of multiple specialties, interests, and concerns is challenging and often nonproductive in getting agreement, eliciting deeper questions, and securing agreements on follow-up actions. Dividing up the groups based on specialties and getting partial agreements sometimes becomes useful toward making progress in the architecture development process.

| Model Layout | Description |
| --- | --- |
| Tabular | Models that present data arranged in rows and columns, which includes structured text as a special case. Corresponds to the TOGAF 9 matrix artifacts. |
| Structural | Includes diagrams describing the structural aspects of architecture. Corresponds to the TOGAF 9 diagram artifacts. |
| Behavioral | Includes diagrams describing the behavioral aspects of architecture. Corresponds to the TOGAF 9 diagram artifacts. |
| Mapping | Provides matrix (or similar) mappings between two different types of information. Corresponds to the TOGAF 9 matrix artifacts. |
| Ontology | Extend the underlying modeling (metamodel) ontology for a particular architecture. |
| Pictorial | Free-form pictures, in which no constraints are generally applicable to the symbols, the layout of the symbols, or graphics connecting the symbols. |
| Timeline | Includes diagrams describing the schedule and programmatic aspects of an architecture. |

**Table 7-2**  Standard Model Layouts

Here are some points to remember when presenting architecture representations to different audiences:

- *People usually care about only the things that concern them and in which they have an interest or stake.* Presenting a number of views that are not relevant to your audience is pointless. Select the right views to present to an audience in order to elicit feedback, comments, agreement, and assistance in formulating next steps toward implementation.

- *People understand at the rate of comprehension they are accustomed to.* Presenting diagrams with several cryptic symbols and connections does not engage everyone. Walkthroughs and progressive buildups are required to carry audiences across the comprehension bridge. An ill-understood model is effort wasted.

- *A diagram must be self explanatory to the maximum extent possible.* Legends cue audiences to the meaning of content. Titles describe the subject of the diagram as well as the architecture view that it represents. Strive for uniformity of colors, styles, and themes to accustom the eyes of the audience to the content rather than the container.

- *The goal of an architecture presentation is to describe the results of discovery and analysis and to recommend courses of action.* The presenter must be able to describe these elements of the presentation succinctly, and to provoke debate and discussion and potentially agreement on the way forward using the specific selection chosen from a number of alternatives.

- *Though hierarchy is a way to break down complex representations into a number of simpler ones, hierarchical presentations may also serve to disconnect the audience from the big picture.* As a result, they may become involved in discussion detours when the architecture must be assessed as a whole. Often we present a single-page complex diagram at the risk of comprehension to provide a bigger picture than would be provided by a series of hierarchical diagrams.

- *Architecture terms usually represent the language of the architect.* Architecture languages are standardized by frameworks such as the DoDAF. However, when presenting architecture representations that depict views of the business model, the architect must use the language of the business; when presenting views of the operating model, the architect must use the language of the operations staff; and when presenting views of technology, the architect must use the language of the technology and infrastructure support personnel.

# Delivery of Dissemination

In this section, we discuss the various ways in which architecture information can be disseminated.

## Web Delivery

By far, the most convenient and popular delivery of repository content is through the Internet, with a web server at one end and a simple web browser application at the other. Web-site publishing is supported by many architecture tools in the marketplace. They generate a collection of hypertext markup language (HTML) files that are linked through cross-file references. A home or index page is provided, generally with a navigation structure that has links to the various views that make up the integrated architecture. Navigation is accomplished via elements of one view to elements of other views. Web output is also combined with interpretive text that describes architecture elements.

The generation of HTML web pages with embedded graphics and text representing the views that are disseminated results in snapshots of the architecture. If the contents of the architecture repository were to be updated, they would not automatically be reflected in the web site until a new web site is generated and published. For architectures that are released relatively infrequently, this is still a good solution.

More sophisticated web delivery systems use scripts to generate the web pages automatically on the fly from active repository content. Any changes to repository data are instantly reflected in the web pages. These systems tend to be repository side applications rather than features of the architecting tool, because the scripts need knowledge of the repository schema.

## Architecture Web Site/Web Portal

The static web generation of architecture views for an integrated architecture, as discussed earlier, is easily accomplished by commercial architecture tools. But architecture dissemination often requires more than just the dissemination of views. In an architecture community of practice, other items such as reference models, policy and guidance, templates, and other information need to be disseminated. An architecture web site or an architecture portal is often built to service a community of architecture team members as a minimum and for an extended community of stakeholders when mature.

Architecture web sites must follow all the rules of good web site design:

- Clear "floor plan"
- Consistent layout of topics and navigation paths
- Appropriate use of fonts, colors, and emphasis
- Design unity with complementary web sites
- Consistent look and feel
- Comprehensive search capabilities
- Facilities for zooming and panning large graphical images
- Appropriate density of information

Architecture web sites and portals can also be built with capabilities for wikis and social networking and provide a collaboration workspace for some tasks such as these:

- Refining vocabulary and terminology
- Refining taxonomies/classification schemes
- Critiquing and improving architecture views
- Suggesting improvements to the architecture program
- Validating views

## Discovery Services

In contemporary computing, discovery services are an important part of net-centric operations. In net-centric operations, information and software services are dispersed over a network. A using or invoking application uses "discovery services" to find appropriate data and services that it can use to accomplish its purpose. Discovery services require that the owner of the information or service "advertise" these services in a transparent manner to the discovery services. The advertising of data and services is done in much the same way as libraries once advertised their holding using index cards. The index cards that "exposed" information and services were formatted in a consistent manner per some predefined metadata standards. One such standard is the DoD's Defense Discovery Metadata Specification (DDMS).

Architecture repositories can expose their information and services to the world outside (or at least the entitled and authorized world outside) using metadata specifications. The burden of searching, discovering, and materializing the data or invoking the service is the responsibility of consuming applications.

## Repository Services

Repository web services are a way to provide dissemination for external applications or web users. Repository web services must be published and registered on a service broker such as a Universal Description, Discovery, and Integration (UDDI) registry. Repository services can run unattended and provide 24/7 services.

Operating repository services imposes a supplier's burden on the architecture repository and the architecture team. This burden is expressed as a commitment to a service level agreement to make repository services available as advertised.

Offering repository services is generally undertaken after an architecture effort has reached a maturity stage that warrants continuous availability of dissemination as a web service. Chapter 8 introduces the concepts of governance and describes the stages of maturity of architecture management.

# Dissemination to Computerized Systems

An architecture description can be viewed as an integrated collection of blueprints stored as electronic documents or as information in an architecture repository. This information may be disseminated through two types of computerized systems:

- Dissemination of EA data between automated computer systems applications, such as architecture modeling tools (see Chapter 6 for examples)
- Dissemination of EA data and views to a receiving enterprise repository or registry

We distinguish between these two types of dissemination because each of them has different needs for semantic and structural data standards for the exchange to be successful.

## Dissemination Between Automated Computer Systems Applications

This form of dissemination requires agreed upon protocols for information semantics as well as information formats. In addition to these, it also may require automated services at either end, one to push information and the other to pull the information in.

The most common form of dissemination between automated computer systems is the dissemination of architecture data from one modeling tool/repository to another. These exchanges are supported by bilateral agreements between pairs of senders and receivers, by custom software, or by a common exchange standard that is used by all tools.

The DoDAF and related defense frameworks are moving toward the Unified Architecture Framework/Profile (UAF/P) to support exchanges between UML- and SysML-based architecture development tools. Once both UML tools have been customized to the UAF profile, architecture data can be exchanged using XML.

An example of an older format for exchange of information between automated tools is the Common Data Interchange Format (CDIF). Another one for exchange of IDEF0 Activity Models is the IDL or IDEF0 Description Language.

## Dissemination to Another Receiving Enterprise Repository or Registry

This form of dissemination requires agreed-upon protocols for information semantics as well as information formats. Consider the following examples.

The Federal Enterprise Architecture (FEA) reference models are disseminated by the OMB through the use of XML. The tags for the FEA reference models are standardized and the semantics published so that an organization receiving the information can decode the contents. The use of this dissemination is to enable agencies to comply with the federal mandate for mapping their agency EAs as well as their planned investments and initiatives to the FEA reference models.

The DoDAF recommends that enterprises implementing their architectures register the Overview and Summary information (AV-1) model with the Defense Architecture Registry System (DARS). The DARS specifies a XML format for submissions of architecture summaries. These are kept in DARS and available as a ready resource for interested stakeholders and modelers.

## Export/Import Files

Traditional forms of dissemination of architecture data has relied on import/export capabilities within architecture tools and architecture repositories. These capabilities produce electronic files of architecture data. The files can be formatted in many ways. Here are a few examples:

- **Tab, comma separated, or some form of delimited data file**   These are the most popular because the format is both general and transparent and enables ready use of the disseminated information.

- **Extensible Markup Language (XML) files**   These are popular because the data is self-identifying. XML tags inside the file specify the nature of the data that is enclosed between tags. The format also enables parsing as well as schema constraint enforcement—important when tools and repositories also allow imports using the same file format.

- **Standardized architecture data exchange specification**   These standards are established by standards bodies such as Object Management Group, Organization for the Advancement of Structured Information Standards (OASIS), or large volume buyers of tools and repositories with an interest in establishing data exchange standards such as the DoD or financial services firms.

- **Binary files**   These are proprietary format files that can be understood only by the applications for which they are created. They cannot be used in any other context.

- **Microsoft Office**   MS Office has become a de facto standard for word processing, spreadsheet, and presentation software in many organizations. Disseminating architecture data in these formats will provide analysts with easy-to-understand, ready-to-use architecture data for their own value-added tasks. Disseminating images using PowerPoint enables audiences to build briefings from readily available, previously constructed models.

- **Acrobat PDF**   Dissemination of architecture data that must not be altered is accomplished by generating Adobe Acrobat PDF files.

# Summary

Architecture representations are primarily built for promoting common understanding of the enterprise and its various facets. Dissemination of architecture representations is key to sharing that understanding with a broader audience than simply the architecting team. In this chapter, we discuss the aspects to be considered about the dissemination of the EA to an audience that can use it as a knowledge base to support creative efforts, perform detailed analysis, plan actions, make decisions, communicate, solve problems and establish governance, to name a few uses. The process for dissemination starts with identifying the audience for the EA. We discuss various common techniques for presenting the architecture in a format that the appropriate audience is used to. We discuss methods by which architecture representations and narratives are delivered to the intended audience as well as methods to exchange architectural data with other repositories and automated systems that can consume that information for various purposes.

# Questions

1. What are the steps you would take to market the adoption of EA in your enterprise? Who are the key decision-makers? Influencers? Stakeholders? Potential SMEs?

2. What are some of the steps you would use to raise the awareness of EA in your organization?

3. What are the different methods for disseminating the architecture views and information about the architecture development project? Discuss the pros and cons of each method. What method is most applicable to your own organization and why?

4. Build a simple EA marketing and communications plan for your own enterprise. Assume that your enterprise is at a preinception stage in the diagram presented earlier in this chapter. What are the risks inherent to the plan? How do you plan to address, mitigate, or eliminate these risks?

5. Identify the stakeholders for enterprise architecture in your enterprise. Describe their roles briefly and their interest in the architecture. Describe the various architecture viewpoints that are useful for each type of stakeholder; use any of the frameworks discussed in this book to define these viewpoints.

6. What is a Fit-for-Purpose view? Describe some examples of customized views or displays you could use from an IDEF0 activity model that shows the flow of resources between activities as well as a description of the performers of the activity. Hint: Think of RACI matrices.

7. Starting with any subset of the DODAF views described in this book, what kinds of Fit-for-Purpose views would be useful to your organization? How would you construct them from the standard views built during the course of the architecture project?

8. What are the issues in managing the configuration of released architectures? How will you address configuration management of your own architectures? What is your strategy for approaching change control? How will you control changes and keep track of the changes for historical purposes?

9. What are the ways in which you plan to communicate the views you have built using architecture tools? How will you ensure that the intended audience does not need the specialized architecture development tools that you have used to build the views?

10. Discuss the issues that arise when architecture work has to be exported from one repository to another? What are the issues related to methodology mismatch? To metamodel mismatch between the sending and receiving repository systems? What are issues related to non-standard uses of architecture terminology? How do you plan to address your own enterprise's submissions of architecture data and pictures to another collaborating enterprise? To a reporting enterprise?

11. Discuss the applicability of the presentation/dissemination development cycle presented in this chapter to your own enterprise. How would you streamline and standardize this process for your enterprise?

12. Provide some examples of the types of Fit-for-Purpose views discussed in this chapter. Which type of view is useful for which type of audiences?

13. What are some examples of formats for standardized views? What is the usefulness of having standardized views? Discuss the correspondence between standardized views and standard types of models that are prescribed by methodologies such as the Rational Unified Process, Integration Definition for Information Modeling (IDEF1X), or business process modeling notation (BPMN). What are the pros and cons of using standard models prescribed by methodologies versus defining models that are tailored for a specific audience?

14. What are the different methods of disseminating architecture data? How would you plan a distributed dissemination scheme for multiple departments in your enterprise when they do not have access to the same repository?

15. What are some of the pros and cons of providing architecture discovery services so that people interested in your architectures can search, discover, and help themselves? What are some of the security issues? Authorization issues? Entitlement issues? What types of policies would you recommend for such a service-based dissemination strategy?

# References

Barnlund, D.C. 1968. *Interpersonal Communication: Survey and Studies.* Boston: Houghton Mifflin.

Chapanis, A. 1961. "Men, Machines, and Models." *American Psychologist*, 16(3)113–31.

CIO Council. 2001. "A Practical Guide to Federal Enterprise Architecture, Version 1.0." www.gao.gov/assets/590/588407.pdf.

Department of Defense. 2009. Department of Defense Architecture Framework Version 2.0. http://dodcio.defense.gov/Library/DoD-Architecture-Framework.

Deutsch, K. 1952. "On Communication Models in the Social Sciences." *Public Opinion Quarterly*, 16: 356–80.

Education, Audiovisual & Culture Executive Agency, University of Macedonia. 2009. "EA Training 2.0: Innovative Enterprise Architecture Education and Training Based on Web2.0 Technologies." http://eacea.ec.europa.eu/LLP/projects/public_parts/documents/ict/2008/mp_143434_ict_FR_eatrain2_.pdf.

Gerbner, G. 1956. "Toward a General Model of Communication." *Audio-Visual Communication Review*, vol. IV: 171–99.

Kaplan, A. 1964. *The Conduct of Inquiry: Methodology for Behavioral Science.* San Francisco: Chandler.

Lackman, R. 1960. "The Model in Theory Construction." *Psychological Review*, 67(2): 113–29.

Sereno, K.K. and C.D. Mortensen. 1970. *Foundations of Communication Theory*. New York: Harper & Row.

The Open Group. 2011. "TOGAF Version 9.1." The Netherlands: Van Haren Publishing.

Watzlawick, P., J. Beavin, and D. Jackson. 1967. *Pragmatics of Human Communication*. New York: Norton.

# Maintaining the Enterprise Architecture

There is a common aphorism among project managers that "all projects are under budget and on schedule on the first day." Without maintenance, enterprise architecture descriptions (view representations) are valid exactly once, if even that, at the time they were built. Truth is, architecture views are snapshots of reality and will require updating to continue to reflect reality.

The EA is, by definition, a set of views that collectively describe the current enterprise and its future. Its value to the business operations is more than just IT investment decision management. The EA is the primary tool used to reduce the response time for impact assessment, tradeoff analysis, strategic plan redirection, and tactical reaction. Consequently, the EA must remain current and must reflect the reality of the organization's enterprise. The EA needs regular upkeep and maintenance—a process as important as its original development.

## Rate and Degree of Change of Architecture Elements

Determining the frequency with which different elements of the enterprise need to be examined for change and then reflecting the changes into the EA is complex. The frequency of change depends on a number of factors.

### Variation by Architecture Object Type

The rate of change of architecture elements within an EA is not uniform for all the various types of elements. Enterprise locations tend to be long-lived, as do the mission and vision of the enterprise. Objectives change over the years, as do strategies. Given a constant mission, the products and services of an enterprise may not change. This is especially true of federal agencies that are chartered by law for their mission where any change in mission requires amendments to the law or new laws to be passed before the changes can be undertaken. The change in products and services of an enterprise may reflect different characteristics and employ different technologies for manufacture and delivery, but the utility as well as the target market for these may not change much.

Following are a few examples to illustrate why the frequency of change of architecture object types varies from one type to another.

## Mission

For federal agencies, mission is based on chartering legislation. Enterprises such as the Securities and Exchange Commission, Nuclear Regulatory Commission, Offices of the Inspector General, Office of the Chief Financial Officer, and Office of the Chief Information Officer in the federal government can all trace their origins to founding legislation. Without drastic changes in legislation, the mission of these types of enterprises rarely changes. Similarly, for established commercial enterprises, such as IBM and AT&T, with enduring markets and customers, the overall mission rarely changes. For conglomerates that are bound by a financial mission of returning profit and meeting revenue objectives, the mission also rarely changes.

## Objectives

Objectives change from time to time but are relatively stable throughout the time frame that they have been set up for. Sometimes, however, commercial enterprises have been accused of changing their objectives to coincide with their actual performances!

## Capability

The master capability list for an enterprise is generally a function of its mission, its business areas, and its lines of business. To be able to durably support delivery of products, enterprises have to establish supply chain capabilities, manufacturing capabilities, testing and integration capabilities, sales and marketing capabilities, as well as delivery and fulfillment and customer support capabilities. If the area of business and the lines of business are fairly stable, the master capability list is also fairly stable. However, the technologies, systems, services, and standards selected to implement the capabilities may change as the options for solutions increases, driven by new technologies, new techniques, or new suppliers of outsourced services.

## Performers, Organizations, and Business Partners

Organizational structures do tend to change periodically, but functional organizational structures rarely change if the enterprise is engaged in providing the same products and services. External performers may change as the enterprise deals with a changing external context. New business partners may be introduced as business strategy changes from in-sourcing to out-sourcing and may replace all or part of internal organizations.

## Locations, Facilities, and Systems

Specific physical locations and facilities do change. Functional or notional locations, however, tend to remain stable. External locations may change as partners change the places where they do business or are replaced by new business partners. With newer hosted technologies such as cloud technology, location independence of the underlying technology infrastructure is a desirable attribute.

## Activities

Activities are steps within a business process. In a continuously improving business process regime, these should and will change. Activities, when modeled as decompositions, tend to change at lower levels or leaf levels because of specific changes in the way the upper-level activity is realized. Mechanisms change when new systems or automated techniques are applied to a previously manual activity. Controls change when policy, directives, and constraints change. Activity sequences may be changed as well as the way activities are partitioned among performers.

## Variation by Enterprise Nature

The nature of the enterprise also determines the rate of change of architecture elements. Smaller, growing enterprises that use disruptive innovation to change their world order use change as a strategic weapon. Such enterprises are constantly growing through innovation, acquisitions, and mergers, thus metamorphosing in terms of market position, market offerings, and organizational structures. As a consequence, their EA must and will change frequently. Enterprise architecture patterns are a powerful form of knowledge that enables startups to analyze and emulate or disrupt their competitors. By understanding the pattern, they can devise counter-patterns or borrow the best practices that are manifested in the patterns. For example, if a multinational retail hypermarket store relies on its supply chain strength, especially for suppliers from China, a counter-pattern may be a strategy based on distributed suppliers of one-of-a-kind merchandise or a supply chain based on local manufacture.

## Variations Introduced by Nonlinear Events

Huge shifts may occur in both business and government enterprises. Think, for example, of two very large airlines that merge, or the formation of U.S. Air Force Air Mobility Command that merged functionality from the erstwhile Strategic Air Command, the Tactical Airlift Command, and the Military Airlift Command at the end of the Cold War. Such tectonic shifts can render previous architecture work inaccurate, but still useful as a basis for creating a new version of the architecture that reflects the transformation. From an internal perspective (operating model), mergers result in major functionality aggregation and the pressing out of redundant capabilities, activities, organizational structures, personnel, systems, and locations. Mergers can significantly change the architecture elements of both original enterprises. From an external perspective (business model), mergers result in reconciliation of offerings to customers and markets, such as product lines, services, or other propositions that bring revenue to the enterprise. From the perspective of shared infrastructure between the merging enterprises, duplication in information assets, systems, and system roles, among others, need to be pressed out or reconciled. In divestitures of parts of one enterprise to another, the architecture has to shrink to accommodate architecture elements that are no longer part of the remaining enterprise.

## A Change Response Model for Reference Models

At a larger granularity than the architecture element types, the "Federal Enterprise Architecture Reference Model Maintenance Process" [Federal Enterprise Architecture Program Management Office 2005] and now the "Consolidated FEA Reference Model Document" in FEAF2 [Federal Enterprise Architecture Program Management Office 2007] describe the natural relative rate of change of each of the FEA reference models, as shown in Figure 8-1, from the Office of Management and Budget.

The intent of the reference models in the Federal Enterprise Architecture Framework (FEAF) is to present government-wide taxonomies that can be used by any agency to instantiate its own architecture against general classification schemes. Such reference models provide a common "schema" that can be used to aggregate and compare architectures from multiple federal agencies from the vantage point of the OMB, which is tasked with managing and controlling expenditure on information technology for the entire federal government.

The message of Figure 8-1 is that the business reference model (BRM) tends to be stable and long lived (at least for federal agencies), as the charter of these enterprises is based on founding legislation, and their highest level organization structure and duties are spelled out in federal law. The data reference model (DRM) tends to be stable because the types of information tend to be the same if the area of business and line of business remain the same. On the other hand, the services reference model (SRM) may be less

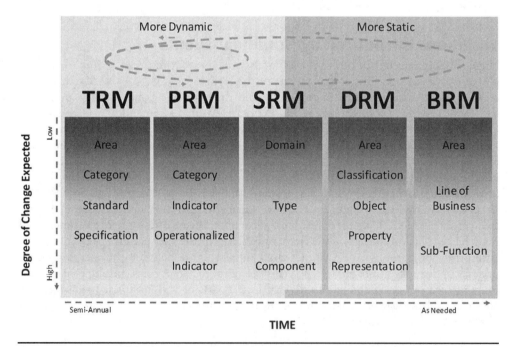

**Figure 8-1** Degree of change of various FEA reference models (graphic from the OMB)

**Figure 8-2**
Enterprise
architecture
transition

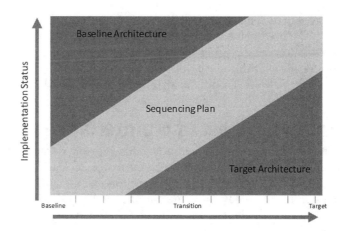

static as new or improved services become available that improve the way processes are implemented. The performance reference model (PRM) will change as new performance measure types need to be introduced as a result of initiatives such as balanced score card (BSC) and other complex measurements of enterprise performance.

Figure 8-1 also shows, within each reference model, what aspect of that reference model changes more rapidly than others.

The "Practical Guide to Federal Enterprise Architecture" [CIO Council 2001] describes how an architecture description must change, showing a decreasing emphasis on maintaining or extending elements of the baseline architecture, focusing on growing the target architecture. Figure 8-2 shows this decreasing emphasis on the baseline architecture as implementation of the transformation process is rolled out according to the sequencing plan and as the target architecture becomes the new baseline. As a historical note, the "Practical Guide" was written at a time when federal agencies were undergoing very large modernization attempts (often after failed previous attempts). By perpetuating the elements of the baseline architecture, the assumption was that the target architecture would be starved of resources and would never come to be.

The sequencing plan (that is, the transition plan) stays constant throughout the transition time frame unless there is a need to resequence activities because of unforeseen circumstances, budget issues, or a stretching out of the timelines.

# Who Is Responsible for Maintenance?

Maintaining the EA should be accomplished within the enforcement structure and configuration control mechanisms of the organization. Chapter 9 deals with these governance issues.

EA maintenance is generally the responsibility of the CIO, chief architect, and the enterprise architecture program office, often through a delegated chain of architecture team members. Under a system of oversight processes and independent verification, the architecture core team periodically assesses the EA and aligns it to reflect ever-changing business practices and technology insertions.

The EA should remain aligned with the organization's modernization projects and vice versa. The management controls to accomplish EA maintenance are the same ones established to initiate the program and to develop the EA. The chief architect may want to establish liaisons with the enterprise groups whose decisions may impact the EA, such as the strategic planning group, the investment review board, and key business managers.

# Planning the Cost of Maintenance

EA maintenance must be planned and budgeted for. Because EA projects themselves compete for resources against enterprise initiatives, a clear business case must be made for both the initial EA development and the follow-on maintenance funding required to keep the architecture data up to date and useful. The EA itself is and should be treated as a capital asset that depreciates without maintenance. Maintenance is used to retain asset value.

Out-of-date architecture data can have an extremely detrimental effect on planning. The assumptions implicit in the architecture also form the basis of assumptions for road-maps and transition plans. The DoDAF Overview and Summary Information (AV-1) or the TOGAF statement of architectural work (first created in the Vision Phase of the Architecture Development Methodology (ADM)) must explicitly specify assumptions, constraints, and the validity for the architecture time frame.

## The Business Case for EA Maintenance

If the EA is not kept current, it will quickly become "shelf-ware"—yet another well-intentioned but unused or underused plan for improving the enterprise. Perhaps even more damaging, if the EA fails to embody the agency's most current strategy, this failure may limit the organization's ability to meet its goals and achieve its mission. A specific organizational and process structure that will ensure the currency of EA content over time is necessary. The EA should reflect the impact of ongoing changes in business function and technology on the enterprise, and in turn support capital planning and investment management in keeping up with those changes. Consequently, each component of and product in the EA-baseline architecture, target architecture, and sequencing plan, need to be maintained and kept accurate and current.

# Periodic Architecture Reassessment

An EA is a living description of the state of the enterprise and its plans for the future. As such, it needs to be periodically reviewed against the real state of the enterprise and enterprise plans to ensure that it still reflects them appropriately.

## The Need for Periodic Reassessment

It is periodically necessary to revisit the vision that carried the organization to the current point in time and to reenergize the enterprise to realize that vision. Typically, the EA should be reviewed in conjunction with the capital planning and investment control (CPIC) process (see Chapter 10), to ensure the following:

- The current or baseline architecture accurately reflects the current status of the business strategy, business operations, and technology infrastructure.

- The target architecture accurately reflects the business vision of the enterprise and appropriate technology advances that have occurred since the last architecture release.

- The sequencing or transition plan reflects the prevailing priorities of the enterprise and the resources that will realistically be available.

The results of this review should generate an updated release of the EA and corresponding changes in dependent projects. The baseline should continue to reflect actions taken to implement the sequencing plan and actions otherwise taken to upgrade the legacy environment as the enterprise evolves. The EA assessment and update should be managed and scheduled to support the update of the agency strategic plan and the process for selecting system investments.

## Models Must Reflect Reality—Always

An enterprise is a business entity that remains responsive to business drivers, emerging technologies, and opportunities for improvement. For government agencies, business drivers include new legislation and executive directives. The EA reflects the evolution of the enterprise and should continuously reflect the current state (baseline architecture), the desired state (target architecture), and the long- and short-term strategies for managing the change (the sequencing or transition plan). Figure 8-2 illustrates the type of continuous changes that should be reflected in the EA. At no time will a specific target architecture ever be achieved with each iterative update of the EA. Instead, all three components shown in the Figure 8-2 and the timeline are recast. The target architecture is a vision of the future that evolves in advance of it being achieved.

## Leverage Solution Architectures to Grow the EA

Figure 8-3 shows that enterprises can adopt one of three strategies for enterprise architecting:

- *Drive the development of solution architectures in a top-down manner by first defining the Enterprise Level architecture.* See, for example, the OMB EA life cycle discussed in Chapter 6. This approach is not usually feasible for enterprises that have been operational for many years. More often, EA is a conversion of the implicit aspects of a working enterprise to an explicit representation that can support planning and transformational activities.

- *Drive the development of the EA in a bottom-up manner by aggregating elements from all the various solution architectures.* This is an acknowledgment that the enterprise is actually viewed as the sum total of its solutions. This approach grandfathers any architectural disconnects and mismatches that exist across solutions and generates an as-is EA that reflects the issues in the current state of the enterprise. If portions of the enterprise do not currently have any solution architectures defined, this approach will ignore the missing solutions in representing the enterprise.

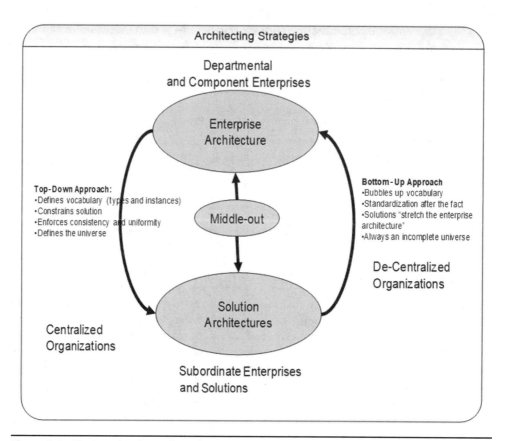

**Figure 8-3** The iterative dependence between EA and solution architectures

- *Blend top-down and bottom-up using a middle-out approach.* In this approach, the top-down architecture is built at the same time as the solution architectures are baselined. The gap between the current state and the target state is used to drive transformational activities.

In the second (bottom-up) and third (middle-out) strategy approach, discovery of as-yet-unincluded elements from solution architectures is flowed back to the EA (in a more abstract manner consistent with the level of the EA) to "grow" the EA.

## Ensure that Business Direction and Processes Reflect Operations

A critical responsibility for the chief architect and architecture core team is to monitor the changes in the business operations that affect the organization, the business processes, and the strategic direction of the business. Changes in business processes that were initiated by process improvement, organizational change, or enterprise mandate should be reflected in the business artifacts of the baseline architecture. Business unit management and SMEs should report changes in their organizations and initiatives to the chief architect and architecture core team. Correspondingly, the chief architect ensures that the architecture core team gains sufficient insight into the evolution of the operations. Plans and expectations may change as priorities shift over time, and these changes need to be reflected in modifications to the target architecture. Priority shifts and the realities of budget constraints need to be reflected in the sequencing plan. Thus, EA maintenance will be both reactive and proactive.

## Ensure that Current Architecture Reflects System Evolution

Despite the best operational management and systems maintenance planning, the current IT architecture and infrastructure may need unanticipated changes. As each new system is deployed and each legacy system reaches a maintenance milestone (such as renewal of maintenance contracts), the baseline for the current architecture changes. In addition, as system versions are updated and system design changes are implemented to respond to high-priority change requests, the baseline architecture should be updated. The requisite information can sometimes be identified from system development life cycle (SDLC) review reports, change control board reports, and post-implementation reviews (PIRs) reports (see Chapter 10).

## Evaluate Legacy System Maintenance Requirements Against the Sequencing Plan

As the current architecture evolves, new information may emerge that will change the maintenance plans for legacy systems and impact subsequent organizational and systems transition. For example, system vendors may unexpectedly cease supporting critical components of the enterprise's infrastructure. Alternative actions should be weighed and decisions made regarding replacing these components, paying for additional specialized contractor support, or changing the timing for phasing in other components in the target architecture. The total cost of ownership of the system versus alternative systems or outsourcing may need to be considered. All of these considerations, alternatives, and decisions may dramatically alter the sequencing plan.

## Maintain the Sequencing Plan as an Integrated Program Plan

The development of the sequencing plan is linked to the acquisition and enterprise engineering processes. The architects work in partnership with managers who understand the evolving business objectives as well as with individual program management offices that oversee the acquisition and development of new IT systems. The sequencing plan should be continuously maintained, reviewed, validated, and approved to reflect the organization's mission and vision just as any product in the architecture package and plan. The sequencing plan delineates the IT management scheme for systems insertion in support of the organization's long-term business strategies.

## Continue to Consider Proposals for EA Modifications

While the enforcement process (see Chapter 9) helps to ensure that the EA guidance is followed, it is unreasonable to assume that new business priorities and new technologies, funding issues, or project challenges will not require modification to the plans, baselines, and products incorporated in the EA. Emerging technologies will continue to impact the enterprise. Many of the considerations for changes to the EA are the same considerations that needed to be addressed during its development. Also, the architectural principles need to be continuously reviewed.

Proposals for modifying the architecture should address the following questions, among others:

- How does the proposed modification support the enterprise in exploiting IT to increase the effectiveness of its organizational components?

- How does the proposed modification impact information-sharing and interoperability among organizational components?

- What are the security implications? For example, will business modifications require changes in security requirements or will technology changes require certification or recertification of new or enhanced systems?

- Does the proposed modification fit within the standards and technology constraints of the enterprise? For example, some enterprises require the use of proven technologies and conforming COTS products to satisfy requirements and deliver IT services. Are these technologies and related standards in the industry mainstream, thereby reducing the risk of premature obsolescence?

- Does the acceptance of this proposal position other standards or products for obsolescence? If so, identify them.

- What is the impact of the proposed modification on the organization and suborganizations if the proposal is not accepted? What is the result of the cost-benefit analysis?

- What external organizations or systems will be affected? What action will external partners have to take?

- What is the estimated overall programmatic cost of the proposed changes, including changes to the EA and/or redirection of impacted projects?

- What alternatives have been considered and why were they not recommended?

- What testing, and by whom, should be completed prior to the operational implementations that will result from acceptance of the proposal?

- What is the recommendation of the enterprise change control board?

Proposals requesting modifications to the EA need to address these issues explicitly. The proposal should be presented to and reviewed by a technical review committee (TRC) (for review by architectural team and SMEs) and by a business review committee (BRC) as necessary and passed to the EA executive steering committee (EAESC) or equivalent review board with recommendations. In cases where the EAESC cannot reach a consensus, a working group may be tasked to investigate and propose recommended actions.

# TOGAF 9.2 ADM Phase H: Architecture Change Management

The DoDAF does not provide any guidance on EA change management, but the TOGAF provides some valuable guidance in this area. Although an overview of TOGAF is provided in Chapter 22, we include details of the TOGAF change management guidance here. Take care to adjust the TOGAF guidance for EA, since the TOGAF is focused on architecting solutions that are driven from the IT organization rather than a pure business-driven architecture that is IT solution agnostic. Additional change management guidance is provided in Chapter 7.

TOGAF 9.2, Phase H (Architecture Change Management) of the Architecture Development Methodology (ADM), addresses the issues of maintaining an architecture once it has been developed. TOGAF 9.2 identifies three types of architecture changes: simplification of an architecture, incremental evolution of an architecture, and rearchitecting. Each of these can be handled incrementally or through partial traversal of the ADM, or it may require an entire iteration through the ADM (rearchitecting).

For TOGAF, the objectives of performing architecture change management are as follows:

- Ensure that baseline architectures are fit for purpose.
- Assess the performance of the architecture and make recommendations for change.
- Assess changes to the framework and principles.
- Establish an architecture change management process for the new EA baseline.
- Maximize business value from the architecture.
- Operate within the governance framework.

The steps recommended for architecture change management from TOGAF are described here:

1. *Establish a value realization process.* Establish a process that ensures that business projects realize value from the EA. This step also involves formulating direct and indirect metrics to correlate the outcomes of the project in terms of the EA context.

2. *Deploy monitoring tools.* Deploy tools for monitoring various aspects, such as technology changes, business changes, and enterprise architecture capability maturity. Deploy tracking tools such as asset management and quality of service tracking.

3. *Manage risks.* Assess EA risks and develop plans to deal with those risks.

4. *Provide analysis for architecture change management.* Conduct various types of analyses on the architecture effort as well as the scope and content of the architecture to determine whether changes should be made.

5. *Develop change requirements to meet performance targets.* Determine changes needed to the architecture to meet the enterprise performance targets that are driven by business requirements.

6. *Manage the governance process.* Conduct the architecture board processes.

7. *Activate the process to implement change.* Initiate the activities needed to produce architecture change such as architecture change requests and investment requests for projects to implement accepted change requests. Ensure that all change requests and architecture change implementation projects are registered in the architecture repository.

## Summary

This chapter focuses on the process of maintaining the enterprise architecture once it has been developed. The EA is an asset that can lose value if it is not updated. Though maintaining the EA may seem like a daunting task, some parts of the EA do not change very often. We outline the architecture elements such as Mission, Objectives, and Capability that do not change often once a business has been established. This rate of change is consistent with the relative stability of WHAT an enterprise does. HOW the enterprise does what it does may change from time to time based on reorganization, continuous improvements, business process re-engineering and constant assessment of best practices to name a few factors. We also discuss exceptions where the nature of a business, its stage of evolution in the enterprise birth to death lifecycle, and the effects of competition may result in the need to change fundamental WHATs of the business.

Rates of change in reference models, such as those provided in the FEAF are also reviewed. Reference Models that establish a standard taxonomy for various types of architecture elements provide a degree of commonality for component enterprises to report against. Amongst the various types of Reference Models, the Business Reference Model tends to change relatively more slowly as federal organizations are chartered by legislation and any change in business scope, activities, authority and services has to be driven by changes in the corresponding legislation.

The chapter includes guidance on change management—who is responsible for maintenance, how to plan the cost of maintenance, needs for periodic re-assessment of architecture elements, changes introduced by non-linear (often deemed disruptive) events. We also show how the EA can be built incrementally rather than monolithically, by flowing in discoveries of new architecture elements and relationships into a growing EA while working on solution projects. Change management has to be treated as a project or program component in much the same way software maintenance is usually planned along with software acquisitions. Details of TOGAF guidance on change management are included because the DoDAF does not provide guidance in this area.

# Questions

1. Do all the architecture elements modeled in the EA change at the same rate with time? Are there types of architecture elements that change more rapidly than others? Why?

2. Discuss the maintainability of business functions versus the maintainability of activities used in business processes. Remember that business functions tend to be very stable if the mission of an enterprise has not changed.

3. What is the effect of the nature of an enterprise on the rate of change of architecture representations? What types of changes may occur in a hypothetical startup enterprise that result in needs to change the EA?

4. If you were to build an EA repository maintenance process for your own enterprise with the granularity of quarterly time periods (three monthly maintenance periods), what types of architecture elements would be maintained at what frequency on the schedule? Why?

5. In your own enterprise, who is responsible for maintaining the EA? How frequently is it updated? Are there any policies related to maintenance frequency, schedule, responsibility, and oversight? How does your enterprise plan for the cost of maintenance?

6. What are the symptoms of a poorly maintained EA? How are these symptoms manifested to the enterprise? What is the effect of a poorly maintained EA on the planning aspects of the enterprise? On the operational aspects? The systems aspects?

# References

CIO Council. 2001. "A Practical Guide to Federal Enterprise Architecture, Version 1.0." www.gao.gov/assets/590/588407.pdf.

Federal Enterprise Architecture Program Management Office. 2007. "FEA Consolidated Reference Model Document Version 2.3." www.reginfo.gov/public/jsp/Utilities/ FEA_CRM_v23_Final_Oct_2007_Revised.pdf.

Federal Enterprise Architecture Program Management Office, Federal CIO Council Architecture and Infrastructure Committee, and E-GOV. 2005. "Federal Enterprise Architecture Reference Model Maintenance Process." www.immagic.com/eLibrary/ ARCHIVES/GENERAL/US_OMB/F050600R.pdf.

The Open Group. 2018. "TOGAF Version 9.2, revised educational edition." The Netherlands: Van Haren Publishing.

# Governing the Enterprise Architecture

Our primary concern in this chapter is the governance of the enterprise architecture as opposed to how the EA assists in the governance of other enterprise processes. The interaction of EA and the enterprise business processes are discussed in Chapter 10.

The purpose of EA governance—that is, the control and oversight of the EA—is to ensure that the EA development, implementation, and maintenance practices are being followed, and to remedy any situations or circumstances where they are not and action is warranted. Control and oversight are continuous, ongoing functions performed throughout the EA life cycle. Effective control and oversight are key to ensuring EA program success and involve identifying authorities and responsibilities for control and oversight. Through governance, accountable decision-makers have the information they need to ensure that effective EA development, implementation, and maintenance activities are being performed and that EA program goals are being met on schedule and within budgets.

Though specific organizations adopt specific governance strategies, some of the considerations that generally apply to all governance strategies are as follows:

- **Assessing the maturity of an enterprise's EA implementation**   This involves assessing where a particular enterprise's EA efforts lie when benchmarked with other enterprises. Some of the available EA maturity models are listed at the end of this chapter.

- **Assessing the effectiveness of EA through metrics**   In enterprises, metrics such as return on assets, return on investment, and others are frequently used to assess the cost-benefit equation for initiatives. EA metrics is an emerging field; it aims to quantify the value of architecture as a capitalized or expensed asset or as a knowledgebase that supports enterprise prioritization, planning, and transformational efforts but may not necessarily be quantifiable in benefit.

- **Managing access to the EA itself and dealing with security- and authorization-related matters**   The EA is especially a vulnerable target for competition and for disgruntled internal personnel. At the same time, widespread access to the EA is desired for promoting enterprise coherence, consistency, and transparency of architecture elements in order for diverse groups to collaborate effectively. This tension between the needs for transparency and communication and the needs for security and access control must be carefully managed.

- **Enforcing EA standards**   An EA program must itself adopt standards for modeling, methodologies, viewing artifacts, managing repository meta-model structures, and managing repository and architecture tool exchange standards for the EA to be both a long-lived asset and one that can interact with architectures, tools, and methodologies used by partner and subenterprises. Standards provide the ability to share architectures, exchange views among multiple organizations, and increase the transparency through broadly available symbology and semantics.

- **Managing the configuration of the EA**   Chapter 8 discussed the issues and concerns related to configuration management of the EA, releasing increments in an evolutionary manner and controlling updates and changes by authorized stewards. The EA, to act as a durable knowledge resource, must continue to be kept up to date. Different aspects of the EA change at different rates. For example, the architecture's business reference model and business functions may not change unless the mission and the lines of business of the enterprise changes. The technology architecture may change more frequently as advances in products make previous versions obsolete.

- **Defining and developing EA policy and EA procedures**   Policy is often perceived as burdensome by operational staff. EA policy must complement existing policies and not add undue burden. The EA is often most valuable to the management of an enterprise and may be perceived as an obstacle by implementers of solutions or subcontractors who see it as a barrier.

To explain some of these concepts further and recognizing that individual enterprises have differences in the ways they govern their architectures, we use a generalized governance framework using a model from the Infosys white paper "Enterprise Architecture: A Governance Framework." [Aziz et al. 2005]

# Governance Framework

Figure 9-1 describes the various components of a governance framework. Each of these components must be addressed in order to achieve EA governance. The annotations of terms that appear next to the circles represent an overlay of the familiar military tenets of DOTMLPF—Doctrine, Organization, Training, Materiel, Leadership, Personnel, and Facility.

The following sections discuss several components important to the governance framework. At the end of each section is a paragraph describing how the component applies to the case study of RMN Airport.

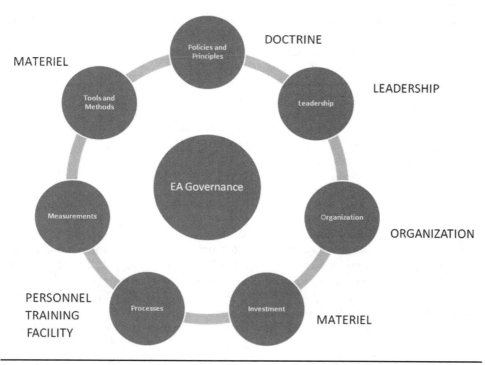

**Figure 9-1**   Governance components

## Leadership

Leadership provides the drive needed to propel architecting efforts forward and to get widespread acceptance. EA should be a key part of planning and prioritization for upper management. Without strong leadership, the interest of the enterprise's holistic view is often sacrificed for immediate (and sometimes noncritical) needs. Leadership from executive management and other sponsors, in addition to full support from the CIO, is essential for a successful EA strategy. To achieve buy-in from management, the chief architect and the CIO have to "sell" the benefits of EA and demonstrate early results and payoffs from the EA program. Governance involves specifying explicit roles for executive management and sponsors within the EA effort and at different stages of the EA life cycle.

> *The chief architect and CIO at RMN Airport have the sponsorship and support of their command chain all the way up to the airport authority. There is tremendous interest not as much in the EA as in the desired outcomes promised by the CIO and chief architect.*

## Investment

The EA program is often a significant investment by an organization. John Zachman asserts that the resulting architecture is an asset that keeps on giving—to every meaningful activity of the enterprise. However, because of the inevitable changes in the information that are represented in the architecture over time, the architecture becomes a perishable asset that needs to be constantly refreshed. An enterprise making the initial investment in the development of an EA must also be ready to invest in the maintenance and evolution of the EA. This readiness is exhibited in planned investments for EA in a phased and multiyear manner. Governance involves displaying commitment to a phased and funded investment strategy for the EA life cycle.

> *RMN Airport has decided to designate a stated percentage of planned investment projects as dedicated to enterprise architecting. These investments are pooled together to set up and operate the EA program. The architects themselves are on staff and available to the enterprise as resources.*

## Organization

A set of formal structures or organizations is needed to oversee EA development, maintenance, and use. In most enterprises, these formal bodies take the form of councils, review boards, working groups, and integrated project teams. A formal organizational structure requires a charter; criteria for membership; roles, authorities, and responsibilities; a calendar for working meetings; and a framework for decision-making. The formal organization structure also includes mechanisms for accountability for the various roles concerned and forms the basis for collecting metrics needed for control.

Governance involves detailing an organizational structure that lays out specific organizations, their roles, responsibilities, and authorities with respect to the EA life cycle.

In "A Practical Guide for the Federal Enterprise Architecture," [CIO Council 2001] the suggested governance organizational structure, at a minimum, within a federal agency includes the following:

- Enterprise architecture executive steering council (EAESC)
- The chief information officer (CIO)
- The chief architect

Some of the roles and responsibilities of the EAESC and chief architect have been identified in Chapter 6, while the roles and responsibilities of the CIO for federal agencies is outlined in OMB Circular A-130 [OMB 2015] and Federal Information Technology Acquisition Reform Act (FITARA). [United States Congress 2015]

> *RMN Airport has appointed an architecture review board comprising the CIO, chief architect, and lead functional managers for various airside and landside functions to whom the domain architects for airside and landside report. The Chair for the ARB is the chief architect.*

## Principles and Policies

Principles are enduring guiding tenets that establish the fundamental backbone of the EA program in an enterprise. Principles should be few in number and general enough to be unspecific to a situation or time frame. Policies are guiding principles that are measurable and enforceable in terms of compliance. Explicit guidance is essential for requiring compliance. Principles and policies must therefore be explicitly published and communicated to stakeholders. Governance involves publishing explicit principles and policies for the various steps of the EA life cycle. Thus, the roles responsible for publishing the principles and policies must be identified as well as the roles with the authority to establish the principles and policies.

> *RMN Airport has tasked the ARB to establish principles for the RMN Airport enterprise architecture. Enduring principles are related to promotion of cost effectiveness, maximum throughput, competitive advantage, and stakeholder benefit.*

## Processes

Processes that are well thought out and documented are essential to the development, maintenance, use, and evolution of the EA. These processes should be simple and streamlined, yet comprehensive. Any issues and defects that arise from improper execution of the steps must be analyzed to determine how improvements can be made to the overall process. The EA-related process must not be burdensome to the stakeholders. Process definition includes the sequence of detailed steps for various aspects of the EA life cycle—from setup of an EA program office; to the development of views, roadmaps, and plans for the maintenance of the EA information; to use of this information in business processes of the enterprise; and to the actual assessment of maturity metrics and effectiveness metrics for the EA program. Governance involves documented and communicated business processes, with steps and major phases, identification of roles and responsibilities of the various players, and controls for monitoring and governing the activity.

One of the processes that is essential to document and communicate is the process for controlling the EA life cycle. The EA program, like any major program, establishes expectations of results, deliverables, and outcomes at the beginning of the program. As the program continues, course corrections may need to be made and expectations reset based on actual experience versus the initial hopes and assumptions that were built into the planning. Independent program reviews by a quality assurance function or by verification and validation (V&V) agents are used to identify deviations from expectations. These deviations may be related to the program management plan, such as omission of work tasks, delays in the completion of work tasks, or additional costs to complete work tasks; or they may be related to management function, such as not following change control procedures, not adhering to the selected EA framework, or not engaging subject matter experts and domain owners within business and technical areas.

> *The RMN Airport architecture review board is traveling to various similar-sized airports with similar aspirations that have already implemented and maintained EA programs to determine what best practices should be adopted in their own case. The ARB has the responsibility for publishing and communicating the EA processes.*

## Tools and Methods

The life cycle of an architecture requires the use of automated tools such as those used to build views; to manage repositories of architecture information for data quality, consistency, accuracy, and timeliness; and to support analysis and reporting. The development of views must follow some consistent and standard methodologies. By applying standard methodologies, the views that are built are consistent across development efforts and also can be easily understood by personnel who are trained in those methodologies. Examples of some standard methodologies are Integrated Definition Language (IDEF0 and IDEF1X), Business Process Modeling Notation (BPMN), and Business Process Execution Language (BPEL). Most commercial architecture development tools provide support for some subset of standard methodologies. Governance involves establishing the roles that have the authority and responsibility to decide on clear criteria for standards and for selection of tools, methods, and repositories for the EA life cycle.

> *The RMN Airport chief architect and her team have been looking at various modeling methodologies and integrated tools and techniques for architecting. They are looking for tools built around the use of industry standards for architecting and an integrated repository that avoids overt or tacit duplication of architecture elements due to independent stove-piped model building. The chief architect has the authority and responsibility for EA standards and selection of tools, methods, and repositories.*

## Measurements

In the words of the Government Accountability Office, "The ability to effectively manage any activity (e.g., architecture development, maintenance, and use) depends upon having meaningful measures of that activity in relation to some standard. Such measurement permits managers to assess progress toward the desired end and to take corrective action to address unacceptable deviations." [GAO 2003]

Measurement is essential for control. Measurements provide a way to determine whether desired results are forthcoming, and they provide a basis for analysis and for devising a course of actions that will provide more favorable outcomes. Measurement can be performed informally through reports (oral, written, and ad hoc) and formal and informal reviews. Measurement can also be performed by periodic or surprise audits.

Governance includes establishing the roles that are responsible for selecting the appropriate measures and for conducting and reporting the required measurements as well as the role that has authority to determine when corrective action is needed.

> *The RMN Airport chief architect is responsible for selecting the measures and the EA development team is responsible for collecting and reporting the measurements to the chief architect, who shares results with the ARB. In this case the EA "development team" may be interpreted in its widest meaning to include QA and IV&V personnel. The chief architect has the authority to determine when corrective action is needed.*

# Security, Access, and Privacy Issues

Another key aspect of governance is to define and manage security controls on the EA. Arguably, the aggregation of many elements of information creates an asset that is of larger value as a whole than the sum of its parts. Governance includes establishing the roles with the authority to approve security policies and the roles with the responsibility for developing, publishing, enforcing, and measuring compliance with security policies for the EA.

Security measures are easier to enforce when the EA resides in a central repository or a system of repositories. It is more difficult to enforce when the architecture development is scattered over a number of tools. Security is enforced either at the database level through mechanisms embedded inside the repository database or through common authorization and access control services that are invoked by all repository applications and tools.

Following are some of the considerations that guide the formulation of specific policies for security:

- Balancing the need for widespread dissemination and transparency of EA information against vulnerabilities and threats

- Promoting cross-business domain integration, federation, and aggregation of architecture elements while securing information against misuse

- Compliance with regulatory directives such as the Federal Information Security Act (FISMA) and the Privacy Act to drive policy that governs security classification needs for encryption and handling of personally identifying information (PII)

# EA Standards Compliance

Another aspect of EA governance is the need to identify the roles with the authority to establish and update EA-related standards and policy as well as the roles with the responsibility to enforce compliance with these standards. The processes for enforcing compliance also need to be established. EA standards are simply a subset of a larger group of standards that must be adopted by enterprises for interoperability and to leverage market forces.

Here are some of the areas for EA standards policy, if applicable:

- Architecture framework
- Repository/metamodel
- Tool import/export standards
- Architecture data exchange standards
- Architecture data translation/mediation standards
- Controlled vocabularies and ontology standards
- Use of standard taxonomies
- Metadata specifications for architecture elements
- Integrated architecture development
- Federated architecture development

# EA Maturity Assessment

From the components of governance, we could construct a simple but serviceable EA maturity framework by assigning a level or degree of maturity that each component has achieved and assigning some type of scoring to determine a maturity index, as illustrated in Table 9-1.

The simple matrix in Table 9-1 is an example of the more sophisticated EA maturity assessment models that are available. All of the more formal models include elements of governance as criteria for achieving the various levels of maturity. Thus, these EA maturity models are useful in estimating the maturity of EA governance.

Maturity assessment of EA management has been approached from various perspectives. Traditional methods have been based on the maturity of process and governance mechanisms. There are two maturity models designed for government agencies:

- **GAO EA Management Maturity Assessment Framework (EAMMF) version 1.1** The EAMMF is a classic five-stage maturity model, with the stages ranging from Stage 1: Creating EA Awareness, to Stage 5: Leveraging the EA to Manage Change.

- **OMB Enterprise Architecture Assessment Framework (EAAF) version 3.1** The EAAF identifies the measurement areas and criteria by which agencies are expected to use the EA to drive performance improvements. The EAAF uses key performance indicators (KPIs) to measure the effectiveness of EA relative to the three EA capabilities areas of completion, use, and results.

There are also two maturity models oriented more toward commercial enterprises:

- **Ross/Weill/Robertson model** This model from the book *Enterprise Architecture as Strategy* [Ross et al. 2006] is a four-stage maturity model that focuses on moving an enterprise from a stove-piped, functional orientation to IT toward an enterprise orientation of shared IT and data with reusable modules.

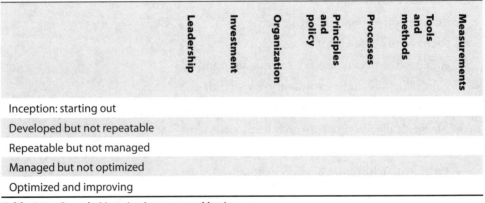

| | Leadership | Investment | Organization | Principles and policy | Processes | Tools and methods | Measurements |
|---|---|---|---|---|---|---|---|
| Inception: starting out | | | | | | | |
| Developed but not repeatable | | | | | | | |
| Repeatable but not managed | | | | | | | |
| Managed but not optimized | | | | | | | |
| Optimized and improving | | | | | | | |

**Table 9-1** Sample Maturity Assessment Matrix

- **Gartner EA Maturity Assessment Framework**   Gartner developed its Architecture Program Maturity Assessment (APMA) [Burke and James 2005] for its clients that measure various aspects of the EA program through surveys. The aspects that are surveyed are architecture scope and authority, stakeholder involvement, architecture definition process, business context, architecture content, future state realization, architecture team resources, and architecture impact.

# Architecture Governance in TOGAF (TOGAF 9.2)

The DoDAF does not provide any guidance on EA governance because this topic is covered by other defense directives and regulations and by the military chain of command. However, the TOGAF provides some valuable guidance regarding governance issues. Although the overall review of the TOGAF is covered in Chapter 22, we include details of TOGAF governance guidance here.

TOGAF 9.2 defines architecture governance as "the practice of monitoring and directing architecture-related work. The goal is to deliver desired outcomes and adhere to relevant principles, standards, and roadmaps (TOGAF 9.2, p 23)." Governance ensures that business is conducted properly. TOGAF draws upon the definition from the basic principles of corporate governance from the Organization for Economic Co-operation and Development. The corporate governance structure specifies the distribution of rights and responsibilities among different participants and spells out the rules and procedures for decision-making on corporate affairs. It also provides the structure through which company objectives are set, and the means of attaining those objectives and monitoring performance.

Architecture governance includes the following:

- Installing and managing controls on the creation and monitoring of components and activities, ensuring introduction, implementation and evolution of architectures

- Ensuring compliance with internal and external standards and regulatory obligations

- Supporting management of the compliances

- Ensuring accountability to external and internal stakeholders

Architecture governance in TOGAF lies at the lowest level of a governance hierarchy that includes the following (listed from broadest to narrowest in scope):

- Corporate governance
- Technology governance
- IT governance
- Architecture governance

Note that this hierarchy is in keeping with the TOGAF's focus on architecting solutions that are driven from the IT organization rather than a pure business-driven architecture that is IT-solution agnostic. This IT focus must be kept in mind when applying TOGAF guidance to EA governance.

## Organizational Structure for Architecture Governance

TOGAF 9.2 describes a typical organizational structure for an architecture organization that supports architecture governance for solution architectures, as shown in Figure 9-2.

In the figure, the chief information officer/chief technology officer is ultimately responsible for governance through all stages of IT solution delivery (development, implementation, and deployment). At each of these stages, different groups of people are responsible for governance. Enterprise architects and domain architects are responsible for developing the architectural aspects of the solution that ensure that the solution is compliant with enterprise standards and fits correctly into the context of the larger enterprise. Using the parlance of the housing industry, the architects are responsible for ensuring that the design conforms to "building codes, zoning regulations, and other regulations."

The program management office entrusted with delivering the solution is responsible for governance of construction practices and use of predefined implementation patterns that ensure a quality solution implementation. The program office is also responsible for ensuring that the implementation follows the architecture guidance from the development phase.

The service management organization that is responsible for releasing and deploying the solution and overseeing maintenance and customer support activities is also responsible for governance of solution changes and continued conformance with the implementation patterns and the architecture guidance from the previous phases.

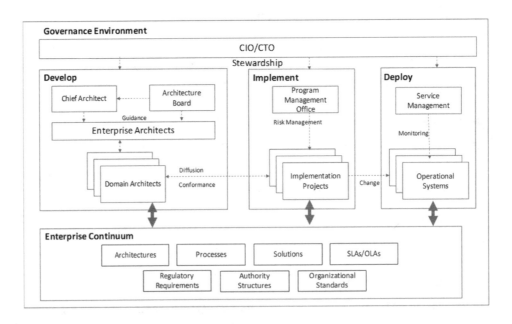

**Figure 9-2** TOGAF 9.2 organizational structure for supporting governance (graphic based on TOGAF 9.2)

All three phases draw upon the resources from the TOGAF Enterprise Continuum (see Chapter 22 for details of the Enterprise Continuum).

# Key Architecture Governance Processes

Governance processes are required to identify, manage, audit, and disseminate all information related to architecture management, contracts, and implementation. These governance processes will be used to ensure that all architecture artifacts and contracts, principles, and operational-level agreements are monitored on an ongoing basis with clear auditability of all decisions made. The key architecture governance processes described by TOGAF 9.2 are covered in the following subsections.

## Policy Management and Take-On

All architecture amendments, contracts, and supporting information must come under governance through a formal process in order to register, validate, ratify, manage, and publish new or updated content. These processes will ensure the orderly integration with existing governance content such that all documents, contracts, and supporting information are managed and audited.

## Compliance

Compliance assessments against service level agreements (SLAs), operational level agreements (OLAs), standards, and regulatory requirements will be implemented on an ongoing basis to ensure stability, conformance, and performance monitoring. These assessments will be reviewed and either accepted or rejected depending on the criteria defined within the governance framework.

## Dispensation

A compliance assessment can be rejected when the subject area (design, operational, service level, or technology) is not compliant. In such circumstances, interim conformance can be achieved in one of two ways:

- The subject area can be adjusted or realigned to meet the compliance requirements.
- The subject area can request a dispensation.

Dispensations are granted for a given time period, during which a set of identified service and operational criteria must be enforced. Dispensations are not granted indefinitely, but are used as a mechanism to ensure that service levels and operational levels are met while providing a level of flexibility in their implementation and timing. The time-bound nature of dispensations ensures that they are a major trigger in the compliance cycle.

## Monitoring and Reporting

Performance management is required to ensure that both the operational and service elements are managed against an agreed-upon set of criteria. This will include monitoring against service- and operational-level agreements, feedback for adjustment, and reporting.

### Business Control

Business control relates to the processes invoked to ensure compliance with the organization's business policies.

### Environment Management

The environment management process identifies all the services required to ensure that the repository-based environment underpinning the governance framework is effective and efficient. These services include physical and logical repository management, access, communication, and accreditation and the training of all users.

The governance environment will have a number of administrative processes defined to facilitate a managed service and process environment. These processes will include user management, internal SLAs (defined in order to control its own processes), and management information reporting.

## Summary

This chapter focuses on the authorities and responsibilities for the control and oversight of the EA. This control and oversight ensures EA development, implementation, and maintenance practices are followed, and action is taken to remedy any situations or circumstances that may arise in the process. A generic governance framework is presented and discussed in detail to provide a basic introduction to EA governance components. Because the DoDAF does not provide specific governance guidance, a summary of TOGAF 9.2 EA governance guidance is provided. However, care must be taken when applying TOGAF guidance to business driven EAs since TOGAF guidance is oriented towards IT driven architectures.

## Questions

1. Does your enterprise have a CIO and a chief architect? If so, what are their EA governance responsibilities and authorities? If not, outline what you think their EA governance responsibilities and authorities should be.

2. Outline the elements of an EA governance organization that your enterprise has or what you think they should be.

3. What EA-related measurements does your enterprise use? Who decides what these measurements should be? What processes are used to collect and report the measurements, and who is responsible for executing these processes?

4. What EA standards does your enterprise have? Who decides what the standards should be? What processes are used to ensure that the standards are complied with? Who is responsible for executing these processes?

5. How is the content of your EA managed? What are the processes and tools for version management? Are there processes and tools for full configuration management? If full configuration management is used, who is the change authority (such as the Chair of the configuration control board)? What groups are responsible for executing the CM processes?

6. What are the policies for managing access to EA information? Who decides what these policies are? Who is responsible for enforcing these policies?

7. Has your enterprise developed any EA principles? If so, are these documented and available to the architecture development team? If not, what do you think some example EA principles could be?

8. Has your enterprise used one of the EA maturity assessment models? If so, what was the result of the assessment? What does this assessment say about the maturity of your EA governance? If not, look at one of the assessment models and make your own assessment as to where your enterprise would rate.

9. Who provides the leadership of your enterprise's EA efforts? Are some of these leaders executive management? If not, how would you plan to get high-level management involved?

# References

Aziz, Sohel, Thomas Obitz, Reva Modi, and Santonu Sarker. 2005. "Enterprise Architecture: A Governance Framework." Paper presented at InfoSys Knowledge Sharing Series web seminar, August 3 and September 6, 2005.

Burke, Brian, and Greta James. 2005. "The Maturity of your Enterprise Architecture Is Key to Its Success." www.gartner.com/doc/486481/maturity-enterprise-architecture-key-success.

CIO Council. 2001. "A Practical Guide to Federal Enterprise Architecture, Version 1.0." www.gao.gov/assets/590/588407.pdf.

Environmental Protection Agency (EPA). 2005–15. "Enterprise Architecture Governance Procedures." EPA Classification Number: CIO 2122-P-01.1. www.epa.gov/sites/production/files/2013-11/documents/cio-2122-p-01.1.pdf.

Government Accountability Office. 2003. "Information Technology. A Framework for Assessing and Improving Enterprise Architecture Management. Version 1.1." (GAO-03-584G).

Office of Management and Budget. 2009. "Enterprise Architecture Assessment Framework (EAAF) 3.1." https://obamawhitehouse.archives.gov/omb/E-Gov/eaaf.

Office of Management and Budget. 2015. OMB Circular A-130: "Managing Information as a Strategic Resource." https://obamawhitehouse.archives.gov/sites/default/files/omb/assets/OMB/circulars/a130/a130revised.pdf.

Organization for Economic Co-operation and Development (OECD). (2004). "OECD Principles of Corporate Governance." www.oecd.org/dataoecd/32/18/31557724.pdf.

Ross, Jeanne W., Peter Weill, and David C. Robertson. 2006. *Enterprise Architecture as Strategy: Creating a Foundation for Business Execution.* Brighton, Massachusetts: Harvard Business School Press.

The Open Group. 2018. "TOGAF Version 9.2." The Netherlands: Van Haren Publishing.

United States Congress. 1974. "Privacy Act of 1974." www.gpo.gov/fdsys/pkg/USCODE-2012-title5/pdf/USCODE-2012-title5-partI-chap5-subchapII-sec552a.pdf.

United States Congress. 2002. "Federal Information Security Management Act of 2002 (FISMA)." Title III of the E-Government Act of 2002 (Pub.L. 107–347, 116 Stat. 2899).

United States Congress. 2015. "Federal Information Technology Acquisition Reform Act (FITARA) – part of the National Defense Authorization Act for Fiscal Year 2015" Title VIII, Subtitle D, H.R. 3979.

# Using the Enterprise Architecture

In Chapter 5, we described three types of conceptual models that are informally used to describe the enterprise in the commercial world. Here's a review:

- **Business model**   Answers the question, "In what ways do we plan to make money or achieve the reasons why our enterprise is in existence?" This model relates to expected revenues, outputs, outcomes, or desired effects from the enterprise in terms of provided goods, services, and value propositions to the target markets and customers. In the military world, the business model is primarily couched in war-fighting capabilities, and competitive advantage is defined as the ability to win a war over an adversary. In fact, capabilities are the unit of planning for military strategic investments.

- **Operating model**   Answers the question, "What are the processes, activities, roles, controls and governances, and other factors that will be brought to bear to produce these goods, services, or value propositions to customers and markets?" The operating model is associated with costs to the enterprise. For a profitable enterprise, the revenues projected by the business model must be in line with and more than the costs anticipated by the operating model and the technology and infrastructure model. In the military world, operational activities are set up around the execution and support of the military mission. The operational model is that of the mission.

- **Technology and infrastructure model**   This model addresses a set of technologies, including information technology as well as the infrastructure of services, networks and transport mechanisms that enable and create new revenues in the business model, and support current operations in the operating model. In the military world, based on Doctrine, Organization, Training, Materiel, Leadership and Education, Personnel, Facilities and Policy (DOTMLPF-P), technology and infrastructure are covered under materiel (military materials and equipment).

In this chapter, we describe how the EA can be used to develop analytical models, support decision-making, and answer questions that are posed against the business model, the operating model, and the technology and infrastructure model. Each of these models poses different issues, concerns, and opportunities for different groups of stakeholders.

- The business model–related aspects are important to business strategists, executive staff, sales and marketing, customer support, and investors, among others.

- The operating model–related aspects are important for management and administration, quality control, engineering, manufacturing, service delivery staff, and service and product help desk staff, among others.

- The technology and infrastructure model–related aspects are important for IT managers; facility managers; and the infrastructure and support organizations for logistics/supply chains and information technology, including communications, applications, data and information storage and movement, transaction processing, customer help desk, and support.

# Some Classes of Enterprise Problems

Though the areas of uses for EA are vast, as are the types of problems enterprises face, we will try to abstract some non-exhaustive classes of problems to illustrate how EA can provide benefits for planning a solution strategy. We also present some subclasses of specific problems under these abstract classes.

## Aligning Technology Infrastructure with Operating Models

In the past, exploding costs for information technology have driven up the cost of IT to a point where its value and benefits need to be balanced against rising cost. One of the earliest federal mandates for IT governance, the Information Technology Reform Act of 1996, recognized this need for alignment and stipulated the role of a CIO as a person reporting the alignment of an agency's IT investments to its business model through development of an EA that showed relationships between the two. Here are some subclasses of this problem:

- Alignment of systems to operational functions, operational activities, and business processes
- Alignment of systems to support of mission-related roles and skills
- Alignment of networks to operational locations
- Alignment of platforms to systems requirements
- Alignment of IT and infrastructure to mobile operational platforms

## Aligning Business Model with Data and Information

An interesting inversion is beginning to occur. In the past, the business model and the operating model drove the capture of data and information required by the business. Today, the large volume of market, customer, operational, and transactional data itself is a source of analysis and discovery. In fact, the collection of data and information is also the driver for predictive analysis—predictions of future behavior of customers and markets—thus driving the ability to shape future enterprise offerings that are capable of taking advantage of that prediction. The EA provides a key representation of the types of information that are collected by the enterprise with relationships to the context in which that information was collected. Here are some subclass problems:

- Definition of new products, services, and value propositions based on observed and analyzed data
- Modifications to current products, services, and value propositions based on observed data
- Rationalizing of product lines based on observed common needs and behaviors

## Modernizing Technology

In today's world of fast emerging threats and discovery of past vulnerabilities, enterprises are constantly forced to upgrade their technology and infrastructure investments. The need to upgrade an investment always brings up several questions: What business aspects (products, services, customers, and markets) are affected by the change? What operating aspects (activities, processes, roles, skill requirements, policies, regulations, and controls) are affected by the change? An EA provides fact-based information on the relationships among business, operations, and IT that support impact analysis of IT changes.

Technology modernization may be as restricted as updating a version of an operating system or as vast as consolidating 16 systems into a single enterprise resource planning (ERP) system. Here are some subclasses of this problem:

- Modernization of computing equipment and software
- Consolidation of systems
- Migration of applications to cloud technology
- Implementation of shared service across multiple enterprises
- Migration to service orientation using services and microservices
- Adoption of cloud technologies to convert capital investment to expense and to benefit from scaling, demand elasticity, and other cloud benefits
- Enablement of a mobile workforce
- Enablement of teleworking on an enterprise-wide scale
- Consolidation of data and information management capabilities

- Facilitation of enterprise-wide structured and unstructured data access, search, aggregation, and content transformation
- Management of data sets tending to infinity
- Protection of enterprise-wide e-mails and messaging
- Implementation of an information security strategy
- Facilitation of upgrades of interoperability for data exchange, interconnection, and application handshaking
- Adoption of industry and de facto technology standards across the enterprise

## Modernizing Process

As new ways of business emerge, as new types of equipment become available, and as new opportunities for offloading previously performed services arise, enterprises begin to consider process modernization by upgrading portions or entire operations. Drivers for these come from increasingly prohibitive cost structures for existing processes; technology obsolescence of equipment; pressure from customers to provide cheaper, faster, better services and products; or changes in the value proposition because of sclerotic processes. The EA records current business processes, functions, and activities with varying levels of detail on performers of activities, inputs, and outputs, enabling mechanisms such as equipment and skill sets, job families and relationships among performers, and roles and skill sets, to cite a few examples. Here are some subclasses of problems under this category that are informed and whose resolution can be assisted by the EA:

- Reengineering business processes
- Retraining the workforce and building skills
- Replacing and upgrading capital equipment
- Changing the enterprise culture
- Shuffling and redistributing process ownership
- Shuffling and redistributing responsibilities

## Capital Planning and Investment Control (CPIC)

As a capital investment, IT assets are durable and capitalized for multiyear service. IT assets do not stand independently but have to interact with and depend on a number of other IT investments. A capital plan for IT is therefore complicated and has to reflect the effect of these dependencies on previous and other future-intended investments. [EPA 2015] Many enterprises have adopted a portfolio management approach for technology and infrastructure capital investments. The portfolio establishes a set of baseline information technology assets that are currently supporting the enterprise: trimming the portfolio as needed to absorb decreases in capital availability, and expanding the portfolio to add new investments that are required based on the needs of the business and operating models. Replacement of investments occurs when elements become obsolete, when vendor support for upgrades ceases, or when performance becomes inadequate because of old technology that is unable to keep up with expectations of performance from the operating or business models. Portfolio management decisions are all affected by dependencies and cost and benefits of the various investment items. The EA provides the required relationships between IT investments and the operating and business model elements they support. Here are some subclasses of the CPIC problem:

- Portfolio management of IT assets on a dashboard
- Development of a capital plan with rationales and justifications for investment decisions
- Development of a capital replacement and improvement roadmap

## Establishing Credible Business Case Analysis for Capital Investments

A business case is a documented justification for a planned new or incremental investment in some capital asset. The capital asset is justified by demonstrating its continued value across its expected lifetime. Developing a business case involves cost-benefit analysis. For example, developing the cost of an IT system involves estimating costs for migration of legacy functions and data; the need for interfaces to provide data from other systems; maintenance and sustainment costs; added burdens on networks, computing, storage capabilities, and added capacity; and skills for the current workforce, to cite a few examples. All of these factors are modeled in the EA and help develop a realistic cost estimate that can be plugged into the capital plan.

Establishing value and benefits for a business investment involves relating the value to specific business functions, operational capabilities, or infrastructure needs—all documented within the EA. By setting up a business case within the context of an EA, the proposer can establish a clearer justification. By rolling up several business cases into a common justification structure, the decision-maker can adjudicate the specific investments that will be funded.

## Changing Enterprise Topology

We use the term "topology" to describe how the enterprise's functions, facilities, people, resources, data and information, computing infrastructure, and network infrastructure are all connected together with links or relationships. Changing the topology can be disruptive to the competition and provide advantage, but it can also cause internal disruption. For example, the DoD has embarked on the concept of a net-centric enterprise—one where everything is connected by digital networks and the war fighter is at "the edge" of the network with authorized access to resources within the network. This is a significant change from isolated groups of war fighters, isolated caches of materiel, and isolated databases of information to a net-centric technology, where users are unknown but need to be authenticated and authorized and where security protections and logical firewalls replace physical isolation. Without the EA representation of the many moving parts, even planning and architecting (and finally implementing in a phased manner) such a transformation is an impossible challenge at the conceptual level. Here are some subclasses of this problem:

- Migrating to IP/VX—from one generation of Internet Protocol standard to a new one
- Changing from a distributed topology to a centralized topology
- Changing from a centralized topology to a distributed topology
- Changing from centralized control to federated control
- Networking for a mobile workforce
- Networking for a teleworking workforce
- Integrating international divisions
- Inserting Wi-Fi technology to replace hardwired networking
- Developing mixed networks of Wi-Fi and wired connections

## "Dissolving" Innovation into the Enterprise

Embracing innovation involves introducing change [Bellman et al. 2016], whether it is in the development of new products, services, or propositions in the business model; improvements in the operating model due to changed processes, locations, resources, or people; or improvements in the technology and infrastructure model due to technology modernization, embracing of standards, cleanup of data and information, or consolidation of systems. Introducing change requires impact assessment and mitigation and change management strategies before change is forced upon the enterprise. EA provides a "breadboard" to superimpose the architecture elements of the planned innovation on to the current EA to assess the impact of change. An impact mitigation and change management plan is created as an outcome of analysis.

## Planning for Enterprise Security

In an environment of global connectedness, and the clear and present danger of foreign actors, local actors, and disgruntled employees wreaking havoc on systems that the enterprise has come to rely upon, security awareness pervades all aspects of planning and implementation in the enterprise. Physical security involves securing physical access to facilities, equipment, and locations. Securing personnel against social engineering and other attacks requires understanding the nature of roles, allocation of specific people to roles, and the association of roles to other aspects of the enterprise. Data and information security may deal with encrypted transmissions, encrypted storage, and imposition of security controls on data access, data transfer, and other means. The EA provides a "big picture" context for defining a security strategy that is more comprehensive than one restricted to information security alone. The three types of security controls—preventative, detective, and reactive—may then be implemented across the entire architecture. (A highly recommended source for security is Sherwood's book *Enterprise Security Architecture: A Business-Driven Approach* published in 2005. Users of SABSA developed an association with yearly conferences and its own certification process. SABSA has been accepted by The Open Group and TOGAF as a standard for security.)

## Reorganizing or Reallocating Responsibilities

Changing the organizational structure of an enterprise is sometimes a necessary component of enterprise transformation. Trying to change entrenched cultures, reassign responsibilities in a manner more suited to the roles of the players, and reassigning functions that were assigned reactively when events and changes adversely impacted the enterprise—these are all situations that have a cascading impact on a number of factors such as new needs for skills, training, process changes, information requirement changes, and corresponding changes in information flows and work products, to name a few. Using the EA provides the planner with knowledge of relationships that radiate from specific roles and performers to various architecture elements of the enterprise.

## Managing Information Asset Inventory

As enterprises grow in size and complexity, the number of information assets start to multiply. As responsibilities get diffuse and distributed, locations grow more remote, and assets are spread throughout the enterprise, keeping track of and managing information assets becomes increasingly difficult. When these assets include multimillion-dollar systems and a mix of systems currently used, systems that are being phased out, and systems that are being planned, the importance of keeping an up-to-date inventory of information assets—typically called an information resource catalog—becomes increasingly important. Every item in the inventory requires contextual data such as the owning organization, points of contact, last upgrades and activities performed, and so on. This in turn requires an inventory of organizations and persons who need to be uniquely identified and serve as metadata for information assets. The EA naturally provides all the dimensions of metadata that are required to locate and interpret information asset inventories.

## Summary of Problem Classes

All of these problem classes (and subclasses) fall into two major categories: effective transformation of the enterprise from a current state to a desired target state and effective management of the enterprise in terms of efficiencies, effectiveness, control, and evolution. Another category—enterprise creation and evolution for startup enterprises—is the subject for another book. In subsequent sections, we characterize various uses of DoDAF viewpoints and views for enterprise transformation, management, and planning for the classes of problems discussed previously.

# DoDAF Viewpoints and Uses

In the DoDAF, what we commonly and approximately called the business model, the operating model, and the technology and infrastructure model are divided up into many specific individual views that are categorized by the eight standard DoDAF viewpoints.

The commercial strategic activities, such as competitive assessment, definition/recognition of markets and customer sets, definition of products and services for commercial benefit, and so on, are outside the purview of the DoDAF. Military analogies in the strategic world, such as worldwide threat assessments, doctrine formulation, and coalition strategies are undertaken at high levels of the executive branch and involve planning through multiagency collaboration. In essence, the business model for the military community is handed down from the highest chains of command including the commander in chief, the President of the United States and the executive chain of command commonly called the National Command Authority (NCA). The strategic focus of the DoDAF is on identifying and developing military capabilities through a Project Viewpoint and a Capability Viewpoint and relating their relevance to the Operational and other Viewpoints that deal with details of military missions and processes.

Nonetheless, the DoDAF is very relevant for commercial enterprises in the area of the operating model, where capability acquisition from multiple vendors, capability need identification, and capability integration is as much an imperative as the understanding of business processes, and supply chains/logistics of inbound goods and outbound goods and services. The DoDAF also provides strong support for modeling and analyzing the technology and infrastructure model, including embracing current and emerging technology standards and interoperability challenges, projecting vendor support for platforms in the future, inventorying IT assets, standardizing procurements of commodity items, and so on.

The use of each of the DoDAF views for analysis and decision-making varies by viewpoint, interests, and concerns. Specific details of the various viewpoints and views are presented in Part III of this book. In this section, we concentrate on examples of how views can be used for enterprise benefit both in terms of what specific views do and in terms of how sets of views can be used to address specific issues. Note that views from multiple viewpoints can be used together to address specific issues.

## Use of the Capability Viewpoint

The primary functions of the Department of Defense are to train, equip, and organize the military forces. (War fighting is a joint responsibility.) The specifics of how these activities are accomplished are driven by the military capabilities that need to be acquired. Acquiring similar but disparate capabilities independently by each of the military services can significantly increase costs, promote integration challenges and handicap the ability to interoperate in a joint forces environment. The primary purpose of the Capability Viewpoint is to mitigate and overcome these issues prior to the acquisition phase of capabilities through proper planning.

For the planner, the Capability Viewpoint provides the language, architecture elements, and relationships to articulate capability needs, decompose them into a well-ordered taxonomy (CV-2: Capability Taxonomy), relate them to how they support the vision of warfare outcomes and effects (CV-1: Vision) and military activities (CV-6: Capability to

Operational Activities Mapping), and relate capability development to sponsoring organizations (CV-5: Capability to Organizational Development Mapping). When capabilities are delivered as services, CV-7: Capability to Services Mapping enables traceability of a capability requirement to the services that deliver the capability.

Here are some of the uses for Capability Viewpoint views with respect to specific issues:

- **Decomposing complex capability needs**   Breaking down a large, granular, complex capability need into smaller grain capabilities; performing an analysis of smaller capabilities to determine if they are already available and can be integrated to deliver the larger grain capability. Relevant views: CV-1: Vision

- **Sequencing capability development**   Analyzing dependencies between capabilities to determine the order of development for the capability; analyzing the process of development of capabilities to determine whether dependency constraints are violated, and make qualitative assessments of the industrial base that is developing the capabilities to see if the capabilities can be delivered in a timely manner. (Can vendors scale up production? Are they forming a cartel? What are the past histories of delivery?) Relevant views: CV-3: Capability Phasing, CV-4: Capability Dependencies, CV-5: Capability to Organizational Development Mapping

- **Operational impact of capabilities**   Analyzing the relationships between planned capabilities and elements of the operating model that they impact, enable, or eliminate. Relevant views: CV-6: Capability to Operational Activities Mapping

## Use of the Project Viewpoint

Military materiel acquisition is performed through military acquisition programs that often run for multiple years, involve many players, consume millions of dollars, and are complex and complicated (Chapter 2). Acquisition programs comprise a number of projects that produce capability increments as an output. For the sponsor, the program manager, and the acquisition community, the Project Viewpoint deals with a portfolio of related projects that are used to acquire materiel and contains the models that relate projects enumerated within the portfolio to the managing organizations (PV-1: Project Portfolio Relationships) and to the capabilities they develop (PV-3: Project to Capability Mapping) as well as identify project dependencies (PV-2: Project Timelines).

Here are some of the uses for Project Viewpoint views with respect to specific issues:

- **Decomposing complex development projects**   Decomposing a large complex program into a portfolio of smaller independent projects that collaborate to produce the capabilities of the large program. Relevant views: PV-1: Project Portfolio Relationships

- **Sequencing project starts and schedules**   Understanding which project delivers which increment of capability and using the understanding of capability dependencies to detect sequencing anomalies in the project portfolio (because a dependent capability should be developed *after* the capability it is dependent upon). Relevant views: PV-2: Project Timelines, CV-4: Capability Dependencies

- **Understanding project-delivered capability relationships**   Understanding, within a large complex program or across several projects, the capability configurations that the complex of projects produce; this helps the developers of capabilities to perform industrial base analysis (ensuring that there is a viable and sustaining industrial base capable of enduring supply and scale-up) related to supplier capabilities, supplier records, and supplier histories. Relevant views: PV-3: Project to Capability Mapping

## Use of the Operational Viewpoint

Military operations are supported by clearly defined chains of command and by specialized and skill-dependent activities that are performed by experienced and skilled personnel and governed by a set of doctrines, policies, rules, and regulations. For the mission planner, the process planner, and process analyst, the Operational Viewpoint provides the language, architecture elements, and relationships for the creation of mission activity models (OV-5a: Operational Activity Decomposition Tree, OV-5b: Operational Activity Model), the examination of collaborative efforts with coalition forces (OV-5a: Operational Activity Decomposition Tree, OV-6c: Event-Trace Description), the understanding of the handoff of one set of activities from one set of performers to another, and the understanding of information flows between performers in the context of the activities they are performing (OV-2: Operational Resource Flow Description, OV-3: Operational Resource Flow Matrix). The Operational Viewpoint also provides the information needed to analyze operations tempo (the rate at which mission activities burn up resources and stress performers, OV-6c: Event-Trace Description) and analyze and break down the LPRG (law, policy, regulation, and guidance) constraints that limit the scope of an activity (OV-6a: Operational Rules Model). In addition, a pictorial representation of military operations is also supported as OV-1: High-Level Operational Concept Graphic.

Here are some of the uses for Operational Viewpoint views with respect to specific issues:

- **Providing a management overview of operations**   Understanding at a glance the elements of a process, operation, complex activity, or mission. Relevant views: OV-1: High-Level Operational Concept Graphic

- **Identifying performers and resource flows**   Understanding the various players who are involved in a process, operation, or complex activity or mission as well as the players in collaborative/coalition missions; understanding the nature of resources that flow between these players in the context of the activities they are performing. Relevant views: OV-2: Operational Resource Flow Description, OV-3: Operational Resource Flow Matrix, OV-4: Organizational Relationships Chart, OV-6c: Event-Trace Description

- **Identifying the elements of a specific process, mission or operation** Understanding the specific activities, performers, inputs, outputs, constraints for a complex activity, process, mission, or operation. Relevant views: OV-5a: Operational Activity Decomposition Tree, OV-5b: Operational Activity Model

- **Analyzing resource flows** Understanding rate of flows and latencies of resources between performers in the context of activities. Relevant views: OV-6c: Event-Trace Description

- **Analyzing external and internal constraints** Understanding the impact of laws, policies, regulations, and guidance on specific activities, performers, locations, events, and data and information. Relevant views: OV-6a: Operational Rules Model

# Use of the Services Viewpoint

The Services Viewpoint looks at the delivery of functionality as a service. A service is self-contained, does not have implicit dependencies such as shared resources that are not owned by the service, and is treated as a self-standing unit of solution for a capability requirement. Services can represent offerings by the enterprise to customers in a market, it can represent a set of services that are acquired and consumed by the enterprise to support the operating model, or it can represent both. Services themselves can be composed using other services through a process called orchestration. The Services Viewpoint looks at the enterprise's services as a portfolio that delivers the capability requirements described in the Capability Viewpoint (CV-7: Capability to Services Mapping). Large-grain services can be composed of many smaller grain services orchestrated together (SvcV-4: Services Functionality Description); services can exchange resources such as information, materiel, and outputs (SvcV-1: Services Context Description, SvcV-3a: Systems-Services Matrix, SvcV-3b: Services-Services Matrix, SvcV-6: Services Resource Flow Matrix); or they can be sequenced to determine latency and duration factors (SvcV-10c: Services Event-Trace Description). Services can be upgraded or consolidated (SvcV-8: Services Evolution Description). The Services Viewpoint is general in that the services are not restricted to information technology services but can extend to business services—business activities, processes, and functions that are procured as independent units of business capability, such as payroll services.

Here are some of the uses for Services Viewpoint views with respect to specific issues:

- **Decomposing "large grain" services** Breaking a large granular service down into smaller services that can be orchestrated together. Relevant views: SvcV-4: Services Functionality Description, SvcV-1: Services Context Description

- **Analyzing service reusability** Examining the reusability of services across solutions. By maintaining a service taxonomy, identification of reusable services can be accomplished. Relevant views: SvcV-4: Services Functionality Description

- **Understanding service needs and measures** Understanding the relationship between a service and the operational model to develop service level agreements and service quality measures. Relevant views: SvcV-5: Operational Activity to Services Traceability Matrix

- **Analyzing service implementation**  Understanding the underlying transport platforms that host and enable the service; for business services, these include ports, throughput constraints, and others, and can be used for bottleneck flow analysis and detection of choke points in transport. Relevant views: SvcV-2: Services Resource Flow Description

## Use of the Systems Viewpoint

Informally, a system is a collection of capabilities that are implemented to provide value to the enterprise. Systems may comprise smaller systems or may interact with peer systems to collaborate on providing functionality. The Systems Viewpoint is used to understand the entire collection of systems that an enterprise has invested in, as well as interactions of these systems with other systems to draw upon resources such as data and information and trigger collaborative actions (ecosystem). Here are some examples of the types of information in some of the Systems Viewpoint views:

- **SV-1: Systems Interface Description, SV-3: Systems-Systems Matrix, SV-6: Systems Resource Flow Matrix**  How systems within the enterprise interface with each other to exchange information among themselves as well as external systems.

- **SV-2: Systems Resource Flow Description**  How systems and their ecosystem of interfaces are implemented on operating platforms such as servers, networks, and communication links.

- **SV-4: Systems Functionality Description**  What the system functionality is.

- **SV-7: Systems Measures Matrix**  What the system specifications are in terms of performance and other parameters.

- **SV-8: Systems Evolution Description**  How system upgrades, migrations, or consolidations from multiple systems to one or more new systems have been planned.

- **SV-9: Systems Technology and Skills Forecast**  How systems are dependent on vendor product versions and the future roadmap of such investments and dependencies including needed skills upgrades or changes.

- **SV-10a: Systems Rules Model**  What rules constrain system implementation and system operations.

- **SV-10c: Systems Event-Trace Description**  How to trace latency and delays within a system as well as in a System of Systems.

Here are some of the uses for Systems Viewpoint views with respect to specific issues:

- **Decomposing complex systems**  Understanding how to break down a large complex system into subsystems and trace how functionality is divided among these subsystems. Relevant views: SV-4: Systems Functionality Description

- **Determining functional patterns across systems**    Understanding the commonality of the same functions across multiple systems to detect anomalies in business rules or methods of computation. Relevant views: SV-4: Systems Functionality Description

- **Understanding resource dependencies between systems**    Understanding the dependency of one system on other systems to provide resources such as data and information as well as understanding the degree of (or lack of) standardization for interfaces between systems and issues of throughput and bottlenecks and latency. Relevant views: SV-1: Systems Interface Description, SV-6: Systems Resource Flow Matrix

- **Understanding alignment of system function to operational need** Understanding the relationships between the system functionality (automation) and the operations model processes and activities that use the system functions. Relevant views: SV-5a: Operational Activity to Systems Function Traceability Matrix, SV-5b: Operational Activity to Systems Traceability Matrix

- **Analyzing system communication needs**    Understanding how a system uses a combination of network and communication links to deliver functionality to users and connect to other systems from which it draws or for which it provides resources. Relevant views: SV-2: Systems Resource Flow Description

- **Consolidating and simplifying of systems portfolios**    Developing a consolidation strategy for systems that reduces the variety and diversity of multiple systems and combines their functionality into a smaller number of homogenous systems. Relevant views: SV-8: Systems Evolution Description, SV-4: Systems Functionality Description

- **Simplifying platform proliferation and diversity**    Analyzing platform differences across systems in an effort to reduce platform diversity and vendor diversity, and increase the degree of standardization of the infrastructure model. Relevant views: SV-9: Systems Technology and Skills Forecast

- **Assessing cloud migration potential**    Analyzing cloud platform migration potential for systems that are currently running on in-house servers. Relevant views: SV-1: Systems Interface Description, SV-2: Systems Resource Flow Description, SV-6: Systems Resource Flow Matrix, SV-7: Systems Measures Matrix, SV-8: Systems Evolution Description, SV-9: Systems Technology and Skills Forecast

## Use of the Data and Information Viewpoint

Enterprises today are critically dependent on data to formulate and fine-tune the business model; support the activities, processes, and events in the operational model; and provide plumbing for the various systems, applications, and services in the technology and infrastructure model. Data is produced and consumed by several elements in these models, such as activities, systems, functions, and decision points. Data may be replicated or uniquely stored in several locations. The Data and Information Viewpoint is useful for identifying the various types of data required by the business in terms of business terminology that is meaningful in the context of the business model and the operational models (DIV-1: Conceptual Data Model), breaking up a complex business term into fundamentally distinct and standardized components and relationships (DIV-2: Logical Data Model), and providing a blueprint for implementing databases that are stored and processed through machine interactions and encoded binary representations (DIV-3: Physical Data Model).

Here are some of the uses for Data and Information Viewpoint views with respect to specific issues:

- **Producing a "map" of meaningful data**   Recording and representing a map of distinct conceptual data that is required by the business and operational model. These are typically represented as a business glossary and can be traced to specific activities and processes that consume or produce them. Relevant views: DIV-1: Conceptual Data Model

- **Engineering data for quality**   Performing data engineering to reduce business concepts into their lowest common denominator concepts and standardizing these to provide data integrity, prevent inconsistent updates, and maintain unambiguous records. Relevant views: DIV-2: Logical Data Model

- **Managing regulatory compliance for data**   Developing strategies for storing unstructured business data objects and managing records, responding to Freedom of Information Act requests, complying with regulations such as privacy, and protecting individual PII records. Relevant views: DIV-1: Conceptual Data Model

- **Resolving data inconsistencies**   Understanding and analyzing problems that arise in data management due to erroneous, inconsistent, or incomplete rules that prevent data from being stored. Relevant views: DIV-3: Physical Data Model

- **Consolidating and aggregating data from multiple databases**   Understanding the schemas of database systems to develop strategies for data warehousing, predictive data analysis, and other nontransactional data initiatives that work on aggregated and summarized data. Relevant views: DIV-2: Logical Data Model, DIV-3: Physical Data Model

- **Blueprinting data organizational structures**   Generating blueprints for database storage (schemas) and messaging systems that can be implemented as data management solutions or message communication services and maintained as such. Relevant views: DIV-3: Physical Data Model

## Use of the Standards Viewpoint

The Standards Viewpoint is concerned with issues of standards for everything within the enterprise, including IT and non-IT elements. Standards are fundamental to interoperability and collaboration with other enterprises that need to work with your enterprise.

Here are some of the uses for Standards Viewpoint views with respect to specific issues:

- **Consolidating standards across the enterprise**   Developing a map of international, national, industry, and de facto standards that is applicable to the enterprise and can be used to specify requirements when acquiring equipment, software, or materials, for example. Relevant views: StdV-1: Standards Profile

- **Forecasting the direction of standards**   Recording the forecast for standards in technologies of interest to the enterprise to determine timing for technology investments in terms of maturity and standards evolution. Relevant views: StdV-2: Standards Forecast

- **Timing a technology migration risk**   Calibrating the risk of adopting innovative technology by surveying technology forecasting specialists to determine the right time to jump in. Relevant views: StdV-2: Standards Forecast

- **Planning system technology upgrades**   Developing a strategy for systems upgrade in conjunction with a technology upgrade map that is consistent with the enterprise standards and the technology forecast. Relevant views: SV-9: Systems Technology and Skills Forecast, StdV-1: Standards Profile, StdV-2: Standards Forecast

## Use of the All Viewpoint

The DoDAF also defines an eighth viewpoint that does not neatly fit with the other seven viewpoints in terms of usefulness to the business, operating, or technology and infrastructure models. The All Viewpoint serves the needs of the architecture community in communicating the context of an architecting effort and documenting assumptions and constraints. The All Viewpoint summarizes the architecture project to sponsors, other architects, and the enterprise at large by describing the scope, purpose, and deliverables of the architecture effort and provides any conclusions or recommendations from analysis. The architecture AV-1: Overview and Summary Information and the AV-2: Integrated Dictionary serve to provide comprehensive documentation on the architecture project itself and make the architecture understandable.

# Summary

Remember that an EA is a tool for supporting decision-making. In reality, problems are solved by decision-makers, planners, and implementers who can use the EA as a common knowledgebase and a set of shared terminology and vocabulary to communicate effectively. Viewpoints and views are specific mechanisms to convey the scope of various aspects of a large problem to a specific set of stakeholders who have a specific set of questions, issues, and concerns.

This chapter has reviewed some of the common ways in which EA is used, by describing various classes of problems that can benefit from EA assistance. There are many other ways in which EA can be used. Many times the various architecture stakeholders (users of the architecture) have different decisions that they will be using the EA to support. This multiplicity of uses is the reason that planning for your EA is so important. Understanding the various ways in which the stakeholders plan to use EA information and how that information will be used in decision-making processes is vital to generating a useful EA.

## Questions

1. Who are the architecture users in your organization? What decisions are made with input from an architecture? What level of architecture (enterprise, segment, or solution) is this input from?

2. Which of the classes of enterprise problems does your enterprise face? Are there other classes of problems as well? Which viewpoints do those problem classes require?

3. What classes of problems described in this section are touched by an enterprise business process engineering or reengineering effort?

4. How would you use the EA to address security planning for the enterprise?

5. What is portfolio management of IT assets? How does EA help manage the portfolio? What are the steps to add new investments, discontinue existing investments, or rebalance the portfolio?

6. How does your organization manage organizational change—that is, what is the process for revising or developing new organizational structures? Is EA information used in this process? What EA data is or would be useful in this process?

7. Does your organization use a business process reengineering process when business processes need to be upgraded or changed? If so, does this process address reorganization? What EA information is used in the process and how are the multiple domains of change coordinated?

8. Have you participated in any transition planning activities for your own organization or for any customers? If so, how many domains of change were involved? How many intermediate stages were used to help phase the transition? What types of architecture data were used in transition planning? Would the existence of a documented architecture have helped with the planning process?

## References

Bellman, Beryl, Ann Reedy, and Prakash Rao. 2016. "Enterprise Architecture Patterns for Innovation," XXVII ISPIM Innovation Conference, Porto Portugal, 19–22 June 2016. http://ispim.org/members/proceedings/ISPIM2016/documents/745928996_Paper.pdf.

Department of Defense. 2009. Department of Defense Architecture Framework Version 2.0. http://dodcio.defense.gov/Library/DoD-Architecture-Framework.

Environmental Protection Agency (EPA). 2015. "Capital Planning and Investment Control Procedures for the Office of Management and Budget Exhibits." EPA Classification Number: CIO 2120-P-02.1 www.epa.gov/sites/production/files/2015-12/documents/cio_2120-p-02.1.pdf.

Federal Enterprise Architecture Program Management Office. 2006. "The Federal Enterprise Architecture Security and Privacy Profile Version 2.0." http://bettergovernment.jp/resources/Security_and_Privacy_Profile_v2.pdf.

Government Accountability Office. 2003. "Information Technology. A Framework for Assessing and Improving Enterprise Architecture Management. Version 1.1." (GAO-03-584G). www.gao.gov/products/GAO-03-584G.

Government Accountability Office. 2004. "Information Technology Investment Management: A Framework for Assessing and Improving Process Maturity, Version 1.1" (GAO-04-0394G) www.gao.gov/assets/80/76790.pdf.

National Institute of Standards and Technology (NIST). 2013. SP 800-53: "Security Controls for Federal Information Systems." https://nvlpubs.nist.gov/nistpubs/specialpublications/nist.sp.800-53r4.pdf.

Office of Management and Budget. 2015. OMB Circular A-130: "Managing Information as a Strategic Resource." https://obamawhitehouse.archives.gov/sites/default/files/omb/assets/OMB/circulars/a130/a130revised.pdf.

Office of Management and Budget. 2016. OMB Circular A-11: "Preparation, Submission, and Execution of the Budget." https://obamawhitehouse.archives.gov/sites/default/files/omb/assets/a11_current_year/a11_2016.pdf.

Ovans, Andrea. 2015. "What Is a Business Model?" *Harvard Business Review*, January 23, 2015. Retrieved 11/9/2017 from https://hbr.org/2015/01/what-is-a-business-model.

Sherwood, John, Andrew Clark, and David Lynas. 2005. *Enterprise Security Architecture: A Business-Driven Approach*. San Francisco: CRC Press.

Songini, Marc. 2005. "Irish Agency Halts Work on Two SAP Application Projects." *Computerworld*, Oct. 17, 2005. www.computerworld.com/article/2558350/app-development/irish-agency-halts-work-on-two-sap-application-projects.html.

United States Congress. 1996. "Information Technology Reform Act of 1996 (Clinger Cohen Act.)" Public Law 104-106 February 10, 1996. http://dodcio.defense.gov/Portals/0/Documents/ciodesrefvolone.pdf.

Zachman, John A. "About the Zachman Framework." www.zachman.com/about-the-zachman-framework.

# PART III

# Viewpoints and Views

# Introduction to Viewpoints and Views

Chapters 12 through 20 provide a detailed look at the DoDAF viewpoints and views and include example views based on our case study from Chapter 3. This chapter provides a quick overview of the DoDAF viewpoints and views that were introduced in Chapter 4, an introduction to the format and content of Chapters 12–20, plus some context for the case study examples. An introduction to the entities of the DoDAF ontology (the DoDAF Metamodel 2, or DM2) is also included to set the stage for view integration discussions that are included in Chapters 12–20. Most of these entities have already been introduced in Chapter 4.

## Views, Models, Pictures, and Artifacts

In Chapter 1 we introduced the concept of pictures and drew the distinction between models and pictures. Pictures in themselves are not a universal means of communication, though they are often used to surmount the barriers of the spoken or written language. The symbols and the semantic objects that the symbols represent are not readily understood or obvious unless conventions are used to enforce commonality of interpretation. Architecture frameworks such as the DoDAF, FEAF2, and TOGAF recommend specific types of views to promote commonality of architecture representations. Because these frameworks also tend to be methodology agnostic (they do not prescribe use of any particular methodology that is specific to the framework), they offer a choice of methodologies for constructing the views. For example, enterprises are free to use Business Process Modeling Notation (BPMN) or ICAM Definition for Functional Modeling (IDEF0) to develop OV-5b: Operational Activity Models (DoDAF), a process flow diagram (TOGAF), or a business process diagram (FEAF2).

In Chapter 1, we also introduced the concept of architecture frameworks that comprise multiple viewpoints, each containing multiple views. Viewpoints and views serve to provide representations that answer questions for different groups of stakeholders. The views may also be overlapped to indicate related concerns between two different groups of stakeholders. In Chapters 12–19, we discuss in detail the viewpoints and views of the DoDAF as well as equivalent views within TOGAF and FEAF2. In Chapter 20, we discuss how the standard viewpoints and views within a framework can be extended to incorporate additional viewpoints and views that overlap with the elements of the existing framework.

## Tailoring of Views

A view is an architectural representation that addresses the concerns of a specific type of stakeholder. Tailoring a view involves the following:

- Adding properties to specify items such as measures to support the intended analysis for the architecture
- Adding relationships that are required to provide a fuller picture than the basic scope of the view

The availability of a large number of views within an architecture framework discourages tailoring, where one type of view with tailoring may replace another existing view.

The DoDAF allows for definition of custom views, called Fit-for-Purpose (FFP) views that enable architects to combine architecture elements in a manner that serves to explain various aspects of the architecture. A FFP view is not intended to replace the standard views of the DoDAF, nor is it intended to violate the relationships between architecture elements as established in the DoDAF metamodel.

# Review of DoDAF Viewpoints and Views

The DoDAF includes eight viewpoints, each of which contains two or more views. These viewpoints are listed here, together with the number of views they contain. The DoDAF also allows for FFP views that are constructed by combining one or more views to provide an aggregated or consolidated picture for stakeholder audiences. This list summarizes the material in Table 4-1 in Chapter 4.

- **All Viewpoint**    Provides overall information for the architecture, including an executive-level overview and detailed definitions of all terms used in the architecture. This viewpoint is used by all architecture stakeholders. Contains two views.

- **Capability Viewpoint**    Documents the desired or required capabilities of the enterprise, their relationships, delivery timing, and deployment context, as well as the relationship of capabilities to operational activities and services. This viewpoint is of primary interest to executive management. Contains seven views.

- **Project Viewpoint**    Documents project portfolios, project interdependencies, and relationships to the capabilities. This viewpoint is of primary interest to executives and business and portfolio managers. Contains three views.

- **Operational Viewpoint**    Documents both the structural aspects of operational processes and the behavioral aspects of operations in terms of scenarios, rules, and state transitions. This viewpoint is of primary interest to the business manager and operational personnel. Contains six overall views, with views 5 and 6 having subparts.

- **Systems Viewpoint**   Documents the enterprise's systems, their functions, their dynamic behaviors, how they are interconnected, what resources they exchange, when they become available, and how they relate to operational activities. This viewpoint is of primary interest to IT personnel. Contains ten views, with views 5 and 10 having subparts.

- **Services Viewpoint**   Documents the business and IT services of the enterprise, including service functions, service behavior, service interfaces and service level agreements (SLAs), service interconnections, resources exchanged, and time of availability. This viewpoint is of primary interest to business managers (for business services) and IT personnel (for IT services). Contains ten views, with views 3 and 10 having subparts.

- **Data and Information Viewpoint**   Documents conceptual, logical, and physical models for shared, structured enterprise data. This viewpoint may be of interest to business managers, operational personnel, and IT personnel, depending on the level of detail included. Contains three views.

- **Standards Viewpoint**   Documents the enterprise technical standards including the systems or services these standards should apply to and the time frames within which the standards should be applied. This viewpoint is of primary interest to IT personnel and to business managers involved in acquisition. Contains two views.

The new Object Management Group (OMG) Unified Architecture Framework (UAF) will be covered briefly in Chapter 20. The new and different viewpoints it appears to contain are based on the ontology the UAF provides. This ontology supports DoDAF and other related defense frameworks, such as the NATO Architectural Framework (NAF), by using appropriate profiles.

# Organization of the Viewpoint Chapters

Each of Chapters 12–19 covers a DoDAF viewpoint and contains examples, based on the RMN Airport Case Study, of all the views or subparts in that viewpoint. Each view example includes a discussion of what the view or subpart is used for, what sort of options or tailoring might be used with the view, and how the view should integrate with the other views in the architecture.

## View Information at a Glance

A filled-in version of the following table is provided for each view in a viewpoint. The View Short Name area provides the code for the view, such as "CV-1" for the Capability Viewpoint first view, Vision. Remember that the ordering of the views within a viewpoint is arbitrary and has no hidden significance. The Other Names and Alternatives area lists alternative names for the views from DoDAF-related frameworks such as MODAF and similar views from other frameworks such as TOGAF and FEAF2. The Formal Modeling Methodology area provides information on the usual representation technique for the view, including any formal modeling techniques used. The contents of the Integration section is discussed in the following paragraphs.

| View Information at a Glance |
| --- |
| View Short Name |
| Name |
| Other Names and Alternatives |
| Viewpoint |
| View Intent |
| View Audience |
| Formal Modeling Methodology |
| Integration of View with other Views |

## View Integration

This notion of integration is key to achieving a useful architecture. Integration involves consistency: for example, if you see a view with system entities in it, then any time you see another view with system entities in it, the names of the system entities in both views should be the same or should align in a reasonable manner. If you have two views, say SV-1 and SV-2, and the system names are not the same (or cannot be identified as being the subsets of one another by looking in the AV-2: Integrated Dictionary), then the architecture is not integrated. Nonintegrated views depict disjoint representations of reality and identify a problem with the architecture; until the problem is resolved, the architecture cannot be used for decision-making.

You can use the integration relationships when reviewing architectures for consistency and completeness. When reviewing a specific view, check to see if it is integrated with the other views contained in the architecture as it is supposed to be. If the views aren't integrated, then there is a consistency problem with the architecture. Similarly, if the architecture, or in some cases an overarching architecture (an enterprise- or segment-level architecture) does not contain any of the other views the specific view is supposed to integrate with, then the architecture is probably incomplete. In other words, the architecture contains at least one view that is not related to any other view in the architecture. The architecture needs to be integrated to present consistent and sufficiently complete information to support decision-making.

## Review of Ontology Entities

We introduced the DoDAF ontology—DM2—in Chapter 4 through a series of diagrams (Figures 4-4 through 4-8), which showed the basic entity names and relationships. As a review, we provide a list the DM2 entities (types) here. Their relationships become clear through a study of the views.

The DM2 contains the core concepts of the DoDAF:

- **Activity** Work, not specific to a single organization, weapon system, or individual that transforms inputs (resources) into outputs (resources) or changes their state.
- **Resource** Data, information, performers, materiel, or personnel types that are produced or consumed.
  - **Materiel** Equipment, apparatuses, or supplies that are of interest, without distinction as to their application for administrative or combat purposes.
  - **Information** The state of a something of interest that is materialized—in any medium or form—and communicated or received.
  - **Data** Representation of information in a formalized manner suitable for communication, interpretation, or processing by humans or by automatic means. Examples could be whole models, packages, entities, attributes, classes, domain values, enumeration values, records, tables, rows, columns, and fields.
  - **Person Type** A category of persons defined by the role or roles they share that are relevant to an architecture.
- **Architectural description** Information describing an architecture, such as OV-5b: Operational Activity Model.
- **Performer** Any entity—human, automated, or any aggregation of human and/or automated—that performs an activity and provides a capability.
- **Organization** A specific real-world assemblage of people and other resources organized for an ongoing purpose.
- **System** A functionally, physically, and/or behaviorally related group of regularly interacting or interdependent elements.
- **Service** A mechanism to enable access to a set of one or more capabilities, where the access is provided using a prescribed interface and is exercised consistent with constraints and policies as specified by the service description. The mechanism is a performer. The capabilities provided are access to resources—information, data, materiel, performers, and locations.
- **Capability** The ability to achieve a desired effect under specified (performance) standards and conditions through combinations of ways and means (activities and resources) to perform a set of activities.
- **Condition** The state of an environment or situation in which a performer performs.
- **Desired effect** A desired state of a resource.
- **Measure** The magnitude of some attribute of an individual.
- **Measure type** A category of measures.
- **Location** A point or extent in space that may be referred to physically or logically.

PART III

- **Guidance** An authoritative statement intended to lead or steer the execution of actions.

- **Rule** A principle or condition that governs behavior; a prescribed guide for conduct or action.

- **Agreement** A consent among parties regarding the terms and conditions of activities that said parties participate in.

- **Standard** A formal agreement documenting generally accepted specifications or criteria for products, processes, procedures, policies, systems, and/or personnel.

- **Project** A temporary endeavor undertaken to create resources or desired effects.

- **Vision** An end that describes the future state of the enterprise, without regard to how it is to be achieved; a mental image of what the future will or could be like.

- **Skill** The ability, resulting from one's knowledge, practice, aptitude, and so on, to do something well.

Figure 11-1 shows the conceptual data model for the DM2 that represents these entities in terms of key relationships.

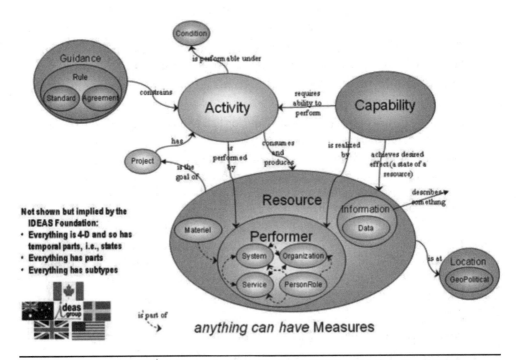

**Figure 11-1** Diagram of DIV-1: Conceptual Data Model for DM2 (graphic from the DoDAF)

# Case Study Example Context

The view examples in Chapters 12–19 will all be based on the RMN Airport Case Study. The view examples may come from the RMN Airport Enterprise Level architecture, the Passenger Management Segment Level architecture, or the Passenger Identification Solution Level architecture, depending on a level appropriate for the viewpoint or view. So, for example, the Capability Viewpoint and Project Viewpoint view examples will be based on the RMN Airport Enterprise Level architecture. The view examples may be simplified or partial because of space and scope considerations, as many of the complete examples would be large and complex.

# Summary

This chapter provides a quick overview of the DoDAF vewipoints and views plus other material that sets the context of and presents the format for material in Chapters 12–20. This additional material includes an overview of the organization of the viewpoints in Chapters 12–20, including a review of the concept of architecture integration; a review of the DoDAF Metamodel entities; and an identification of the specific architecture levels that the view examples in Chapters 12–20 will be drawn from.

# References

Department of Defense. 2009. DoD Architecture Framework Version 2.0. "Volume 1: Introduction, Overview, and Concepts." http://dodcio.defense.gov/Portals/0/Documents/DODAF/DoDAF%20V2%20-%20Volume%201.pdf.

Department of Defense. 2009. DoD Architecture Framework Version 2.0. "Volume 2: Architectural Data and Models." http://dodcio.defense.gov/Portals/0/Documents/DODAF/DoDAF%20V2%20-%20Volume%202.pdf.

Department of Defense. "DM2 – DoDAF Meta-Model: The DM2 Conceptual Data Model." http://dodcio.defense.gov/Library/DoD-Architecture-Framework/dodaf20_conceptual/. Retrieved on 1/12/2018.

**PART III**

# CHAPTER 12

# All Viewpoint

This viewpoint is called the All Viewpoint for good reason—it provides all the information you need to understand and interpret all the other viewpoints included in an architecture. The All Viewpoint provides an executive summary of the architecture and development effort and detailed definitions and explanations of all the terms used in the architecture. The All Viewpoint provides essential support to the repository that must hold all the architecture data from all the viewpoints and to the architecture development team that has to develop an integrated architecture and must coordinate and integrate many viewpoints and views.

The All Viewpoint is where we state the scope of an architecture effort in terms of coverage, the types of questions it is supposed to answer, and the key stakeholders involved in terms of the sponsors of the architecture effort. These sponsors and stakeholders participate in the architecture development and ultimately in its deployment as a solution or a collection of solutions to business problems.

The All Viewpoint content corresponds to information developed in the TOGAF Architecture Vision phase of the Architecture Development Methodology (ADM) that includes views such as the solution concept diagram, the stakeholder map matrix, and the value chain diagram. (See Chapter 22.)

The All Viewpoint content also corresponds to information developed in step 1 of the Collaborative Planning Methodology in the FEAF2. In step 1, the scope and purpose of the architecture is defined and the stakeholders and their needs are identified. This step is responsible for identifying the major drivers for change and defining, validating, and prioritizing the operational realities of the mission and goals with leadership, stakeholders, and operational staff. (See Chapter 23.)

## Introduction to the Views in the All Viewpoint

The All Viewpoint contains two views: AV-1: Overview and Summary Information and AV-2: Integrated Dictionary. These views are introduced in this section. Details of the All Viewpoint views and examples are provided in subsequent sections.

## AV-1: Overview and Summary Information

The Overview and Summary Information view (see Figure 12-1) is a living document that contains a current overview of the architecture form and contents. As such, it contains much of the information developed in the first four steps of the Six-Step Process, such as the architecture purpose, the scope of the architecture, and the views contained in the architecture (see Chapter 5). The AV-1 describes the assumptions and constraints that bound the architecture effort. The AV-1 is usually started as the first view of the architecture development, and it should be updated as the development proceeds and iteration through the Six-Step Process results in changes to the views being developed or changes to their details. As releases of the architecture occur, the AV-1 should be updated with the findings and recommendations associated with the release. The AV-1 usually also has a high-level schedule outlining the planned release dates for the architecture.

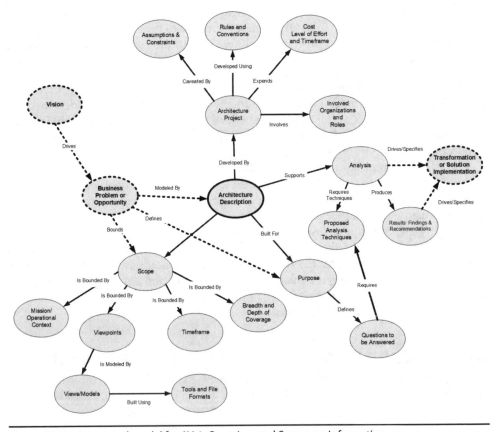

**Figure 12-1**   Integrated model for AV-1: Overview and Summary Information

The AV-1 acts simultaneously as an advertising document, an informative abstract, and an executive summary for the architecture. It also describes the types of planned analysis during development or after the architecture is developed, and at the end of each release of the architecture effort, it is used for recording analysis results, findings, and recommendations for future actions. The AV-1 is also frequently expanded to provide the development plan for the architecture, including such information as configuration management, versioning, and release.

## AV-2: Integrated Dictionary

The Integrated Dictionary view is an authoritative and integrated dictionary for all architecture elements or terms used in all views that support all viewpoints (see Figure 12-2). The AV-2 is not a simple glossary nor is it restricted to a single view, although extracts from the AV-2 may be presented with each view in hard-copy documents to make reading easier. The integrated dictionary forces disparate elements from multiple views to be resolved by the modeling teams and presents consistent and distinct architecture elements. The AV-2 may also contain taxonomies (classification schemes) for architecture elements to provide abstraction hierarchies that enable integration of detailed views with abstract views. The AV-2 may also contain semantic relationships. The AV-2 is the place for the architect to document any additional information he or she believes is important for understanding the architecture elements.

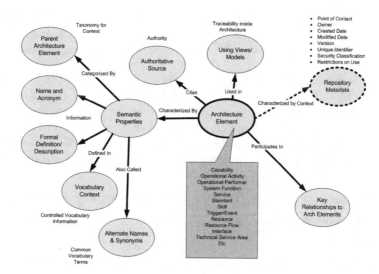

**Figure 12-2**
Integrated
model for AV-2:
Integrated
Dictionary

The AV-2: Integrated Dictionary view is usually generated in a tabular format with a long list of architecture elements, their acronyms expanded, their descriptions, authoritative sources that are the origins of the definitions, and a cross-reference of usage of architecture elements in the various views of the architecture description. Many architecture tools automatically generate the AV-2 as a byproduct of architecture development but the ultimate burden of ensuring an integrated architecture, that is, the consistent use of architecture elements across views, still falls on the architect. This is also true for architecture repositories that generate the AV-2 automatically for a specific architecture. The AV-2 is one of the most labor-intensive views in the architecture, even with automated support. This means that entries should be developed or updated as the other views are developed, with conflicts resolved as quickly as possible.

The AV-2 is a valuable tool for the architecture integrator—the person or persons responsible for delivering an integrated architecture. When the same architecture element is named differently in different views, integration does not occur. Analysis will be faulty, as the intersection of common elements across views will not occur and any searching and querying method returns incomplete information. It is recommended that the AV-2 be continuously generated throughout the architecture development and efforts expended to ensure that the architecture elements are constantly reviewed for consistency, especially if multiple people are developing different views at different locations and bringing them together for integration.

## Alternative Views

In TOGAF 9.2, additional views are recommended to support the Preliminary phase and the Architecture Vision phase of the Architecture Development Methodology (ADM), where the All Viewpoint views are developed. The additional views are listed here:

- **Architecture Vision**  Created early on in the project life cycle and provides a high-level, aspirational view of the end architecture product. The purpose of the vision is to agree at the outset what the desired outcome should be for the architecture, so that architects can then focus on the critical areas to validate feasibility. Providing an Architecture Vision also supports stakeholder communication by providing an executive summary version of the full architecture definition.

- **Principles Catalog**  Lists the guiding principles for architecture development.

- **Stakeholder Map Matrix**  Depicts the stakeholders and their roles in the architecture.

In the TOGAF, the architecture repository plays the part of and stores the Integrated Dictionary (AV-2). In addition, the architecture requirements specification is an important document that acts as a companion to the Overview and Summary Information (AV-1). The architecture roadmap lists individual increments of change and lays them out on a timeline to show progression from the baseline architecture to the target architecture. The architecture roadmap forms a key component of transition architectures and is incrementally developed throughout phases B, C, D, E, and F within the ADM.

Another important view that supports the All Viewpoint is the request for architecture work (TOGAF) or a statement of work (federal) that describes the tasks that are to be performed during the architecture development. "The Statement of Architecture Work defines the scope and approach that will be used to complete the architecture development cycle. The Statement of Architecture Work is typically the document against which successful execution of the architecture project will be measured and may form the basis for a contractual agreement between the supplier and consumer of architecture services" (TOGAF Version 9.2, p 363).

# AV-1: Overview and Summary Information

The AV-1 can be short and provide the minimum metadata related to an architecture development. It can also be a long and comprehensive description of the context of the architecture with a detailed description of the problem that is being addressed by and the details of the architecture development. Many enterprises standardize the format of the AV-1 to enable uniform registration of multiple architectures using similar attributes. An integrated architecture repository that is used to automatically generate the text-based AV-1 will also enforce this discipline.

| View Information at a Glance | |
| --- | --- |
| View short name | AV-1 |
| Name | Overview and Summary Information |
| Other names | Business problem statement (federal) <br> Architecture definition document (TOGAF) |
| Viewpoint | All |
| View intent | Summarize the purpose, scope, and viewpoints and views of the architecture; present results of analysis, findings, and recommendations for actions based on analysis; can include architecture project-related details such as duration, involved personnel, and level of effort |
| View audience | Sponsors of the architecture effort; all people with an interest in getting a broad and brief view of the overall architecting effort |
| Formal modeling methodology | None. Usually a text-based document that is unstructured and descriptive. An enterprise-wide standard template will help standardize recording of the AV-1 and facilitate the loading of repositories with homogenous data structures. A structured version of the AV-1 can be used to store architecture descriptions inside a registry for supporting discovery of architectures. This method is employed by the Defense Architecture Registry System (DARS) to collect and publish architecture descriptions of various architectures developed throughout the DoD. |
| Integration of view with other views | Describes elements of scope that are shared by all other architecture viewpoints and views. The span of performers, activities, capabilities, services, systems, locations, and other architecture elements must match the contents. |

Table 12-1 shows an example short-form template for the AV-1.

| *Architectural Description Identification* |
|---|
| Name of the architecture |
| Name of the architect |
| Name of the organization developing the architectural description |
| List of assumptions and constraints |
| Approval authority |
| Architecture completion date |
| Description of the level of effort required |
| *Scope* |
| Viewpoints addressed by the architecture representation |
| Views developed (with option details) |
| Time frame addressed by architecture such as by specific years or by designations such as "current," "target," or transitional |
| Organizational entities that fall within the scope of the architectural description |
| *Purpose and Perspective* |
| The need that drives the development of the architectural description |
| The types of analyses that will be applied to the architecture |
| Who is expected to perform the analyses |
| What decisions are expected to be made based of each form of analysis |
| Who is expected to make those decisions |
| What actions are expected to result |
| The perspective from which the architectural description is developed |
| *Context* |
| Mission addressed by the architecture |
| Doctrine |
| Relevant goals and vision statements |
| Concepts of operation |
| Scenarios |
| Information assurance context (such as types of system or service data to be protected, such as classified or sensitive but unclassified, and expected information threat environment) |
| Other threats and environmental conditions |
| Geographical areas addressed, where applicable |

**Table 12-1**   AV-1 Sample Architecture Overview and Summary Template

Authoritative sources for the standards, rules, criteria, and conventions that are used in the architecture

Any linkages to related architecture efforts

**Status**

Status of the architecture at the time of publication or development of the AV-1 (which might precede the architectural development itself); status includes creation, update, validation, and assurance activities.

**Tools and File Formats Used**

Tool suite used to develop the architectural description

Filenames and formats for the architectural views if appropriate

**Architecture Development Schedule**

Start date

Development milestones and release dates

Date completed

**Findings**

Findings and recommendations that have been developed based on the architectural effort. Examples of findings include identification of shortfalls, recommended system implementations, and opportunities for technology insertion.

**Costs**

Architecture budget

Cost projections, or actual costs that have been incurred in developing the architecture and/or undertaking the analysis, which may include integration costs, equipment costs, and other costs.

**Table 12-1**    AV-1 Sample Architecture Overview and Summary Template *(continued)*

When views are identified in the AV-1, the information on the view should not just identify the name of the view (in terms of the selected framework) but also the specific format or formal modeling technique being used. If an unusual modeling technique or format is used, a reference to a description of the technique or format should be included. The intent of this element of the AV-1 is to let the reader understand what to expect in terms of the architecture contents and what background or expertise may be necessary to read, understand, and interpret the views.

## Example: Richard M Nixon Airport Enterprise Architecture (RMN-EA) Overview and Summary Information

The following example shows an AV-1 for the RMN Airport Enterprise Level architecture. This AV-1 is intended to be a foundational document for a multiyear enterprise transformation. The primary purpose of the AV-1 is to establish a lasting and living directional document for EA development and for communications with executive and business management as well as other stakeholders. General background for the RMN Airport Case Study can be found in Chapter 3.

## Architectural Description Identification

**Name of architecture:** Richard M. Nixon International Airport Enterprise Level Architecture (RMN-ELA)

**Name of the architect:** Chief Architect, RMN Airport

**Name of the organization developing the architectural description:** RMN Airport Enterprise Architecture Department

**List of assumptions and constraints:**

- **Assumptions** RMN must comply with regulations from the following organizations: Federal Aviation Administration for Flight Safety and Air Traffic Management; Department of Homeland Security and Transportation Safety Administration for Passenger, Baggage, and Cargo–related constraints as well as requirements for airport terminal safety; state, county, and city regulations for local ordinances related to noise pollution, traffic, and other items; Environmental Protection Agency for hazardous cargo, pollution, disposals; OSHA for occupational safety and health of airport staff and contract personnel; Sarbanes-Oxley for fiscal and operational transparency of RMN operations.

- **Constraints** For the first version of the EA, only limited access to stakeholders and subject matter experts is available because of unavailable time or access and insufficient resources to canvass and arrange interviews and set up post-processing of interview results. RMN is an ongoing operation where execution of activities takes precedence to EA and planning-related activities that are perceived as peripheral and potentially counterproductive. Until the EA can produce results that command attention, this will remain a culture issue. For the first version of the EA, the culture of treating EA and planner interactions as a low priority item compared to addressing the operational challenges of the day will remain a barrier.

**Approval authority:** RMN Airport Authority

**Architecture completion date:** 1/1/2018

**Description of the level of effort required:** 6 staff months

## Scope

**Viewpoints addressed by the architecture description:** Capability Viewpoint, Project Viewpoint, Operational Viewpoint

**Views developed:**

- **CV-1: Vision** Multiphase version with strategic vision, phases, capabilities, and goals; objectives and measures documented in the AV-1

- **CV-2: Capability Taxonomy** Hierarchical list

- **CV-3: Capability Phasing**   Graphic showing capability versus capability configurations (using system-related project names) on a three-year timeline
- **CV-4: Capability Dependencies**   Graphic showing capability dependencies with dependent capabilities at the arrow tail and capabilities they depend on at the head of arrows
- **CV-5: Capability to Organizational Development Mapping**   Graphic showing organizations versus capabilities with capability configurations and interfaces between them for the mid- to late-phase 1 time frame
- **PV-1: Project Portfolio Relationships**   Table of projects, description, and start and stop dates organized by owning organizations
- **PV-2: Project Timelines**   Graphic showing one timeline per project with relevant delivery milestones and showing dependencies of each project on deliveries from other projects
- **PV-3: Project to Capability Mapping**   Matrix of projects versus capabilities showing which projects contribute to which capabilities
- **OV-4: Organizational Relationships Chart**   RMN organizational chart showing internal RMN organizations plus enterprise context organizational chart showing all the organizations involved in operating the airport

**Time frame addressed:** 15-year, three-phase, RMN transformation period

**Organizational entities in scope:** All the organizations involved in operating the airport including the RMN Airport internal organizations

## Purpose and Perspective

**The need:** Provide a roadmap for transforming RMN Airport from a general aviation field into an international airport providing an alternative (reliever airport) to LAX and other Los Angeles area airports

**The types of analyses:** Financial analyses on funding sources (bonds and operational revenue) versus expected costs of capability development

**Who is expected to perform the analyses:** RMN Airport Finance Division with assistance from contractors as necessary

**What decisions are expected to be made based on each form of analysis:** Prioritization of capability development

**Who is expected to make those decisions:** RMN Airport Authority

**What actions are expected to result:** Updates/changes to RMN Airport capability portfolios both in terms of content and timing; updates to RMN-ELA

**The perspective from which the architectural description is developed:** The perspective used is that of RMN executive management.

## Context

**Mission addressed by the architecture:** RMN transformation

**Doctrine:** N/A, although some FAA regulations and requirements may approach doctrine

**Relevant goals and vision statements:** Vision (from RMN Airport Master Plan) – Upgrade RMN Airport to become a viable alternative to LAX for passengers as an en route point or a destination all within a 15-year time frame

**Concepts of operation:** Implied by FAA, TSA, CBP, ICE, and law enforcement standards and procedures

**Scenarios:** N/A

**Information assurance context:** Security requirements specified by FAA, NIST, federal, and law enforcement standards as well as state and local regulations on privacy

**Other threats and environmental conditions:** TBD

**Geographical areas addressed:** RMN Airport grounds, airspace, and business offices

**Authoritative sources:** As noted previously for security requirements; FAA standards for airport planning, runways, airport equipment and instrumentation, air traffic personnel, airline staff, and air crew; state and local regulations for zoning, noise, and traffic; relevant regulations from involved federal agencies (such as TSA, CBP, and ICE) and law enforcement; OSHA regulations

**Any linkages to related architecture efforts:** RMN Airport will also be developing a Segment Level architecture for passenger management and a Solution Level architecture for passenger identification.

## Status

**Current Status:** Draft RMN-ELA version 0.5 completed

## Tools and File Formats

**Tool suite used:** MS Office products

**Filenames and formats:** N/A - hard copy

## Architecture Development Schedule

**Start date:** 6/1/2017

**Development milestones:** Draft version 0.5 complete 1/1/2018

**Date completed:** TBD

## Findings

**Findings and recommendations:** TBS (to be supplied)

## Costs

**Architecture budget:** 12 staff months

**Cost projections:** 12 staff months

# AV-2: Integrated Dictionary

Before the DoDAF was developed, architecture projects delivered several models, each of which was accompanied by its own glossary. Each glossary defined the architecture elements specific to a single model. The DoDAF is designed to produce an integrated architecture where the architecture elements of the same name have the same definition regardless of the view in which it appears. Similarly, any two elements with the same definition should have the same name. The AV-2 is a mechanism to get architects to resolve name conflicts and definitional issues across views and provides a single, consistent dictionary for the architecture as a whole.

| View Information at a Glance | |
| --- | --- |
| View short name | AV-2 |
| Name | Integrated Dictionary |
| Other names | Integrated model glossary, glossary |
| Viewpoint | All |
| View intent | Provide authoritative (sourced) definitions for architecture elements. Resolve inconsistencies between disparate definitions and names across different models of an integrated architecture. |
| View audience | All readers and users of the architecture |
| Formal modeling methodology | None. Usually provided as an alphabetized list. |
| Integration of model with other views | The AV-2 must define every term in every model that represents an architecture element. In addition, the AV-2 must expand acronyms and abbreviated terms for all architecture elements. |

## Example: Integrated Dictionary Sample Entries

The following example provides sample entries for different types of architecture elements taken from RMN Airport architectures (Enterprise, Segment, or Solution Level). AV-2 entries can be tailored by adding more information as well as alternative terms for the same architecture element (synonyms). Additional dictionary entries are provided in Chapters 13–19 for elements in various views.

| Name | Type | Acronym/ Short Name | Description | Used In |
| --- | --- | --- | --- | --- |
| Handle domestic commuter flights for West coast and Denver | Capability | Handle domestic commuter flights | The ability to handle domestic commuter flights for the West coast and adjacent states, including California, Oregon, Washington, Nevada, and Arizona at a minimum, with potential for service to Colorado (Denver) | CV-1, CV-2 |

(continued)

| Name | Type | Acronym/ Short Name | Description | Used In |
|---|---|---|---|---|
| Be competitive as a commuter airport in the LA area | Goal | None | Measure: Number of flights per day; one flight is a single aircraft into and out of the airport. Objective: A minimum of 5 flights per day at the end of 18 months Objective: A minimum of 15 flights per day at the end of 5 years | CV-1 |
| Screener | Performer | None | TSA or contract employee who performs the initial screening of passengers in the security area | OV-1, OV-2, OV-3, OV-5, OV-6c |
| Airline reservation and ticketing system | System | ARTS | Manages bookings, ticketing, generation of boarding passes and baggage tags | SV-1, SV-2, SV-3, SV-4, SV-5, SV-6, SV-8, SV-9 |
| identifyPAX | Service | None | Uses PaxIS to retrieve and check passenger identity from multiple places in the airport | All SvcV views |
| Gate | Data entity type | None | Provides the abstraction for all the data instances for airport gates. Gates have attributes including gate number, terminal location, size of airplanes that it can handle, and access mode such as ramp or staircase | DIV-2, DIV-3 |

# Summary

The All Viewpoint has two views and is used by all stakeholders and readers of the architecture. The AV-1: Overview and Summary Information provides an executive level summary of the purpose and contents of the architecture as well as providing conclusions and recommendations based on the current release of the architecture. More than just a glossary, the AV-2: Integrated Dictionary provides a consistent set of definitions and other information for all of the architecture elements and terms used in the architecture. The AV-2 provides the basis for ensuring the architecture is integrated and provides a place to document information about architecture elements that may be needed to fully interpret the architecture.

# Questions

1. For which types of stakeholders does the All Viewpoint provide benefits?

2. What are the challenges you foresee in developing an AV-1 for your own project in the following areas:

   - Identifying and stating the problem that needs to be solved by using the architecture development as a representational and clarifying exercise?

   - Identifying the stakeholders who are involved and must sponsor, collaborate, support, and be the audience for the architecture development?

   - Identifying the types of questions the architecture must answer as well as the types of analysis that must be performed? The data that is needed by the analyses?

   - Identifying, specifying, and restricting yourself to a stated scope to prevent project or program creep?

3. True or False? Provide clarifying statements to support your answer.

   A. The AV-1 is the very first model (or artifact) that is built in order to establish the scope, purpose, viewpoints, and models that will be covered by the architecture effort.

   B. The AV-1 is the very last model to be completed, because at the end of an architecture development, the architecture team records its findings and recommendations inside the AV-1.

4. What is the advantage of an integrated architecture dictionary (a single one for an entire architecture development effort) versus having a separate model glossary for each model that is built? What are the pros and cons?

5. What are the dimensions of scope that are described inside an AV-1? (Hint: breadth of architecture modeling domain and numbers and types of models built and many others.)

6. For your own enterprise, who would be the various stakeholders in the enterprise architecture? What are the types of models you would build to provide value to them?

7. What is the purpose of including architecture development time frames, costs, levels of effort involved, and development organizations inside the AV-1?

8. What are the pros and cons of using the AV-1 as an "index card" to contain information about your architecture in some larger architecture library or registry? The Defense Architecture Registry System (DARS) is one such registry. What would you recommend as a method or mechanism to transmit, store, and manage the AV-1 in such a registry? How would someone use "discovery" techniques to browse such a registry?

9. What are the types of architecture elements documented in the AV-2: Integrated Dictionary?

**10.** What is the purpose of the Integrated Dictionary?

**11.** What are some of the challenges in integrating AV-2 dictionaries across different enterprises? Discuss some of the problems with structural integration such as data formats as well as semantic integration—differences in vocabularies and meanings.

# References

Department of Defense. 2009. DoD Architecture Framework Version 2.0. "Volume 1: Introduction, Overview, and Concepts." http://dodcio.defense.gov/Portals/0/Documents/DODAF/DoDAF%20V2%20-%20Volume%201.pdf.

Department of Defense. 2009. DoD Architecture Framework Version 2.0. "Volume 2: Architectural Data and Models." http://dodcio.defense.gov/Portals/0/Documents/DODAF/DoDAF%20V2%20-%20Volume%202.pdf.

Department of Defense. "DoDAF Viewpoints and Models: All Viewpoint." http://dodcio.defense.gov/Library/DoD-Architecture-Framework/dodaf20_all_view/.

The Open Group. 2018. "TOGAF Standard Version 9.2." The Netherlands: Van Haren Publishing.

# CHAPTER 13

# Capability Viewpoint

Because different architecture frameworks deal with representing the elements of enterprise strategy differently, we present an abstract view of strategy that may vary in the specifics across different frameworks. For example, in the DoDAF, strategy is reflected in the CV-1: Vision, which ties the capability requirements to the enterprise vision and goals. In the FEAF2 strategy is represented explicitly in the strategic sub-architecture domain. In the TOGAF, strategy is part of the business architecture, albeit first addressed during the Vision Phase (A) of the ADM. The important thing is to ensure that for coherence, strategy provides the compass against which capability, operations and infrastructure must be aligned. The differences in how strategy is represented in the different frameworks is a reflection of how strategic planning is performed in military, government and commercial enterprises. We will use the term Strategic/Capability Viewpoint as an abstraction that incorporates the differences.

The Capability Viewpoint, sometimes called the Strategic Viewpoint, is a key viewpoint of Enterprise Level architectures. It is useful primarily to executive management and enterprise planners who have a longer window of planning than "firefighting" and support of current operations. For example, in the federal government, this planning window must extend to at least five years, and the strategic plan must be revised at least once in three years. [OMB 1993] The Capability Viewpoint identifies the enterprise vision or strategy and defines the enterprise's desired capabilities and their relationship to the enterprise vision and to each other. The Capability Viewpoint also identifies what organizations will use the capabilities and how the systems or projects that provide the capability will evolve over time. This viewpoint provides the context for laying out projects and initiatives that are consistent with the goals and objectives of the enterprise.

## Federal Government Planning Requirements

The federal government's planning cycle is based on programs and initiatives that are related to goals and objectives and the mission of a specific agency. Federal law requires the ability to relate the mission of the enterprise to its goals and objectives. Each of these goals and objectives must relate to the major functions and operations of the enterprise; the achievement of goals and objectives must be tied to the use of operations, skills, and resources of the enterprise, and investments in programs and initiatives must also be traceable to the goals and objectives that they support.

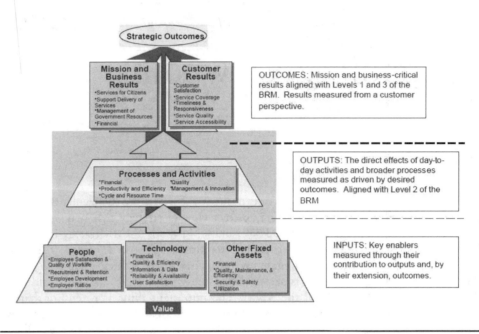

**Figure 13-1**   Line of sight (graphic from the OMB)

In addition, the Office of Management and Budget (OMB) requires that agencies use the FEAF2 performance reference model (PRM), which describes the cause-and-effect relationship between inputs, outputs, and outcomes. Inputs to an agency are typically resources such as people, skills, and technology. These enable the processes of the agency. The processes and activities of the agency deliver outputs and results. The outputs and results impact the outcomes such as mission, business, and customer results. Figure 13-1 shows the depiction of this "line of sight." See Chapter 23 for more information on the FEAF2 PRM.

# DoD Planning Requirements

Even though the Department of Defense (DoD) is required to conform externally to the same requirements as the other federal agencies, the DoD planning cycle is driven by capability needs for readiness to face and overcome emerging threats to the nation. In a constantly changing world, the planning cycle is focused on the acquisition/development of capabilities as well as the closing of capability gaps that are evident from lessons learned from ongoing exercises and battle.

Identification of capabilities is a fundamental step in planning for requirements in the DoD. The DoD Joint Capabilities Integration and Development System (JCIDS) was a departure from requirements-based planning to capabilities-based planning. The Department of Defense Architecture Framework (DoDAF) defines capability as "the ability to achieve a Desired Effect under specified [performance] standards and conditions through combinations of ways and means [activities and resources] to perform a set of activities."

A capability is a way to couch an enduring requirement without defining the solution in a very restrictive and specific manner. Requiring a capability to fly through the atmosphere, for example, does not predicate a specific type of flying vehicle. In general, a capability can be satisfied by many solutions, with each having different costs and complexities and entailing different types of tradeoffs. A specific capability may require the availability of another capability before it can be realized. For example, the ability to get on a bicycle, get off a bicycle, and stay on a bicycle is essential before embarking on a bicycle journey toward a destination.

A *capability configuration* is a set of related capabilities that must all be planned together to ensure that critical dependencies are not missed. While planning an airframe, for example, the engine, the landing gear, and a host of other subsystems must all be planned together. Typically, complex large-scale capabilities are delivered in increments and in pieces by multiple projects working often in multiple locations under multiple enterprises. Without a carefully planned strategy to manage the capability configuration and the orchestration of capability development projects, the odds of successfully delivering a complex integrated capability are very low.

# Views in the Capability Viewpoint

The following views make up the Capability Viewpoint. Although these views are couched in capability language, they can also be easily interpreted and used in a requirements-based approach to strategic planning.

- **CV-1: Vision**  The CV-1 is a key view that provides "line of sight" traceability of capability needs back to the vision and goals of the enterprise. By examining capability mappings to the goals, prioritization can be made during a capability-based acquisition process in which capability needs are submitted by multiple contenders for funding and resourcing. The CV-1 is similar in scope and intent to views in federal government and commercial industry that require that transformation initiatives be mapped back to strategic goals and objectives in the strategic plan and to key ingredients of strategy that support the vision.

- **CV-2: Capability Taxonomy**  The CV-2 is used to decompose a complex capability need into smaller granularity, simpler capability needs that can then be mapped to a capability development timeline. The decomposition is arranged as a tree, and the leaf nodes of the tree may be associated with specific measures of performance or effectiveness for the leaf-level capability.

- **CV-3: Capability Phasing**  The CV-3 takes the capability configuration concept to its logical conclusion. If all the component capabilities of the CV-2 were to be developed in disparate projects, how do we orchestrate the delivery of capabilities from each of these projects in an orderly manner to assemble the larger grain capability? The CV-3 maps capability developments to time phases and projects to describe what capability will be available in what time frames.

- **CV-4: Capability Dependencies**   The CV-4 explicitly represents dependencies of a specific capability on another. Knowledge of capability dependencies is essential to orchestrate capability developments in such a manner that a predecessor capability is developed first before trying to develop a successor capability that depends on it.

- **CV-5: Capability to Organizational Development Mapping**   The CV-5 traces capabilities to the organizations that use them within a given time frame. This view enables traceability of capabilities to the organizations that use them.

- **CV-6: Capability to Operational Activities Mapping**   In acquiring capabilities, it is important to represent the mission or business activity that will use and benefit from that capability. The CV-6 establishes mappings between a capability configuration and the set of operational activities (business processes) that will harness the capability.

- **CV-7: Capability to Services Mapping**   The solutions for problems may lie in the procurement of outsourced business services or in automation—use of automated software services. The Services Viewpoint (SvcV) views address the modeling of the service-based views. The CV-7 provides traceability of service-based solutions back to the original capabilities that were planned. The CV-7 also supports capability audits that trace capabilities down to the solutions that provide the capability.

## Capability Viewpoint Element Overview

All the Capability Viewpoint views share the capability architecture element, as shown in Figure 13-2. Many of the views provide "gateway" relationships to other viewpoints to ensure that these viewpoints integrate with the Capability Viewpoint.

Here are some examples of such gateway relationships:

- CV-5 relates the Capability Viewpoint to the organizational user by mapping the capabilities to the organizations that use the capabilities.

- CV-6 relates the Capability Viewpoint to the Operational Viewpoint to ensure that capabilities that are being acquired by the enterprise support some named enterprise activity specifically.

- CV-7 relates the Capability Viewpoint to the Services Viewpoint to ensure that business or software services are traceable to the capability they implement.

- CV-1 implies a relationship to a Strategic Viewpoint if one existed that deals with the vision, goals, strategies, and objectives of the enterprise and is of interest to the strategic planner.

The DoDAF's scope does not include representing a strategic viewpoint as its purpose was to drive the core DoD processes. Strategy at the DoD is conducted at high levels and

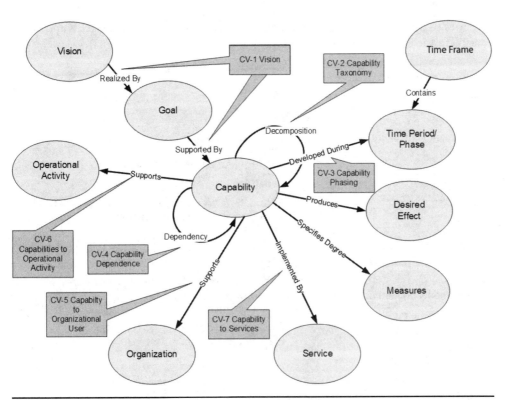

**Figure 13-2**  Integrated view set for the Capability Viewpoint

handed down to the planner. The Capability Viewpoint aligns the proposed capabilities to the declared strategy.

# CV-1: Vision

The purpose of the CV-1: Vision view is to provide an overview of the capabilities that are important to the enterprise and how they relate to the enterprise strategy and desired effects (goals and objectives). The CV-1 can also be used to outline the long-term transformation phase plan and how the capabilities and their related measures change as the transformation evolves.

The CV-1 goals define the ends, and the related capabilities provide the means to achieve those ends. The operational activities described in the Operational Viewpoint represent the ways, or the hows. Although the operational activities can be included in the CV-1, the explicit relationship between the capabilities and activities is captured in the CV-6: Capability to Operational Activities Mapping. The CV-1 can link the activities to the capabilities (ways and means) and the capabilities to the goals and vision (means to the ends).

| View Information at a Glance | |
|---|---|
| View short name | CV-1 |
| Name | Vision |
| Other names and alternatives | Strategic Plan (FEAF2)<br>Business Capability Map (TOGAF 9.2)<br>Capability Assessment (TOGAF 9.2) |
| Viewpoint | Capability |
| View intent | Record the strategic drivers for enterprise capabilities and document the relationships between these drivers and the capabilities. |
| View audience | Planners at the enterprise level that must deal with prioritization of capability development within resource and schedule constraints |
| Formal modeling methodology | None. Contains elements from standard strategic planning with relationships to capabilities |
| Integration of view with other views | Capabilities in CV-1 must be consistent with capabilities in all other CV views. |

The CV-1 can be used to show a single phase of transformation or to describe a multi-phased approach to transformation. The strategy or vision statement in the CV-1 should come from an authoritative source, and that source should be documented in the AV-2: Integrated Dictionary entry for the vision statement. Measures should be included in the CV-1 either in the graphic or in the AV-2 documentation to show how the achievement of objectives will be measured. In other words, each goal associated with the vision statement should have associated measurable objectives, and both the objectives and the measures should be included in the AV-2 if nowhere else.

It is important to remember that capabilities must reflect something of business or mission value and not specific technologies. The technologies that are used to provide the capabilities are identified through the CV-7: Capability to Services Mapping view.

## Example: RMN Airport Enterprise CV-1

Figure 13-3 illustrates a partial CV-1: Vision view for RMN Airport. The RMN Airport CV-1 depicts a phased transformation for achieving the airport's vision of becoming a viable alternative to Los Angeles International for passengers using it as an en-route point or as a destination, within a 15-year time frame. Measures and other elements of the CV-1, such as the explicit description of the capabilities, can be documented in the AV-2: Integrated Dictionary if there is no space to include them in the graphic. The description of the capability in the AV-2 is critical because it is difficult to determine exactly what the capability entails from the short phrase that is typically all that will fit in the graphic. (See Chapter 12 for an example of AV-2 entries for capabilities and goals for the RMN Airport Enterprise Vision CV-1.)

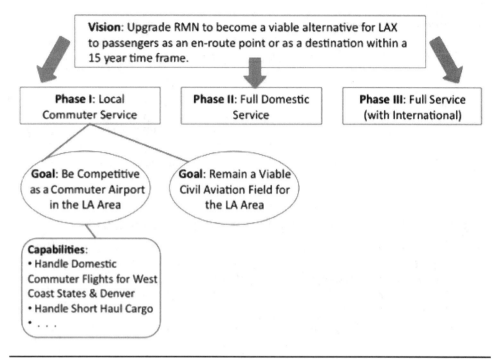

**Figure 13-3**  RMN Airport Enterprise Vision CV-1

# CV-2: Capability Taxonomy

This view is important for the Capability Viewpoint, because most of the other views use the capabilities defined in the CV-2.

| View Information at a Glance | |
| --- | --- |
| View short name | CV-2 |
| Name | Capability Taxonomy |
| Other names and alternatives | Capability Hierarchy, Master Capability List, Joint Capability Area (DoD) Function Decomposition Diagram (TOGAF 9.2) Capability Assessment (TOGAF 9.2) |
| Viewpoint | Capability |
| View intent | Depicts a specialization (supertype-subtype) hierarchy for capabilities that shows how a higher level capability can be built using combinations of lower-level capabilities. Level denotes granularity and scope. |

*(continued)*

| View Information at a Glance | |
| --- | --- |
| View audience | Planners at the enterprise level who are interested in elaborating abstract capabilities in terms of concrete capabilities that can form the basis for projects to develop those capabilities |
| Formal modeling methodology | None. This view is a specialization (subtype-supertype) hierarchy. It is frequently represented in a tree form or as an indented list. Measures can be included for the lowest-level capabilities. |
| Integration of view with other views | Capabilities in CV-2 must be consistent with capabilities in all other CV views. |

## Example: Handle Domestic Commuter Flights CV-2

Figure 13-4 shows a partial taxonomy for the high-level capabilities identified for the phase 1 transformation in the RMN Airport Enterprise Vision CV-1. It provides a decomposition of one of these high-level capabilities.

**Figure 13-4**
Handle domestic commuter flight CV-2

- Domestic Commuter Flights
  - Host Airline Operations
    - Support Commuter Airline Aircraft Operations
    - Support Airline Passenger Operations
  - Handle Domestic Passengers
    - Support Security Screening for Domestic Passengers
    - Provide Vendor Services for Passengers
    - Handle Baggage for Domestic Passengers
  - . . .

- Short Haul Cargo
  - . . .

# CV-3: Capability Phasing

The CV-3: Capability Phasing view lays out the capability configurations that provide the various capabilities and how the capability configurations evolve over time. Frequently, the capability configurations are designated by project names instead of detailed system or service names. The CV-3 shows time frames in terms of years within or across phases. Note that this view does not make sense for Solution Level architectures.

| View Information at a Glance | |
|---|---|
| View short name | CV-3 |
| Name | Capability Phasing |
| Other names and alternatives | Capability Roadmap<br>Project Context Diagram (TOGAF 9.2) |
| Viewpoint | Capability |
| View intent | Shows when new/upgraded capabilities become available through the duration of the project/capability configurations that provide the capability. Useful in planning the succession of projects and identifying time gaps when no projects have been planned to provide the required capability configurations. |
| View audience | Planners and acquisition managers at the enterprise level, interested in ensuring orderly development of capabilities and succession of programs and projects |
| Formal modeling methodology | None. Whatever representation is chosen, it should be one where gaps in capability coverage are easy to identify. |
| Integration of view with other views | Any capabilities named in CV-3 must be consistent with capabilities in all other CV views. Project/capability configurations named must be consistent with PV views. Time frames and phases must be consistent with architecture time frame and phases (CV-1) as well as the time frames described in the Project Timelines (PV-2) and the Systems, Services, and Standards Viewpoint views. |

PART III

## Example: RMN Airport Transformation Phase 1 CV-3

Figure 13-5 provides a partial example CV-3: Capability Phasing for the first phase of the RMN Airport transformation. The gaps (indicated by the dark arrows) in any row of the figure indicate times when a capability configuration may not exist. For example, the Domestic Passenger Check-in capability may not be fully supported immediately after an airline upgrades its Airline Reservation and Ticketing System (ARTS) and forces an update to the Passenger Intelligence Services (PaxIS) interface to that ARTS. This

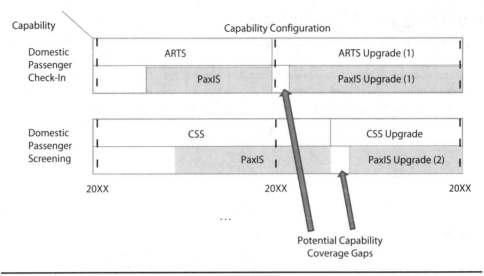

**Figure 13-5** CV-3: Capability Phasing for Phase I of the RMN Airport transformation

gap highlights a potential risk that management needs to consider and potentially move to mitigate. The gap indicates that the interfaces between PaxIS and the various airline ARTS systems need to be examined for the existence of standards or other mechanisms that may be used to ensure that upgrades to ARTS will not interfere with the ARTS system interface to PaxIS.

# CV-4: Capability Dependencies

The CV-4: Capability Dependencies view provides important information used in the orchestration of development projects that deliver capabilities. The dependent capabilities need to be developed after the capabilities they depend upon.

| Information at a Glance | |
| --- | --- |
| View short name | CV-4 |
| Name | Capability Dependencies |
| Other names and alternatives | Business Footprint Diagram (TOGAF 9.2) |
| Viewpoint | Capability |
| View intent | Depict explicitly the development or operational dependencies between capabilities to reflect the fact that one capability may need the completed development or performance of another. |

| Information at a Glance | |
|---|---|
| View audience | Planners and acquisition managers at the enterprise level, interested in ensuring orderly development of capabilities based on identified dependencies and project schedules (PV views) |
| Formal modeling methodology | None. Either a diagram or a tabular format may be used to represent the view. |
| Integration of view with other views | Capabilities in CV-4 must be consistent with capabilities in all other CV views. The subtype and supertype relationships from CV-2 should also be reflected in the CV-4. |

## Example: RMN Airport Capability Dependencies CV-4

Figure 13-6 shows a partial set of capability dependencies for RMN Airport capabilities. The capability at the head of the arrow is dependent on the capability at the tail of the arrow. So the ability to handle baggage depends on the ability to check-in and the ability to screen passengers. In other words, baggage handling needs to know what the passenger's trip itinerary is in order to tag and route baggage successfully, and baggage handling needs to know if the passenger has been successfully screened either before loading baggage or before the airplane is allowed to leave the gate. If a passenger fails screening and is not allowed to board the airplane, any baggage for that passenger that has been loaded on the airplane must be removed before the airplane is allowed to leave the gate.

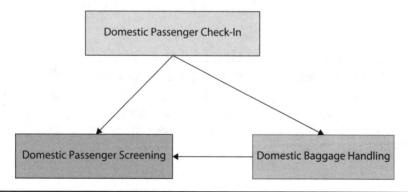

**Figure 13-6**   RMN Airport Capability Dependencies CV-4

# CV-5: Capability to Organizational Development Mapping

The CV-5: Capability to Organizational Development Mapping view shows planned (by phase) capability deployment to organizations and relationships among the capability implementations.

| View Information at a Glance | |
| --- | --- |
| View short name | CV-5 |
| Name | Capability to Organizational Development Mapping |
| Other names and alternatives | Business Footprint Diagram (TOGAF 9.2)<br>Business Interaction Matrix (TOGAF 9.2) |
| Viewpoint | Capability |
| View intent | Show the relationships between capabilities and the organizations that use the capabilities during a specific time frame. It can also show interfaces between the various capability configurations. |
| View audience | Planners at the enterprise level, interested in ensuring orderly development of capabilities for operational organizations. |
| Formal modeling methodology | None. A matrix or other simple graphic can be used to represent this type of view. |
| Integration of view with other views | Capabilities in CV-5 must be consistent with capabilities in all other CV views. The organizations included should be consistent with the organizations in the OV-4: Organizational Relationships Chart. |

## Example: Organizational Use of Capabilities During RMN Airport Phase 1 Transformation CV-5

Figure 13-7 provides an example CV-5 for the RMN Airport during Phase I of the transformation outlined in CV-1: Vision. Again, the capability configurations are identified by project names. The dark lines indicate interfaces among the systems across the capability configurations.

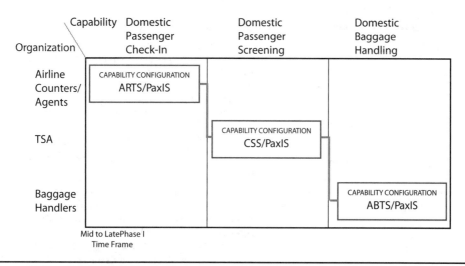

**Figure 13-7**   CV-5 for RMN Airport Phase I transition

# CV-6: Capability to Operational Activities Mapping

The CV-6: Capability to Operational Activities Mapping view can be included in Solution Level architectures only if there is an overarching Enterprise or Segment Level architecture that defines capabilities in a CV-1 or CV-2, or, in the absence of these, an authoritative document that provides an accepted set of capabilities for the enterprise. The Solution Level architect should not define capabilities on his or her own.

| View Information at a Glance | |
| --- | --- |
| View short name | CV-6 |
| Name | Capability to Operational Activities Mapping |
| Other names and alternatives | Business Footprint Diagram (TOGAF 9.2)<br>Value Chain Diagram (TOGAF 9.2)<br>Value Stream/Capability Matrix (TOGAF 9.2) |
| Viewpoint | Capability |
| View intent | Depict the relationship between capabilities and the activities they enable. Capabilities provide abilities for an activity to be performed. The activity may be viewed as a target "application" for the capability. An activity is a unit of mission accomplishment. By relating capabilities to activities, we can assess the value of a capability not in isolation, but within a mission context. |

*(continued)*

| View Information at a Glance | |
| --- | --- |
| View audience | Portfolio managers at the enterprise level assessing the relative value of each capability within a capability portfolio and ensuring that the activities performed during operations actually relate to the desired capabilities and enterprise strategy. Project managers at the solution level documenting the relationship of the activities their systems/services support to the desired capabilities and enterprise strategy. |
| Formal modeling methodology | None. A simple matrix can be used to represent this type of view. |
| Integration of view with other views | Capabilities in CV-6 must be consistent with capabilities in all other CV views. Activities must be consistent with the operational activities in the Operational Viewpoint. These activities should also be consistent with the activities performed by the organizations identified as using the capability in CV-5: Capability to Organizational Development Mapping. |

## Example: Domestic Passenger Identification CV-6

| | Capability | | |
| --- | --- | --- | --- |
| Activity | Passenger Check-In | Passenger Screening | Baggage Handling |
| Sell ticket | X | | |
| Issue boarding pass | X | | |
| Authenticate identity | X | X | X |
| Screen carry-on baggage | | X | |
| Screen passenger | | X | |
| Perform secondary screening | | X | |
| Remove passenger | | X | |
| Retrieve passenger checked baggage | | X | |
| Tag baggage | X | | X |
| Screen checked baggage | | | X |
| Route checked baggage | | | X |
| Load checked baggage | | | X |
| Unload checked baggage | | | X |
| Route baggage to baggage claim | | | X |
| Display baggage claim information | | | X |

This view is limited to Phase 1 RMN Airport Transformation

# CV-7: Capability to Services Mapping

The CV-7: Capability to Services Mapping can be included in Solution Level architectures only if an overarching Enterprise or Segment Level architecture defines capabilities in a CV-1 or CV-2, or, in the absence of these, an authoritative document that provides an accepted set of capabilities for the enterprise. Solution Level architect should not define capabilities on his or her own.

| View Information at a Glance | |
| --- | --- |
| View short name | CV-7 |
| Name | Capability to Services Mapping |
| Other names and alternatives | Goal/Objective/Service Diagram (TOGAF 9.2) Business Footprint Diagram (TOGAF 9.2) |
| Viewpoint | Capability |
| View intent | Depict the relationship between a capability as a requirement and a service as a solution. |
| View audience | Project managers and service developers can trace the services they are developing back to desired enterprise capabilities and enterprise strategy. Portfolio managers can follow a capability down to its implementation as a business or software service. |
| Formal modeling methodology | None. A simple matrix can be used to represent this type of view. |
| Integration of view with other views | Capabilities in CV-7 must be consistent with capabilities in all other CV views. Services must be consistent with the services represented inside the Services Viewpoint views. The services should also be consistent with services used by any organization identified as using the capability in CV-5: Capability to Organizational Development Mapping. |

## Example: Domestic Passenger Identification CV-7

| Service | Capability | | |
| --- | --- | --- | --- |
| | Passenger Check-In | Passenger Screening | Baggage Handling |
| Capture passenger information | X | | |
| Check passenger against watch lists | X | | |
| Check passenger TSA Pre status | X | | |
| Capture trip information | X | | |
| Capture payment information | X | | |
| Process payment | X | | |

*(continued)*

| | Capability | | |
|---|---|---|---|
| **Service** | **Passenger Check-In** | **Passenger Screening** | **Baggage Handling** |
| Issue boarding pass | X | | |
| Verify ticket at gate | X | | |
| Check boarding pass | | X | |
| Retrieve passenger police record | | X | |
| Retrieve passenger trip information | | | X |
| Issue baggage tag | | | X |
| Route checked baggage to airplane | | | X |
| Track baggage by tag number/ passenger name | | | X |
| Plan baggage distribution to baggage claims | | | X |
| Route checked baggage to baggage claim | | | X |
| Display baggage claim information | | | X |

This view has same limitations as CV-6.

# Alternatives

Two additional approaches for the Capability Viewpoint that may be useful come from the TOGAF 9.2 and the balanced score card. These alternative approaches are discussed very briefly next.

## TOGAF 9.2 Support for Capability and Strategy

Before embarking upon a detailed architecture definition, TOGAF suggests that you should understand the baseline and target capability level of the enterprise. To do this, you perform a capability assessment that requires answering the following questions:

- What is the capability level of the enterprise as a whole? Where does the enterprise want to increase or optimize capability? What are the architectural focus areas that will support the desired development of the enterprise?

- What is the capability or maturity level of the IT function within the enterprise? What are the likely implications of conducting the architecture project in terms of design governance, operational governance, skills, and organization structure? What is an appropriate style, level of formality, and amount of detail for the architecture project to fit within the culture and capability of the IT organization?

- What is the capability and maturity of the architecture function within the enterprise? What architectural assets are currently in existence? Are they maintained and accurate? What standards and reference models need to be considered? Are there likely to be opportunities to create reusable assets during the architecture project?

- Where capability gaps exist, to what extent is the business ready to transform in order to reach the target capability? What are the risks to transformation, cultural barriers, and other considerations to be addressed beyond the basic capability gap?

The outputs of the capability assessment include the following types of products:

- **Business capability assessment**   Includes identification of baseline capabilities, capability gaps and future capability needs from a business perspective

- **IT capability assessment**   Assesses from the IT perspective

- **Architecture maturity assessment**   Determines the level of maturity of the architecture development effort and identifies gaps in scope (depth and breadth) and coverage as well as in the use and dissemination

- **Business transformation capability assessment**   Determines the capabilities needed as well as the readiness of the enterprise in undertaking transformations

# FEAF2 Support for Strategic/Capability Viewpoint

The Federal Enterprise Architecture Framework Version 2 (FEAF2) describes an explicit strategy sub-architecture domain that also recommends a set of artifacts to support a strategic viewpoint:

- **Strategic Plan (S-2)**   A description of the organization's vision and strategic objectives, a prioritization of the desired outcomes from achieving those objectives, the measurements that will demonstrate achievement, and the resources to be used to achieve them. This artifact combines the elements of the DoDAF CV-1: Vision, CV-2: Capability Taxonomy, CV-3: Capability Phasing, CV-5: Capability to Organizational Development Mapping, and CV-6: Capability to Operational Activities Mapping.

- **Strengths, Weaknesses, Opportunities, and Threat Analysis (S-4)**   Presents the strengths, weaknesses/limitations, opportunities, and threats involved in a project or in a business venture including risks and impacts. There is no equivalent in the DoDAF.

- **Performance Measures Scorecard (S-5)**   A strategic performance management tool that can be used by managers to keep track of the performance metrics associated with the execution of activities by the staff within their control and to identify the performance gaps and consequences arising from these gaps.

The FEAF2 also provides a performance reference model (PRM), illustrated in Figure 13-8, that contains the types of measures used to assess performance in the federal arena. Historically, agencies reported performance information in an anecdotal, non-standard manner that made it difficult to link information management investments and activities. The PRM establishes mechanisms to link directly to the authoritative performance elements published in compliance with the law by agencies and provides the means for use of future developments in the mandated central performance web site, www.Performance.gov.

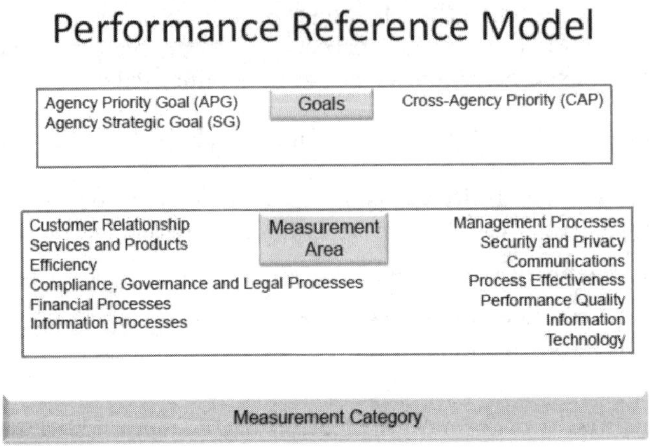

**Figure 13-8**
FEAF2 performance reference model (graphic from the OMB)

Performance Reference Model

Agency Priority Goal (APG)    Goals    Cross-Agency Priority (CAP)
Agency Strategic Goal (SG)

Customer Relationship    Measurement    Management Processes
Services and Products    Area    Security and Privacy
Efficiency    Communications
Compliance, Governance and Legal Processes    Process Effectiveness
Financial Processes    Performance Quality
Information Processes    Information
    Technology

Measurement Category

## Balanced Score Card

The BSC is a strategic planning and management system that is used extensively in business and industry, government, and nonprofit organizations worldwide to align business activities to the vision and strategy of the organization, improve internal and external communications, and monitor organization performance against strategic goals. It was originated by Drs. Robert Kaplan (Harvard Business School) and David Norton as a performance measurement framework that added strategic nonfinancial performance measures to traditional financial metrics to give managers and executives a more "balanced" view of organizational performance. While the phrase "balanced score card" was coined in the early 1990s, the roots of this type of approach are deep and include the pioneering work of General Electric on performance measurement reporting in the 1950s and the work of French process engineers (who created the *Tableau de Bord*—literally, a dashboard of performance measures) in the early part of the 20th century.

The BSC has evolved from its early use as a simple performance measurement framework to a full strategic planning and management system. The "new" BSC transforms an organization's strategic plan from an attractive but passive document into the marching orders for the organization on a daily basis. It provides a framework that not only provides performance measurements, but helps planners identify what should be done and measured. It enables executives to truly execute their strategies.

## Summary

The Capability Viewpoint provides key information for enterprise level managers, planners, and acquisition specialists in ensuring the linkage of identified enterprise needs, either in terms of capabilities or requirements, to stated enterprise vision and strategy. This viewpoint supports the prioritization, selection, and orchestration of acquisitions and development projects based on the enterprise vision and strategy and assists in the clear statement of performance measures for assessing progress toward meeting goals and objectives based on the enterprise strategy.

While the Capability Viewpoint is oriented towards the DoD's readiness-based planning on capabilities, it is easily adapted to a requirements-based approach. The same care must be taken to document the enterprise vision and its relationship to the capabilities/requirements (CV-1: Vision), decompose the capabilities/requirements into manageable pieces (CV-2: Capability Taxonomy), and identify dependencies (CV-4: Capability Dependencies). Acquisition and development of capabilities/requirements must be phased based on dependencies and care taken that there are no gaps in capability/requirement support (CV-3: Capability Phasing). Capabilities/requirements need to be traced to who uses them (CV-5: Capability to Organizational Development Mapping) and how they support business processes and activities (CV-6: Capability to Operational Activities Mapping) as well as to the services that provide the solution to the needs (CV-7: Capability to Services Mapping).

TOGAF provides some additional guidance in this area and FEAF2 provides additional views. In addition, the business community provides the balanced score card approach to support the measured linkage of enterprise vision and strategy to both financial and non-financial business activities.

# Questions

1. Who is the audience for the Capability Viewpoint? In your own enterprise, who performs the planning function that requires this viewpoint?

2. Discuss the pros and cons of capability-based acquisition versus requirements-based acquisition.

3. What is the difference between the federal government approach and the Defense Department's approach to capabilities? Discuss whether the nature of the DoD enterprise (readiness based) is fundamentally different from the federal government (legislation and strategic plan based) and is fundamentally different from commercial enterprise (profit based). Do these fundamental drivers affect how capabilities are viewed, measured, and assessed for effectiveness?

4. What is line of sight? Why is it important?

5. What is the balanced score card? Discuss the pros and cons of using a balanced score card approach to drive the enterprise's motivation. What would be the dimensions of your own enterprise's BSC? What should they be?

6. What is a capability configuration? Why is it important to manage a capability configuration in terms of investments and schedule? What types of Capability Viewpoint views will help you manage a capability configuration? Explain why.

7. What is the CV-1? How would you use it in your own enterprise? Who would/should be using the CV-1 to communicate the enterprise vision?

8. What is the CV-2? A capability name is usually a compound phrase of a verb and a noun. Discuss the pros and cons of developing capability decomposition (CV-2) around the verb phrase and the noun phrase, respectively.

9. How does the CV-3: Capability Phasing help orchestrate multiple capability developments? What is the impact of not developing a CV-3 to assist in a major acquisition of a new multimillion-dollar airframe development?

10. How can you use the CV-3: Capability Phasing and CV-4: Capability Dependencies together to identify and resolve issues with orchestrating capability developments?

11. What are the pros and cons of not developing a CV-5: Capability to Organizational Development Mapping?

12. What are the pros and cons of not developing a CV-6: Capability to Operational Activities Mapping?

13. What are the pros and cons of developing services around capabilities rather than around specific stated business needs of a specific consumer (requirements)? How will the CV-7: Capability to Services Mapping help in analyzing redundant services across the enterprise?

# References

Balanced Score Card Basics, Balanced Scorecard Institute, Strategic Management Group, www.balancedscorecard.org/BSC-Basics/About-the-Balanced-Scorecard

CIO Council. 2013. "Federal Enterprise Architecture Framework, Version 2." https://obamawhitehouse.archives.gov/sites/default/files/omb/assets/egov_docs/fea_v2.pdf.

Defense Acquisition University (DAU). *ACQuipedia: An Encyclopedia of Acquisition Terms for the Defense Acquisition Community.* www.dau.mil/acquipedia/Pages/Default.aspx.

Department of Defense. 2009. DoD Architecture Framework Version 2.0. "Volume 2: Architectural Data and Models." http://dodcio.defense.gov/Portals/0/Documents/DODAF/DoDAF_v2-02_web.pdf.

Department of Defense. 2001. Quadrennial Defense Review Report. http://archive.defense.gov/pubs/qdr2001.pdf.

Office of Management and Budget (OMB). 1993. Government Performance Results Act (GPRA). https://obamawhitehouse.archives.gov/omb/mgmt-gpra/.

The Open Group. 2018. "TOGAF Standard Version 9.2." The Netherlands: Van Haren Publishing.

# CHAPTER 14

# Project Viewpoint

As the old saying goes, "Rome wasn't built in a day!" Complex capability developments or complex and prolonged transformation efforts [GAO 2006] are seldom accomplished through single projects. For the manager who is managing a portfolio of such projects or initiatives [EPMC 2009], the task of orchestrating the deliverables of each project in synchronization with the needs of other projects is tricky and challenging. The Project Viewpoint provides the portfolio manager with a set of views that enables him/her to orchestrate the combined planning and management of multiple projects. The operative words here are "multiple projects," because of the various dependencies between projects that affect the delivered capabilities and the need to plan the deliverables carefully in keeping with the dependencies as we have seen earlier in the views CV-3: Capability Phasing and CV-4: Capability Dependencies in Chapter 13. The Project Viewpoint is not concerned as much with the detailed tasks, schedules, and resources for individual projects as it is with the concerns of managing a group of coordinated projects that must collaborate to deliver a complex deliverable.

In the federal government arena, projects or initiatives are used to transform government or to improve the current state of the enterprise while remaining consistent with strategic goals and objectives. A family or portfolio of projects is used to deliver a collection of related initiatives that support enterprise transformation or a phase of enterprise transformation.

In the DoD arena, projects are collections of tasks that deliver capabilities within the framework of a larger initiative called a *program* or *acquisition program*. A collection of systems or services that, together with operational processes and human and other organizational resources, delivers a capability is called a *capability configuration*. To be effective, a program must deliver all of the component parts of the capability configuration in a consistent and orchestrated manner. A typical DoD program is responsible for the acquisition of large-scale, complex weapons systems or automated information systems as well as sustainment and maintenance of the systems once they are acquired and deployed. Programs tend to run for multiple years and are funded in increments based on various metrics that determine the health of the program and the viability of the capabilities that are produced.

The concept of portfolios is applicable to non-DoD enterprises such as the federal government as well. A transformation may be viewed as a collection of initiatives. Each of these initiatives has dependencies with other initiatives. Portfolios of projects that are responsible for delivering the collection of initiatives need to reflect and factor in the dependencies among the initiatives.

In the commercial world, every initiative is deemed an investment and is measured in terms of payback or return. A collection of initiatives is therefore seen as a portfolio of investments. A project or family of projects is related to single or multiple investments. The principles and view types described in the DoDAF Project Viewpoint are applicable, adaptable, and customizable to the commercial domain as well, given a change in terminology and a shift in focus. In the commercially oriented TOGAF 9, the formulation of opportunities and solutions is performed in Phase E of the Architecture Development Methodology (ADM). It is during this phase that a project context diagram similar to the PV-1: Project Portfolio Relationships described in this chapter is developed.

As we saw earlier with the Capability Viewpoint, we have the ability to model capability dependencies, capability taxonomies, relationships of capabilities to using organizations, to solution services, and to operational activities the capabilities enable. The Project Viewpoint view of a project is something that is responsible for delivering clearly stated capabilities. These capabilities are consistent with those defined in the Capability Viewpoint. The Project Viewpoint views must be consistent with and reflect capability dependencies. (See Figure 5-12 in Chapter 5, which shows the relationships among the Capability Viewpoint views and the Project Viewpoint views.) The multiple projects in a portfolio must be orchestrated consistent with capability dependencies, and projects must deliver independent upstream configuration components earlier than dependent downstream configuration components.

A capability configuration is a collection of interdependent capability components that must be planned together. Because each of these capability components may be developed by a different project, it is important that the project portfolio responsible for developing the entire capability configuration be orchestrated to reflect capability dependencies and the orderly development of capabilities in a manner that is consistent with those dependencies.

## Views in the Project Viewpoint

The Project Viewpoint contains three views:

- **PV-1: Project Portfolio Relationships**   The PV-1 is used to depict the grouping of projects into portfolios and the mapping of the portfolios to the responsible development organizations or portfolio managers.

- **PV-2: Project Timelines**   The PV-2 acts like an aggregated Gantt chart for a portfolio of projects and allows a very quick view of the various timelines of the component projects and their dependencies.

- **PV-3: Project to Capability Mapping**   The PV-3 illustrates the relationship of a project to the capabilities it delivers. Together with the CV-3, it helps identify anomalies such as redundant capability development or the identification of capability gaps that are not covered by any project.

Figure 14-1 shows how all the elements of the Project Viewpoint fit into the views. See Figure 4-4 in Chapter 4 for an alternative view that shows how elements of the Capability Viewpoint and Project Viewpoint relate.

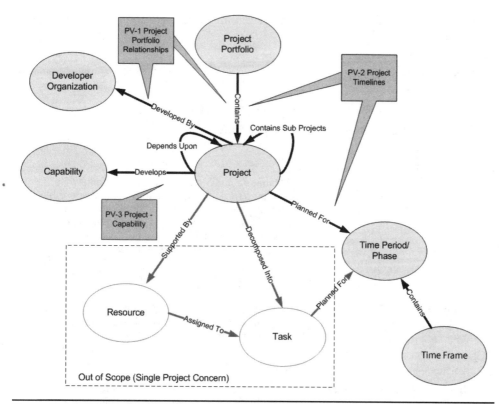

**Figure 14-1**    Integrated views set for the Project Viewpoint

Though not explicitly represented by a DoDAF-described type, the project portfolio is a composition structure that describes the families of projects that form the enterprise project portfolio.

All the Project Viewpoint views must consistently reference the same project list.

# PV-1: Project Portfolio Relationships

Traditional project management tools do a great job of supporting single projects using work breakdown structures, cost, schedule, resources, and tasks. However, enterprise architecture is concerned with the management and coordination of multiple projects. The concept of project portfolios is basic. Some commercial project management tools [Microsoft 2011] address portfolio representation using a *master project* approach that provides active links to several smaller subprojects. The PV-1 provides a technique for representing the groupings of multiple projects into portfolios. In TOGAF 9 (see Chapter 22), the formulation of opportunities and solutions is performed in Phase E of the TOGAF ADM. It is during this phase that a Project Context Diagram, similar to the PV-1, is developed. The Project Context Diagram can be used as an alternative to the PV-1.

The PV-1 shows how acquisition or development projects are grouped in terms of organizational ownership.

| View Information at a Glance | |
| --- | --- |
| View short name | PV-1 |
| Name | Project Portfolio Relationships |
| Other names and alternatives | Project Portfolio<br>Project Context Diagram (TOGAF 9.2) |
| Viewpoint | Project |
| View intent | Manage a family of projects as a portfolio while keeping track of which organization is responsible for which project. The hierarchical nature of the PV-1 enables an enterprise to represent its projects as a well-formed hierarchy of portfolios and assign organization responsibilities to each level of the hierarchy. In complex multi-organization, multirole, multiproject situations, the PV-1 is an invaluable representation tool. |
| View audience | Portfolio managers managing definition of projects and assignment of responsibility to project owners; high-level decision-makers interested in project outcomes desirous of identifying responsibility |
| Formal modeling methodology | None |
| Integration of view with other views | Capabilities in the PV-1 must be consistent with capabilities mentioned in the Capability Viewpoint and in all other Project Viewpoint views. Organizations in PV-1 must be consistent with OV-4: Organizational Relationships Charts. Individual views in the Project Viewpoint must be consistent with other views in the Project Viewpoint and with views in the Capability Viewpoint as indicated in Figure 5-12 in Chapter 5. |

## Example: RMN Passenger Management PV-1

This example references the systems in Figure 16-3 and "Example: Passenger Identification SV-2" in Chapter 16. The focus is on the projects that are under the control of RMN Airport. Projects to develop the systems provided by organizations external to the airport, such as the airlines and TSA, are not included. The time frame reflected in this view is that of the first years of the initial phase (phase 1) of transformation, where RMN Airport starts to support scheduled commuter airlines. (See Figure 13-3 and "Example: RMN Airport Enterprise CV-1" in Chapter 13.) The assumptions implicit in the example are that a small airport supporting only domestic flights will not need customs and border protection (CBP), immigration, and some of the other functions that will need to be added toward the end of phase 1 as the airport approaches phase 2 of transformation.

However, it will still need interfaces to the Transportation Security Agency's Common Screening System (CSS). It is also assumed that each airline will use a different Airline Reservation and Ticketing System (ARTS) that potentially requires a different interface to Passenger Intelligence System (PaxIS) and that upgrades to externally supplied systems will not necessarily be coordinated with RMN. This example includes facilities development projects as well as IT development projects.

| Project | Description | Owner | Start | End |
|---|---|---|---|---|
| Interface development and upgrade for PaxIS | PaxIS needs to interface with systems supplied by enterprises external to RMN such as ARTS (multiple versions) from airlines, CSS from TSA, and ABTS Commercial. Since upgrades to these external systems are not developed in conjunction with RMN, upgrades to the PaxIS interface may be required after the external system upgrade is installed. | RMN Development & Maintenance | Q2 YR2 | Open ended |
| Application secure LANS | Three secure networks need to be developed for RMN: airline secure LAN (multiple); FEDLAN secure LAN for federal and law enforcement users such as TSA and Customs and Border Protection (CBP); and RMN MAN. | RMN Information & Communication Technology | Q1 YR1 | Q1 YR2 |
| PaxIS LAN and firewalls | PaxIS needs its own LAN with firewalls to communicate with the airline secure LAN, FEDLAN secure LAN, and RMN MAN. | RMN Information & Communication Technology | Q3 YR1 | Q4 YR1 |
| PaxIS | The PaxIS is the centralized repository of passenger information for RMN. Its main functions are to support passenger identification, tracking, and management. | RMN Development & Maintenance | Q1 YR1 | Q3 YR2 |
| Passenger terminal construction | As RMN begins to provide regularly scheduled passenger airline operations and as the airport grows, RMN must develop and expand passenger terminal spaces and facilities. | RMN Development & Maintenance | Q1 YR1 | Q1 YR3 |
| RMN operations center upgrade | Before PaxIS can be installed, appropriate facilities need to be provided. | RMN Development & Maintenance | Q1 YR1 | Q4 YR2 |

## PV-2: Project Timelines

Just as the PV-1 shown earlier is a view that represents the composition of a project portfolio in terms of constituent projects and project owners, the PV-2: Project Timelines view represents a time-based schedule that depicts how these projects must be orchestrated in order for one project to provide timely deliverables to another.

The PV-2 references a time frame and phases and milestones. The planning window must be represented by these time frames, phases, and milestones, be consistent throughout the architecture and align with time frames, phases, and milestones in other roadmap type views such as the CV-3: Capability Phasing, SV-7: Systems Measures Matrix, SvcV-7: Services Measures Matrix, SvcV-8: Services Evolution Description, SvcV-9: Services Technology and Skills Forecast, SV-8: Systems Evolution Description, SV-9: Systems Technology and Skills Forecast, and StdV-2: Standards Forecast for example. These time frames and phases will also likely be described by the AV-1 as the applicable time frames overall for the architecture.

| View Information at a Glance | |
|---|---|
| View short name | PV-2 |
| Name | Project Timelines |
| Other names and alternatives | Application Migration Diagram (TOGAF 9.2) |
| Viewpoint | Project |
| View intent | The PV-2 is intended as a timeline chart for a collection of projects. Project management tools provide Gantt charts for a project in terms of tasks and schedule. The PV-2 serves a project portfolio with a similar representation—representing entire projects from a portfolio on a phased timeline. Some of the uses of the PV-2 are project management and control (including delivery timescales), project dependency risk identification, management of dependencies, and project portfolio management. |
| View audience | Project portfolio managers, executive management looking at the portfolio of projects and their respective schedules and risks on a dashboard-like display |
| Formal modeling methodology | None. |
| Integration of view with other views | Projects in PV-2 must be consistent with projects in all other Project Viewpoint models. The time frames and phases must be consistent with the architecture time frame and also roadmap-type views such as the SV-7: Systems Measures Matrix, SV-8: Systems Evolution Description, SV-9: Systems Technology and Skills Forecast, and StdV-2: Standards Forecast. See Figure 5-12 in Chapter 5 for integration with the CV-5: Capability to Organizational Development Mapping and PV-1: Project Portfolio Relationships. |

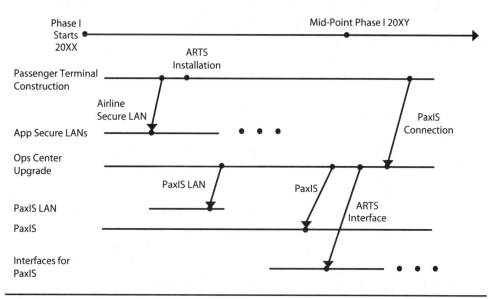

**Figure 14-2**   Example RMN passenger management PV-2

The PV-2 shows project start and stop dates, how project durations relate to each other, and project dependencies. Note that the PV-2 is not intended for use with Solution Level architectures because it is designed for managing multiple projects with dependencies. (Standalone schedules for single projects are of interest only to the single project manager.)

## Example: Passenger Management PV-2

Figure 14-2 shows an example PV-2, a partial set of timelines for early RMN Airport transition phase 1. In the figure, the arrows show the dependencies, with the tail of each arrow indicating the dependent project and the head of each arrow pointing to the project that should supply the needed component. The positioning of the arrows indicates the expected time when the needed component should be available. The assumptions are that early in phase 1, there will be only one airline serving RMN Airport. The focus is on the dependencies around the integration of the airline-supplied basic ARTS system and PaxIS. The example would be more complex if the timelines covered more of phase 1 and if more than one airline was involved.

# PV-3: Project to Capability Mapping

In a project portfolio of multiple projects whose primary purpose is to deliver a capability or a set of capabilities, the PV-3: Project to Capability Mapping view maps each individual project to the capabilities it provides components for. In other words, a project may provide only some components for a capability configuration, a complete capability configuration, or, in rare cases, more than one complete capability configuration. This view is useful for detecting whether multiple projects are delivering the same capability configuration or whether some projects do not contribute to any capabilities. It can also show whether some component of a capability configuration is not being developed by any project.

| View Information at a Glance | |
| --- | --- |
| View short name | PV-3 |
| Name | Project to Capability Mapping |
| Other names and alternatives | Project Context Diagram (TOGAF 9.2) |
| Viewpoint | Project |
| View intent | The PV-3 can be used to identify capability redundancies and shortfalls, highlight phasing issues, expose organizational or system interoperability problems, and support program decisions, such as when to phase out a legacy system. |
| View audience | Portfolio managers and planners |
| Formal modeling methodology | None. The view can be represented using a tabular format. |
| Integration of view with other views | Projects in PV-3 must be consistent with projects in all other Project Viewpoint views. Capabilities in PV-3 must be consistent with capabilities in the CV-2: Capability Taxonomy. |

## Example: Domestic Passenger Identification PV-3

In this example, most of the projects provide components for each of the three identified capabilities. It is assumed that in the early phase 1 transition for RMN Airport, the passenger terminal construction project does not address facilities for TSA and baggage handling or baggage claims. (For example, the early passenger terminal may consist of portable temporary structures.) The projects for these facilities have not been included in this set of examples.

| | Capability | | |
| --- | --- | --- | --- |
| **Project** | **Passenger Check-In** | **Passenger Screening** | **Baggage Handling** |
| Interface development and upgrade for PaxIS | X | X | X |
| Application secure LANs | X | X | X |
| PaxIS LAN and firewalls | X | X | X |
| PaxIS | X | X | X |
| Passenger terminal construction | X | | |
| RMN operations center upgrade | X | X | X |

# Summary

The Project Viewpoint views are designed to support portfolio managers and planners in the management of investment portfolios. The Project Viewpoint views integrate with the Capability Viewpoint views and these two viewpoints provide the majority of the recommended core views for Enterprise Level architectures. The Project Viewpoint includes only three views—PV-1: Project Portfolio Relationships allows tracking of portfolio projects to the organization managing the portfolio; PV-2: Project Timelines allows the tracking of critical deliverable dependencies among the projects in a portfolio or across portfolios; and PV-3: Project to Capability Mapping allows the tracking of project contributions to the development of desired capabilities.

# Questions

1. Discuss the challenges of managing a family of projects versus managing a single project. Will the project management tools that help manage single projects also help you manage multiple projects? How will they handle the determination of dependencies of tasks across projects?

2. What Capability Viewpoint views can help you manage a family of products? How would you use the CV-3: Capability Phasing and CV-4: Capability Dependencies to help you analyze the project portfolio?

3. Does your enterprise distinguish between programs, projects, and initiatives? Explain what these terms mean in the context of the federal government, DoD, and commercial enterprises.

4. Where are the financial aspects of a project, program, or initiative reflected (or not) inside the Project Viewpoint views depicted in this chapter?

5. What are the pros and cons of not developing a PV-3: Project to Capability Mapping?

6. Who is the audience for the Project Viewpoint?

7. Discuss the analysis aspects related to the costs, paybacks, and benefits of:

    a. A new system being developed and viewed as a capital investment

    b. A project viewed as a budgeted expense that represents a sunken investment

    c. An initiative that is opportunistic and represents a gamble on the payoff

# References

The Enterprise Portfolio Management Council, Pennypacker, James, and San Retna, eds. 2009. *Project Portfolio Management: A View from the Management Trenches.* Hoboken, NJ: John Wiley & Sons.

Government Accountability Office. 2005. *Best Practices: Better Support of Weapons System Program Managers Needed to Improve Outcomes.* GAO-06-110. www.gao.gov/new.items/d06110.pdf.

Government Accountability Office. 2006. *Defense Acquisitions: Major Weapons Systems Continue to Experience Cost and Schedule Problems Under DoD's Revised Policy.* GAO-06-368. www.gao.gov/new.items/d06368.pdf.

Microsoft Corporation. 2011. *Plans Within Plans: Master Projects and Subprojects.* http://office.microsoft.com/en-us/project-help/plans-within-plans-master-projects-and subprojects-HA001226035.aspx#BM#2.

# Operational Viewpoint

The Operational Viewpoint serves the interest of an audience concerned with the business processes, activities, and tasks that are performed by an enterprise or enterprise segment or that provide the context for a business solution. The Operational Viewpoint is concerned with the here and the now, as opposed to the Capability (strategic) Viewpoint, which is concerned with planning for the future.

In military operations, the Operational Viewpoint models and represents the concept of operations (CONOPS). The military mission drives the military operation. The operation involves tasks and/or activities that are conducted by one or more performers. The Operational Viewpoint represents how military tasks are orchestrated by multiple performers to achieve the desired effect or end result of the mission. A military operation also has to consider threats, battlefield conditions, and other context information that materially affect an operation.

In civilian government and commercial operations, the Operational Viewpoint represents the business processes, their decompositions into specific activities and steps, as well as the orchestration of activities required to achieve the purpose of the process. The Operational Viewpoint involves both human and automated processes that fulfill and support the mission of the enterprise.

An operational viewpoint that represents as-is architecture elements may represent current processes with current automated and nonautomated performers that enable specific activities within the process. An operational viewpoint that represents to-be, or target, architecture elements should avoid depicting solutions and focus on defining the future state only in operational terms. Deferring the decision to design the solution but focus on identifying and representing the business problem provides what the programming community calls "late binding"—offering a wider canvas for implementation as newer technologies and solution techniques become available.

Frequently, there is much debate among the architects and stakeholders on the distinctions between a business function that represents *what* is required in terms of the mission needs as activity, and the business process that depicts *how* the function is accomplished today. For example, in RMN Airport passenger identification, there is a function that must be accomplished to entitle passengers to access and to services: the process that checks badges, alien registration cards, passports, and other passenger identification documents is specific to today's needs as well as those in the future. But the primary difference between functions and processes is that functions are enduring when the mission is enduring, but processes can change with reorganizations, technology modernization, improved business processes, or efficiency speedups. In the DoDAF, a capability is akin to the commercial function, in that they both indicate *what* is needed, not *how* it is resolved or addressed. Commercial organizations that in the past defined a purely functional enterprise are beginning to take a capability-based view of their enterprise along with its implications for service-based solutions.

# Architecting Concerns for the Operational Viewpoint

The Operational Viewpoint addresses some of the architecting concerns and discipline related to operations:

- **Communicating the "big picture" to decision-makers**  The many details of real-world operations serve to cloud a deeper understanding of the big picture. The OV-1: High-Level Operational Concept Graphic view is a simple freeform graphical representation of the operation, depicting key players, key locations, key activities, key outcomes and results, and linkages between these. Aimed at the high-level decision-maker who has little time but great capacity to absorb and understand well-drawn pictures in briefings, the OV-1 view is essential for the architect to tell his or her operational story.

- **Understanding command relationships**  In large and complex organizations, people's roles are clearly defined in terms of authority and responsibility. An organizational chart depicts the roles and responsibilities and reporting relationships formally. At the same time, in collaborative operations involving people from multiple enterprises, formal memorandum of understanding, formal rules of engagement, or contracts must be put in place to ensure that collaboration will occur. The OV-4: Organization Relationships Chart view is a recording of all of these mechanisms for ensuring collaboration. In many operations, teams may be temporarily constituted for a specific purpose and be disbanded once the purpose is accomplished. In many governance and administrative operations, standing teams are put in place to function as oversight, steering, or coordination bodies. Each of these types of teams must be represented in the OV-4 view along with the permanent roles or organizational assignments that members have in addition to their team roles.

- **Breaking down task complexity**  A complex task involves many activities and performers, many exchanges of resources, and the need for a more detailed breakdown. The OV-5a: Operational Activity Decomposition Tree view represents the orderly decomposition of activities that support an operation or process. Depending on the type of actual modeling methodology used, such models can also depict the following:

- Refinement of a larger grain activity into smaller grain activities using decomposition (OV-5a)

- Sequencing of predecessor and successor activities to indicate temporal dependencies (OV-5b)

- Resource flows (including information flows) from one activity to another (OV-5b: Operational Activity Model in conjunction with OV-2 and OV-3–Operational Resource Flow Description and Matrix)

- Constraints, rules, and guidance used to control and guide activities (OV-5b in conjunction with OV-6a: Operational Rules Model)

- Measures associated with activity performance, resource expenditure (OV-5b in conjunction with measure types and measures)

- **Knowing where to start architecting**  The activity model is one of the first models to build in an integrated architecture, since all dynamics in an architecture come from activities and tasks. The activity model defines the span of an operational life cycle and hence serves to set the scope for the rest of the architecture. Omitting an activity also results in omitting the performers of that activity, the locations where the activity is performed, and the resource flows going in and out of the activity. Setting architecture scope frequently involves controlling the scope of the activity model. The start of an activity-focused operational viewpoint is usually through a IDEF0 context diagram (OV-5b) along with optional ancestor diagrams that show the broader context in which the key activity is placed.

- **Understanding resource flows**  In a complex interconnection of players, understanding of resource supply lines and flows is essential, particularly if some of the players are external to the enterprise and require agreements for supply. The OV-2: Operational Resource Flow Description view is used to identify the need for resource flows between activities. Since activities are associated with performers, the OV-2 also depicts the resource flows between performers associated with the activities they are performing. The OV-3: Operational Resource Flow Matrix view is a detailed representation of all resource flows between performer pairs in the context of the activities they are performing. The OV-2 and OV-3 views therefore primarily support the interests of an audience that is interested in who the players are in the Operational Viewpoint and what the needs for information/resource exchange between the players are. In the OV-2, players can also be marked to indicate that they represent an external enterprise or another player who is external to the scope of the architecture. The OV-2 is a valuable model for providing a very quick pictorial view of the key players in an architecture and their needs to exchange resources.

- **Understanding the effect of planned and unplanned behaviors**  The OV-6a: Operational Rules Model, OV-6b: State Transition Description, and OV-6c: Event-Trace Description views all model the dynamic behavior of the operation. All of the other operational models described depict static configurations of architecture elements for performing some role in the Operational Viewpoint.

- **Flowing behavioral constraints down from guidance**   Guidance is related to establishing constraints on behaviors (and sometimes structures). Examples of guidance such as laws, policies, and regulations all result in rules that must be obeyed by the operations. The OV-6a: Operational Rules Model represents these rules as well as their traceability to the guidance that established the rules. These rules may be tied to operational activities through the activity model controls as in IDEF0. In Business Process Modeling Notation (BPMN), the rules that guide decision points are described in the OV-6a, while the activity model itself is modeled as a OV-5b.

- **Establishing structural constraints in a database**   Structural rules establish database constraints, for example. A rule can constrain and assert how many instances of one entity can be related to how many instances of others; for example, a passenger can have only one passport, or a passenger may have multiple passports (dual citizens).

- **Understanding activity sequencing and handoffs**   One of the key concerns in a mission or business process is the exact sequence in which activities are to be performed. Activity models (OV-5b) such as those built using the BPMN or flowcharts represent sequences of activities. The combination of activity performer pairs that are sequenced with other activity performer pairs shows the handoffs from one performer to another.

- **Understanding event sequences**   Event sequencing is an important part of analyzing operational architectures in terms of the information flow and the ability to process information within certain windows of event sequences. Event sequences based on scenarios are represented in OV-6c. Events occur within the scope of some activity. The activities that are represented in the OV-6c are consistent with the activities in other views.

- **Understanding state transitions**   An architecture object retains its state unless an activity or event changes that state. Understanding how the behaviors of activities and events can change the state of architecture objects is an important part of impact analysis—the study of desirable and undesirable side effects. The OV-6b provides the view needed to perform state-change analysis. The architecture objects, activities, and events in the OV-6b are consistent with other architecture objects within the scope of the architecture.

# Operational Viewpoint Integrated Models

The Operational Viewpoint describes a set of tightly coupled models that must share many common elements such as activities, resource flows/information flows, rules and constraints, performers, and so on. A few examples of the needs for consistency between models in an integrated architecture are listed here:

- If the OV-1 depicts performers and activities, they must be consistent with performers and activities in the OV-2, OV-3, OV-5, OV-6a, and OV-6c.

- Resource flows, if depicted in the OV-2, must be consistent with OV-3 and OV-6c.

- Activities, performers, and resource flows in OV-5 must be consistent with OV-2, OV-3, and OV-6c.

- Triggering events in OV-3 must be consistent with events in OV-6c.

# Operational Focus

One of the biggest challenges in architecting is to establish a viable scope. Many architecture projects find out very late in the process that the scope was too large for the development time frames. The Operational Viewpoint arguably provides the key controls over the scope. In this section, we describe a few methods to show how the scope for an architecture project may be maintained by focusing on some key architecture elements. When enterprise transformation involves focus on the Capability Viewpoint, the management of scope may be restricted to those parts of the operations that may need to change because of changes in strategy or the availability or loss of capabilities.

## Operational Activity

Figure 15-1 shows the operational activity in the center of the diagram. This tends to imply that we start with defining activities based on a predefined mission or business process. Activities are "scope cuts" that also limit the performers, resources, locations, events, and other architecture elements that are related to that activity. We can take this

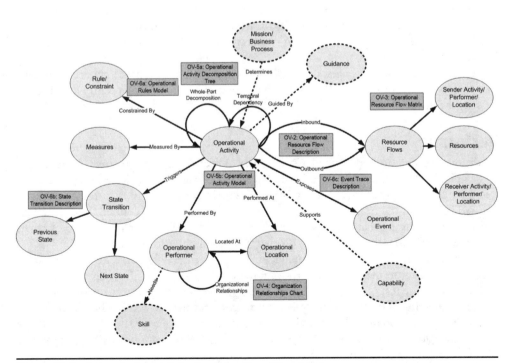

**Figure 15-1**  Integrated models for the Operational Viewpoint

to the next step and define the scope of an architecture as described and represented by a life cycle of activities. Often this is perceived as a value-added process by which raw materials and other inputs are transformed into a value-added product at the end of the life cycle.

In the RMN Airport, for example, we could model the life cycle of passenger processing to understand the various stages and activities involved from the time the passenger enters the airport to the time he or she departs on an outbound flight; or we could model the life cycle of a passenger car entering the airport terminal, dropping off passengers, and parking in one of the airport operated parking ramps.

## Operational Event

Another method of modeling can start with an event that sets in motion a chain of responses. By making the operational event the focus, we can then define the activities that are involved in responding to the event.

In the RMN Airport, a key event may be the event of an aircraft fire while an aircraft is parked at the gate. The modeling of the scenario starts with this event and lays out the various responses in crowd management, passenger and crew management, emergency firefighting, law enforcement activities, and other elements of disaster recovery.

## Operational Location

In some architectures, location becomes a key focus for defining the expanse of the architecture scope. Notional locations such as air bases, operational centers, data centers, or military camps are all potential locations of focus. Sometimes a combination of locations and performers such as an integrated operations center becomes the focus of the architecture.

In the airport, the passenger terminal or the operations center are generic locations that may be the focus for an architecture that is focused on operations center activities or passenger terminal activities.

## Performer

Traditional command and control architectures are centered on performer. A performer is assigned responsibility and accountability and is allocated or assigned various activities. In the federal government, key positions are defined by law and their responsibilities defined in acts. In the military, key roles as well as their duties are defined in joint operations. Sometimes, especially in future architectures, the performer may not be known and is replaced with a business function that is a placeholder for the performer.

In the airport, the concessions manager is a performer who may be of interest in defining a small enterprise around airport concessions. The scope of the architecture will be focused on the responsibilities, duties, and activities around the concessions manager such as managing activities, performers, resources, and events within the airport's collection of concessionaires that provide food, parking, gift shop, shoeshine, overnight accommodation, showers, and other passenger amenities that are not directly related to the core domain of aviation.

# Views in the Operational Viewpoint

The Operational Viewpoint contains nine views:

- **OV-1: High-Level Operational Concept Graphic**   The OV-1 is a key communication tool to show how the operational concept works. The OV-1 is a free-form pictorial representation of the various elements of the operation and their relationships, and its primary aim is to communicate at a high level the operational concepts to decision makers, planners, and architects. The OV-1 can describe a mission, a class of missions, or scenarios. It is primarily used to represent the elements of an operational solution.

- **OV-2: Operational Resource Flow Description**   The OV-2 depicts flows of resources between activities also showing the performers of those activities. The OV-2 is a DoDAF-described model that requires a formal representation that is defined by the DoDAF. It can be used to show flows of funding, personnel, and materiel in addition to information. The OV-2 does not show how resources are exchanged, but simply what is exchanged between activities with their corresponding performers. In the OV-2, given the constraints of diagrammatic representation, resource flows are represented in an aggregated manner for compactness. The OV-2 acts as a communication tool to depict resource flows across the scope of the architecture.

- **OV-3: Operational Resource Flow Matrix**   The OV-3 details the compact resource flows depicted in the OV-2 in the form of a matrix that shows the exchange activities with their performers, as well as a breakdown of the aggregated resources and descriptions of the resource elements. The OV-3 may contain contextual attributes and performance attributes/requirements for the resource flows within an operational context for the operations. The OV-3 may also contain attributes for information assurance such as security classification and identification of privacy requirements. The OV-3 is the operational blueprint for a detailed description of resource exchanges. It can be used to determine if there are any exchange requirements that have been omitted or not detailed with attributes such as exchange timeliness requirements, security classification, or throughput requirements.

- **OV-4: Organizational Relationships Chart**   The OV-4 shows the relationships among organizations that are acting as performers in the operational architecture. Based on the nature of the organizations involved, these may range from a command relationship to one defined by contractual agreements. The OV-4 may also depict temporary force structures as well as permanent organizations. The OV-4 is used to ensure that the command and organizational relationships are consistent with other aspects of the architecture such as resource flows that require prior establishment of formal relationships to occur effectively and repeatedly.

- **OV-5a: Operational Activity Decomposition Tree**   The OV-5a is a hierarchy diagram that systematically breaks down a complex activity into its components. A common technique in activity modeling methods such as IDEF0 (or pools and performer swim lanes in process models), the OV-5a depicts the scope of a complex activity through its decomposition. The OV-5a acts like a summary explanation of how a complex activity can be broken down into simpler ones and is a good communication and validation tool to determine if there are any holes in understanding.

- **OV-5b: Operational Activity Model**   The OV-5b is focused on detailing activities with the input and output resources they transform, their performers, and the constraints and drivers (controls) that guide their execution. In formal modeling techniques such as IDEF0, the OV-5a and OV-5b are part of the same model set—the decomposition of the activities is also followed by the decomposition of inputs, outputs, controls, and performers. The OV-5b is a complete characterization of the activity that describes and explicitly represents all aspects required for an implementation.

- **OV-6a: Operational Rules Model**   The OV-6a tabulates the business rules that are constraints on the way that business is done in the enterprise. At the enterprise level, these may represent laws, regulations, policies, and rules that guide and constrain the enterprise. At the mission or scenario level, these may be specific rules that flow down from the laws, policies, and regulations that are applicable to the specific scenario. The OV-6a is useful to ensure that governance can be effectively applied to the operations and compliance is explicitly represented in the architecture.

- **OV-6b: State Transition Description**   The OV-6b is a formal mathematical model for describing the state or status transitions of some operational architecture element that has interesting state. The combination of the object's current state and triggering event (usually caused by an activity) causes a transition to the object's next state. A simple application of the OV-6b is to describe the status changes in a work product as it travels through a workflow process. The key to OV-6b is to identify the object that has state. Actions can be associated with transitions.

- **OV-6c: Event-Trace Description**   Each OV-6c includes a textual scenario that illustrates a critical sequence of events, such as a performance or security critical sequence. It can also be used to illustrate details of a concept of operations in a way similar to a use case. The OV-6b also includes a graphic that traces the sequence of events in terms of the series of resource exchanges from the OV-3 involving performers and activities triggered by the events as described in the scenario. This modeling technique is designed for modeling discrete events.

# OV-1: High-Level Operational Concept Graphic

| View Information at a Glance | |
| --- | --- |
| View short name | OV-1 |
| Name | High-Level Operational Concept Graphic |
| Other names | Graphical CONOPS (concept of operations)<br>Concept Overview Diagram (FEAF2)<br>Business Footprint Diagram (TOGAF)<br>Business Model Diagram (TOGAF)<br>Valuestream Map (TOGAF) |
| Viewpoint | Operational |
| View intent | Provide a graphical depiction of what the architecture is about and an idea of the players and operations involved. An OV-1 can be used to orient and focus detailed discussions. Its main use is to aid human communication, and it is intended for presentation to high-level decision-makers. |
| View audience | High-level decision-makers—anyone who needs a quick briefing on an architecture |
| Formal modeling methodology | None. This model uses freeform graphics and is primarily intended for communication and not analysis. |
| Integration of view with other views | The OV-1 abstracts the performers in OV-2, OV-3, OV-5, and OV-6c, as well as activities in OV-5, OV-3. It may also abstract locations in OV-2, SV-1, and SvcV-1; systems in SV-1; and services in SvcV-1. It may also depict desired effects associated with the capabilities in the Capability Viewpoint. |

## Example: Passenger Identification OV-1

Figure 15-2, drawn as an unstructured picture, simply depicts that a common form of identification process will be used for the passenger at multiple locations—a significant improvement from the current situation, where each location is performing its own passenger identification—with mixed results!

Because of the free form of expression, the architect has the freedom to choose the focus of the OV-1. In geographic military operations, for example, the backdrop of the OV-1 may be the terrain inside the theater. In phased activities, the OV-1 may have a life cycle "arrow" depicting the phases and their sequence with markings for specific activities and players. The OV-1 is therefore really a picture and not a "Model" because of this creative freedom it offers.

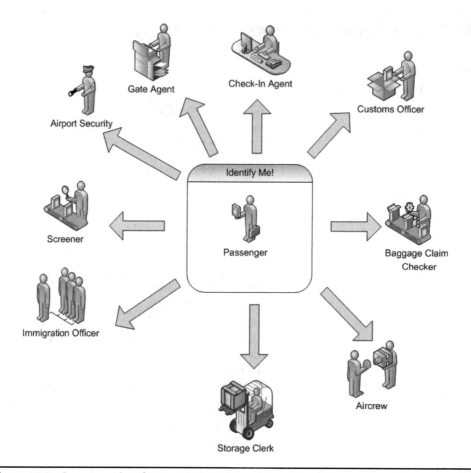

**Figure 15-2**   Passenger identification OV-1: High-Level Operational Concept Graphic

## OV-2: Operational Resource Flow Description

| View Information at a Glance | |
| --- | --- |
| View short name | OV-2 |
| Name | Operational Resource Flow Description |
| Other names | Operational Node Connectivity Description (Old)<br>Business Node Connectivity Description<br>Business Interaction Matrix (TOGAF 9) |
| Viewpoint | Operational |

| View Information at a Glance | |
|---|---|
| View intent | A specific application of the OV-2 is to describe a logical pattern of resource (information, funding, personnel, or materiel) flows among performers. The purpose of an OV-2 model is to describe a logical pattern of resource flows. The logical pattern need not correspond to specific organizations, systems or locations, allowing resource flows to be established without prescribing the way that the resource flows are handled and without prescribing solutions. |
| View audience | Any planner with an interest in analyzing resource flows such as logistics planners (materiel flows), communications network planners (information flows), and staffing and deployment planners (personnel flows) |
| Formal modeling methodology | None. At its simplest, the OV-2 can be represented as a simple matrix of performers, with each intersection representing a resource flow. The OV-2 can also be depicted graphically with performers at the end points of an arrow describing a resource flow and annotations to depict activities and locations related to the performers. |
| Integration of view with other views | OV-2 performers must be consistent with OV-3 senders and receivers, OV-5 performers, and OV-6c performers. |

## Example: Passenger Identification OV-2

The OV-2 is a structured graphic (Figure 15-3) view depicting need lines—needs for resource exchange between the end points—typically performers, activities, and location combinations. The solid lines represent the current (as-is) resource flows. The dotted lines represent the envisioned future state resource flows. The OV-2 is a topological map of resource flows, an abstract graph where the vertices represent performers, activities, and locations and the edges represent need lines or needs to exchange resources. Optionally the flow lines can be annotated with specific resources that are flowing between the end points—information elements, materiel, personnel, or funds. It is one of the simplest models to build and provides a quick overview of key players and key operational need line interfaces. It can also be more compactly depicted as a matrix with the two axes both representing performers and the intersecting cells representing whether there is a need line requirement between the performers in the X and Y axes for that cell.

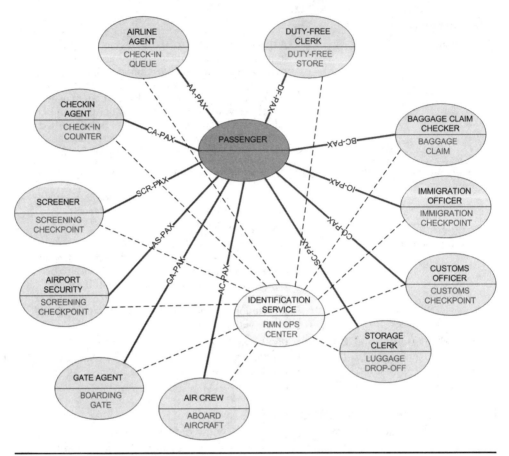

**Figure 15-3** Passenger identification OV-2: Operational Resource Flow Description

## OV-3: Operational Resource Flow Matrix

| View Information at a Glance | |
| --- | --- |
| View short name | OV-3 |
| Name | Operational Resource Flow Matrix |
| Other names | Operational Information Exchange Matrix (Old)<br>Business Information Exchange Matrix<br>Data Entity/Business Function Matrix (TOGAF 9.2)<br>Business Interaction Matrix (TOGAF 9.2)<br>(Business) Service/Information Diagram (TOGAF 9.2) |
| Viewpoint | Operational |

| **View Information at a Glance** | |
|---|---|
| View intent | Depicts resource flows (including information exchanges) between operational activities in different locations, organizations, or performers. The OV-3 depicts key attributes of the resource flows and represents a logistics network for resource flow. |
| View audience | People interested in flow of resources outside the boundaries of their organizations or locations to other organizations or locations based on the activities that need to be performed at both places. These flows have to be set up with explicit agreements and rules of engagement. |
| Formal modeling methodology | None. This view is usually represented as a matrix. |
| Integration of view with other views | Performers, locations, and activities in OV-3 must be consistent with performers, locations, and activities in OV-2 and OV-5. Resource flows in OV-3 must be consistent with need lines in OV-2 and input/output flows in activity models (OV-5b). Resource flows in OV-3 must be consistent with messages exchanged between lifelines in OV-6c. |

## Example: Passenger Identification OV-3

The following table shows the OV-3 as an elaboration of the need lines depicted inside the OV-2. Each specific resource flow for each specific need line in the OV-2 is detailed with a description of the sender, receiver, sending activity, receiving activity, as well as the resource and resource type that are exchanged.

| Need Line from OV-2 | ID | Sender | Sender Activity | Receiver | Receiver Activity | Resource | Resource Type |
|---|---|---|---|---|---|---|---|
| AA-PAX | 1 | Passenger | Enter passenger queue | Airline agent | Check entitlement | Boarding pass | Information |
| | 2 | Passenger | Enter passenger queue | Airline agent | Check identity | Identity document | Information |
| | 3 | Airline agent | Record entitlement | Passenger | Enter queue | Stamped boarding pass | Information |
| DF-PAX | 4 | Passenger | Pay for purchase | Duty-free clerk | Check entitlement | Boarding pass | Information |
| | 5 | Passenger | Pay for purchase | Duty-free clerk | Check identity | Identity document | Information |
| | 6 | Passenger | Pay for purchase | Duty-free clerk | Validate payment | Payment artifact | Information |
| | 7 | Passenger | Pay for purchase | Duty-free clerk | Record payment | Payment | Funds |

*(continued)*

| Need Line from OV-2 | ID | Sender | Sender Activity | Receiver | Receiver Activity | Resource | Resource Type |
|---|---|---|---|---|---|---|---|
| | 8 | Duty-free clerk | Acknowledge payment | Passenger | Receive acknowledgment | Receipt artifact | |
| | 9 | Duty-free clerk | Dispatch merchandise | Passenger | Pick up merchandise | Merchandise | Materiel |

The OV-3 may also show attributes of the resource flow (not shown in example), such as throughput, measurement units, and so on. In the case of information flows, attributes such as personally identifying information (PII) or security classification are important to define operationally in the OV-3 before jumping in and implementing systems exchanges that could compromise these attributes.

## OV-4: Organizational Relationships Chart

| View Information at a Glance | |
|---|---|
| View short name | OV-4 |
| Name | Organizational Relationships Chart |
| Other names | Org Chart Organization/Actor Catalog (TOGAF 9.2) Role Catalog (TOGAF 9.2) Actor/Role Matrix (TOGAF 9.2) Organization Decomposition Diagram (TOGAF 9.2) |
| Viewpoint | Operational |
| View intent | Depict formal and informal organization relationships to determine whether architectural linkages such as resource flows are supported by organizational relationships. |
| View audience | All people interested in how the stakeholders or players in an architecture are related. Most enterprises control and publish their formal organization charts, and joint military operations are accompanied (and coordinated) by formal organization relationship structures. |
| Formal modeling methodology | None. Organization charts are typically tree-structured, matrix-oriented, or combinations of tree structures with nondirect relationships between organizations. |
| Integration of view with other views | OV-4 provides the context for all organizational performers in an integrated architecture and must be consistent with performers depicted in other Operational Viewpoint models such as OV-1, OV-2, OV-3, OV-5, OV-6a (authorization rules), and OV-6c (lifelines). Any role-based, as opposed to organization-based, performers must be mapped to OV-4 organizations in the AV-2 if nowhere else. |

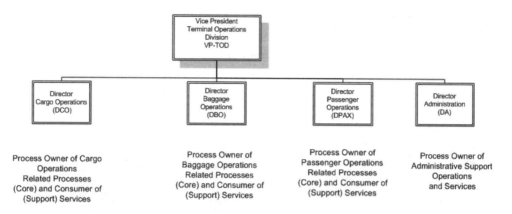

**Figure 15-4**   Terminal operations OV-4: Organizational Relationships Chart

## Example 1: RMN Terminal Operations Division Organization Relationships Chart

The RMN Terminal Operations Division (TOD) chart (Figure 15-4) depicts the formal reporting relationships that are useful to understand in the context of the terminal operations Segment Level architecture. Not shown on this organization relationships charts are organizations external to the TOD. These will be added as the OV-2 gets fleshed out. This example includes information on lower-level organizations from the AV-2.

The example OV-4 is very simple. In reality, the OV-4 encompasses all types of organizational relationships and is not restricted to the formal reporting structures. In fact, the OV-4 is a very useful model to clarify relationships between standing organizations (permanent structures) and temporary organizations constructed for some purpose such as task forces, working groups, committees, and oversight and review boards. Frequently, members of the permanent organizations are also assigned roles in these temporary structures and must be represented in the OV-4 to gain a fuller insight into their interactions.

## Example 2: Passenger Identification OV-4

This OV-4 (Figure 15-5) depicts in great detail the roles and organizations that surround the passenger in the context of passenger identification. Notice that these relationships are governed by many considerations: contracts and agreements, formal reporting authority, customer-supplier relationships, and legal and regulatory forces to comply. This model is more realistic of a real-world situation. The OV-4 may also be overlaid with relationships that are based on real-world aberrations as well to recognize that these relationships do influence the behavior of the architecture.

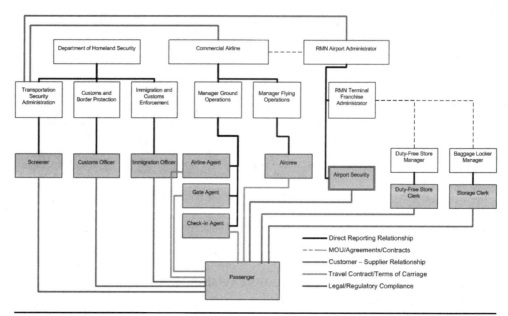

**Figure 15-5**   Passenger identification OV-4: Organizational Relationships Chart

## OV-5a: Operational Activity Decomposition Tree
## OV-5b: Operational Activity Model

| View Information at a Glance | |
| --- | --- |
| View short name | OV-5a, OV-5b |
| Names | Operational Activity Decomposition Tree (OV-5a)<br>Operational Activity Model (OV-5b) |
| Other names | Activity Model (IDEF0)<br>Function Decomposition (SADT)<br>Process Model<br>Workflow Model (IDEF3)<br>Swim Lane Model (BPMN)<br>Activity Based Costing Model (ABM)<br>Process/Event/Control/Product Catalog (TOGAF 9.2)<br>Functional Decomposition Diagram (TOGAF 9.2)<br>Process Flow Diagram (TOGAF 9.2) |
| Viewpoint | Operational |
| View intent | The OV-5a and the OV-5b describe the operations that are normally conducted in the course of achieving a mission or a business goal. They describe operational activities (or tasks), input/output flows between activities, and to/from activities that are external (outside the scope of the architectural description). |

| View Information at a Glance | |
| --- | --- |
| View audience | Process engineers, process improvement specialists, operational analysts |
| Formal modeling methodology | Several activity/process modeling methodologies are applicable: IDEF0 activity models, BPMN, and ABM are all good techniques for representing activity models. |
| Integration of view with other views | The OV-5a and OV-5b activities must be consistent with all operational activities used in all the views such as OV-1, OV-2, OV-3, OV-6a (process-based rules), OV-6b (agents for state transition), and OV-6c. |

## Example 1: Functional Decomposition of RMN Airport's Enterprise Business Functions

Though we have described the difference between business functions and process activities, we will use the OV-5a view to depict the decomposition of business functions at RMN Airport (Figure 15-6).

Core Mission Operations
Mission Support Operations

**RMN International Operations – As-Is Business Reference Model**

**Airport Operations**
  Airport Security
  Motor Vehicle Operations
  Fire Safety Operations
  Airport Operating Permits

**Airfield Operations**
  Airfield Permits
    Air Carrier Operating Permit
    Single Use Operating Certificate
    Non-Exclusive License Agreement
    Motor Vehicle Permit Monthly
    Motor Vehicle Operating Permit
    Fuel Delivery Permit
    Off-Site In-Flight Catering Permit
  Airfield Surface Movement Operations
    Airfield Bus Operations
    Service Vehicle Operations
    Aircraft Movement Area Operations

**Architecture and Civil Engineering**
  Permits
  Civil Engineering Projects

**Facilities and Equipment Management**
  Facility Maintenance
  Equipment Maintenance

**Terminal Operations**
  Passenger Information Services
    Visitor Information and Services Unit
    LAX Ambassador Program
  Terminal Cargo Operations
  Terminal Passenger Operations
    Passenger Checkin
    Passenger Screening
    Passenger Seating
    Public Address Operations
    Wireless Hot Spot Operations
    Restroom Operations
    Left Luggage Operations
  Gate/Ramp Operations
    TBIT Ramp Safety
    Planeside Loading/Unloading Operations
    Mobile Ramp Operations
    Gate Operations
  Baggage Handling Operations
    TBIT/T3 Baggage Handling System
    Lost Baggage Services
    Oversize Baggage Handling
    HAZMAT/Special Baggage Handling
    Baggage Tracking
    Baggage Screening
  TBIT Refurbishment
  Secure In Line Baggage Screening Services
    Northside Inline Project
    Southside Inline Project
  Terminal Solicitation Management Services
    GM Solicitation Program

**Landside Operations**
  Parking Services
    Parking Garage Services
    Public Parking Services
    Airport Employee Parking Services
    Airport Vehicles Parking Services
    Vendors and Delivery Parking Services
    Cargo Delivery and Pickup Parking Services
  Delivery Mode
    Overflow Parking Lots
    Short Term Parking Areas
    Long Term Parking
    Valet Parking
  LAX ShuttleLAX
  FlyAway
  Ground Transportation Permit Program
    Vendor Delivery Parking Permit
    LAX Employee Parking Program
  Ground Transportation Services
    Airport Terminal ShuttleTrain
    Terminal Services
    Taxi and Limousine Services
    Rental Car Services

**Administration**
  Franchisory Oversight
  Financial Administration
  Facility Administration
  Policy and Procedures

**Human Resource Management**
  Benefits Administration
  Payroll Recruitment and Outprocessing
  Union Liaison
  Performance Management
  Ombudsman/Mediation/Arbitration

**Aircraft Operations**
  Noise Abatement
  Engine Test Operations
  Maintenance Operations
  Refueling Operations
  Loading/Unloading Operations
  Flight Kitchen/Catering Operations
  Deicing Operations
  Disinfection Operations

**IT Operations**
  Data Center Operations
  Network Operations
  Infrastructure Operations
  Chief Information Officer
  Systems Program Offices

**Financial Operations**
  Financial Planning
  Accounts Management
  Contracts and Leases
  Budget Planning and Execution
  Investment Management

**Security Operations**
  Airport Security
  Landspace Security
  Aircraft Movement Area Security
  Terminal Building Security
  In line Screening Area Security
  Law Enforcement

**Figure 15-6**  RMN enterprise business reference model OV-5a: Operational Activity Decomposition Tree

The example depicts the functional decomposition of RMN Airport's business functions as a hierarchy (OV-5a). Core mission functions of operating an airport are distinguished from supporting functions that are required to ensure that core mission functions can be accomplished. A business reference model such as this is very useful for representing the span of an enterprise's functions and can be augmented to display top-level business processes under those functions.

### Example 2: Passenger Identification OV-5a: Operational Activity Decomposition Tree

In Figure 15-7, the example OV-5a is shown as activity decompositions from a variety of contexts. The figure shows the decompositions from the viewpoints of the immigration officer, the duty-free store clerk, the customs officer, and the storage clerk, for example. Because each of these roles (viewpoints) can see only their own activities, we wind up with a clump of decompositions that must later be orchestrated by a threading activity model, as shown in the next example.

### Example 3: Passenger Identification OV-5b: Operational Activity Model

In this model (Figure 15-8), we represent each of the viewpoints shown in the OV-5a as a swim lane. The activities inside the swim lane represent those that are visible to the respective performer. The lines are used to trace the control flow or handoffs of activities.

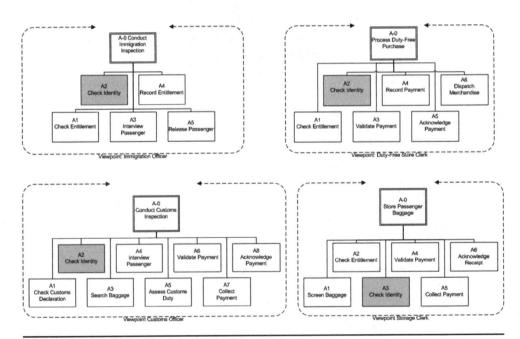

**Figure 15-7**   Passenger identification OV-5a: Operational Activity Decomposition Tree

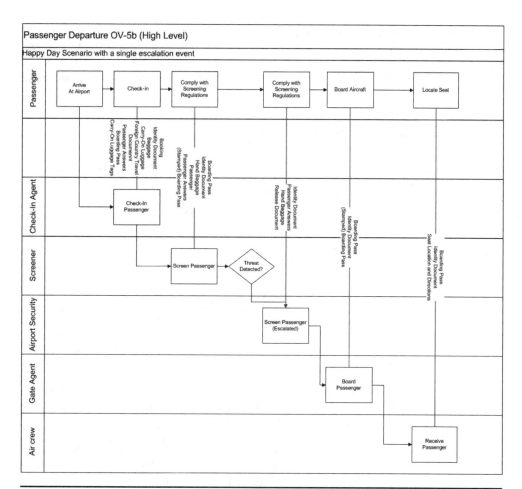

**Figure 15-8**  Passenger identification OV-5b: Operational Activity Model

The straight vertical lines show the information flows as annotations. The OV-5b information flows must be consistent with the OV-3 in the same architecture, which also shows information flows between the performers. Notice that the OV-3 can be easily derived from an annotated BPMN activity model that shows data flows.

We talk about "Happy Day scenarios" as activity sequences that do not have exceptions and that flow smoothly. In real life, we need to take into account all outcomes of the decision boxes in an activity model and handle the processing of those decisions appropriately.

The popular and widely used IDEF0 technique is excellent for progressive refinement and exposition of activities as well as their inputs, controls, outputs, and mechanisms (ICOMS), but it is not so good at representing orchestration of many activities by many performers in one diagram such as the swim lane or BPMN method does. Some modeling techniques are good at representing the hand-off of one activity to another (control flow), while others are better at depicting input-output flows. Each modeling technique has its strengths and weaknesses, and thorough discussion of activity modeling is outside the scope of this book.

## OV-6a: Operational Rules Model

| View Information at a Glance | |
|---|---|
| View short name | OV-6a |
| Name | Operational Rules Model |
| Other names | Rules Model<br>Decision Tree<br>Decision Table |
| Viewpoint | Operational |
| View intent | Specifies operational or business rules that are constraints on the way that business is done in the enterprise. At the mission-level, OV-6a may be based on business rules contained in doctrine, guidance, rules of engagement, and so on. At lower levels, OV-6a describes the rules that activities or other elements of the architecture behave under specified conditions. Rules are frequently required for executable models. |
| View audience | Process modelers, doctrine and policy making organizations, data modelers, performance and execution analysts. Because of its granularity, OV-6a is best applied to specific solution architectures rather than enterprise or segment architectures. |
| Formal modeling methodology | Decision tree, first order predicate logic, structured English, or other mathematical languages for expressing constraints. Rules are declarative (not procedural) and should be atomic, distinct, independent constructs. |
| Integration of view with other views | The rules must be associated with other elements of the architecture—that is, the rules apply to activities, state transitions, or other elements of the architecture. The terms used in business rules must be consistent with similar terms used in other models of the same integrated architecture. This varies from rule to rule. For example, authorization rules must be consistent with performers defined in other models. Actions in if-then-else (action assertion rules) must be consistent with operational activities; data elements used in formulae (derivation rules) must be consistent with data attributes in DIV models. |

# Example: Passenger Identification OV-6a: Operational Rules Model (Fragment)

The following example contains the form of rules found in source documents. These would need to be translated into some formal rules notation to become useful for behavior modeling. For example, the TSA guidance listing the types of acceptable passenger identification documents would be translated into at least 16 separate formal rules (since rules need to be atomic).

| Rule Group | Rule Statement | Source |
|---|---|---|
| Passenger Identification Document | Effective June 21, 2008, adult passengers (18 and over) are required to show a U.S. federal or state-issued photo ID that contains name, date of birth, gender, expiration date, and a tamper-resistant feature in order to be allowed to go through the checkpoint and onto their flight. | TSA Guidance: ID Requirements for Airport Checkpoints www.tsa.gov/travelers/airtravel/ acceptable_documents.shtm |
| Passenger Identification Document | Acceptable identification documents include U.S. passport DHS "Trusted Traveler" card U.S. passport card NEXUS SENTRI FAST U.S. military ID (active duty or retired military and their dependents and DoD civilians) Permanent resident card Border crossing card DHS designated enhanced driver's license Drivers licenses or other state photo identity cards issued by Department of Motor Vehicles or equivalent that meets REAL ID benchmarks An airline or airport issued ID (under TSA-approved security plan) Foreign government–issued passport Canadian provincial driver's license or Indian and Northern Affairs Canada (INAC) card Transportation Worker Identification Credential (TWIC) | TSA Guidance: ID Requirements for Airport Checkpoints www.tsa.gov/travelers/airtravel/ acceptable_documents.shtm |
| Passenger Identification Document | Non-U.S./Canadian citizens are not required to carry their passports if they have documents issued by the U.S. government such as permanent resident cards. Those who do not should be carrying their passports while visiting the United States. | TSA Guidance: ID Requirements for Airport Checkpoints www.tsa.gov/travelers/airtravel/ acceptable_documents.shtm |

It is important to cite the authority for rules. In the rules model, rules are generally tied to activities and performers though they can be associated with measurement, assessment, formulae for transforming values, and so on. A tailored form of the OV-6a can be used to associate rules with architecture elements. The DoDAF categorizes rules into the following major categories:

- **Structure assertion rules**   These rules constrain structural or existential relationships. Examples of such rules are definitions of customer, transaction, and so on. Structure assertion rules are used to build the logical data model for database implementation and often reflect data relationships.

- **Action assertion rules**   These rules constrain operational behaviors. They are frequently represented by decision boxes that apply to branching of an activity sequence based on the evaluation of conditions.

- **Derivation rules**   These rules determine how computations are performed to derive data from other data. Examples of these are equations, formulas, and lookup functions.

## OV-6b: State Transition Description

| View Information at a Glance | |
|---|---|
| View short name | OV-6b |
| Name | State Transition Description |
| Other names | Object State Transition Network (OSTN) Finite State Model, Harel State Chart |
| Viewpoint | Operational |
| View intent | The OV-6b is a formal mathematical model for describing how an object class or object (frequently a data entity) responds to various events (results of activities) by changing state or status. This model describes dynamic behavior. |
| View audience | The OV-6b, like the other behavioral models OVB-6a and OV-6c, is best applied to solution architecture descriptions and is not as applicable at the enterprise or segment architecting level. Solution architects and people interested in simulation and ensuring that behaviors are bounded in well-understood states are the audience for OV-6b. |
| Formal modeling methodology | UML State Chart, Harel State Chart, Finite State Model |
| Integration of view with other views | Activities and events in OV-6b must be consistent with activities and events in other Operational Viewpoint models. The architecture element that has state must appear in some other Operational view. |

## Example: Passenger Identification OV-6b

The state transition diagram (Figure 15-9) represents the state of a passenger through his or her movement through the terminal. A passenger is assumed to have a prior booking. The completion of the check-in activity transforms the passenger from a booked passenger state to a checked-in passenger state. Once the passenger enters the security screening area, he or she becomes subject to the screening process. If the screening process proceeds without any exceptions—that is, no triggering of any monitors or any selection of the passenger for additional screening—the passenger is cleared. If the additional screening fails to uncover some threat, the passenger is cleared. Cleared passengers go on to board their aircrafts with the agents scanning their boarding passes at the gate. If additional screening uncovers some confirmed threat, a passenger is detained.

The example serves to illustrate the technique in a deceptively simple and readable manner in a very contained scenario. In reality, state charts can get complicated with decision boxes, nested states, and concurrent transitions that have to meet at the same point. Not every object or class has interesting state. This technique is best used when the understanding of state and state transitions is important to understanding how business is done.

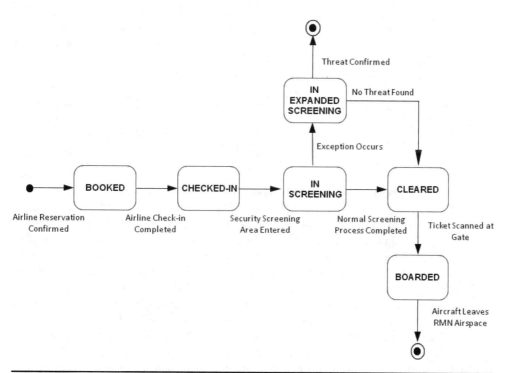

**Figure 15-9**   Passenger identification OV-6b: State Transition Description

# OV-6c: Event-Trace Description

| View Information at a Glance | |
| --- | --- |
| View short name | OV-6c |
| Name | Event-Trace Description |
| Other names | Event Diagram (TOGAF)<br>Rational Unified Process (UML) Sequence Diagram |
| Viewpoint | Operational |
| View intent | Enables the tracing of resource exchanges in a scenario or critical sequence of events. OV-6c can be used by itself or in conjunction with OV-6b: State Transition Description to describe the dynamic behavior of business activities or a mission/operational thread. An operational thread is defined as a set of operational activities, with sequence and timing attributes of the activities, and includes the resources needed to accomplish the activities. |
| View audience | Process designers, process modelers, simulation analysts who are interested in tracing the timing aspects of the sequence of events, performers, actions, and exchange of resources. |
| Formal modeling methodology | The associated scenario text can use document structures from use case approaches. A similar graphical technique is described in most real-time texts. |
| Integration of view with other views | OV-6c must be consistent with performers in OV-2, with resource flows from OV-3, and with activities in OV-5. It may be associated with rules from OV-6a (authorization rules). |

## Example: Passenger Identification OV-6c: Event-Trace Description

Each OV-6c view should have associated text that describes the scenario it is based on. The scenario in the passenger identification event/trace description is based on a passenger moving through the airport to catch a flight (Figure 15-10). This scenario is familiar to all who have experience with air travel and may need only a short description for such audiences. However, for readers who are not familiar with air travel or with U.S. airport practices, the scenario might require a much more detailed description. For example, the first step is for the passenger to check in with the airline desk agent and present baggage to be checked and carried on, identity documents, and booking information. In this case, the passenger is bound for a foreign destination and has the necessary documents. The check-in agent confirms the passenger's identity, reviews the travel documents, and confirms the passenger's destination. The passenger then receives his or her baggage tags and boarding pass and can proceed to the security screening area.

Like its counterparts in behavioral modeling, such as the OV-6a and OV-6b, the OV-6c: Event-Trace Description model is very useful in elaborating specific scenarios and tracing the behavior of an operational situation.

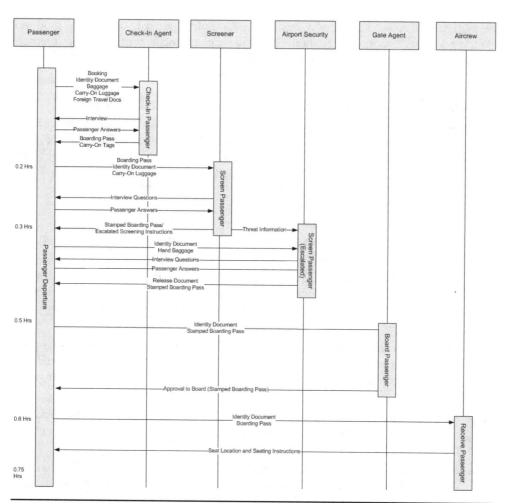

**Figure 15-10** Passenger identification OV-6c: Event-Trace Description

Sometimes, with a few changes, one type of model can be transformed into another. For example, if we were to turn the OV-6c on its side, it looks like a swim lane diagram—the lifelines in the OV-6c are transformed into swim lane roles; but the swim lane diagram misses the timing and event sequence that characterizes the OV-6c, which is a specific scenario or sequence of events, while the swim lane diagram is usually generic activities. The OV-3 also contains information that can be used to construct the OV-5b in a swim lane fashion or the OV-6c as a sequence diagram or event-trace style model. This requires that the OV-3 contain triggering events that start, or trigger, the resource flow represented by a row of the OV-3: Operational Resource Flow Matrix.

The advantage of an integrated architecture is that all models consistently model the same baseline or planned reality. The importance of integrating your models can never be understated. As we have learned, using the AV-2: Integrated Dictionary to hold our evolving architecture models guarantees that we can reconcile conflicts in architecture elements across models and modeling efforts.

# TOGAF Support for the Operational Viewpoint

The business architecture (developed in Phase B of the ADM) in TOGAF represents the Operational Viewpoint. TOGAF recommends the construction of various types of models to represent various facets of the business architecture using a rich set of model types:

- **Organization/actor catalog** Lists all participants that interact with IT, including users and owners of IT systems.

- **Driver/goal/objective catalog** References cross-organizationally how an organization meets its drivers in practical terms through goals, objectives, and (optionally) measures.

- **Role catalog** Provides a listing of all authorization levels or zones within an enterprise. Frequently, application security or behavior is defined against locally understood concepts of authorization that create complex and unexpected consequences when combined on the user desktop.

- **Business service/function catalog** Provides decomposition in a form that can be filtered, reported on, and queried, as a supplement to graphical functional decomposition diagrams. The CV-2: Capability Taxonomy is an equivalent view in the DoDAF.

- **Location catalog** Lists all locations where an enterprise carries out business operations or houses architecturally relevant assets, such as data centers or end-user computing equipment.

- **Process/event/control/product catalog** Provides a hierarchy of processes, events that trigger processes, outputs from processes, and controls applied to the execution of processes. This catalog provides a supplement to any process flow diagrams that are created and enables an enterprise to filter, report, and query across organizations and processes to identify scope, commonality, or impact. The collection of OV-3: Operational Resource Flow Matrices across the set of processes will yield a similar collection of inputs, outputs, activities, and events.

- **Contract/measure catalog** Lists all agreed service contracts and (optionally) the measures attached to those contracts. It forms the master list of service levels agreed to across the enterprise. The SvcV-7: Services Measures Matrix is an equivalent to this artifact.

- **Business interaction matrix** Depicts the relationship interactions between organizations and business functions across the enterprise. The CV-5: Capability to Organizational Development Mapping provides the relationship between a capability and a developing organization.

- **Actor/role matrix**   Shows which actors perform which roles, supporting definition of security and skills requirements.

- **Business footprint diagram**   Describes the links between business goals, organizational units, and business functions and services, and maps these functions to the technical components delivering the required capability. This artifact is similar to the OV-1: High-Level Operational Concept Graphic.

- **Business service/information diagram**   Shows the information needed to support one or more business services. Shows what data is consumed by or produced by a business service and may also show the source of information. This artifact is more appropriately represented in the DoDAF Services Viewpoint views.

- **Functional decomposition diagram**   Shows on a single page the capabilities of an organization that are relevant to the consideration of an architecture. By examining the capabilities of an organization from a functional perspective, we can quickly develop models of what the organization does without being dragged into extended debate on how the organization does it. The equivalent view in the DoDAF is the CV-2: Capability Taxonomy.

- **Product life cycle diagram**   Assists in understanding the life cycles of key entities within the enterprise. Understanding product life cycles is becoming increasingly important with respect to environmental concerns, legislation, and regulation where products must be tracked from manufacture to disposal. The life cycle of a System or Service is depicted in the SV-8/SvcV-8: Systems/Services Evolution Description views.

- **Goal/objective/service diagram**   Defines the ways in which a service contributes to the achievement of a business vision or strategy. Services are associated with the drivers, goals, objectives, and measures that they support, enabling the enterprise to understand which services contribute to similar aspects of business performance. This artifact is equivalent to a combination of the DoDAF CV-1: Vision and CV-7: Capability to Services Mapping views, which enable a trace of services back to the capability and the vision for which they implement as a solution.

- **Business use-case diagram**   Displays the relationships between consumers and providers of business services. Business services are consumed by actors or other business services and the business use-case diagram provides added richness in describing business capability by illustrating how and when that capability is used. This artifact is more appropriately reflected in the Services Viewpoint.

- **Organization decomposition diagram**   Depicts organizational relationships and whole-part composition relationships between organizations, boards, councils, committees, and working groups. This artifact is identical to the OV-4: Organizational Relationships Chart.

PART III

- **Process flow diagram**   Depicts the flow of data and control between the activities that participate in a business process. It shows sequential flow of control between activities and may use swim-lane techniques to represent ownership and realization of process steps. In addition to showing a sequence of activity, process flows can also be used to detail the controls that apply to a process, the events that trigger or result from completion of a process, and the products that are generated from process execution. This artifact is equivalent to the OV-5a: Operational Activity Decomposition Tree and OV-5b: Operational Activity Model views in the DoDAF.

- **Event diagram**   Traces the sequence of events, the occurrence of activities, the mapping of performers to activities, and the messages and interactions between the performers in the context of the performed activity. This artifact is very similar to the OV-6c: Event-Trace Description.

# FEAF2 Support for Operational Viewpoint

The FEAF2 business subarchitecture domain corresponds to the DoDAF Operational Viewpoint. The artifacts of this domain that are counterparts to the Operational Viewpoint views are listed here:

- **Business process diagram (B-1)**   Presents the hierarchical structure of organizational activities and activities performed by organizational performers to consume and produce resources. This artifact corresponds to the OV-5a and OV-5b (activity models) in the DoDAF.

- **Business operating plan (B-2)**   A plan that shows on a timeline, changes to the business service catalog, organizational chart, and business process model to transition from the current state of the enterprise to the target or objective state.

- **Business service catalog (B-3)**   Presents the business services taken from the business reference model (BRM) that are provided within the scope of the architecture and may also indicate business services that are consumed or used internally within the architecture. Business services are discussed as part of the Services Viewpoint in Chapter 17.

- **Organization chart (B-4)**   Presents the composition and relationships among organizational performers. This artifact corresponds to the OV-4: Organizational Relationships Chart in the DoDAF.

- **Use-case narrative and diagram (B-5)**   Describes a set of possible sequences of interactions between systems and users in a particular environment and related to a particular goal.

- **Business case/alternatives analysis (B-6)**   Summarizes the planning, budgeting, acquisition, and management of federal capital assets sufficient to determine if investment funding should be recommended or continued.

# Summary

The Operational Viewpoint represents views that incorporate the elements of tasks and activities, operational performers, and resource flows between activities. The Operational Viewpoint uses a combination of formal models (e.g., OV-5b: Operational Activity Model), tables/matrices of detailed information (e.g., OV-3: Operational Resource Flow Matrix), and structured narratives (OV-6a: Operational Rules Model) to represent different views for different types of planners. An integrated architecture ensures that the specific architecture element in each view is consistent with the same element in other views. The purpose of the operational architecture is to present an integrated set of plans that consider all aspects of the operation and ensure that they dovetail and work effectively together. At the enterprise level, the Operational Viewpoint may simply consist of high-level business functions that collectively run the enterprise. At a mission, scenario, or class of mission level, the elements are restricted to those that are relevant to the architecture scope.

# Questions

1. How is the Operational Viewpoint different from the Capability (strategic) Viewpoint? Who are the stakeholders for each of these?

2. The DoDAF views the Operational Viewpoint from the perspective of military operations. Compare and contrast this perspective against the needs of federal agencies and commercial enterprises for business processes.

3. In systems engineering, there is a renewed interest in the use of repeatable patterns to shorten the design cycle. Are there operational patterns that are reusable also? Discuss operational patterns in the context of a reusing enterprise such as a fast-food franchise.

4. Can you identify reusable operational patterns (a collection of activity types, role types, location types, resource types, and so on, that form a logical unit of mission or operation) in your own enterprise?

5. What is the purpose of the OV-1: High-Level Operational Concept Graphic? Is the OV-1 a model or a picture using our earlier definitions elsewhere in this book? Why?

6. What are the pros and cons of using a highly tailored OV-1 for a specific audience? Are there communication risks in doing so?

7. What are some of the techniques you would use in your OV-1s for involving architecture stakeholders in your enterprise?

8. How would you indicate the difference between internal and external performers in your OV-2: Operational Resource Flow Description? What other operational model will provide validation of the ability to satisfy a need line relationship? Hint: Reporting relationships or formal rules of engagement need to be established.

9. What is the relationship between the OV-2: Operational Resource Flow Description and the OV-3: Operational Resource Flow Matrix?

10. To comply with Privacy Act requirements for protecting personal information, what attributes would you add to the OV-3 to indicate that certain resource flows will need appropriate handling for compliance? For determining the need for protecting classified information in some of the resource exchanges in the OV-3, how would you tailor the OV-3 with additional columns?

11. What types of organizational relationships are represented in the OV-4? Is the OV-4 restricted to the formal organization chart of an enterprise? If not, why not?

12. Does the OV-4 represent only permanent organizations such as business units, departments, and divisions, or does it also represent temporary working groups, task forces, and councils comprising people staffed from permanent organizations for a specific charter or purpose?

13. What is the OV-5a? Why do you think there are two types of models, OV-5a and OV-5b, for representing configurations of operational activities? When is each type of model useful?

14. What is a swim lane activity model? What advantages are provided by a swim lane model over an IDEF0 representation? What disadvantages?

15. What is the OV-6a: Operational Rules Model? Why is it useful in architecting? How (through what mechanisms) are rules implemented in enterprises?

16. How would you organize the many rules in your enterprise?

17. What is the OV-6b: State Transition Description model? How are the states of a process or an object represented within an information system?

18. Discuss the applicability of state models to business needs such as providing in-process visibility (IPV).

19. Discuss and build a state model for the states of a package during its transmission from a web retailer to your home using a popular package express carrier.

20. Compare and contrast the TOGAF artifact types against the DoDAF views described in this chapter.

21. Compare and contrast the FEAF2 artifact types against the DoDAF views described in this chapter.

22. How would you analyze the relationships between subordinate activities within a business process? What artifact/view would you use?

# References

Appleton, Daniel. 1993. *Corporate Information Management: Process Improvement Methodology for DoD Functional Managers,* 2nd Edition. Boston: D. Appleton & Company.

CIO Council. 2013. "Federal Enterprise Architecture Framework, Version 2." https://obamawhitehouse.archives.gov/sites/default/files/omb/assets/egov_docs/fea_v2.pdf.

Department of Defense. 2010. DoD Architecture Framework Version 2.02. http://dodcio.defense.gov/Library/DoD-Architecture-Framework/.

Fowler, Martin, and Kendall Scott. 1997. *UML Distilled: Applying the Standard Object Modeling Language.* Boston: Addison-Wesley.

Hill, Steven C., and Lee A. Robinson. 1994. *A Concise Guide to the IDEF0 Technique: A Practical Technique for Business Process Reengineering.* Enterprise Technology Concepts Press.

National Institute of Standards and Technology (NIST). 1993. Draft Federal Information Processing Standards, Publication 183: "Announcing the Standard for Integration Definition for Function Modeling (IDEF0)." www.idef.com/wp-content/uploads/2016/02/idef0.pdf.

National Institute of Standards and Technology (NIST). 1993. Federal Information Processing Standards, Publication 184: "Announcing the Standard for Integration Definition for Information Modeling (IDEF1X)." www.niatec.iri.isu.edu/GetFile.aspx?pid=59.

Object Management Group. 2018. Business Process Modeling Notation (BPMN). www.bpmn.org.

Object Management Group. 2018. Organization home page. www.omg.org.

Ring, Steven J., Dr. Bruce Lamar, Jacob Heim, and Elaine Goyette. 2005. "Integrated Architecture-Based Portfolio Investment Strategies." Paper presented at 10th International Command and Control Research and Technology Symposium: The Future of C2. www.mitre.org/sites/default/files/pdf/05_0571.pdf.

Ross, Ronald G. 2003. *Principles of the Business Rule Approach.* Boston: Addison-Wesley Information Technology Series.

Sharp, Alec, and Patrick McDermott. 2001. *Workflow Modeling: Tools for Process Improvement and Application Development.* Norwood, MA: Artech House.

The Open Group. 2018. "TOGAF Standard Version 9.2." The Netherlands: Van Haren Publishing.

**PART III**

# CHAPTER 16

# Systems Viewpoint

The Systems Viewpoint serves the interests of people involved with the planning, design, implementation, deployment, and maintenance of automated systems. Automated information systems are a subset of automated systems in general. The DoDAF generalizes information as a resource, and the Systems Viewpoint is therefore applicable to all systems, resource processing, and human and automated performers in the general case. Earlier versions of the DoDAF were restricted to information processing systems that were directed toward supporting C4ISR (Command, Control, Computers, Communications, Intelligence, Surveillance and Reconnaissance). The Systems Viewpoint can embrace a single system and its context, a Family of Systems (FoS), or a System of Systems (SoS).

Systems engineering of complex systems requires architecture models that can deal with the complexity. A complex system can be characterized (albeit circularly!) as one whose development and maintenance is complex, one whose behavior is complex, or usually both.

Often, the term "enterprise-wide" is used to characterize a complex system. This term can signify a global business enterprise as well as collections of systems that interact across their individual boundaries to achieve some common goal.

Some salient features of complex systems, as described within MITRE and in the literature, include the following:

- Complex systems are usually enterprise-wide systems that are constructed by the integration of multiple separate systems.

- Participants using these systems must merge their individual goals and behaviors to meet the goals of the enterprise to which they belong.

- Many participants have existing systems, cultures, or practices in place that are in conflict with those of other participants and are not easy to change.

- The requirements for the system are not precisely known at the start and dynamically change with time.

- Interaction among the system's components and with its environment can produce behavior that is not always predictable or explainable from observing the behavior.

The views presented in the Systems Viewpoint other than the SV-10a, 10b, and 10c are static views of systems. The SV-10a, 10b, and 10c provide modeling techniques for the behavior of the system.

With the recent interest in and promises of cloud computing and service-oriented solutions, there is belief that all systems architecting will be replaced with service-based modeling methods and that the need for a Systems Viewpoint will be shortly and quickly replaced by a Services Viewpoint. But the preponderance of systems in today's solution environment will guarantee that the Systems Viewpoint is here to stay for a long time to come, and attempts at migration of current infrastructures to new target architecture will require representation of legacy systems mixed in with services and the need for modeling the encapsulation of legacy functions into services.

# Purposes of the Systems Viewpoint Views

The Systems Viewpoint enables analysis of systems from many aspects. Each of the SV views has a different purpose for the system analyst. Some of these aspects follow.

## System Resource Flows/Information Exchanges

The counterpart to the Operational Viewpoint view OV-2: Operational Resource Flow Description is the Systems Viewpoint view SV-1: Systems Interface Description. The SV-1 replaces the operational performers, locations in the OV-2 with systems performers and systems hosting locations and replaces the operational need lines that indicated needs for exchange of information/flow of resources with interfaces that also indicate a need to exchange information/resources between systems performers. If every operational performer were to be supported by a single system, the layout of the SV-1 would perfectly match the layout of the OV-2. But in reality, multiple systems support a single performer, and non-automated activities in the operational realm do not have a system counterpart in the systems realm. The SV-3: Systems-Systems Matrix is a compact view that represents some aspect of interaction between pairs of systems. The SV-3 may also be used as a compact view for representing the many interfaces in a large and complex SV-1. Other systems resource flow models such as the SV-6: Systems Resource Flow Matrix focus on the details of the information exchanges/resource flows between specific systems in the context of specific system functions being performed by the systems.

## Systems Functionality

Just as the operational activity was the prime ingredient for changing operational behavior, the system function is the prime ingredient that describes system behavior. The SV-4: Systems Functionality Description models the system functions that have been implemented or are planned for a system as a well-ordered taxonomy.

- The SV-4 can be used to decompose system functions progressively into smaller units of functionality. Decomposition is a technique to address system complexity by breaking down the system into components that are easier to analyze.

- The SV-4 is useful to compare systems functions across multiple systems, looking for duplication and overlaps. Military organizations have tried to standardize the list of system functions to enable consolidation of systems for joint operations or for savings from reuse of existing systems across multiple organizations.

- The SV-4 also models the input/output behavior of system functions in terms of the information/resources they consume, transform, or produce. The system resources comprise data/information and materiel resources. The resource flow diagram is a generalization of the classic data flow diagram, where the data flows are generalized to reflect any form of resource exchange.

- The SV-4 can be used to examine the orchestration of information exchanges/resource flows between multiple systems. The resource flow diagram can describe an orderly flow of information in an architectural scenario from system function to system function prior to the allocation of system functions to systems.

## Systems Need for Connectivity

The interfaces that demonstrate the need for information exchange/resource flows between systems inside the SV-1 need to be implemented physically using communication paths that connect the systems together and provide a means for transmitting and receiving information/resources. In the IT sense, these are represented by paths through communication links, communication equipment, and computer networks. In the more general sense, these represent logistic chains that channel resources between systems such as concourses in airports, baggage conveyor belts, and so on.

The SV-2: Systems Resource Flow Description models the physical paths that are travelled by information/resources between systems. Because the physical path may have several intermediate links that are purely to route communications and resource transfer, the SV-1 may not have an exact correspondence with the SV-2, even though the end points for the path must coincide. The SV-2 is a depiction of the physical transfer path for information/resources that is depicted in the interfaces in the SV-1.

In the past, connectivity was achieved only through physical media connections by wire and fiber-optics. Today, physical connectivity can be achieved by wireless and broadcast means such as Wi-Fi and Bluetooth technologies, and connections can be achieved through software rather than through hardware with the network topology being established by software commands. All of these communication means contribute communication elements for an SV-2 diagram to indicate how the data interfaces in the SV-1 and the data exchanges between systems in the SV-6: Systems Resource Flow Matrix are accomplished through physical transfer of digital information.

## Systems Traceability to Operational Usefulness

Too often, systems are built with many features that were required at the time by business or military operations. As time goes on, some of these features may not be very useful as changes in the operating environment or technology occur, or they may represent obsolete functions. Systems may also be built with architected capabilities and resulting functionality that was planned but never used. These functions impose a maintenance burden that may be unnecessary. They may also create unknown vulnerabilities that are never exposed when the functions are never used except by bad actors.

The SV-5a: Operational Activity to Systems Function Traceability Matrix and SV-5b: Operational Activity to Systems Traceability Matrix map systems and system functions to the operational activities they support. This is a useful view for analyzing the impact of change of either the operational activity or the system function on each other. For future planned systems, it also provides an explicit plan of which operational activities will be enabled/facilitated or automated by a system function. For a system, the SV-5 views also provide a coverage map of usefulness of system function to operational activity. In an IDEF0-style activity model, the relationship between the system and the activity it enables is reflected in the activity-mechanism relationship, as the system is represented as a mechanism for an activity.

## Systems Performance Specification

Another useful view, the SV-7: Systems Measures Matrix, is used to specify the acceptable performance measures for a system or the specifications that drive the acquisition of systems. The specification of performance measures early in a system specification enables the creation of tradeoffs during the design process and also establishes minimum acceptance criteria for various components as well as the system itself. The SV-7 uses system parameters that are represented in some form of measure type taxonomy. Developing a standard taxonomy of measures enables comparisons of performance (benchmarking) between competing or alternate systems for similar measures.

## Systems Evolution

For planners, one of the important models to build is a roadmap of systems evolution. The SV-8: Systems Evolution Description view offers the representation in two formats—evolution of features and functions for systems in planned release increments, and migration of multiple systems into one or more target systems. The SV-8 is a useful view for planning modernization initiatives as well as for allocating feature evolution to system increments. The time frames for the SV-8 must be consistent with the time frames described in the AV-1: Overview and Summary Information.

## Systems Operating Platforms

No system runs by itself without the need for underlying system software such as operating system support, support from commercial-off-the-shelf (COTS) software such as electronic mail, document creation and rendering, and so on. For technology infrastructure staff, it is important to map systems to the operating platforms that they need to run on and to lay out roadmaps of their evolution based on available vendor information.

The SV-9: Systems Technology and Skills Forecast view provides the capability of expressing a platform migration strategy for specific systems. A portfolio of SV-9 views can then be used at the enterprise level to determine mismatches in migration strategy or missed migrations, for example. As adoption of cloud computing increases, many of the operating platforms are provisioned in the cloud, and platform vendors provide a roadmap of how their cloud platform offerings will evolve. Planning the SV-9 must be done in coordination with such roadmaps, as availability is restricted to those offerings if the same cloud provider is to be selected. Alternatively, a cloud platform vendor with limited offerings and no roadmap may not be the best provider of platform services for applications that must stay up to date with vendor's latest patches, updates, and releases to avoid vulnerabilities.

The SV-9 also provides a format for representing the needs for skills as operating platforms are added/modified to support the enterprise's systems. Military organizations have a standardized skills taxonomy that spells out the training, certification, and validation and classifications for skill credentials.

## Systems Behavioral Models

For detailed modeling of systems behavior, the SV-10a: System Rules Model, the SV-10b: Systems State Transition Description, and the SV-10c: Systems Event-Trace Description are available as counterparts of the OV-6a, OV-6b, and OV-6c operational behavioral models (see Chapter 15). These are useful for providing detailed representation of orchestration sequences of system functions, information/resource exchanges, and triggering events (SV-10c: Systems Event-Trace Description) or detailed representation of algorithmic behavior used to implement system functions, or for establishing structural constraints among data in a systems database (SV-10a), or establishing detailed representation of the state transitions of a system or system function in the face of triggering events and activities.

# Systems Viewpoint Integrated Views

For brevity, a partial subset of the Systems Viewpoint is shown in Figure 16-1 to illustrate the concepts of integrated views in the context of the Systems Viewpoint (missing are the SV-9, SV-10a, SV-10b, and SV-10c).

The Systems Viewpoint also represents a tight coupling of views for consistency purposes. Views share many common elements such as systems, systems functions, system locations, and data flows.

Some examples of the needs for consistent use of architecture elements between Systems Viewpoint views are given here:

- SV-1 systems must be consistent with systems in all the systems views. SV-1 interfaces must be consistent with SV-4 data-flows and SV-6 data exchanges between the same end-point systems.

- SV-4 system functions must be consistent with SV-5 system functions.

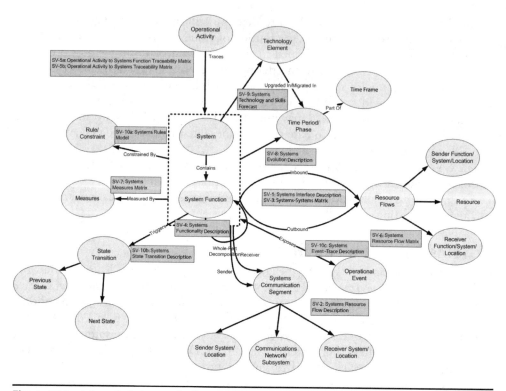

**Figure 16-1**    Integrated view set for Systems Viewpoint

In addition to the integration needs of models within the Systems Viewpoint, there are integration needs implicit inside the models to other viewpoints:

- SV-5 maps the systems functions and systems to operational activities defined inside the Operational Viewpoint. SV-5b maps the systems to operational activities (systems to operations alignment).

- SV-9 must be consistent in the evolution of system technology to the elements defined in the StdV-1: Standards Profile and the StdV-2: Standards Forecast (systems to technology alignment).

# SV-1: Systems Interface Description

| View Information at a Glance | |
|---|---|
| View short name | SV-1 |
| Name | Systems Interface Description |
| Other names | A-1 Application Interface Diagram (FEAF2)<br>Interface Catalog (TOGAF 9 Catalog) |
| Viewpoint | Systems |
| View intent | The SV-1 depicts all systems of interest within the scope of the architecture together with their locations and the interfaces representing resource flows between systems. Usually represented as a simple network. |
| View audience | Capability configuration planners who must consider all aspects of performers, systems, locations, and resource flows to implement a capability requirement. |
| Formal modeling methodology | None. SV-1 is built as a network graph with the vertices representing combinations of systems, locations, performers, and activities and the edges representing resource flows. |
| Integration of view with other views | The systems in SV-1 must be consistent with systems in all other SV views. The resource flows in SV-1 must be consistent with SV-4 resource flows and SV-6 resource flows. |

## Example: Passenger Identification SV-1

The SV-1 is the systems counterpart of the OV-2: Operational Resource Flow Description. The human and organizational performers who represent the end points of the need lines in the OV-2 are replaced by systems representing their automation counterparts in the SV-1 as shown in Figure 16-2. The need lines of the OV-2 are transformed into the interfaces between the systems of the SV-1.

In the general case, if every operational performer had one and only one system representing it, and every need line had one and only one systems interface counterpart, the SV-1 would be topologically the same as the OV-2. But in reality, many human and organizational activities may or may not have automated counterparts, and there may be systems whose only purpose is to relay the interface and do not play a vital part in the operations. In the example we presented, the OV-2 and SV-1 are very similar.

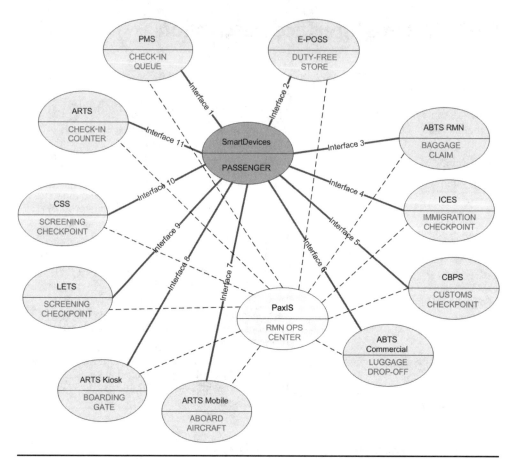

**Figure 16-2** Passenger identification in the SV-1: Systems Interface Description

# SV-2: Systems Resource Flow Description

| View Information at a Glance | |
|---|---|
| View short name | SV-2 |
| Name | Systems Resource Flow Description |
| Other names | Systems Connectivity Description (Old)<br>A-2 Application Communication Diagram (FEAF2)<br>Application Communication Diagram (TOGAF 9)<br>Communications Engineering Diagram (TOGAF 9)<br>Processing Diagram (TOGAF 9)<br>Platform Decomposition Diagram (TOGAF 9) |

| View Information at a Glance | |
|---|---|
| Viewpoint | Systems |
| View intent | Specifies the communication paths between systems and may also list the protocol stacks used in connections. A SV-2 DoDAF-described model is used to give a precise specification of a connection between systems. This may be an existing connection, or a specification for a connection that is to be made. A SV-2 comprises systems, their ports, and the resource flows between those ports. The architect may choose to create a diagram for each resource flow for all systems or to show all the resource flows on one diagram if possible. |
| View audience | Resource flow planners, communications and networks analysts (connectivity analysis). Because of the complexity of the resource flow paths, SV-2 is more applicable to solution architecture than for enterprise or segment architecture, though major "resource" highways may still be representable at these scales of architecting. |
| Formal modeling methodology | None. SV-2 is represented as a network diagram with the vertices representing end points for resource flows and a sequence of links that make up connectivity paths between vertices. |
| Integration of view with other views | Systems represented in SV-2 must be consistent with systems objects in other SV views. Locations represented at each vertex of an SV-2 must be consistent with locations in other SV views such as SV-1. |

## Example: Passenger Identification SV-2

The SV-2 represents the physical connectivity and actual resource flow (communication) paths that achieve the interfacing represented inside the SV-1. The SV-2 provides a graphical view of these paths and enables the analyst to annotate communication and transmission standards and protocols, bandwidth, and capacity constraints and readily determine issues such as bottlenecks and capacity constraints or mismatched protocols, for example. The SV-2 (Figure 16-3) represents physical communication links and elements needed to support the requirement for exchange of resources depicted in the SV-1.

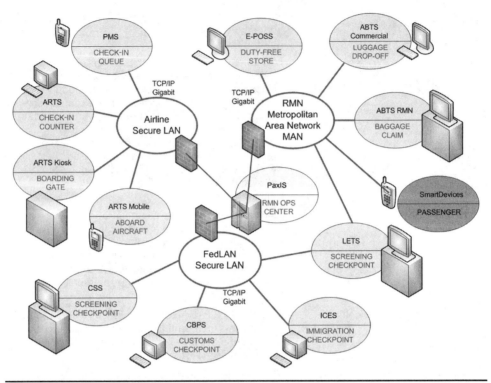

**Figure 16-3**  Passenger identification SV-2: Systems Resource Flow Description

# SV-3: Systems-Systems Matrix

| View Information at a Glance | |
| --- | --- |
| View short name | SV-3 |
| Name | Systems-Systems Matrix |
| Other names | S2 Matrix<br>SXS Matrix<br>A-3 Application Interface Matrix (FEAF2)<br>Application Interaction Matrix (TOGAF 9) |
| Viewpoint | Systems |

| View Information at a Glance | |
|---|---|
| View intent | Enables a quick overview of all the system resource interactions specified in one or more SV-1: Systems Interface Description views. The SV-3 provides a tabular summary of the system interactions specified in the SV-1 for the architectural description. The matrix format supports a rapid assessment of potential commonalities and redundancies (or, if fault-tolerance is desired, the lack of redundancies). The SV-3 can be organized in a number of ways to emphasize the association of groups of system pairs in context with the architecture's purpose. |
| View audience | Executive level planners who must digest the aggregation of many SV-1s for high-level analysis. The matrix simplifies the aggregation of many and large SV-1s. The intersections cells of the matrix can be tailored to a specific interest for the planner or analyst. |
| Formal modeling methodology | None. SV-3 uses a simple tabular matrix format. |
| Integration of view with other views | Systems in SV-3 must be consistent with system objects in other SV views. |

## Example: Passenger Identification SV-3

The SV-3 in a matrix format summarizes all the interfaces across all the systems within the scope of the architecture and provides a compact "at a glance" view of interfaces, along with codes in the intersection cells that provide additional information about the interfaces, as shown in Table 16-1. The SV-3 can be tailored to provide a range of codes that may depict interface development status or other attributes of the interface.

| Sending System | Acronym | Receiving System | | | | | | | | | | | | |
|---|---|---|---|---|---|---|---|---|---|---|---|---|---|---|
| | | ARTS | ARTS (Kiosk) | ARTS(Mobile) | ABTS (Commercial) | ABTS (RMN) | CSS | CBPS | E-POSS | ICES | LETS | PaxIS | PMS | Smart Devices |
| Airline Reservation and Ticketing System | ARTS | | C | C | C | | | | | | | | | C |
| Airline Reservation and Ticketing System (Kiosk) | ARTS (Kiosk) | C | | C | C | | | | | | | | | C |

**Table 16-1**   Passenger Identification SV-3: Systems-Systems Matrix

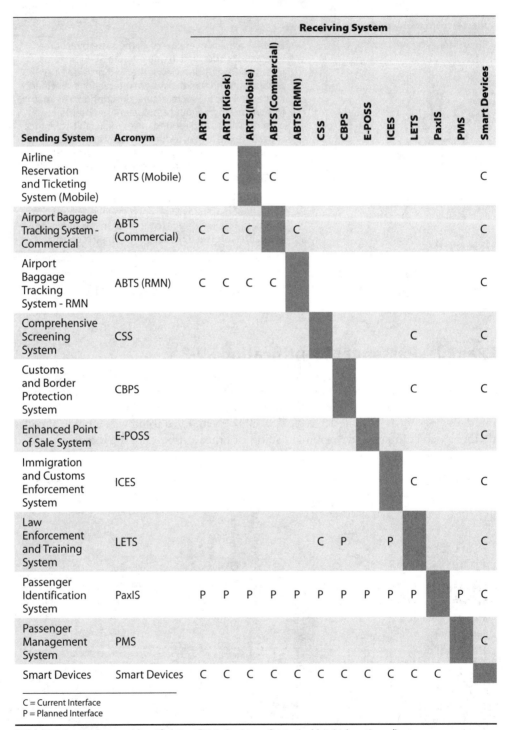

| Sending System | Acronym | Receiving System | | | | | | | | | | | | |
|---|---|---|---|---|---|---|---|---|---|---|---|---|---|---|
| | | ARTS | ARTS (Kiosk) | ARTS(Mobile) | ABTS (Commercial) | ABTS (RMN) | CSS | CBPS | E-POSS | ICES | LETS | PaxIS | PMS | Smart Devices |
| Airline Reservation and Ticketing System (Mobile) | ARTS (Mobile) | C | C | | C | | | | | | | | | C |
| Airport Baggage Tracking System - Commercial | ABTS (Commercial) | C | C | C | | C | | | | | | | | C |
| Airport Baggage Tracking System - RMN | ABTS (RMN) | C | C | C | C | | | | | | | | | C |
| Comprehensive Screening System | CSS | | | | | | | | | | C | | | C |
| Customs and Border Protection System | CBPS | | | | | | | | | | C | | | C |
| Enhanced Point of Sale System | E-POSS | | | | | | | | | | | | | C |
| Immigration and Customs Enforcement System | ICES | | | | | | | | | | C | | | C |
| Law Enforcement and Training System | LETS | | | | | | C | P | | P | | | | C |
| Passenger Identification System | PaxIS | P | P | P | P | P | P | P | P | P | P | | P | C |
| Passenger Management System | PMS | | | | | | | | | | | | | C |
| Smart Devices | Smart Devices | C | C | C | C | C | C | C | C | C | C | C | | |

C = Current Interface
P = Planned Interface

**Table 16-1**　Passenger Identification SV-3: Systems-Systems Matrix *(continued)*

# SV-4: Systems Functionality Description

| View Information at a Glance | |
|---|---|
| View short name | SV-4 |
| Name | Systems Functionality Description |
| Other names | System Function List (Enterprise Catalog)<br>Master System Function List (Enterprise Catalog)<br>A-10 Application Inventory (FEAF2 Catalog)<br>Application Portfolio Catalog (TOGAF 9 Catalog) |
| Viewpoint | Systems |
| View intent | Addresses human and system functionality. The SV-4 is the Systems Viewpoint view counterpart to the OV-5b: Operational Activity Model of the Operational Viewpoint and has the same tree decomposition structure as the OV-5a. Like the OV-5b, it can also be used to define the resource flows (information exchanges) between system functions. |
| View audience | Solution architects, portfolio managers, solution planners |
| Formal modeling methodology | Dataflow diagrams (SADT, De Marco, etc.), system function decomposition tree (SADT).<br><br>The taxonomic functional hierarchy shows a decomposition of functions depicted in a tree structure and is typically used where tasks are concurrent but dependent, such as a production line.<br><br>The data flow diagram shows functions connected by data flow arrows and data stores. |
| Integration of view with other views | The system functions in SV-4 must be consistent with system functions in other SV views such as the SV-5b, SV-6, SV-7, SV-8, SV-10b, and SV-10c. (The SV-5 views map system functions in SV-4 to the Operational Viewpoint activities in OV-5 and represent a solution-to-requirement mapping.) |

## Example: Passenger Identification SV-4

Table 16-2 shows a hierarchy of system functions for a hypothetical information broker system that integrates airline, hospitality, and airport data for passengers. The example table also contains descriptions of the system functions from the AV-2. The SV-4 also allows for a data/resource flow representation that depicts the output of a system function shown as an input of another system. This view represents inputs from human resource/data sources (external resource providers) as well as outputs that go into a storage mechanism for resources/information (sinks). The dataflow version of the SV-4 is not shown here.

| System | System Acronym | System Function | System Function Description |
|---|---|---|---|
| Passenger management | PMS | Verify passenger identity | Verify passenger identity based on identity document supplied by passenger against information located from trusted sources. |
| | | Display passenger name record (PNR) | Display previously stored passenger information using the airline standard PNR format. |
| | | Search flight | Search for flight number by destination, time, date, airline, and gate. |
| | | Search gate | Search for gate by destination, airline, date, time, and flight number. |
| | | Display passenger special request | Display any special requests for passenger such as wheelchair, unaccompanied minor, special meals, and so on. |
| | | Display travel award information | Display award level in frequent flyer program for entitlement to enhanced services. |
| | | Display club entitlement information | Display entitlement to airline-operated clubs and lounges. |
| | | Request wheelchair service | Request wheelchair services from common pool of wheelchair services operated by RMN. |
| | | Request special service | Request special service for hearing impaired, visually impaired, diabetic, or other passengers. |
| | | Print meal voucher | Print meal voucher to compensate for airline-caused delays. |
| | | Print hotel voucher | Print hotel voucher to compensate for airline-caused delays. |
| | | Entitle delayed passenger for hotel | Mark passenger PNR for delayed flight entitlement to hotel accommodation. |
| | | Entitle delayed passenger for meals | Mark passenger PNR for delayed flight entitlement to refreshments. |

**Table 16-2** Passenger Management System SV-4: Systems Functionality Description

# SV-5a: Operational Activity to Systems Function Traceability Matrix
# SV-5b: Operational Activity to Systems Traceability Matrix

PART III

| View Information at a Glance | |
| --- | --- |
| View short name | SV-5a, SV-5b |
| Name | Operational Activity to Systems Function Traceability Matrix (SV-5a)<br>Operational Activity to Systems Traceability Matrix (SV-5b) |
| Other names | Application/Function Matrix (TOGAF 9)<br>Process/Application Realization Diagram (TOGAF 9) |
| Viewpoint | Systems |
| View intent | Addresses the linkage between system functions described in SV-4: Systems Functionality Description and operational activities specified in OV-5a: Operational Activity Decomposition Tree or OV-5b: Operational Activity Model. The SV-5a depicts the mapping of system functions and, optionally, the capabilities and performers that provide them to operational activities. The SV-5a identifies the transformation of an operational need into a purposeful action performed by a system or solution. |
| View audience | Portfolio planners, solution architects, process analysts. The SV-5a is more useful for segment and enterprise architecting because of the lesser degree of granularity; the SV-5b is useful for solutions architecting. |
| Formal modeling methodology | None. The SV-5a and SV-5b vary in degree of detail but are both represented as tabular matrices. |
| Integration of view with other views | Systems in the SV-5a and SV-5b must be consistent with systems in other SV views such as SV-1, SV-2, SV-3, SV-4, SV-6, SV-7, SV-8, SV-9, and SV-10c. System functions in the SV-5a must be consistent with system functions in other SV views such as SV-4, SV-7, SV-8, SV-10b, and SV-10c. The operational activities in both SV-5a and SV-5b should be consistent with the activities in the OV-5. |

## Example: Passenger Identification SV-5a

Table 16-3 shows the relationships between systems and operational activities. This correspondence is very useful to determine which system functions are useful for which operational activities and which system functions are not useful in a specific operational context. The SV-5a provides a valuable model for portfolio analysis of system functions across the spectrum of operational activities.

**System Names**

| Operational Activities | Passenger Management System (PMS) | Comprehensive Screening System (CSS) | Law Enforcement and Training System (LETS) | Airline Reservation and Ticketing System (ARTS) | Airline Reservation and Ticketing System (ARTS) (Mobile) | Airline Reservation and Ticketing System (ARTS) (Kiosk) | Airport Baggage Tracking System (ABTS) - Commercial | Customs and Border Protection System (CBPS) | Immigration and Customs Enforcement System (ICES) | Airport Baggage Tracking System (ABTS) - RMN | Enhanced Point of Sale System (E-POSS) | Smart Devices | Passenger Identification System (PaxIS) |
|---|---|---|---|---|---|---|---|---|---|---|---|---|---|
| Check in passenger | X | | | X | | | | | | | | X | X |
| Screen passenger | | X | X | | | | | | | | | X | X |
| Board passenger | | | | | X | | | | | | | X | |
| Receive passenger | | | | | | X | | | | | | X | X |
| Conduct immigration inspection | | | | | | | | | X | | | X | X |
| Conduct customs inspection | | | | | | | | X | | | | X | X |
| Store passenger baggage | | | | | | | X | | | | | X | X |
| Process duty-free purchase | | | | | | | | | | | X | X | X |
| Deliver baggage | | | | | | | | | | X | | X | X |

**Table 16-3**  Passenger Identification SV-5a: Operational Activity to Systems Function Traceability Matrix

# Example: Passenger Identification SV-5b

The SV-5b provides a more detailed view of the relationships between systems and operational activities and provides the mapping between specific system functions and operational activities, as shown in Table 16-4. This extends the usefulness of the SV-5a to provide more fine-grained analysis of system function redundancy and system function applicability to the operational context.

| System Functions / Operational Activities | PMS | | | | | | | | | | | | | ARTS | | | | | | | |
|---|---|---|---|---|---|---|---|---|---|---|---|---|---|---|---|---|---|---|---|---|---|
| | Verify Passenger Identity | Display Passenger Name Record (PNR) | Search Flight | Search Gate | Display Passenger Special Request | Display Travel Award Information | Display Club Entitlement Information | Request Wheelchair Service | Request Special Service | Print Meal Voucher | Print Hotel Voucher | Entitle Delayed Passenger for Hotel | Entitle Delayed Passenger for Meals | Verify Booking | Print Boarding Pass | Print Ticket | Print Ticket Receipt | Display Passenger Name Record (PNR) | Check No Fly List | Transmit PNR to SFPD | Verify Passenger Identity |
| **Check in passenger** | | | | | | | | | | | | | | | | | | | | | |
| –Check booking | | X | X | X | X | X | X | | | | | | | X | | | | X | | | |
| –Check identity | X | | | | | | | | | | | | | | | | | | | | X |
| –Check in baggage | | | | | | | | | | | | | | | | | | | | | |
| –Validate carry-on size | | | | | X | | | | | | | | | | | | | | | | |
| –Validate foreign country entry authorization | | | | | | | | | | | | | | | | | | | | | |
| –Interview passenger | | | | | | | | | | | | | | | | | | | | | |
| –Entitle passenger | | | | | | | X | | | X | X | | | | X | X | X | | | | |

**Table 16-4**   Passenger Identification SV-5b: Operational Activity to System Traceability Matrix (Extract)

PART III

# SV-6: Systems Resource Flow Matrix

| View Information at a Glance | |
|---|---|
| View short name | SV-6 |
| Name | Systems Resource Flow Matrix |
| Other names | Systems Data Exchange Matrix (Old)<br>A-4 Application Data Exchange Matrix (FEAF2)<br>Interface Catalog (TOGAF 9 Catalog) |
| Viewpoint | Systems |
| View intent | Specifies the characteristics of resource flow exchanges between systems. The SV-6 is the physical equivalent of the logical OV-3 table and provides detailed information on the system connections that implement the resource flow exchanges specified in OV-3. Non-automated resource flow exchanges, such as verbal orders, are also captured. System resource flow exchanges express the relationship across the three basic architectural data elements of a SV (systems, system functions, and system resource flows) and focus on the specific aspects of the system resource flow and the system resource content. |
| View audience | Resource flow analysts interested in capacity, throughput analysis, design of systems resource flow networks, and analysis of flows that cross enterprise boundaries to touch external systems. |
| Formal modeling methodology | None. Represented as a tabular matrix. |
| Integration of view with other views | Producer and consumer systems in SV-6 must be consistent with systems in other SV views. Resource flows in SV-6 must be consistent with resource flows in SV-1, SV-4 (resource flow model version), and SV-10c. |

## Example: Passenger Identification SV-6

Table 16-5 depicts the flow of resources between systems (and optional locations). The resource type exchanged in the example is data. The system function being performed and attributes of the resource exchange may also be recorded. This example presents data standards that govern the data being exchanged as well as a format and a size for communications personnel to use in assessing the burden on the communications network.

| Sender | | Receiver | | Resource | | | Transaction | | |
| --- | --- | --- | --- | --- | --- | --- | --- | --- | --- |
| **System** | **Location** | **System** | **Location** | **Name** | **Type** | **Format** | **Standard** | | **Size (bytes)** |
| ARTS kiosk | Boarding gate kiosk | ARTS | Airline data center | Passenger boarding pass record | Data | Encrypted binary | ICAO Universal Boarding Pass Standard | | 356 |
| ARTS kiosk | Boarding gate kiosk | ARTS | Airline data center | Passenger booking record | Data | Encrypted binary | Airline PNR Standard | | 512 |
| ARTS kiosk | Boarding gate kiosk | ARTS | Airline data center | Passenger identity submission record | Data | Encrypted binary | NIEM Identity Data Standard | | 1024 |
| ARTS mobile | On-board aircraft | ARTS | Airline data center | Passenger identity submission record | Data | Encrypted binary | NIEM Identity Data Standard | | 1024 |
| ARTS mobile | On-board aircraft | ARTS | Airline data center | Passenger boarding pass record | Data | Encrypted binary | ICAO Universal Boarding Pass Standard | | 356 |

**Table 16-5**  Passenger Identification SV-6: Systems Resource Flow Matrix

# SV-7: Systems Measures Matrix

| **View Information at a Glance** | |
| --- | --- |
| View short name | SV-7 |
| Name | Systems Measures Matrix |
| Other names | Systems Performance Parameters Matrix (Old) A-6 Application Performance Matrix (FEAF2) |
| Viewpoint | Systems |
| View intent | Depicts the current and desired future values of architecture-specific metrics for system architecture elements. The Systems Measures Matrix expands on the information presented in an SV-1 by depicting the characteristics of the architecture elements such as systems, systems functions, locations, and resource flows. |
| View audience | Systems and solution planners, designers, and analysts for documenting current and specifying target performance objectives. |
| Formal modeling methodology | None. The SV-7 is laid out as a tabular grid with progressively growing time frames generally specifying increasing targets for performance measures. |
| Integration of view with other views | Systems in SV-7 must be consistent with SV-1. Interfaces or resource flows in SV-1 must be consistent with performance measures for resource flows in SV-7. The target time frames identified in SV-7 should be consistent with the system evolution time frames in SV-8 and SV-9. |

# Example: Passenger Identification SV-7

Table 16-6 shows an SV-7 performance measure specification for some system functions that are in scope for the passenger identification solution architecture.

| | Architecture Element | Type | Measure | Demo Baseline | IOC Objective | FOC Target |
|---|---|---|---|---|---|---|
| 1 | Check no-fly list | System function | Response time on positive determination | < 20 sec | < 10 sec | Near real-time* |
| | | | Response time on negative | < 30 sec | < 20 sec | Near real-time |
| 2 | Detect chemicals and hazmats | System function | Sensitivity | 100 ppm | 50 ppm | 20 ppm |
| 3 | Detect concealed weapons | System function | Ferrous weapon detection accuracy | 80% | 90% | 100% |
| | | | Plastic weapon detection accuracy | 60% | 80% | 100% |
| 4 | Detect explosives | System function | Sensitivity | 5 ppm | 3 ppm | 1 ppm |
| 5 | Detect inflammable material | System function | Sensitivity | 10 ppm | 8 ppm | 5 ppm |
| 6 | Detect metal objects | System function | Detection accuracy | 80% | 90% | 100% |
| 7 | Detect sharp objects | System function | Lethal weapon detection accuracy | 80% | 90% | 100% |
| | | | Nonlethal sharps | 70% | 80% | 80% |
| 8 | Display bag dimensions | System function | Dimensional accuracy | 85% | 90% | 99% |
| 9 | Generate coded locker key | System function | Key generation time | 20 sec | 10 sec | Near real-time |
| 10 | Print baggage storage barcode label | System function | Printing barcode time | 20 sec | 10 sec | Near real-time |
| 11 | Print baggage storage ticket | System function | Printing time | 20 sec | 10 sec | Near real-time |

**Table 16-6**  Passenger Identification SV-7: Systems Measures Matrix

| Architecture Element | Type | Measure | Demo | IOC | FOC |
|---|---|---|---|---|---|
| | | | Baseline | Objective | Target |
| 12 Print boarding pass | System function | Printing time | 30 sec | 20 sec | 10 sec |
| 13 Register active baggage | System function | Transaction end to end time | 10 sec | 8 sec | 5 sec |
| 14 Transmit arc information | System function | Transmission time | 10 sec | 5 sec | Near real-time |
| 15 Transmit credit card information | System function | Transmission time | 10 sec | 5 sec | Near real-time |
| 16 Transmit DHS entry card information | System function | Transmission time | 10 sec | 5 sec | Near real-time |
| 17 Transmit DL information | System function | Transmission time | 10 sec | 5 sec | Near real-time |
| 18 Transmit passport information | System function | Transmission time | 10 sec | 5 sec | Near real-time |
| 19 Transmit PNR to SFPD | System function | Transmission time | 10 sec | 10 sec | 10 sec |
| 20 Verify boarding pass | System function | Verification time | <30 sec | <20 sec | < 10 sec |
| 21 Verify passenger identity | System function | Positive identification | <30 sec | <20 sec | < 10 sec |
| | | Negative identification | <1 min | <30 sec | <20 sec |
| 22 Weigh and display bag weight | System function | Weight accuracy | 95% | 98% | 100% |
| | | Weight result display time | 10 sec | 10 sec | Near real-time |

*Near real-time as <= 3 seconds

**Table 16-6**   Passenger Identification SV-7: Systems Measures Matrix *(continued)*

# SV-8: Systems Evolution Description

| View Information at a Glance | |
|---|---|
| View short name | SV-8 |
| Name | Systems Evolution Description |
| Other names | A-7 System/Application Evolution Diagram (FEAF2) Application Migration Diagram (TOGAF 9) |
| Viewpoint | Systems |

*(continued)*

PART III

| View Information at a Glance | |
|---|---|
| View intent | When linked together with other evolution views, such as CV-3: Capability Phasing and StdV-2: Standards Forecast, provides a rich definition of how the enterprise and its capabilities are expected to evolve over time. In this manner, the view can be used to support an architecture evolution project plan or transition plan. |
| | An SV-8 can either describe historical (legacy), current, or future system capabilities against a timeline. Two styles of SV-8 are defined—one is focused on how capabilities of systems are merged over a time frame and how new systems emerge from merging or splitting system functions from legacy configurations; the other is focused on displaying, for a single system, the evolution of system capabilities over a planning time frame. |
| View audience | Planners, systems program managers, portfolio managers |
| Formal modeling methodology | None. A tabular or a graphical method (such as a fishbone chart) can be used to display the evolution of a systems migration strategy for multiple systems or a single system's evolving capabilities over time. |
| Integration of view with other views | Systems in SV-8 must be consistent with all other SV views depicting systems such as SV-1, SV-2, SV-3, SV-4, SV-5, SV-6, SV-7, SV-9, and SV-10c. System functions depicted in SV-8 must be consistent with system functions in other SV views such as SV-4, SV-5, and SV-10c. |

## Example: Passenger Identification SV-8

The SV-8 is generally drawn as a graphic. Table 16-7 shows a tabular rendering of the evolution of the various systems in terms of functions that will be added in system increments over a period of time. (We use "Current Year" for this example. The view should contain the specific years for which the evolution is planned.)

| System | Current Year | Current Year + 1 | | | Current Year + 2 | | |
|---|---|---|---|---|---|---|---|
| | 4Q | 1Q | 2Q | 3Q | 1Q | 2Q | 3Q |
| PMS | | | | | Freq. flyer entitlement | PaxIS upgrade | |
| ARTS | | | | | | PaxIS upgrade | |
| CSS | | | | | | PaxIS upgrade | |
| LETS | | | | | | PaxIS upgrade | |
| ARTS-mobile | | | | | PaxIS upgrade | | |

**Table 16-7** Passenger Identification SV-8: Systems Evolution Description

| System | Current Year | Current Year + 1 | | | Current Year + 2 | | |
|---|---|---|---|---|---|---|---|
| | 4Q | 1Q | 2Q | 3Q | 1Q | 2Q | 3Q |
| ARTS-kiosk | | | | | PaxIS upgrade | | |
| ABTS-commercial | | | | | | | PaxIS upgrade |
| CBPS | | | | | | PaxIS upgrade | |
| ICES | | | | | | PaxIS upgrade | |
| ABTS - RMN | | | | | | PaxIS upgrade | |
| E-POSS | | | | | PaxIS upgrade | | |
| Smart devices | Smart reader | Machine-readable passports | RFID passports | All magnetic stripe devices | | | |
| PaxIS | | | IOC | FOC | | | |

**Table 16-7** Passenger Identification SV-8: Systems Evolution Description (continued)

# SV-9: Systems Technology and Skills Forecast

| View Information at a Glance | |
|---|---|
| View short name | SV-9 |
| Name | Systems Technology and Skills Forecast |
| Other names | Systems Technology Forecast (Old) System Technology Matrix (TOGAF 9) |
| Viewpoint | Systems |
| View intent | Maps technology forecasts against an adoption timeline for the scope of the architecture system elements. This includes, for example, mapping for each system the planned infusion of new technology. The technology depiction may be general or specific to vendor products. Identifies any personnel skill upgrades or changes associated with the new technology. |
| View audience | Technology and HR planners, systems program offices, standards personnel, investment review boards |
| Formal modeling methodology | This view is usually a textual document. |
| Integration of view with other views | The technology classification scheme in SV-9 must be consistent with the taxonomy of the StdV-1 and StdV-2 service areas and services. Any standards used in SV-9 must also be consistent with StdV-1 and StdV-2 standards. Systems represented in SV-9 must be consistent with systems in other SV views such as SV-1, SV-2, SV-3, SV-4, SV-6, SV-7, SV-8, and SV-10c. |

PART III

## Example: Passenger Identification SV-9

Table 16-8 shows the planned technology upgrades and migrations for various systems over a planning time frame. Note that the SV-9 shows actual upgrades of technology instances (vendor products) rather than planned adherence to technical standards such as compliance to FIPS 127 SQL Standard. The StdV-1 focuses more on technical profiles (service areas, services and standards) while the SV-9 is focused more on a planned migration of specific technologies. This example does not include comments on skill upgrade needs.

| | 2010 | 2011 | | | | 2012 | |
|---|---|---|---|---|---|---|---|
| System | 4Q | 1Q | 2Q | 3Q | 4Q | 2Q | 3Q |
| PMS | Windows 7 Server | | | | | | |
| ARTS | Windows 7 Server | | Oracle 11 | | SQL Server YYY | | |
| CSS | Windows 7 Server | | | | | | |
| LETS | Windows 7 Server | | | Oracle 11 | | | |
| ARTS-mobile | Windows 7 Server | | | SQL Server YYY | MySQL | | |
| ARTS-kiosk | Windows 7 Server | | | | SQL Server YYY | | |
| ABTS-commercial | Windows 7 Server | | | | | | |
| CBPS | Windows 7 Server | | | Oracle 11 | | | |
| ICES | Windows 7 Server | | Oracle 11 | | | | |
| ABTS - RMN | Windows 7 Server | | | | | | |
| E-POSS | Windows 7 Server | | | SQL Server YYY | | | |
| Smart devices | Windows Mobile | ISO XXX | ISO XXX | ISO XXX | | | |
| PaxIS | Apache Web Server | | IOC | FOC | | | |

**Table 16-8**   Passenger Identification SV-9: Systems Technology and Skills Forecast

# SV-10a: Systems Rules Model

| View Information at a Glance | |
| --- | --- |
| View short name | SV-10a |
| Name | Systems Rules Model |
| Other names | Rules Model |
| Viewpoint | Systems |
| View intent | Rules that control, constrain, or otherwise guide the implementation aspects of the architecture. System rules are statements that define or constrain some aspect of the business, and may be applied to system and human performers, resource flows, system functions, system ports, and data elements. |
| View audience | Systems and solution architects. The SV-10a is a fine-grained model that may not be applicable to enterprise and segment architecting and must be driven by various systems scenarios. |
| Formal modeling methodology | The model is represented using English text or formal mathematical notation, like the OV-6a: Operational Rules Model. |
| Integration of view with other views | Any architecture elements referenced by a rule must be consistent with the corresponding model elements in SV views such as system performers in SV-1, SV-2, SV-3, SV-4, SV-6, SV-7, SV-8, SV-9, and SV-10c, or resource flows in SV-1, SV-4, SV-6, and SV-10c. |

The SV-10a: Systems Rules Model is similar to the OV-6a: Operational Rules Model in that it describes the rules that constrain systems or system functions. These rules are embedded inside the logic of the system function, or they may also represent constraints that govern the operator interface and permission sets:

- **Structure assertion rules**   Embedded inside the database as constraints. For example, a rule may be "A passenger is a person who has a boarding pass" to distinguish people who have simply made a booking from those that are actually travelling.

- **Action assertion rules**   Generally in the form "If (A is true) then (B is true) else (C is true)"; these rules provide criteria for use in decision points of the processing logic of system functions.

- **Derivation rules**   Provide algorithms to compute, at run time, needed values from other available data. These rules are embedded into the processing logic.

Here are some more examples of unstructured systems rules that constrain system behavior:

- All systems performing passenger identification shall be able to read machine-readable passports complying with ICAO Document 9303 (endorsed by the International Organization for Standardization and the International Electrotechnical Commission as ISO/IEC 7501-1). If a system encounters a nonmachine-readable passport, it shall notify the system operator with an error message indicating failure to read nonmachine-readable passport.
- All systems shall maintain an access control table that maps the roles of users to permissible system functions.
- The system shall authenticate the user first and the role second before attempting to match permissions to requested system functions. No information about system functions shall be provided to end users.
- Though the system user can potentially assume one of many roles, at any point in the use of a system, a system user shall enter and remain in the system using one and only one selected role.

# SV-10b: Systems State Transition Model

| View Information at a Glance | |
| --- | --- |
| View short name | SV-10b |
| Name | Systems State Transition Description |
| Other names | UML State Chart<br>Harel State Chart<br>Finite State Model |
| Viewpoint | Systems |
| View intent | Depicts the state transitions of a system architecture element, usually a system or subsystem. This model is frequently used to describe the functioning of control systems based on sensor inputs. The next state of the system element is determined by its current state and a triggering event that causes the transition to the next state. |
| View audience | Systems and Solution architects, simulation analysts. The SV-10b is a fine-grained model that is not readily applicable to enterprise and segment architectures. |
| Formal modeling methodology | UML state chart, Harel Chart, finite state model |
| Integration of view with other views | Actions in SV-10b must be consistent with system functions in other SV views such as SV-4 and SV-5. |

The SV-10b: Systems State Transition Description is similar to the OV-6b: State Transition Description. In its simplest form it describes the change in state of a system due to system functions or system/external events. The objective of state transition diagrams is to observe the behavior of a system in terms of desired and undesired states, detect undesirable possible cycling between states, and ensure that the states are bounded and well understood when the system is deployed.

# SV-10c: Systems Event-Trace Description

| View Information at a Glance | |
|---|---|
| View short name | SV-10c |
| Name | Systems Event-Trace Description |
| Other name | UML Sequence Diagram |
| Viewpoint | Systems |
| View intent | Each SV-10c includes a textual scenario that illustrates a critical sequence of system/external events, such as a performance or security-critical sequence. The SV-10c also includes a graphic that traces the sequence of events in terms of the series of resource exchanges from the SV-6 involving systems and system functions triggered by the events as described in the scenario. This modeling technique is designed for modeling discrete events. |
| View audience | Systems and solution architects. The SV-10c is not readily applicable to enterprise or segment architecting and is best used in conjunction with scenarios. |
| Formal modeling methodology | UML sequence diagram is used to model object class interactions. A similar graphical technique is described in most real-time texts. |
| Integration of view with other views | Systems in SV-10c must be consistent with systems in other SV views. Resource flows in SV-10c must be consistent with (but not necessarily identical in level of abstraction) with resource flows in SV-1, SV-4 and SV-6. |

The SV-10c: Systems Event-Trace Description is similar to the OV-6c: Event-Trace Description in that it models the sequence of resource exchanges between system functions in a scenario or contained situation. It also depicts the exchange of resources in the context of timing so that the architect can observe and determine timing-related issues. The SV-10c is very useful in examining a detailed scenario in terms of sender systems and receiver systems, the functions they are performing at the time of the resource exchange, the type of information/resource that forms the subject of the interaction, and timing information associated with the exchange. The SV-10c complements the SV-6: Systems Resource Flow Matrix by laying out the data exchanges on a timeline and representing the exact sequence with which the resources are sent and received. Though we have discussed the SV-10c as a view for representing data exchange, it can also be generalized to represent the exchange of any type of resource such as funds, people, and materiel.

# TOGAF Information Systems Architecture

Though many of the artifacts that support the data architecture are data-oriented rather than system-oriented, the following artifacts represent aspects of the Systems Viewpoint that depict the relationship between systems and data entities:

- **Application/data matrix**  The application/data matrix depicts the relationship between the applications and the data entities that are accessed and updated by them. The entry in the intersection cells contain one or more of the following codes: (C) If the application creates instances of the data entity; (R) if it references/reads instances of the data entity; (U) if the application updates properties of instances of the data entity; and (D) if the application can delete instances of the data entity. This artifact is sometimes commonly known as a CRUD Matrix. The CRUD Matrix is akin to a summary matrix compiled from several SV-4 data flow diagrams from the DoDAF and is useful to summarize and concentrate the information from the several diagrams into a matrix that provides an overview of all data interactions by all applications in a compact format.

- **Data dissemination diagram**  The data dissemination diagram shows the relationship between data entity, business service, and application components. At the center of the diagram is a business service connected with arrows to the applications that provide data or consume data in the context of the business service along with specific data entities that are referenced by the business service. There is no equivalent view in the DoDAF.

The TOGAF (within the applications architecture corresponding to the DoDAF Systems Viewpoint) recommends the development of the following artifacts:

- **Application portfolio catalog**  The application portfolio catalog takes inventory of all the applications used throughout the enterprise. The catalog serves as a tool to assess the impacts of any changes on the applications and to anticipate unintended consequences that may result from lack of that knowledge. The catalog contains "logical" application components that may actually comprise multiple applications in realization, "physical" or individual specific application components, as well as information services that supply information in response to requests. There is no equivalent in the DoDAF Systems Viewpoint as an architecture view, but in the DoD, the central application portfolio catalog is the Defense IT Portfolio Registry (DITPR).

- **Interface catalog**   The interface catalog is an inventory of all the interfaces between applications within the enterprise. Interfaces impose a dependency between applications. The interface catalog is akin to the universe of all the SV-1: Systems Interface Description views within the DoDAF all stored within a single repository. The interface catalog also contains descriptions of the interface in terms of the exchange protocols, throughput, information security requirements and classification levels, and other properties in addition to the end-point applications.

- **Application/organization matrix**   This artifact depicts the relationship between applications and organizational units within the enterprise. The intersection cell is assigned an "X" if an application component is used by an organization or left blank if not. The matrix provides a summary of application usefulness by organization units. There is no equivalent view in the DoDAF. The matrix also provides a rapid gap analysis to determine organizations that need to be served by applications but are currently not being served. It also provides a quick view of the collection of application components used by a specific organization.

- **Role/application matrix**   This matrix depicts the relationship between applications and the business roles that use them within the enterprise. The intersection cells within the matrix contain an "X" if an application component is used by a specific role or left blank if not. This is an important matrix to use in security planning and in determining what roles need what types of access to what applications. It can also be used for gap analysis when roles may need to be enabled to specific application components. Role usage may also drive the need to customize application interfaces to be convenient, efficient, and effective for those specific roles. There is no equivalent view in the DoDAF, though in the SV-10a: Systems Rules Model, assertions of which roles are enabled for which applications can be represented as authorization rules.

- **Application/function matrix**   This matrix depicts the relationship between applications and business functions within the enterprise. The matrix establishes a direct correspondence between an application component and the business function that it supports. The matrix is a useful tool in performing gap analysis for business functions that may need additional application support, or the potential for redundancy of applications that support the same business function. The SV-5a: Operational Activity to Systems Function Traceability Matrix and SV-5b: Operational Activity to Systems Traceability Matrix serve the same purpose as this matrix.

- **Application interaction matrix**   This matrix represents dependencies between two applications. This artifact is identical to the SV-3: Systems-Systems Matrix and serves a similar purpose in analyzing system dependencies.

- **Application communication diagram**   This diagram depicts application components and interfaces between them. Communications are shown as logical arrows and depict intermediary technology only when it is architecturally relevant. Though similar in name to the DoDAF SV-2: Systems Resource Flow

Description, the DoDAF view is concerned with networking components such as communication links, routers, firewalls, and hubs in addition to the application components. The application communication diagram may also be represented as follows:

- **N2 model or node connectivity diagram**   This is similar to the SV-1: Systems Interface Description.

- **Information exchange matrix**   This is similar to the DoDAF SV-6: Systems Resource Flow Matrix.

- **Application and user location diagram**   This diagram depicts clearly the business locations from which business users typically interact with the applications, but also the hosting location of the application infrastructure. The usefulness of the diagram is in answering questions related to deployment of an application to multiple locations; set user types in terms of quantities, licensing, estimation of support needed; and to help plan the selection of system management tools and application management suites. There is no equivalent view in the DoDAF.

- **Application use case diagram**   This diagram represents the interaction between a user role and the system and its functions that are exercised in a particular usage scenario. A use case diagram may depict multiple application components that are exercised within a scenario as well as multiple user roles that may participate in a specific use case scenario. There is no direct equivalent for this artifact in the DoDAF, although a hybrid OV-6c/SV-10c can be used in a similar way.

- **Enterprise manageability diagram**   This artifact shows how one or more applications interact with the components that support operational management of a solution. The usefulness of this artifact is in determining disconnected and discordant system management components that can be consolidated or unified in capability to provide a more comprehensive and effective overall system management strategy. There is no equivalent DoDAF view for this artifact.

- **Process/application realization diagram**   This diagram depicts the sequence of events when multiple applications are involved in executing a business process. The benefit of using this artifact is to gain insight into handoffs between applications, sequencing constraints, and the flows of data between application components all laid out in a timeline. The equivalent view within the DoDAF is the SV-10c: Systems Event-Trace Description.

- **Software engineering diagram**   This artifact breaks applications down into packages, modules, services, and operations from a development perspective. It supports planning through decomposition of a complex objective into smaller, simpler objectives that can be scheduled and resourced in a systematic manner. It also acts as a management tool for complex development environments. The DoDAF does not have an equivalent view.

- **Application migration diagram** This artifact represents the migration of legacy and current applications to future applications that will replace them. This artifact is identical to the DoDAF SV-8: Systems Evolution Description and serves the same purpose.

- **Software distribution diagram** This optional diagram is a composite of the software engineering diagram and the application-user location diagram. There is no DoDAF equivalent view that corresponds to this diagram.

# FEAF2 Applications Subarchitecture Domain

The Applications subarchitecture domain corresponds to the DoDAF Systems Viewpoint within the Common Approach/FEAF2 Framework, though the focus of the FEAF2 is primarily on government IT business systems, while the DoDAF is generalized to encompass embedded electronic systems, command and control systems, intelligence and reconnaissance systems in addition to war fighting and business support. The concerns that are addressed in the Application subarchitecture domain are similar to the ones that are addressed by the DoDAF systems views:

- Which systems and applications will be needed to generate, share, and store the data, information, and knowledge that the business services need?

- How can multiple types of IT systems, services, applications, databases, and web sites be made to work together where needed?

- How can configuration management help to create a cost effective and operationally efficient common operating environment (COE) for systems and applications?

- What are the workforce, standards, and security issues for applications and systems development and deployment?

The following artifacts are recommended in the FEAF2 to support the Application subarchitecture domain/Systems Viewpoint:

- **Application Interface Diagram (A-1)** (core requirement) The representation of application resource flows and their composition in terms of resource elements. This artifact is equivalent to the DoDAF SV-1: Systems Interface Description.

- **Application Communication Diagram (A-2)** The representation of the underlying communications means through which resource flows shown in the application interface diagram are implemented. This artifact is equivalent to the DoDAF SV-2: Systems Resource Flow Description.

- **Application Interface Matrix (A-3)** The interface relationships between systems represented as a matrix. This artifact is equivalent to the DoDAF SV-3: Systems-Systems Matrix.

- **Application Data Exchange Matrix (A-4)**   This artifact represents the details of resource flows among systems: the business activities performed, the resources exchanged, and the attributes (rules and measures) associated with these exchanges. This artifact is equivalent to the DoDAF SV-6: Systems Resource Flow Matrix.

- **Application Service Matrix (A-5)**   This table represents the relationship between systems and services. This artifact is equivalent to the SvcV-3a: Systems-Services Matrix and the SvcV-3b: Services-Services Matrix.

- **Application Performance Matrix (A-6)**   This table of measures is associated with an application's performance. These measures are used as specifications to plan or benchmark an application in terms of desirable properties such as availability and latency of user response to application response. This artifact is equivalent to the DoDAF SV-7: Systems Measures Matrix.

- **System/Application Evolution Diagram (A-7)**   This timeline chart depicts planned incremental steps toward migrating a suite of systems/applications to a more efficient suite or toward evolving a current system or application to a future implementation. This artifact is equivalent to the DoDAF SV-8: Systems Evolution Description.

- **Application Maintenance Procedure (A-9)**   This artifact describes how to modify software to provide error corrections, enhancements of capabilities, deletion of obsolete functionality, and optimization of behaviors and structures. There is no DoDAF equivalent to this artifact.

- **Application Inventory (A-10)**   This is a registry of applications and services: the system functions or service activities they perform and, optionally, their prioritization ranking. There is no equivalent for this artifact within the DoDAF, but the TOGAF Application Portfolio Catalog is an exact equivalent.

- **Software License Inventory (A-11)**   A list of COTS and open-source software assets with details about each (installation date, original cost, condition, and such).

# Summary

The Systems Viewpoint serves the interests of people involved with the planning, design, implementation, deployment, and maintenance of automated systems. The concepts presented in this chapter apply equally to automated information processing systems as well as automated systems that process generalized resources. The set of architecture views that support the Systems Viewpoint range from simple interface diagrams that represent the need to exchange resources by lines between systems (SV-1) to more complex views that support the evolution of a system's technology platforms (SV-9), migration and consolidation of systems (SV-8), model systems behaviors (SV-10a, SV-10b, SV-10c), specify a system's functionality (SV-4), and develop performance specifications (SV-7).

Though today's trend is to move away from monolithic systems and provide application functionality through a service-oriented architecture and infrastructure through cloud computing, the planning aspects from the systems viewpoint still remain—such as the challenge of orchestrating services, planning migration of services, understanding the relationship between services and some of the rules that are embedded within them to name a few!

# Questions

1. What audience is served by the Systems Viewpoint?

2. Discuss how your enterprise would use the Systems Viewpoint views to move to a service-oriented architecture. Which are the Services Viewpoint counterparts for the Systems Viewpoint views? (See Chapter 17 for the Services Viewpoint views)

3. Which of the Data and Information Viewpoints is complementary to the Systems Viewpoint views? Why?

4. Distinguish between a system function and a service.

5. What is the SV-1: Systems Interface Description? Would you expect to find all the systems of the enterprise in your SV-1? Why or why not?

6. What is the SV-2: Systems Resource Flow Description? Would you expect to find items such as networks, routers, modems, and firewalls depicted inside the SV-1? Inside the SV-2?

7. What is the relationship between the SV-1 and the SV-2? What common architecture elements do they share?

8. What is the SV-3? How can your enterprise tailor an SV-3 to depict interfaces that are already implemented as well as planned interfaces?

9. What is the SV-4? The example in Table 16-2 shows a simple functional decomposition, but the SV-4 can also show data flows between system functions. How would you depict these data flows in a diagram? How would you accommodate operators typing data into a system or data flowing into a database? (Hint: See "Data Flow Diagrams," DoDAF Volume II.)

10. How can the SV-5a and SV-5b be used to determine the composition of a systems portfolio? What are the risks in using the SV-5 to determine redundancy?

11. How can you tailor the SV-6 to include needs to capture data security classification, personal identification information, and throughput?

12. What are performance measures for systems functions that are commonly used in your enterprise? What other measures are applicable to other architecture elements?

13. The SV-8: Systems Evolution Description can be rendered in two ways: in a system evolution of an individual system in terms of evolution of features and functions over a time frame, or in a migration style diagram that shows which systems are merged or split to form a new systems portfolio. Discuss the applicability of these two styles of SV-8 to your own enterprise.

14. What are the elements of forecast for technology in an SV-9? Are they technical standards or are they specific vendor products? Why?

# References

CIO Council. 2013. "Federal Enterprise Architecture Framework, Version 2." https://obamawhitehouse.archives.gov/sites/default/files/omb/assets/egov_docs/fea_v2.pdf.

Department of Defense. 2009. DoD Architecture Framework Version 2.0. "Volume 1: Introduction, Overview, and Concepts." http://dodcio.defense.gov/Portals/0/Documents/DODAF/DoDAF%20V2%20-%20Volume%201.pdf.

Department of Defense. 2009. DoD Architecture Framework Version 2.0. "Volume 2: Architectural Data and Models." http://dodcio.defense.gov/Portals/0/Documents/DODAF/DoDAF_v2-02_web.pdf.

Federal Enterprise Architecture Program Management Office, OMB. 2007. "FEA Practice Guidance." www.whitehouse.gov/sites/default/files/omb/assets/fea_docs/FEA_Practice_Guidance_Nov_2007.pdf.

Norman, Douglas O., and Michael L. Kuras. 2004. "Engineering Complex Systems." The MITRE Corporation. www.mitre.org/publications/technical-papers/engineering-complex-systems.

Object Management Group. 2013. Unified Profile for DoDAF and MODAF Specification Version 2.1. www.omg.org/spec/UPDM/2.1/.

Object Management Group. 2018. "About the Unified Modeling Language Specification Version 2.5.1." www.omg.org/spec/UML/About-UML/.

SysML.org. 2018. "SysML Open Source Specification Project: What Is SysML?" SysML.org at www.sysml.org/.

The Open Group. 2011. "Sample Catalogs, Matrices and Diagrams," Version 3, TOGAF Enterprise Edition Version 9.2. Microsoft PowerPoint presentation. www.togaf.info/togaf9/togafSlides91/TOGAF-V91-Extra-Catalogs-Matrics-Diagrams-v3.pdf.

The Open Group. 2018. "TOGAF Version 9.2." The Netherlands: Van Haren Publishing.

# CHAPTER 17

# Services Viewpoint

The world is changing at an ever faster rate. Traditional methods of architecting both business functions and software functionality cannot keep up with the pace of this rapid rate of change. The luxury of crafting custom functionality in systems to tailor them to an enterprise's specific needs is being overtaken by investment in commodity software. Enterprises are either changing business processes to adapt to the software or customizing the software to fit the business. Internal software development must also be leveraged. A change in the style with which traditional requirements-driven monolithic software was being developed is occurring. In this style of architecting, functional capabilities are implemented in modular, decoupled, scalable services that are individually implemented, and larger grain business functionality is achieved by composing multiple services, some home-grown, others purchased.

## Conventional Information Technology Services

With the widespread adoption of cloud technology and the view of information technology services as a utility that can be purchased and expensed as a scalable collection of services from providers outside the enterprise, architecting services have become ever more important. Conventionally, services have been divided into the following, starting from the business end to the information technology components end:

- Business Services
- Software as a Service (SaaS)
- Platform as a Service (PaaS)
- Infrastructure as a Service (IaaS)

## Business Services

In the area of business functions, vertically integrated enterprises that develop their own business functions are often outpaced by nimbler competitors that offload the functions to service providers and concentrate on managing the interfaces with these service suppliers. Even small businesses are outsourcing their payment transactions to card payment processing services that take over once a credit card is swiped. Enterprises are increasingly focused on their "core competencies" and offload mission support functions to business partners whose own core competency is providing that function. These offloaded business functions are deemed services, although any packaged business function that is loosely coupled and governed by agreement or contract between the provider and consumer may be deemed a business service.

The design of a service therefore requires architecture decoupling of interrelationships so that the service can be treated as a black box, whose behavior and performance can be negotiated as a level of delivery of service. It also requires clear definition of service interfaces—how the service looks to the consumer—that is independent of the internal implementation of the service. Atomic services by themselves are also stateless—their invocation processes maintain the state information needed to successfully orchestrate a collection of services needed to achieve a business objective or mission.

Business services for the consumer simply represent an undertaking by a provider to deliver service at an agreed upon grade, quality, and price through a service agreement (SLA). The service agreement also defines how the service will be delivered, how acceptance and payment is to be made, how to seek redress, as well as caveats, restrictions, and limitations.

The provider of the service, on the other hand, has to deal with many issues that surround the development, standing up, and delivery of a service to consumers. Business services encapsulate data, algorithms/process steps, and business rules as constraints, computational formulas, or guidance for decision-making. Services also need to be managed as secured objects that require controls for access and traceability of usage. For services that require transparency, they also need controls to enable auditing and logging. Services may also have to comply with regulations and concerns related to data privacy.

## Software as a Service (SaaS)

In the area of software development, a similar solution based on vertically integrated software relies on in-house development of software functions that are tightly tied to the software solution being developed. Such tightly integrated systems are immune to adaptability, because the impact of change requires widespread change to the solution. At the same time, the enterprise cannot take advantage of market forces for a software component that can be purchased, leased, or supplied by external providers. Software services are standalone, loosely coupled, defined with clear published interfaces, and stateless providers of functionality that are used as building blocks to build software applications.

Service-oriented architecture (SOA) is a paradigm for organizing and utilizing distributed capabilities that may be under the control of different ownership domains. A key characteristic of SOA is modularity that facilitates/enables service reuse across processes and organizational boundaries. A service that is designated for reuse or as an enterprise service, such as authentication, must reside in an environment that is discoverable, reliable, maintainable, and monitorable. An overarching architecture is needed to contain these services as they are developed and implemented.

SaaS is a natural evolution of thin client, fat server technology, where a web browser serves as a client and services are delivered by a cloud-based server that may or may not be owned or controlled by the enterprise but is managed through SLAs between the enterprise and the service provider—usually a third party. SaaS is the most ubiquitous model of services today with widespread adoption of cloud-based software providing e-mail, word processing, business presentation, spreadsheet, accounting, and tax preparation capabilities. As acceptance for the concept of "renting" software from businesses and users grows, more and more traditional installed commercial-off-the-shelf (COTS) software is being delivered as a service.

## Platform as a Service (PaaS)

Gartner defines a PaaS offering as a broad collection of application infrastructure (middleware) services (including application platform, integration, business process management, and database services).

Microsoft Corporation (https://azure.microsoft.com/en-us/overview/what-is-paas/). defines PaaS as "a complete development and deployment environment in the cloud, with resources that enable you to deliver everything from simple cloud-based apps to sophisticated, cloud-enabled enterprise applications. You purchase the resources you need from a cloud service provider on a pay-as-you-go basis and access them over a secure Internet connection."

PaaS, like IaaS, includes infrastructure—servers, storage, and networking—but also middleware, development tools, business intelligence (BI) services, database management systems, and more. PaaS is designed to support the complete web application life cycle: building, testing, deploying, managing, and updating.

PaaS is built on top of virtualization technology. Enterprises can requisition virtual resources as they need them, scaling up as demand grows or scaling down when demand shrinks.

## Infrastructure as a Service (IaaS)

According to Gartner, IaaS is a "standardized, highly automated offering, where compute resources, complemented by storage and networking capabilities, are owned and hosted by a service provider and offered to customers on-demand. Customers are able to self-provision this infrastructure, using a web-based GUI that serves as an IT operations management console for the overall environment. API access to the infrastructure may also be offered as an option."

# Architecting a DoDAF Solution Through Service Components

Regardless of the type of individual component services in use, a business or technology solution typically requires several service components that must be brought together and integrated. A *service composition* is an aggregate of services that automate a particular task or business process. Integrating the invocation of multiple services in a planned manner requires orchestration. Some of the architecture needs related to issues and concerns regarding the Services Viewpoint follow:

- **Realize capability need through service solutions**   Capabilities represent the statement of generalized needs to enable outcomes or achieve desired effects. Capabilities are used by the planner to determine what needs to be acquired. Services represent solutions that satisfy the capability need. The DoDAF CV-7: Capability to Services Mapping establishes an explicit association between the capability need and the service solution that guides the capability planner to specify what services will deliver desired capability.

- **Identify service performers**   In a SOA, services are provided by a service provider and used or consumed by a service consumer. Intermediary performers such as service brokers provide value-added services. Service performers, service brokers, and service consumers are tied together through service agreements that specify terms of provision and consumption of services, quality of services, and other parameters that govern how the service will be delivered on an ongoing basis. The key transactions between the performers are the request for service from a consumer and the ultimate provision of the service by the provider. The transactions are performed through a messaging infrastructure. In the DoDAF, services can result in transfer of resources other than information, in addition to transfer of information for notifications.

- **Specify services functionality**   Just as the operational activity was the prime ingredient for changing operational behavior, the service operation is the prime ingredient that describes service behavior. The SvcV-4: Services Functionality Description models the service operations that have been implemented or are planned for a system as a well-ordered taxonomy. The SvcV-4 is useful to compare services functions across multiple services, looking for duplication and overlaps. It also helps to establish a composition map for larger grain services in terms of smaller grain service components. The SvcV-4 also models the input/output behavior of service operations in terms of the information/resources they consume, transform, or produce. The SvcV-4 can be used to examine the orchestration of information exchanges/resource flows between multiple services and to drive the development of service specifications at the implementation level using specification languages such as the Web Services Description Language (WSDL).

- **Analyze service resource flow/information exchange requirements**   The counterpart to the OV-2: Operational Resource Flow Description is the SvcV-1: Services Context Description. The SvcV-1 replaces the operational performers and locations in the OV-2 with services performers and services hosting locations, and it also replaces the operational need lines that indicated needs for exchange of information/flow of resources with interfaces that indicate a need to exchange information/resource flows between services performers. If every operational performer were to be supported by a single service, the layout of the SvcV-1 would perfectly match the layout of the OV-2. But in reality, multiple services support a single performer, and nonautomated activities in the operational realm do not have a service counterpart in the services realm. The SvcV-3b: Services-Services Matrix is a compact model that represents some aspect of interaction between pairs of services. The SvcV-3b may also be used as a compact model for representing the many interfaces in a large and complex SvcV-1. Other services resource flow models such as the SvcV-6: Services Resource Flow Matrix focus on the details of the information exchanges/resource flows between specific services in the context of specific service operations being performed by the services.

- **Analyze services connectivity** The interfaces that demonstrate the need for information exchange/resource flows between services inside the SvcV-1 need to be implemented physically using communication paths that connect the services together and provide a means for transmitting and receiving information/resources. In the IT sense, these are represented by paths through communication links, communication equipment, and computer networks. In the more general sense of resource flows, rather than simply information flows, these represent logistic chains that channel resources between services such as concourses in airports, baggage conveyor belts, and so on. The SvcV-2: Services Resource Flow Description models the physical paths that are travelled by information/resources between services. Since the physical path may have several intermediate links that are purely to route communications and resource transfer, the SvcV-1 may not have an exact correspondence with the SvcV-2 even though the end points for the path must coincide. The SvcV-2 is a depiction of the physical transfer path for information/resources that is depicted in the interfaces in the SvcV-1.

- **Trace services to operational usefulness** Too often, services are built with many features that were required at the time by business or military operations. As time goes on, some of these features may not be very useful or may represent obsolete functions. The SvcV-5: Operational Activity to Services Traceability Matrix maps services and service operations to the operational activities they support. This is a useful view for analyzing the impact of change of either the operational activity or the service operation on each other. For future planned services, it also provides an explicit plan of which operational activities will be enabled/facilitated or automated by a service operation.

- **Moving from a business process–focused approach to a business service–based approach** Enterprises that are contemplating migrating internally performed business processes to one or more business services need a plan to identify which service or collection of services would replace a specific business process. The SvcV-5 can be used as a mapper for a business service to an operational process to support the representation/replacement of a current internally performed business process with a candidate/actual business service that will provide the same functionality. Using a business service approach "detaches" a business process and provides the ability to outsource it to a service provider without worrying about the internals and focusing instead on outputs and outcomes.

- **Specify service performance** Another useful view is the SvcV-7: Services Measures Matrix used to specify the measurements for acceptance of a service or specifications that drive the acquisition of service capabilities. The specification of performance measures early in a service specification enables tradeoffs to be made during the design process and establishes minimum acceptance criteria for various components as well as the service itself. Service measures are a key part of service agreements that bind providers and consumers to service levels and quality of service.

- **Develop services evolution roadmap** For planners, one of the important models to build is a roadmap of services evolution. The SvcV-8: Services Evolution Description view offers the representation in two formats: evolution of features and functions for services in planned release increments, consolidation, and migration of multiple services into one or more target services. The SvcV-8 is a useful view for planning modernization initiatives as well as for allocating feature evolution to service increments.

- **Map services to operating platforms** For technology infrastructure staff, it is important to map services to the operating platforms that they need to run on. The SvcV-9: Services Technology and Skills Forecast view provides the capability of expressing a platform migration strategy for specific services. A portfolio of SvcV-9 models can then be used at the enterprise level to determine mismatches in migration strategy or missed migrations, for example. Service platforms themselves provide technology services. Database platforms provide query services; operating systems platforms provide file retrieval services.

- **Model service behaviors** For detailed views of services behavior, the SvcV-10a: Services Rules Model, SvcV-10b: Services State Transition Description, and the SvcV-10c: Services Event-Trace Description are available as counterparts of the OV-6a, OV-6b, and OV-6c operational behavioral views. These are useful for providing detailed representation of orchestration sequences of internal service operations, information/resource exchanges, and triggering events (SvcV-10c), or for detailed representation of constraints or algorithmic behavior used to implement service operations (SvcV-10a), or for detailed representation of the internal state transitions of a service in the face of triggering events and activities.

## Services Viewpoint Views

This section discusses the various views associated with the DoDAF Services Viewpoint. Each of these views addresses some specific concern from the Services Viewpoint. Remember that within the Services Viewpoint, the issues and concerns of a service consumer may be different from those of a service provider.

For brevity, a partial subset of the Services Viewpoint is shown in Figure 17-1 to illustrate the concepts of integrated models in the context of the Services Viewpoint (missing are SvcV-9, SvcV-10a, SvcV-10b, and SvcV-10c). Figure 17-1 shows a simplistic view of the various elements that are visible in the Services Viewpoint. The figure is more a picture than a formal model, and the arrow in the relationships provides a reading order

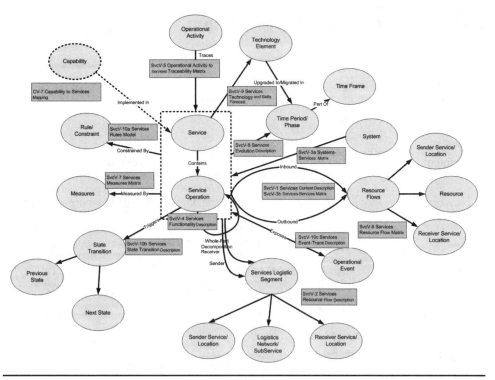

**Figure 17-1** Integrated view of the Services Viewpoint

for the name of the relationship using the start concept of the arrow with the name on the arrow and the end concept of the arrow.

The Services Viewpoint also has a tight coupling of models for consistency purposes. Views share many common elements such as services, services functions, service locations, data flows, and so on.

Following are some examples of the needs for consistent use of architecture elements between Services Viewpoint views:

- SvcV-1 services must be consistent with SvcV-2 services. SvcV-1 interfaces must be consistent with SvcV-4 data flows and SvcV-6 data exchanges between the same end point services.

- SvcV-4 service operations must be consistent with SvcV-5 service operations.

In addition to the integration needs of views within the Services Viewpoint, there are integration needs implicit inside the views to other viewpoints. Here are examples:

- SvcV-5 maps the services functions and services to operational activities defined inside the Operational Viewpoint.

- SvcV-9 must be consistent in the evolution of system technology to the elements defined in the StdV-1: Standards Profile and the StdV-2: Standards Forecast.

# SvcV-1: Services Context Description

| View Information at a Glance | |
| --- | --- |
| View Short Name | SvcV-1 |
| Name | Services Context Description |
| Other names | None |
| Viewpoint | Services |
| View intent | In addition to depicting services (performers) and their structure, the SvcV-1 addresses service resource flows, which indicate that resources pass between one service and the other. In the case of services, this can be expanded into further detail in SvcV-2: Services Resource Flow Description view. A services resource flow is a simplified representation of a pathway or network pattern, usually depicted graphically as a connector (a line with possible amplifying information). The SvcV-1 depicts all resource flows between resources that are of interest. |
| View audience | SOA architects, portfolio planners, solution architects |
| Formal modeling methodology | None |
| Integration of view with other views | Services in SvcV-1 must be consistent with services in all other SvcV views such as SvcV-2, SvcV-3a, SvcV-3b, SvcV-4, SvcV-6, and SvcV-10c. |

## Example: Passenger Identification SvcV-1

In the SvcV-1: Services Context Description (Figure 17-2), we have shown the services at different locations. The locations also represent different types of activities that are being performed by various performers at those locations.

The diagram shows the as-is interfaces in the circles along the outside of the figure. In the as-is situation, the various services are independently invoking their own passenger identification operations internally (not shown). The double-arrowed lines show the proposed interface configuration where a single passenger identification service (processIdentifyPAX) is provided centrally from the RMN Operations Center and can service each of the locations from a single point. The proposed solution will eliminate differing business rules in the separate implementations of passenger identification and provides uniform updates for all stakeholders.

The lines with single arrows indicate the as-is need for interaction between services representing independent passenger identification capabilities and the double arrow-headed lines the proposed configuration, with a centralized service processIdentifyPAX at the RMN Operations Center that provides identification services to all invoking services located at the various locations.

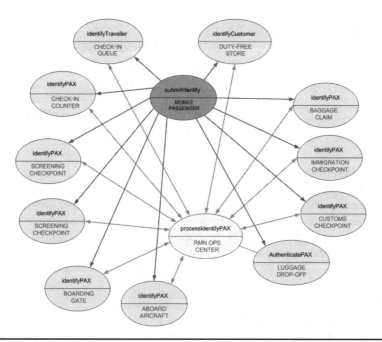

**Figure 17-2**    Passenger identification SvcV-1: Services Context Description

# SvcV-2: Services Resource Flow Description

| View Information at a Glance | |
| --- | --- |
| View short name | SvcV-2 |
| Name | Services Resource Flow Description |
| Other names | None |
| Viewpoint | Services |
| View intent | The SvcV-2 specifies the resource flows between services and may also list the protocol stacks used in connections. The SvcV-2 DoDAF-described model is used to give a precise specification of a connection between services. This may be an existing connection or a specification of a connection that is to be made in the future. |
| | For a network data service, the SvcV-2 comprises services, their ports, and the service resource flows between those ports. The SvcV-2 may also be used to describe non-IT type services such as search and rescue. The architect may choose to create a diagram for each service resource flow and the producing service, each service resource flow and consuming service, or all the service resource flows on one diagram, if this is possible. |

*(continued)*

| View Information at a Glance | |
|---|---|
| View audience | Service designers, SOA architects, resource planners |
| Formal modeling methodology | None |
| Integration of view with other views | The services in SvcV-2 must be consistent with services used in other SvcV views such as SvcV-1, SvcV-3a, SvcV-3b, SvcV-4, SvcV-6, SvcV-7, SvcV-8, SvcV-9, and SvcV-10c. |

## Example: Passenger Identification SvcV-2

The SvcV-2 shown in Figure 17-3 is for architecting the boarding gate kiosk. The kiosk allows a passenger to insert a combination of magnetically encoded identification cards and/or machine readable passports. The kiosk invokes a common service validateIdentityDocument provided by the RMN data center to all consumers who want to validate magnetic cards and machine readable passports.

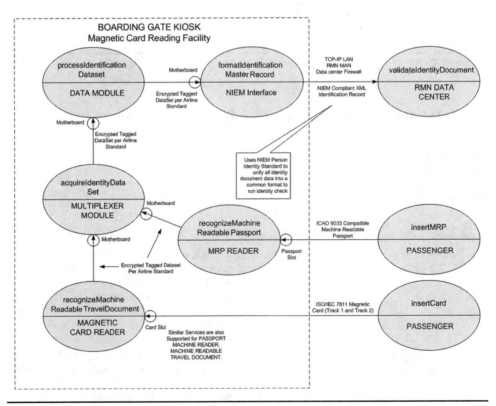

**Figure 17-3**  Passenger identification SvcV-2: Services Resource Flow Description

# SvcV-3a: Systems-Services Matrix
# SvcV-3b: Services-Services Matrix

| View Information at a Glance | |
|---|---|
| View short name | SvcV-3a, SvcV-3b |
| Name | Systems-Services Matrix (SvcV-3a)<br>Services-Services Matrix (SvcV-3b) |
| Other names | Service-Service Matrix |
| Viewpoint | Services |
| View intent | The SvcV-3a enables a quick overview of all the system-to-service resource interactions specified in one or more SvcV-1: Services Context Description views. The SvcV-3a provides a tabular summary of the system and services interactions specified in the SvcV-1 for the architectural description. This view can be useful in supporting existing systems that are transitioning to provide services. The matrix format supports a rapid assessment of potential commonalities and redundancies (or, if fault-tolerance is desired, the lack of redundancies).<br><br>An SvcV-3b enables a quick overview of all the services resource interactions specified in one or more SvcV-1: Services Context Description views. The SvcV-3b provides a tabular summary of the services interactions specified in the SvcV-1 for the architectural description. |
| Model audience | Service portfolio managers, planners, SOA architects, solution architects |
| Formal modeling methodology | None |
| Integration of view with other views | The services in SvcV-3 must be consistent with services used in other SvcV views such as SvcV-1, SvcV-2, SvcV-4, SvcV-6, SvcV-7, SvcV-8, SvcV-9, and SvcV-10c. |

## Example: Passenger Identification SvcV-3a

The SvcV-3a shown in Table 17-1 depicts current interfaces between systems and services as well as the planned interfaces. We notice clearly the planned transition of all systems to a single consistent identifyPassenger service that will eliminate the inconsistencies, ambiguities, and inaccuracies that are evident in the current multiplicity of independent interfaces to independent services. We show the time frame for the migration that is implied inside the SvcV-3a in the SvcV-8: Services Evolution Description. The advantage of each of these views is that they elaborate some aspect of the architecture, but each view adds a different dimension for a different audience. Without integration, the views would very quickly become inconsistent.

| System | Service identifyCustomer | identifyPassenger (To-Be) | identifyPAX (Airline) | identifyPAX (Airport) | identifyPAX (Customs) | identifyPAX (Immigration) | identifyPAX (Screening) | identifyTraveller |
|---|---|---|---|---|---|---|---|---|
| Airline reservation and ticketing system | C | P | C | | | | | |
| Airline reservation and ticketing system (kiosk) | | P | C | | | | | |
| Airline reservation and ticketing system (mobile) | | P | C | | | | | |
| Airport baggage tracking system (commercial) | | P | C | | | | | |
| Airport baggage tracking system (RMN Airport) | | P | C | C | | | | |
| Comprehensive screening system | | P | | | C | | C | C |
| Customs and border protection system | | P | | | C | | C | |
| Enhanced point of sale system | C | P | | | | | | |
| Immigration and customs enforcement system | | P | | | | C | C | |
| Law enforcement and training system | | P | | | | | C | C |
| Passenger identification system | | P | | | | | | |
| Passenger management system | | P | C | C | | | | C |
| Smart devices | | P | | | | | | C |

Legend: P = Planned Interface, C = Current Interface

**Table 17-1**  Passenger Identification SvcV-3a: Systems-Services Matrix

The SvcV-3b expresses relationships between services in much the same way the SvcV-3a showed the relationship between systems and services. The cell intersections can carry any information that is a characteristic of the association between system and service (or service and service) such as planned/actual as we have chosen to do in the SvcV-3a example.

The SvcV-3 views provide a compact representation for interactions between systems and services and also between services themselves. The meaning of the intersection cell is left to the modeler and must be described in a legend accompanying the view. The SvcV-3 views can be used to display compactly the information in a large and complex SvcV-1 in a single matrix instead of a large diagram running into several pages.

# SvcV-4: Services Functionality Description

| View Information at a Glance | |
|---|---|
| View short name | SvcV-4 |
| Name | Services Functionality Description |
| Other names | Service Component Reference Model (SRM) |
| Viewpoint | Services |
| View intent | • Develop a clear description of the necessary data flows that are input (consumed) by and output (produced) by each resource. <br><br> • Ensure that the service functional connectivity is complete (that a resource's required inputs are all satisfied). <br><br> • Ensure that the functional decomposition reaches an appropriate level of detail. <br><br> The SvcV-4 is the Services Viewpoint counterpart to the OV-5b: Operational Activity Model of the Operational Viewpoint. |
| View audience | SOA architects for planning the service decomposition tree and for analyzing composition and orchestration issues. Service planners and portfolio managers for the system decomposition. |
| Formal modeling methodology | Based on dataflow diagram methodology for systems. |
| Integration of view with other views | The services in SvcV-4 must be consistent with services used in other SvcV views such as SvcV-1, SvcV-2, SvcV-3a, SvcV-3b, SvcV-6, SvcV-7, SvcV-8, SvcV-9, and SvcV-10c. |

## Example: Passenger Identification SvcV-4

Notice in Figure 17-4 that the way we have broken down the large grain "Read Identity Document" into various sub-functions of smaller grain services is by using two techniques:

- Breaking down the life cycle of the larger grain service into component services that form the life cycle steps such as Recognize Identity Document Type, Acquire Identity Dataset, Process Identification Dataset, and Format Identification Master Record.

- Specializing a type of service into subservices that perform the same function on different payloads because of business rule differences or the need to reach out to different external resources. In this example, the larger abstraction Recognize Identity Document Type is specialized into Recognize Drivers License, Recognize Machine Readable Passport, and Recognize Machine Readable Travel Document.

**Figure 17-4**

Passenger
identification
SvcV-4: Services
Functionality
Description

1. **Read Identity Document**
   1.1 Recognize Identity Document Type
        1.1.1 Recognize Drivers License
        1.1.2 Recognize Machine Readable Passport
        1.1.3 Recognize Machine Readable Travel Document
   1.2 Acquire Identity Dataset
        1.1.4 Acquire Magnetic Card Dataset
        1.1.5 Acquire Machine Readable Passport Dataset
        1.1.6 Acquire Machine Readable Travel Document Dataset
   1.3 Process Identification Dataset
        1.3.1 Process Driver License Dataset
        1.3.2 Process US Passport Dataset
        1.3.3 Process Foreign Passport Dataset
        1.3.4 Process Travel Document Dataset
   1.4 Format Identification Master Record
        1.4.1 Load Identification Master Record
        1.4.2 Store Identification Master Record
2. **Validate Identity Document**
   2.1 Validate US Passport Identity
   2.2 Validate Foreign Passport Identity
   2.3 Validate US Drivers License Identity
   2.4 Validate Travel Document Identity
        2.4.1 Validate DHS Travel Document Identity
        2.4.2 Validate BIA Travel Document Identity
        2.4.3 Validate Canadian Travel Document Identity
3. **Alert Airport Security (TBD)**
4. **Alert First Responders (TBD)**

# SvcV-5: Operational Activity to Services Traceability Matrix

| View Information at a Glance | |
|---|---|
| View short name | SvcV-5 |
| Name | Operational Activity to Services Traceability Matrix |
| Other names | None |
| Viewpoint | Services |
| View intent | Addresses the linkage between service functions described in SvcV-4 and operational activities specified in OV-5a: Operational Activity Decomposition Tree or OV-5b: Operational Activity Model. The SvcV-5 depicts the mapping of service functions (optionally the capabilities and performers that they implement) to operational activities and thus identifies the transformation of an operational need into a purposeful action performed by a service solution. |
| View audience | Portfolio managers to assess relevance of services to the mission as represented by operational activity mappings, planners, SOA architects |
| Formal modeling methodology | None |

**View Information at a Glance**

| | |
|---|---|
| Integration of view with other views | The services in SvcV-5 must be consistent with services used in other SvcV views such as SvcV-1, SvcV-2, SvcV-3a, SvcV-3b, SvcV-6, SvcV-7, SvcV-8, SvcV-9, and SvcV-10c. The activities in SV-5 must be consistent with operational activities in OV-1, OV-2, OV-3, OV-5a, OV-5b, and OV-6c. |

## Example: Passenger Identification SvcV-5

In Table 17-2, although it appears that the intersections of services are for all operational activities (within the scope of this SvcV-5 view), the important finding is that the reuse potential for the services is extremely high, since identity documents are read and validated in every context in which determining a passenger's identity through an identification document is important.

In general, the SvcV-5 view enables the service architect to establish correspondence between a service and the operational context in which it is useful. Planning a family of services is similar to a product planning exercise where the planner is determining the product features that maximize market coverage and minimize development investments.

## SvcV-6: Services Resource Flow Matrix

**View Information at a Glance**

| | |
|---|---|
| View short name | SvcV-6 |
| Name | Services Resource Flow Matrix |
| Other names | None |
| Viewpoint | Services |
| View intent | Express the relationship across the three basic architectural data elements of an SvcV—services, service functions (Operations), and service resource flows—and focus on the specific aspects of the service resource flow and the service resource content. These aspects of the service resource flow exchange can be crucial to the operational mission and are critical to understanding the potential for overhead and constraints introduced by the physical aspects of the implementation, such as security policy and communications and logistics limitations. |
| View audience | SOA architects and service planners for planning the resource flows |
| Formal modeling methodology | None. The model is represented in a tabular format. |
| Integration of view with other views | The services in SvcV-6 must be consistent with the services in other SvcV views such as SvcV-1, SvcV-2, SvcV-3a, SvcV-3b, SvcV-5, SvcV-7, SvcV-8, SvcV-9, and SvcV-10c. The service functions must be consistent with the service functions in SvcV-4, SvcV-5, SvcV-8, and SvcV-10c. The resource flows/information exchanges must consistent with those in SvcV-1, SvcV-2, SvcV-4, and SvcV-10c. |

| Services | Operational Activities | | | | | | | | |
|---|---|---|---|---|---|---|---|---|---|
| | Check-In Passenger | Screen Passenger | Board Passenger | Receive Passenger | Conduct Immigration Inspection | Conduct Customs Inspection | Store Passenger baggage | Process Duty-Free Purchase | Deliver Baggage |
| **1. Read Identity Document** | X | X | X | X | X | X | X | X | X |
| 1.1 Recognize Identity Document Type | | | | | | | | | |
| 1.1.1 Recognize drivers license | | | | | | | | | |
| 1.1.2 Recognize machine readable passport | | | | | | | | | |
| 1.1.3 Recognize machine readable travel document | | | | | | | | | |
| 1.2 Acquire Identity Dataset | | | | | | | | | |
| 1.2.1 Acquire magnetic card dataset | | | | | | | | | |
| 1.2.2 Acquire machine readable passport dataset | | | | | | | | | |
| 1.2.3 Acquire machine readable travel document dataset | | | | | | | | | |
| 1.3 Process Identification Dataset | | | | | | | | | |
| 1.3.1 Process driver license dataset | | | | | | | | | |
| 1.3.2 Process US passport dataset | | | | | | | | | |
| 1.3.3 Process foreign passport dataset | | | | | | | | | |
| 1.3.4 Process travel document dataset | | | | | | | | | |

1.4 Format Identification Master Record

1.4.1 Load identification master record

1.4.2 Store identification master record

**2. Validate Identity Document** — X X X X X X X X

2.1 Validate US Passport Identity

2.2 Validate Foreign Passport Identity

2.3 Validate US Drivers License Identity

2.4 Validate Travel Document Identity

2.4.1 Validate DHS travel document identity

2.4.2 Validate BIA travel document identity

2.4.3 Validate Canadian travel document identity

**3. Alert Airport Security (TBD)** — X X

**4. Alert First Responders (TBD)** — X X

**Table 17-2**  Passenger Identification SvcV-5: Operational Activity to Services Traceability Matrix

### Example: Passenger Identification SvcV-6

Table 17-3 shows a sample resource flow matrix that corresponds to the SvcV-2 view presented earlier. The SvcV-6 tabulates the resource flows (in this case, data exchanges) and also optionally depicts standards, formats, media types, criticality, and other attributes of the resource exchange that help the architect assess and promote interoperability between the exchanging services. This example does not include service functions.

## SvcV-7: Services Measures Matrix

| View Information at a Glance | |
| --- | --- |
| View short name | SvcV-7 |
| Name | Services Measures Matrix |
| Other names | None. |
| Viewpoint | Services |
| View intent | Depicts the current and desired future values of architecture-specific metrics for service architecture elements. The measures are selected by the end user community and described by the architect. Performance parameters include all performance characteristics for which requirements can be developed and specifications defined. The complete set of performance parameters may not be known at the early stages of architectural description, so it is to be expected that this view is updated throughout the specification, design, development, testing, and possibly even its deployment and operations life cycle phases. |
| View audience | SOA architects for planning the performance requirements, services planners, service development program managers, service users |
| Formal modeling methodology | None |
| Integration of view with other views | SV-7 elements such as service and service operation must be consistent with their counterparts in other SvcV views. |

| Sender Service Provider | Sender Service | Receiver Service Provider | Receiver Service | Resource | Resource Type | Standard | Format |
|---|---|---|---|---|---|---|---|
| Boarding Gate Kiosk | insertCard | Magnetic Card Reader | recognizeMachine ReadableTravel Document | Magnetic Card Travel Document | Materiel | ISO/IEC 7811 Magnetic Card (Track1 and Track 2) | Encoded Magnetic Stripe |
| Magnetic Card Reader | recognizeMachine ReadableTravel Document | Multiplexer Module | acquireIdentity DataSet | Encrypted and Tagged Passenger Information Dataset | Data | ICAO Airline Agreement | Encrypted Digital DataStream |
| Multiplexer Module | acquireIdentity DataSet | Data Module | processIdentification DataSet | Encrypted and Tagged Passenger Information Dataset | Data | ICAO Airline Agreement | Encrypted Digital DataStream |
| Data Module | processIdentification DataSet | NIEM Interface | formatIdentification MasterRecord | Encrypted and Tagged Passenger Information Dataset | Data | ICAO Airline Agreement | Encrypted Digital DataStream |
| NIEM Interface | formatIdentification MasterRecord | RMN Data Center | validateIdentity Document | NIEM-Compliant Passenger Identification XML Document | Data | National Information Exchange Model Passenger Identification Standard | Encrypted Digital DataStream |

**Table 17-3**   Passenger Identification SvcV-6: Services Resource Flow Matrix

| Service | Measure | Baseline | Threshold | Objective |
|---|---|---|---|---|
| identifyPassenger | Availability | 98.00% | 99.00% | 99.9999% |
| identifyPassenger | Response Time | 2.0 sec | 1.5 sec | 1.0 sec |
| identifyPassenger | Accuracy | 95.0% | 98.0% | 99.5% |

**Table 17-4**   Passenger Identification Service Measures Matrix SvcV-7

## Example: Passenger Identification SvcV-7

In Table 17-4, the SvcV-7 specifies baseline (current), threshold (acceptable), and objective (desired) performance parameters for the identifyPassenger service. In reality, an SLA is used to specify service levels for both business and software services and acts as a durable agreement between service provider and service consumer that guarantees a level of service under contractual penalties.

# SvcV-8: Services Evolution Description

| View Information at a Glance | |
|---|---|
| View short name | SvcV-8 |
| Name | Services Evolution Description |
| Other names | None |
| Viewpoint | Services |
| View intent | Depicts the evolution of a portfolio of services over time showing margining or splitting of functionality between services and rearrangement of service boundaries. Depicts the evolution of a service in terms of functionality over time. |
| View audience | Service planners, SOA architects, service development program managers, portfolio managers, services roadmap developers |
| Formal modeling methodology | None. View can be represented graphically with a timeline backbone or as a table. |
| Integration of view with other views | The services in SvcV-8 must be consistent with services used in other SvcV views such as SvcV-1, SvcV-2, SvcV-3a, SvcV-3b, SvcV-5, SvcV-6, SvcV-7, SvcV-9, and SvcV-10c. |

## Example: Passenger Identification SvcV-8

Figure 17-5 shows the evolution of the IdentifyPassenger service and the migration of independent services currently used by various systems (as shown in the SvcV-3a: Systems-Services Matrix) to a common IdentifyPassenger service that incorporates common algorithms and business rules, and researches a comprehensive data sources to provide a single unified, consistent service.

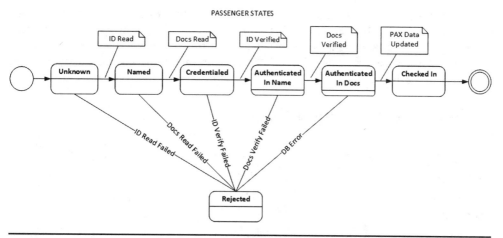

PASSENGER STATES

**Figure 17-5**   Passenger Identification Services Evolution Description SvcV-8

The SvcV-8 can be built using one of two styles:

- Migration style diagram that shows how multiple services are migrated over time into one or more services, as shown in the example.

- Evolution style (not shown) that generally describes how a service or collection of services from a single provider evolves in terms of functionality over a time period.

# SvcV-9: Services Technology and Skills Forecast

| View Information at a Glance | |
|---|---|
| View short name | SvcV-9 |
| Name | Services Technology and Skills Forecast |
| Other names | None |
| Viewpoint | Services |
| View intent | Models the insertion of technology (and consequent need to acquire skills) into services on a timeline. The specific types of technologies may be couched generically in terms of the service areas, services, and standards or specifically in terms of vendor products. |
| View audience | Technology roadmap planners, service development program office, SOA planners, service planners |
| Formal modeling methodology | None. |
| Integration of view with other views | The services in SvcV-9 must be consistent with services used in other SvcV views such as SvcV-1, SvcV-2, SvcV-3a, SvcV-3b, SvcV-5, SvcV-6, SvcV-7, SvcV-8, and SvcV-10c. The technology classification scheme must be consistent with the one used in StdV-1 and StdV-2. |

PART III

The SvcV-9: Services Technology and Skills Forecast (not shown) is similar to the SV-9: Systems Technology and Skills Forecast and depicts the planned insertion of technology into a collection of services over a period of time. It may also depict the need to acquire and insert skills for operators, developers, and maintainers of these services at the same time to ensure that skill development is orchestrated with service upgrades.

# SvcV-10a: Services Rules Model

| View Information at a Glance | |
|---|---|
| View short name | SvcV-10a |
| Name | Services Rules Model |
| Other names | None |
| Viewpoint | Services |
| View intent | Describes the rules that control, constrain, or otherwise guide the implementation aspects of the architecture. Service rules are statements that define or constrain some aspect of the business, and may be applied to:<br><br>• Performers (services)<br>• Resource flows<br>• Service functions<br>• System ports<br>• Data elements |
| View audience | Service designers/developers, solution architects, service planners |
| Formal modeling methodology | Rules languages, structured English, first order logic, pseudo code, algorithmic languages |
| Integration of view with other views | Any architecture elements referenced by a rule must be consistent with the corresponding view elements in SvcV views such as service performers in SvcV-1, SvcV-2, SvcV-3a, SvcV-3b, SvcV-4, SvcV-6, SvcV-7, SvcV-8, SvcV-9, and SvcV-10c, or resource flows in SvcV-1, SvcV-4, SvcV-6, and SvcV-10c. |

## Example: Passenger Identification SvcV-10a

Service rules constrain some aspect of the service such as behavior. Service rules are embedded inside the logic that implements the service. For business services, service rules may be provided as a constraint specification by the business entity that is sponsoring the service. Typically, these may be rules that must flow through to service providers such as in regulatory scenarios or in compliance with requirements of policy. Table 17-5 shows an example.

| Service | Rule ID | Rule | Authority/Source Reference |
|---------|---------|------|----------------------------|
| Read Identity Document | RID-001 | Identity documents that are implemented in magnetic cards must comply with ISO/IEC 7811 standards. | ICAO DOC-9303 |
| | RID-002 | Machine readable passports must comply with the ICAO 9303 Part 1 standards for fonts, printing, sizing, and proportions. | RMN Identification Procedures Manual 2010 |
| | RID-003 | If an identity document cannot be read automatically by a machine, then an audible machine signal is necessary. All audible machine signals are capable of being turned off. | RMN Identification Procedures Manual 2010 |
| | RID-004 | If three attempts at reading a machine readable identify document are unsuccessful, then an alternative form of identification must be available. | RMN Identification Procedures Manual 2010 |
| | RID-005 | Machine attempts at reading machine readable documents must be nondestructive. | RMN Identification Procedures Manual 2010 |
| | RID-006 | If a machine accidently alters a machine readable document, the operator is required to provide an alternative form of identification that is acceptable to airport authorities. | RMN Identification Procedures Manual 2010 |

**Table 17-5**   Passenger Identification SvcV-10a: Services Rules Model

## SvcV-10b: Services State Transition Description

| View Information at a Glance | |
|------------------------------|--|
| View short name | SvcV-10b |
| Name | Services State Transition Description |
| Other names | UML State Chart Harel State Chart |
| Viewpoint | Services |

*(continued)*

PART III

| View Information at a Glance | |
| --- | --- |
| View intent | Depicts the internal state transitions of a service architecture element, such as a service or service function for technical services or data/information element for a business service. The next state of the service element is determined by its current state and a triggering event that causes a transition to the next state. This model can be simulated. |
| View audience | Service designers, SOA architects, simulation analyst |
| Formal modeling methodology | UML State Chart, Harel State Chart, Finite State modeling techniques |
| Integration of view with other views | The granularity of the SvcV-10b generally will not match that of the other non-behavior-related larger grained models, but the element that has state must appear in at least one other SvcV view and any activity included in the model or related to an event in the model must be consistent with service operations in SvcV-4, SvcV-6, or SvcV-10c. |

## Example: Free Wi-Fi Kiosk Service SvcV-10b

Figure 17-6 represents the states of a hypothetical kiosk service that entitles passengers (PAX) to free Wi-Fi services for Internet connectivity. In this example, we insert a few conditions that are to be fulfilled before a passenger receives Wi-Fi services. (1) A passenger is required to identify himself/herself to the service through a contactless identity document. Without valid identification, Wi-Fi access is denied. (2) He/she is also required to provide a travel document such as a boarding pass that shows that they have arrived or are departing within the space of twenty-four hours from the time of the Wi-Fi request.

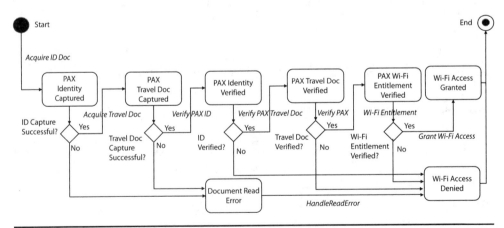

**Figure 17-6**   Passenger Kiosk Free Wi-Fi Service SV-10b: Services State Transition Description

(3) The passenger should not have previously availed themselves of the Wi-Fi service within the last twenty-four hours. If these conditions are satisfied, the service will provide four hours of free Wi-Fi access through the kiosk that also has a built-in web browser to connect to the worldwide web.

## SvcV-10c: Services Event-Trace Description

| View Information at a Glance | |
| --- | --- |
| View short name | SvcV-10c |
| Name | Services Event-Trace Description |
| Other names | Sequence diagrams<br>Timing diagrams<br>Event scenarios |
| Viewpoint | Services |
| View intent | Provides a time-ordered examination of the interactions between services functional resources. Each event-trace diagram should have an accompanying description that defines the particular scenario or situation. The SvcV-10c specifies the sequence in which resource flow elements are exchanged in context of a resource or service port. The components of an SvcV-10c include functional resources (services) or service ports, owning performer (provider), as well as the port that is the subject for the lifeline. |
| View audience | Service designers, SOA architects, performance analysts |
| Formal modeling methodology | UML sequence diagram, use case techniques (for business services and providing scenario text) |
| Integration of view with other views | The services in SvcV-10c must be consistent with services used in other SvcV views such as SvcV-1, SvcV-2, SvcV-3a, SvcV-3b, SvcV-5, SvcV-6, SvcV-7, SvcV-8, and SvcV-9. Resource flows/information exchanges must be consistent with those in SvcV-4 and SvcV-6. |

The SvcV-10c: Services Event-Trace Description (not shown) is similar to the SV-10c: Systems Event-Trace Description, except that the lifelines depict services (and service providers) and the exchange of messages represents interactions between the services as depicted over a timeline. The SvcV-10c enables the architect to describe detailed interactions between services to examine issues related to timing as well as responsibility. The SvcV-10c is typically used to elaborate a scenario or contained situation and is generally too fine-grained for enterprise-level architectures. In much the same way activities performed by their performers are depicted on the lifelines, service operations performed by the respective services may also be depicted on the lifelines.

# DoD View of Services (DoD Information Enterprise Architecture)

The Department of Defense Information Enterprise Architecture (DoD IEA) version 2.0 was approved by the DoD Chief Information Officer on August 10, 2012 for immediate use and supersedes the previous DoD IEA v1.2. It provides the common vocabulary for describing the capabilities, activities and services to achieve the Joint Information Environment (JIE).

The DoD IEA uses the DoDAF to represent the views that describe (i) a set of common capabilities that are required to support the JIE, (ii) the operational activities that are required to stand up and sustain the information enterprise, (iii) a common vocabulary for the types of services that will be provided to support the JIE from the viewpoint of the Joint enterprise, (iv) relationships between these architecture elements to provide an integrated architecture. The DoD IEA provides the roadmap for services that will be delivered to DoD applications and systems enterprise-wide to promote consistency and uniformity between independently developed applications that are required to work together in a peacetime and wartime environment.

# TOGAF View of Services

TOGAF 9 distinguishes business functions from business services from information system services using the following definitions:

- **Function**  A thing that a business does. Services support functions, are functions, and have functions, but functions are not necessarily services. Services have more specific constraints than functions.

- **Business service**  A thing that a business does that has a defined, measured interface and has contracts with consumers of the service. A business service is supported by combinations of people, processes, and technologies.

- **Information system service**  A thing that a business does that has a defined, measured interface and has contracts with consumers of the service. Information system services are directly supported by applications and have associations to SOA service interfaces.

## TOGAF Service Artifacts

The business architecture developed in Phase B of the TOGAF Architecture Development Method (ADM) contains the following artifacts relevant to the Services Viewpoint:

- **Business Service/Function Catalog**  Contains a catalog of organizational units, business functions, business services, and information system services, and relationships among these.

- **Business Service/Information Diagram**  Shows the information needed to support one or more business services. Shows what data is consumed or produced by a business service and may also show the data source for that information. Similar to the DoDAF SvcV-4: Services Functionality Description.

- **Goal/Objective/Service Diagram**  Defines the ways in which a service contributes to the achievement of a business vision or strategy. Services are associated with the drivers, goals, objectives, and measures that they support. Useful for making the business case for a service. Similar to the DoDAF CV-1: Vision combined with the CV-7: Capability to Services Mapping.

- **Business Footprint Diagram**  Describes the links between business goals, organizational units, business functions, and services and establishes line of sight from service to goal. Each line of sight is represented on a swim lane for each organizational unit. Useful for planning services and making a business case and identifying sponsors.

- **Business Use Case Diagram**  Displays the relationships between consumers and providers of business services. Business services are consumed by actors or other business services. The business use-case diagram provides added richness in describing business capability by illustrating how and when that capability is used. The artifact is similar to the CV-7: Capability to Services Mapping with added information about consumers and providers.

The application architecture developed in Phase C of the ADM contains the following artifacts relevant to the Services Viewpoint:

- **Application Portfolio Catalog**  Intended to identify and maintain a list of all applications in the enterprise. It contains instances of logical application components, physical application components, and information systems services as well as relationships among these.

- **Interface Catalog**  Scopes and documents the interfaces between applications to establish overall dependencies between applications to be scoped as early as possible. This artifact can be tailored to reflect service interface agreements between information system services. The functionality of the artifact is similar to the SvcV-1: Services Context Description.

- **Application/Organization Matrix**  Depicts the relationship between applications and organizational units that use the applications. This can be tailored to include information system services used by organizations and also add relationships that reflect ownership/stewardship/responsibility for provision concerns.

- **Role/Application Matrix**  Depicts the relationship between applications and the business roles that use them within the enterprise. This artifact can be tailored to reflect relationships between user roles and information system services to support an access control strategy for such services. The function of this artifact can be accomplished by authorization rules in the DoDAF SvcV-10a: Services Rules Model.

- **Information Exchange Matrix**   Documents the information exchanges between applications (tailored for information system services) showing source, destination, unique label, the data that is exchanged, and the triggering (business) event. This artifact is similar in scope to the DoDAF SvcV-6: Services Resource Flow Matrix.

- **Enterprise Manageability Diagram**   Shows how one or more applications (tailored to be information system services) interact with application and technology components that support operational management of a solution. This is a useful artifact for supporting a service management framework.

- **Process/Application Realization Diagram**   Depicts the sequence of events when multiple applications are involved in executing a business process. The artifact is similar to a swim lane process diagram where the performers can be either applications, systems, or information system services. The DoDAF SvcV-10c: Services Event-Trace Description is similar to this artifact.

- **Software Engineering Diagram**   Breaks applications into packages, modules, services, and operations from a development perspective and is a bill of materials for driving the development of applications and information system services.

- **Application Migration Diagram**   Identifies application migration from baseline to target application components. When tailored to represent information system services, this artifact becomes similar to the SvcV-8: Services Evolution Description.

The technology architecture developed in Phase D of the ADM contains the following artifacts relevant to the Services Viewpoint:

- Technology Standards Catalog
- Technology Portfolio Catalog
- System/Technology Matrix
- Platform Decomposition Diagram
- Networked Computing/Hardware Diagram

## TOGAF Technical Reference Model

The TOGAF Technical Reference Model is part of the TOGAF foundation architecture (compare reference architecture discussions in Chapter 1). The TOGAF foundation architecture is an architecture of generic services and functions that provides a foundation on which more specific architecture and architectural components can be built. The foundation architecture has two main elements: The technical reference model (TRM), which provides a model and taxonomy of generic platform services, and the standards information base, which provides a database of standards that can be used to define the particular services and other components of an organization specific architecture. Figure 17-7 depicts the TRM.

**Figure 17-7**
Technical
Reference Model
(used with
permission from
TOGAF)

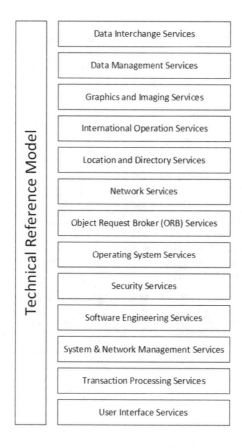

# FEAF2 and Federal View of Services

## Service-Oriented Framework

The Services Viewpoint caters to the interest of people responsible for planning, architecting, developing, implementing, and deploying service-oriented solutions. This is an evolutionary field that is arguably more well defined toward the construction of software services but less so in the planning and architecture realms.

Figure 17-8 depicts the layers of an agile enterprise based on a service-oriented paradigm [CIO Council 2008]:

- **Service-oriented enterprise** (SOE)   The business, management, and operational processes, procedures, and policies that support a services model. In essence this is an organizational behavior model aligned with the service model and designed to facilitate and govern its effective maturation. Organizational behavior drives the enterprise to seek a services-oriented solution approach to capability needs rather than the all-encompassing, integrated, monolithic solution of the day (purchased or developed) that is difficult and expensive to extend, evolve, customize, or modularize.

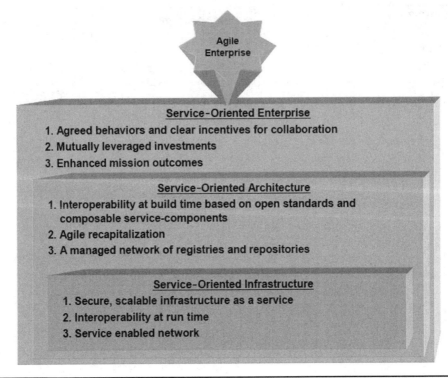

**Figure 17-8** Service-oriented framework (graphic from the Federal CIO Council)

- **Service-oriented architecture** (SOA)   Enhanced architecture practices that leverage robust models to capture and facilitate service architecture engineering best practices. SOA is the application of the service model from EA, through segment architectures to solution architectures. Today there is much interest in micro-services—small units of functionality delivered as a service that have more universal reuse potential than larger granularity domain-specific services.

- **Service-oriented infrastructure** (SOI)   The service-enabling environment, itself delivered as a collection of robust enterprise services that enable runtime connectivity and interoperability. SOI represents the operational environment that supports the service model. Today's infrastructure of choice is based on cloud deployment, concentration of data centers, virtualization of computing facilities, and a utility services view of infrastructure investments rather than as capital investments.

# FEAF2 Service Artifacts

The business subarchitecture domain in the FEAF2 recommends the following artifact that is relevant to the Services Viewpoint:

- **Business Service Catalog (B-3)**    Presents the business services, taken from a business reference model that are provided within the scope of the architecture and may also indicate business services that are consumed or used internally within the architecture.

The applications subarchitecture domain in the FEAF2 recommends the following artifacts that are relevant to the Services Viewpoint:

- **Application Interface Diagram (A-1)**    The identification of application (service) resource flows and their composition. This artifact is similar to the SvcV-1: Services Context Description.

- **Application Communication Diagram (A-2)**    The means (communication paths) by which resource flows between applications (services) occur. This is equivalent to the SvcV-2: Services Resource Flow Description in the DoDAF.

- **Application Interface Matrix (A-3)**    The interface relationships among systems (services). This is equivalent to the DoDAF SvcV-3a: Systems-Services Matrix and SvcV-3b: Services-Services Matrix.

- **Application Data Exchange Matrix (A-4)**    The details of resource flows among systems (services), the activities performed, the resources exchanged, and the attributes (rules and measures) associated with these exchanges. This artifact is similar to the DoDAF SvcV-6: Services Resource Flow Matrix.

- **Application Service Matrix (A-5)**    Interface relationships between services and applications. This artifact is similar to the DoDAF SvcV-3a: Systems-Services Matrix and SvcV-3b: Services-Services Matrix.

- **Application Performance Matrix (A-6)**    The measures (metrics) of applications tailored also to define measures of service delivery and performance. This artifact is similar to the DoDAF SvcV-7: Services Measures Matrix.

- **System/Application Evolution Diagram (A-7)**    The planned incremental steps toward migrating a suite of systems and/or applications and/or services to a more efficient suite, or toward evolving a current system or application to a future implementation. This artifact is similar to the SvcV-8: Services Evolution Description.

- **Enterprise Service Bus Diagram (A-8)**    Describes the interaction and communication between mutually interacting software applications in a SOA.

- **Application Inventory (A-10)**    A registry of applications and services and the system functions or service activities they perform, which are, optionally, prioritized or ranked.

## FEAF2 Business Reference Model

The business reference model (BRM) is a classification taxonomy used to describe the types of business functions and services that are performed in the federal government. The BRM provides a standard classification scheme under which business services are listed. These services may also represent application services that provide business/mission support capabilities. The expectation by OMB is that by using a common taxonomy for services, agencies can compare their needs to the availability of services from other agencies or offer their own services for sharing across the government.

The structure of the BRM is three layered, as shown in Figure 17-9:

- **Mission Sector**   Identifies the ten business areas of the federal government in the common approach to EA
- **Business Function**   Describes what the federal government does at an aggregated level, using the budget function classification codes provided in OMB Circular A-11
- **Service**   Further describes what the federal government does at a secondary or component level

By using the BRM service categories and classification schemes as attributes for the services in their service catalogs, agencies can align and report on their services to a standardized rubric.

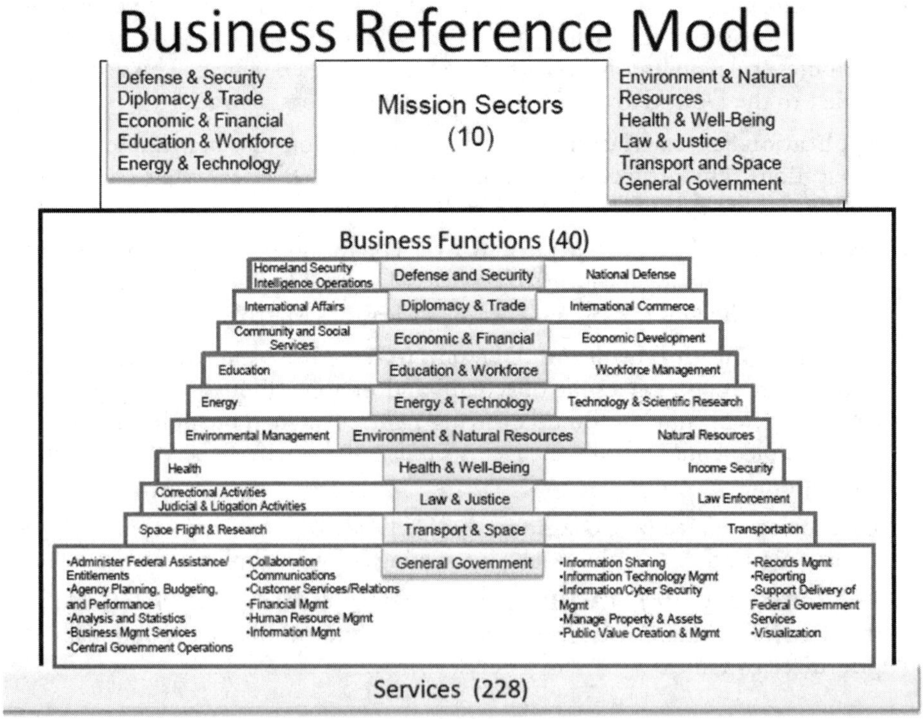

**Figure 17-9**   FEAF2 BRM (graphic from the OMB)

# Summary

The Service Viewpoint is becoming increasingly attractive as enterprises move away from monolithic systems that are complex, often undocumented and updated multiple times in their history to packaged services that can be independently invoked to provide capabilities. Service-oriented architectures are architected using the principles of separation of concerns and loose coupling. As enterprises adopt cloud computing, the scope of service-based implementation extends to software, platforms, infrastructures, and other capabilities that were traditionally purchased as capital items. The Service Viewpoint represents the solution counterpart to the requirements described within the Capability Viewpoint. The Capability to Services Mapping (CV-7) explicitly relates the capability requirement to the service solution.

In this chapter we describe the views that are described in the DoDAF for representing the concerns of service architects. The chapter describes views that present the overview of services that are developed within the scope of an architecture and the needs for orchestration and interactions between services and systems (SvcV-1, SvcV-2, SvcV-3a, SvcV-3b); the specific detailed functionality provided by the services (SvcV-4); the relationship between operational activities and the services that assist/augment/perform them (SvcV-5a, SvcV-5b); the protocols and resource exchanges between services (SvcV-6); performance specifications typically used for service level agreements (SvcV-7); the consolidation, migration, deprecation of services over time (SvcV-8); the evolution of technology and skill requirements over time needed to sustain services (SvcV-9); and representation of behavioral aspects of services such as rules and constraints that are embedded in the service algorithms, or constrain the use of the service (SvcV-10a), state transitions of services during the execution life cycle (SvcV-10b), and event trace of messaging on a timeline between services to understand latency, delay and timeliness issues (SvcV-10c).

TOGAF and the FEAF also address the service viewpoint with artifacts that extend the types of views described in this chapter. The area of service modeling and representation is constantly evolving, especially in the area of what is popularly termed, "the Internet of Things (IoT)." As the traditional boundary between hardware and software starts to disappear, service orientation provides a modular way to deliver functionality that is generally free of side effects and provides pin-pointed functionality for parts of a capability requirement from providers who specialize in that part.

# Questions

1. What is a service? Distinguish between a business service and a software service.

2. What are the issues and concerns of a service consumer? What are the issues and concerns of a service provider? How do they differ?

3. What is a service level agreement? Which of the Services Viewpoint views describes the elements of a service level agreement?

4. How are operational performers such as service providers reflected in the Services Viewpoint? Which views represent service providers?

5. True or false?

   a. Service models can be represented from the view of the service provider or the service consumer. These views are different. (Why?)

   b. A service can be provided by more than one provider.

   c. A service can be provisioned from more than one location.

   d. The SvcV-2 view can represent service brokers because they are intermediaries and are not involved in the providing or consumption of the service directly.

6. What is the usefulness of the SvcV-1?

7. Which view would you develop to forecast and plan for platform migrations for a family of services?

8. Which view would you use to develop and refine service functionality and represent in detail, the decomposition of services down to the level of WSDL operations?

9. Which view would you use to compactly represent the interfaces between services?

10. Which view would you use to describe the data exchange protocols between services using message templates and automated data exchanges?

11. How would you restrict the scope of detailed, fine-grain behavioral modeling such as for the SvcV-10b and SvcV-10c?

12. What is the relationship between the SvcV-6 and the SvcV-10c? Which elements are required to be consistent for the views to be part of the same integrated architecture?

13. Which view would you use to trace a service back to the operational activities that it supports?

14. Which view would you use to trace the service back to a capability that was identified as a requirement by the enterprise?

15. Compare and contrast the SvcV-1: Services Context Description, the SvcV-6: Services Resource Flow Matrix, and the SvcV-10c: Services Event-Trace Description. All of these views depict resource flow exchanges between services. Which type of view is useful for what purpose?

# References

Architecture and Infrastructure Committee, Federal Chief Information Officers Council (CIO Council). 2008. "Enabling the Mission: A Practical Guide to Federal Service Oriented Architecture, Version 1.1." https://s3.amazonaws.com/sitesusa/wp-content/uploads/sites/1151/2016/10/Enabling-the-Mission-A-Practical-Guide-to-Federal-Service-Oriented-Architecture-1.pdf.

CIO Council. 2013. "Federal Enterprise Architecture Framework, Version 2." https://obamawhitehouse.archives.gov/sites/default/files/omb/assets/egov_docs/fea_v2.pdf.

Department of Defense. 2009. DoDAF Architecture Framework Version 2.0, "Volume 2: Architectural Data and Models, Architect's Guide." http://bea.osd.mil/bea11/products/dodaf_volume_II.pdf.

DoD Information Enterprise Architecture. Retrieved 6/17/2018 from https://dodcio .defense.gov/IntheNews/DoDInformationEnterpriseArchitecture.aspx

Erl, Thomas. 2004. *Service-Oriented Architecture: A Field Guide to Integrating XML and Web Services.* Upper Saddle River, NJ: Pearson Education/Prentice Hall.

Erl, Thomas. 2005. *Service-Oriented Architecture: Concepts, Technology, and Design.* Boston: Pearson Education.

Erl, Thomas. 2016. *SOA: Principles of Service Design.* Boston: Prentice Hall.

Gartner Research. *IT Glossary.* Retrieved 12/5/2017 from www.gartner.com/it-glossary.

Microsoft Corporation. "What Is PaaS? Platform as a Service." Microsoft Azure web site. Retrieved 12/5/2017 from https://azure.microsoft.com/en-us/overview/what-is-paas.

The Open Group. "The TOGAF Standard, Version 9.2, Part VI: Architecture Capability Framework, Architecture Contracts." Retrieved 12/5/2017 from http://pubs.opengroup .org/architecture/togaf9-doc/arch/chap43.html.

# CHAPTER 18

# Data and Information Viewpoint

The Data and Information Viewpoint caters to all producers, consumers, and managers of the data that is generated by and consumed by operations, systems, and services. From the point of view of these stakeholders, data is consumed or transformed by activities, represents the state of something at a point in time, or is required by an activity or a person for decision-making.

## Representing Data

Data is a digital representation of some aspect of reality. Problems occur when the same reality results in different data representations for different activities or people. Standardizing data definitions is important if consistency and uniformity of data is to be promoted. In much the same way a spoken language like English is used to communicate thoughts, intents, directives, and descriptions, data is used in businesses to communicate intent, observations, measurements, commands, and descriptions, using a combination of human and automated processes. Just as dictionaries and thesauri describe and relate the collection of words in the English language, data dictionaries are used to describe and relate data elements across the enterprise.

Data is also stored in computer databases in digital format. When data is stored by one group of people or systems and retrieved by another, the ability to convey standard meaning becomes important, because the data has to carry that meaning independent of the system or person who stored the data. Organizations of data, called *schemas*, are used as maps for stored data. When data is duplicated and spread across a database, anomalies can occur when one instance is updated and another is not, or when not all instances are deleted at the same time.

Methods of "normalizing" the data have addressed the update and delete anomaly problems of duplicated data storage by storing every piece of data in one place, once. This step of data engineering changes the "map" of the data and sometimes makes the organization structure of the data difficult for people to understand (as the original schema is exploded into atomic components and reconstituted), though the original purpose of normalization is to preserve data quality.

All of these representational issues bring the need for multiple ways of representing maps of data: conceptual models that are closer to human understanding of the types of data that are consumed by business activities and information systems, logical data models that are a result of data engineering (normalization of concepts and addition of identifiers to identify unique pieces of data), and precise models that become a blueprint for physical database construction. These models have built-in capabilities for data quality enforcement through structural constraints, format representation, and behavioral rules, all of which make the database cleanse itself at time of data entry.

In this chapter, we restrict ourselves to the issues and concerns of representing data as an architectural exercise. Many processes surround how data is collected, organized, distributed, secured, archived, and administered. Management of data is entrusted to dedicated functions in enterprises such as data administration, information security, data governance, and records management, to cite a few examples. The scope of this chapter is to describe the DoDAF Data and Information Viewpoint and the related views as well as to compare and contrast these with the corresponding FEAF2 and TOGAF approaches.

## Data at Rest and Data in Motion

An important distinction is the one between *data at rest* and *data in motion*, which is like the difference between water held in a tank versus water in a flowing river. Data at rest is not actively moving from device to device or network to network. Such data may be stored in a hard drive, laptop drive, or flash drive, or archived and stored in some other manner. Data in motion is actively moving from one location to another, such as across the Internet or through the private network. Data flows in motion in response to requirements for data as inputs to activities, service operations, and system functions.

The Data and Information Viewpoint in the DoDAF deals with the views of data at the conceptual, logical, and physical levels. When applied to data at rest, these views relate to the design of databases and the interpretation of the meaning of data in such databases. When applied to data in motion, the DoDAF views relate to the schemas that define the semantics and format representations of messages between operational activities and performers. These views are still representational in nature, in that they specify a set of meanings and formats for all types of data exchanges.

It is important to remember that the DoDAF Data and Information Viewpoint views (DIV-1, DIV-2, and DIV-3) are representational (or schematic) in nature. These types of views are free of scenario, operational, or system context. They are intrinsic to the information they represent. Other DoDAF models such as the SV-4: Systems Functionality Description, SV-6: Systems Resource Flow Matrix, SV-10c: Systems Event-Trace Description, and the OV-3: Operational Resource Flow Matrix model the actual flow of data between systems functions or operational activities and performers, to cite an example. These are appropriate views to use to model data in motion. They use the context of the performer and the operational activity or system function in which data is consumed or produced and results in a flow between producers and consumers.

## Historical Time Varying Data

Another important distinction is between data that has been collected over a period of time (data warehouse) versus the data that is required for ongoing transactions of the business (online transaction processing, or OLTP). The benefit of collecting historical data is to support analysis. Using analytical tools that process historical data, enterprises are able to recognize patterns of behavior or trends that enable planning and decision-making activities based on that knowledge. Managing historical data has a number of challenges, including the fact that the data was collected under an evolving database organization structure over the years. Aggregation and summarization of data requires cleaning up data to "connect the dots." Data needs to have associated meta-data that identifies its source and the context in which it was collected.

Data warehousing is the progressive storage of historical data for analytical purposes. Data warehousing has become a very important technology for analytics and predictive exercises, where past behavior is indicative of future performance, or for the detection of patterns of behaviors that are evident from the data. Analytical techniques based on statistical methods, algorithmic reasoning, or combinations of these are used to convert large volumes of data into actionable information for further actions or decision support. The topic of architecture views for data warehousing is beyond the scope of this book. The topic of time varying data and data warehouses is not addressed by the DoDAF views.

## Structured Data vs. Unstructured Data

The traditional "data processing" view of data is based on storage of the data on some medium in an organized manner. The data was described by an organizational structure called the *schema*. Through the prism of the schema, the semantics of the data could be ascertained, and search and retrieval of data could occur. On the other side of the coin, unstructured data was stored simply as narratives with little or no structure to the way it was organized. The bulk of enterprise knowledge is stored as unstructured data. Methods of search and retrieval do not have a schema organization but have to rely on searching the actual content inside the narratives for specific keywords, phrases, or patterns of symbols. In recent times, multiple technologies have been brought to bear on the processing of unstructured data to speed up and make the search and retrieval process more efficient.

The scope of the DoDAF, TOGAF, and FEAF2 currently does not cover these technologies for unstructured data as they fit the category of enterprise engineering rather than enterprise architecture. The upper level views/models such as the conceptual data model are still valid as semantic targets for searching unstructured data. The discussion of unstructured data management is beyond the scope of this book.

## Data vs. Information

Both data and information represent knowledge. Data is the lowest or rawest form in which that knowledge is stored and managed, such as in a database, an electronic file, or even as text on a paper document. Information results from processing data to extract meaning. Information provides the level of knowledge needed to drive action.

Information is modeled using semantic models. Data is modeled using structural models. One example is the use of a logical data model to elevate the meaning of the tables in a relational database schema. In fact, both data and information are two points in the conventional information management continuum:

*Data -> Information -> Knowledge -> Wisdom (DIKW)*

In this continuum, informally, data represents observations, objective discrete facts that are verifiable; information represents the meaning, usually provided by the context in which the data was collected; knowledge is a more elusive concept of applying information to some activity or purpose; and wisdom is a set of capabilities to increase effectiveness through collections of accumulated knowledge. Though DIKW has many detractors and the levels of knowledge and wisdom depend on many cultural, experiential, factors, in addition to what can be gleaned only from the information, data and information have been conventionally separated as distinct and concrete concepts.

Here's an example: *Data* is a fact represented by a number, 30 minutes. *Information* is that this is the expected delay at Chicago's O'Hare airport for an average flight on a particular day in September. *Knowledge* is knowing that this delay is likely to increase over time as flights start to pile up. *Wisdom* is knowing that, historically, the airport has been able to "catch up" late at night and start the next day with no delays.

Modeling data in the past has been an exercise in understanding the data plumbing—a database management system is akin to a cistern holding water, while messaging is like the pipes that carry water to consuming systems. Much effort has been spent in standardizing the layout of the cisterns and planning the sizes and data types. The task of standardizing data formats and relational database schemas has been the responsibility of the database administrator. Only in recent times has the focus shifted to the content of the pipes—the meaning of the data. The data administrator has been responsible for standardizing the meaning and interpretation of the data in terms of "logical" data standards that are focused more on the meaning and less on the data representation.

Today, the data administrator also needs to become the information administrator—with the skills needed to understand the science of meaning, of information concepts and relationships (ontology), and of classification techniques (taxonomy), as well as understanding that different groups of people often define their own set of terms and definitions (vocabularies) that are specific to their own domain but may have different meanings and interpretations in other domains.

The Data and Information Viewpoint must cater to the interests and needs of data management personnel as well as data administration personnel who are charged with developing standards for information representation. We will present a few terms before we launch into the detailed models that the DoDAF includes in the Data and Information Viewpoint. For readers who are well versed in traditional data modeling techniques such as Integration Definition for Information modeling (IDEF1X), information engineering Entity-Relationship modeling techniques, or object class modeling techniques, the concepts presented next are a departure from the familiar and will initially need a change in worldview from structured data management and data engineering techniques to the recognition of the existence of information in all forms and representations that need different treatment than the traditional approaches.

The concepts of ontology are based on existence of information and methods to represent this existence. Arguably, traditional approaches have tried to "coerce" information into a format suitable for machine processing. The result of that coercion is to drive data schemas into a format that few people outside of the data management and application development community understood. The focus of the newer approaches to information management is to provide a form of data representation that is more easily and universally understood—especially across the World Wide Web. The semantic web is commonly perceived as the next leap forward in information transparency and ubiquitous use. Without the semantic models of information, traditional models need to be accompanied by applications that transform the internal models of data into information.

## Ontology

*Ontology* is an explicit formal specification of the concepts in a domain and the relationships among them. Implicit in this definition is the existence of a contained or restricted domain of applicability called a *domain of discourse* and a formal specification of the concepts and relationships between the concepts. One example of a formal specification is the Web Ontology Language (OWL)—a standard sponsored by the World-Wide Web Consortium (W3C).

Ontologies are very useful for compressing large volumes of instance knowledge using abstract relationships to form compact schemas that can be applied to more instances. The following table illustrates the organizing of information into an ontological framework:

| Instance Knowledge | Abstract Conceptual Model |
| --- | --- |
| <ul><li>Flight XY 27 leaves from Gate 34.</li><li>Flight PQ 46 leaves from Gate 56.</li><li>Gate 34 is located in the Red Concourse.</li><li>Gate 56 is located on the Green Concourse.</li><li>Terminal 1 contains the Red Concourse.</li><li>Terminal 2 Contains the Green Concourse.</li><li>Gate 34 does not have a jet bridge.</li><li>Gate 56 has a jet bridge.</li></ul> | <ul><li>Flights leave from gates (association).</li><li>Gates are located in concourses (composition).</li><li>Terminals contain concourses (composition).</li><li>Airport contains terminals (composition).</li><li>Gates may have jet bridges (association).</li></ul> |

Notice that relationships themselves can be grouped into compositions, instantiations, and associations in this example. Also notice that items such as Flight XY 27 and Gate 34 represent specific instances (proper nouns) while concepts like Flights and Gates are quite general and describe classes of objects that are encountered in airports. Abstracting one level higher, we recognize that everything in the world is either a proper noun instance ("thing") or a category of real world objects ("types") and that broad classes of relationships exist between these and each other (generalization, aggregation, instantiation, and association, for example). The language that is used to express this "upper level" set of things and types, and relationship types, is called a *foundation ontology* in much the same way that alphabets are used to construct words and words are used to make sentences.

PART III

International Defence Enterprise Architecture Specification (IDEAS) is the foundation ontology that provides the building blocks for the DoDAF Metamodel DM2; the Unified Modeling Language represents a foundation ontology for several UML profiles such as the Universal Profile for DoDAF and MoDAF (UPDM).

It is beyond the scope of this book to cover the details and use of ontologies, but it is useful to know that architecture frameworks such as DoDAF 2.0 are based more on the use of ontologies to represent knowledge of architecture elements and less about the specific modeling technique metamodels as earlier architecture techniques tended to be. In fact, the Zachman Framework, one of the first architecture frameworks, provided a conceptual mechanism for representing meaningful architecture elements independent of modeling technology.

Architectural representations are used to represent real world objects and concepts using terms and symbols. Because different viewpoints address different groups of people with their own language and vocabularies, there is a risk that the same architecture term or symbol may be represented differently in different views. An ontology allows for resolution and identification of the same object even when it is represented differently in many places. As reiterated many times in this book, an integrated architecture presses out such redundancies and is an accurate representation of the real world that it models.

## Taxonomy

*Taxonomy* is the science of classification. A taxonomy is a specific classification of entities (in a domain of interest) based on an ordering imposed by the "is-a-type-of" (or "is-a-member-of") relationship. Taxonomy consists of a set of *taxa*—categories. The set of taxa form a *hierarchy* (a "tree"). Each level—formally called a *rank*—of the hierarchy is usually given a name. The set of *taxon* names (or categories) is the classification. The levels (or ranks) establish the "is-a-type-of" relationship among the taxa.

A taxonomy of a domain can be derived from an ontology of that domain by selecting all entities of interest that stand in an "is-a-type-of" relationship to one another. A taxonomy can also be developed independently of any explicit ontology for a domain of interest and only later incorporated into an explicit ontology of the domain.

An example taxonomy for airport operating revenues is shown here [Graham 2007]:

**1. Aeronautical Revenues/Fees**
    1.1 Landing Fees
    1.2 Passenger Fees
    1.3 Aircraft Parking Fees
    1.4 Handling Fees (if airport operator provides)
    1.5 Other Aeronautical Fees
        1.5.1 Air Traffic Control Fees
        1.5.2 Lighting Fees
        1.5.3 Airbridge Use Fees

### 2. Nonaeronautical Revenues/Fees

2.1 Concessions

2.2 Rents

2.3 Direct Sales (shops, catering, and other services provided by airport operator)

2.4 Car Park (if provided by airport operator)

2.5 Recharges (for gas, water, electricity, etc.)

2.6 Other Non-aeronautical Revenue

    2.6.1 Consultancy

    2.6.2 Visitor and Business Services

    2.6.3 Property Development, etc.

Ontologies and taxonomies can serve several purposes. For example, they can serve to formalize and standardize the vocabulary of a domain, facilitating communication and understanding among domain users and system developers. The process of developing a domain ontology and associated taxonomies can inform the development of other domain artifacts such as architectures and data models or be used to constructively analyze existing domain artifacts. A formal ontology is a prerequisite for automated (machine) reasoning and is necessary to realize the vision of the semantic web.

## Controlled Vocabularies

A *vocabulary* is a collection of terms and definitions used by a community to describe real-world and abstract concepts. Because vocabularies evolve without conscious control and new terms are coined to represent existing concepts, resolution of terms and their meanings becomes increasingly difficult over time. Understanding the meaning of terms without ambiguity is essential for the architectural representations that will be built based upon that understanding. Vocabulary control (ANSI/NISO Z.39.19-2005) is the process of organizing a list of terms to indicate which of two or more synonymous terms is authorized for use to distinguish between homographs—one of two or more words that have the same spelling but different meanings and origins—and to indicate hierarchical and associative relationships among terms in the context of a controlled vocabulary or subject heading list.

## Data Element Naming

In domains such as the decennial US census, or in capturing complex measurement information, the actual value of the data element is sometimes a simple number that only has meaning through the name of the data element that describes it. For example, the value of the average temperature in the month of June in the Great Lakes region of the United States would simply be a number representing the value of the temperature in degrees Fahrenheit. However, the interpretation of that number requires the fact the name of the data element is GREAT-LAKES-REGION-JUNE-AVERAGE-TEMPERATURE-FAHRENHEIT, to make up an example! The construction of such data element names and data element registration standards such as the ISO 11179

Information Technology—Metadata Registries are beyond the scope of this book but illustrate how difficult it is to assign meaning to data elements that helps us understand the simple values they describe and how the context described by metadata is essential to interpret data as information.

# Data and Information Viewpoint Views

The Data and Information Viewpoint provides three levels of abstraction for representing data and information in a common and consistent format across systems, services and operations: (1) A conceptual view that represents information irrespective of its data implementation or the engineering needed to promote data quality during the process of creating, updating, or deleting data by a automated system. The conceptual view is represented using business language and is meant to be comprehensible to the people running the enterprise. (2) A logical or engineered view of data that ensures that data is consistently processed by automated systems in a manner where data integrity is maintained. This view is targeted at the data engineer and is not meant to be used for a quick understanding of the semantics of data for a broader audience though it conveys limited meaning as well. (3) A physical view that shows how data is represented and implemented in an automated system that processes, stores, and manages the data. This view is targeted towards the database designer and for machine data exchange and data processing. The physical view is not generally comprehensible to a broad audience and is subject to the constraints of the implementation technology such as lengths and character sets.

## DIV-1: Conceptual Data Model

The DIV-1: Conceptual Data Model (or semantic data model) represents the business concepts that apply to the domain and scope of the architecture. These concepts represent real-world and abstract items of information that must be managed by the enterprise. The purpose of the DIV-1 is to document and describe the information concepts in terms of model elements that can be easily recognized by the business in real-world terms. The DIV-1 caters to the data administrator's interests as well as the interests of the business analyst. The model is easily validated by subject matter experts who understand the model elements and can provide constructive feedback to improve and finalize the model.

In the unstructured data management world, the DIV-1 is also used to define the *concepts* that can be associated with unstructured data to provide context, although the representation of the unstructured data format (such as a document outline structure) can be considered a physical representation (DIV-3: Physical Data Model). For example, document section names can be associated with the semantic concepts that they document. The DIV-1 can also be used as a high-level "subject area" classification for more detailed DIV-2: Logical Data Model modeling efforts. In such a use, the DIV-1 becomes a taxonomy scheme for categorizing logical data entities.

The DIV-1 can be used to construct a business glossary. If the proliferation of terms is controlled and managed by a registration and stewardship process, the business glossary can also become an enterprise vocabulary. Constructing an enterprise vocabulary will require resolving differences of meanings across different parts of the same enterprise. For example, "tank" for a civil engineer is a container for fluids; "tank" for a Army commander is a armored vehicle capable of shooting at the enemy.

## DIV-2: Logical Data Model

The DIV-2: Logical Data Model (key-based/fully attributed logical data model) is the first step toward engineering the information representation for implementation as a data management schema. In the logical model, independent concepts are identified and separated. Trying to identify independent concepts often involves looking at properties of some of the business entities in the DIV-1: Conceptual Data Model and determining whether they should be independent concepts in their own right or subordinate attributes of an entity. Identifiers are assigned to each of these independent concepts to enable machine identification of instances of such concepts and to enforce relationship integrity. Indeterminate relationships (many-to-many relationships) are resolved into associative entities. The resulting model (key-based logical data model) has the graphical topology of the ultimate DIV-2.

Finally, attributes are added to the key-based logical data model to create a fully attributed logical data model.

The entity relationship style logical data model DIV-2 tends to be more applicable to the design of data management solutions for transaction-based systems and does not in general lend itself to the complex and rich set of relationship models typically found in unstructured data sources or in complex data elements that intersect with many concepts. For example, a single complex data element used in a census survey may report on the average income of an undivided American family resident in the continental United States (CONUS) for the period 2000–2010.

## DIV-3: Physical Data Model

The DIV-3: Physical Data Model is a detailed representation of the physical data formats. Using our earlier analogy, the DIV-3 does model the data plumbing and enforces the needs for consistency, uniformity, and compatibility of data formats to ensure successful data management of the physical data.

Because different types of technologies are used to implement data management solutions, the DIV-3 is specific to the technology of the implemented database and organization. The DIV-3 view must obey the constraints of the technology used to implement it and reflect a real-world implementation. Some examples of DIV-3 representation are Structured Query Language (SQL) and Data Definition Language (DDL) statements, Extensible Markup Language (XML) schemas, and US Message Text Format (USMTF) templates.

**PART III**

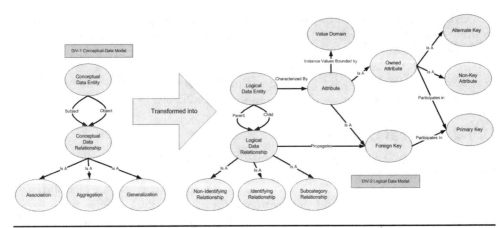

**Figure 18-1**   Integrated model set for data and information viewpoint

## Relationships Among the Data and Information Viewpoint Integrated Views

For simplicity, Figure 18-1 depicts the DIV-1 as a business dictionary with informal ontology relationships and taxonomy, DIV-2 as an entity relationship model, and DIV-3 as a relational database management schema instance. Other forms of technology representations, such as OWL for representing DIV-1 and XML Schema Definition (XSD) language for representing DIV-3, are also applicable.

The Data and Information Viewpoint, rather than require exact match of architecture elements, requires a transformation consistency and the need to be able to trace back from, say, the DIV-3: Physical Data Model to the DIV-2: Logical Data Model.

There is traceability between the DIV-1 to the DIV-2, to the DIV-3, as follows:

- The information representations in the DIV-1 are transformed into the data representations in the DIV-2. The DIV-1 information representations can range in detail from concept lists to structured lists (that is, whole-part, super-subtype), to interrelated concepts. At the DIV-1 level, any relationships are simply declared, and then at the DIV-2 level they are made explicit and attributed. Similarly, attributes (or additional relationships) are added at the DIV-2 level.

- The DIV-3's performance and implementation considerations usually result in standard modifications of the DIV-2, and so it traces quite directly. In other words, no new semantics are introduced going from the DIV-2 to the DIV-3.

Figure 18-2 shows the traditional steps involved in transforming a semantic data model (DIV-1: Conceptual Data Model) to a key-based and fully attributed DIV-2: Logical Data Model and then to a DIV-3: Physical Data Model in a structured data management regime.

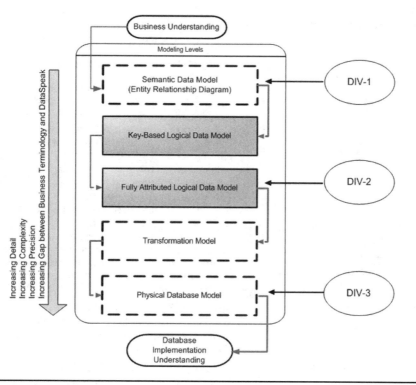

**Figure 18-2** Transformation steps in data and information modeling

# DIV-1: Conceptual Data Model

| View Information at a Glance | |
| --- | --- |
| View short name | DIV-1 |
| Name | Conceptual Data Model |
| Other names | Business Data Model<br>Entity Relationship Model<br>Ontology Model<br>Data Reference Model<br>Class Diagram (UML)<br>Class Hierarchy Diagram (TOGAF 9)<br>Semantic Data Model |

*(continued)*

| View Information at a Glance | |
| --- | --- |
| Viewpoint | Data and Information |
| View intent | Addresses the information concepts at a high level on an operational architecture. The DIV-1 is used to document the business information requirements and structural business process rules of the architecture. Included are information items, their attributes or characteristics, and their interrelationships. Unlike the DIV-2 and DIV-3 models that are arranged to support automated data processing, the DIV-1 describes data in terms of the business language. The DIV-1 is independent of how and where the data is used in applications or business processes or how the data is represented inside a computer. It is meant to be a representation of data semantics. The DIV-1 is used to establish the business ontology and taxonomy for the enterprise as well as the vocabulary of business terms. It is frequently combined with a business glossary that defines the data concepts (or included in the AV-2 for an architecture). |
| View audience | Business analysts, data administrators, data standards personnel, logical data modeling personnel (as a higher level context for more detailed logical data models). |
| Formal modeling methodology | Ontology modeling using OWL, RDF, entity-relationship modeling, object class modeling |
| Integration of view with other views | The DIV-1 concepts and relationships must be consistent with their transformation into DIV-2 entities and relationships and DIV-3 technology data objects such as relational tables and columns or XML simple types and complex type definitions. |

# Example: Passenger Identification DIV-1

Figure 18-3 depicts a subtype hierarchy of data concepts. The names of the concepts are couched in simple business terms. The model distinguishes between the various types of passenger identification documents to enable more detailed analysis of the data structures that need to be constructed for both messaging and data storage downstream.

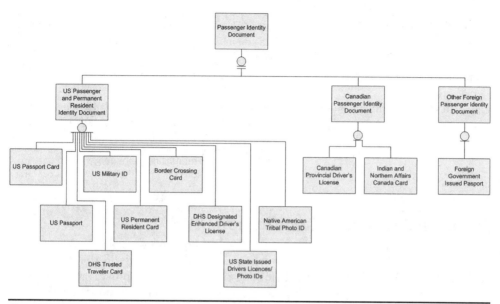

**Figure 18-3**  Passenger identification DIV-1: Conceptual Data Model

# DIV-2: Logical Data Model

| View Information at a Glance | |
| --- | --- |
| View short name | DIV-2 |
| Name | Logical Data Model |
| Other names | Key-Based Logical Data Model<br>Fully Attributed Logical Data Model<br>Class Diagram (UML)<br>Class Diagram (TOGAF 9) |
| Viewpoint | Data and Information |
| View intent | Transforms business concepts into data management concepts that are compatible with principles that promote data quality such as normalization and referential integrity. The DIV-2 provides a data representation that can be implemented in multiple messaging and storage technologies and is independent of technology. It also establishes a data dictionary and definitions for shared data in a data management function for the enterprise. The DIV-2 is also free of context—how and where the data is used by processes and systems. It provides an engineering blueprint for unique identification of data items and freedom from update and delete anomalies that result from multiple data copies. |

(continued)

| View Information at a Glance | |
| --- | --- |
| View audience | Data administrators, database administrators, application developers |
| Formal modeling methodology | IDEF1X, UML object class diagram, generalized Chen E-R modeling, information engineering |
| Integration of view with other views | The DIV-2 entities, attributes, and relationships must be consistent with the higher level business ontology expressed in the DIV-1. They must also be consistent with transformed physical data objects in DIV-3 that are used to implement data management and data communication solutions. |

## Example: Passenger Identification DIV-2

In this model (Figure 18-4), we have started to elaborate on the conceptual model by separating out independent and dependent parts of the concepts in the DIV-1. The construction of the DIV-2 starts by examining the DIV-1: Conceptual Data Model and separating out candidate logical data entities. These are then examined to determine and separate the independent entities from the dependent entities. Relationships are established to reflect this dependence. Relationships are characterized by cardinality and can express a 0 to Many, 1 to Many, or Many to Many set of relationships between two entities (not shown in the model).

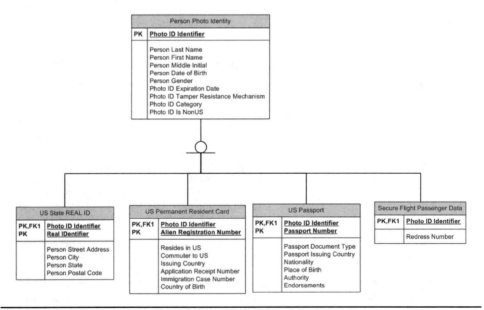

**Figure 18-4** Passenger identification DIV-2: Logical Data Model

During the construction of the DIV-2, we also start establishing identifiers—unique attributes of an entity that help to identify an instance of that entity. Identifiers form the primary key for an entity. Sometimes a natural and human-recognizable attribute of an entity can be used as a primary key by itself, but in most cases, a single attribute may not serve to identify an entity instance uniquely. A surrogate key is a made-up identifier that serves as a unique identifier in databases but has no intrinsic meaning to a human being by itself.

Designing a logical data model is a specialty skill. It is outside the scope of this book to discuss detailed data modeling techniques such as the IDEF1X or the UML object class modeling techniques. There are several good books on data modeling such as Tom Bruce's seminal book on the IDEF1X technique, *Designing Quality Databases with IDEF1X Information Models*, or Martin Fowler's *UML Distilled*.

# DIV-3: Physical Data Model

| View Information at a Glance | |
|---|---|
| View short name | DIV-3 |
| Name | Physical Data Model |
| Other names | Database Schema<br>XML Schema Document<br>RDBMS Schema<br>Message Template |
| Viewpoint | Data and Information |
| View intent | Represents data and information at the systems level for use by automated application systems or services. DIV-3 transforms the abstract DIV-2: Logical Data Model into an implementable technology model such as a RDBMS schema or a XML schema document or a USMTF message template. |
| View audience | Database administrators, application developers, messaging and communication standards designers |
| Formal modeling methodology | Technology specific. Examples are relational database/ Structured Query Language, XML schema document (XSD), COBOL file, record, field structures, Object-Oriented Design (OOD) object class structures, Common Object Request Broker Architecture (CORBA) Interface Definition Language (IDL) interfaces. |
| Integration of view with other views | The DIV-3 data objects must be consistent with the DIV-2 logical data entities and attributes, which in turn must be consistent with the DIV-1 ontological concepts. |

PART III

## Example: Passenger Identification DIV-3

The example shown in Figure 18-5 represents a physical schema for implementation in an Oracle database management system. The DIV-3 is dependent on the implementation technology because it deals with detailed specifications for data representations including data formats, physical constraints, and grammars for representation. To illustrate the technology dependence of the DIV-3, we will present another example of a DIV-3 using XML schema document (XSD), shown in Figure 18-6.

The XSD example represents a small fragment of a physical schema built to model the data elements, simple types, and complex types. Notice the difference in style between the cross-connected (network graph) RDBMS schema and the hierarchical definition of the XML schemas (tree graph).

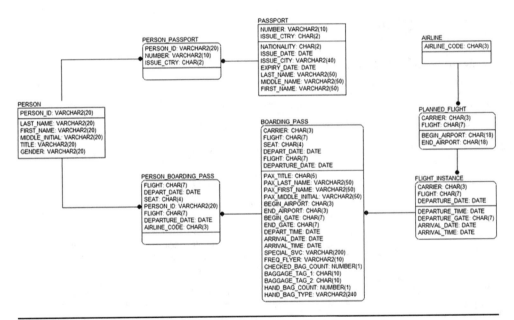

**Figure 18-5**   Passenger identification DIV-3: Physical Data Model

```
<?xml version="1.0" encoding="UTF-8"?>
<xs:schema xmlns:xs="http://www.w3.org/2001/XMLSchema">
    <xs:simpleType name="T_MIDDLE_INITIAL">
        <xs:restriction base="xs:string">
            <xs:enumeration value="Q"/>
        </xs:restriction>
    </xs:simpleType>
    <xs:complexType name="T_Passenger">
        <xs:sequence>
            <xs:element ref="PNR"/>
            <xs:element ref="LAST_NAME"/>
            <xs:element ref="FIRST_NAME"/>
            <xs:element ref="MIDDLE_INITIAL"/>
            <xs:element ref="TITLE"/>
            <xs:element ref="GENDER"/>
            <xs:element ref="PASSPORT" maxOccurs="unbounded"/>
            <xs:element ref="BOARDING_PASS" maxOccurs="unbounded"/>
        </xs:sequence>
    </xs:complexType>

    <xs:complexType name="T_PASSPORT">
        <xs:sequence>
            <xs:element ref="ISSUE_CTRY"/>
            <xs:element ref="ISSUE_CITY"/>
            <xs:element ref="ISSUE_DATE"/>
            <xs:element ref="NUMBER"/>
            <xs:element ref="NATIONALITY"/>
        </xs:sequence>
    </xs:complexType>
    <xs:complexType name="T_HAND_BAGGAGE">
        <xs:sequence>
            <xs:element ref="BAG_TYPE" maxOccurs="unbounded"/>
        </xs:sequence>
        <xs:attribute ref="COUNT" use="required"/>
    </xs:complexType>
```

**Figure 18-6**   Passenger identification DIV-3: Physical Data Model (XSD)

# FEAF2 Data Subarchitecture Domain Artifacts

In the FEAF2, artifacts supporting the data subarchitecture domain comprise individual models as well as catalogs of data objects. In addition, FEAF2 artifacts can also be plans that relate to data strategy, data quality management, knowledge management, data flows, state transitions, and so on. Unlike the DoDAF, which treats data representations as independent of applications and processes, the FEAF2 treats the data architecture domain in its entirety. The following artifacts (models, plans, matrices, catalogs, and diagrams) document the data subarchitecture domain in the FEAF2:

- **Logical Data Model (D-1)**   This artifact is identical to the DoDAF DIV-2: Logical Data Model.

- **Knowledge Management Plan (D-2)**   This plan shows how knowledge, information, and data are shared across the enterprise between systems, applications, knowledge warehouses, and databases.

- **Data Quality Plan (D-3)**   This plan shows how data quality assurance is to be accomplished.

- **Data Flow Diagram (D-4)**   This artifact is identical to the DoDAF SV-4: Systems Functionality Description or the SvcV-4: Services Functionality Description.

- **Physical Data Model (D-5)**   This artifact is identical in scope and purpose to the DoDAF DIV-3: Physical Data Model.

- **CRUD Matrix (D-6)**   This presents resources that are consumed and produced by activities performed by organizational performers. This artifact is identical in scope and purpose to the DoDAF OV-3: Operational Resource Flow Matrix but is summarized in the form of a relationship between business processes and data entities: creator, referencer, updater, or deletor.

- **State Transition Diagram (D-7)**   This artifact is identical to the DoDAF SV-10b: Systems State Transition Description or the SvcV-10b: Services State Transition Description.

- **Event Sequence Diagram (D-8)**   This artifact is identical to the DoDAF SV-10c: Systems Event-Trace Description or the DoDAF SvcV-10c: Services Event-Trace Description.

- **Data Dictionary (D-9)**   This is similar to the TOGAF data entity/component catalog and is a central repository of information about data such as name, type, range of values, source, and authorization for access for each data element in the enterprise's files and databases.

- **Object Library (D-10)**   This is a collection of computer programs in the form of relocatable instructions that reside on, and maybe read from, a mass storage device. Objects encapsulate data and function.

# FEAF2 Data Reference Model (DRM)

Unlike the other reference models in the FEAF2, the Data Reference Model (Figure 18-7) is a specification of how to characterize data from a specific agency in such a manner that it can be compared to data from other agencies across the federal government. In defining a standardized classification scheme, the expectation is that individual agencies will use the categories to describe their own data assets. The DRM is a fluid taxonomy that can evolve with the addition of new subjects and topics as and when they are discovered and found not to overlap with existing ones.

The FEAF2 describes three methods of standardization for data across the federal government that help one agency understand another's data assets and determine its opportunities for data exchange, sharing, and reusability through a COI, a community of interest that shares common goals and missions:

- Data context

- Data description

- Data sharing

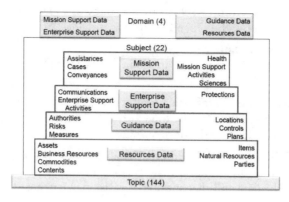

**Figure 18-7**
FEA Data Reference Model—areas of standardization (graphic from the OMB)

## Data Context

Data is always captured in some context—by some organization for some specified purpose at a specified time period in connection with specified activities, to name a few contextual items. Context often takes the form of a set of terms (words or phrases) that are, themselves, organized in lists, hierarchies, or trees. *Data context* is any information that provides additional meaning to data and an understanding to the purposes for which it was created. The data context method can also be called categorization or classification.

Agencies and organizations participating in COIs are called upon to categorize their data. Once shared in data registries, these categorizations become vehicles for discovering data that offers value for data sharing. For an agency, the DRM taxonomy can be used to categorize core data sources (such as data bases, data warehouses, files) that support a particular business function.

## Data Description

A *data description* provides a means to describe data uniformly, thereby supporting its discovery and sharing. Traditionally, a data description was solely focused on organizing and describing structured data. With unstructured data as the largest focus of agencies' data management challenges, the DRM description component has been revised to focus on the larger topic of metadata, which includes both traditional structured data and unstructured data descriptions. Techniques for describing data representations recommended in the FEAF2 include the following:

- **Integration Definition for Information Modeling (IDEF1X)**   The IDEF1X modeling technique is used to define a logical data model when the target deployment is known to be a relational database.

- **The Open Group Architecture Framework (TOGAF) 9.2**   A framework sponsored by The Open Group that provides artifacts for data description.

- **Unified Modeling Language (UML)**   A mature and widely adopted technology independent, modeling language that supports the application development life cycle sponsored by the Object Management Group.

- **Department of Defense Architecture Framework v2.02 (DoDAF v2.02)**   A framework sponsored by the Chief Information Officer, Department of Defense that includes models for describing data.

- **ISO/IEC 11179**   An international standard sponsored by the International Standards Organization that specifies the kind and quality of metadata needed to describe data and that specifies how to manage metadata in a metadata registry.

- **Dublin Core**   A core metadata vocabulary sponsored by the Dublin Core Metadata Initiative intended to facilitate discovery and management of resources.

## Data Sharing

*Data sharing* is the use of information by one or more consumers that is produced by another source other than the consumer. It supports the access and exchange of data and is enabled by capabilities provided by both the data context and data description standardization areas.

The methods listed here describe the current best practices used for information sharing:

- **National Information Exchange Model (NIEM)**   NIEM is a federated information exchange framework that enables interoperability across multiple mission areas or domains, with each domain managing its data models and content standards separately, while benefiting from central investment in tools, training, model management, and governance.

- **Data.gov**   The purpose of Data.gov is to increase public access to high value, machine-readable datasets generated by the executive branch of the federal government. It provides descriptions of the federal datasets (metadata), information about how to access the datasets, and tools that leverage government datasets.

- **Linked Open Data**   Refers to a set of best practices for publishing and connecting structured data on the Web. Key technologies that support Linked Open Data are URIs (a generic means to identify entities or concepts in the world), HTTP (a simple yet universal mechanism for retrieving resources, or descriptions of resources), and RDF (a generic graph-based data model with which to structure and link data that describes things in the world).

- **Information Sharing Environment Building Blocks**   The Information Sharing Environment Building Blocks guidance helps organizations promote responsible information sharing. The Federal Information Sharing Environment (ISE) is designed to facilitate the sharing of terrorism and homeland security information among all relevant entities through the combination of information sharing policies, procedures, and technologies. The ISE helps to combat terrorism and protecting information privacy in the course of increased information access and collaboration across and among ISE participants.

# TOGAF Data Architecture Artifacts

The following artifacts document the data architecture as recommended by the TOGAF:

- **Data entity/data component catalog**   Identifies and maintains a list of all the data use across the enterprise, including data entities and the data components where data entities are stored. Data components such as data stores and databases (physical names and logical names) are system components in the DoDAF. The data entities are elements of the DIV-1: Conceptual Data Model or DIV-2: Logical Data Model. The catalog artifact is a static location map for data. Data stores are represented in the SV-4: Systems Functionality Description in the DoDAF.

- **Data entity/business function matrix**   Depicts the relationship between data entities and business functions. This relationship can take two forms—ownership for the data or a requirement for input or output of data by a business function. This artifact enables modeling data in motion. It also enables establishment of governance and ownership of data by business function. The OV-3: Operational Resource Flow Matrix describes the relationships between data and function in DoDAF, but in the context of specific performers and activities. The TOGAF artifact may be considered a high-level summary of the two parts of the OV-3 (sending and receiving ends).

- **Application/data matrix**   Depicts the relationship between applications and the data entities that are accessed and updated by them. Applications will create, read, update, and delete specific data entities that are associated with them. This artifact summarizes data in motion in terms of the applications that consume, transform, or produce data. The closest DoDAF counterpart is the DoDAF SV-4: Systems Functionality Description, which models application data input output relationships.

- **Conceptual data diagram**  The key purpose of the Conceptual Data diagram is to depict the relationships between critical data entities within the enterprise. This diagram is developed to address the concerns of business stakeholders. Techniques used include Entity relationship models and Simplified UML class diagrams. The Conceptual data diagram is identical to the DIV-1 (if modeled as a business entity representation). The purpose of the conceptual data diagram is to support the concerns of business stakeholders.

- **Logical data diagram**  Identical to the DIV-2: Logical Data Model (if modeled as a normalized representation) counterpart in the DoDAF. The diagram is independent of context but is intrinsic to the data and relationships among data entities. This artifact supports representation of data at rest and addresses the concerns of application developers and database designers.

- **Data dissemination diagram**  Shows the relationship between data entities and business services and application components. It shows how logical entities are to be physically realized by application components such as database interfaces or data services. The closest equivalent is the DoDAF SvcV-4: Services Functionality Description.

- **Data security diagram**  Depicts which actor (person, organization, or system) can access which enterprise data. This artifact enables the setup of role-based access control systems at the granularity of the data. In the DoDAF, these are couched as authorization rules using the OV-6a: Operational Rules Model or the SV-10a: System Rules Model. The artifact can also be rendered as a matrix.

- **Data migration diagram**  Traces the steps and flow of data from a legacy source application to the intended target new application. Data migration is a necessary requirement for application modernizations or transformations. This artifact provides a blueprint and a map for the data migration and enables systematic tracing of legacy data entities inside the transformation's new systems.

- **Data life cycle diagram**  An essential part of managing business data throughout its life cycle from conception until disposal. This artifact aids data governance requirements for "live" data versus "archived data" and for analyzing requirements of records management. There is no DoDAF equivalent, though the SV-8: Systems Evolution Description shows the application's step-by-step migration into a transformed system (merger, split, or replacement).

## Summary

In this chapter we discuss the representation of data and information as shared resources that transcend individual activities, systems or system functions, or services. The collection of data that is consumed or produced by these collectively is the subject of this viewpoint. Data encodes measurements and observations in a digital format. Data that has meaning in a specific context is information. Without context or semantic content, data representations have no meaning. The uniform representation of the same data across multiple systems, services, and activities is essential for an enterprise's effective functing. The mapping of data representations to higher level semantics is essential for understanding the data.

The subject of data modeling is very extensive and specialized. We have tried to present concepts that are important for the enterprise architect to know. Like all aspects of modeling for enterprise architecture, effective enterprise architecting is best done in teams with skilled and trained data/object class modelers, process modelers, systems and network modelers, and business modelers. Data and information modeling create a reusable shared information asset that can be used by multiple operations, systems, and services. Data and information provide the backbone of the information processing segment of the enterprise.

# Questions

1. What is the difference between data and information? What transformations need to be made to data to convert it into information?

2. What is an ontology? Why is the understanding of ontology fundamental to communications and language? Provide an example of a language used for modeling ontologies.

3. Discuss how ontology can be used for compressing knowledge representation.

4. (Advanced) Compare ontology representation in OWL against the representation of object classes in UML.

5. What is a taxonomy? Why are taxonomies useful in architecture work? How does a taxonomy organize knowledge?

6. What is a vocabulary? What is a controlled vocabulary? How is the proliferation of terms controlled in a controlled vocabulary? Name a standard that governs controlled implementations for monolingual vocabularies.

7. Discuss the various techniques recommended for data description. What are they and how do they differ from each other?

8. What is the difference between data context and data description in the FEAF2 Data Reference Model?

9. How does your specific enterprise approach the need for an enterprise data model? How are data standards developed, promulgated, and implemented?

10. What is the DIV-1: Conceptual Data Model? What are the steps you would use to construct a conceptual data model inside your enterprise? How would you start to organize and layout the model?

11. What is the DIV-2: Logical Data Model? How is it useful to the enterprise? What are some of the transformations that need to be made to a DIV-1: Conceptual Data Model to convert it into a DIV-2: Logical Data Model?

12. What is the cardinality of a relationship inside a DIV-2: Logical Data Model?

13. What is the primary key for a Person, Passport, or Boarding Pass? (Remember two countries can issue passports with identical passport numbers.) Make any reasonable assumptions you want on the attributes.

14. What is the DIV-3: Physical Data Model? Why is it technology dependent?

15. If you were to specify the exact format of message templates to define interoperability between two systems, which model would you build and why: DIV-1, DIV-2, or DIV-3?

16. Compare and contrast the TOGAF artifacts against the DoDAF Data and Information Viewpoint views.

17. Compare and contrast the TOGAF artifacts against the FEAF2 artifacts.

18. Compare and contrast the FEAF2 artifacts against the DoDAF Data and Information Viewpoint views.

# References

Baca, M., ed. 2002. "Metadata Standards." *Library Technology Reports*, 38(5): 19–41.

Bargmeyer, Bruce. 2007. "Practical Semantics: Challenges and Uses." Presented at Integrating Standards in Practice, 10th Open Forum on Metadata Registries, July 9–11, 2007, New York.

Bernstein, J. H. 2009. "The data-information-knowledge-wisdom hierarchy and its antithesis." In Jacob, E. K. and Kwasnik, B., eds. *Proceedings North American Symposium on Knowledge Organization Vol. 2*, Syracuse, NY: 68–75.

Blaha, Michael. 2010. *Patterns of Data Modeling (Emerging Directions in Database Systems and Applications)*. Boca Raton, FL: CRC Press.

Bruce, Thomas A., M.D. 1991. *Designing Quality Databases with IDEF1X Information Models*. New York: Dorset House.

Chang, Daniel, and Elisa Kendall. "Metamodels for RDF Schema and OWL." nd. http://citeseerx.ist.psu.edu/viewdoc/download?doi=10.1.1.184.7990&rep=rep1&type=pdf.

CIO Council. 2001. "A Practical Guide to Federal Enterprise Architecture," Version 1.0. https://www.gao.gov/assets/590/588407.pdf.

CIO Council. 2013. "Federal Enterprise Architecture Framework, Version 2." https://obamawhitehouse.archives.gov/sites/default/files/omb/assets/egov_docs/fea_v2.pdf.

CJCSI 6241.02, Chairman of the Joint Chiefs of Staff, United States Message Text Formatting Policy and Procedures.

Department of Commerce. 1993. "Integration Definition for Information Modeling," (IDEF1X) FIPS PUB 184.

Department of Defense. nd. "Essential Elements of the Net-Centric Environment Ontology and Taxonomies." NCOW Reference Model.

Department of Defense. 2010. "Discovery Metadata Specification (DDMS), Version 3.0."

Department of Homeland Security Federal Information Sharing Environment Privacy and Civil Liberties Policy. https://www.dhs.gov/publication/department-homeland-security-federal-information-sharing-environment-privacy-and-civil.

Department of Transportation. nd. "Common Terms in Air Travel." Retrieved 12/4/2017 from https://cms.dot.gov/sites/dot.gov/files/docs/CommonTermsAirTravel.pdf.

Dublin Core Metadata Initiative. nd. "Dublin Core Metadata Element Set, Version 1.1: Reference Description." www.dublincore.org/documents/dces/.

Duval, E. 2001. "Metadata Standards: What, Who & Why." *Journal of Universal Computer Science*, (7)7: 591–601.

English, Larry P. 2009. *Information Quality Applied: Best Practices for Improving Business Information, Processes and Systems*. Indianapolis: Wiley.

Extensible Markup Language (XML), Worldwide Web Consortium (W3C), https://www.w3.org/XML/.

Federal Aviation Administration. "Glossary of Airport Acronyms Used in FAA Documents: Airports." Retrieved 12/4/2017 from www.faa.gov/airports/resources/acronyms.

Federal Enterprise Architecture Program Management Office. 2005. "The Data Reference Model Version 2.0" xml.coverpages.org/FEA-DRMv20Final-2005.pdf.

Fowler, Martin. 2003. *UML Distilled: A Brief Guide to the Standard Object Modeling Language*, 3rd Edition. Boston: Addison-Wesley Professional.

Graham, Anne. 2007. *Managing Airports: An International Perspective*, 5th Edition. New York: Routledge.

Gruber, Thomas R. 1995. "Toward Principles for the Design of Ontologies Used for Knowledge Sharing." *International Journal of Human-Computer Studies - Special issue: the role of formal ontology in the information technology*, (43)5–6: 907–28.

Hay, David C. 1996. *Data Model Patterns: Conventions of Thought*. New York: Dorset House.

Hay, David C. 2006. *Data Model Patterns: A Metadata Map*. San Francisco: Morgan Kauffman.

Hoberman, Steve. 2016. *Data Modeling Made Simple: A Practical Guide for Business and IT Professionals*, 2nd Edition. Basking Ridge, NJ: Technics Publications.

International Air Transport Association (IATA). 2018. "Industry Data Model." Retrieved 12/4/2017 from www.iata.org/whatwedo/passenger/Pages/industry-data-model.aspx.

International Air Transport Association (IATA). 2018. "Passenger and Airport Data Interchange Standards (PADIS) Board." Retrieved 12/4/2017 from www.iata.org/whatwedo/workgroups/Pages/padis.aspx.

International Organization for Standardization. "Information technology – Metadata registries (MDR) – Part 3: Registry metamodel and basic attributes." https://www.iso.org/standard/50340.html.

International Organization for Standardization. "Information technology – Metadata registries (MDR) – Part 5: Naming principles." https://www.iso.org/standard/60341 .html.

Lacy, Lee W. 2005. *OWL: Representing Information Using the Web Ontology Language.* Victoria, BC: Trafford.

Lambe, Patrick. 2007. *Organising Knowledge: Taxonomies, Knowledge and Organisational Effectiveness.* Oxford, UK: Chandos Publishing.

National Information Standards Organization (NISO). 2004. *Understanding Metadata.* Baltimore, MD: NISO Press.

National Information Standards Organization. 2005. "Guidelines for the Construction, Format and Management of Monolingual Controlled Vocabularies," ANSI/NISO Z.39.19-2005. https://groups.niso.org/apps/group_public/download.php/12591/z39-19-2005r2010.pdf.

National Information Exchange Model (NIEM) Website: https://www.niem.gov/

OASIS. 2009. "UIMA Base Type System Namespace," Version 1.0. http://docs.oasis-open.org/uima/ns/base.ecore.

Patel-Schneider, Peter, Patrick Hayes, and Ian Horrocks, eds. 2004. "OWL Web Ontology Language Semantics and Abstract Syntax: W3C Recommendation." www.w3.org/TR/owl-semantics/.

Ross, Ronald G. 2003. Principles of the Business Rule Approach. Boston: Addison-Wesley Professional.

Ross, Ronald G. 2005. *Business Rule Concepts: Getting to the Point of Knowledge,* 2nd Edition. Houston, TX: Business Rule Solutions.

Simsion, Graeme C. 2005. *Data Modeling Essentials,* 3rd Edition. San Francisco: Morgan Kauffman.

The Open Group. 2018a. TOGAF 9.2 Standard, Version 9.2: A Pocket Guide, Revised Educational Edition. The Netherlands: Van Haren Publishing.

The Open Group. 2018b. TOGAF 9.2 Standard, Version 9.2 Foundation and Certified (Level 1 & 2). The Netherlands: Van Haren Publishing.

Vojvodić, K. 2008. "Airport Concessions." Department of Economics and Business Economics, University of Dubrovnik. Retrieved 12/4/2017 from https://hrcak.srce .hr/file/41698.

Weinberger, David. 2010. "The Problem with the Data-Information-Knowledge-Wisdom Hierarchy." *Harvard Business Review*, February 2, 2010. Retrieved 12/3/2017 from https://hbr.org/2010/02/data-is-to-info-as-info-is-not.

# CHAPTER 19

# Standards Viewpoint

The Standards Viewpoint is responsible for answering several questions: "Which standards do we currently adopt or aspire to adopt?" "Which standards are changing or being superseded and when?" "Which standards are forecasted to be in widespread use and which standards are still trying to gain traction?" The answers to the first question can be documented in a standards forecast and the answers to the second two questions can be documented in a standards forecast. For larger organizations or enterprises with commercial interests in a standard or vested interests in proprietary products and services that either depend on a standard or standards or threaten to become a standardized commodity, these questions may need to be answered: "What are emerging standards?" "Which standards bodies are working on which standards that may have a direct impact on our business?" The answers to these questions can be documented in a standards profile.

The scope of standards spans not just the technology aspects but rather all the viewpoints of the enterprise. Operational standards may be conventions for codes and values that are agreed upon by an industry association or body. Three-letter codes for countries are established by the International Organization for Standardization (ISO). Domain-specific standards are established by bodies that govern the domain.

In the DoDAF, the Standards Viewpoint was originally intended to deal with technology standards. However, it can also be used to document business standards such as standard operating procedures, relevant laws and regulations, and security standards. The technology standards may be *de jure* standards developed and published by standards organizations such as the American National Standards Institute (ANSI), Institute of Electrical and Electronics Engineers (IEEE), ISO, and Object Management Group (OMG), or the technical standards may be proprietary offerings that have become *de facto* standards, such as Microsoft Windows. The Standards Viewpoint can also deal with enterprise-specific standards including such things as the standard technology configurations for workstations or servers.

The need for standards, especially technical standards, is driven by the need for interoperability. The world runs smoothly on standards. When you swipe a credit card inside the card reader on the gas pump, the use of a common standard guarantees that the card reader reads the magnetic stripe and retrieves the encoded information that was stored by your bank or credit card provider. When you slide the boarding pass issued by one airline into a card reader operated and used by another airline, your flight and booking information travels smoothly to the carrier and you are authenticated and welcomed into the aircraft.

The Standards Viewpoint (StdV) provides the minimal set of rules governing the arrangement, interaction, and interdependence of system or service parts or elements. The StdV provides the technical systems implementation guidelines upon which engineering specifications are based, common building blocks are established, and product lines are developed. It includes a collection of the technical standards and standards options that can be organized into profile(s) that govern systems and system or service elements in a given architectural description.

The Standards Viewpoint caters to the need of people responsible for interoperability, integration and federation-related activities and supports acquisition. For example, operational interoperability requires common semantic vocabularies between multiple performers. In an emergency response scenario, first responders use an abbreviated (terse) form of communication that is understood by everyone who is familiar with and using that standard. A standard used in the past are 10-codes by police and citizens band radio operators.

The lack of standards can result in significant breakdown of communications in an urgent operational scenario. In the tragedy at Charlottesville, Virginia, involving protest events in 2017, one of the failures of standards involved Charlottesville Police Department (CPD) and Virginia State Police (VSP) operating on separate communications channels. CPD zone commanders could not communicate with assigned VSP personnel via radio during the height of violence on July 8, 2017 [Hunton & Williams 2017].

We are all familiar with the effect of standards on interoperability. Major advances in widespread proliferation of computer communications began to occur after the majority of vendors adopted TCP/IP. The HTTP and XML standards are other examples of communications protocols that have been behind the explosive adoption of the World Wide Web. In the area of data standards, financial institutions have established interbank funds transfer standards to enable disparate banks to conduct financial transactions automatically through messaging.

The Standards Viewpoint provides the following:

- A plan to enhance interoperability by publishing enterprise-wide guidance that requires adherence to standards for items such as business processes; military operations; systems hardware and software components or interfaces; communication devices, protocols, and links; and materiel that is used by processes

- A documentation of the disparate standards currently in use with an intent of reducing variety and fostering more uniformity and consistency in the future

We draw the distinctions between standards profiles that describe the list of applicable standards and inventories of technology assets that record actual instances of technology use in the enterprise. The DoDAF Standards Viewpoint is geared toward a profile-based approach. The Defense Information Standards Registry records these profiles.

Systems Viewpoint and Services Viewpoint views such as the SV-9: Systems Technology and Skills Forecast or the SvcV-9: Services Technology and Skills Forecast list actual technology instances that are used by systems or services and their projected lives and replacement strategies.

# Views of the Standards Viewpoint

The Standards Viewpoint is supported by two views, both of which are based on the profile rather than actual instances of technology:

- **StdV-1: Standards Profile**   Lists the various standards that are used by an enterprise. These standards relate not only to technology but also elements of the operations such as airport codes, aircraft types, and country codes and are used to promote interoperability across operations and systems.
- **StdV-2: Standards Forecast**   Shows a predictive view of where the standards are going within the windows of the architecture time frame.

The StdV-1 and StdV-2 views must share the same classification scheme and standards coding scheme to enable traceability and for integration. The StdV-1 and StdV-2 are sometimes combined into a comprehensive standards reference that shows the current standards with the dates when they will no longer be accepted in new systems or services and when they must be removed from all operational systems and services. It also shows the future standards and the dates when they must be used in all new systems or services.

## Standards Profile View

The StdV-1: Standards Profile records the current list of standards that are used within an enterprise organized by a normative classification scheme that is sometimes called the technical reference model (TRM), plus operational standards. The StdV-1 provides engineers with an opportunity to identify duplicative or overlapping standards and to identify opportunities for improvement by reducing the number of standards or justifying the need for multiple standards based on mission needs.

The importance of using the same classification scheme for standards across cooperating and collaborating enterprises is that they can lay their StdV-1 models side-by-side and make comparisons that find potential conflicts in their standards postures. Because of the sheer magnitude of the lists of standards that are applicable to an enterprise, a commonly understood and adopted classification scheme is necessary to make comparisons easy and to reduce errors.

Federal agencies must use the FEAF2 TRM (see Chapter 23) as the overarching technical standards categorization scheme. Individual agencies may develop their own standards profiles that extend the FEAF2 TRM and may also list agency standard technology configurations in addition to technology standards.

Department of Defense enterprises must use the Defense IT Standards Registry (DISR) provided by the DoD both for a standard classification scheme as well as the list of registered standards. In general, not all standards that are used by all DoD enterprises are available in the DISR—only those that are common to multiple enterprises.

There are other classification schemes for technology standardization. Standards bodies such as ANSI, IEEE, ISO, and International Civil Aviation Organization (ICAO) have also developed standards using committees and working groups that are laid out according to their own internal grouping schemes.

## Standards Forecast View

The StdV-2: Standards Forecast view supports planner's needs for developing roadmaps for future standards adoption and implementation. The StdV-2 collects projections of standards maturity over a time period to determine which standards will become obsolete, which standards will be supplemented with newer versions, and which new standards will emerge within the time frame of interest.

## Standards Viewpoint Integrated Views

The Standards Viewpoint views tend to stand alone, more as guidance for the enterprise in the acquisition process and to promote interoperability as early as possible. However, the SV-9: Systems Technology and Skills Forecast and SvcV9: Services Technology and Skills Forecast, both must be consistent with the StdV-1: Standards Profile and StdV-2: Standards Forecast. Figure 19-1 provides the integrated view set for the Standards Viewpoint.

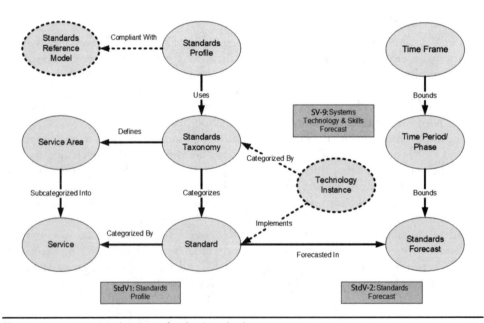

**Figure 19-1**    Integrated view set for the Standards Viewpoint

# StdV-1: Standards Profile

| View Information at a Glance | |
| --- | --- |
| View short name | StdV-1 |
| Name | Standards Profile |
| Other names | Technology Reference Model (TRM)<br>Technical Profile (Old Name)<br>Technology Standards Catalog (TOGAF 9)<br>Technology Portfolio Catalog (TOGAF 9) |
| Viewpoint | Standards |
| View intent | Defines the technical, operational, and business standards, guidance, and policy applicable to the architecture being described.<br><br>The StdV-1 view is as applicable to the enterprise architecture as it is to solution architectures. The StdV-1 compiles all applicable standards. At an enterprise level, this may be too large a number and a proper taxonomy or grouping scheme is required to provide a way to understand the complexity. A standards reference model (TRM) is useful for performing this categorization. The DISR provides a standard service area/service/standard categorization scheme for DoD. Other enterprises may have their own categorization scheme. For comparisons and understanding the differences in standards, especially in the presence of a large volume of standards, common taxonomies are essential. |
| View audience | Standards personnel, integration and cross functional interoperability groups, acquisition managers |
| Formal modeling methodology | None. The DoD DISR and the FEAF2 TRM are two examples of formal well-established classification schemes for technology standards. |
| Integration of view with other views | The StdV-1 elements must be consistent with SV-9, SvcV-9, and StdV-2 elements. StdV-1 standards should be traceable to the operational system, services, or infrastructure elements that they should apply to. This traceability can be documented in the AV-2: Integrated Dictionary entries for each standard included. |

Dictionary entries for each standard should include a brief outline of the features of the standard and should specify any options of the standard that are required.

Because the categorization scheme is used to group literally thousands of standards in large enterprises, the importance of standardizing the categorization scheme itself is considered a very important exercise in architecting the enterprise.

The Department of Defense maintains a standard technology classification using the DISR, which is intended to provide a common classification model for all defense enterprises. This means that DoD StdV-1s can be unified and aggregated at higher levels within DoD. The FEAF2 TRM provides a standard list of categories under which technology standards can be grouped. TOGAF also provides for a TRM that implementing organizations can use to categorize their technology standards. The technology architecture for an enterprise is one of the important TOGAF 9 components of architecture. The TOGAF distinguishes between technology standards such as POSIX or FIPS 127 Structured Query Language that are modeled in the technology standards catalog from the actual instances of technology such as an Oracle Database or a Microsoft Server, which are modeled inside the technology portfolio catalog.

The StdV-1 may also be tailored to show cross-reference to the architecture elements that use or reference a specific standard. The following example shows the issue date (year) of the standard as well as the status of the standard at the time the architecture was built.

## Example: Passenger Identification StdV-1

In this example, we have invented a classification scheme for RMN Airport that has a progressive three-level structure: Service Area, Service, and Subservice. Standards are then categorized by this three-level classification scheme.

| RMN Service Area | | Standard | | | | |
|---|---|---|---|---|---|---|
| RMN Service | RMN Subservice | Number | Authority | Title | Issue Date | Status |
| Identification | | | | | | |
| Machine Identification | | | | | | |
| | Magnetic Identification Cards | | | | | |
| | | ISO 7810 | ISO/IEC | Physical characteristics of credit card size document | 2003 | Current |
| | | ISO 7811-1 | ISO/IEC | Part 1: Embossing | 2002 | Current |
| | | ISO 7811-2 | ISO/IEC | Part 2: Magnetic Stripe – Low Coercivity | 2001 | Current |
| | | ISO 7811-3 | ISO/IEC | Part 3: Location of Embossed Characters | 1995 | Withdrawn |
| | | ISO 7811-4 | ISO/IEC | Part 4: Location of Tracks 1 and 2 | 1995 | Withdrawn |
| | | ISO 7811-5 | ISO/IEC | Part 5: Location of Track 3 | 2001 | Withdrawn |
| | | ISO 7811-6 | ISO/IEC | Part 6: Magnetic Stripe – High Coercivity | 2008 | Current |
| | | ISO 7813 | ISO/IEC | Financial transaction cards | 2006 | Current |

| RMN Service Area | | Standard | | | | |
| | | | | | | |
| RMN Service | RMN Subservice | Number | Authority | Title | Issue Date | Status |
|---|---|---|---|---|---|---|
| **Optical Character Recognition** | | | | | | |
| | **Alphanumeric Character Recognition** | | | | | |
| | | ISO 1073/II | ISO/IEC | Alphanumeric character sets for optical recognition – Part 2: Character Set OCR-B – Shapes and dimensions of the printed image | 1976 | Withdrawn |
| | | ISO 1831 | ISO/IEC | Printing specifications for optical character recognition | 1980 | Current |
| | | ISO 3166-2 | ISO/IEC | Codes for the representation of countries and their subdivision: Part 1: Country Codes | 2007 | Current |
| | | ISO/IEC 7810 | ISO/IEC | Identification cards – physical characteristics | 2003 | Current |
| | | ISO 8601 | ISO | Data Elements and Data Interchange Formats – Information Interchange – Representation of dates and times. | 2001 | Current |

**PART III**

# StdV-2: Standards Forecast

| View Information at a Glance | |
|---|---|
| View short name | StdV-2 |
| Name | Standards Forecast |
| Other names | Technology Reference Model (TRM) Technical Profile (Old Name) |
| Viewpoint | Standards |
| View intent | Tracks the evolution of existing standards and the emergence of new standards of interest. |
| View audience | Standards personnel, integration and cross-functional interoperability groups, systems and services planners |
| Formal modeling methodology | None. The DoD DISR and the FEAF2 TRM are two examples of formal well-established classification schemes for technology standards. |
| Integration of view with other views | The StdV-2 elements must be consistent with SV-9 and SvcV-9. StdV-2 should use the same classification scheme used by the StdV-1. StdV-2 standards should be traceable to the systems, services, or infrastructure elements that they may apply to or that they may impact. This traceability can be documented in the AV-2: Integrated Dictionary entries for each standard included. |

Dictionary entries for each standard should include a brief outline of the features of the standard and specify any options of the standard that should be required.

## Example: Passenger Identification StdV-2

In this StdV-2 example, we depict a timeline of ten years with short-term, mid-term, and long-term forecasts for each standard of interest. The purpose of the StdV-2 is to assist in developing a standards roadmap for RMN Airport that will lay out a blueprint for architects that clearly shows some of the assumptions for standards evolution and will guide stakeholders in making acquisition-, design-, and development-related decisions.

| RMN Service Area / RMN Service | RMN Subservice | Standards Forecast | | |
|---|---|---|---|---|
| | | Short Term (<2 Years) | Mid Term (1–5 Years) | Long Term (5–10 Years) |
| **Identification** | | | | |
| **Machine Identification** | | | | |
| | Magnetic card identification | Expected to use heavily in 80% of identification cases. Solid, reliable, and established. | Shift to in-biometric techniques. Still expected to use in 40% of identification cases. | Eliminate all non-biometric methods because they can be taken by force from owners. |
| | Barcode identification | Very limited use (<10%). Single-dimensional bar code information density not acceptable. | Expect to use two-dimensional bar codes in 5% of identification cases. | Eliminate all non-biometric methods because they can be taken by force from owners. |
| | Smart chip identification | Currently used in U.S. passports and select country passports. | Increasing use of non-contact RF detection and interrogation methods (60%) with photo image information. | Augmented to also contain biometric information. |

# Alternatives

The TOGAF and FEAF2 have alternative approaches to the DoDAF Standards Viewpoint.

## TOGAF Technology Architecture

The TOGAF recommends the following type of artifacts to represent the technology architecture. Note that some of these artifacts are at a much lower level of abstraction and detail than those included in the DoDAF.

- **Technology Standards Catalog**   This catalog documents the agreed-upon standards for technology across the enterprise covering technologies and versions, the technology life cycles, and the refresh cycles for the technology. This catalog is an extended version of the StdV-1: Standards Profile view of the DoDAF.

- **Technology Portfolio Catalog**   This catalog identifies and lists all the technology in use across the enterprise, including hardware, infrastructure software, and application software. An agreed-upon technology portfolio supports life cycle management of technology products and versions and also forms the basis for definition of technology standards. It contains the following metamodel entities: Platform Service, Logical Technology Component, and Physical Technology Component. The Technology Portfolio Catalog is an instance catalog while the Technology Standards Catalog is a list of standards.

- **Application/Technology Matrix**    This artifact documents the mapping of applications to the technology platform.

- **Environments and Locations Diagram**    This artifact depicts the relationships between enterprise locations and the applications they host. It also identifies what technologies are used at which locations.

- **Platform Decomposition Diagram**    This artifact depicts the technology platform that supports the operations of the information systems architecture. A platform is associated with a *stack*—a set of interdependent technology items that collectively provide the platform's capabilities.

- **Processing Diagram**    This artifact focuses on deployable units of code and how these are deployed on the processing platforms.

- **Networked Computing/Hardware Diagram**    This artifact depicts how logical application components are deployed in a distributed network computing environment.

- **Communications Engineering Diagram**    This artifact maps the logical interfaces between application components to the physical networks, boundaries, and communications infrastructure. It is similar to the SV-2: Systems Resource Flow Description or the SvcV-2: Services Resource Flow Description in the DoDAF.

# FEAF2 Approach to Standards

The FEAF2 deals with standards both in the infrastructure subarchitecture domain and in the infrastructure reference model (IRM) as described in the following sections.

## FEAF2 Infrastructure Subarchitecture Domain

The infrastructure subarchitecture domain within the FEAF2 contains the elements of information technology that support the execution of applications and services. However, the DoDAF Standards Viewpoint covers standards not only for technology but also for supporting operational activities. For example, the ICAO's list of airport codes may be a relevant standard for RMN Airport, as does the specifications from the FAA for airport minimum functions or runway lengths and airport classification categories. The following artifacts are recommended for the infrastructure subarchitecture domain:

- **Network Diagram (I-1)**    Describes the means that implement the resource flows in an architecture. The DoDAF SV-2: Systems Resource Flow Description and SvcV-2: Services Resource Flow Description are equivalent views.

- **Hosting Concept of Operations (I-2)**    Presents the high-level functional architecture, organization, roles, responsibilities, processes, and metrics and strategic plan for hosting and use of hosting services.

- **Technical Standards Profile (I-3)**    Collects the various system standard rules that implement/constrain choices in the design and implementation of the architecture. This artifact is equivalent to the DoDAF StdV-1: Standards Profile.

- **Technology Forecast (I-4)**   The emerging technologies, software/hardware products, and skills that are expected to be available in a given set of time frames and that will affect future infrastructure development. This artifact is equivalent to the DoDAF SV-9: Systems Technology and Skills Forecast or the SvcV-9: Services Technology and Skills Forecast views.

- **Cable Plant Diagram (I-5)**   Diagrams the wires and connectors used to tie a network together. (Not included in DoDAF architectures.)

- **Wireless Connectivity Diagram (I-6)**   Diagrams a communications network that provides connectivity to wireless devices. (Not included in DoDAF architectures.)

- **Rack Elevation Diagrams (I-7)**   Two-dimensional elevations drawn to scale and show everything that needs to be placed in a certain area, which describe the organization of specific equipment on a rack. (Not included in DoDAF architectures.)

- **Data Center/Server Room Diagram (I-8)**   Diagrams the layout and contents of a data center or server room. (Not included in DoDAF architectures.)

- **Wiring Closet Diagram (I-9)**   Diagrams the layout and contents of a wiring closet. (Not included in DoDAF architectures.)

- **Point of Presence Diagram (I-10)**   Not described in FEAF2. A point of presence (PoP) is an artificial demarcation point or interface point between communicating entities. The PoP indicates where an external carrier such as a telecommunication company enters the locations of the enterprise such as a data center. An Internet point of presence typically houses servers, routers, network switches, multiplexers, and other network interface equipment. It is typically located in a data center. ISPs typically have multiple PoPs.

- **Asset Inventory (I-11)**   Lists infrastructure assets with details about each asset (installation date, original cost, condition, and so on). (Not included in DoDAF architectures.)

- **Facility Blueprints (I-12)**   Represents technical drawings of the facility. (Not included in DoDAF architectures.)

## FEAF2 Infrastructure Reference Model

In the FEAF2, the IRM is the taxonomy-based reference model for categorizing IT infrastructure and the facilities and network that host the IT infrastructure. The IRM supports definition of infrastructure technology items and best-practice guidance to promote positive outcomes across technology implementations. The generic (underlying) platform consists of the hardware, software, and delivery platform upon which specific/customized capabilities (solutions, applications) may be deployed. In addition to providing a categorization schema for IT infrastructure assets, the IRM enables analysis of IT infrastructure assets at a department or an agency level as well as at a federal government level. In the federal context, the IRM is adopted and used to conduct government-wide analysis of IT infrastructure assets and to identify consolidation initiatives. In the department or agency

# Infrastructure Reference Model

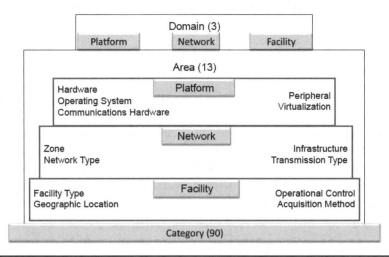

**Figure 19-2**   Infrastructure reference model (used with permission from TOGAF)

context, the IRM is used to drive good IT infrastructure asset management practices such as identifying end-of-life assets before they affect the mission of an organization and to identify opportunities for sharing and consolidating infrastructure.

The IRM taxonomy is intended to provide a categorization scheme for physical IT assets, the operating systems and firmware that run them, and the locations or facilities that host the assets. The IRM is divided into three levels, as shown in Figure 19-2:

- **Level 1, Domain**   Consists of 3 entities, Platform, Network, and Facility, which are linked and related to each other to enable analysis of IT assets across the three dimensions.

- **Level 2, Area**   Consists of 13 total areas (such as Hardware) linked to the three domains in Level 1.

- **Level 3, Category**   Consists of 90 total categories (for example, Personal Computer – Laptop) linked to the 13 areas in Level 2.

# Summary

The StdV-1: Standards Profile and StdV-2: Standards Forecast views are useful for base-lining existing standards (profile) and planning future investments in products and service platforms with an understanding of where these are headed (forecast). Industry consulting organizations such as the Gartner Group or the Forrester Group, which are consultants for technology strategy, surveille technology trends and provide forecasts that drive entire segments of industry toward emerging standards. The StdV-1: Standards Profile is useful for looking at the enterprise's current baseline of standards, determining whether a shift is necessary, and planning an orderly migration strategy toward contemporary or emerging standards (Standards Forecast). The migration path for an individual system may be represented using the SV-9: Systems Technology and Skills Forecast in the case of the DoDAF.

# Questions

1. Why are standards important to the enterprise? Who is the audience for the Standards Viewpoint? Why?

2. Why are standards important across enterprises? Name some examples of scenarios where multiple enterprises are involved and where the lack of standards is a serious impediment to interoperability.

3. What is a technical reference model? Why is a common standards classification scheme important for various parts of the enterprise to interoperate?

4. What is a standards profile? How does your enterprise generate a standards profile? Does the enterprise standards profile match one of the reference models mentioned in this chapter—National Institute of Standards and Technology (NIST), the FEAF2 TRM, or the Defense Department's DISR? Does your enterprise standardize the classification scheme and categories and standards specifications or does it categorize vendor platforms such as IBM DB2 or Oracle for RDBMS, IBM Web Server for web services, and so on? Why?

5. What is a standards forecast? How does your enterprise generate standards forecasts? For what time frames? How do the time frames in the StdV-2 tie in to/be consistent with other time frame models such as the SV-9: Systems Technology and Skills Forecast?

6. What is the relationship between the StdV-1: Standards Profile, the StdV-2: Standards Forecast, the SV-9: Systems Technology and Skills Forecast, and the SvcV-9: Services Technology and Skills Forecast views?

7. Contrast the FEAF2 infrastructure standards approach to the more general Standards Viewpoint of the DoDAF. How will you describe operational standards through the FEAF2 artifacts? Which artifacts?

8. Compare and contrast the TOGAF technical architecture artifacts against the FEAF2 artifacts.

9. Compare and contrast the TOGAF technical architecture artifacts against the DoDAF Standards Viewpoint views.

# References

American National Standards Institute (ANSI). Home page. www.ansi.org/.

CIO Council. 2013. "Federal Enterprise Architecture Framework, Version 2." https://obamawhitehouse.archives.gov/sites/default/files/omb/assets/egov_docs/fea_v2.pdf.

Department of Defense. 2010. DoD Architecture Framework Version 2.02. http://dodcio.defense.gov/Library/DoD-Architecture-Framework/.

Department of Homeland Security, FEMA. "Plain Language Guide: Making the Transition from Ten Codes to Plain Language." www.fema.gov/media-library/assets/documents/25461.

Fernandes, James. 2005. Academic Dictionary of Internet. Isha Books, p. 316.

Hunton & Williams. "Final Report: Independent Review of the 2017 Protest Events in Charlottesville, Virginia." www.hunton.com/images/content/3/4/v2/34613/final-report-ada-compliant-ready.pdf, p.79.

Institute of Electrical and Electronics Engineers (IEEE). Home page. www.ieee.org.

International Organization for Standardization (ISO). Home page. www.iso.org/iso/home.html.

National Institute of Standards and Technology (NIST). Home page. www.nist.gov/index.html.

The Open Group. 2011. "Sample Catalogs, Matrices and Diagrams," Version 3, TOGAF Enterprise Edition Version 9.1. Microsoft PowerPoint presentation. www.togaf.info/togaf9/togafSlides91/TOGAF-V91-Extra-Catalogs-Matrics-Diagrams-v3.pdf.

# CHAPTER 20

# Extension Viewpoints

In Chapter 1 we introduced the concept of viewpoints. Viewpoints are frames of reference for a particular group of stakeholders in terms of what they want to see in the enterprise architecture. These stakeholders are driven by their own concerns and vocabularies and the architecture scope from their vantage points. Within these viewpoints are views, each of which addresses a subset of the concerns of the stakeholder.

The architecture frameworks we have reviewed in this book all support the concept of a core set of viewpoints and views that are recommended and standardized by the framework specifications. This core set of viewpoints may be considered in general for all architecture-related concerns and is underlain by the fundamental ontology for describing architecture elements in the general sense. These elements, such as activity, performer, location, motivation, events, information, and data, are fundamental elements that are needed to represent enterprise structure and enterprise behavior.

This chapter is unique in that the concepts presented here are intended for the architect responsible for extending or changing the scope of the architecture framework to support additional viewpoints and views that were not part of the core framework but are required for the architecture to support analyses and additional types of decision-making, or to assist the reification process of taking concepts to implementation.

## The Need for Extension Viewpoints

In an ideal world, the core set of viewpoints will be sufficient to represent all the concerns of all types of stakeholders. But because of the need to abstract the core architecture elements to a high enough level that they serve to cover multiple situations, the abstraction level of the core elements may detract from the communication required by the architecture to stakeholders. Stakeholders want to see architecture elements they recognize and not some abstracted label that has little meaning to them!

Another need for extensions to the architecture elements, relationships, views, and viewpoints is to reflect special concerns related to specific business processes. The core architecture views and architecture elements should not be comingled with the architecture elements that support, say, procurement and acquisition, or governance or security. Adding more viewpoints and views that address these added concerns to the architecture representation may require extensions to the viewpoints, views, and the underlying metamodel itself.

Extension viewpoints are used to extend the collection of standard viewpoints in an architecture framework to support some specific interests and concerns for decision-making that may require architecture information beyond what can be currently represented in the standard framework. So when enterprise architecture is used to support decision-making for specific domains, additional sets of viewpoints may need to be defined. These viewpoints address domain-specific concerns that refine and specialize the architecture elements that are already defined within the core set of viewpoints.

To ensure an integrated architecture, the new elements in the extension viewpoints:

- Should not duplicate architecture element types that already exist in the core set of viewpoints. New elements may be subtypes or specializations of core elements but they should not be parallel in meaning to the elements that are already present.

- Should integrate with the core set of elements by establishing relationships from the added elements to the existing elements.

## TOGAF Extension Example

Figure 20-1 shows how the TOGAF core content metamodel is extended to support the concerns for governance, service-oriented architectures, details of processes, infrastructure consolidation considerations, and strategic and motivation concerns.

## DoDAF Extensions

The DoD Architecture Framework provides the architecture development guidance to support decision making in the six key processes: Joint Capability Identification and Development System (JCIDS); Defense Acquisition System (DAS); Systems Engineering (SE); Programming, Planning, Budgeting and Execution (PPBE); and Net-Centric Integration and Portfolio Management (PfM). Figure 20-2 shows how DoDAF 2.0 and 2.02 contain extensions to incorporate the concerns of the six DoD core processes from earlier versions of the DoDAF and C4ISR architecture framework specifications.

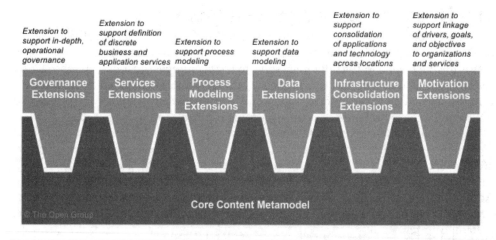

**Figure 20-1**   TOGAF core content metamodel with extensions (used with permission from TOGAF)

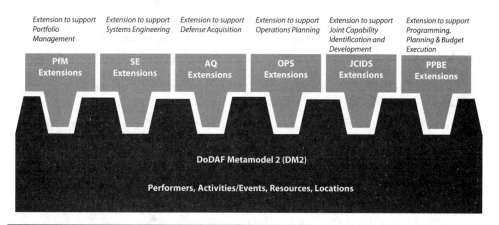

**Figure 20-2** DoDAF V2 incorporated extensions

To support the Joint Capabilities Integration and Development System (JCIDS), the Capability Viewpoint was added to the previous version of the DoDAF. To accommodate the concerns of acquisition program planning, monitoring, and control, the Project Viewpoint was added. The obvious relationships between the capabilities in the Capability Viewpoint and the projects in the Project Viewpoint were added to integrate the newly added extension viewpoints. The capabilities were also related to the operational activities in the Operational Viewpoint and the services in the Services Viewpoint to ensure traceability from the capabilities to their implementations and to ensure a line of sight.

# Extending a Standard Framework

Extending an existing framework is an exercise akin to voiding the warranty when we open up the internals of some complex equipment we have purchased. Customers of enterprise resource planning systems (ERPs) have recognized that customizations come at a great price, not only from the initial customization investment but in terms of continuing maintenance, as new releases need to be customized over and over again. Framework extensions are best left to standards bodies that deliberate changes to the core framework to accommodate new concerns and issues that are not represented in the current framework. However, in the interests of integration or supporting unique needs, large enterprises may undertake the task of extending the framework viewpoints and views through the techniques described next.

How do we extend the standard architecture framework such as the DoDAF, or the TOGAF, that have well-established viewpoints, views and content metamodels? The following list explains:

- *Identify the concerns and types of stakeholders that need to use the core architecture for a specific purpose.* For example, financial analysis is an important enterprise function that simply abstracts architecture elements as items of asset or items of expense. Financial analysts are not as much concerned with the details of operations or infrastructure as they are concerned with items such as investment management, cost management, and financial strategy. Hypothetically, by abstracting architecture elements as asset or cost items, financial analysts may concentrate on measures as properties of these assets or cost items to support financial analysis in terms of time and dollars. The focus on activity inputs and outputs is replaced by viewing activities as having a financial transaction component that is of interest to the financial analyst.

- *Determine whether new entities need to be added to support extension views.* These entities represent the elements of the concern and should not already be present in the framework metamodel. For example, in the financial view, we may want to introduce notions of a financial transaction and subtype it as a financial investment or a financial expense. We may want to call out resource flows coming in from sources (performers) external to the enterprise as income and resource flows going to external resources as expenses. The resource in all cases is money/currency.

- *Relate extension entities to existing core entities in the framework to ensure that integration is preserved.* In our example, a superclass called Asset or Investment may be defined to encompass any type of architecture element that can be subclassed and viewed as an asset or investment by a financial analyst.

- *Define a viewpoint with a recognizable and standardized name and establish a subject area of the framework metamodel that depicts entities, relationships, and properties of metamodel elements that support the viewpoint.* A narrative that describes the viewpoint, content model, subject area metamodel subset, stakeholders, and concerns supported is completed.

- *Develop views or standard artifacts that reference the extended metamodel.* In our case, some of the standard financial statements such as a balance sheet, income statement, or cash flow statement can be defined based on the extensions to the metamodel for assets, investments, income, expense, and so on, that we have now built into the standard framework as extensions.

- *Extend tools to accommodate the extensions.* For tools built on UML profiles, such as the Unified Profile for DoDAF and MODAF (UPDM), changes to the profile are necessary to accommodate the extensions. Traditional architecting tools built on an abstract metamodel can accommodate the specification of extensions by simply altering the personalization file that subclasses the abstract metamodel inside the tool engine to specific content profiles.

## Ontology Extensions

There is another way to deal with needed extensions: by working with the underlying ontology or metamodel of the framework. The metamodel of a framework such as the Content Metamodel for TOGAF or the DoDAF Metamodel (DM2) are based on ontology concepts. Understanding the ontological model is fundamental to understanding where changes are to be made to support extension viewpoints. Adding new entity concepts can be done by subtyping elements from the foundation ontology (underlying meta-metamodel) or by subclassing existing entities in the ontology. Working with an ontology is also a way for tool vendors to build tools that support multiple frameworks. The following paragraphs discuss some of the ontologies that are or have been used to support architecture frameworks.

## IDEAS Foundation Ontology

The International Defence Enterprise Architecture Specification (IDEAS) is a formal ontology foundation developed by the defense departments and ministries of the United States, United Kingdom, Canada, Australia, and Sweden in coordination with the North Atlantic Treaty Organization (NATO). IDEAS is an "uber" ontology that is universal in coverage not only for military/defense architectures but for all other types of architectures as well. The IDEAS foundation ontology is very similar to the foundation ontology of the Unified Modeling Language (UML) that abstracts everything that can be modeled as classes and objects. Just as UML profiles are used to restrict the scope of classes to enable restricted modeling for a specific domain, the DoDAF and some other defense frameworks can be seen as profiling mechanisms for IDEAS. Providing extension views involves altering or extending the profile—the foundation ontology is unaltered and new profile elements should neatly fit under the foundation ontology.

Figure 20-3 depicts the IDEAS ontology as a simplified class diagram without providing details of cardinality/multiplicity of the relationships.

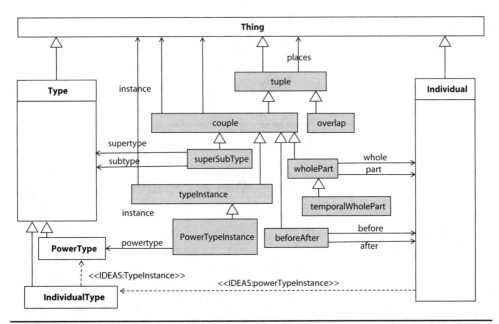

**Figure 20-3**　IDEAS simplified ontology diagram

In the figure, the highest abstraction in the IDEAS ontology comes from Thing broken down into three type of subclasses: Type, Individual, and tuple (relationship). That is, classifiers, instances, and relationships are all treated as Things. A collection of types is called a PowerType and a collection of individuals is called an IndividualType. Collections of instances of type are called PowerTypeInstance. Collections enable us to model groups of similar objects and enumerate them as sets and work with the set as a whole.

Relationships can represent an overlap between two Things in space and time. They can represent a generalization relationship (supertype or subtype). They can represent a composition relationship (wholePart), and the composition can either be structural or temporal. Finally, relationships can represent precedent/antecedent relationships (before/after).

With these constructs, IDEAS is able to provide a foundation ontology (overarching shorthand notation) that is expressive enough to describe the DM2.

## DoDAF Metamodel (DM2)

Figure 20-4 depicts the conceptual entities of the DM2. (The diagram does not show relationships other than simple subtyping, nor does it reflect the fact that measures can be associated with all entities and relationships.) The DM2 is an ontology model that inherits directly from the IDEAS ontology—a universal or "foundation" ontology that is abstract enough to encompass all objects in all domains of discourse. The DM2 specializes IDEAS and adds subtypes that are semantically richer than the abstract Thing or Thing Type.

Adding an extension entity involves placing it at the top of the hierarchy as a subclass of type, assuming we can make a stipulation that the new entity does not duplicate the semantics of existing entities.

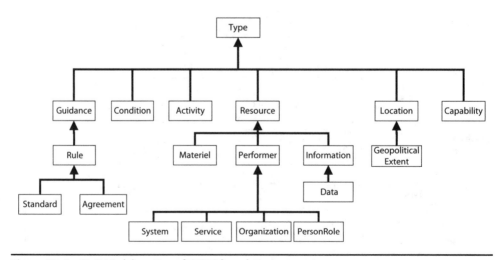

**Figure 20-4**  DoDAF elaboration of IDEAS foundation concepts

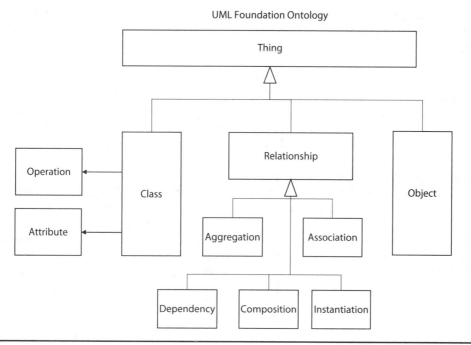

**Figure 20-5**   Simplified view of UML foundation ontology

## UML Foundation Ontology

The UML is also specified using abstract higher level classifiers (metaclasses) along the lines of the IDEAS approach by implementing a foundation ontology that enables a rich set of specializations. Figure 20-5 illustrates the UML ontology.

In UML every Thing is either a Class or an Object. Relationships associate classes to classes and classes to objects. Relationships can establish aggregation of dissimilar classes or objects, composition of homogenous classes or objects, nonspecific associations between classes or objects, existential dependency relationships representing preconditions, and instantiation relationships that represent the instantiation of a class into one or more objects.

### UML Profiles

Profiling is the technique used in UML to restrain the scope of classifiers and establish relationships that are meaningful, and to constrain the establishment of arbitrary associations to those that are allowed by the profile specification. A profile in UML provides a generic extension mechanism for customizing UML models for particular domains and platforms. Extension mechanisms enable the refinement of standard semantics in a strictly additive manner, preventing them from contradicting standard semantics.

Profiles are defined using stereotypes, tag definitions, and constraints that are applied to specific model elements, such as Classes, Attributes, Operations, and Relationships. A profile is a collection of such extensions that collectively customize UML for a particular domain (such as aerospace, healthcare, or financial) or platform (relational database).

The DoDAF is implemented as a profile in UML through the Unified Profile for DoDAF and MODAF (UPDM). A UML-based modeling tool loads the UPDM specification and behaves like a DoDAF-compliant modeling tool as the UPDM profile constrains random instantiations or associations. Extensions applied to DoDAF while using UPDM require the extension of the UPDM specifications. As far as the tool user is concerned, applying a revised UPDM specification to a tool automatically creates an extended version of the DoDAF. In a multitool, multiarchitect architecture development environment, controlling and managing the configuration of the changed UPDM profile is essential if consistency of architecting is to continue with extensions applied.

## Unified Architecture Framework

UPDM has been evolved to keep up with the evolution of DoDAF and the evolution of MODAF. As MODAF has been merged into the NATO Architectural Framework (NAF), UPDM has been superseded by the Unified Architecture Framework (UAF). Despite its name, UAF is not an architecture framework in the usual sense, but an ontology built on UML and SysML. UAF is designed as a UML tool profile to support all the DoDAF-related defense frameworks, even though these frameworks use different names for the same concepts and may have disjoint or overlapping viewpoints. The Unified Architecture Framework Profile (UAFP) allows a SysML tool to support DoDAF architecture development.

UAF is described in terms of viewpoints and views, where the viewpoints are as follows:

- Actual Resources
- Dictionary
- Operational
- Personnel
- Projects
- Requirements
- Security
- Services
- Standards
- Strategy
- Summary and Overview

Despite some of the viewpoint names, they frequently don't exactly correspond to the DoDAF viewpoints of a similar name. For example, the view that most closely corresponds to the DoDAF OV-1: High-Level Operational Concept Graphic shows up in the UAF Summary and Overview viewpoint.

Some of the UAF viewpoints, such as the Security and Actual Resources viewpoints, have concepts that are not currently in the DoDAF. For example, the Security viewpoint illustrates the security assets, security constraints, security controls, families, and measures required to address specific security concerns. This viewpoint addresses the security constraints and information assurance attributes that exist on exchanges between resources. The intended audience is security architects, security engineers, systems engineers, and operational architects. The Actual Resources viewpoint illustrates the expected or achieved actual resource configurations and actual relationships between them. So this viewpoint focuses on more concrete entities than the more abstract entities used in the DoDAF. The Actual Resources viewpoint addresses the concerns of resource analysis—such as the evaluation of different alternatives, what-if, trade-offs, or verification and validation (V&V) on the actual resources. The intended audience is solution providers, systems engineers, business architects, and human resources.

# Summary

We have reviewed the potential need to extend an architecture framework and two approaches to achieving that extension. For single frameworks, we provided a process for extending the framework while retaining the ability to develop an integrated architecture. However, there is an alternative approach, especially if the desire is to provide tools that support multiple related, but overlapping, frameworks. The alternative approach is to develop an ontology that can underlie all the desired frameworks while providing a way, such as via profiling, to limit the general ontology to the scope of each individual framework. Then it is easy to extend any of the supported frameworks to include concepts from one of the other frameworks.

# Questions

1. The Federal Aviation Administration wants to standardize on an IT Application Portfolio Management extension to the DM2 (to be used in all the IT departments) that involves the following: A IT Application Portfolio is an aggregate of Systems and Services. The Portfolio needs to associate performers in the role of Owners of Systems or Services, Steward for Systems and Services, and Certification & Accreditation Authority for Systems and Services. The Portfolio also needs to associate measures with systems and services that help decision-makers make decisions on what to drop/end game, what to augment or extend, and what to add. The portfolio must also be associated with activities of the enterprise. How would you go about examining the DM2 for places to extend, and what types of extensions would you contemplate?

2. What is a UML profile? How does it enforce standardization of architecting?

3. What is the Universal Profile for DoDAF and MODAF? What is the connection between the DoDAF Metamodel (DM2) and the UPDM?

4. What is the relationship between UPDM and the Unified Modeling Language?

5. How would UML tools deal with extensions applied to the UPDM? How would users be affected?

**6.** What are the added viewpoints in the Unified Architecture Framework? Compare and contrast these Viewpoints with the DoDAF 2.0 Viewpoints as well as the TOGAF artifacts.

**7.** What are the various ways in which viewpoints in a framework may be extended?

# References

Department of Defense. 2010. DoD Architecture Framework Version 2.02, "DM2: DoDAF Formal Ontology." http://dodcio.defense.gov/Library/DoD-Architecture-Framework/dodaf20_ontology1.

Department of Defense. 2010. DoD Architecture Framework Version 2.02, "Introduction." https://dodcio.defense.gov/Library/DoD-Architecture-Framework/dodaf20_background/.

The IDEAS Group. "Overview." Retrieved 1/8/2018 from www.ideasgroup.org/1Overview.

Larman, Craig. 2001. *Applying UML and Patterns: An Introduction to Object-Oriented Analysis and Design and Iterative Development.* Englewood Cliffs, NJ: Prentice-Hall.

Object Management Group. 2018. "About the Unified Modeling Language Specification Version 2.5.1." www.omg.org/spec/UML/About-UML/.

Object Management Group. "Unified Architecture Framework (UAF) Version 1.0." Retrieved on 1/8/2018 from www.omg.org/spec/UAF/1.0/pdf.

# PART IV

# Comparative Frameworks

# CHAPTER 21

# The Zachman Framework

John A. Zachman is widely recognized for establishing the historical foundation for enterprise architecture. Although he is (and remains) a major influence on EA, most of his writings comprise only a few articles, a co-authored book, and several prefaces to other books. Instead, he has maintained his own organization and published on his web site [Zachman International] in the forms of blogs and other entries.

Zachman developed the first version of his framework in the mid-1980s and published it in the *IBM Systems Journal* [Zachman 1987] as "A framework of information systems architecture." This effort was an extension of his work begun in 1984, when he developed the first three-column "Information System Architecture" inspired by work from Peter Chen and Charles Bachman. The 1987 publication still retained the three columns, as it represented only information systems. In 1992, Zachman expanded the concept to include rows for planner, owner, designer, builder, subcontractor, and the enterprise view. In 2008, and more recently in 2011, Zachman developed the framework to the most current iteration—a six-by-six matrix. The 2011 representation is a clarification involving a renaming of the rows in the framework ontology. On the vertical axis are rows representing six *perspectives*, and on the horizontal axis are six columns of *interrogatives* addressed by each of the respective perspectives.

## The Zachman Framework as an Ontology

Zachman calls his framework an "ontology," which he defines on his web site as "a theory of the existence of a structured set of essential components of an object for which explicit expressions is necessary and perhaps even mandatory for creating, operating, and changing the object." The scope of the objects the framework can address is "an Enterprise, a department, a value chain, a 'sliver,' a solution, a project, an airplane, a building, a product, a profession or whatever." Zachman states that his framework is not a methodology for creating the implementation (an instantiation) of the object. Instead, he says, the "Framework IS the ontology for describing the Enterprise. The Framework (ontology) is a STRUCTURE whereas a methodology is a PROCESS. A Structure is NOT a Process. A Structure establishes definition whereas a Process provides Transformation."

The Zachman Framework is therefore a comprehensive and structured categorization scheme that enables the architect to discover, record, and categorize the real-world objects and abstractions that are involved within a transformation process. The word "ontology" is used to describe concepts and relationships. The two-dimensional ontology arises from the scheme of columns and rows that are used to label the category of a specific architecture object.

The Zachman Framework, as illustrated in Figure 21-1, is represented as a two-dimensional grid, where the columns represent interrogatives and the rows represent perspectives. The interrogatives are the six questions—What, How, Where, Who, When, and Why. These are used to describe with completeness any narrative as stated by philosophers and taught today in courses on journalism, like the opening lines of the Rudyard Kipling poem *I Keep Six Honest Serving Men*:

> I keep six honest serving-men
>   (They taught me all I knew);
> Their names are What and Why and When
>   And How and Where and Who.

Figure 21-1 shows the most recent Zachman Framework 3.0 picture provided at the Zachman International web site.

As with any other narrative, an architecture narrative can be described by answering the six questions and tabulating the results of the corresponding questions.

Zachman realized that the question Why? may have different answers to different stakeholders. In other words, getting a consistent and reliable set of answers to the six interrogatives may not always be possible when you talk to many people who have their own ideas of what the answers are.

For example, when the question Why? is posed to the airport authority for RMN Airport, the following answers result:

- Develop the local economy around the airport.
- Develop a revenue-generation engine for the three municipalities surrounding the airport.
- Provide employment for the local citizenry.

But when the Why? question is posed to an airline that uses the airport as an origin or destination, the answers are different:

- Provide runways for safe landings and takeoffs.
- Provide terminal facilities for safety and comfort of passengers.
- Provide refueling and maintenance capabilities.

Though both stakeholders are talking about the same airport and the reasons why it is in existence, each of them has different concerns, issues, needs, and even language to catalog the architecture objects that they describe.

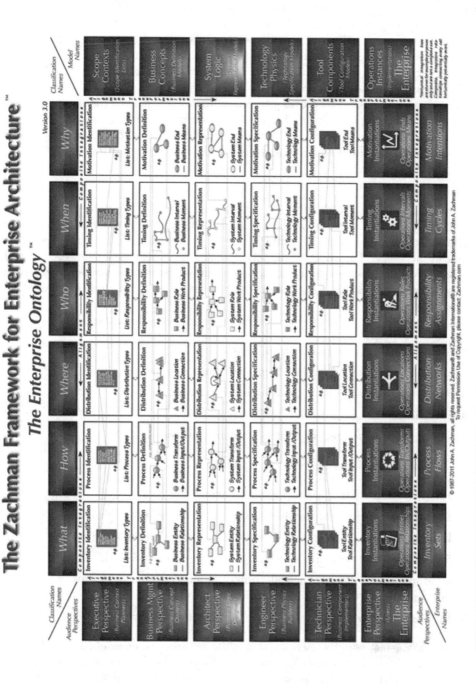

PART IV

**Figure 21-1** The Zachman Framework of the Enterprise Ontology (used with permission from Zachman International)

The problem of classifying architecture elements becomes more complex when architecture elements are used loosely in descriptions. Is *USA* a location (Where) or is it a role (Who)? Depending on the usage of the architecture element, we can resolve whether the term is used as a location or a role. Repository storage of *USA* may require two distinct elements: USA (geo-location) and USA (geo-political entity). The Zachman interrogatives force resolution of such ambiguities because a tabulation of Where? or Who? is required for the *USA* in this example.

Recognizing that each stakeholder group has different answers to the same question, often couched in their own terms, Zachman stipulated that there should be rows that correspond to the perspective of such diverse stakeholder groups. Thus, the perspectives correspond loosely to the viewpoint concepts found in other frameworks.

## Reification

How then to systematically identify who these stakeholders are so that the row structures can be standardized? Zachman's analysis initially looked at the stages through which a building is constructed, from the planning stage to the physical construction stage, and the role of the architect amid all of these stages. Later, he generalized the stages involved in any endeavor that involves converting concepts into implementations through a series of transformations using the general steps of problem-solving. This process is what he calls *reification*.

Zachman identified the following transformation steps in a logical sequence:

1. **Identification** is transformed into **Definition**.

2. **Definition** is transformed into **Representation**.

3. **Representation** is transformed into **Specification**.

4. **Specification** is transformed into **Configuration**.

5. **Configuration** is transformed into **Implementation**.

Each of the six reification stages is defined as follows:

- **Identification**   Identify the problem (Owner).
- **Definition**   Define the variables of the problem (Planner).
- **Representation**   Represent the variables and relationships (Architect).
- **Specification**   Specify the elements of the solution (Designer).
- **Configuration**   Specify the collection of elements and relationships to be implemented for the solution (Acquirer).
- **Implementation**   Implement the solution (Implementer).

These are abstractions that have more specific meaning when applied to a problem domain and a specific enterprise. We consider reification in the context of the problem of verifying the identity of the people at RMN Airport, establishing their entitlement to the services they might be requesting, and verifying their authorization to be in the area where they are currently located or attempting to enter.

- The CIO has *identified* the problem of the inability to identify anyone walking around in the airport—from airline employees, to airport concessionaires, to passengers, to service personnel, to airport administration staff, to TSA staff, to aircrew and others—and the potential consequences for disastrous events.

- The *definition* of the problem and the staging of solution capabilities are performed at the planning staff level. The needed capabilities and their scopes are laid out and allocated to specific projects.

- The *representation* of specific identification processes—data, roles, and events— and time periods is performed by the enterprise architect.

- The *specification* for acquiring these capabilities is performed by the design team.

- The *configuration* of multiple acquisitions and project oversight is performed by a program manager.

- The actual *implementation* is performed by contractors for specific projects and a systems integrator responsible for the needed interoperability across the projects.

# The Perspectives

Zachman's perspectives correspond to the stakeholders within the six reification steps described. It is important to note that the standard Zachman Framework perspectives are articulated based on an assumption of reification as the intent of the framework.

 **NOTE** The authors have discovered that multiple tribal perspectives exist in an enterprise even during nonreification transformations (emergence) and that these tribal perspectives are not conscious acts of planning and execution but are forced on the enterprise from the external environment or from internal forces. These are the subject of ongoing work by the authors.

Here are the perspectives shown from top to bottom in Figure 21-1:

- **Executive Perspective** Referred to as the Planner's Perspective in earlier versions of the framework, provides the scope of the enterprise. This viewpoint represents the group that manages the business of the enterprise at the highest level, defines the scope of the project, and operates at a relatively high level of abstraction.

- **Business Management Perspective** Referred to at the Owner's Perspective in earlier versions of the framework, represents the viewpoint of the business area managers in the enterprise. Once the executive identifies the scope, the business area owner/manager gives more detail about business-specific aspects that provide materials to be used by the architect or designer of the enterprise in the next rows.

- **Architect Perspective**   Referred to as the Designer's Perspective in earlier versions of the framework, is the viewpoint of those who represent the business in a disciplined manner and complete the strategic view of the enterprise. The architect also relates the business needs of the enterprise identified in the first two rows to the solution and technical viewpoints of the following two rows. The architect as designer provides the logical structure for data and architects the whole enterprise. Note that specific solutions are not identified at this level. These solutions are determined in the engineer's or builder's view in the following row.

- **Engineer Perspective**   Referred to as the Builder's Perspective in earlier versions of the framework, provides the viewpoint of those who identify specific technology solutions to solve business problems identified in the previous perspectives. After the designers create the designs for the architecture, the builder implements the design and is responsible for providing solutions in the form of products, which may be commercial-off-the-shelf (COTS) or custom-built. This creates what Zachman refers to as the "enterprise physics."

- **Technician Perspective**   Referred to as the Subcontractor's Perspective in earlier versions of the framework, is the viewpoint of those hired or tasked with implementation of the solutions. It is here that the specific products are implemented according to the enterprise physics determined in the previous row.

- **Enterprise Perspective**   Referred to as the Functioning Enterprise in earlier versions of the framework, is the physical representation of the system itself.

# The Interrogative Columns

Each of the perspectives has six different aspects depicted as columns. These are based on the classic six interrogatives: What, How, Where, Who, When, and Why. By addressing each of these questions for the respective rows, we have a complete understanding of the subject.

- *What* is the data column and addresses the understanding of the enterprise data.
- *How* is the function column describing the various processes entailed in dealing with data columns.
- *Where* is the network column describing the locations and logistics between entities.
- *Who* is the people or roles column characterizing those who participate in the organizational activities.
- *When* is the timing column describing when a function is to be performed.
- *Why* is the motivation column characterizing the end goals, constraints, rules, and regulations involved.

# Classification Schema

The intersection of six interrogative columns with six perspective *rows* columns creates a matrix of thirty-six cells, as the intersection between the two classifications of interrogatives and the six stages of transformation or reification. According to Zachman, each cell is a single variable (distinct representation) containing only one type of enterprise component and the relationships with all other components of the same type in the enterprise. In Zachman's terms, the 36 variables that contain values of architecture elements completely describe the ingredients of transformation within the reification process.

The Zachman Framework is considered to be an ontological or thought tool for organizing and classifying enterprise knowledge. It is methodologically independent of other frameworks (such as DoDAF, FEAF2, and TOGAF) and is an accompaniment to them. The usefulness of the Zachman Framework is in the systematic manner in which architecture elements can be cataloged and related. The Zachman Framework can be equally used to identify capabilities and performers in the DoDAF, to identify requirements in the TOGAF, or to identify processes, roles, and inputs and outputs in the FEAF2.

The power of reification is that it captures all the steps of a major transformation, from identification to implementation, and is therefore a powerful alignment tool to understand how the identification is mapped to the implementation. These types of alignments are required across the enterprise. For example, business strategy should map to operational processes, operational processes should map to information systems and automation, and information systems and automation should map to the infrastructure computing platforms and networks.

# Primitives and Composites

Having standardized the rows and columns of his framework, Zachman set out to standardize (in an abstract manner) what types of architecture objects are represented within each of the 36 cells. He used an analogy to the periodic table of elements that codifies the chemical elements with symbols and a location within the table ordered by certain criteria. He called the architecture elements in the Zachman Framework cells "primitives" and reasoned that "composites" of architecture elements were similar to chemical molecular structures that comprise multiples of the same element or combinations of diverse elements described by a distinct formula. Just as the exact formula reflects constraints such as valency, relationships between architecture objects described in composites are also constrained by manmade rules, existential constraints or the laws of nature.

Each Zachman Framework cell therefore contains primitives analogous to the elements in the periodic table. These primitive elements are invariant structures that make up all enterprises. The combinations of elements or primitives into composites are "snapshot" structures that characterize a particular enterprise at a given moment in time. These are variant structures dependent on the context and nature of the technologies and business. The invariant primitives are characteristic independent variables defining the nature of any enterprise.

Table 21-1 describes the primitive elements or "models" within each cell of the matrix.

| | Data/What | Function/How | Network/Where | People/Who | Time/When | Motivation/Why |
|---|---|---|---|---|---|---|
| **Executive** | Inventory Identification: List: Inventory Types | Process Identification: List: Process Types | Distribution Identification: List: Distribution Types | Responsibility Identification: List: Responsibility Types | Timing Identification: List: Timing Types | Motivation Identification: List: Motivation Types |
| **Business/ Management** | Inventory Definition: Business Entities and Relationships | Process Definition: Business Transform and Inputs/Outputs | Distribution Definition: Business Location and Connections | Responsibility Definition: Business Role and Work Product | Timing Definition: Business Interval and Moment | Motivation Definition: Business End and Means |
| **Architect** | Inventory Representation: System Entity and Relationship | Process Representation: System Transform and Inputs/Outputs | Distribution Representation: System Location and Connections | Responsibility Representation: System Role and Work Product | Timing Representation: System Interval and Moment | Motivation Representation: System End and Means |
| **Engineer** | Inventory Specification: Technology Entity and Relationship | Process Specification: Technology Transform and Inputs/Outputs | Distribution Specification: Technology Location and Connections | Responsibility Specification: Technology Role and Work Product | Timing Specification: Technology Interval and Moment | Motivation Specification: Technology End and Means |
| **Technician** | Inventory Configuration: Tool Entity and Relationship | Process Configuration: Tool Transform and Inputs/Outputs | Distribution Configuration: Tool Location and Connections | Responsibility Configuration: Tool Role and Work Product | Timing Configuration: Tool Interval and Moment | Motivation Configuration: Tool End and Means |
| **Enterprise (functioning)** | Inventory Instantiations: Operational Entities and Relationships | Process Instantiations: Operational Transforms and Inputs/Outputs | Distribution Instantiations: Operational Locations and Connections | Responsibility Instantiations: Operational Roles and Work Products | Timing Instantiations: Operational Intervals and Moments | Motivation Instantiations: Operational Ends and Means |

**Table 21-1**  Zachman Framework Primitives

In summary, in the Zachman Framework, row 1 deals with scope:

- The WHAT of row 1 are high-level data classes.
- The HOW is the high-level business process types.
- The WHERE is the location types.
- The WHO are the roles or responsibility types.
- The WHEN are the timing types.
- The WHY are the types of motivations.

Row 2 focuses on business models:

- The WHAT is the business data model.
- The HOW is the business process models.
- The WHERE is the location models.
- The WHO is the business role models.
- The WHEN is the business timing model.
- The WHY are the business ends and means.

Row 3 focuses on system models:

- The WHAT is system data models and data relationships.
- The HOW is logical representations of information systems and their relationships.
- The WHERE is logical representations of the distributed system location architecture.
- The WHO is logical representation systems roles and work products.
- The WHEN is logical system timing.
- The WHY are system ends and means.

Row 4 contains the technology models as physical models of solutions:

- The WHAT involves technology level data physical data models.
- The HOW is specifications of applications technology.
- The WHERE is specifications of network locations and connections.
- The WHO is specification of technology roles.
- The WHEN is the specification of technology timing.
- The WHY is technology ends and means.

Row 5 is the as-built and deployment of business components or tools:

- The WHAT is the tool data models.
- The HOW is coded program functions (tool transforms).
- The WHERE is tool locations and connections.
- The WHO is tool roles.
- The WHEN is tool timing definitions coded to sequence activities on particular platforms and technologies.
- The WHY are the tool ends and means.

Row 6 is the operational enterprise and affords evaluation. This is the functioning enterprise:

- The WHAT is data values stored in actual databases—the operational data entities and relationships.
- The HOW is the operational processes.
- The WHERE is the operational locations and connections.
- The WHO is the operational roles and work products.
- The WHEN involves operational timing definitions operating to sequence activities.
- The WHY are operational ends and means.

# Rules for the Use of the Zachman Framework Ontology

To establish the effectiveness of the framework, Zachman defines several rules that need to be followed. Note that the term "model" is used more loosely here than in other frameworks such as DoDAF.

- *Rows or columns are not to be added to the framework.* WHO, WHAT, WHERE, WHY, and HOW are the only primitive interrogatives accepted. This provides a full comprehensive set for understanding a subject. All are required. Adding or removing any of these would result in either duplication or discontinuities. This rule specifies that the framework rows and columns cannot be modified.
- *Each column contains a simple generic model.* For example, the WHAT column focuses on data and relationships. These are single and independent aspects of the enterprise.
- *Each cell model is specific to its column's generic model.* As each column has a simple and generic model, each cell provides information on the perspective specific to the row. Thus, each cell model is a specific version of the generic model for each column.

- *No meta concept (such as the element type chemical symbol in the periodic table analogy) can be classified into more than one cell.* Each row is unique, as is each column. Each cell is unique. Each meta concept is specific to the cell, and it is logical that none of the meta concepts can be classified into more than one cell.

- *One must not create diagonal relationships between cells.* A diagonal relationship relates a cell in one perspective to a cell in another. Each perspective defines its own semantics for its columns. Thus, creating diagonal relationships will lead to semantically incomplete communication. This can lead to significant misunderstandings and communication breakdowns.

- *The names of the rows and columns should not be changed.* Any change would not be acceptable as a corruption of the basic framework.

- *The logic involved in the framework is generic and recursive.* The framework can be applied equally appropriately to a parent enterprise as to smaller component enterprises within that parent enterprise. The framework is considered generic enough to classify descriptive representations of anything, and the framework is enough to analyze all aspects relative to the architectural composition of anything.

## Summary

The Zachman Framework is a tool used for classifying artifacts and providing the logic for aligning information systems and business. It is a generic framework that works for all scopes and is intended as a resource for other frameworks such as DoDAF, TOGAF, and FEAF2. Although the Zachman Framework provides perspectives that reflect stakeholder viewpoints, it does not specify specific models or views. Rather, the framework cells focus on versions of generic models or primitives based on both a perspective and an interrogative. The Zachman Framework does not and was not intended to provide a methodology for a step-by-step process for creating an EA. Instead, it proffers a holistic view that gives a complete classification system of architecture elements and a structure to categorize architecture objects in a systematic manner that reflects the actual process of transformation.

## Questions

1. What is the relationship of the first two rows of the framework to the bottom three rows, and the significance of the architect's perspective?

2. Although Zachman changed the labels for the perspectives, what is the basis for the rule that the names now used should not be revised?

3. How are you able to distinguish between primitives and composites? Why are primitives invariant while composites are conditioned by business contexts and the current state of an enterprise?

4. How are you able to create a composite view of some entity out of a combination of enterprise primitives?

5. Why does the Zachman Framework use a two-dimensional ontology to categorize architecture objects?

6. What are some problems that do not fit into the reification category?

7. How would you organize the DoDAF Metamodel 2 (DM2) metamodel classes into the Zachman Framework?

8. How would you organize the requirements-gathering framework of TOGAF and the architecture objects of TOGAF's metamodel into the Zachman Framework?

9. Can you identify the various perspectives of the Zachman Framework for your own enterprise?

## References

Kipling, Rudyard. *I Keep Six Honest Serving Men,* from *Just So Stories.* Free Book Series, Gutenberg.org. Retrieved 12/13/2017 from www.gutenberg.org/ebooks/2781.

Zachman International. www.zachman.com.

Zachman, John A. 1987. "A framework for information systems architecture." *IBM Systems Journal,* 26 (3).

Zachman, John A. 1993. Foreword to *Enterprise Resource Planning,* by Steven Spewak. New York: Wiley.

Zachman, John A. 2011. Foreword to *FEAC Certified Enterprise Architect CEA Study Guide* by Prakash Rao, et al. New York: McGraw-Hill.

Zachman, John A. 2016. "The Concise Definition of the Zachman Framework." www.zachman.com/about-the-zachman-framework.

Zachman, John P. 2009. "The Zachman Framework Evolution." Zachman International. www.zachman.com/ea-articles-reference/54-the-zachman-framework-evolution.

# TOGAF: The Open Group Architecture Framework

In this chapter, we cover a basic overview of the concepts involved in The Open Group Architecture Framework (TOGAF) and provide additional references to The Open Group documents as well as books dedicated specifically to TOGAF. The Open Group itself is a vendor- and technology-neutral industry consortium, with more than 500 member organizations. Though The Open Group is vendor-neutral, many of its members are vendors and provide information on their products so they can be integrated into TOGAF as reusable solution building blocks. TOGAF is only one of the products and standards developed and maintained by The Open Group. The Open Group is also the certifying authority for TOGAF.

TOGAF is the systematic development of an architecture representation and solution requirements based on an iterative process using a set of architectural assets. It was first developed in 1995 based on pre-DoDAF DoD technical architecture work and has its origins in the Joint Technical Architecture (JTA) standards. Since then, TOGAF has continued to evolve and incorporate a more general non-defense stance and a broadening from a technology focus to an overall coverage of the environment around the technology. Various versions of TOGAF have evolved, leading to its current major iteration, TOGAF 9.0 in 2009. Since that time, TOGAF has been revised twice, with versions 9.1 in 2011 and most recently to 9.2 on April 16, 2018.

TOGAF 9 was designed for a broad range of different types of architectures and is used along with elements of other frameworks focused on vertical sectors such as government, telecommunications, manufacturing, defense, finance, and more. According to *TOGAF 9.2 Standard, Version 9.2: A Pocket Guide,* the major changes in the new version are described as "an update to the TOGAF 9.1 standard providing improved guidance, correcting errors, improving the document structure, and removing obsolete content. Key enhancements made in this version include updates to the Business Architecture and the Content Metamodel." [The Open Group 2018a, p. 7] We provided a discussion of changes in the TOGAF content metamodel in the context of our discussions of comparisons with DoDAF and other framework models or artifacts in previous chapters.

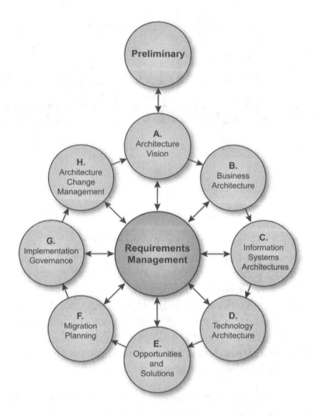

**Figure 22-1**
Phases of
the ADM (used
with permission
from TOGAF)

The Open Group Standard TOGAF Version 9.2 "is an architecture framework that provides the methods and tools for assisting in the acceptance, production, use, and maintenance of an enterprise architecture. It is based on an iterative process model supported by best practices and a re-usable set of existing architecture assets." [The Open Group 2018a, p. 9] At the heart of TOGAF is the Architecture Development Method (ADM), sometimes metaphorically called "the crop circle" because of its signature graphic, which is illustrated in Figure 22-1. This graphic outlines the iterative phases of the ADM.

## TOGAF Documentation

The ADM is one of six parts of the TOGAF that, together with the introduction, correspond to the sections of the TOGAF Standard and manual. The non-introduction sections of the TOGAF manual describe the major components of the TOGAF and are illustrated in Figure 22-2.

The six TOGAF document parts cover the following material:

- **Introduction**   Provides a high-level introduction to the major or key concepts of EA using the TOGAF approach.

- **Architecture Development Method**   Describes the ADM.

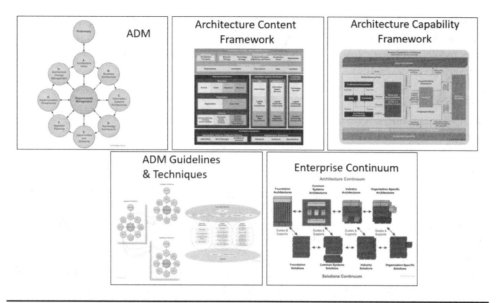

**Figure 22-2** Major components of the TOGAF (used with permission from TOGAF)

- **Application of the ADM**   Offers guidelines and techniques.
- **Architecture Content Framework (ACF)**   Includes a structural metamodel for the TOGAF architectural artifacts and reusable architecture building blocks. Includes a discussion of typical architectural deliverables or contracted capabilities (that is, contractual requirements) that a given architecture is to provide. (Note that TOGAF uses the term "capability" more informally than DoDAF does.) Although TOGAF provides its own content framework, the use of the artifacts contained is only recommended because TOGAF is meant to work with artifacts (views) from any other major framework (such as FEAF, DoDAF, MODAF, and NAF), even though these "borrowed" artifacts have their own names and forms of representation. The artifacts from these other frameworks can be mapped to the TOGAF ACF.
- **Enterprise Continuum**   Addresses architecture building blocks and tools. This continuum is a library repository organized from the most general to organizational specific reusable building blocks and reference models. This repository includes an architecture continuum of enterprise functionalities and desired capabilities mapped to a solutions continuum: either COTS solutions or built or customized realizations of the requirements identified in the architecture continuum.
- **Architecture Capability Framework**   Describes processes, skills, roles, and responsibilities needed to create and operate an architecture function within the enterprise.

The phases of the ADM provide the basic methodology for creating TOGAF, with the other sections providing resources for iteratively deploying the architecture. We summarize each of the sections of the TOGAF (except the introduction) next.

# The ADM

We review the phases of the ADM and the Requirements Management process as illustrated in Figure 22-1.

## The Preliminary Phase

In the Preliminary phase, the organization prepares for architecture development projects. This phase involves the preparation for and initiation of activities in response to the business directive for a new enterprise architecture. These activities entail the definition of an organization-specific architecture framework and tools based on TOGAF and the definition of architecture principles. During this phase, decisions and plans are made for how architecture activities and process will be performed in the context of the enterprise involved. The result of this phase is the establishment of the architecture capability for the organization. The architecture team and responsibilities are identified, governance is established, and architecture and business principles are identified. TOGAF is tailored and related to other frameworks as necessary.

As inputs to this stage are reference materials archived in the TOGAF Library (https://publications.opengroup.org/togaf-library/), the outputs are the organizational model for the EA projects, the initial repository, and a request for a Statement of Architecture Work.

## Phase A: Architecture Vision

The Preliminary phase continually iterates with Phase A (Architecture Vision), as the Preliminary phase activities provide support for the vision for the architecture to be developed. The objectives of Phase A are to develop a vision of the capabilities to be developed by the architecture and to obtain a Statement of Architecture Work in response to the request for work developed in the Preliminary phase. The Statement of Architecture Work defines the scope and approach that will be used to complete an architecture development cycle. The Statement of Architecture Work is typically the document against which successful execution of the architecture project will be measured and may form the basis for a contractual agreement between the supplier and consumer of architecture services.

The activities involved in Phase A are as follows:

1. Establish the architecture practice.
2. Identify relevant stakeholders and their concerns.
3. Evaluate capabilities.
4. Assess business transformation readiness.

5. Scope the work to be done.

6. Confirm architecture and business principles.

7. Develop the architecture vision.

8. Define key performance indicators for the architecture that can support completeness and traceability for audit.

9. Identify transformation risks and develop mitigations.

10. Secure approval for the Statement of Architecture Work.

## Phase B: Business Architecture, Phase C: Information Systems Architecture, and Phase D: Technology Architecture

These three phases of the ADM address the four major domains found in all enterprise architectures: business, data, application, and technology. In TOGAF Phase C combines data and application architecture into a single phase as Information Systems Architecture. During Phases B, C, and D, a high-level baseline or as-is architecture is described and related to a high-level target or to-be architecture of each for the major domains: business, data, application, and technology. A high-level gap analysis is conducted between the as-is and to-be architectures for each of the major domains. Each of these analyses is then refined. The analyses are combined in Phase E (Opportunities and Solutions) and used during Phase F (Migration Planning).

In Phase B, the focus is on business; the technique based on business scenarios is key. This technique is first used in Phase A but it also provides support for Phase B (Business Architecture). This technique involves a description of a business process or the applications enabled by the architecture. The description includes the business and technology environment, the actors (both human and computer) involved, and the desired outcomes. The development of the scenarios is governed by the SMART criteria: the scenarios are to be specific, measurable, actionable, realistic, and time-bound. Using this scenario-based technique, a clear business vision can be articulated for the particular iteration of the EA involved. The primary objective of Phase B is to develop the target business architecture to achieve the business goals and strategic drivers identified in Phase A. Once the detailed business target architecture has been developed, a detailed gap analysis is performed to determine what needs to be accomplished for the transformation.

As phases B, C, and D relate to each of the four primary architectural domains of EA, the steps involved for each phase are consistent:

1. Select reference models, viewpoints, and tools.

2. Develop baseline (as-is) descriptions.

3. Develop target (to-be) descriptions.

4. Conduct gap analyses.

5. Define candidate roadmap components.

6. Resolve impacts across the entire architecture landscape.

7. Conduct formal stakeholder reviews.

8. Finalize the respective portions of the architecture and incorporate these into the ongoing development of the architecture definition document.

## Phase E: Opportunities and Solutions

After completing phases B, C, and D, Phase E begins the implementation of the architecture by identifying the projects involved in transformation. The objective is to develop a first take on the complete version of the architecture roadmap as based on the combined gap analyses from Phases B, C, and D, and to determine whether to use an incremental approach involving transition architectures. Here are the steps:

1. Identify key change attributes and any constraints.

2. Consolidate gap analyses.

3. Review requirements.

4. Confirm readiness and risks involved in transformation.

5. Formulate an implementation strategy.

6. Create major work packages including any transition architectures.

7. Create the roadmap and the implementation and migration plan.

## Phase F: Migration Planning

Phase F is concerned with Migration Planning. The objective is to finalize the architecture roadmap and the implementation and migration plan. Here are the steps:

1. Develop a management approach for the implementation and migration plan.

2. Assign business value to work packages in terms of the vision and architecture iteration goals.

3. Develop a plan estimating resource requirements, timings, and how to deliver the architecture deliverables.

4. Prioritize migration projects.

5. Confirm the roadmap and architecture definition document.

6. Complete the architecture development cycle.

## Phase G: Implementation Governance

Phase G is about Implementation Governance. Its objective is to ensure conformance with the target architecture by the implementation projects and to establish governance functions for architecture change management. Here are the steps:

1. Confirm the scope of the deployment.

2. Guide the development of the solutions.

3. Perform compliance reviews.

4. Implement new and updated business and IT operations.

5. Conduct post-implementation reviews.

The outputs of Phase G include the signed contract(s) (the architecture contracts) for the implementation of the architecture and the start-up and the continuing monitoring of the implementations. These contracts are the joint agreements between development partners and sponsors on the deliverables, quality, and fitness-for-purpose of an architecture. Successful implementation of these agreements will be delivered through effective architecture governance.

## Phase H: Architecture Change Management

Phase H is the final phase of the ADM and deals with Architecture Change Management. Because enterprises and their environments are not static and must respond to changes in both the business and technological landscapes, an organization's EA must be adapted to the changing environment either by revisions to the existing architecture or through a full new iteration of the ADM. Hence, the objective of architecture change management is to ensure the architecture is maintained and to provide for any adaptations to meet changing requirements. Here are the activities in Phase H:

1. Use monitoring tools.

2. Review risk management analysis and mitigation strategies.

3. Develop change requests to meet performance targets.

4. Manage the governance process.

5. Initiate and monitor the process to implement needed changes.

Thus, this phase interacts with the governance in Phase G and may initiate a new cycle of the ADM through a revised or new architecture vision. The "ADM Guidelines and Techniques" section later in the chapter provides guidance on how Phase G and Phase H interact.

## Requirements Management

At the center of the ADM is Requirements Management, which interacts with each of the phases and continually updates requirements. The objective is to ensure that the Requirements Management process operates during all the phases of the ADM and that the requirements are available throughout the phase processes. Each architecture domain (Phases B, C, and D) generates its own detailed requirements, and there is traceability between the phases and the requirements. The outputs of Requirements Management are the updated and/or new requirements at the end of each phase, along with impact analyses or assessments identifying any phases of the ADM that are impacted by changed requirements and need to be revisited.

PART IV

# Architecture Content Framework

The Architecture Content Framework (ACF) provides a recommended set of artifacts relevant to each of the ADM phases. To make the TOGAF compatible with all other architectural frameworks discussed in this book, the views described in these other frameworks (such as the DoDAF and FEAF) can be substituted for the artifacts in the ACF.

As illustrated in Figure 22-3, the Architecture Content Framework is organized into sections that map to the parts of the ADM.

Each of the sections of the ACF can be populated by specific artifacts in the form of catalogs, matrices, and diagrams. These artifacts in turn constitute the deliverables contained in an Architecture Definition Document provided to the client for the architecture. For instance, an Architecture Definition Document is a deliverable that documents an architecture description. The Architecture Definition Document contains artifacts that are views relevant to the architecture. In this manner, a process flow diagram is a type of artifact that might be created to describe a target call handling process as a building block. This type of artifact (a process flow diagram) can likewise be used to identify other building blocks, for instance the actors involved in the process (such as a customer services representative). A deliverable is the contractually specified part of the architecture that is provided to the client.

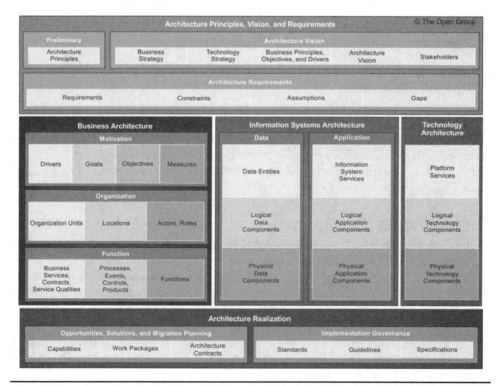

**Figure 22-3**   The Architecture Content Framework (used with permission from TOGAF)

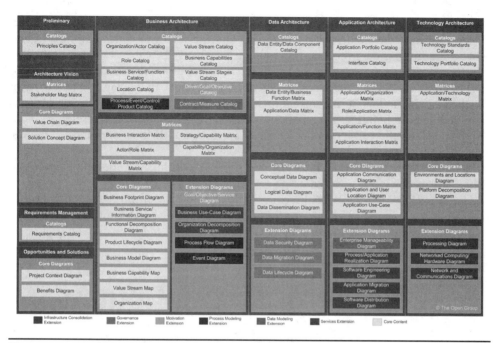

**Figure 22-4** Artifacts of the Architecture Content Framework (used with permission from TOGAF)

The full list of the artifacts suggested in TOGAF 9.2 corresponding to each of the ACF sections is shown in Figure 22-4. These lists include both core and extension artifacts for each phase.

The artifacts in Figure 22-4 are flexible, suggested, and not specifically mandated because the TOGAF is designed to be used in conjunction with other frameworks. The artifacts or views of DoDAF, MODAF, FEAF, UAF, Zachman, and other frameworks can be used instead of those in the ACF. These alternative artifacts can be mapped to the artifact types comprising the Architecture Content Metamodel, part of the ACF. The Architecture Content Metamodel has both a core and extensions. The core metamodel provides a minimum set of architectural content to support traceability across artifacts. The metamodel extensions provide additional concepts that enable focus in specific areas of specific interest.

# The Enterprise Continuum

TOGAF recommends that building blocks be stored in an architectural repository. In this way, when creating a new EA, the architect can search for reusable building blocks for any current project. If no building blocks are found, they must be created, and once developed, they are stored within the repository for future reference.

Such a repository is referred to an *enterprise continuum*, which comprises two interrelated continua: the architectural continuum and the solutions continuum. The architectural continuum describes the functions to be involved in the desired EA, and the solutions continuum comprises actual products or solutions that are either purchased (COTS) or created to satisfy the requirements. For instance, there may be a requirement specified in the architecture continuum for a database management system (DBMS) as an architecture building block (ABB), which is then actualized in the solutions continuum as a specific COTS product such as an Oracle DBMS as a solutions building block (SBB).

In Figure 22-5, both the architecture and solution continua can be read from left to right in terms of general to specific.

The arrows in Figure 22-5 represent a bidirectional relationship between categories and architectures in the enterprise continuum. The left end of each continuum addresses enterprise needs and business requirements, while the right end is focused on leveraging

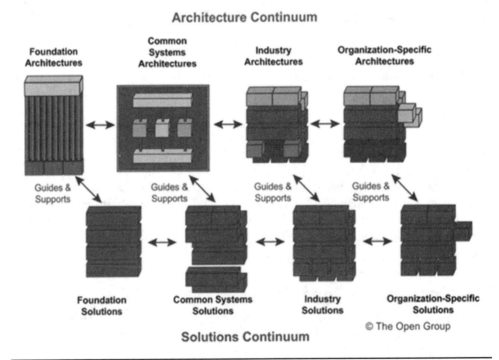

**Figure 22-5** TOGAF enterprise continuum (used with permission from TOGAF)

architectural components and building blocks. The architect searches for reusable architectural elements moving to the left of the continuum. When not found, the requirements for the missing elements are passed to the left of the continuum for incorporation.

The four architecture categories illustrated in the architecture continuum indicate the range of different types of architecture that may be developed at different points in the continuum; they are not fixed stages in a process. Many different types of architecture may occur at points between those shown in the figure.

Although the enterprise continuum does not represent a formal process, it represents a progression at several levels: logical to physical, horizontal, or IT technology focused to vertical or business focused, generalization to specialization, taxonomy to complete particular architecture specification. At each point in the continuum, the architecture is devised in terms of the design concepts and building blocks available and relevant to that point. The solutions continuum represents implementations of architectures at the corresponding parts of the architecture continuum. The solution continuum is composed of SBB that are either purchased (COTS) representing the solution to a particular enterprise's business needs. Together these two continua form an inventory of solutions that can be reused in developing an EA in the IT environment.

# TOGAF Reference Models

The reference models were once part of the architecture continuum but in TOGAF 9.2 are located in the TOGAF Library as a Series Guide. TOGAF recommends the use of two reference models: the Technical Reference Model (TRM) and the Integrated Information Infrastructure Model (III-RM, or 3 IRM). The TRM relates to the Foundation Architecture; it is a taxonomy and is represented by a graphic depicting generic platform services, illustrated by Figure 22-6. This is now located as part of the TOGAF Library, cited earlier. A Foundation Architecture is an architecture of building blocks and corresponding standards supporting all the Common Systems Architectures and, therefore, the complete operating environment. Thus, the TRM describes a fundamental architecture that forms the basis for more specific architectures.

The III-RM is related to the Common Systems Architecture and is a model for business applications and infrastructure applications in support of the TOGAF trademarked vision of Boundaryless Information Flow. III-RM is considered a subset of the TRM in terms of scope and expands parts of the TRM for business applications and infrastructure applications parts. The III-RM is a taxonomy and is represented by Figure 22-7.

There are both human and computing actors in the business environment who act as information consumers who require information, and there are both human and computing actors who have information and act as information providers. Information consumers require technology services to request information. Information providers need services to enable them to provide the information in their control in response to requests. In this manner, the III-RM distinguishes information consumer services and information provider services. In addition, there are types of information consumers

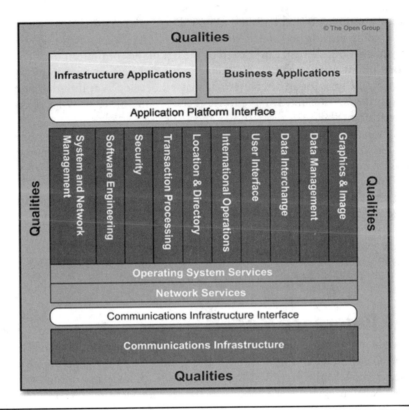

**Figure 22-6** The TOGAF Technical Reference Model (used with permission from TOGAF)

and providers that are shown as Brokering services in the reference model. Also in the business environment are development organizations, both outsourced or in-house, and management organizations. These organizations are supported by tools and utilities that support the management of the information services described in the III-RM. Because both people and information are distributed and mobile, there is a need for a directory. The directory is provided to the tools, utilities, and services through the directory services in the reference model.

In addition, the business environment must be secure, be mobile, perform to meet the business needs, and be manageable. These nonfunctional requirements are depicted by the associated qualities that the reference model must support. The III-RM model is focused on only those tools, utilities, and services that develop, manage, or provide access to integrated information. It assumes an underlying technology platform of operating systems, networks, and middleware contained in the TRM.

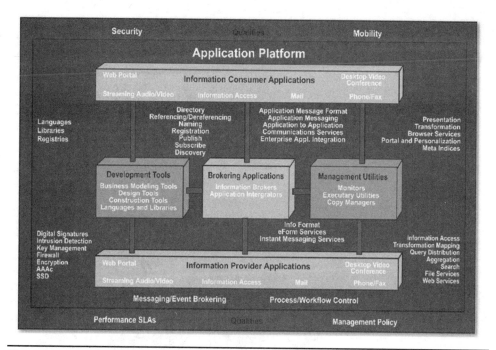

**Figure 22-7** TOGAF III-RM (used with permission from TOGAF)

# ADM Guidelines and Techniques

The Guidelines and Techniques section of the TOGAF covers both the application of the ADM as an iterative process and various tools and types of information relevant to an architecture. This section provides guidelines for adapting the ADM to such areas as security, service-oriented architecture (SOA), and other techniques for architecture development. This section of the TOGAF also provides guidelines for interacting and coordinating between related phases of the ADM.

TOGAF identifies several types of iteration for the ADM. The ADM is a process that can be used both to develop a comprehensive architecture landscape (the state of the EA at a given point in time) and to evolve an EA through multiple ADM cycles according to various initiatives related to various requests for architecture work. The ADM guidelines describe the integrated process of creating an architecture where the activities in different ADM phases interact. The ADM guidelines also describe the process of managing change to the organization's architecture capability. These iteration and integration guidelines are summarized in Figure 22-8.

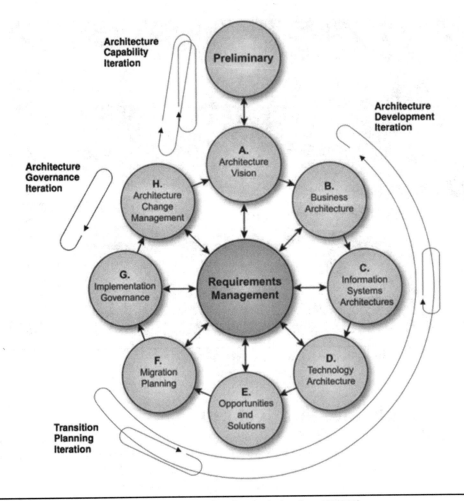

**Figure 22-8**   ADM iteration guidelines (used with permission from TOGAF)

The Architecture Capability Iteration in Figure 22-8 shows the interaction between the Preliminary Phase and Phase A (Architecture Vision) as an architecture capability is identified, planned, and supported. Figure 22-8 also shows an iteration between Phase H (Architecture Change Management) and the Preliminary Phase for a new iteration of the ADM cycle. There is an architecture development iteration linking Phases B, C, and D (dealing with each of the architecture domains) and Phases E (Opportunities and Solutions) and F (Migration Planning). Phases E and F are also involved in the Transition Planning Iteration. Phases G (Implementation Governance) and H (Architecture Change Management) together constitute the Architecture Governance Iteration.

Also in the ADM Guidelines and Techniques section is advice on how to develop and establish architecture principles, on approaches for stakeholder management, on how to identify and create architecture patterns, on establishing interoperability requirements, and on conducting risk management. This section also includes techniques on developing business scenarios (particularly in Phases A and B), conducting gap analyses (at Phases B, C, and D) and consolidated gap analysis (in Phase E), and engaging in capability based planning (discussed further in the upcoming "Architecture Capability Framework" section).

Consistent with the iteration of the ADM is the concept of how different iterations can be developed in concert with partitioning of architectures. TOGAF provides examples of types of architecture partitions to allow for cost and complexity management. These partitions divide the enterprise into sections that can be worked on in parallel by different teams and still result in a fully integrated architecture. These types of architecture partitions are illustrated in Figure 22-9.

The top level in Figure 22-9 shows a strategic architecture that reflects the corporate capability. The strategic architecture offers a foundation for operational and change activity targeted especially for an executive-level audience. The lower levels of the architecture can then be developed in different segments. This partitioning of architecture provides for better management of portions of an EA that in the end can be combined into the full architecture. Different project teams can develop these segments and align themselves under the direction of a chief architect as part of implementation governance. The segment architecture approach provides a foundation for operational and change

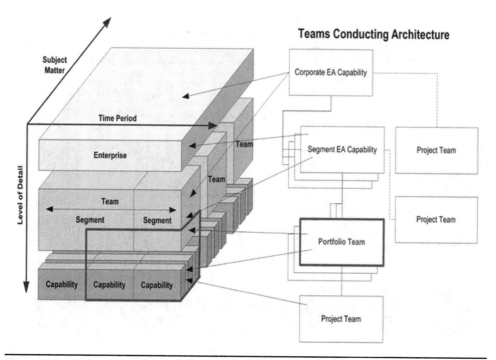

**Figure 22-9** Types of architecture partitioning (used with permission from TOGAF)

activity while giving direction for architecture roadmaps at the program and portfolio levels. The capability architecture provides an organizing mechanism and roadmap for managing different capability increments that exist within and between segments. The assignment of teams and their relationships are normally established during the Preliminary phase of the ADM.

# Architecture Capability Framework

The Architecture Capability Framework is a set of reference materials for establishing an architecture function for the enterprise. The framework is used at each phase of the ADM to assess what architecture capability is required for each of the four architecture domains (business, data, application, and technology). The Architecture Capability Framework provides guidance in establishing an architecture practice in terms of architecture capabilities. Examples of such capabilities include financial management, performance management, service management, risk management, resource management, communications and stakeholder management, quality management, supplier management, configuration management, and environment management.

The framework includes what is necessary for the assessment, planning, and implementation of an enterprise architecture capability, including the resources and training required for those involved in conducting the various processes involved. The content of the Architecture Capability Framework is illustrated in Figure 22-10.

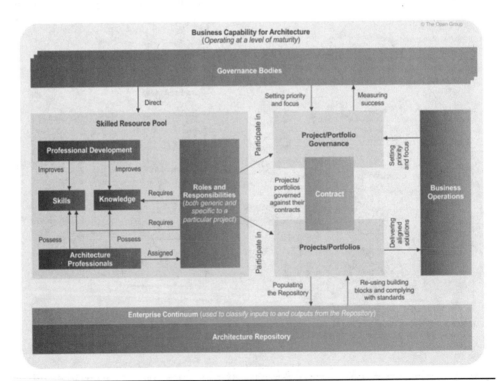

**Figure 22-10**   The Architecture Capability Framework (used with permission from TOGAF)

Figure 22-10 shows how to establish an architecture capability, including the following:

- Creating the governance process with an architecture board
- Providing approaches and metrics to insure compliance
- Providing structure for architecture contracts
- Assessing the readiness and status of the architecture in the enterprise using maturity models (based on the CMMI)
- Providing a skills framework for implementation and training for those involved

## Summary

We summarize the characteristics of TOGAF in terms of the architecture concepts introduced in Chapter 1.

TOGAF is an enterprise architecture framework that provides viewpoints (business, data, application, and technology) and views (in the Architecture Content Framework). However, the views themselves may be "borrowed" from other frameworks such as the DoDAF, as long as the view contents can be mapped to the Architecture Content Metamodel. TOGAF is process or methodology based and has at its heart its multiphase Architecture Development Method (ADM). The ADM provides processes for architecture planning and development, including migration planning, as well as for governance, change management, and requirements management.

TOGAF provides guidance on partitioning architectures to allow for cost and complexity management. TOGAF allows for Enterprise, Segment, and Solution Level architectures and provides support for reusable solution building blocks as well as reusable architecture building blocks. TOGAF recommends the use of two coordinated reference models: the TRM and the III-RM. These reference models are integrated into TOGAF's repository for reusable building blocks. The TRM provides a taxonomy of generic platform services describing a complete operating environment. The III-RM is a subset of the TRM in terms of scope and expands parts of the TRM for business applications and infrastructure applications parts. TOGAF also provides guidance on how to identify and create architecture patterns.

In addition to these common concepts, TOGAF provides additional concepts, materials, and guidance. Included are techniques and guidance to support the processes in the ADM; a repository approach for organizing, searching, and managing the reusable building blocks (the Enterprise Continuum); and a set of reference materials, including advice and guidelines, for establishing an architecture function for the enterprise (the Architecture Capability Framework).

## Questions

1. Beginning with the Preliminary phase through Phase H, what are outputs for each phase?

2. What is the relationship of Requirements Management to each of the phases?

3. What is the structure of the enterprise continuum? What is the relationship between the architecture continuum and the solutions continuum?

4. Where are the TRM and IIIRM references models located, and how do they relate to each other?

5. What are the distinctions between a deliverable, artifact, and a building block? Provide an example of a deliverable and its constituent building blocks and deliverables.

6. How is the Architecture Content Metamodel organized and what types of artifacts are recommended?

7. Name five sources from which you can obtain data within your enterprise for each of the architecture domains (business, data, applications, and technology).

8. Under what conditions through Phase H would a governance body in concert with the architecture team recommend a modification to an existing ADM versus a new iteration of the ADM cycle?

9. What is architecture partitioning? Describe what types of partitions are relevant to your enterprise.

10. What is meant by architecture iteration? Describe how projects exercise iteration through the entire ADM cycle, and provide an example of how this would work in your enterprise.

# References

The Open Group. 2018a. *TOGAF 9.2 Standard, Version 9.2: A Pocket Guide*, Revised Educational Edition. The Netherlands: Van Haren Publishing.

The Open Group. 2018b. *TOGAF 9.2 Standard, Version 9.2: Foundation and Certified (Level 1 & 2)*. The Netherlands: Van Haren Publishing.

# Common Approach and FEAF2

While the U.S. Department of Defense started its EA efforts because of interoperability and architecture comparability issues, the EA guidance for federal agencies as a whole is driven by reporting requirements from the Office of Management and Budget (OMB). The OMB is responsible for oversight and management of the budget, approval of capital investments and expenditures, and other duties to ensure that government monies are spent responsibly and effectively. (The federal guidance applies only to DoD at the highest level. Thus, DoD has its own internal architecture requirements for the military services, defense, and intelligence agencies.) The focus of this chapter is on the most recent guidance for federal agencies contained in two documents:

- "The Common Approach to Federal Enterprise Architecture" (May 12, 2012)
- The "Federal Enterprise Architecture Framework, Version 2" (January 29, 2013)

These two documents contain overlapping sets of guidance, with the FEAF Version 2 document providing more detailed guidance on the methodology and use of the consolidated reference models. We will refer to the combined guidance in these two documents as FEAF2. Figure 23-1 summarizes the contents of these two documents.

The material from these two documents is presented in the same order as the framework concepts in Chapter 1, with additional summary material at the end of this chapter.

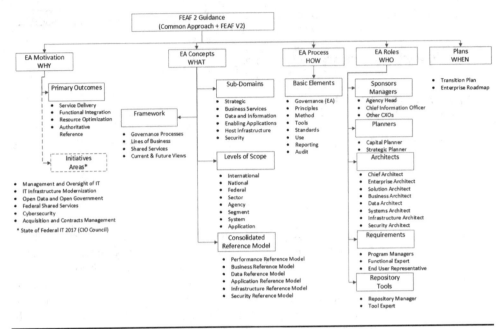

**Figure 23-1** Combined contents of the Common Approach and FEAF2 documents

# Background

The focus of enterprise architecture at the federal level is on the executive branch of the government. The executive branch is the part of the government that is responsible for day-to-day operational delivery of services to the citizen. The cabinet departments are divided functionally into divisions that have different but complementary missions. Cabinet departments are large organizational units (such as the Department of Defense) that have several smaller enterprises under their umbrella.

The diversity of the federal government is high. There are more than 300 organizational entities of differing size, scope, and complexity, which include departments, administrations, bureaus, commissions, agencies, and boards. These entities collectively employ more than 2.6 million people and spend more than $3.4 trillion each year to perform their mission functions. More than $80 billion of annual federal spending is devoted to various forms of information technology. Each of these diverse agencies is focused on its own missions that flow from the U.S. Constitution and public laws. Their budgets are rolled up and managed by the Executive Office of the President of the United States.

The origins of enterprise architecting in the federal government stemmed from rapidly increasing information technology (IT) expenses without a corresponding ability to determine whether these increasing costs were in line with agency missions and functions and a corresponding inability of OMB to determine effectiveness of IT investments. The Clinger-Cohen Act of 1996 (also called the Information Technology Management

Reforms Act, ITMRA) first established the EA as mechanism for assessing this alignment of IT-to-agency mission/functions. Clinger-Cohen established the "three pesky questions" for determining whether additional IT was required:

- Should the agency perform the function?
- Should the function be performed by the private sector or another agency?
- Should the business process be redesigned to improve efficiency (before adding additional IT support)?

Clearly, before an agency spends money on IT, the first question needs to be answered "Yes" and the second two questions should be answered "No."

Clinger-Cohen also requires that every agency has a position for the chief information officer (CIO), who is responsible for reporting on the IT spending aligned by the EA. This law was implemented through OMB Circular A-130, "Managing Information as a Strategic Resource." The EA information was also key in developing an agency's budget request as required by OMB Circular A-11. While the specific requirements have evolved over time, the agency's EA has continued to be a key element in reporting to OMB and in submitting budget requests.

To guide agencies in developing enterprise architectures in a consistent manner, the Federal CIO Council developed the Federal Enterprise Architecture Framework (FEAF) in 1999. The FEAF was a concept document based on some of the earliest EA work, techniques, and approaches developed by Spewak (1995) and Zachman (1992). A few years later, OMB developed the Federal Enterprise Architecture (FEA) that consisted of the initial set of reference models. The FEAF and the reference models have evolved into the Common Approach and the FEAF2.

# Levels of Scope (Levels of Enterprise)

The Common Approach describes eight levels of scope for architectures. These levels of scope are designed to improve architecture consistency and standardize the various degrees of complexity used by agencies across the federal enterprise. In the Common Approach, the goal is to use architectures to enable shared services in a collaborative approach. The architecture representations identify the consumer and producer of services; represent common requirements; and define agreements for enablement, sharing, exchange of resources, and service level agreements for multiple stakeholders. Architecture becomes most important when more than one consumer of a shared service is involved, be it another agency, another nation, another mission partner, or another mission support organization. The Common Approach is geared toward enabling shared services that are documented by architectures.

Figure 23-2 depicts a view of the executive branch of the government through sub enterprises that can be modeled to address different types of concerns. The Office of Management and Budget deals with functional areas such as budget, policy, management and governance, and guidance for the executive branch agencies. Cross-agency enterprises that represent overlap among multiple organizations coordinate and provide collaboration among multiple agencies at the national level, at the federal level, at the

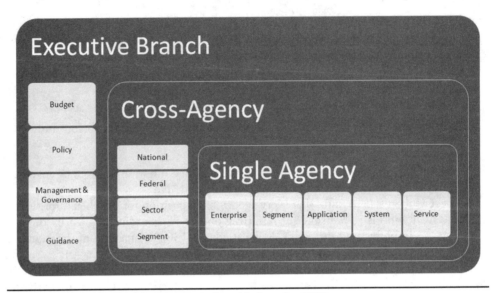

**Figure 23-2**   Levels of architecture scope (graphic from the OMB)

sector level, and at the functional segment level. Within a single agency, the entire agency can be represented architecturally as a single enterprise, or as multiple enterprises at the functional segment level, or as specific application, system, or service solutions at the program/project level.

Figure 23-3 depicts the distinction between the various levels of architecture scope.

| Architectural Level | Scope | Mission Impact | Planning Detail | Audience |
|---|---|---|---|---|
| International | U.S. & Other Governments | Global Outcomes | Low | All Stakeholders |
| National | U.S. - Wide | National Outcomes | Low | All Stakeholders |
| Federal | Executive Branch | Government Outcomes | | |
| Sector | Multiple Agencies | Mission Outcomes | Medium | Business Owners |
| Agency | One Agency Organization | Mission Outcomes | Medium | Business Owners |
| Segment | One or More Business Units | Business Outcomes | | |
| System | One or More Systems | Functionality | High | Users and Developers |
| Application | One or More Applications | Functionality | High | Users and Developers |

**Figure 23-3**   Levels of architecture scope and impact (graphic from the OMB)

The various levels of architecture scope are described here:

- **International** Architectures whose scopes include international partnerships of the federal government with other governments, global industry, nonprofits, and other groups. These architectures often center on how shared services enable collaboration and how these shared services are governed by *agreements that cross national boundaries.*

- **National** Architectures that include all federal, state, tribal, and local government agencies within the United States and its territories. These architectures center on national needs for *coordination of nationwide capabilities* that are performed in the national interest and that cut across any individual agency. Examples of such capabilities are first responder coordination, disaster notification, and telecommunications and transportation infrastructure.

- **Federal** Architectures that focus on services and systems that *serve the entire executive branch* of the federal government. These cut across individual agency boundaries and provide common services and support for federal-wide "lines of business" (or LOB, as defined in the business reference model, or BRM, discussed later in the chapter). OMB channels mission and mission support services through designated LOB providers. These architectures are used to define the roles of consumers and providers of common services and represent the requirements for such LOB services.

- **Sector** Architectures that focus on systems and services *within one particular mission sector* of the executive branch of the federal government. The architectures may cut across multiple agencies but they are focused on a single mission sector. An example of such a mission sector is International Trade.

- **Agency** Architectures that represent an *overview of an entire department/agency* and provide consistent, decomposable views of all subagencies/bureaus, business units, programs, systems, networks, and mission and mission support services. The architectures at the agency level of scope are broad and are intended to provide information for support of planning and decision-making as prioritized in the context of the agency's strategic and operating plans. Additional detail is assembled by providing drill-down capabilities from the agency architecture to various segment, system, and application architectures.

- **Segment** Architectures that focus on a particular *service area of a business unit* within an agency. If used to represent services between agencies, it is used to represent a limited scope that is not federal-, sector-, or agency-wide in nature.

- **System** Architectures that represent *one particular IT system* that supports the delivery of one or more services within or between segments and agencies. These architectures are used to document all aspects of the systems functionality and configuration including strategic drivers, business requirements, applicable standards, workflow processes, information exchanges, software applications, host infrastructure, remote access, and security/privacy controls.

PART IV

- **Application**   Architectures that represent the structure and behavior of *software applications* that are part of one or more system(s)/service(s) in one or more organizations.

# Subarchitecture Domains (Viewpoints)

The FEAF2 has six subarchitecture domains that reflect the different issues and concerns from different stakeholders. There are overlaps across subarchitecture domains and there are also relationships that connect the elements of the subarchitecture domains. Figure 23-4 illustrates the six subarchitecture domains.

## Subarchitecture Domain Artifacts (Views)

Each subarchitecture domain organizes a set of artifacts. In the discussion that follows, the name of each artifact is preceded by a shorthand identifier consisting of a subarchitecture domain identifying letter and the number of the artifact. This shorthand artifact identifier is similar in style to the view identifiers used in DoDAF. Where applicable, DoDAF views that are similar to the FEAF2 artifacts are referenced. The DoDAF viewpoints that align with the subarchitecture domains are also provided. The asterisk indicates that the artifact is a core requirement for representing the subarchitecture domain.

### Strategy Artifacts

For any scope of enterprise, the Strategy subarchitecture domain identifies the mission, vision, and goals of the enterprise being documented. Strategic drivers are also identified and initiatives are mapped to strategic goals. The Strategy domain corresponds to the

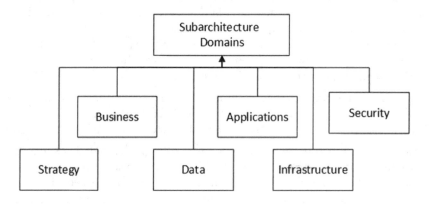

**Figure 23-4**   Subarchitecture domains

DoDAF Capability and Project Viewpoints, where Capability Viewpoint goals are replaced by capability requirements and the relationship of a capability need to an implementing project becomes the relationship of a strategic initiative to a strategic goal. The core (marked with an asterisk) and optional artifacts that support the domain are listed here:

- S-1: Concept Overview Diagram*
- S-2: Strategic Plan
- S-3: Concept of Operations Scenarios (CONOPS)
- S-4: Strengths, Weakness, Opportunities, Threats (SWOT) Analysis
- S-5: Performance Measures Scorecard

The performance reference model (PRM) from the FEAF2 reference models provides a taxonomy of performance measures. The S-5: Performance Measures Scorecard provides indicators for performance measures using techniques such as the balanced score card (BSC).

## Business Artifacts

The Business subarchitecture domain represents elements of the operating model for the enterprise. Elements include the key business units or organizational players, key locations, key business processes, and the mission and support services used within a business unit and between business units. The Business domain corresponds to the Operational Viewpoint in the DoDAF. The core (marked with asterisk) and optional artifacts that support the domain are

- B-1: Business Process Diagram* (similar to DoDAF OV-5a/b)
- B-2: Business Operating Plan
- B-3: Business Service Catalog (compare to a combination of DoDAF SvcV-1, SvcV-4, and SvcV-8 elements)
- B-4: Organization Chart (similar to DoDAF OV-4)
- B-5: Use Case Narrative and Diagram (similar to DoDAF OV-6c)
- B-6: Business Case/Alternatives Analysis

## Data Artifacts

The Data subarchitecture domain addresses the issues and concerns with the representation of data and information (logical and physical data models), flows of data and information between services and systems and organizations (data flow diagrams, event sequence diagrams), standardized meanings of data and information (data dictionary), reusable application data structures (object library), promotion of data quality improvements, and knowledge management (beyond data, information). The Data domain contains all the same views as the Data and Information Viewpoint in the DoDAF but also overlaps some of the views for Operational, Systems, and Services Viewpoints such as the flow models and the event trace models. The core (marked with asterisk) and optional artifacts that support the domain are

- D-1: Logical Data Model* (similar to DoDAF DIV-2)
- D-2: Knowledge Management Plan
- D-3: Data Quality Plan
- D-4: Data Flow Diagram (similar to DoDAF SV-4 or SvcV-4)
- D-5: Physical Data Model (similar to DoDAF DIV-3)
- D-6: CRUD Matrix
- D-7: State-Transition Diagram (similar to DoDAF OV-6b, SV-10b, and SvcV-10b)
- D-8: Event Sequence Diagram (similar to DoDAF OV-6c, SV-10c, and SvcV-10c)
- D-9: Data Dictionary
- D-10: Object Library

## Applications Artifacts

The Applications subarchitecture domain reflects the interests and concerns related to software applications. It helps answer questions such as these:

- Which systems and applications will be needed to generate, share, and store the data, information, and knowledge that the business services need?
- How can multiple types of IT systems, services, applications, databases, and web sites be made to work together where needed?

Some of the artifacts that are developed to support this domain describe how applications interface, how applications communicate through networks and communications links, what data is exchanged between applications, what services are invoked by applications, what performance parameters characterize the execution of an application, how services communicate through an enterprise service bus, and how the applications inventory is cataloged. The Application subarchitecture domain is similar to the combination of the Systems and Services Viewpoints of the DoDAF and reflects the same types of issues and concerns. Here are the core (marked with asterisk) and optional artifacts that support the domain:

- A-1: Application Interface Diagram* (similar to DoDAF SvcV-1, SV-1)
- A-2: Application Communication Diagram (similar to DoDAF SV-2, SvcV-2)
- A-3: Application Interface Matrix (similar to DoDAF SV-3)
- A-4: Application Data Exchange Matrix (similar to DoDAF SV-6 or SvcV-6)
- A-5: Application Service Matrix (similar to DoDAF SvcV-3)
- A-6: Application Performance Matrix (similar to DoDAF SV-7)
- A-7: System/Application Evolution Diagram (similar to DoDAF SvcV-8 or SV-8)
- A-8: Enterprise Service Bus Diagram

- A-9: Application Maintenance Procedure
- A-10: Application Inventory
- A-11: Software License Inventory

## Infrastructure Artifacts

The Infrastructure subarchitecture domain is concerned with the network and processing infrastructure needed to support voice, data, and video transmission and processing across the enterprise. The infrastructure also includes servers and other hosting elements. As enterprises start to move their processing nodes to the cloud, the cloud architecture, cloud providers, and the concerns related to availability, sustainability, single points of failure, and sourcing become important in addition to the classic concerns about reachability (does a connection exist), performance (speed of transfer, latency), and standards (protocols and stacks). The Infrastructure subdomain overlaps the DoDAF Systems, Services, and Standards Viewpoints. Here are the core (marked with asterisk) and optional artifacts that support the domain:

- I-1: Network Diagram* (similar to DoDAF SV-2 which has a system-centric approach, not an infrastructure-centric approach)
- I-2: Hosting Concept of Operations
- I-3: Technical Standards Profile (similar to DoDAF StdV-1)
- I-4: Technology Forecast (similar to DoDAF StdV-2)
- I-5: Cable Plant Diagram
- I-6: Wireless Connectivity Diagram
- I-7: Rack Elevation Diagrams (front and back)
- I-8: Data Center/Server Room Diagram
- I-9: Wiring Closet Diagram
- I-10: Point of Presence Diagram
- I-11: Asset Inventory
- I-12: Facility Blueprints

## Security Artifacts

The Security subarchitecture domain addresses concerns of security: how to counter threats from bad actors inside and outside the enterprise and how to prevent or mitigate vulnerabilities in business processes and activities, applications and services, infrastructure networks, and processing nodes. Here are the core (marked with asterisk) and optional artifacts that support the domain:

- SP-1: Security Controls Catalog* (combination of DoDAF OV-6a, SvcV-6a, and SV-6a)
- SP-2: Security and Privacy Plan
- SP-3: Certification & Accreditation Documentation

- SP-4: Continuous Monitoring Procedures (can use DoDAF OV-5a/b to document)
- SP-5: Disaster Recovery Plan
- SP-6: Continuity of Operations Plan

# Reference Models

In earlier federal approaches, standard taxonomies, called reference models, were developed from the vantage point of the entire federal government. From that vantage point, it was possible for OMB to request submissions of individual agency elements as categorized by the standard taxonomies. The taxonomies were deemed part of the Federal Enterprise Architecture (and not the Framework) as they instantiated classes of architecture elements into categories of more restrictive classes. For example, specific LOBs were enumerated in a standard manner for use across all agencies in the BRM. Each agency then identified its own responsibility for one or more LOBs against the standard taxonomy. Standardizing categories served to align reporting to OMB in a way that OMB could aggregate or compare items under the same category to make investment decisions and tradeoff analyses against competing demands for money.

In the FEAF2, the Framework and the Federal Enterprise Architecture are now under the same roof. The FEAF2 continues the approach of defining standard taxonomies of architecture categories. The consolidated reference model is the collection of six reference models that are described in the FEAF2 as standard taxonomies for the FEA. Figure 23-5 shows the consolidated reference model.

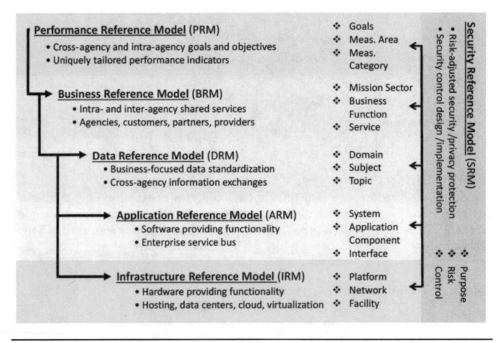

**Figure 23-5** FEAF2 consolidated reference model (graphic from the OMB)

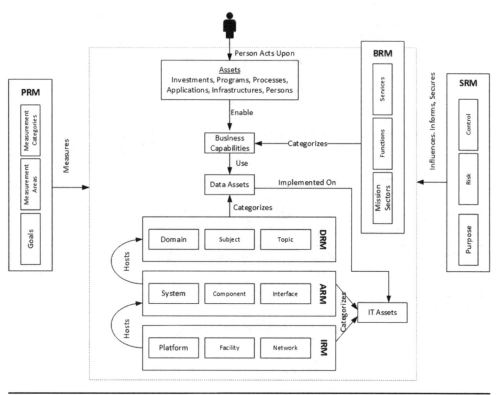

**Figure 23-6** FEA V2 reference model relationship diagram (graphic from the OMB)

The reference models are not isolated from one another. They are used to categorize various data and IT assets using a common classification scheme and align these in terms of the business capabilities across the Federal enterprise. Figure 23-6 shows the relationships between the reference model classification schemes and the assets they categorize.

## Performance Reference Model (PRM)

The PRM defines standard terms and approach for reporting performance measures for an enterprise throughout the executive branch. The taxonomy is hierarchical (Figure 23-7) and is progressively broken down from measurement area, at the broadest, to category, grouping, and indicator in a progressively narrowing manner. The reference model does not contain specific performance measures, but discusses only types of performance measures. One of the primary concerns addressed by the PRM is a standardization of measures needed to assess performance. An important concept for government efficiency is the *line of sight*—the tracing of explicit performance relationships from agency *inputs*, to the *outputs* they produce, to the *outcomes* they lead to (Figure 23-8). Agencies are measured on outcomes for the purposes for which they were established.

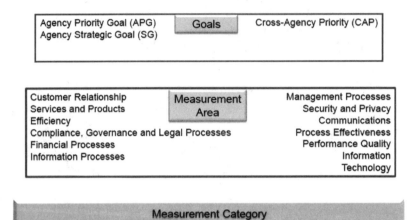

**Figure 23-7**   Performance reference model taxonomy structures (graphic from the OMB)

**Figure 23-8**
Line-of-sight
diagram (graphic
from the OMB)

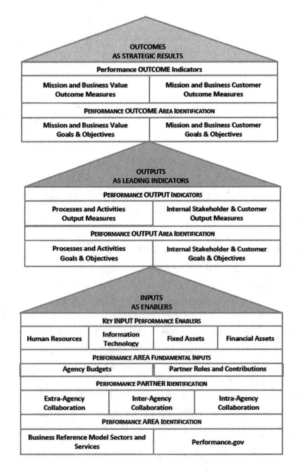

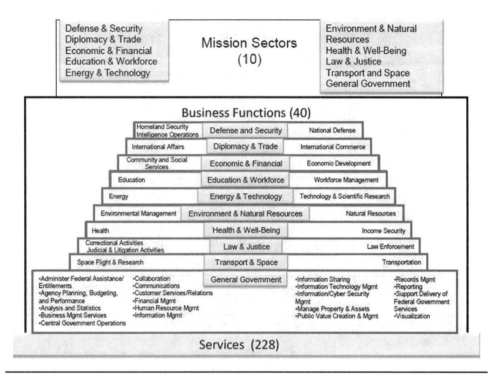

**Figure 23-9** BRM taxonomy structures (graphic from the OMB)

Enterprises can then select the appropriate hierarchical path in the PRM to report the actual value or goals of those performance measurements. The terminology is consistent with the requirements of the Government Performance and Results Modernization Act of 2010 (GPRA). The PRM is an essential tool for agency performance reporting and contributions to federal scorecards, dashboards, assessments, and evaluations of health and improvements.

## Business Reference Model

The BRM is a taxonomy designed to standardize the labeling of business reporting across the executive branch (Figure 23-9). The BRM provides a functional view through taxonomy groupings such as lines of business, business functions, and business services. The BRM is an essential tool for identifying commonality of need, opportunities for identifying and building shared services, and seeking leveraging of common activities and services to reduce government cost.

## Data Reference Model (DRM)

The purpose of the DRM (Figure 23-10) is to provide a taxonomy of information categories that answer two core questions: What information is available for sharing and reuse across agencies and within an agency? What are the information gaps that need to be filled or corrected? The DRM provides a standard method to describe, categorize,

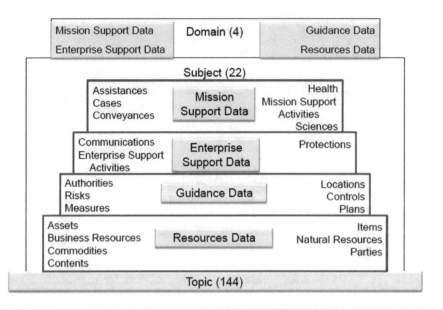

**Figure 23-10** DRM taxonomy structures (graphic from the OMB)

and share data. Data description provides a way to describe data uniformly to convey meaning. Data context facilitates discovery of data through searching authoritative data sources that are registered according to a taxonomy. Data sharing supports the access and exchange of data where access consists of ad hoc requests and exchange consist of fixed, recurring transactions between parties. The DRM is essential to the construction of a shared data enterprise that has few silos, tremendous transparency, and availability of meaningful data through authoritative sources using standard means of access.

## Application Reference Model (ARM)

The ARM supports analysis and reporting of service and application architectures (Figure 23-11). The component-driven taxonomy of the ARM standardizes the systems and application-related standards and technologies that support and enable the delivery of service components and capabilities. The purpose of the ARM is to leverage a common standardized vocabulary to enable interagency discovery, collaboration, and interoperability of applications. The ARM is essential for leveraging licenses of standard components, collapsing the varieties of standards across the federal enterprise, and leveraging purchasing and maintenance capabilities. In the future, the ARM will be used as a governance tool to prevent needless proliferation of variety.

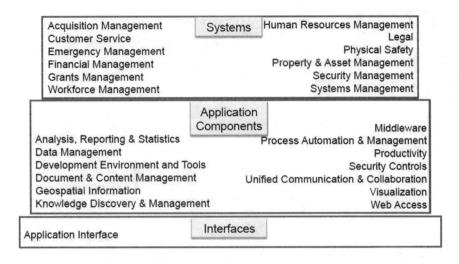

**Figure 23-11** ARM taxonomy structures (graphic from the OMB)

## Infrastructure Reference Model (IRM)

The IRM (Figure 23-12) is a component-driven taxonomy that categorizes the network- or cloud-related standards and technologies to support and enable the delivery of voice, data, video, and mobile service components, and technical capabilities. The IRM also unifies existing agency infrastructure portfolios and guidance on standard desktop configurations by providing a foundation to advance the reuse and standardization of technology and service components from a federal government perspective.

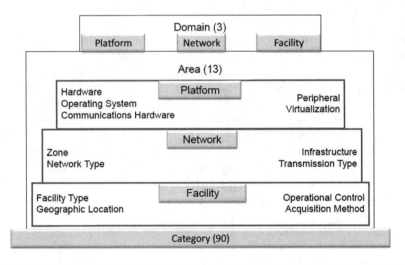

**Figure 23-12** IRM taxonomy structures (graphic from the OMB)

**Figure 23-13**
SRM taxonomy
structures
(graphic from
the OMB)

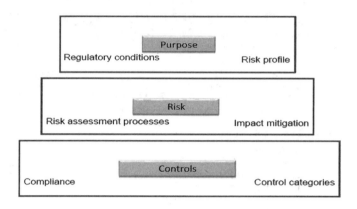

## Security Reference Model (SRM)

The SRM provides a common language for discussing security and privacy in the context of federal agencies' business and performance goals (Figure 23-13). The SRM provides a taxonomy for the itemization of security controls in an architecture and the overall EA, as well as a scalable, repeatable and risk-based methodology for addressing information security and privacy requirements within and across systems, segments, agencies, and sectors. The SRM is an essential tool for planning security of new systems as well as for reporting and mitigating vulnerabilities in existing services, systems, and applications at the architecture level.

# Enterprise Roadmap

In addition to specific views, the FEAF2 provides guidance on an enterprise roadmap and the information, including current (as-is) and future (to-be) architectures, that should be contained in it. In the FEAF2, there is one enterprise roadmap for the overall enterprise and one transition plan/two views for each architecture project.

Figure 23-14 shows how the current (as-is) architecture of the enterprise is transformed to the target or future (to-be) state through a set of initiatives. These initiatives are time-bound, clearly specified in terms of expected outputs, and have associated work breakdown schedules and funding. In addition, an initiative should have contract support if it is to be contracted out of the enterprise. If these initiatives have dependencies, then architecture analysis is necessary, using information from the Strategy subarchitecture domain (or the DoDAF Capability and Project Viewpoints) to validate that key outputs are available in a timely manner for dependent or consuming initiatives from producing initiatives. The views of the current architecture as well as the future architecture must be described in terms of architecture elements from all six subarchitecture domains.

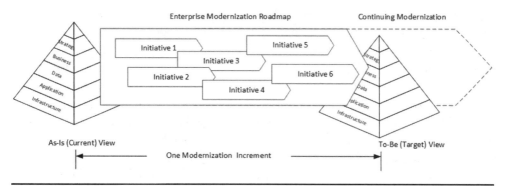

**Figure 23-14** Enterprise transformation

These architectures contain artifacts selected from the subdomains based on the questions posed during planning, risk assessment, costing, and requirements preparation for the proposals related to acquiring the initiatives. The collection of initiatives forms the stated implementation of the enterprise's stated strategy.

The enterprise roadmap provides the line of sight from the organization's strategic goals to the business services, which in turn relate to technology solutions across all of an agency's LOB. The roadmap is a structured, living document that is updated periodically. The roadmap has multiple sections that describe the overall EA with a summary of the current and future architecture and identify performance gaps, resource requirements, planned solutions, and transition plans. The roadmap also describes the EA governance process, the implementation methodology, and the documentation framework.

The roadmap is archived in the online EA repository to support easy access to information and to promote the linkage of EA to other management and technology processes. Each agency is required to submit its enterprise roadmap to OMB annually for use as an authoritative reference for IT portfolio reviews and program level analysis and planning.

## Roles and Responsibilities

An important part of the roadmap documents the roles and responsibilities of the various stakeholders. The following is a list of potential stakeholders and their typical roles and responsibilities:

- **Agency head**   The executive sponsor for the EA program, who champions the EA program both as a valuable methodology and as an authoritative reference. The agency head approves resources for the EA program and assists in resolving high-level architecture issues and conflicts.

- **Chief information officer (CIO)**   Provides executive leadership and decision-making. The CIO works with the agency head, CXOs, business unit managers, and program managers to gain and maintain support for the EA program. The CIO provides guidance and resources to the chief architect, leads resolution of high-level EA issues, and integrates EA into other areas of business and technology governance.

PART IV

- **Other CXOs** Provide executive support, participate in EA program governance, and promote the EA as an authoritative reference. They use EA information and products in planning/decision-making.

- **Chief architect** Manages the EA program, identifies methods and standards, coordinates architecture projects, and leads the configuration management process.

- **Enterprise architect** Responsible for architecture integration. In coordination with the chief architect, each enterprise architect works with executive managers and staff to identify requirements and solutions in all domains and levels of scope.

- **Solution architect** Performs problem-solving in coordination with the chief architect and/or an enterprise architect. Solution architects do architecture analysis and documentation and work collaboratively with stakeholders to identify solutions for business and technology requirements.

- **Strategic planner** Provides direction and prioritization. In coordination with agency leadership and other stakeholders, including the chief architect, strategic planners work to update strategic plans, prioritize goals, and identify linkages to program activities.

- **Business architect** Performs business process analysis, design, and documentation. In coordination with the chief architect and other architects, business architects work collaboratively with stakeholders to create, improve, or reengineer business processes and identify enabling IT.

- **Data architect** Performs data analysis, design, and documentation. In coordination with the chief architect and other architects, data architects work collaboratively with stakeholders to provide technical analysis and design for data-level solution architecture projects and data-related business and technology requirements. Data architects ensure that data solutions meet integration, interoperability, and privacy requirements.

- **Systems architect** Performs systems analysis, design, and documentation. In coordination with the chief architect and other architects, system architects work collaboratively with stakeholders to provide technical analysis and design support for systems-level architecture projects. System architects ensure that IT systems meet integration and interoperability requirements.

- **Infrastructure architect** Performs network analysis, design, and documentation. In coordination with the chief architect and other architects, infrastructure architects work collaboratively with stakeholders to provide technical analysis and design support for infrastructure-level architecture projects. Infrastructure architects ensure that IT network and data center hosting solutions meet integration and interoperability requirements.

- **Security architect** Performs security and privacy analysis, design, and documentation. In coordination with the chief architect and other architects, security architects work collaboratively with stakeholders to provide technical analysis and design for security-related architecture projects and security or privacy-related business and technology requirements. Security architects ensure that security and privacy solutions support risk mitigation plans.

- **Line of business managers**   Identify business requirements. Line of business managers support the EA program and ensure that program managers participate in architecture projects by identifying business and IT requirements for program activities.

- **Program managers**   Identify program requirements. Program managers participate in architecture projects and configuration management activities and identify business and IT requirements for program activities.

- **Capital planner**   Performs investment analysis. Capital planners use EA information to support the development of alternatives analysis and to make investment decisions.

- **Functional experts**   Provide subject matter expertise. Functional experts participate in architecture projects to provide subject matter expertise in a functional requirement area.

- **End-user representatives**   Identify requirements. These representatives participate in architecture projects. They identify business and IT requirements for systems/applications.

- **Tool experts**   Provide EA documentation support and maintenance of EA tools. Tool experts support architecture projects and the EA repository.

- **Repository manager**   Provides EA repository support through maintenance of the EA web site and repository, associated EA content, and links to other web sites as needed.

Remember that these represent roles and not actual people. In a smaller organization, these roles may be assigned to a few employees. In larger enterprises, they may well be individuals, and the EA program may become quite large with increases in the needs for communications, teamwork, and coordination of deliverables across a large staff that does not have line reporting responsibilities.

## Repositories and Metamodels

The FEAF2 requires an EA repository—preferably an online, web-based repository such as that recommended for the enterprise roadmap. There is more about support and responsibilities for the EA repository mentioned in the FEAF2 overview and the EA program office material discussed in the following section.

Unlike the DoDAF or TOGAF, the FEAF2 does not provide an overall metamodel or ontology for its architecture concepts and elements.

## Methodology/Process

The Common Approach recommends a common methodology called the Collaborative Planning Methodology (CPM). The CPM is intended as a full planning and implementation life cycle that includes EA as one of the involved planning disciplines. This methodology represents "a simple repeatable process that consists of integrated, multi-disciplinary analysis that results in recommendations formed in collaboration with leaders, stakeholders, planners and implementers" [POTUS 2012] and is part of the FEAF2 basic elements of a EA program office.

The CPM consists of two major phases: Organize and Plan, and Implement and Measure, as illustrated in Figure 23-15. Though the figure shows the phases as if they were sequential, in reality there are frequent and important iterations within and between the phases.

In the Organize and Plan phase, the role of the architect is to facilitate collaboration between leadership and various stakeholders to clearly identify and prioritize needs, research other organizations facing similar needs, and formulate a set of integrated plans that define an enterprise roadmap (including architectures) that will address the needs through changes that are planned in an orchestrated manner.

In the Implement and Measure phase, the architect's role is participatory, supporting other key personnel working to implement and monitor the change-related activities. The architect also facilitates interpretation of the plans and needs identified in the Organize and Plan phase. As part of the second phase, the architect supports investment, procurement, implementation, and performance measurement actions and decisions.

The CPM is stakeholder-centered in that the leadership and key stakeholders drive the needs with the architect as a facilitator and provider of leverage through knowledge of other efforts within the enterprise and outside the enterprise. Ultimately, the CPM helps planners work with leadership and stakeholders to clearly articulate a roadmap that defines needs, what will be done to address those needs, when actions will be taken, how much it will cost, what benefits will be achieved, when those benefits will be achieved, and how those benefits will be measured.

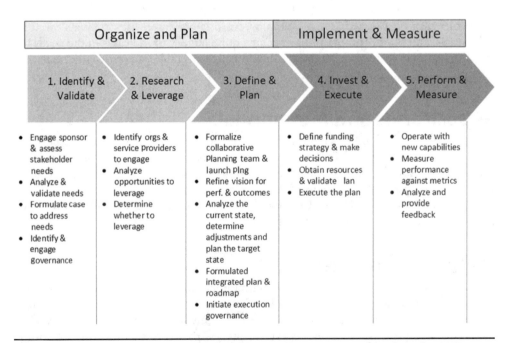

**Figure 23-15** Collaborative Planning Methodology (CPM) overview (graphic from the OMB)

# Overview of the Common Approach

The overall concept of the Common Approach is illustrated in Figure 23-16. The document refers to this figure as the "metamodel" although this terminology is not the same as that we are using in our discussions of EA frameworks.

## Primary Outcomes

The outside ring of Figure 23-16 identifies the primary outcomes for the Common Approach: Service Delivery, Functional Integration, Resource Optimization, and Authoritative Reference, as well as the levels of scope that were discussed previously. The primary outcome concepts are defined as follows:

- **Service Delivery**  The ability to deliver agency mission-related services that are mandated by law and enabled by shared IT services and related, embedded information technologies. By developing architectures that are constructed according to a federal services development strategy, the ability to deliver complex services through shared IT services and orchestration is significantly enhanced.

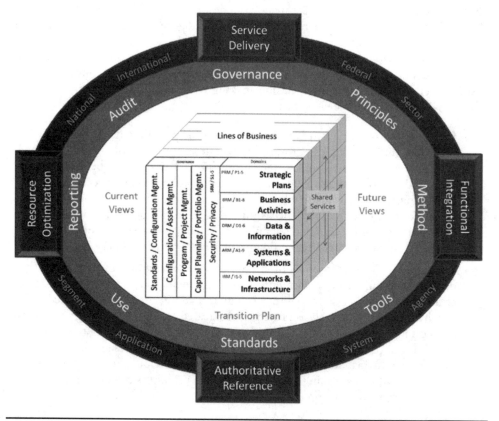

**Figure 23-16**  Metamodel for the Common Approach to FEA (graphic from the OMB)

- **Functional Integration** There is interoperability among programs, systems, and services, which requires knowledge of the business context (meta-context) as well as adherence to standards. The EA provides the business context as well as a listing of standards that enable functional integration.

- **Resource Optimization** Decisions can be made in the context of accurate and complete enterprise resource information. The EA evolves over time to document several harmonized views of the enterprise variables that are essential for analysis. Asset management and configuration management are important elements of resource optimization that EA also enables.

- **Authoritative Reference** The EA is used for the design and documentation of systems and services. With the EA, issues of ownership, management, resourcing, and performance goals can be resolved in a more consistent and effective manner. The EA also provides the information needed for designing security strategies that are more comprehensive than controls provided at the individual system level.

## Basic Elements of FEA

Federal agencies perform enterprise architecting under an EA program office are generally charged with delivering architecture documentation and architecture data needed for IT planning and governance, as well as data regarding alignment of IT investments to the OMB and other governance organizations.

The Common Approach recommends a set of eight basic elements that are required by a EA program within an agency as a best practice for EA program implementation to support effective planning and decision-making within an agency. The inside ring of Figure 23-16 lists these basic elements:

- **Governance** The EA program must identify the planning, decision-making, and oversight processes and groups that will determine how the EA is developed, verified, versioned, used, and sustained over time. The EA must be managed and measured in terms of completeness, consistency, coherence, and accuracy from the perspectives of all stakeholders. (Additional discussion of governance concepts can be found in Chapter 9.) The Common Approach provides details of the interrelationships between federal guidance, agency governance processes, and the programs that implement that guidance in an integrated manner.

- **Principles** The Common Approach describes a variety of principles that drive decision-making for IT investments. General principles represent the overarching criteria against which potential investment and architectural decisions are weighed. Design and analysis principles are geared toward promoting a consistent and common way of practicing EA across federal agencies by using the same principles across agencies. These design and analysis principles are broken down into three domains: Strategic Principles, Business Principles, and Technology Principles. More details on the specifics of these principles can be found in the Common Approach document.

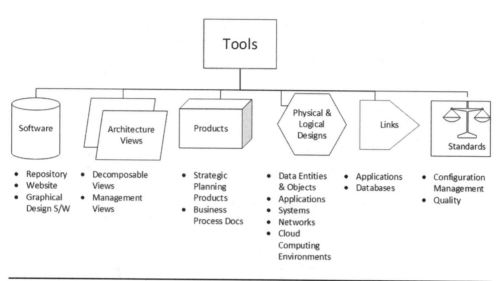

**Figure 23-17** Types of tools

- **Method**  The Collaborative Planning Methodology has been discussed earlier.

- **Tools**  Figure 23-17 shows the types of tools that are recommended by the Common Approach for an EA program to support EA documentation and analysis activities. The word "tool" is used in the general sense that it applies to software applications and repositories as well as to conceptual mechanisms such as products and views that are required to communicate architecture representations to stakeholders.

- **Standards**  Architecture practice, be it in the building industry, the engineering industry, or in any design effort, is built on top of the use of standards. Architecture standards apply to all areas of EA practice. Standards are fundamental to achieving interoperability and resource optimization as they represent agreements between multiple parties to adhere to a set of documented, accepted practices that relate to structural and behavioral constraints. Example (de jure) standards bodies include the National Institute of Standards and Technology (NIST), the Institute of Electrical and Electronics Engineers (IEEE), the International Organization for Standardization (ISO), European Committee for Standardization (CEN), and the American National Standards Institute (ANSI). In addition to the de jure standards are standards that are instituted internal to an enterprise of any scale. In much the same way that home builders build to the basic floor plan of a few select model homes and offer customizations to individual home purchasers, enterprises define reference architectures that form the general blueprint for specific implementations. These reference architectures embed the standards of construction and rules of interconnection to provide guidelines for a starting implementation. Enterprises may also try to standardize components of architectures across multiple systems or service developments and implementations.

- **Use** Often, the act of developing an architecture exposes questions that must be answered and problems that must be solved. These questions and problems may require a deeper understanding of the architecture elements that are currently supporting the enterprise and the changes that need to be made to transform the enterprise or achieve the desired end state of the project. Multiple architecture projects may be needed to roll up into the overall EA. At present, planning at the enterprise level has to rely on these rollups for sufficient information to make decisions related to future planned investments, develop a coherent roadmap for projects, and understand at varying levels of granularity and specificity the types of changes that must be made to architectural elements. Analysis of the architecture will also expose bottlenecks in process latency and information flows, lack of connectivity, and potential for vulnerabilities from outside attacks, to name a few examples. The EA is used in many ways by the agency when viewed as an authoritative source of knowledge about the enterprise. By the same token, if the EA is not maintained as an authoritative source, planners must seek alternative methods for getting the needed information. At a minimum, the EA can provide catalogs of objects of interest to planners such as systems catalogs, shared service catalogs, taxonomies of business functions, organization charts and responsibilities, catalogs of skills and job families, catalogs of data sources, databases, and message standards, to cite a few examples. The EA may also provide categorization schemes for these items to allow for orderly maintenance of information assets by grouping them according to these standard taxonomies.

- **Reporting** The EA program not only provides a self-serve mechanism such as an electronic repository of architecture artifacts, plans, catalogs, taxonomies, solutions, and other information, but it should also provide regular reports on capabilities and options through the "lens" of the architecture. These reports should be delivered in a standardized way such as dashboards to communicate the overall health and progress of projects, initiatives, investments, and improvements.

- **Audit** Audits should be performed periodically to ensure that EA programs are performing quality work, are using consistent methods, and are constantly increasing their capability and maturity. These audits are performed by internal and external experts to ensure that proper methods are being followed, information is accurate, and value is being produced by the EA program. Audits provide recommendations to the agency CIO for further action.

## The FEAF2 Framework

The cube in the center of Figure 23-16 represents the FEAF2 framework, the principle elements of which have been discussed in this chapter. The cube shows the architecture subdomains using shared services in the context of the enterprise LOBs (from the BRM) and of other governance activities such as program management, configuration management, and capital planning.

# Summary

In summary, the FEAF2 and the Common Approach as a combined framework are collections of concepts, motivations, and methods to provide, literally, a "common approach" to the process of setting up and operating an enterprise program office at the federal agency or program level. The combined framework provides these program offices an approach to develop architectures that can be aligned, aggregated, compared, and reported on. However, the integration level provided by the Common Approach is at the artifact level. No attempt is made to define data standards for the contents of these artifacts that allows for integration and federation at a more fundamental granularity of architecture element. The lack of content level standards for the ontology of architecture elements precludes computational methods for processing architecture data. Thus, exercises in analysis tend to be by hand and vary from one architecture to another. The lack of a standardized ontology also prevents easy analysis and promotion of interoperability or the opportunity of aggregating federated architectures or even defining reference architectures (templates that can be reused across the federal enterprise). However, based on the varying levels of maturity in federal organizations, the Common Approach provides a starting point based on artifacts that are roughly prescribed (as shown in this chapter for each architecture subdomain) but do not have the rigor supported by the DoDAF metamodel. The Common Approach borrows upon and builds on many of the views of the DoDAF. In fact, any of those views can be used to generate artifacts in support of federal architecting.

# Questions

1. What are the changes between the first version of the FEAF (2001) and FEAF2 (2013)? What is the change in focus that could have caused the changes?

2. How can the EA help shared service identification? Which reference model would you use to identify shared services in your own agency? With other agencies?

3. How would you use the PRM to report performance results to OMB? What are the performance measure categories or types in the PRM that are relevant to your agency?

4. What are the lines of businesses in your agency? Can you find them or align them to the LOBs in the BRM? What are your observations on the granularity of the LOB in your agency and the one in the BRM? Are they comparable or identical?

5. How would you use the ARM to identify common component applications such as MS Office that are used in your agency? How would you use the Application subarchitecture domain for your enterprise to determine strategies for commodity application licensing?

6. What is data context with reference to the DRM? How will it help standardize the metadata for a data element?

7. What are the types of attributes you would capture in a systems inventory? Why? How do they compare with other enterprises' system catalogs?

8. How does a CRUD matrix help in determining the sequence in which applications are to be developed?

9. What is an enterprise roadmap? How often must it be updated? What are the elements in the enterprise roadmap? Where is the enterprise roadmap kept? By whom?

10. What are the different roles involved in enterprise architecting at the federal enterprise? Which of these roles relate to management and planning? Which of these roles relate to building architecture models inside a tool?

11. How does (or does not) the FEAF2 support integration of architecture elements? Compare and contrast FEAF2 architecting with the requirement for the AV-2: Integrated Dictionary in the DoDAF. How is the Data Dictionary in FEAF2 different from the Integrated Dictionary in DoDAF?

# References

CIO Council. 2001. "A Practical Guide to Federal Enterprise Architecture, Version 1.0." https://www.gao.gov/assets/590/588407.pdf.

CIO Council. 2013. "Federal Enterprise Architecture Framework, Version 2." https://obamawhitehouse.archives.gov/sites/default/files/omb/assets/egov_docs/fea_v2.pdf.

CIO Council. 2017. CIO.gov web site. www.cio.gov/.

CIO Council. 2017. "State of Federal Information Technology." https://s3.amazonaws.com/sitesusa/wp-content/uploads/sites/1151/2017/05/CIO-Council-State-of-Federal-IT-Report-January-2017-1.pdf.

Executive Office of the President of the United States (POTUS). "The Open Government Initiative." https://obamawhitehouse.archives.gov/open.

Executive Office of the President of the United States (POTUS). 2012. "The Common Approach to Federal Enterprise Architecture." https://obamawhitehouse.archives.gov/sites/default/files/omb/assets/egov_docs/common_approach_to_federal_ea.pdf.

Executive Office of the President of the United States (POTUS). 2017. "Budget for FY2018: Chapter 16. Information Technology." www.whitehouse.gov/sites/whitehouse.gov/files/omb/budget/fy2018/ap_16_it.pdf.

Government Accountability Office. 2016. "GAO-16-325: Cloud Computing - Agencies Need to Incorporate Key Practices to Ensure Effective Performance." www.gao.gov/assets/680/676395.pdf.

Kundra, Vivek. 2011. "Federal Cloud Computing Strategy." https://obamawhitehouse.archives.gov/sites/default/files/omb/assets/egov_docs/federal-cloud-computing-strategy.pdf.

Office of Management and Budget. 2015. "OMB Memorandum M-15-14: Management and Oversight of Federal Information Technology." www.nrc.gov/public-involve/open/digital-government/fitara-06-10-2015.pdf.

Office of Management and Budget. 2016. OMB Circular A-11: "Preparation, Submission, and Execution of the Budget." https://obamawhitehouse.archives.gov/sites/default/files/omb/assets/a11_current_year/a11_2016.pdf.

Office of Management and Budget. 2015. OMB Circular A-130: "Managing Information as a Strategic Resource." https://obamawhitehouse.archives.gov/sites/default/files/omb/assets/OMB/circulars/a130/a130revised.pdf.

Scott, Tony. 2016. "M-16-19 Data Center Optimization Initiative (DCOI)." https://obamawhitehouse.archives.gov/sites/default/files/omb/memoranda/2016/m_16_19_1.pdf.

Sowa, J.F. and J.A. Zachman. 1992. "Extending and formalizing the framework for information systems architecture." IBM Systems Journal, 31 (3). https://www.zachman.com/images/ZI_PIcs/ibmsj1992.pdf retrieved on 7/1/2018.

Spewak, Stephen. 1995. *Enterprise Architecture Planning.* New York: Wiley.

United States Congress. 2015. "Federal Information Technology Acquisition Reform Act (FITARA) – part of the National Defense Authorization Act for Fiscal Year 2015" Title VIII, Subtitle D, H.R. 3979.

United States Office of Personnel Management (OPM). 2016. "Sizing up the Executive Branch: Fiscal Year 2015." www.opm.gov/policy-data-oversight/data-analysis-documentation/federal-employment-reports/reports-publications/sizing-up-the-executive-branch-2016.pdf.

U.S. Digital Service. 2017. "Digital Services Playbook." https://playbook.cio.gov.

**PART IV**

# CHAPTER 24

# Summary Comparison of Frameworks

In this chapter, we compare the four frameworks: DoD Architecture Framework (DoDAF), Federal Enterprise Architecture Framework Version 2 (FEAF2), The Open Group Architecture Framework (TOGAF), and the Zachman Framework. This comparison is particularly useful when an enterprise is trying to select a framework as one of the first tasks undertaken by an enterprise architecture (EA) program. Each of the frameworks we have discussed has its own merits and limitations. Each was designed for a different purpose and is strong in the factors that benefit the stakeholders it was designed to benefit.

We briefly summarize the four frameworks before making a detailed comparison between them, after presenting a comparison rubric.

## DoD Architecture Framework

The DoDAF is a general architecting framework that scales up to the multiorganizational enterprise and scales down to the systems engineering project. It was designed for DoD decision-makers to support critical decision points in the following six DoD core processes:

- **Joint Capability Identification and Development System (JCIDS)** Used for acquiring military capabilities that range widely from war-fighting capabilities to business-support capabilities. The Capability Viewpoint of the DoDAF directly supports JCIDS.

- **Defense Acquisition System (DAS)** Used for acquiring solutions for capability requirements. These solutions are in the form of acquisition programs and projects that need to collaborate and coordinate with one another to ensure interoperability between the procured solutions. The Capability and Project Viewpoints directly support the Program of Programs approach for DAS.

- **Systems Engineering (SE)** Used for analysis, design, and integration of solutions. The Systems, Services, Data and Information, Operational, and Standards Viewpoints directly support SE.

- **Planning, Programming, Budgeting, and Execution (PPBE)**   Used for planning future programs that require processes for identification of needed military capabilities, for program planning, and for resource estimation, as well as allocation decisions.

- **Portfolio Management (PfM)**   Used for reviewing a collection of investments in capabilities as a portfolio that needs to be periodically reviewed and either trimmed or grown to meet anticipated future needs. Each portfolio is managed using the architecture plans, risk management techniques, capability goals and objectives, and performance measures.

- **Operations (OPS)**   Used for repetitive planning and execution of military operations. A high degree of process orientation for stateside operations and a high degree of training on tactics, techniques, and procedures for theater operations are the hallmark of operations. The DoDAF Operational Viewpoint directly supports the operational views that represent the activities, event sequences, and goal-directed activities of operations.

Figure 24-1 depicts the various scopes of architecting against the needs of the six DoD core processes.

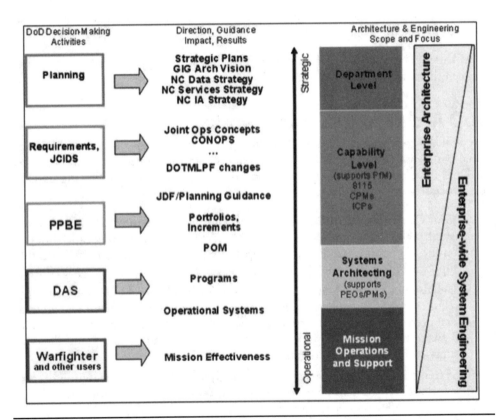

**Figure 24-1**   DoDAF support for DoD core processes (graphic from the DoDAF)

The DoDAF started with roots in the Joint Technology Architecture and Command Control, Communications, Computers, Intelligence, Surveillance, and Reconnaissance (C4ISR) with their concentration on computing, communication and networking, data and information exchanges, and activities and events that relate to triggering of information exchanges. As it evolved, the DoDAF was expanded to support decision-making for the six core DoD processes. Today, the DoDAF is capable of supporting the modeling of not only information technology but also the more general resource processing technology. Information exchanges are replaced with a more general resource flow/exchange. Performers are generalized to perform any activity, not simply IT-focused ones. Projects can be general and are not specific to IT. For example, acquisition of a new weapons system is also a project, though modern weapons systems are highly IT intensive. Contrast the DoDAF's general nature of architecting to the more IT-focused frameworks such as TOGAF and FEAF2 that are squarely aimed at the IT project and the IT enterprise.

The DoDAF is nonprescriptive in the step-by-step process for developing architectures. The Six-Step Process is a broad meta-process that can be customized by specific organizations with specific roles, tools, and techniques and intermediary inputs and outputs. The DoDAF does not provide the specificity of the TOGAF Architecture Development Method (ADM) or the Collaborative Planning Method (CPM) of the FEAF2.

The DoDAF, on the other hand, defines a specific ontology for architecture elements as specified in the DoDAF Metamodel (DM2). The TOGAF references views but does not specify a common set of metamodel objects. The ArchiMate tool for TOGAF implementations does, however, implement a metamodel that is used to drive the diagrams and artifacts that are created by it. The FEAF2 does not specify a metamodel and leaves architects considerable freedom for staying within the specification of views that are prescribed.

The DM2 contains the core concepts of the DoDAF: Activity, Resource (Materiel, Information, Data, Person Type), Architectural Description, Performer, Organization, System, Service, Capability, Condition, Desired Effect, Measure, Measure Type, Location, Guidance, Rule, Agreement, Standard, Project, Vision, and Skill, in addition to other concepts.

# Federal Enterprise Architecture Framework

The FEAF2 is focused on two major areas:

- *Standardizing the process of IT architecting across the federal government.* The goal is slowly to incorporate the capability to compare, aggregate, and federate diverse architectures when the needs of the mission require such interoperability. The Common Approach has the following objectives:

  - Standardizing the service-oriented manner in which IT is implemented to leverage resources across the government.

  - Standardizing the commercial off-the-shelf (COTS) technologies that can be leveraged by multiple agencies.

- Promulgation of federal-wide standards for interoperability to assist the planning of future systems and services.

- *Defining overarching taxonomies that span the entire government to be used for governance, for alignment of reporting, and for budget analysis of investments.* The use of a common taxonomy has long been practiced in accounting to ensure that diverse spending enterprises report their spending using a common categorization scheme. This common reporting scheme allows for higher level oversight and governance functions needed for work with aggregated investments. This is done through the FEAF2 Reference Models: Business Reference Model, Performance Reference Model, Service Reference Model, Application Reference Model, Technology Reference Model, and Security Reference Model.

The FEAF2 provides an alignment approach for any specific agency by providing reference models. The DoDAF does not provide reference models, though the DoD Information Technology Portfolio Repository (DITPR) is a catalog of DoD systems (providing a taxonomy to support the Systems Viewpoint) and applications, and the Defense Information Technology Standards Repository (DISR) is a catalog of standards throughout the DoD (providing a taxonomy for the Standards Viewpoint). The Joint Capability Areas (JCAs) provide a reference model for capability types (providing a taxonomy of capabilities to support the Capability Viewpoint). The Joint Common System Function List is a taxonomy of automated functions (providing a taxonomy for the Systems Functions in the Systems Viewpoint). The DoD Information Enterprise Architecture contains a number of reference taxonomies related to IT. These are not part of the DoD Architecture Framework, however. The DoDAF is used as a language to express these taxonomies through standardized views such as the CV-2, SvcV-4, SV-4, and StdV-1.

The FEAF2 recommends the Collaborative Planning Methodology (CPM) for developing and using architecture representations in the overall context of federal IT-shared services and IT project developments. The FEAF2 also recommends a set of views contained in each of various architecture subdomains that are akin to DoDAF viewpoints and TOGAF artifacts, but it does not specify an overarching ontology model at this time.

# The Open Group Architecture Framework

The Open Group is a consortium of IT vendors such as IBM and Oracle as well as a worldwide group of IT customers and consumers committed to open standards for IT systems. TOGAF, in its initial version, was focused on technology and based on an early (pre-DoDAF) DoD architecture document. Over time, TOGAF has evolved into a broader coverage of the business processes that are enabled by IT and the strategic drivers that drive those business processes. Today, TOGAF provides a very detailed methodology for architecture development (ADM) and governance that can be used for individual projects, a project of projects, or a portfolio of IT projects. The core focus of the Architecture

**Figure 24-2**
TOGAF ADM
(used with
permission from
TOGAF)

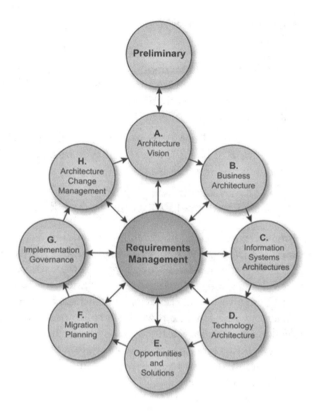

Development Method (ADM) in TOGAF is the holistic gathering of requirements to drive complete implementations as depicted in Figure 24-2. The TOGAF recommends a fairly detailed architecting methodology in the ADM.

In addition to the ADM, TOGAF also describes a standardized terminology for concepts through the Core Content Metamodel. The core concepts of TOGAF in this metamodel are Actor, Application Component, Business Service, Data Entity, Function, Information System Service, Organization Unit, Platform Service, Role, and Technology Component in addition to other concepts.

# Zachman Framework

The Zachman Framework is not easily comparable to the other frameworks described here. This framework's primary focus is to represent all the architecture elements that are involved in an enterprise of any size using a systematic, mutually exclusive, two-dimensional ontological structure made up of six interrogatives as the columns and the six perspectives as the rows.

The Zachman Framework does not:

- Provide any specific viewpoints like the Capability Viewpoint in the DoDAF, or the Security subarchitecture domain in the FEAF2. It does not provide prescribed views such as the CV-1 or OV-1 in the DoDAF or artifacts like the BV-1 in the FEAF2. However, the Zachman Framework does provide the perspectives as stakeholder viewpoints.

- Have the specificity of the DM2 as a metamodel. The definition of the cells is made in the form of larger "models" rather than specific semantic objects that are standardized by the framework.

- Recommend an architecture development methodology like the ADM in TOGAF, the CPM in the FEAF, or the Six-Step Process in the DoDAF.

The Zachman Framework is, however, an underlying data discovery mechanism that enables an architect to ask the right questions from the right people and tabulate the architecture elements that he/she discovers into a format where they are uniquely defined and categorized. It is a good way to develop a worksheet for a architecture project coupled with the right questions for stakeholders. The authors are currently working on a "scaffolding approach," where separate rows of six columns are used to develop the strategic and operational viewpoints for specific groups of stakeholders we call "corporate tribes."

The Zachman Framework can be used in conjunction with any of the other frameworks to discover, tabulate, and relate primitives and develop reusable architecture composites, as described in Chapter 21.

# Normalizing Comparison Criteria

To be able to make more rigorous comparisons between the three frameworks of DoDAF, FEAF2, and TOGAF, we define a structure that can be used to perform an apples-to-apples comparison. Figure 24-3 illustrates the analysis rubric by dissecting

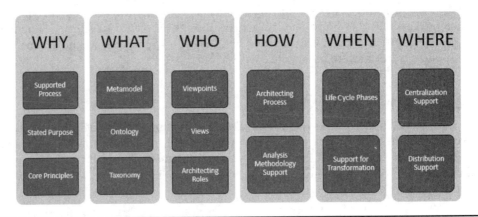

**Figure 24-3** Framework analysis components

and expanding on the six interrogatives with respect to architecting. The rubric also serves as a comparison matrix across frameworks to look for similarities and differences. We have organized the rubric using the six Zachman interrogatives:

- **WHY**   Relates to the motivation factors that drove the development of the framework involved. What core or business process was the framework designed to support? What is the stated purpose of the framework in the view of the sponsoring organization? What are the core principles that are specified by the framework?

- **WHAT**   Relates to the data and information aspects of the framework. Does it specify a standard metamodel that can be used universally for architecture information exchange and for aggregating or federating architectures from multiple architecture efforts? Does the framework support an ontological representation that has meaning as opposed to a technical model whose semantics are not comprehensible to the average stakeholder? Does the framework offer standard taxonomies of terms that can be used to categorize architecture elements or offer classes of elements that can be used as placeholders?

- **WHO**   Relates to the types of stakeholders, their issues, and their concerns that are addressed by the framework. Does the framework offer standardized viewpoints? Does the framework offer standardized views for the appropriate groups of stakeholders? Does the framework specify architecting roles that are performers during the course of an architecting effort?

- **HOW**   Relates to the process, methodology, or sequence of steps that is recommended by the framework. Does the framework specify an architecting process? Does the framework support specific types of analysis methodologies such as IDEF1X, IDEF0, or BPMN, for example?

- **WHEN**   Relates to the life cycle phases recommended by the framework for the architecting process. Does the framework specify phases within the architecting process? Does the framework provide explicit support for baseline (as-is) and target (to-be) architectures?

- **WHERE**   Relates to whether the framework supports both centralized and distributed architecting approaches for enterprises that are spread out and autonomous. Does the framework support centralization of architecting efforts? Does the framework support distributed architecting efforts?

Tables 24-1 through 24-6 provide a comparison of the four frameworks: DoDAF, TOGAF, FEAF2, and Zachman organized along the six Zachman interrogatives.

| WHY | DoDAF | TOGAF | FEAF2 | Zachman |
|---|---|---|---|---|
| Supported Core Processes | • Portfolio Management (PfM)<br>• Systems Engineering (SE)<br>• Acquisition (DAS)<br>• Planning, Programming, Budgeting, & Execution (PPBE)<br>• Joint Capabilities Integration & Development System (JCIDS)<br>• Operations (OPS) | • Process Integration<br>• Automation Integration<br>• Integration of legacy systems | • Capital Planning and Investment Control<br>• Shared Service Planning<br>• Leveraging Services across the Government<br>• Security Controls for Information Technology<br>• Infrastructure Investment & Management | • Enterprise Transformation<br>• Enterprise Engineering |
| Stated Purpose | "Enabling the development of architectures to facilitate the ability of Department of Defense (DoD) managers at all levels to make key decisions more effectively through organized information sharing across the Department, Joint Capability Areas (JCAs), Mission, Component, and Program boundaries." | "The purpose of enterprise architecture is to optimize across the enterprise the often fragmented legacy of processes (both manual and automated) into an integrated environment that is responsive to change and supportive of the delivery of the business strategy." | • Service Delivery<br>• Functional Integration<br>• Authoritative Reference<br>• Resource Optimization | "The Zachman Framework is the fundamental structure for enterprise architecture and thereby yields the total set of descriptive representations relevant for describing an enterprise." |

| Core Principles | | | |
|---|---|---|---|
| • V2.0 focuses on architectural data, rather than on developing individual products, as described in previous versions.<br><br>• Enables architectural content that is fit-for-purpose as an architectural description consistent with specific project or mission objectives.<br><br>• Serves as the principal guide for development of integrated architectures. The term *integrated* means that data required in more than one instance in architectural views is commonly understood across those views. | • Provide a methodology driven approach to architecting that produces consistent results (ADM).<br><br>• Provide a holistic requirements–gathering framework for IT projects. | • Provide a collaborative planning methodology–driven approach.<br><br>• Provide a looser structural framework for architecture views. | • The first is the fundamentals of communication found in the primitive interrogatives: What, How, When, Who, Where, and Why.<br><br>• The second is derived from reification, the transformation of an abstract idea into an instantiation: Identification, Definition, Representation, Specification, Configuration, and Instantiation.<br><br>• The interrogatives and reification steps together as axes, form a 36-cell matrix for categorization of architecture elements (primitives). |

**Table 24-1** Comparison of WHY Dimensions of Frameworks

PART IV

| WHAT | DoDAF | TOGAF | FEAF2 | Zachman |
|---|---|---|---|---|
| **Metamodel & Ontology** | • Foundation ontology called IDEAS—a set of metaclasses and relationships that instantiate the DM2 elements<br>• DoDAF Metamodel (DM2) | • Core Content Metamodel<br>• Extension Content Metamodel | • No formal integrated metamodel is defined.<br>• A non-integrated metamodel can be inferred from the types of artifacts that must be used to represent the architecture. | • The rows and columns form the super classes.<br>• A cell inherits from both the row and the column it is associated with.<br>• Every cell has its own metamodel independent of the other cells.<br>• Does not indicate in detail the individual cell metamodels but refers to them as "models." |
| **Taxonomy** | • As a pure architecting framework, does not specify standard taxonomies.<br>• Other joint/DoD guidance and practices are responsible for defining formal taxonomies such as the JMETL, JCA, JCSFL, and so on. | • Defines a detailed Platform Taxonomy Model that breaks down application platform services into detailed subcategories.<br>• The Technology Reference Model is also a standard taxonomy defined in the TOGAF. | • Performance Reference Model<br>• Business Reference Model<br>• Data Reference Model<br>• Application Reference Model<br>• Infrastructure Reference Model<br>• Security Reference Model | No reference models are described. It serves as a ontology model though potentially one can theoretically define 36 taxonomy models, one for each cell. |

**Table 24-2** Comparison of WHAT Dimensions of Frameworks

PART IV

| WHO | DoDAF | TOGAF | FEAF2 | Zachman |
|---|---|---|---|---|
| Viewpoints | Standard Viewpoints are<br>• Capability Viewpoint<br>• Project Viewpoint<br>• Operational Viewpoint<br>• Services Viewpoint<br>• Systems Viewpoint<br>• Data and Information Viewpoint<br>• Standards Viewpoint<br>• All Viewpoint | Though TOGAF does not formally call out standard viewpoints, we can infer the following:<br>• Architecture Principles, Requirements, and Roadmap—corresponding to the DoDAF All Viewpoint<br>• Business Architecture<br>• Application Architecture<br>• Technology Architecture | The subarchitecture domains correspond to viewpoints:<br>• Strategy subarchitecture domain<br>• Business subarchitecture domain<br>• Data subarchitecture domain<br>• Applications subarchitecture domain<br>• Infrastructure subarchitecture domain<br>• Security subarchitecture domain | Perspectives akin to the viewpoints in the other frameworks. From a reification perspective, these are<br>• Identification<br>• Definition<br>• Representation<br>• Specification<br>• Configuration<br>• Instantiation |
| Views | • All Viewpoint: 2 views<br>• Capability Viewpoint: 7 views<br>• Project Viewpoint: 3 views<br>• Operational Viewpoint: 9 views<br>• Services Viewpoint: 13 views<br>• Systems Viewpoint: 13 views<br>• Data and Information Viewpoint: 3 views<br>• Standards Viewpoint: 2 views | • Architecture Principles, Requirements, and Roadmap (compare to All Viewpoint): 7 artifacts<br>• Business Architecture: 18 artifacts<br>• Data Architecture: 9 artifacts<br>• Application Architecture: 14 artifacts<br>• Technology Architecture: 8 artifacts | • Strategy subarchitecture domain: 5 artifacts<br>• Business subarchitecture domain: 6 artifacts<br>• Data subarchitecture domain: 10 artifacts<br>• Applications subarchitecture domain: 11 artifacts<br>• Infrastructure subarchitecture domain: 12 artifacts<br>• Security subarchitecture domain: 6 artifacts<br>• CPM artifacts: Many to support project (compare to All Viewpoint) | None. Allows the definition of arbitrary composites that are combinations of primitive architecture elements but based on rules of combination, as described in Chapter 21. |

**Table 24-3** Comparison of WHO Dimensions of Frameworks

| WHO | DoDAF | TOGAF | FEAF2 | Zachman |
|---|---|---|---|---|
| **Architecting Roles** | • Enterprise architect<br>• Solutions architect<br>• Sponsor<br>• Program manager<br>• Organization manager<br>• Subject matter experts<br>• Solution architect<br>• Capability portfolio manager<br>• Program executive office | • Planners<br>• Program managers<br>• Line managers<br>• Enterprise architects<br>• Solution architects<br>• Sponsors<br>• Stakeholders<br>• Users<br>• Governance<br>• Service providers | • Corporate functions: CXO, enterprise security, program mgmt office, QA/standards, procurement, HR<br>• End-user organizations: executives, line mgmt, business domain experts, data owners<br>• Project organizations: executives, line mgmt, business process/functional experts, product specialist, technical specialist<br>• System operations: IT service mgmt, service desk, application mgmt, infrastructure mgmt, data/voice communications<br>• Enterprise architect<br>• Solutions architect<br>• External roles: suppliers, regulatory bodies | • Business context planners (row 1)<br>• Business concept owners (row 2)<br>• Business logic designers (row 3)<br>• Business physics builders (row 4)<br>• Business component implementers (row 5)<br>• Users (row 6) |

**Table 24-3** Comparison of WHO Dimensions of Frameworks (*continued*)

| HOW | DoDAF | TOGAF | FEAF2 | Zachman |
|---|---|---|---|---|
| **Architecting Process** | Six-Step Process approach is more of a metaprocess that defines the stages of architecting to solve any general or specific military problem. | Architecture Development Method (ADM) is prescribed as a consistent, step-by-step approach to gathering holistic requirements and building an architecture description. | Collaborative Planning Methodology (CPM) is a fairly detailed collaborative methodology in two phases: Planning and Execution of projects. The architect's role is as an enabler and a facilitator for the business during planning and the contractor during implementation. | No methodology specified. In fact, Zachman states that the framework is not a methodology. However, the framework supports use of any of the other methodologies such as the Six-Step, ADM, and CPM. |
| **Analysis Methodology Support** | Analysis methodology agnostic. Views are prescribed to contain some key concepts from the DM2 regardless of the analysis methodology. | Describes a set of artifacts but not the underlying analysis methodology. The content metamodel requires specific concepts. | Does not prescribe analysis methodologies and allows the use of multiple analysis techniques for representation of the artifacts described for the various subarchitecture domains. | No analysis methodology specified or prescribed. Any of the classic analysis techniques can be used against the information captured using framework for an architecture description. However, these analysis techniques require building composites. |

**Table 24-4**   Comparison of HOW Dimensions of Frameworks

| WHEN | DoDAF | TOGAF | FEAF2 | Zachman |
|---|---|---|---|---|
| **Life Cycle Phases** | The Six-Step Process specifies how architectures are developed to address specific business or operational questions but does not go beyond the end result of answering the decision support questions through the architectural analysis. The architecture life cycle, including maintenance of the architecture, is up to the implementing organizations. | The ADM does address the architecture life cycle, including maintenance of the architecture and governance processes to ensure that change controls are applied. | The CPM does not directly discuss architecture life cycle or architecture maintenance. | Does not deal with an architecture life cycle or maintenance of the architecture description that is captured through the framework. |
| **Support for Transformation Phases** | The architecture project defines the transformation sequence that can be captured through a CV-1 and outlined in the AV-1. There is no intrinsic property of architecture elements that determines whether they exist in the current or target state. The time frame of elements are attributes that must be maintained inside the architecture repository or AV-2. | The ADM supports transformation phases by specifying as-is and to-be architecture elements in the ADM Phases B, C and D and arranges the retained as-is elements and the chosen to-be elements together as part of the to-be road-map in Phase E Opportunities and Solutions. | The FEAF2 approach is transformative, but there is no intrinsic specification for maintaining transformation state properties. | The framework can express both current and future state architecture elements, but denoting these states is the responsibility of repository storage. |

**Table 24-5**   Comparison of WHEN Dimensions of Frameworks

| WHERE | DoDAF | TOGAF | FEAF2 | Zachman |
|---|---|---|---|---|
| **Centralization Support** | Can be used to manage the architectures centrally under the control of a specific organization (USTRANSCOM, air mobility command, and so on). | Lends itself ideally to a project-oriented architecting approach. Centralized development can hamper agile developments. | FEAF2 does not lend itself to a centralized approach, though large agencies may be able to maintain centralized repositories of common elements that can be reused by component organizations. | A centralized repository would provide needed integration for managing architecture elements that are captured by the framework. |
| **Distribution Support** | "Index Cards" such as the AV-1 metadata can be stored centrally for distributed architectures to provide information for search and retrieval. | TOGAF provides catalogs of reusable artifacts that are shared through central repositories. | FEAF2 artifacts are not standardized around a metamodel making it hard to share and reuse objects and to resolve inconsistencies across methodologies and analysis techniques that may use different names for the same architecture object. | Because of the specific contextual meanings of the cells, the reuse of objects is independent of cell affiliations but must rather be based on their existence in the real world |

**Table 24-6**   Comparison of WHERE Dimensions of Frameworks

## Summary

We have made a comparison among the various selected frameworks to assist the architect in selecting the right framework for the right purpose. Choice of framework is an impactful decision that has many implications down the pike when architecture projects are under way. Identifying the right framework for an enterprise makes it possible to standardize the architecting process and the architecting language, tools, repositories, and data exchanges. It also enables aggregation and federation of architectures as well as comparison of architectures and the development of "notional" reference architectures that act as templates for instantiation. These reference architectures provide a jumpstart for solution projects that can leverage this generic solution architecture as a starting point.

## Questions

1. Which frameworks support a prescriptive step-by-step methodology for development of architectures?

2. Compare and contrast the FEAF CPM against the TOGAF ADM.

3. What is the metamodel for TOGAF? Can one develop a metamodel from the knowledge of the artifacts? Is the metamodel integrated across artifacts—similar items with similar labels in different types of artifact?

4. Can an enterprise use more than one framework to set up an architecture program? Explain your answer. Are there contradictions that may arise?

5. The Zachman Framework is comprehensive and can do everything the other frameworks do. True or False? Explain your answer.

6. Which framework provides ontological guidance in an explicit manner? What is a foundation ontology (hint: IDEAS or the UML Class metamodel)?

7. Compare and contrast the key metamodel elements from the DoDAF DM2 and the TOGAF Core Content Model.

8. Compare and contrast the DoDAF Six-Step Process against the TOGAF ADM.

## References

CIO Council. 2013. "Federal Enterprise Architecture Framework, Version 2." https://obamawhitehouse.archives.gov/sites/default/files/omb/assets/egov_docs/fea_v2.pdf.

Common Approach Executive Office of the President of the United States (POTUS). 2012. "The Common Approach to Federal Enterprise Architecture." https://obamawhitehouse.archives.gov/sites/default/files/omb/assets/egov_docs/common_approach_to_federal_ea.pdf.

Department of Defense. 2009. Department of Defense Architecture Framework Version 2.0. http://dodcio.defense.gov/Library/DoD-Architecture-Framework.

Martin, James, Kevin Kreitman, Jeff Diehl, and Scott Bernard. 2004. "Exploring the Differences Between Enterprise and System Architectures – A Look at the Different Methods, Tools, and Techniques." Ground System Architectures Workshop Breakout Session. http://csse.usc.edu/GSAW/gsaw2004/s10b/martin.pdf.

Rao, Prakash C. 2011. "Is God Too Large to Fit into One Religion?" Presented at the FEAC Alumni Symposium Conference 2011, Enterprise Architecture Conference, Washington, DC. www.academia.edu/35137192/Is_God_Too_Large_to_Fit_into_One_Religion.

Rao, Prakash C. 2013. "Selecting FEAF II/DoDAF Views and Models for Use in Shared Service Projects, Their Integration & Analysis." Presented at the Enterprise Architecture Conference, Washington, DC. www.academia.edu/35137003/Selecting_FEAF_II_DoDAF_Views_and_Models_for_Use_in_Shared_Service_Projects_Their_Integration_and_Analysis.

The Open Group. "Welcome to the TOGAF Standard, Version 9.2." Section 1.3: Executive Overview. http://pubs.opengroup.org/architecture/togaf9-doc/arch.

Zachman, John A. "About the Zachman Framework." www.zachman.com/about-the-zachman-framework.

This glossary defines the terms used in the book. Because the scope of this book covers multiple architecture frameworks, the same term appears more than once with the definition that is taken from the appropriate framework. The context citation at the end of each entry contains the context to be used for interpreting the description.

**actionable**  Architecture analysis and documentation that is used by executives, managers, and staff to support resource planning, decision-making, and management. (Context: Common Approach/FEAF2)

**activity**

Work, not specific to a single organization, weapon system, or individual, that transforms inputs (resources) into outputs (resources) or changes their state. (Context: DoDAF 2.02)

Work that may comprise an entire business process or a task within a business process. (Context: TOGAF 9)

**activity-based costing**  Analysis process that determines the costs of a specific business process, including personnel, equipment, and facility costs. (Context: General)

**actor**  A person, organization, or system whose role initiates or interacts with activities— for example, a sales representative who travels to visit customers. Actors may be internal or external to an organization. In the automotive industry, an original equipment manufacturer would be considered an actor by an automotive dealership that interacts with its supply chain activities. (Context: TOGAF 9)

**actor/role matrix**  A matrix that shows which specific actors perform which abstract roles, in support of the definition of security and skills requirements. (Context: TOGAF 9)

**Actual Resources Structure (Ar-Sr) domain**  The analysis (evaluation of different alternatives, what-ifs, trade-offs, verification, and validation) of the actual resource configurations. It illustrates the expected or achieved actual resource configuration. (Context: Unified Architecture Framework)

**ADM phase**  A phase of the Architecture Development Methodology/Method (ADM); the TOGAF-recommended approach to developing enterprise architectures. (Context: TOGAF 9)

**agency**  Any executive or military department, bureau, government corporation, government-controlled corporation, independent regulatory agency, or other organization in the Executive Branch of the United States government. (Context: Common Approach/ FEAF2)

**agency level**  A level of architecture that provides an overview of the entire department/agency and consistent, decomposable views of all subagencies/bureaus, business units, programs, systems, networks, and mission or support services. The depth of documentation in any particular area of an agency's architecture is determined by the need to support planning and decision-making, prioritized in the context of the agency's strategic goals and business operating plans. Drill-down is accomplished through the completion of segment-, system-, and application-level architectures. (Context: Common Approach/FEAF2)

**agreement**  A consent among parties regarding the terms and conditions of activities that said parties participate in. (Context: DoDAF 2.02)

**airfield**  The portion of an airport that contains the facilities necessary for the operation of aircraft. (Context: RMN Airport Case Study)

**airport authority**  A quasi-governmental public organization responsible for setting the policies governing the management and operation of an airport or system of airports under its jurisdiction. (Context: RMN Airport Case Study)

**airport layout plan**  A scaled drawing of the existing and planned land and facilities necessary for the operation and development of an airport. (Context: RMN Airport Case Study)

**airport master plan**  The airport's concept of the long-term development and use of an airport's land and facilities. (Context: RMN Airport Case Study)

**airport sponsor**  The entity that is legally responsible for the management and operation of an airport, including the fulfillment of the requirements of laws and regulations related thereto. (Context: RMN Airport Case Study)

**airside**  The portion of an airport that contains the facilities necessary for the operation of aircraft. (Context: RMN Airport Case Study)

**alignment**
Conformance to a policy, standard, and/or goal. (Context: Common Approach/FEAF2)

The enterprise word for "quality." The definition of quality is "producing products that meet the requirements as defined by the customer." In enterprise terms, "producing Enterprise implementations (Row 6) that meet the requirements (Row 1/2) as defined by Management." (Context: Zachman)

**All Viewpoint (AV)**  Describes the overarching aspects of the architecture context that relate to all DoDAF viewpoints. (Context: DoDAF 2.02)

**application**
A level of architecture that focuses on the development, update, or integration of one or more software applications that are part of one or more system(s)/service(s) in one or more organization(s). This includes web sites, databases, e-mail, and other mission or support applications. (Context: Common Approach/FEAF2)

A deployed and operational IT system that supports business functions and services—for example, a payroll. Applications use data and are supported by multiple technology components but are distinct from the technology components that support the application. (Context: TOGAF 9)

**application and user location diagram** A diagram that shows the geographical distribution of applications that can be used to show where applications are used by the end user; the distribution of where the host application is executed and/or delivered in thin client scenarios; the distribution of where applications are developed, tested, and released; and so on. (Context: TOGAF 9)

**application architecture** A description of the structure and interaction of the applications as groups of capabilities that provide key business functions and manage the data assets. (Context: TOGAF 9)

**application communication diagram** A diagram that depicts all models and mappings related to communication among applications in the metamodel entity. (Context: TOGAF 9)

**Application Communication Diagram (A-2)** The means by which resource flows between applications occur. Equivalent to the DoDAF SV-2: Systems Resource Flow Description and SvcV-2: Services Resource Flow Description. (Context: Common Approach/FEAF2)

**application component** An encapsulation of application functionality aligned to implementation structure—for example, a purchase request processing application. (Context: TOGAF 9) *See also* logical application component *and* physical application component.

**Application Data Exchange Matrix (A-4)** The details of resource flows among systems, the activities performed, the resources exchanged, and the attributes (rules and measures) associated with these exchanges. Similar to the DoDAF SV-6: Systems Resource Flow Matrix and SvcV-6: Services Resource Flow Matrix. (Context: Common Approach/FEAF2)

**application/data matrix** Depicts the relationship between applications (application components) and the data entities that are accessed and updated by them. (Context: TOGAF 9)

**application/function matrix** Depicts the relationship between applications and business functions within the enterprise. (Context: TOGAF 9)

**application interaction matrix** Represents dependencies between two applications. This artifact is identical to the SV-3: Systems-Systems Matrix and serves a similar purpose in analyzing system dependencies. (Context: TOGAF 9)

**Application Interface Diagram (A-1)** The identification of application resource flows and their composition. Similar to the DoDAF SV-1: Systems Context Description. (Context: Common Approach/FEAF2)

**Application Interface Matrix (A-3)**  The interface relationships among systems DoDAF. Equivalent to the DoDAF SvcV-3a: Systems-Services Matrix and SvcV-3b: Services-Services Matrix. (Context: Common Approach/FEAF2)

**Application Inventory (A-10)**  A registry of applications and services, the system functions, or the service activities they perform, which are optionally prioritized or ranked. (Context: Common Approach/FEAF2)

**Application Maintenance Procedure (A-9)**  Describes how to modify software to provide error corrections, enhancements of capabilities, deletion of obsolete capabilities, and optimization of behaviors and structures. (Context: Common Approach/FEAF2)

**application migration diagram**  Identifies application migration from baseline to target application components. It enables a more accurate estimation of migration costs by showing precisely which applications and interfaces need to be mapped between migration stages. (Context: TOGAF 9)

**application/organization matrix**  Depicts the relationship between applications and organizational units within the enterprise. (Context: TOGAF 9)

**Application Performance Matrix (A-6)**  A table of measures is associated with an application's performance. These measures are used as specifications to plan or benchmark an application in terms of desirable properties such as availability and latency of user response to application response. This artifact is equivalent to the DoDAF SV-7: Systems Measures Matrix and SvcV-7: Services Measures Matrix. (Context: Common Approach/FEAF2)

**application portfolio catalog**  Identifies and maintains a list of all the applications in the enterprise, which helps to define the horizontal scope of change initiatives that may impact particular kinds of applications. An agreed-upon application portfolio enables a standard set of applications to be defined and governed. (Context: TOGAF 9)

**application reference model (ARM)**  Categorizes the system- and application-related standards and technologies that support the delivery of service capabilities, enabling agencies to share and reuse common solutions and benefit from economies of scale. (Context: Common Approach/FEAF2)

**Application Service Matrix (A-5)**  Interface relationships between services and applications. Similar to DoDAF SvcV-3a: Systems-Services Matrix and SvcV-3b: Services-Services Matrix. (Context: Common Approach/FEAF2)

**application/technology matrix**  Documents the mapping of applications to technology platform. This matrix should be aligned with and complement one or more platform decomposition diagrams. (Context: TOGAF 9)

**application use-case diagram**  Displays the relationships between consumers and providers of application services. Application services are consumed by actors or other application services, and the diagram provides added richness in describing application functionality by illustrating how and when that functionality is used. (Context: TOGAF 9)

**Applications subarchitecture domain**   In the applications subarchitecture domain of the EA framework asks the following questions: Which systems and applications will be needed to generate, share, and store the data, information, and knowledge that the business services need? How can multiple types of IT systems, services, applications, databases, and web sites be made to work together where needed? How can configuration management help to create a cost-effective and operationally efficient common operating environment (COE) for systems and applications? What are the workforce, standards, and security issues in this subarchitecture view? What are the workforce, standards, and security issues in this domain? (Context: Common Approach/FEAF2)

**apron**   A specified portion of the airfield used for passenger, cargo, or freight loading and unloading, aircraft parking, and the refueling, maintenance, and servicing of aircraft. (Context: RMN Airport Case Study)

**architectural description (AD)**
   Information describing an architecture. (Context: DoDAF 2.02)

   A collection of products to document an architecture. (Context: IEEE Std 1471-2000)

**architectural model**   A view may comprise one or more architectural models, each of which is developed using the methods established by its associated architectural viewpoint. An architectural model may be included in more than one view. (Context: IEEE Std 1471-2000)

**architecture**
   A systematic approach that organizes and guides design, analysis, planning, and documentation activities. (Context: Common Approach/FEAF2)

   The fundamental organization of a system, embodied in its components, their relationships to each other and the environment, and the principles governing its design and evolution. (Context: IEEE Std 1471-2000 and ISO/IEC 42010:2007)

   A formal description of a system, or a detailed plan of the system at component level, to guide its implementation. (Source: ISO/IEC 42010: 2007) (Context: TOGAF 9)

   The structure of components, their interrelationships, and the principles and guidelines governing their design and evolution over time. (Context: TOGAF 9)

   A structured set of descriptive representations relevant to describing an object and being employed such that an instance of the object can be created and such that the descriptive representations serve as the baseline for changing an object instance. (Context: Zachman)

**architecture building blocks**   A constituent of the architecture model that describes a single aspect of the overall model. (Context: TOGAF 9)

**architecture capability**   Defines the parameters, structures, and processes that support governance of the architecture repository. (Context: TOGAF 9)

**Architecture Continuum** Part of the Enterprise Continuum, this repository of architectural elements offers increasing detail and specialization. This continuum begins with foundational definitions such as reference models, core strategies, and basic building blocks. From there it spans industry architectures all the way to an organization's specific architecture. (Context: TOGAF 9)

**architecture definition document** A deliverable container for the core architectural artifacts created during a project. It spans all architecture domains (business, data, application, and technology) and also examines all relevant states of the architecture (baseline, interim state(s), and target). (Context: TOGAF 9)

**Architecture Development Method/Methodology (ADM)** The core of TOGAF, this is a step-by-step approach to develop and use an enterprise architecture for developing architectures, which includes establishing an architecture framework, developing architecture content, transitioning, and governing the realization of architectures. All of these activities are carried out within an iterative cycle of continuous architecture definition and realization that enables organizations to transform their enterprises in a controlled manner in response to business goals and opportunities. (Context: TOGAF 9)

**architecture domain** The architectural area being considered. Within TOGAF, there are four architecture domains: business, data, application, and technology. (Context: TOGAF 9)

**architecture framework** A conceptual structure used to develop, implement, and sustain an architecture. (Context: TOGAF 9)

**architecture landscape** The architectural representation of assets deployed within the operating enterprise at a particular point in time. The landscape is likely to exist at multiple levels of abstraction to suit different architecture objectives. (Context: TOGAF 9)

**architecture levels of scope** The Common Approach to Federal Enterprise Architecture (FEA) defines eight levels of scope that describe the span and coverage of the architecture: international, national, federal, sector, agency, segment, system. and application. (Context: Common Approach/FEAF2)

**architecture maturity assessment** Determines the level of maturity of the architecture development effort and identifies gaps in scope (depth and breadth) and coverage as well as in the use and dissemination. (Context: TOGAF 9)

**architecture metamodel** Describes the organizationally tailored application of an architecture framework, including a metamodel for architecture content. (Context: TOGAF 9)

**architecture principles**

A specific class of normative principles that direct the design of an enterprise, from the definition of its business to its supporting IT. (Context: General)

A qualitative statement of intent that should be met by the architecture, which has at least a supporting rationale and a measure of importance. (Context: TOGAF 9)

**architecture program maturity assessment**    A tool developed by the Gartner Group to measure architecture scope and authority, stakeholder involvement, and the architecture definition process of the EA program through surveys. (Context: Gartner)

**architecture repository**    In support of the Enterprise Continuum, can be used to store different classes of architectural output at different levels of abstraction, created by the Architecture Development Methodology (ADM). In this way, TOGAF facilitates understanding and cooperation between stakeholders and practitioners at different levels. (Context: TOGAF 9)

**architecture requirements specification**    Provides a set of quantitative statements that outline what an implementation project must do to comply with the architecture. Typically forms a major component of an implementation contract or contract for more detailed architecture definition. (Context: TOGAF 9)

**architecture roadmap**    Lists individual increments of change and lays them out on a timeline to show progression from the baseline architecture to the target architecture. (Context: TOGAF 9)

**architecture segment**    A part of the overall EA that documents one or more lines of business, including all levels and threads. (Context: Common Approach/FEAF2)

**architecture vision**    A succinct description of the target architecture that describes its business value and the changes to the enterprise that will result from its successful deployment. It serves as an aspirational vision and a boundary for detailed architecture development. (Context: TOGAF 9)

**artifact**
A documentation product, such as a text document, diagram, spreadsheet, briefing slides, or video clip. (Context: Common Approach/FEAF2)

An architectural work product that describes an aspect of the architecture. (Context: TOGAF 9)

A descriptive representation, usually used for engineering design—primitive models in the context of the Zachman Framework. An artifact could be a descriptive formalism for any object including buildings, airplanes, computers, or any Industrial Age products. (Context: Zachman)

**as-is architecture**    An architecture that represents the current state of the enterprise. Sometimes this is the as-planned architecture that includes any changes that are funded in the current budget. (Context: General)

**asset inventory**    A list of assets with details about each (installation date, original cost, condition, and such) asset register. (Context: Common Approach/FEAF2)

**assumption**    A statement of probable fact that has not been fully validated because of external constraints. For example, it may be assumed that an existing application will support a certain set of functional requirements, although those requirements may not yet have been individually validated. (Context: TOGAF 9)

**authoritative reference**    Like building blueprints, this reference provides an integrated, consistent view of strategic goals, mission and support services, data, and enabling technologies across the entire organization, including programs, services, and systems. When the EA is recognized as the authoritative reference for the design and documentation of systems and services, issues of ownership, management, resourcing, and performance goals can be resolved in a consistent and effective manner. EA also serves as a reference to promote the achievement and maintenance of desired levels of security and trust in an agency's business and technology operating environment. EA's contribution to security protection is accomplished through the integrated use of federal methods during process or resource design activities to identify and implement controls to address potential vulnerabilities with users, processes, systems, applications, and networks. (Context: Common Approach/FEAF2)

**balanced score card (BSC)**    A strategic planning and management system used extensively in business and industry, government, and nonprofit organizations worldwide to align business activities to the vision and strategy of the organization, improve internal and external communications, and monitor organization performance against strategic goals. (Context: Common Approach/FEAF2)

**baseline architecture**    The set of products that portray the existing enterprise, the current business practices, and the technical infrastructure. Commonly referred to as the as-is architecture. (Context: Common Approach/FEAF2)

**benefits diagram**    Shows opportunities identified in an architecture definition, classified according to their relative size, benefit, and complexity. Can be used by stakeholders to make selection, prioritization, and sequencing decisions on identified opportunities. (Context: TOGAF 9)

**building block**    Represents a (potentially reusable) component of business, IT, or architectural capability that can be combined with other building blocks to deliver architectures and solutions. Building blocks can be defined at various levels of detail, depending on what stage of architecture development has been reached. For instance, at an early stage, a building block can simply consist of a name or an outline description. Later on, a building block may be decomposed into multiple supporting building blocks and may be accompanied by a full specification. Building blocks can relate to architectures or solutions. (Context: TOGAF 9)

**business architecture**    A description of the structure and interaction between the business strategy, organization, functions, business processes, and information needs. (Context: TOGAF 9)

**business capability assessment**    Identifies baseline capabilities, capability gaps, and future capability needs from a business perspective. (Context: TOGAF 9)

**business case**    A collection of descriptive and analytic information about an investment in resource(s) and/or capabilities. (Context: Common Approach/FEAF2)

**business case/alternatives analysis (B-6)**   A summary of the planning, budgeting, acquisition, and management of federal capital assets sufficient to determine whether investment funding should be recommended or continued. Equivalent to OMB Exhibit 300: Capital Asset Plan and Business Case Summary. (Context: Common Approach/FEAF2)

**business case analysis**   Analysis process or resulting report that provides the business case for a specific proposed investment or project; exact format may vary by business organization. (Context: Common Approach/FEAF2)

**business concepts**   The set of Row 2 models of the Zachman Framework that constitute management's perceptions of the design and operation of the enterprise. (Context: Zachman)

**business footprint diagram**   Describes the links between business goals, organizational units, business functions, and services, and maps these functions to the technical components delivering the required capability. (Context: TOGAF 9)

**business function**   Delivers business capabilities closely aligned to an organization, but not necessarily explicitly governed by the organization. (Context: TOGAF 9)

**business interaction matrix**   Depicts the relationship interactions between organizations and business functions across the enterprise. (Context: TOGAF 9)

**business model**   Answers the question, "In what ways do we plan to make money or achieve the reasons why our enterprise is in existence?" (Context: General)

**business operating model**   The combination of roles, skills, structures, processes, assets, and technologies that an organization uses to deliver products and services to its customers. (Context: General)

**business operating plan (B-2)**   Describes, from a timeline perspective, the changes to the business service catalog, organizational chart, and business process model to transition from the current state to the objective state. Similar to DoDAF PV-2: Project Timelines, Business Transition Plan. (Context: Common Approach/FEAF2)

**business problem statement**   The conglomeration of key elements into one expression to convey the issue at hand. After the business has decided a problem is worth pursuing in its analysis, the business analyst creates a problem statement. (Context: General)

**business process diagram (B-1)**   Presents the hierarchical structure of organizational activities and activities performed by organizational performers to consume and produce resources DoDAF OV-5a: Operational Activity Decomposition Tree, Operational Activity Diagram, and OV-5b: Operational Activity Decomposition Model, Business Process Model. (Context: Common Approach/FEAF2)

**Business Process Modeling Notation (BPMN)**   A graphical notation that depicts the steps and the end-to-end flow of a business process. Processes can be coordinated from behind, within, and over organizations natural boundaries. (Context: BPMN Organization)

**business process reengineering (BPR)**   A business management strategy originally pioneered in the early 1990s that focuses on the analysis and design of workflows and business processes within an organization. BPR aims to help organizations fundamentally rethink how they do their work to improve customer service, cut operational costs, and become world-class competitors. (Context: General)

**business reference model (BRM)**   A classification taxonomy used to describe the type of business functions and services that are performed in the federal government. By describing the government using standard business functions rather than an organizational view, the BRM promotes cross-government collaboration. (Context: Common Approach/FEAF2)

**business service**   Supports business capabilities through an explicitly defined interface and is explicitly governed by an organization. (Context: TOGAF 9)

**business service catalog (B-3)**   Presents the business services, taken from the BRM, that are provided within the scope of the architecture, and may also indicate business services that are consumed or used internally within the architecture. Included in DoDAF SvcV-1: Services Context Description. (Context: Common Approach/FEAF2)

**business service/function catalog**   Provides a functional decomposition in a form that can be filtered, reported on, and queried as a supplement to graphical functional decomposition diagrams. (Context: TOGAF 9)

**business service/information diagram**   Shows the information needed to support one or more business services, shows what data is consumed by or produced by a business service, may also show the source of information. (Context: TOGAF 9)

**Business subarchitecture domain**   Represents elements of the operating model for the enterprise, such as the key business units or organizational players, key locations, key business processes, and the mission and support services used within a business unit and between business units. Corresponds to the Operational Viewpoint in the DoDAF. Provides answers for the following questions: What is the business plan (operating plan)? How does this relate to the strategic plan's goals and metrics? What are the business units (usually depicted in the organization chart)? What are the mission and support services within and between the business units? How do we measure the effectiveness and efficiency of the line of business processes (input/output measures) and their contribution to strategic goals (outcome measures)? Do any of these business services or manufacturing processes need to be reengineered/improved before they are made to be part of the future architecture? (Context: Common Approach/FEAF2)

**business transformation capability assessment**   Determines the capabilities needed as well as the readiness of the enterprise in undertaking transformations. (Context: TOGAF 9)

**business use case diagram**   Displays the relationships between consumers and providers of business services, which are consumed by actors or other business services. The diagram provides added richness in describing business capability by illustrating how and when that capability is used. (Context: TOGAF 9)

**cable plant diagram (I-5)**   Diagrams the wires and connectors used to tie a network together. (Context: Common Approach/FEAF2)

**capability**

The ability to achieve a desired effect under specified (performance) standards and conditions through combinations of ways and means (activities and resources) to perform a set of activities. (Context: DoDAF 2.02)

A business-focused outcome that is delivered by the completion of one or more work packages. Using a capability-based planning approach, change activities can be sequenced and grouped to provide continuous and incremental business value. (Context: TOGAF 9)

The ability to perform a desired business function that creates business value. (Context: TOGAF 9)

An ability that an organization, person, or system possesses, typically expressed in general and high-level terms and typically requiring a combination of organization, people, processes, and technology to achieve—for example, marketing, customer contact, or outbound telemarketing. (Context: TOGAF 9)

**capability architecture**   A highly detailed description of the architectural approach to realize a particular solution or solution aspect. (Context: TOGAF 9)

**capability assessment**   An articulation of baseline and target capability levels of the enterprise on several levels, which is created before embarking upon a detailed architecture definition. (Context: TOGAF 9)

**capability configuration**   A collection of systems or services that, together with operational processes and human and other organizational resources, delivers a capability. (Context: MODAF)

**Capability Dependencies (CV-4)**   The dependencies between planned capabilities and the definition of logical groupings of capabilities. (Context: DoDAF 2.02)

**capability increment**   A discrete portion of a capability architecture that delivers specific value. When all increments have been completed, the capability has been realized. (Context: TOGAF 9)

**Capability Phasing (CV-3)**   The planned achievement of capability at different points in time or during specific periods of time. The CV-3 shows the capability phasing in terms of the activities, conditions, desired effects, rules complied with, resource consumption and production, and measures, without regard to the performer and location solutions. (Context: DoDAF 2.02)

**capability roadmap**   Alternative name for the Capability Phasing view. (Context: DoDAF 2.02)

**Capability Taxonomy (CV-2)**   Used to decompose a complex capability need into smaller granularity, simpler capability needs that can then be mapped to a capability development timeline. (Context: DoDAF 2.02)

**Capability to Operational Activities Mapping (CV-6)**   Establishes mappings between a capability configuration and the set of operational activities (business processes) that will harness the capability. (Context: DoDAF 2.02)

**Capability to Organizational Development Mapping (CV-5)**   The fulfillment of capability requirements shows the planned capability deployment and interconnection for a particular capability phase. The CV-5 shows the planned solution for the phase in terms of performers and locations and their associated concepts. (Context: DoDAF 2.02)

**Capability to Services Mapping (CV-7)**   Provides traceability of service-based solutions back to the capabilities they implement. (Context: DoDAF 2.02)

**Capability Viewpoint (CV)**   Articulates the capability requirements, the delivery timing, and the deployed capability. (Context: DoDAF 2.02)

**capital improvement plan**   In the RMN Airport Case Study, the airport sponsor's plan for the capital needs of the airport, typically including its planned capital funding sources. This is separate and distinct from the FAA's Airports Capital Improvement Plan (ACIP), which indicates how to allocate AIP funds. (Context: RMN Airport Case Study)

**capital planning and investment control (CPIC)**   Also known as capital programming. A decision-making process for ensuring IT investments integrate strategic planning, budgeting, procurement, and the management of IT in support of agency missions and business needs. The term comes from the Clinger-Cohen Act of 1996 and generally is used in relationship to IT management issues. CPIC includes a management process for ongoing identification, selection, control, and evaluation of investments in IT. The CPIC process links budget formulation and execution, and is focused on agency missions and achieving specific program outcomes. (Context: Common Approach/FEAF2)

**catalog**   A list of building blocks of a specific type, or of related types, that is used for governance or reference purposes (for example, an organization chart, showing locations and actors). As with building blocks, catalogs carry metadata according to the metamodel, which supports query and analysis. (Context: TOGAF 9)

**cell**   According to the Zachman Framework, the intersection between two classifications that have been used by humanity for thousands of years, the six primitive interrogatives, and the six stages of transformation of reification. The cell is one category, one classification of facts relevant to the existence of the enterprise. Each cell is a single-variable—that is, it contains only one and only one type of enterprise component and the relationships with all other components of the same type in the enterprise. (Context: Zachman)

**change management**   The process of setting expectations and involving stakeholders in how a process or activity will be changed, so that the stakeholders have some control over the change and therefore may be more accepting of the change. (Context: Common Approach/FEAF2)

**chief architect**   The leader and manager of the enterprise architecture effort, who reports to the CIO. (Context: TOGAF 9)

**chief information officer (CIO)**   Also known as the chief digital information officer (CDIO) or information technology (IT) director. A job title commonly given to the most senior executive in an enterprise responsible for the IT and computer systems that support enterprise goals. (Context: General)

**Chief Information Officers Council (CIO Council)**   The principal interagency forum for improving practices in the design, modernization, use, sharing, and performance of federal government agency information resources; established in the E-Government Act of 2002. (Context: Common Approach/FEAF2)

**chief technology officer (CTO)**   Sometimes known as a chief technical officer. An executive-level position in a company or other entity whose occupation is focused on scientific and technological issues within the organization. (Context: General)

**Collaborative Planning Methodology (CPM)**   A simple, repeatable process that consists of integrated, multidisciplinary analysis that results in recommendations formed in collaboration with leaders, stakeholders, planners, and implementers. (Context: Common Approach/FEAF2)

**commercial-off-the-shelf (COTS)**   Commercially available technology that can be purchased and utilized directly without modifications. (Context: General)

**Common Approach**   The Common Approach to Federal Enterprise Architecture accelerates agency business transformation and new technology enablement by providing standardization, design principles, scalability, an enterprise roadmap, and a repeatable architecture project method that is more agile and useful and will produce more authoritative information for intra- and interagency planning, decision-making, and management. (Context: Common Approach/FEAF2)

**common operating picture (COP)**   A single identical display of relevant (operational) information (such as position of own troops and enemy troops, position and status of important infrastructure such as bridges, roads, and so on) shared by more than one command. (Context: General)

**communications engineering diagram**   Describes the means of communication—the method of sending and receiving information—between assets in the technology architecture, insofar as the selection of package solutions in the preceding architectures put specific requirements on the communications between the applications. (Context: TOGAF 9)

**community of interest (COI)**   A gathering (potentially virtual) of people assembled around a topic of common interest. (Context: General)

**community of practice (COP)**   A group of people who share a craft or a profession. (Context: General)

**complex systems**   Any system featuring a large number of interacting components (agents, processes, and so on), whose aggregate activity is nonlinear (not derivable from the summations of the activity of individual components) and typically exhibits hierarchical self-organization under selective pressures. (Context: Indiana University)

**complicated systems**   A system comprising many components that may interact with each other and that are related not only to the scale of the problem, but also to increased requirements around coordination or specialized expertise. Even though complicated systems have many moving parts, their output or outcome can be calculated and predicted with success. (Context: General)

**component**   In the Zachman Framework, one member of a set of components that constitute a primitive model, a single cell. (Context: Zachman)

**composite**
An artifact that uses several documentation modeling techniques and/or represents several types of EA components. (Context: Common Approach/FEAF2)

A descriptive representation (model) comprising different types of components from at least two different primitive cells of the Zachman Framework. Used for manufacturing, implementations. Any implementation must, by definition, be a composite, multivariable model. (Context: Zachman)

**concept of operations (CONOPS) scenarios (S-3)**   A document that organizes business process sequences into scenarios. Similar to DoDAF OV-6c: Event-Trace Description. (Context: Common Approach/FEAF2)

**concept overview diagram (S-1)**   The high-level graphical/textual description of the operational concept. Similar to DoDAF OV-1: High-Level Operational Concept Graphic. (Context: Common Approach/FEAF2)

**conceptual data diagram**   Developed to address the concerns of business stakeholders, it depicts the relationships between critical data entities within the enterprise. (Context: TOGAF 9)

**Conceptual Data Model (DIV-1)**   The required high-level data concepts and their relationships. (Context: DoDAF 2.02)

**concerns**
The key interests that are crucially important to the stakeholders in a system and that determine the acceptability of the system. Concerns may pertain to any aspect of the system's functioning, development, or operation, including considerations such as performance, reliability, security, distribution, and evolvability. (Context: TOGAF 9)

Interests that pertain to the system's development, its operation, or any other aspects that are critical or otherwise important to one or more stakeholders. Concerns include system considerations such as performance, reliability, security, distribution, and evolvability. (Context: IEEE Std 1471-2000)

**condition**   The state of an environment or a situation in which a performer performs. (Context: DoDAF 2.02)

**configuration control board (CCB)**   Also known as a configuration management board. A group that should play an essential role in an organization's overall EA strategy. Typically chaired by the CIO, it usually includes voting representatives from every department in the company. (Context: General)

**configuration management (CM)**

The process of managing updates to business and technology resources (such as processes, systems, applications, and networks) to ensure that security controls are operating effectively and that standards are being followed. (Context: Common Approach/FEAF2)

A systems engineering process for establishing and maintaining consistency of a product's performance, functional, and physical attributes with its requirements, design, and operational information throughout its lifetime. Applied to architecture, the process of keeping the artifacts up to date to reflect a given state of the enterprise architecture. (Context: General)

**connection**   A route of path over which some enterprise inventory is transported from location to location. (Context: Zachman)

**connectivity view type (Cn)**   Describes the connections, relationships, and interactions between the different elements. (Context: Unified Architecture Framework)

**Consolidated Reference Model (CRM)**   Part of the Federal Enterprise Architecture Framework (FEAF), it equips Office of Management and Budget and federal agencies with a common language and framework to describe and analyze investments. It consists of a set of interrelated reference models designed to facilitate cross-agency analysis and the identification of duplicative investments, gaps, and opportunities for collaboration within and across agencies. Collectively, the reference models comprise a framework for describing important elements of federal agency operations in a common and consistent way. Through the use of the FEAF and its vocabulary, IT portfolios can be better managed and leveraged across the federal government, enhancing collaboration and ultimately transforming the federal government. (Context: Common Approach/FEAF2)

**constraint**   An external factor that prevents an organization from pursuing particular approaches to meet its goals. For example, if customer data is not harmonized within the organization, regionally or nationally, it constrains the organization's ability to offer effective customer service. (Context: TOGAF 9)

**constraints view type (Ct)**   Details the measurements that set performance requirements constraining capabilities. Also defines the rules governing behavior and structure. (Context: Unified Architecture Framework)

**continuity of operations plan (SP-6)**   A plan that describes all aspects of recovery from an incident that temporarily disables the operational capabilities of the enterprise and requires relocation. (Context: Common Approach/FEAF2)

**continuous monitoring plan (SP-4)** Describes the organization's process of monitoring and analyzing the security controls and reporting on their effectiveness. (Context: Common Approach/FEAF2)

**contract** An agreement between a service consumer and a service provider that establishes functional and nonfunctional parameters for interaction. (Context: TOGAF 9)

**contract/measure catalog** Provides a list of all agreed-upon service contracts and (optionally) the measures attached to those contracts. It forms the master list of service levels agreed to across the enterprise. (Context: TOGAF 9)

**control** A decision-making step with accompanying decision logic used to determine execution approach for a process or to ensure that a process complies with governance criteria—for example, a sign-off control on a purchase request processing process that checks whether the total value of the request is within the sign-off limits of the requester, or whether it needs escalating to higher authority. (Context: TOGAF 9)

**core views** The DoDAF views that are recommended by the authors for Enterprise Level, Segment Level, and Solution Level architectures. (Context: General)

**crosscutting segment** Serves several lines of business within or between agencies. Examples include e-mail systems that serve the whole enterprise and financial systems that serve several lines of business. (Context: Common Approach/FEAF2)

**CRUD matrix (D-6)** Create, Read, Update or Delete. Presents resources that are consumed and produced by activities performed by organizational performers. Similar to DoDAF OV-3: Operational Resource Flow Matrix, Business Data Mapped to Key Business Processes (CRUD). (Context: Common Approach/FEAF2)

**culture** The beliefs, customs, values, structure, normative rules, and material traits of a social organization. Evident in many aspects of how an organization functions. (Context: Common Approach/FEAF2)

**current view** A collection of artifacts that represent processes and technologies that currently exist in the enterprise. (Context: Common Approach/FEAF2)

**data**
Refers to an elementary description of things, events, activities, and transactions that are recorded, classified, and stored, but not organized to convey any specific meaning. Data items can be numeric, alphabetic, figures, sounds, or images. A database consists of stored data items organized for retrieval. (Context: Common Approach/FEAF2)

Representation of information in a formalized manner suitable for communication, interpretation, or processing by humans or by automatic means. (Context: DoDAF 2.02)

**Data and Information Viewpoint (DIV)** Articulates the data relationships and alignment structures in the architecture content for the capability and operational requirements, system engineering processes, and systems and services. (Context: DoDAF 2.02)

**data architecture**   A description of the structure and interaction of the enterprise's major types and sources of data, logical data assets, physical data assets, and data management resources. (Context: TOGAF 9)

**data center/server room diagram (I-8)**   Diagrams the layout and contents of a data center or server room. (Context: Common Approach/FEAF2)

**data dictionary (D-9)**   A centralized repository of information about data such as name, type, range of values, source, and authorization for access for each data element in the organization's files and databases. (Context: Common Approach/FEAF2)

**data dissemination diagram**   Shows the relationships between data entities, business services, and application components; shows how the logical entities are to be physically realized by application components. This enables effective sizing to be carried out and the IT footprint to be refined. Moreover, by assigning business value to data, an indication of the business criticality of application components can be gained. (Context: TOGAF 9)

**data entity**   An encapsulation of data that is recognized by a business domain expert as a thing. Logical data entities can be tied to applications, repositories, and services and may be structured according to implementation considerations. (Context: TOGAF 9)

**data entity/business function matrix**   Depicts the relationship between data entities and business functions within the enterprise. Business functions are supported by business services with explicitly defined boundaries and will be supported and realized by business processes. (Context: TOGAF 9)

**data entity/data component catalog**   Identifies and maintains a list of all the data use across the enterprise, including data entities and also the data components where data entities are stored. Supports the definition and application of information management and data governance policies and also encourages effective data sharing and reuse. (Context: TOGAF 9)

**data flow diagram (D-4)**   The functions (activities) performed by systems or services, their hierarchical structure, and their resource flows. Similar to DoDAF SV-4: Systems Functionality Description and SvcV-4: Services Functionality Description. (Context: Common Approach/FEAF2)

**data life cycle diagram**   An essential part of managing business data throughout its life cycle from conception until disposal within the constraints of the business process. The data is considered as an entity in its own right, decoupled from business process and activity. Each change in state is represented on the diagram, which may include the event or rules that trigger that change in state. The separation of data from process enables common data requirements to be identified, which enables resource sharing to be achieved more effectively. (Context: TOGAF 9)

**data migration diagram**   Shows the flow of data from the source to the target applications, provides a visual representation of the spread of sources/targets, and serves as a tool for data auditing and establishing traceability. This diagram can be elaborated or enhanced as necessary. For example, the diagram can contain an overall layout of migration landscape or could go into the individual application metadata element–level of detail. (Context: TOGAF 9)

**data model**    An abstract model that organizes elements of data and standardizes how they relate to one another and to properties of the real world entities. (Context: General)

**data quality plan (D-3)**    A systematic approach to data quality assurance. (Context: Common Approach/FEAF2)

**data reference model (DRM)**    One of six reference models of the Federal Enterprise Architecture (FEA) version 2.0, DRM is a classification taxonomy used to describe the context for information exchanges and the type of data entities and attributes in a particular solution architecture at the system, segment, agency, sector, federal, national, or international level. (Context: Common Approach/FEAF2)

**data security diagram**    Depicts which actor (person, organization, or system) can access which enterprise data. This relationship can be shown in a matrix form between two objects or can be shown as a mapping. Data is considered an asset to the enterprise and data security ensures that enterprise data is not compromised and that access to it is suitably controlled. (Context: TOGAF 9)

**Data subarchitecture domain**    After the lines of business and specific business services have been identified, it is important to ask the following: What are the flows of information that will be required within and between service areas in order to make them successful? How can these flows of information be harmonized, standardized, and protected to promote sharing that is efficient, accurate, and secure? How will the data underlying the information flows be formatted, generated, shared, and stored? What are the workforce, standards, and security issues in this domain? (Context: Common Approach/FEAF2)

**Defense Architecture Framework (DAF), Australia**    A DoDAF-related defense architecture framework in Australia. (Context: General)

**Defense Discovery Metadata Specification (DDMS)**    Created in support of the DoD Net-Centric Data Strategy (May 9, 2003), which specifies a set of information fields that are to be used to describe any data or service asset that is made known to the DoD enterprise. The elements in the DDMS are designed to be platform-, language-, and implementation-independent, and the specification is described with an XML schema. (Context: General)

**deliverable**    An architectural work product that is contractually specified and in turn formally reviewed, agreed upon, and signed off by the stakeholders. Deliverables represent the output of projects, and deliverables in documentation form will typically be archived at completion of a project, or transitioned into an architecture repository as a reference model, standard, or snapshot of the architecture landscape. (Context: TOGAF 9)

**Department of National Defense Architecture Framework (DNDAF), Canada** Department of National Defense/Canadian Armed Forces architecture framework started with the DoDAF that has extended it to include security-related issues. (Context: General)

**desired effect** A desired state of a resource. (Context: DoDAF 2.02)

**diagram** A rendering of architectural content in a graphical format that enables stakeholders to retrieve the required information. Can also be used as a technique for graphically populating architecture content or for checking the completeness of information that has been collected. TOGAF defines a set of architecture diagrams to be created (such as an organization chart). Each may be created several times for an architecture with different styles or content coverage to suit stakeholder concerns. (Context: TOGAF 9)

**dictionary** *See* Integrated Dictionary (AV-2). (Context: Unified Architecture Framework)

**disaster recovery plan (SP-5)** A plan that describes all aspects of recovery from an incident that temporarily disables the operational capabilities of the enterprise but does not entail relocation. (Context: Common Approach/FEAF2)

**distribution networks** The Column 3 models of the Zachman Framework descriptive of the locations from which and to which the enterprise acquires, stores, and disposes of its various inventories. At Row 6, the locations and connections instances will have latitudes and longitudes. (Context: Zachman)

**DoD Architecture Framework (DoDAF)** An architecture framework developed by the U.S. Department of Defense that serves as the basis for many other defense frameworks. DoDAF Version 2.0 is the overarching, comprehensive framework and conceptual model that enables the development of architectures to facilitate the ability of DoD managers at all levels to make key decisions more effectively through organized information sharing across the department, Joint Capability Areas (JCAs), and mission, component, and program boundaries. (Context: DoDAF 2.02)

**DoD Architecture Registry System (DARS)** A DoD repository for Overview and Summary Information (AV-1) documents. (Context: DoDAF 2.02)

**DoD Core Data Center reference architecture** Defines the DoD cloud architecture as a reference model to deploy military applications to support net-centric operations. (Context: DIEA)

**DoD Joint Capabilities Integration and Development System (JCIDS)** A U.S. DoD business process to identify capability needs across the military services, prioritize and aggregate these needs, and sponsor the development of military capabilities in support of joint operations. (Context: General)

**DoD Joint Information Enterprise reference architecture**  An overarching view of how DoD information, IT, and cyber environment will be transformed for the future through a collection of a vision, reference architectures, and ways forward. (Context: DIEA)

**DoDAF Metamodel (DM2)**  Defines all the types of DoDAF architecture elements and their intended relationships. (Context: DoDAF 2.02)

**DoDAF viewpoints**  To assist decision-makers, DoDAF provides the means of abstracting essential information from the underlying complexity and presenting it in a way that maintains coherence and consistency. One of the principal objectives is to present this information in a way that is understandable to the many stakeholder communities involved in developing, delivering, and sustaining capabilities in support of the stakeholder's mission. It does so by dividing the problem space into manageable pieces, according to the stakeholder's viewpoint, further defined as DoDAF-described models. (Context: DoDAF 2.02)

**DoDAF views**  Specific representations of the architecture contained as a subset within a viewpoint that provides communication and analytical value to stakeholders whose concerns are addressed by a particular view. (Context: General)

**DOTMLPF**  An acronym that stands for Doctrine, Organization, Training, Materiel, Leadership, Personnel, and Facility, sometimes with a suffix -P signifying Policy. These are used as elements for military planning, equipping, and organizing resources. (Context: DoDAF 2.02)

**driver**  An external or internal condition that motivates the organization to define its goals. An example of an external driver is a change in regulation or compliance rules that require changes to the way an organization operates (such as Sarbanes-Oxley). (Context: TOGAF 9)

**driver/goal/objective catalog**  Provides a cross-organizational reference of how an organization meets its drivers in practical terms through goals, objectives, and (optionally) measures. (Context: TOGAF 9)

**EA basic program elements**  Eight basic elements must be present and be designed to work together in each agency EA program: governance, principles, method, tools, standards, use, reporting, and audit. These elements ensure that agency EA programs are complete and can be effective in developing solutions that support planning and decision-making. (Context: Common Approach/FEAF2)

**EA governance**  The first basic (Program EA Basic) element that identifies the planning, decision-making, and oversight processes and groups that will determine how the EA is developed, verified, versioned, used, and sustained over time with respect to measures of completeness, consistency, coherence, and accuracy from the perspectives of all stakeholders. (Context: Common Approach/FEAF2)

**EA principles**  Provide a basis for decision-making throughout an enterprise and inform how the organization sets about fulfilling its mission. Principles that govern the implementation of the architecture, establishing the first tenets and related guidance for designing and developing information systems. (Context: TOGAF 9)

**EA program office**   An organization with a charter, budget, and mission to provide enterprise architecting services to the enterprise. Can be run as a project or as a standing organization. (Context: General)

**electronic government**   The use by the federal government of Internet applications and other information technologies, combined with processes that implement these technologies, to enhance the access to and delivery of government information and services to the public, other agencies, and other government entities; or to bring about improvements in government operations that may include effectiveness, efficiency, service quality, or transformation. (Context: Common Approach/FEAF2)

**end**   A goal or objective that is significant for motivating the design or operation of the enterprise. (Context: Zachman)

**enterprise**

An organization (or cross organizational entity) supporting a defined business scope and mission that includes interdependent resources (people, organizations, and technologies) that must coordinate their functions and share information in support of a common mission (or set of related missions). (Context: CIO Council 1999)

An area of common activity and goals within an organization or between several organizations, where information and other resources are exchanged. (Context: Common Approach/FEAF2)

A complex, (adaptive) sociotechnical system that comprises interdependent resources of people, processes, information, and technology that must interact with each other and their environment in support of a common mission. (Context: *Ronald Giachetti, Design of Enterprise Systems: Theory, Architecture, and Methods*, CRC Press, 2010)

One or more organizations sharing a definite mission, goals, and objectives to offer an output such as a product or service. (Context: ISO 2000)

An entity that is tightly bounded and directed by a single executive function, or when organizational boundaries are less well defined and where there may be multiple owners in terms of direction of the resources being employed. The common factor is that both entities exist to achieve specified outcomes. (Context: MODAF 2004)

A purposeful combination (such as a network) of interdependent resources (such as people, processes, organizations, supporting technologies, and funding) that interact with each other to coordinate functions, share information, allocate funding, create workflows, and make decisions; and their environment(s) to achieve business and operational goals through a complex web of interactions distributed across geography and time. (Context: Rebovich and White, *Enterprise Systems Engineering: Advances in the Theory and Practice*, CRC Press, 2010)

A collection of organizations that has a common set of goals. Or the highest level (typically) of description of an organization that typically covers all missions and functions. An enterprise will often span multiple organizations. (Context: TOGAF 9)

### enterprise architecture

A strategic information asset base that defines the mission, the information necessary to perform the mission, the technologies necessary to perform the mission, and the transitional processes for implementing new technologies in response to changing mission needs. It includes a baseline architecture, a target architecture, and a sequencing plan. (Context: Common Approach/FEAF2)

A structured set of descriptive representations relevant for describing an enterprise and being employed such that an instance of the enterprise can be created and such that the descriptive representations serve as a baseline for changing the instantiated enterprise. (Context: Zachman)

**enterprise architecture executive steering committee (EAESC)**　A committee of business and executive managers that make the key decisions regarding the enterprise architecture. This group can act as the configuration control board (CCB) for the enterprise architecture. (Context: TOGAF 9)

**Enterprise Continuum**　A categorization mechanism useful for classifying architecture and solution artifacts, both internal and external to the architecture repository, as they evolve from generic foundation architectures to organization-specific architectures. (Context: TOGAF 9)

**enterprise diagnosis**　The process of analyzing enterprise problems to determine their "root" causes based on the enterprise ontology (the Zachman Framework) to prescribe enduring solutions as opposed to putting "band aids" on symptomatic anomalies by trial and error or gut feel. (Context: Zachman)

**enterprise engineering**　The process of creating the single-variable, "primitive" descriptive representations of an enterprise such that they can be used (reused) in producing enterprise implementation "composites" such that the enterprise can be integrated, flexible, interoperable, reusable, aligned, and so on, to accommodate extreme complexity and extreme rates of change. (Context: Zachman)

**Enterprise Level architecture**　An enterprise architecture focused on the executive management-level concerns such as strategy, acquisition, planning, and projects. (Context: Common Approach/FEAF2)

**enterprise manageability diagram**　Shows how one or more applications interact with application and technology components that support operational management of a solution. (Context: TOGAF 9)

**enterprise manufacturing**　The process of creating enterprise implementations, systems, manual or automated, "composites." If components of "primitive" models are employed in the process of creating the implementation composites, the enterprise will be architected. If components of primitive models are not used in creating the implementation "composites," the enterprise will be implemented, but not architected. (Context: Zachman)

**enterprise resource planning (ERP)**   A process by which a company (often a manufacturer) manages and integrates the important parts of its business. An ERP management information system integrates areas such as planning, purchasing, inventory, sales, marketing, finance, and human resources. (Context: Investopedia)

**enterprise roadmap**   A document produced at least annually by the organization responsible for the enterprise (usually a federal agency) that describes the current and future views of the enterprise-wide architecture, how changes occur, and how the EA program functions. (Context: Common Approach/FEAF2)

**enterprise service bus diagram (A-8)**   Describes the interaction and communication between mutually interacting software applications in service-oriented architecture (SOA). (Context: Common Approach/FEAF2)

**enterprise systems engineering (ESE)**   The application of SE principles, concepts, and methods to the planning, design, improvement, and operation of an enterprise. To enable more efficient and effective enterprise transformation, the enterprise needs to be looked at as a system, rather than as a collection of functions connected solely by information systems and shared facilities. Although a systems perspective is required for dealing with the enterprise, this is rarely the task or responsibility of people who call themselves systems engineers. (Context: Systems Engineering)

**Enterprise Transition Plan (ETP)**   A roadmap for the DoD business systems that are new or being modernized, and the governance and strategic framework DoD uses to manage its investments. It describes how those investments are part of the department's overarching management reform efforts, outlines key improvement initiatives for the current fiscal year, and provides specific information regarding each of its business system investments. The ETP is now incorporated into functional strategies, component organizational execution plans, and data in the DoD Information Technology Portfolio Repository (DITPR), Select and Native Programming Data Input Systems for Information Technology (SNaP-IT), Integrated Business Framework Data Alignment Portal (IBF-DAP), and the DoD Information Technology Investment Portal (DITIP). (Context: DoD Change Management Office)

**entity**   A collection of like objects that have identical characteristics but are unique individuals. For example, apples have identical characteristics but each member of the set of apples is a unique individual. There could never be an entity called "apples" that is made up of apples and oranges because apples have completely different characteristics than do oranges. (Context: Zachman)

**environmental impact assessment**   A document required of federal agencies by the National Environmental Policy Act for major projects or legislative proposals affecting the environment. It is a tool for decision-making describing the positive and negative effects of a proposed action and citing alternative actions. (Context: FAA AMP)

**environments and locations diagram**  Depicts which locations host which applications, identifies what technologies and/or applications are used at which locations, and identifies the locations from which business users typically interact with the applications. (Context: TOGAF 9)

**event**
   An organizational state change that triggers processing events. It may originate from inside or outside the organization and may be resolved inside or outside the organization. (Context: TOGAF 9)

   Something that happens at a given place and time; in architecture, a discrete event that causes some action to take place such as an information exchange or a change in state. (Context: General)

**event diagram**  Depicts the relationship between events and process. (Context: TOGAF 9)

**event sequence diagram (D-8)**  A sequence of triggering events associated with resource flows and systems. Similar to DoDAF SV-10c: Systems Event-Trace Description and SvcV-10c: Services Event-Trace Description. (Context: Common Approach/FEAF2)

**Event-Trace Description (OV-6c)**  One of three views used to describe activity (operational activity). It traces actions in a scenario or sequence of events. (Context: DoDAF 2.02)

**executive agency**  The agency defined in section 4(1) of the Office of Federal Procurement Policy Act (41 U.S.C. 403(1)). (Context: Common Approach/FEAF2)

**explicit knowledge**  Knowledge that can be written down or incorporated in computer codes. (Context: Systems Engineering)

**extended enterprise**  A wider organization representing all associated entities—customers, employees, suppliers, distributors, and so on—who directly or indirectly, formally or informally, collaborate in the design, development, production, and delivery of a product (or service) to the end user. (Context: www.businessdictionary.com)

**facility blueprints (I-12)**  Technical drawings of the facility. (Context: Common Approach/FEAF2)

**Family of Systems (FoS)**  A set of separate systems that can be integrated in different ways to provide a variety of mission-related capabilities. (Context: Systems Engineering)

**federal**  This level of architecture focuses on services (and associated systems) that serve the entire Executive Branch of the U.S. government. These federal-wide mission and support services are channeled through OMB-designated "Line of Business" providers, wherein the roles of provider and consumer are detailed and a comprehensive business model for each federal-wide service generates requirements for that architecture. (Context: Common Approach/FEAF2)

**Federal Aviation Administration (FAA)**   A national authority with powers to regulate all aspects of civil aviation in the United States. These include the construction and operation of airports, air traffic management, the certification of personnel and aircraft, and the protection of U.S. assets during the launch or reentry of commercial space vehicles. (Context: General)

**Federal Enterprise Architecture (FEA)**   A business-based documentation and analysis framework for government-wide improvement that enables agencies to use standardized methods to describe the relationship between an agency's strategic goals, business functions, and enabling technologies at various levels of scope and complexity. The FEA comprises a framework for documentation in six domain areas (strategic goals, business services, data and information, systems and applications, infrastructure, and security) and six reference models areas that are designed to facilitate standardized analysis, reporting, and the identification of duplicative investments, gaps, and opportunities for collaboration within and across federal agencies. The FEA method is based on a five-step repeatable method for solution architecture that can be used at various levels of scope and provides current views, future views, and a transition (sequencing) plan. (Context: Common Approach/FEAF2)

**Federal Enterprise Architecture Framework (FEAF) v2**   Describes a suite of tools to help government planners implement the Common Approach. At its core is the consolidated reference model (CRM) that equips OMB and federal agencies with a common language and framework to describe and analyze investments. (Context: Common Approach/FEAF2)

**Federal Information Security Management Act (FISMA)**   U.S. legislation that defines a comprehensive framework to protect government information, operations, and assets against natural or manmade threats. FISMA was signed into law part of the Electronic Government Act of 2002. (Context: General)

**Federal Information Technology Acquisition Reform Act (FITARA)**   Passed by Congress in December 2014, a historic law that represents the first major overhaul of federal IT in almost 20 years. (Context: General)

**Federal IT Dashboard**   A web site enabling federal agencies, industry, the general public, and other stakeholders to view details including performance for federal information technology investments. (Context: Common Approach/FEAF2)

**federated architecture (FA)**   A pattern in enterprise architecture that enables interoperability and information sharing between semiautonomous, decentrally organized lines of business, information technology systems, and applications. (Context: General)

**Fit-for-Purpose (FFP) views**   Customized views included in DoDAF architectures for the purpose of documenting issues not addressed by standardized DoDAF views or communicating with specific stakeholder groups; must be integrated with some set of standard DoDAF views. (Context: DoDAF 2.02)

**foundation architecture** Generic building blocks and their interrelationships with other building blocks, combined with the principles and guidelines that provide a foundation on which more specific architectures can be built. (Context: TOGAF 9)

**framework**

A structure for organizing information that defines the scope of the architecture (what will be documented) and how the areas of the architecture are related. (Context: Common Approach/FEAF2)

A conceptual framework, or frame of reference, for architectural description, that establishes terms and concepts pertaining to the content and use of architectural descriptions. (Context: IEEE Std 1471-2000)

A structure for content or process that can be used as a tool to structure thinking, ensure consistency, and ensure completeness. (Context: TOGAF 9)

A structure, a classification, that is typically misapplied as something generic, abstract, or of imprecise definition rather than a structure. (Context: Zachman)

**function** Delivers business capabilities closely aligned to an organization, but not necessarily explicitly governed by the organization. Also referred to as business function. (Context: TOGAF 9)

**functional decomposition diagram** Shows on a single page the capabilities of an organization that are relevant to the consideration of an architecture. By examining the capabilities of an organization from a functional perspective, it is possible to develop models of what the organization does without being dragged into extended debate on how the organization does it. (Context: TOGAF 9)

**functional integration** Interoperability among programs, systems, and services, which requires a metacontext and standards to be successful. Program, systems, and services interoperability is foundational for federal government organizations to be able to partner successfully in new shared service models that may involve outside providers and new roles for participation (such as consumer, developer, or provider). (Context: Common Approach/FEAF2)

**future view** A collection of artifacts that represent processes and technologies that do not yet exist in the enterprise. (Context: Common Approach/FEAF2)

**GAO EA Management Maturity Assessment Framework (EAMMF)** A classic five-stage maturity model, with the stages ranging from Stage 1, Creating EA Awareness, to Stage 5, Leveraging the EA to Manage Change. (Context: Common Approach/FEAF2)

**gap** A statement of difference between two states. Used in the context of gap analysis, where the difference between the baseline and target architecture is identified. *See* gap analysis. (Context: TOGAF 9)

**gap analysis** Involves the comparison of actual performance with potential or desired performance, the gap between capability needs and current capabilities. If an organization does not make the best use of current resources or forgoes investment in capital or technology, it may produce or perform below its potential. (Context: General)

**general aviation**   The segment of aviation that encompasses all aspects of civil aviation except certified air carriers and other commercial operators such as airfreight carriers. (Context: FAA AMP)

**goal**   A high-level statement of intent or direction for an organization. Typically used to measure success of an organization. (Context: TOGAF 9)

**goal/objective/service diagram**   Defines the ways in which a service contributes to the achievement of a business vision or strategy. TOGAF alternative view of CV-7: Capability to Services Mapping. (Context: TOGAF 9)

**governance**

A group of policies, decision-making procedures, and management processes that work together to enable the effective planning and oversight of activities and resources. (Context: Common Approach/FEAF2)

The practice by which enterprise architectures are managed and controlled. (Context: TOGAF 9)

**governance log**   Provides a record of governance activity across the enterprise. (Context: TOGAF 9)

**Government Accountability Office (GAO)**   This U.S. federal agency that reviews the status of various government projects at congressional request and provides reports on observed status and problems. (Context: Common Approach/FEAF2)

**government publication**   Information published as an individual document at government expense, or as required by law. (44 U.S.C. 1901). (Context: Common Approach/FEAF2)

**guidance**   An authoritative statement intended to lead or steer the execution of actions. (Context: DoDAF 2.02)

**High-Level Operational Concept Graphic (OV-1)**   The high-level graphical/textual description of the operational concept. (Context: DoDAF 2.02)

**horizontal segment**   A crosscutting process, program, or resource that serves several lines of business. (Context: Common Approach/FEAF2)

**hosting concept of operations (I-2)**   Presents the high-level functional architecture, organization, roles, responsibilities, processes, metrics, and strategic plan for hosting and use of hosting services. (Context: Common Approach/FEAF2)

**IDEF (Integration Definition for Information Modeling)**   A family of modeling languages in the field of systems and software engineering; each of these modeling languages is standalone. (Context: General)

**IDEF0**   The IDEF modeling language and methodology for process modeling. (Context: General)

**IDEF1X**  The IDEF modeling language and methodology for data modeling. (Context: General)

**Identity and Access Management (IdAM) reference architecture**  Specifies a standard architecture for identification and access management across the U.S. Army. (Context: U.S. Army)

**implementations**  Usually a running system, manual or automated, that is, in Zachman Framework terms, a Row 6 instantiation. However, any composite, whether it is architected within any row of the Zachman Framework or not architected as an ad hoc or random composite that exists can be an implementation. (Context: Zachman)

**information**
Any communication or representation of knowledge such as facts, data, or opinions in any medium or form, including textual, numerical, graphic, cartographic, narrative, or audiovisual forms. (Context: Common Approach/FEAF2)

The state of a something of interest that is materialized—in any medium or form—and communicated or received. (Context: DoDAF 2.02)

**information life cycle**  The stages through which information passes, typically characterized as creation or collection, processing, dissemination, use, storage, and disposition. (Context: Common Approach/FEAF2)

**information management**  The planning, budgeting, manipulating, and controlling of information throughout its life cycle. (Context: Common Approach/FEAF2)

**information resource catalog**  Up-to-date inventory of information assets. (Context: TOGAF 9)

**information resource management (IRM) strategic plan**  A strategic document that addresses all information resources management of the agency. Agencies must develop and maintain the agency's IRM strategic plan as required by 44 U.S.C. 3506(b) (2). IRM strategic plans should conform to guidance provided annually in OMB Circular A–11, provide a description of how IT management activities help accomplish agency missions delivery area and program decision, and ensure that decisions are integrated with management support areas including organizational planning, budget, procurement, financial management, and HR. (Context: Common Approach/FEAF2)

**information resources**  Resources that include both government information and IT. (Context: Common Approach/FEAF2)

**information resources management**  The process of managing information resources to accomplish agency missions. The term encompasses both information itself and the related resources, such as personnel, equipment, funds, and IT. (Context: Common Approach/FEAF2)

**information security**  Involves all functions necessary to meet federal information security policy requirements. It includes the development, implementation, and maintenance of security policies, procedures, and controls across the entire information life cycle. This includes implementation and activities associated with NIST SP-800-37

Revision 1: Guide for Applying the Risk Management Framework to Federal Information Systems, Security Awareness Training; SP-800-39: Managing Risk from Information Systems; SP-800-53A Revision 4: Assessing Security and Privacy Controls in Federal Information Systems and Organizations; and FISMA compliance reporting, development of security policy, security audits, and testing. (Context: Common Approach/FEAF2)

**information system**   A discrete set of IT, data, and related resources, such as personnel, hardware, software, and associated information technology services organized for the collection, processing, maintenance, use, sharing, dissemination, or disposition of information in accordance with defined procedures, whether automated or manual. (Context: Common Approach/FEAF2)

**information system life cycle**   The phases through which an information system passes, typically characterized as initiation, development, operation, and termination. (Context: Common Approach/FEAF2)

**information system service**   The automated elements of a business service that may deliver or support part or all of one or more business services. (Context: TOGAF 9)

**information technology (IT)**
   1. The life cycle management of information and related technology used by an organization. 2. An umbrella term that includes all or some of the subject areas relating to the computer industry, such as business continuity, business IT interface, business process modeling and management, communication, compliance and legislation, computers, content management, hardware, information management, Internet, offshoring, networking, programming and software, professional issues, project management, security, standards, storage, voice and data communications. Various countries and industries employ other umbrella terms to describe this same collection. 3. Term commonly assigned to a department within an organization tasked with provisioning some or all of the domains described in definition 2. 4. Alternate names commonly adopted include information services, information management, and so on. (Context: TOGAF 9)

   Any equipment or interconnected system or subsystem of equipment that is used in the automatic acquisition, storage, manipulation, management, movement, control, display, switching, interchange, transmission, or reception of data or information by an executive agency. IT is related to the terms capital asset, IT investment, program, project, subproject, service, and system. (Context: Common Approach/FEAF2)

**information technology governance**   Provides the framework and structure that links IT resources and information to enterprise goals and strategies. Institutionalizes best practices for planning, acquiring, implementing, and monitoring IT performance, to ensure that the enterprise's IT assets support its business objectives. (Context: TOGAF 9)

**information technology investment**   The expenditure of IT resources to address mission delivery and management support. May include a project or projects for the development, modernization, enhancement, or maintenance of a single IT asset or group of IT assets with related functionality and the subsequent operation of those assets in a production environment. While each asset or project would have a defined life cycle, an investment that covers a collection of assets intended to support an ongoing business mission may not. (Context: Common Approach/FEAF2)

**information view type (If)**   Addresses the information perspective on operational, service, and resource architectures. Allows analysis of an architecture's information and data definition aspect, without consideration of implementation-specific issues. (Context: Unified Architecture Framework)

**infrastructure reference model (IRM)**   Categorizes the network/cloud–related standards and technologies to support and enable the delivery of voice, data, video, and mobile service components and capabilities. (Context: Common Approach/FEAF2)

**Infrastructure subarchitecture domain**   In the EA framework. it is important to ask the following: What types of voice, data, mobile, and video networks will be required to host the IT systems/applications and to transport associate, data, images, and conversations? What type of physical infrastructure is needed to support the networks (such as buildings, server rooms, points of presence, and other equipment)? Will highly scalable cloud computing environments be needed, and, if so, will the organization be a provider or consumer? How can these networks be integrated to create a cost-effective and operationally efficient hosting environment? Will these networks extend beyond the enterprise? What are the physical space and utility support requirements for the networks? Will cloud-based concepts be used (virtualization, scaling, metering)? What are the workforce, standards, and security issues in this subarchitecture domain? (Context: Common Approach/FEAF2)

**input**
The raw material and/or energy that is transformed by some process into some product or service. (Context: Zachman)

Resources (human, employee time, funding) used to conduct activities and provide services. (Context: ECA)

**Integrated Dictionary (AV-2)**   An authoritative and integrated dictionary for all architecture elements or terms used in all views that support all viewpoints. (Context: DoDAF 2.02)

**integrated product teams (IPTs)**   Temporary teams composed of personnel from various organizations or roles within the enterprise that are established to develop a specific product. In the architecture case, this product would be a part of the architecture. (Context: General)

**integration**
In the context of an architecture, an assurance that the same architecture element is modeled consistently across multiple views. Integration avoids creating multiple representations for a common object that can lead to flaws in analysis and interpretation. (Context: General)

The characteristic of any formalism in which there are no anomalies, no discontinuities, and elements perfectly fit together. (Context: Zachman)

**intelligence community** The collection of federal and military agencies that collaborate and cooperate in national intelligence–related activities. (Context: General)

**Intelligence, Surveillance, and Reconnaissance (ISR)** The coordinated and integrated acquisition, processing, and provision of timely, accurate, relevant, coherent, and assured information and intelligence to support a commander's conduct of activities. (Context: General)

**interaction scenarios view type (Is)** Expresses a time-ordered examination of the exchanges as a result of a particular scenario or between participating elements as a result of a particular scenario. (Context: Unified Architecture Framework)

**interface catalog** Scopes and documents the interfaces between applications to enable the overall dependencies between applications to be scoped as early as possible. (Context: TOGAF 9)

**international** The level of architecture that focuses on international partnerships of the U.S. government with other governments, global industries, non-profits, and other groups. International-level architectures often center on the enablement of shared services, wherein the roles of provider and consumer need to be detailed and a comprehensive business model for the service provides the requirements for the architecture. (Context: Common Approach/FEAF2)

**International Defense Enterprise Architecture Specification (IDEAS)** A formal ontology foundation developed by the defense departments and ministries of the United States, United Kingdom, Canada, Australia, and Sweden in coordination with NATO. (Context: DoDAF 2.02)

**interoperability** The ability of different operating and software systems, applications, and services to communicate and exchange data in an accurate, effective, and consistent manner. (Context: Common Approach/FEAF2)

**interval** A length of time of significance to the enterprise such that its duration in clock time will be recorded at Row 6 of the Zachman Framework. (Context: Zachman)

**inventory** The enterprise (business) name for an entity, a set, things the enterprise counts. Inventories typically have a serial numbers on the instances at Row 6. (Context: Zachman)

**inventory sets** The Column 1 models of the Zachman Framework, descriptive of the inventories that the enterprise manages. At Row 6 the inventory instances likely have serial numbers associated. (Context: Zachman)

**IT capability assessment (TOGAF 9)** Identifies baseline capabilities, capability gaps, and future capability needs from the IT perspective. (Context: TOGAF 9)

**joint asset visibility** Refers to supplies (expendable items) and equipment (nonexpendable items)—on order, in transit, in storage, or on hand—that are owned or destined for the military services, DoD agencies, or coalition partners. (Context: U.S. Army)

**Joint Capability Area (JCA)**   Collections of similar DoD capabilities functionally grouped to support capability analysis, strategy development, investment decision-making, capability portfolio management, and capabilities-based force development and operational planning. JCAs are aligned with functional configuration boards (FCBs). (Context: Defense Acquisition)

**joint mission thread (JMT)**   An operational and technical description of the end-to-end set of activities and systems that accomplish the execution of a joint mission. (Context: Joint Instruction)

**Joint Requirements Oversight Council (JROC)**   Part of the U.S. DoD acquisition process that reviews programs designated as JROC interest and supports the acquisition review process in accordance with law. (Context: General)

**joint task force**   A joint (multiservice) ad hoc military formation. (Context: General)

**knowledge**   Data or information that has been organized and processed to convey understanding, experience, accumulated learning, and expertise as it applies to a current problem or activity. Data that is processed to extract critical implications and to reflect past experience and expertise provides the recipient with organizational knowledge, which has a very high potential value. (Context: Common Approach/FEAF2)

**knowledge management plan (D-2)**   Provides a detailed description of how knowledge, information, and data are shared across the enterprise between systems, applications, knowledge warehouses, and databases. (Context: Common Approach/FEAF2)

**landside**   The portion of an airport that provides the facilities necessary for the processing of passengers, cargo, freight, and ground transportation vehicles. (Context: FAA AMP)

**legacy systems**   In computing, an old method, technology, computer system, or application program of, relating to, or being a previous or outdated computer system. Often a pejorative term, referencing a system as "legacy" means that it paved the way for the standards that would follow it. (Context: General)

**level of effort (LOE)**   Any particular support type activity that customarily does not lend itself to the ultimate establishment via measure of the sum total of discrete accomplishment. (Context: PMBOK)

**life cycle model**   A framework containing the processes, activities, and tasks involved in the development, operation, and maintenance of a software product, which spans the life of the system from the definition of its requirements to the termination of its use. (Context: IEEE Std 1471-2000)

**line of business (LOB)**

A specific operating unit or shared service that exists within or between agencies. LOBs are also OMB-authorized service providers for the federal government, managed by designated executive agencies. (Context: Common Approach/FEAF2)

A general term that refers to a product or a set of related products that serve a particular customer transaction or business need. (Context: General)

**line of sight (LOS)**    Aligning employee goals with a firm's larger strategic goals is critical if organizations hope to manage their human capital effectively and ultimately attain strategic success. An important component of attaining and sustaining this alignment is for employees to have a line of sight with their organization's strategic objectives. (Context: *Harvard Business Review*)

**location**
   A point or extent in space that may be referred to physically or logically. (Context: DoDAF 2.02)

   A place where business activity takes place and that can be hierarchically decomposed. (Context: TOGAF 9)

   A geographic position of significance to the enterprise. At Row 6 of the Zachman Framework, a location would have a latitude and longitude. (Context: Zachman)

**location catalog**    Provides a listing of all locations where an enterprise carries out business operations or houses architecturally relevant assets, such as data centers or end user computing equipment. (Context: TOGAF 9)

**logical application component**    An encapsulation of application functionality that is independent of a particular implementation—for example, the classification of all purchase request processing applications implemented in an enterprise. (Context: TOGAF 9)

**logical data component**    A boundary zone that encapsulates related data entities to form a logical location to be held—for example, external procurement information. (Context: TOGAF 9)

**logical data diagram**    Shows logical views of the relationships between critical data entities within the enterprise. (Context: TOGAF 9)

**logical data model (D-1)**    Presents data requirements that reify the information concepts identified by corresponding conceptual information models. Similar to DoDAF DIV-2: Logical Data Model. (Context: Common Approach/FEAF2)

**Logical Data Model (DIV-2)**    The documentation of the data requirements and structural business process (activity) rules. In DoDAF V1.5, this was the OV-7. (Context: DoDAF 2.02)

**logical technology component**    An encapsulation of technology infrastructure that is independent of a particular product. A class of technology product—for example, supply chain management software as part of an enterprise resource planning (ERP) suite, or a commercial off-the-shelf (COTS) purchase request processing enterprise service. (Context: TOGAF 9)

**major investment**    A program requiring special management attention because of its importance to the mission or function of the agency, a component of the agency, or another organization; has significant program or policy implications; has high executive visibility; has high development, operating, or maintenance costs; is funded through other than direct appropriations; or is defined as major by the agency's capital planning and investment control process. Office of Management and Budget may work with the agency to declare other investments as major investments. Agencies should consult with the respective OMB agency budget officer or analyst about what investments to consider as "major" and "non-major." (Context: Common Approach/FEAF2)

**managing partner** The agency designated as the lead agency responsible for coordinating the implementation of the E-Gov or line of business initiative; also responsible for coordinating and submitting the Exhibit 300 for the initiative, and the Exhibit 300 will be represented as part of the managing partner's budget portfolio. (Context: Common Approach/FEAF2)

**materiel** Equipment, apparatus, or supplies that are of interest, without distinction as to their application for administrative or combat purposes. (Context: DoDAF 2.02)

**matrix/matrices** Grids that show relationships between two or more model entities that are used to represent relationships that are list-based rather than graphical in their usage (for example, a CRUD matrix showing which applications Create, Read, Update, and Delete a particular type of data is difficult to represent visually). (Context: TOGAF 9)

**measure**
The magnitude of some attribute of an individual. (Context: DoDAF 2.02)

An indicator or factor that can be tracked, usually on an ongoing basis, to determine success or alignment with objectives and goals. (Context: TOGAF 9)

**measure type** A category of measures. (Context: DoDAF 2.02)

**meta** Something of a higher or second order form. In a modeling context, a model of something—a model of a model would be a metamodel. Or a concept model that constitutes the basis for the database design of a repository product, a database for storing models, would be a metamodel. (Context: Zachman)

**meta context** The highest level context for understanding an idea, design, enterprise. (Context: Common Approach/FEAF2)

**meta framework** A classification of the descriptive representations relevant to the existence of an enterprise. The Row 2 models of one framework can be meta relative to another framework—that is, they are of a higher or second order in that they operate relative to all the models of the fundamental framework. For example, there is a set of models that are meta relative to the enterprise framework (enterprise architecture), which would constitute the Row 2 models of another complete framework of models. This meta framework of models is descriptive of the community of people who are designing and building the enterprise framework models (enterprise architecture). By the same token, the Row 2 models of the enterprise framework are meta relative to the product framework, and therefore the enterprise framework is a meta framework relative to the product framework. (Context: Zachman)

**metadata domain (Md)**   Captures metadata relevant to the entire architecture. Provides information pertinent to the entire architecture. Presents supporting information rather than architectural models. (Context: Unified Architecture Framework)

**metamodel**   A model that describes how and with what the architecture will be described in a structured way. (Context: TOGAF 9)

**methodology**

Sometimes called approach, refers to the repeatable process by which architecture documentation will be developed, archived, and used, including the selection of principles, a framework, modeling tools, artifacts, repository, reporting, and auditing. (Context: Common Approach/FEAF2)

A defined, repeatable series of steps to address a particular type of problem, which typically centers on a defined process, but may also include definition of content. (Context: TOGAF 9)

A series of steps that if correctly employed result in a definable result, a process that is typically associated with producing a system or an implementation. The inputs and outputs of a methodology for producing systems or implementations are "composites." (Context: Zachman)

**military services**   The U.S. Military Services include the U.S. Army, the U.S. Navy, the U.S. Air Force, the U.S. Marine Corps, and the U.S. Coast Guard. (Context: General)

**Ministry of Defense Architecture Framework (MODAF)**   An architecture framework that defines a standardized way of conducting enterprise architecture, originally developed by the UK Ministry of Defence. (Context: General)

**mission**   A use or operation for which a system is intended by one or more stakeholders to meet some set of objectives. (Context: IEEE Std 1471-2000)

**mission statement**   A succinct description of why the enterprise exists. (Context: Common Approach/FEAF2)

**MODAF**   *See* Ministry of Defense Architecture Framework (MODAF).

**model**   A representation of a subject of interest that provides a smaller scale, simplified, and/or abstract representation of the subject matter. Constructed as a means to an end. In the context of EA, the subject matter is a whole or part of the enterprise and the end is the ability to construct views that address the concerns of particular stakeholders—their viewpoints in relation to the subject matter. (Context: TOGAF 9)

**moment**   A point in time of significance to the enterprise, sufficiently significant that the clock time at Row 6 of the Zachman Framework is recorded. (Context: Zachman)

**motivation**   The reason or rationale for choices that are made in the design and operation of an enterprise. (Context: Zachman)

**motivation intentions**   The Column 6 models of the Zachman Framework descriptive of the ends and means, the objectives and strategies of the enterprise. At Row 6 the ends will have measurements associated and the means will have constraints ("rules") associated for mitigating risk in the event of conflicting objectives. (Context: Zachman)

**national level**   A level of architecture that includes all federal, state, tribal, and local government agencies within the United States and its territories. These architectures are very important to the coordination of nationwide capabilities, such as first-responder coordination, disaster notification, telecommunications, and transportation infrastructure. (Context: Common Approach/FEAF2)

**national security system**   Any telecommunications or information system operated by the United States government, the function, operation, or use of which involves intelligence activities, involves cryptologic activities related to national security, involves command and control of military forces, involves equipment that is an integral part of a weapon or weapons system, or is critical to the direct fulfillment of military or intelligence missions, but excluding any system that is to be administrative and business applications (including payroll, finance, logistics, and personnel management applications). (Context: Common Approach/FEAF2)

**NATO Architecture Framework (NAF)**   North Atlantic Treaty Organization Architecture Framework, another DoDAF-related defense architecture framework. (Context: General)

**network**   An interconnected set of locations from and to which various inventories are transported for storage or disposition. (Context: Zachman)

**network diagram (I-1)**   Describes the means by which resource flows between systems occur. Similar to DoDAF SV-2: Systems Resource Flow Description and SvcV-2: Services Resource Flow Description. (Context: Common Approach/FEAF2)

**network security enterprise reference architecture**   Specifies an overall U.S. Army approach to providing network security. (Context: Defense Information Enterprise Architecture)

**networked computing/hardware diagram**   Shows the "as deployed" logical view of logical application components in a distributed network computing environment. (Context: TOGAF 9)

**new IT investment**   An IT investment and its associated projects newly proposed by the agency that has not been previously funded by the OMB. This does not include investments existing within the agency that have not previously been reported to OMB. (Context: Common Approach/FEAF2)

**Next Generation Air Traffic System (NGATS)**   An ongoing multibillion dollar modernization of the National Airspace System (NAS). The Federal Aviation Administration (FAA) started working on NextGen improvements in 2007 and plans to have all major components in place by 2025. (Context: RMN Airport Case Study)

**non-major investment**   An IT investment not meeting the definition of major as defined in this glossary, but that is part of the agency's IT portfolio. All non-major investments are reported on the agency IT portfolios (Exhibit 53). (Context: Common Approach/FEAF2)

**object library (D-10)**   A collection of computer programs in the form of relocatable instructions, which reside on, and may be read from, a mass storage device. (Context: Common Approach/FEAF2)

**Object Management Group (OMG)**   A standards group comprising industrial, government, and academic participants. (Context: General)

**objective**   A timebound milestone for an organization used to demonstrate progress toward a goal—for example, "Increase capacity utilization by 30 percent by the end of 2021 to support the planned increase in market share." (Context: TOGAF 9)

**Office of Management and Budget (OMB)**   A U.S. executive branch agency that controls budgets for the other executive agencies and uses architecture information to decide which proposed projects get funding or which continuing projects get additional funding. (Context: General)

**OMB Circular A-130**   A memo issued by the OMB that establishes general policy for the planning, budgeting, governance, acquisition, and management of federal information, personnel, equipment, funds, IT resources, and supporting infrastructure and services. (Context: Common Approach/FEAF2)

**OMB Enterprise Architecture Assessment Framework (EAAF)**   Identifies the measurement areas and criteria by which agencies are expected to use the EA to drive performance improvements. (Context: Common Approach/FEAF2)

**ongoing investment**   An investment and its associated assets, including both maintenance projects and operations, that have been through a complete budget cycle with OMB with respect to the president's budget for the current year. (Context: Common Approach/FEAF2)

**ontology**

In computer science and information science, a formal naming and definition of the types, properties, and interrelationships of the entities that really exist in a particular domain of discourse. (Context: General)

A theory of the existence of a structured set of essential components of an object for which explicit expression is necessary for designing, operating, and changing the object, the object being an enterprise, a department, a value chain, a solution, a project, an airplane, a building, a bathtub, and so on. (Context: Zachman)

**operating model**   Answers the question, What are the processes, activities, roles, controls, governances, and other factors that will be brought to bear to produce these goods, services, or value propositions to customers and markets? (Context: General)

**Operational Activity Decomposition Tree (OV-5a)**   The capabilities and activities (operational activities) organized in a hierarchical structure. (Context: DoDAF 2.02)

**Operational Activity Model (OV-5b)**   The context of capabilities and activities (operational activities) and their relationships among activities, inputs, and outputs. Additional data can show cost, performers, or other pertinent information. (Context: DoDAF 2.02)

**Operational Activity to Services Traceability Matrix (SvcV-5)**   A mapping of services (activities) back to operational activities (activities). (Context: DoDAF 2.02)

**Operational Activity to Systems Function Traceability Matrix (SV-5a)**   A mapping of system functions (activities) back to operational activities (activities). (Context: DoDAF 2.02)

**Operational Activity to Systems Traceability Matrix (SV-5b)**   A mapping of systems back to capabilities or operational activities (activities). (Context: DoDAF 2.02)

**operational concept**   A user-oriented document that describes systems characteristics for a proposed system from a user's perspective, also known as a concept of operations (CONOPS). A CONOPS also describes the user organization, mission, and objectives from an integrated systems point of view and is used to communicate overall quantitative and qualitative system characteristics to stakeholders. (Context: Systems Engineering)

**operational domain (Op)**   Illustrates the logical architecture of the enterprise. Describes the requirements, operational behavior, structure, and exchanges required to support (exhibit) capabilities. Defines all operational elements in an implementation/ solution independent manner. (Context: Unified Architecture Framework)

**operational level agreement (OLA)**   Defines the interdependent relationships in support of a service-level agreement (SLA). The agreement describes the responsibilities of each internal support group toward other support groups, including the process and time frame for delivery of their services. (Context: General)

**Operational Resource Flow Description (OV-2)**   A description of the Resource Flows exchanged between operational activities. (Context: DoDAF 2.02)

**Operational Resource Flow Matrix (OV-3)**   A description of the resources exchanged and the relevant attributes of the exchanges. (Context: DoDAF 2.02)

**Operational Rules Model (OV-6a)**   One of three models used to describe activity (operational activity). It identifies business rules that constrain operations. (Context: DoDAF 2.02)

**Operational Viewpoint (OV)**
   Includes the operational scenarios, activities, and requirements that support capabilities. (Context: DoDAF 2.02)

   Both a DoDAF and a UAF viewpoint. (Context: Unified Architecture Framework)

**operations**   The day-to-day management of an asset in the production environment, including activities involved in operating data centers, help desks, data centers, telecommunication centers, and end user support services. Operational costs include the expenses associated with an IT asset that is in the production environment to sustain an IT asset at the current capability and performance levels including federal and contracted labor costs, and costs for the disposal of an asset. (Context: Common Approach/FEAF2)

**operations and maintenance (O&M)**   The phase of an asset in which the asset is in operations and produces the same product or provides a repetitive service. O&M is the same as steady state. (Context: Common Approach/FEAF2)

**operations instances**   The Zachman Framework, Row 6 enterprise implementations. The "as built" instantiations of the enterprise. This is the actual enterprise, not architectural abstractions. (Context: Zachman)

**Organisation for Economic Cooperation and Development (OECD)**   An intergovernmental economic organization with 35 member countries, founded in 1960 to stimulate economic progress and world trade. (Context: General)

**organization**   A specific real-world assemblage of people and other resources organized for an ongoing purpose. (Context: DoDAF 2.02)

**organization/actor catalog**   Captures a definitive listing of all participants who interact with IT, including users and owners of IT systems. (Context: TOGAF 9)

**organization chart (B-4)**   Presents the composition and relationships among organizational performers. Equivalent to DoDAF OV-4: Organizational Relationships Chart. (Context: Common Approach/FEAF2)

**organization decomposition diagram**   Describes the links between actor, roles, and location within an organization tree. (Context: TOGAF 9)

**organization-specific architecture**   An architecture representation that is unique to each type of organization and does not generalize across organizations. (Context: TOGAF 9)

**organization unit**   A self-contained unit of resources with goals, objectives, and measures. Organization units may include external parties and business partner organizations. (Context: TOGAF 9)

**Organizational Relationships Chart (OV-4)**   The organizational context, role, or other relationships among organizations. (Context: DoDAF 2.02)

**output**   The product or service that is the result of some transformation. (Context: Zachman)

**Overview and Summary Information (AV-1)**   A living document that contains an overview of the architecture form and contents. It describes a project's visions, goals, objectives, plans, activities, events, conditions, measures, effects (outcomes), and produced objects. (Context: DoDAF 2.02)

**partner agency**   The agency for an E-Gov or line of business (LOB) initiative designated as an agency that should provide resources (such as funding, FTEs, in-kind) to the management, development, deployment, or maintenance of a common solution. The partner agency is also responsible for including the appropriate line items in its Exhibit 53, reflecting the amount of the contribution for each of the E-Gov or LOB initiatives to which it is providing resources. (Context: Common Approach/FEAF2)

**patterns**   A technique for putting building blocks into context—for example, to describe a reusable solution to a problem. Building blocks are what you use, and patterns can tell you how you use them—when, why, and what tradeoffs you have to make in doing so. (Context: TOGAF 9)

**performance gap**   An identified activity or capability that is lacking within the enterprise, which causes the enterprise to perform below desired levels or not to achieve strategic or tactical goals. (Context: Common Approach/FEAF2)

**performance measurement**   Regular measurement of outcomes and results, which generates reliable data on the effectiveness and efficiency of programs. (Context: ECA)

**performance measures scorecard (S-5)**   A strategic performance management tool that can be used by managers to keep track of the performance metrics associated with the execution of activities by the staff within their control and to identify the performance gaps and consequences arising from these gaps. A balanced scorecard (BSC) is a performance measures scorecard. (Context: Common Approach/FEAF2)

**performance reference model (PRM)**   Links agency strategy, internal business components, and investments, providing a means to measure the impact of those investments on strategic outcomes. (Context: Common Approach/FEAF2)

**performer**   Any entity—human, automated, or any aggregation of human and/or automated—that performs an activity and provides a capability. (Context: DoDAF 2.02)

**person type**   A category of persons defined by the role or roles they share that are relevant to an architecture. (Context: DoDAF 2.02)

**personally identifying information (PII)**   Any data that could potentially identify a specific individual. Any information that can be used to distinguish one person from another. (Context: General)

**personnel domain (Pr)**   Defines and explores organizational resource types. Shows the taxonomy of types of organizational resources as well as connections, interaction, and growth over time. (Context: Unified Architecture Framework)

**Phase A: Architecture Vision**   Describes the initial phase of an architecture development cycle. It includes information about defining the scope of the architecture development initiative, identifying the stakeholders, creating the architecture vision, and obtaining approval to proceed with the architecture development. (Context: TOGAF 9)

**Phase B: Business Architecture**   Describes the development of a business architecture to support the architecture vision. (Context: TOGAF 9)

**Phase C: Information Systems Architecture**  Describes the development of information systems architectures to support the architecture vision. (Context: TOGAF 9)

**Phase D: Technology Architecture**  Describes the development of the technology architecture to support the architecture vision. (Context: TOGAF 9)

**Phase E: Opportunities & Solutions**  Conducts initial implementation planning and the identification of delivery vehicles for the architecture defined in the previous phases. (Context: TOGAF 9)

**Phase F: Migration Planning**  Addresses how to move from the baseline to the target architectures by finalizing a detailed implementation and migration plan. (Context: TOGAF 9)

**Phase G: Implementation Governance**  Provides an architectural oversight of the implementation. (Context: TOGAF 9)

**Phase H: Architecture Change Management**  Establishes procedures for managing change to the new architecture. (Context: TOGAF 9)

**physical application component**  An application, application module, application service, or other deployable component of functionality—for example, a configured and deployed instance of a COTS enterprise resource planning (ERP) supply chain management application. (Context: TOGAF 9)

**physical data component**  A boundary zone that encapsulates related data entities to form a physical location to be held—for example, a purchase order business object comprising purchase order header and item business object nodes. (Context: TOGAF 9)

**physical data model (D-5)**  Presents data elements and data structures that reify the data requirements specified by corresponding logical data models Equivalent to DoDAF DIV-3: Physical Data Model. (Context: Common Approach/FEAF2)

**Physical Data Model (DIV-3)**  The physical implementation format of the logical data model entities, such as message formats, file structures, physical schema. In DoDAF V1.5, this was the SV-11. (Context: DoDAF 2.02)

**physical technology component**  A specific technology infrastructure product or technology infrastructure product instance—for example, a particular product version of a COTS solution, or a specific brand and version of server. (Context: TOGAF 9)

**platform decomposition diagram**  Diagram that depicts the technology platform that supports the operations of the information systems architecture. It covers all aspects of the infrastructure platform and provides an overview of the enterprise's technology platform. It can be expanded to map the technology platform to appropriate application components within a specific functional or process area. This diagram may show details of specification, such as product versions, number of CPUs, and so on, or simply could be an informal "eye-chart" providing an overview of the technical environment. (Context: TOGAF 9)

**platform service**   A technical capability required to provide enabling infrastructure that supports the delivery of applications. (Context: TOGAF 9)

**point of presence (PoP) diagram (I-10)**   An artificial demarcation point or interface point between communicating entities that describes communications inside the enterprise from the PoP of external communications agents. (Context: General)

**policy**
    **a:** a definite course or method of action selected from among alternatives and in light of given conditions to guide and determine present and future decisions; **b**: a high-level overall plan embracing the general goals and acceptable procedures especially of a governmental body. (Context: *Merriam Webster Dictionary and Thesaurus*)

    A guiding principle that is measurable in terms of compliance and enforceable. (Context: General)

**port authority**   In Canada and the United States, a governmental or quasi-governmental public authority for a special-purpose district usually formed by a legislative body (or bodies) to operate ports and other transportation infrastructure. Sometimes known as port district. (Context: General)

**portfolio of investments**   A collection of assets owned by an enterprise. (Context: General)

**post-implementation review (PIR)**   A management review of an installed system that assesses whether the system still meets its proposed purpose and achieves its desired goals or if it should be retired or replaced. PIRs should be held periodically for all installed systems. (Context: DoD Acquisition)

**preliminary phase**   Describes the preparation and initiation activities required to create an architecture capability including customization of TOGAF and definition of architecture principles. (Context: TOGAF 9)

**primary outcomes**   Though there are many positive outcomes to which EA contributes, four outcomes are considered primary, in that they represent areas of direct, positive impact that architectures can make within and between agencies and with customers and partners external to government. These outcomes are service delivery, functional integration, authoritative reference and resource optimization. (Context: Common Approach/FEAF2)

**primitive**
    An artifact that uses one modeling technique to describe one type of EA component. (Context: Common Approach/FEAF2)

    A descriptive representation (model) depicting "normalized" instances and their interrelationships of a single type of component of an enterprise, an ontologically defined set of components. Used for engineering. The contents of single cell of the Zachman Framework. (Context: Zachman)

**principle**

A comprehensive and fundamental law, doctrine, or assumption. (Context: *Merriam Webster Dictionary and Thesaurus*)

A guiding tenet that is enduring and establishes the fundamental backbone of the EA program in an enterprise. (Context: General)

A qualitative statement of intent that should be met by the architecture. Has at least a supporting rationale and a measure of importance. Note that a sample set of architecture principles is defined in Chapter 23. (Context: TOGAF 9)

**principles catalog (TOGAF)**   Lists the guiding principles for architecture development. (Context: TOGAF 9)

**privacy impact assessment (PIA)**   A process for examining the risks and ramifications of using information technology to collect, maintain, and disseminate information in identifiable form from or about members of the public, and for identifying and evaluating protections and alternative processes to mitigate the impact to privacy of collecting such information. Consistent with OMB M–03–22, implementing the privacy provisions of the E-Government Act, agencies must conduct and make publicly available PIAs for all new or significantly altered IT investments administering information in identifiable form collected from or about members of the public. (Context: Common Approach/FEAF2)

**process**

The flow of control between or within functions and/or services (depends on the granularity of definition). Processes represent a sequence of activities that together achieve a specified outcome, can be decomposed into subprocesses, and can show operation of a function or service (at next level of detail). Processes may also be used to link or compose organizations, functions, services, and processes. (Context: TOGAF 9)

A transformation—you take something in, do something to it (process), and send something different out. (Context: Zachman)

**process/application realization diagram**   Depicts the sequence of events when multiple applications are involved in executing a business process. It enhances the application communication diagram. (Context: TOGAF 9)

**process/event/control/product catalog**   Provides a hierarchy of processes, events that trigger processes, outputs from processes, and controls applied to the execution of processes. This catalog provides a supplement to any process flow diagrams that are created and enables an enterprise to filter, report, and query across organizations and processes to identify scope, commonality, or impact. (Context: TOGAF 9)

**process flow diagram (TOGAF)**   Depicts all models and mappings related to the process metamodel entity and shows the sequential flow of control between activities; may utilize swim lane techniques to represent ownership and realization of process steps—for example, the application that supports a process step may be shown as a swim lane. In addition to showing a sequence of activity, process flows can also be used to detail the controls that apply to a process, the events that trigger or result from completion of a process, and the products that are generated from process execution. (Context: TOGAF 9)

**process flows**   The Column 2 models of the Zachman Framework descriptive of the process transformations the enterprise performs. At Row 6 the instances will be actual transformations performed by a person or a machine. (Context: Zachman)

**processes view type (Pr)**   Captures activity-based behavior and flows. It describes activities, their inputs/outputs, activity actions, and flows between them. (Context: Unified Architecture Framework)

**processing diagram**   Focuses on deployable units of code/configuration and how these are deployed onto the technology platform. A deployment unit represents grouping of business function, service, or application components. (Context: TOGAF 9)

**product framework**   The classification of all the descriptive representations that are relevant to the existence of the product—that is, any Industrial Age product. (Context: Zachman)

**product life cycle diagram**   Assists in understanding the life cycles of key entities within the enterprise. Understanding product life cycles is becoming increasingly important with respect to environmental concerns, legislation, and regulation where products must be tracked from manufacture to disposal. Equally, organizations that create products that involve personal or sensitive information must have a detailed understanding of the product life cycle during the development of business architecture to ensure rigor in design of controls, processes, and procedures. Examples of this would include credit cards, debit cards, store/loyalty cards, smart cards, and user identity credentials (identity cards, passports, and so on). (Context: TOGAF 9)

**product output**   The business product of the execution of a process generated by the business. (Context: TOGAF 9)

**program**   An ongoing set of activities and projects managed in a coordinated way. (Context: Common Approach/FEAF2)

**program management office**   A group or department entrusted with delivering the solution of the project. (Context: Systems Engineering)

**program management review (PMR)**   A structured program review that is conducted by the program manager (PM) with all key stakeholders. A PMR might be conducted at a specific milestone on a program or on a predictable scheduled (monthly, quarterly, or semiannually). (Context: Defense Acquisition)

**program or acquisition program**   An initiative that includes a grouping of projects that deliver capabilities. (Context: Defense Acquisition)

**project**
A temporary activity to create a unique product, service, or result. (Context: Common Approach/FEAF2)

A temporary endeavor undertaken to create resources or desired effects. (Context: DoDAF 2.02)

**project and program**   The term "program" is used in various ways in different domains. In some domains a team can be called a program (a customer support team is the business's customer relationship program). In others, an entire business is called a program (a wireless communications business unit program), and in others the whole enterprise is called a program (the Joint Strike Fighter program and the Apollo Space program). And in many cases, the terms "project" and "program" are used interchangeably with no discernible distinction in their meaning or scope. (Context: Systems Engineering)

**project context diagram**   Shows the scope of a work package to be implemented as a part of a broader transformation roadmap. The project context diagram links a work package to the organizations, functions, services, processes, applications, data, and technology that will be added, removed, or impacted by the project. (Context: TOGAF 9)

**project management plan (PMP)**   A formal, approved document used to manage project execution. The PMP documents the actions necessary to define, prepare, integrate, and coordinate the various planning activities and defines how the project is executed, monitored and controlled, and closed. (Context: Project Management)

**Project Portfolio Relationships (PV-1)**   It describes the dependency relationships between the organizations and projects and the organizational structures needed to manage a portfolio of projects. (Context: DoDAF 2.02)

**Project Timelines (PV-2)**   Acts like an aggregated Gantt chart for a portfolio of projects and provides a very quick view of the various timelines of the component projects and their dependencies. (Context: DoDAF 2.02)

**Project to Capability Mapping (PV-3)**   A mapping of programs and projects to capabilities to show how the specific projects and program elements help to achieve a capability. (Context: DoDAF 2.02)

**Project Viewpoint (PV)**   Describes the relationships between operational and capability requirements and the various projects being implemented. Also details dependencies among capability and operational requirements, system engineering processes, systems design, and services design within the Defense Acquisition System process. (Context: DoDAF 2.02)

**projects domain (Pj)**   Describes projects and project milestones, how those projects deliver capabilities, the organizations contributing to the projects, and dependencies between projects. (Context: Unified Architecture Framework)

**quality assurance (QA)**   The systematic monitoring and evaluation of the various aspects of a project, service, or facility to maximize the probability that standards of quality are being attained by the production process. (Context: Common Approach/FEAF2)

**rack elevation diagram (I-7)**   Two-dimensional elevations (both of front and back) drawn to scale and showing everything that needs to be placed in a certain area to describe the organization of specific equipment on a rack. (Context: Common Approach/FEAF2)

**records**   Includes all books, papers, maps, photographs, machine-readable materials, or other documentary materials, regardless of physical form or characteristics, made or received by an agency of the United States government under federal law or in connection with the transaction of public business and preserved or appropriate for preservation by that agency or its legitimate successor as evidence of the organization, functions, policies, decisions, procedures, operations, or other activities of the government or because of the informational value of data in them. Library and museum materials made or acquired and preserved solely for reference or exhibition purposes, extra copies of documents preserved only for convenience of reference, and stocks of publications and of processed documents are not included. (Context: Common Approach/FEAF2)

**records management**   The planning, controlling, directing, organizing, training, promoting, and other managerial activities involved with respect to records creation, maintenance and use, and disposition in order to achieve adequate and proper documentation of the policies and transactions of the federal government and effective and economical management of agency operations. (44 U.S.C. 2901(2)). (Context: Common Approach/FEAF2)

**reference architecture**   An authoritative source of information about a specific subject area that guides and constrains the instantiations of multiple architectures and solutions. (Context: Common Approach/FEAF2 and Reference Architecture OASD 2010)

**reference library**   Provides guidelines, templates, patterns, and other forms of reference material that can be leveraged to accelerate the creation of new architectures for the enterprise. (Context: TOGAF 9)

**reference model**   An abstract framework for understanding significant relationships among the entities of an environment, and for the development of consistent standards or specifications supporting that environment. A reference model is based on a small number of unifying concepts and may be used as a basis for education and explaining standards to a nonspecialist. A reference model is not directly tied to any standards, technologies, or other concrete implementation details, but it does seek to provide common semantics that can be used unambiguously across and between different implementations. (Context: TOGAF 9)

**reference models (FEA)**   There are six reference models in the common approach to federal EA: performance reference model (PRM), business reference model (BRM), data reference model (DRM), application reference model (ARM), infrastructure reference model (IRM), and security reference model (SRM). These taxonomies provide standardized categorization for strategic, business, and technology models and information and support analysis and reporting across agency EAs and each of the documentation domains. (Context: Common Approach/FEAF2)

**relationship**   In a modeling context, the logical connector between two entities. In the Zachman Framework, the relationship between the two meta-entities in each of the cells of Rows 2–6 is not simply a logical connector but an entity in its own right as it has contents. Two meta-entities describe each cell: an entity and a relationship entity. (Context: Zachman)

**repository**   A storage system that manages all of the data of an enterprise, including data and process models and other enterprise information. Hence, the data in a repository is much more extensive than that in a data dictionary, which generally defines only the data making up a database. (Context: TOGAF 9)

**request for architecture work**   A statement of work that defines the scope and approach that will be used to complete an architecture project. (Context: TOGAF 9)

**request for proposal (RFP)**   A document that solicits a proposal, often made through a bidding process, by an agency or company interested in procurement of a commodity, service, or valuable asset, to potential suppliers to submit business proposals. (Context: General)

**requirement**   A quantitative statement of business need that must be met by a particular architecture or work package. (Context: TOGAF 9)

**requirements catalog**   Captures things that the enterprise needs to do to meet its objectives. Requirements generated from architecture engagements are typically implemented through change initiatives identified and scoped during Phase E (Opportunities & Solutions). Requirements can also be used as a quality assurance tool to ensure that a particular architecture is fit-for-purpose (that is, can the architecture meet all identified requirements). (Context: TOGAF 9)

**requirements management**   Examines the process of managing architecture requirements throughout the Architecture Development Methodology (ADM). (Context: TOGAF 9)

**Requirements Viewpoint**   One of the UAF viewpoints. (Context: Unified Architecture Framework)

**resource**   Data, information, performers, materiel, or personnel types that are produced or consumed. (Context: DoDAF 2.02)

**resource optimization**

As custodians of public funds, federal sector organizations have a special responsibility to optimize their use of resources. Additionally, because of a variety of factors that cannot be anticipated or controlled (such as new laws, policies, and regulations; growing/evolving customer needs; new technologies; natural disasters) federal government organizations must often accomplish their mission with less resources than anticipated. (Context: Common Approach/FEAF2)

A means to achieve the goal of maximizing value for the enterprise and its stakeholders. At one extreme, in a product-oriented organization, projects may be responsible for hiring, training, and firing their own staff, as well as managing all assets required for their delivery of products or services. At the other extreme, in a functional organization, the projects delegate almost all their work to functional groups. In between these two extremes is a matrix organization that is used to give functional specialists a "home" between project assignments. (Context: Jeanne Ross, Peter Weill, and David C. Robertson, *Enterprise Architecture as Strategy: Creating a Foundation for Business Execution,* 2006)

**resources domain (Rs)**   Captures a solution architecture consisting of resources, such as organizational, software, artifacts, capability configurations, and natural resources, that implement the operational requirements. Further design of a resource is typically detailed in SysML or UML. (Context: Unified Architecture Framework)

**responsibility assignments**   The Column 4 models of the Zachman Framework descriptive of the roles and responsibilities of the enterprise's people for managing performance. At Row 6 the individual instances will likely have standard industrial classification codes and the work products assigned have physical manifestations. (Context: Zachman)

**return on investment (ROI)**   The analysis process or resulting report that compares the expected investment costs versus the expected business value (the improvement in outcomes) of the investment over time. (Context: General)

**roadmap**   An abstracted plan for business or technology change, typically operating across multiple disciplines over multiple years (for example, technology roadmap, architecture roadmap, and so on). (Context: TOGAF 9)

**roadmap view type (Rm)**   Addresses how elements in the architecture change over time, at different points in time, or at different periods of time. (Context: Unified Architecture Framework)

**role**

The usual or expected function of an actor, or the part somebody or something plays in a particular action or event. An actor may have a number of roles. (Context: TOGAF 9) *See also* actor.

An innate educational or genetic ability possessed by someone to which responsibility for an enterprise work product is assigned. Typically possessing a standard industrial classification code (SIC code) designation. (Context: Zachman)

**role/application matrix**   Depicts the relationship between applications and the business roles that use them within the enterprise. (Context: TOGAF 9)

**role catalog**   Provides a listing of all authorization levels or zones within an enterprise. Frequently, application security or behavior is defined against locally understood concepts of authorization that create complex and unexpected consequences when combined on the user desktop. (Context: TOGAF 9)

**rule**   A principle or condition that governs behavior; a prescribed guide for conduct or action. (Context: DoDAF 2.02)

**runway**   A defined rectangular area at an airport designated for the landing and takeoff of an aircraft. (Context: FAA AMP)

**scenario**   A set of circumstances, events, players, and activities that provide a setting and context for a model or simulation. (Context: General)

**scope context**  The set of Row 1 Lists of the Zachman Framework that constitute the boundary or limit of the enterprise relative to the columnar abstractions. (Context: Zachman)

**sector**  A level of architecture that focuses on a system or service in one particular mission sector of the Executive Branch of the U.S. government. These interagency architectures often include the enablement of mission and/or support shared services, wherein the roles of provider and consumer need to be detailed and a comprehensive business model for the service provides the requirements for the architecture. These architectures may also include private sector participants. (Context: Common Approach/FEAF2)

**security and privacy plan (SP-2)**  A description of the enterprise security and privacy programs, policies, and procedures for the agency. (Context: Common Approach/ FEAF2)

**security authorization documentation (SP-3)**  Compilation of security documents relevant to each system, such as system security plan, risk analysis, security requirements traceability matrix, system security authorization agreement, authority to operate, and so on. (Context: Common Approach/FEAF2)

**security controls catalog (SP-1)**  Describes the total set of security controls from which the developer may choose, which are applicable for the effort. (Context: Common Approach/FEAF2)

**security domain (Sc)**  Defines the hierarchy of security assets and asset owners, security constraints (policy, laws, and guidance) and details where they are located (security enclaves). (Context: Unified Architecture Framework)

**security reference model (SRM)**  Provides a common language and methodology for discussing security and privacy in the context of federal agencies' business and performance goals. (Context: Common Approach/FEAF2)

**Security subarchitecture domain**  Pervades all of the other five areas of the EA framework, because security and privacy controls, to be most effective, need to be built into service workflows, data flows, systems, applications, and host networks. This is also true for standards and workforce skills. (Context: Common Approach/FEAF2)

**segment**  A level of architecture that focuses on a particular service area or business unit within an agency or between agencies that is not federal-, sector-, or agency-wide. Each segment is defined either organizationally (for example, as a business unit and per the organization chart) or functionally (as a vertical or crosscutting mission or support service). Segments are individual elements of the enterprise describing core mission areas and common or shared business services and enterprise services. They provide the core linkage of the IT investment portfolio to the agency's performance management system. As such, segments are designed to be common across programs that support the same mission area. Increasingly, shared segments will be common across the government and agencies should plan to use approved government-wide shared segments as their target architecture. (Context: Common Approach/FEAF2)

### segment architecture

A detailed, results-oriented architecture (baseline and target) and a transition strategy for a portion or segment of the enterprise. (Context: Common Approach/FEAF2)

A detailed, formal description of areas within an enterprise, used at the program or portfolio level to organize and align change activity. (Context: TOGAF 9)

**Segment Level architecture**   One of an integratable component architectures that together make up the decomposition of an Enterprise Level architecture. (Context: Common Approach/FEAF2)

### service

A mechanism to enable access to a set of one or more capabilities, where the access is provided using a prescribed interface and is exercised consistent with constraints and policies as specified by the service description. (Context: DoDAF 2.02)

An element of behavior that provides specific functionality in response to requests from actors or other services. A service delivers or supports business capabilities, has an explicitly defined interface, and is explicitly governed. Services are defined for business, information systems, and platforms. (Context: TOGAF 9)

**service consumer**   An agency or business unit that receives business or technology service(s) from a line-of-business provider. A service consumer may be either internal or external to the organization responsible for providing services. (Context: Common Approach/FEAF2)

**service delivery**   Federal agencies exist to perform a wide spectrum of missions that meet the nation's ongoing needs through a variety of programs and services. These missions, programs, and services are provided in law, administration policy, and agency policy. Increasingly, these mission and support programs/services/systems require joint management and execution by multiple agencies that are enabled through an IT shared service strategy and various embedded information-related technologies. (Context: Common Approach/FEAF2)

**service implementation**   An actual implementation of an abstract service. (Context: Common Approach/FEAF2)

**service level agreement (SLA)**   A document that spells out such items as the performance characteristics promised by the service provider. (Context: Common Approach/FEAF2)

### service-oriented architecture (SOA)

An architectural style that supports service orientation. (Context: TOGAF 9)

A set of principles and methodologies for designing and developing software in the form of interoperable services. (Context: Common Approach/FEAF2)

**service provider** An agency or business unit that provides business or technology service(s) as a line-of-business consumer(s). This includes a discrete set of personnel, IT, and support equipment with the primary function of providing service(s) to more one or more other agencies or business units on a reimbursable basis. (Context: Common Approach/FEAF2)

**service quality** A preset configuration of nonfunctional attributes that may be assigned to a service or service contract. (Context: TOGAF 9)

**Services Context Description (SvcV-1)** The identification of services, service items, and their interconnections. (Context: DoDAF 2.02)

**services domain (Sv)** The service-orientated view (SOV)—a description of services needed to support the operational domain as described in the operational view. A service within MODAF is understood in its broadest sense as a unit of work through which a provider provides a useful result to a consumer. In DoDAF, the service views within the Services Viewpoint describe the design for service-based solutions to support operational development processes and defense acquisition system or capability development within the joint capability areas. (Context: Unified Architecture Framework)

**Services Event-Trace Description (SvcV-10c)** One of three models used to describe service functionality. It identifies service-specific refinements of critical sequences of events described in the Operational Viewpoint. (Context: DoDAF 2.02)

**Services Evolution Description (SvcV-8)** The planned incremental steps toward migrating a suite of services to a more efficient suite or toward evolving current services to a future implementation. (Context: DoDAF 2.02)

**Services Functionality Description (SvcV-4)** The functions performed by services and the service data flows among service functions (activities). (Context: DoDAF 2.02)

**Services Measures Matrix (SvcV-7)** The measures (metrics) of Services Viewpoint elements for the appropriate time frame(s). (Context: DoDAF 2.02)

**Services Resource Flow Description (SvcV-2)** A description of resource flows exchanged between services. (Context: DoDAF 2.02)

**Services Resource Flow Matrix (SvcV-6)** Provides details of service resource flow elements being exchanged between services and the attributes of that exchange. (Context: DoDAF 2.02)

**Services Rules Model (SvcV-10a)** One of three models used to describe service functionality. It identifies constraints that are imposed on systems functionality due to some aspect of system design or implementation. (Context: DoDAF 2.02)

**Services State Transition Description (SvcV-10b)** One of three models used to describe service functionality. It identifies responses of services to events. (Context: DoDAF 2.02)

**Services Technology and Skills Forecast (SvcV-9)**   The emerging technologies, software/hardware products, and skills that are expected to be available in a given set of time frames and that will affect future service development. (Context: DoDAF 2.02)

**Services Viewpoint (SvcV)**   The design for solutions articulating the performers, activities, services, and their exchanges, providing for or supporting operational and capability functions. (Context: DoDAF 2.02)

**Services-Services Matrix (SvcV-3b)**   The relationships among services in a given architectural description. It can be designed to show relationships of interest (such as service-type interfaces, planned versus existing interfaces). (Context: DoDAF 2.02)

**shared service**   A mission or support function provided by one business unit to other business units within or between organizations. (Context: Common Approach/FEAF2)

**single-variable**   Components of a single type, normalized—a primitive. Antonym is multivariable (apples and oranges). (Context: Zachman)

**Six-Step Process**   The DoDAF meta-process for architecture development. (Context: DoDAF 2.02)

**skill**   The ability, coming from one's knowledge, practice, aptitude, and so on, to do something well. (Context: DoDAF 2.02)

**software distribution diagram**   Shows how application software is structured and distributed across the estate. It is useful in systems upgrade or application consolidation projects. (Context: TOGAF 9)

**software engineering diagram**   Divides applications into packages, modules, services, and operations from a development perspective. (Context: TOGAF 9)

**software license inventory (A-11)**   A list of COTS and open source software assets with details about each (installation date, original cost, condition, and so on). (Context: Common Approach/FEAF2)

**solution architecture**

A standardized method of identifying business requirements and viable technology solutions within the context of a single agency's enterprise architecture or a multiagency sector or government-wide/international architecture. Solution architecture includes current and future views as well as transition plans at a number of levels of scope including applications, systems, segments, enterprise, sector, government-wide, national, and international. The Federal Solution Architecture Methodology (FSAM) is the repeatable process for creating solution architecture through projects at various levels of scope in the federal sector. (Context: Common Approach/FEAF2)

A description of a discrete and focused business operation or activity and how IS/IT supports that operation. A solution architecture typically applies to a single project or project release, assisting in the translation of requirements into a solution vision, high-level business and/or IT system specifications, and a portfolio of implementation tasks. (Context: TOGAF 9)

**solution building block**   A candidate solution that conforms to the specification of an architecture building block (ABB). (Context: TOGAF 9)

**solution concept diagram**   A high-level orientation of the solution that is envisaged to meet the objectives of the architecture engagement. In contrast to more formal and detailed architecture diagrams developed in later phases, the solution concept represents a "pencil sketch" of the expected solution at the outset of the engagement. (Context: TOGAF 9)

**Solution Level architecture**   An architecture level focused on a specific business/mission process solution involving a system or service or set of systems or services. (Context: Common Approach/FEAF2)

**solutions continuum**   A part of the enterprise continuum. A repository of reusable solutions for future implementation efforts that contains implementations of the corresponding definitions in the architecture continuum. (Context: TOGAF 9)

**stakeholder**

One who is or will be affected by a program, activity, or resource. (Context: Common Approach/FEAF2)

An individual, team, or organization (or classes thereof) with interests in, or concerns relative to, the outcome of the architecture. Different stakeholders with different roles will have different concerns. (Context: TOGAF 9)

**stakeholder map matrix (TOGAF)**   Depicts the stakeholders and their roles in the architecture. (Context: TOGAF 9)

**standard**

A formal agreement documenting generally accepted specifications or criteria for products, processes, procedures, policies, systems, and/or personnel. (Context: DoDAF 2.02)

A *de jure* standard is developed and published by a standards development group such as ISO, ANSI, IEEE, or OMG. A *de facto* standard is an interface or proprietary product that has become a standard in the marketplace. (Context: TOGAF 9)

**standard protocol**   Protocol implemented by a system port. (Context: General)

**standards domain (Sd)**   In MODAF, technical standards views are extended from the core DoDAF views to include nontechnical standards such as operational doctrine, industry process standards, and so on. In DoDAF, the standards views within the Standards Viewpoint are the set of rules governing the arrangement, interaction, and interdependence of solution parts or elements. (Context: Unified Architecture Framework)

**Standards Forecast (StdV-2)**   The description of emerging standards and potential impact on current solution elements, within a set of time frames. (Context: DoDAF 2.02)

**standards information base**   A database of standards that can be used to define the particular services and other components of an organization-specific architecture. (Context: TOGAF 9)

**Standards Profile (StdV-1)**   The listing of standards that apply to solution elements. (Context: DoDAF 2.02)

**Standards Viewpoint (StdV)**   Articulates the applicable operational, business, technical, and industry policies, standards, guidance, constraints, and forecasts that apply to capability and operational requirements, system engineering processes, and systems and services. (Context: DoDAF 2.02)

**state**   The status of some architecture element such as a data element, performer, or system, that changes based on events caused by activities. (Context: DoDAF 2.02)

**State Transition Description (OV-6b)**   One of three models used to describe operational activity (activity). It identifies business process (activity) responses to events (usually, very short activities). (Context: DoDAF 2.02)

**statement of work (SOW)**   Created as a deliverable of Phase A, an architecture contract between the architecting organization and the sponsor of the enterprise architecture (or the IT governance function, on behalf of the enterprise). (Context: TOGAF 9)

**states view type (St)**   A graphical representation of states of a structural element and how it responds to various events and actions. It captures state-based behavior of an element. (Context: Unified Architecture Framework)

**State-Transition Diagram (D-7)**   Indicates the states systems transition to in response to events. Equivalent to DoDAF SV-10b: Systems State Transition Description and SvcV-10b: Services State Transition Description. (Context: Common Approach/FEAF2)

**strategic architecture**   A summary formal description of the enterprise, providing an organizing framework for operational and change activity, and an executive-level, long-term view for direction setting. (Context: TOGAF 9)

**strategic domain (St)**   Capability management process. Describes the capability taxonomy, composition, dependencies, and evolution. (Context: Unified Architecture Framework)

**strategic plan (S-2)**   A description of the organization's vision and strategic objectives, a prioritization of the desired outcomes from achieving those objectives, the measurements that will demonstrate achievement, and the resources to be used to achieve them. Included in DoDAF CV-1: Vision, CV-2: Capability Taxonomy, CV-3: Capability Phasing, CV-5: Capability to Organizational Development Mapping, and CV-6: Capability to Operational Activities Mapping. (Context: Common Approach/FEAF2)

**Strategic Viewpoint**   Defines the desired business outcome and the capabilities that are required to achieve it. It provides a means to align an enterprise's strategy with the capabilities required to deliver that strategy, identifying any capability gaps that may exist. (Context: MODAF)

**strategy (business)**   The enterprise's working plan for achieving its vision, prioritizing objectives, competing successfully, and optimizing financial performance with its business model. (Context: General)

**Strategy subarchitecture domain** Identifies the mission, vision, and goals of the enterprise being documented. (Context: Common Approach/FEAF2)

**structure view type (Sr)** Describes the definitions of the dependencies, connections, and relationships between the different elements. (Context: Unified Architecture Framework)

**structured analysis and design technique (SADT)** A systems engineering and software engineering methodology for describing systems as a hierarchy of functions. SADT is a structured analysis modelling language that uses two types of diagrams: activity models and data models. (Context: General)

**subarchitecture domain** Represents a specific area of the overall framework. The type and depth of documentation should be guided by the need for detail and answers to questions about requirements, applicable standards, time frames, and available resources. (Context: Common Approach/FEAF2)

**subject matter expert** Personnel with enterprise business or technical expertise, usually operators or performers of enterprise activities. (Context: General)

**Summary and Overview** UAF viewpoint. (Context: Unified Architecture Framework)

**SWOT analysis (S-4)** Presents the strengths, weaknesses/limitations, opportunities, and threats (SWOT) involved in a project or in a business venture, including risks and impacts. (Context: Common Approach/FEAF2)

**system**

A tangible IT asset that comprises hardware devices, software applications, databases, users, processes, and security controls. (Context: Common Approach/FEAF2)

A functionally, physically, and/or behaviorally related group of regularly interacting or interdependent elements. (Context: DoDAF 2.02)

A collection of components organized to accomplish a specific function or set of functions. (Context: IEEE Std 1471-2000)

A set of things working together as parts of a mechanism. In the context of the Zachman Framework, the Row 3 models are a set of things working together that formalize a mechanism to realize the Row 2 enterprise concepts as one stage of reification, transforming the ideas of the enterprise, management's perceptions, into an operational realities. (Context: Zachman)

**system/application evolution diagram (A-7)** The planned incremental steps toward migrating a suite of systems and/or applications to a more efficient suite, or toward evolving a current system or application to a future implementation. Equivalent to DoDAF SV-8: Systems Evolution Description and SvcV-8: Services Evolution Description. (Context: Common Approach/FEAF2)

**system environment**  The environment, or context, that determines the setting and circumstances of developmental, operational, political, and other influences upon that system. The environment can include other systems that interact with the system of interest, either directly via interfaces or indirectly in other ways. The environment determines the boundaries that define the scope of the system of interest relative to other systems. (Context: IEEE Std 1471-2000)

**System Level architecture**  A level of architecture that focuses on one particular information technology system that supports the delivery of one or more services within or between segments and agencies. All aspects of a system's functionality and configuration should be documented, including strategic drivers, business requirements, applicable standards, workflow processes, information exchanges, software applications, host infrastructure, remote access, and security/privacy controls. (Context: Common Approach/FEAF2)

**System of Systems (SoS)**  A set of systems that are the components of a more complex system that shows emergent properties. (Context: General)

**system ports**  Used by a system to send data to external systems. (Context: General)

**system stakeholder**  An individual, team, or organization (or classes thereof) with interests in, or concerns relative to, a system. (Context: IEEE Std 1471-2000)

**systems development life cycle (SDLC)**  Guidance, policies, and procedures for developing systems throughout their life cycle, including requirements, design, implementation testing, deployment, operations, and maintenance. (Context: Common Approach/FEAF2)

**Systems Event-Trace Description (SV-10c)**  One of three models used to describe system functionality. It identifies system-specific refinements of critical sequences of events described in the Operational Viewpoint. (Context: DoDAF 2.02)

**Systems Evolution Description (SV-8)**  The planned incremental steps toward migrating a suite of systems to a more efficient suite, or toward evolving a current system to a future implementation. (Context: DoDAF 2.02)

**Systems Functionality Description (SV-4)**  The functions (activities) performed by systems and the system data flows among system functions (activities). (Context: DoDAF 2.02)

**Systems Interface Description (SV-1)**  The identification of systems, system items, and their interconnections. (Context: DoDAF 2.02)

**Systems Measures Matrix (SV-7)**  The measures (metrics) of systems model elements for the appropriate time frame(s). (Context: DoDAF 2.02)

**Systems Resource Flow Description (SV-2)**  A description of resource flows exchanged between systems. (Context: DoDAF 2.02)

**Systems Resource Flow Matrix (SV-6)**   Provides details of system resource flow elements being exchanged between systems and the attributes of that exchange. (Context: DoDAF 2.02)

**Systems Rules Model (SV-10a)**   One of three models used to describe system functionality. It identifies constraints that are imposed on systems functionality due to some aspect of system design or implementation. (Context: DoDAF 2.02)

**Systems State Transition Description (SV-10b)**   One of three models used to describe system functionality. It identifies responses of systems to events. (Context: DoDAF 2.02)

**Systems Technology and Skills Forecast (SV-9)**   The emerging technologies, software/hardware products, and skills that are expected to be available in a given set of time frames that will affect future system development. (Context: DoDAF 2.02)

**Systems Viewpoint (SV)**   For legacy support, is the design for solutions articulating the systems, their composition, interconnectivity, and context providing for or supporting operational and capability functions. (Context: DoDAF 2.02)

**Systems-Services Matrix (SvcV-3a)**   The relationships among or between systems and services in a given architectural description. (Context: DoDAF 2.02)

**Systems-Systems Matrix (SV-3)**   The relationships among systems in a given Architectural description. It can be designed to show relationships of interest (such as system-type interfaces, planned versus existing interfaces). (Context: DoDAF 2.02)

**tacit knowledge**   Much of the relevant knowledge that exists in people's heads and in the context of relationships that people form with each other (such as team, project, and business level knowledge). The ability of an organization to create value is critically dependent on its employees' tacit knowledge—what they know, how they work together, and how well they are organized and motivated to contribute to the organization's purpose. (Context: Systems Engineering)

**target architecture**   The representation of a desired future state or "to be built" for the enterprise within the context of the strategic direction. (Context: Common Approach/FEAF2)

**taxonomy**   The study of the general principles of scientific classification. (Context: *Merriam Webster Dictionary and Thesaurus*)

**taxonomy of architecture views**   The organized collection of all views pertinent to an architecture. (Context: TOGAF 9)

**taxonomy view type (Tx)**   Presents all the elements as a standalone structure. Presents all the elements as a specialization hierarchy and provides a text definition for each one and references the source of the element. (Context: Unified Architecture Framework)

**technical reference model (TRM)**   As part of TOGAF, the TRM provides a model and taxonomy of generic platform services. (Context: TOGAF 9)

**technical review board or committee (TRB/TRC)**  A committee that ensures the technology choices made by the organization are the best options for all groups and departments. Although many organizations lack an established TRB or review process, establishing and maintaining a TRB process does not need to be overly complicated. (Context: General)

**technical standards profile (I-3)**  Collects the various systems standards rules that implement and sometimes constrain the choices that can be made in the design and implementation of an architecture. Equivalent to DoDAF StdV-1: Standards Profile. (Context: Common Approach/FEAF2)

**technology and infrastructure model**  A set of technologies including IT as well as the infrastructure of services, networks, and transport mechanisms to enable and create new revenues in the business model, and to support current operations in the operating model. (Context: General)

**technology architecture**  A description of the structure and interaction of the platform services, and logical and physical technology components. (Context: TOGAF 9)

**technology component**  An encapsulation of technology infrastructure that represents a class of technology product or specific technology product. (Context: TOGAF 9)

**technology forecast (I-4)**  The emerging technologies, software/hardware products, and skills that are expected to be available in a given set of time frames and that will affect future infrastructure development. Equivalent to DoDAF SV-9: Systems Technology and Skills Forecast and SvcV-9: Services Technology and Skills Forecast. (Context: Common Approach/FEAF2)

**technology portfolio catalog**  Identifies and maintains a list of all the technology in use across the enterprise, including hardware, infrastructure software, and application software. The technology portfolio supports life cycle management of technology products and versions and also forms the basis for definition of technology standards. (Context: TOGAF 9)

**technology standards catalog**  Documents the standards for technology across the enterprise covering technologies, and versions, the technology life cycle, and the refresh cycles for the technology. (Context: TOGAF 9)

**The Open Group Architecture Framework (TOGAF)**  An architecture framework that provides the methods and tools for assisting in the acceptance, production, use, and maintenance of an enterprise architecture. It is based on an iterative process model supported by best practices and a reusable set of existing architecture assets. (Context: TOGAF 9)

**to-be architecture**  Represents the planned state of the enterprise at a specific date in the future. This is sometimes called the vision or target architecture. (Context: General)

**TOGAF** *See* The Open Group Architecture Framework (TOGAF).

**traceability view type (Tr)** Describes the mapping between elements in the architecture—between different viewpoints within domains, between domains, or between structure and behaviors. (Context: Unified Architecture Framework)

**transition architecture** A formal description of one state of the architecture at an architecturally significant point in time. One or more transition architectures may be used to describe the progression in time from the baseline to the target architecture. (Context: TOGAF 9)

**UDDI (Universal Description, Discovery, and Integration) registry** An XML-based registry for businesses worldwide to list themselves on the Internet. Its ultimate goal is to streamline online transactions by enabling companies to find one another on the Web and make their systems interoperable for e-commerce. (Context: General)

**Unified Architecture Framework (UAF)** An ontology that provides a unified ontology for the defense architecture frameworks as well as for commercial enterprise frameworks. UAF is defined in Unified Modeling Language (UML). (Context: Unified Architecture Framework)

**Unified Architecture Framework Profile (UAFP)** A profile for SysML that can be used to customize a UML-based tool for development of DoDAF architecture descriptions. (Context: Unified Architecture Framework)

**Unified Capabilities Reference Architecture** A framework intended to guide and align DoD component instantiation of respective unified capabilities implementation plans and solutions. (Context: Joint Instruction)

**Unified Modeling Language (UML)** A notation used to represent models that is not based on a specific methodology. UML is based on the object-oriented paradigm and is capable of supporting profiles for a variety of metamodels. (Context: Unified Architecture Framework)

**Universal Profile for DoDAF and MODAF** A profile that adapts a UML-based tool to support both DoDAF and MODAF. Unified Architecture Framework is superseding this profile. (Context: Unified Architecture Framework)

**use case narrative and diagram (B-5)** Describes a set of possible sequences of interactions between systems and users in a particular environment and related to a particular goal. (Context: Common Approach/FEAF2)

**value chain diagram** Provides a high-level orientation view of an enterprise and how it interacts with the outside world. In contrast to the more formal functional decomposition diagram developed within Phase B (Business Architecture), the value chain diagram focuses on presentational impact. The purpose of this diagram is to on-board and align stakeholders for a particular change initiative, so that all participants understand the high-level functional and organizational context of the architecture engagement. (Context: TOGAF 9)

**value creation**   The primary purpose of an enterprise is to create value for society, other stakeholders, and for the organizations that participate in that enterprise. (Context: Systems Engineering)

**verification and validation (V&V)**   In software project management, software testing, and software engineering, the process of checking that a software system meets specifications and that it fulfills its intended purpose. It may also be referred to as software quality control. (Context: General)

**view**

A representation of a whole system from the perspective of a related set of concerns. (Context: IEEE Std 1471-2000)

The representation of a related set of concerns, as part of a viewpoint. An architecture view may be represented by a model to demonstrate to stakeholders their areas of interest in the architecture. A view does not have to be visual or graphical in nature. (Context: TOGAF 9)

**viewpoint**

A pattern or template for representing one set of concerns relative to an architecture. A viewpoint provides the formalization of the groupings of models. (Context: IEEE Std 1471-2000)

A definition of the perspective from which a view is taken. It is a specification of the conventions for constructing and using a view (often by means of an appropriate schema or template). A view is what you see; a viewpoint is where you are looking from—the vantage point or perspective that determines what you see. (Context: TOGAF 9)

**vision**   An end that describes the future state of the enterprise, without regard to how it is to be achieved; a mental image of what the future will or could be like. (Context: DoDAF 2.02)

**Vision (CV-1)**   In the Capability Viewpoint, a view that addresses the enterprise concerns associated with the overall vision for transformational endeavors and thus defines the strategic context for a group of capabilities. (Context: DoDAF 2.02)

**vision statement**   The part of a strategic plan that succinctly describes the competitive strategy of the enterprise. (Context: Common Approach/FEAF2)

**web-enabled**   Applications and services that are accessed through a web browser and function through an internal and/or external Internet-protocol based collaboration environment such as the Internet, or local area network, wide area network, public cloud, private cloud, and hybrid cloud). (Context: Common Approach/FEAF2)

**wireless connectivity diagram (I-6)**   Diagrams a communications network that provides connectivity to wireless devices. (Context: Common Approach/FEAF2)

**wiring closet diagram (I-9)**   Diagrams the layout and contents of a wiring closet. (Context: Common Approach/FEAF2)

**work breakdown structure (WBS)**   A key project deliverable that organizes the team's work into manageable sections. (Context: General)

**work package**   A set of actions identified to achieve one or more objectives for the business; can be a part of a project, a complete project, or a program. (Context: TOGAF 9)

**Zachman Framework**   An enterprise ontology and a fundamental structure for EA, which provides a formal and structured way of viewing and defining an enterprise. The ontology is a two-dimensional classification schema that reflects the intersection between two historical classifications. (Context: General)

# INDEX